RACIAL
AND ETHNIC
DIVERSITY

5th EDITION

RACIAL
AND ETHNIC
DIVERSITY

Asians, Blacks, Hispanics, Native Americans, and Whites

BY THE NEW STRATEGIST EDITORS

New Strategist Publications, Inc.
P.O. Box 242, Ithaca, New York 14851
800/848-0842; 607/273-0913
www.newstrategist.com

ISBN 1-885070-71-3

Printed in the United States of America

Table of Contents

List of Tables

Chapter 2. Asians

Income

Labor Force

Living Arrangements

Population

Spending

Chapter 3. Blacks

Education

Health

Housing

Income

Labor Force

Living Arrangements

Population

Living Arrangements

Population

Spending

Wealth

Chapter 6. Total Population

Education

Labor Force

Living Arrangements

Population

Chapter 7. Attitudes and Behavior

Introduction

The U.S. population is growing more diverse much faster than many had predicted. Behind the growing diversity are a number of factors, including immigration, rising fertility rates, and new ways of defining racial categories. The 2000 census counted not only more people than had been projected, but more diversity than had been expected. Now, with the 21st century well underway, the composition of the U.S. population is continuing its rapid change. Hispanics have become the largest minority. Asians are the most affluent segment of the population, surpassing non-Hispanic whites. Blacks are making significant gains in education and earning power. Only by understanding each of these increasingly important segments of the population can policymakers and business people hope to tailor their programs and products to the wants and needs of 300 million Americans.

The fifth edition of *Racial and Ethnic Diversity* is a profile of America as the 21st century unfolds. It provides an all-important update to 2000 census data, revealing the patterns of change that are reshaping our society. It profiles the social and economic wellbeing of American Indians, Asians, blacks, Hispanics, and non-Hispanic whites. It provides a snapshot of each of these populations and allows for contrasts and comparisons.

In addition to detailed estimates and projections of the U.S. population by race and Hispanic origin, the fifth edition of *Racial and Ethnic Diversity* includes the latest socioeconomic data on blacks and Hispanics and more comprehensive information on Asians and American Indians—thanks to expanded efforts by the federal government to collect data on smaller minority groups. This edition of *Racial and Ethnic Diversity* includes spending data for Asian households, a recent addition to the Bureau of Labor Statistics' Consumer Expenditure Survey. It provides updated information on American Indians—including their numbers by state and metropolitan area—from the Census Bureau's American Community Survey, which has replaced the census long form. Results from the new American Time Use Survey are also included in these pages, profiling the similarities and differences in how people allocate their time by race and Hispanic origin.

Understanding the demographics, lifestyles, and attitudes of racial and ethnic groups is of vital importance to researchers and policy makers. *Racial and Ethnic Diversity* provides the key to understanding both the similarities and differences between non-Hispanic whites, blacks, Hispanics, Asians, and American Indians. Whenever possible, the tables in *Racial and Ethnic Diversity* include data that allow researchers to compare characteristics across racial groups.

There's no doubt Americans are more alike than different, and *Racial and Ethnic Diversity* documents our many similarities. But there are also important differences among racial and ethnic groups that, if not taken into account, can derail public policy efforts and business strategies. The living arrangements of Hispanics differ from those of non-Hispanic whites or blacks, for example, and those differences affect not only political attitudes but also consumer behavior. The educational level of Asians distinguishes them from other minorities. The substantial educational, employment, and economic gains made by blacks, documented in these pages, are contrary to popular perception, but they are of utmost importance to policymakers and business leaders.

Racial and Ethnic Diversity is as complete and up-to-date as possible given the constraints of the data. In a perfect world, the tabulations for each racial and ethnic group would be identical, but this is impossible because the government does not collect some types of information for smaller racial and ethnic groups. The Consumer Expenditure Survey, for example, lacks data on the spending of American Indians. The Survey of Consumer Finances has limited data on wealth by race and ethnicity. Despite these limitations, the scope of data provided in the fifth edition of *Racial and Ethnic Diversity* is greater than in any previous edition, providing a comprehensive portrait of each major racial group and Hispanics.

Racial classifications

The 2000 census transformed racial classification in the U.S. The census allowed Americans, for the first time in modern history, to identify themselves as belonging to more than one racial group. This makes the analysis of racial and ethnic diversity more complex—and more rewarding—than ever before. Beginning in 2003, the government required its surveys to include the new racial classification scheme. Consequently, researchers now have a wealth of data available to them broken down by detailed racial and ethnic group.

The federal government's new racial classification system has resulted in a variety of racial and ethnic combinations. Three terms are used to distinguish one group from another. The "race alone" population consists of people who identify themselves as being of only one race. The "race in combination" population consists of people who identify themselves as being of more than one race, such as white and black. The "race, alone or in combination" population includes both those identifying themselves as being of one race and those identifying themselves as being of more than one race. For example, the "black, alone or in combination" population includes those who say they are black alone and those who say they are black and white and those who say they are black, white, and Asian, and so on.

While the new classification system is a goldmine for researchers, the numbers no longer add up. This may frustrate some, but it provides a more accurate picture of each racial group than the previous methodology did, which required the multiracial to align with only one race. Under the new scheme, however, tables showing the "race alone" population exclude the multiracial. Tables showing the "race in combination" population count some people more than once. To make matters even more complex, Hispanics are considered an ethnic group rather than a race and can be American Indian, Asian, black or white. In addition, the non-Hispanic white category is a combination of race and ethnicity. Non-Hispanic whites are those identifying their race as white alone and not Hispanic. Keep these factors in mind as you peruse the numbers.

Whenever possible, the tables in *Racial and Ethnic Diversity* show the "race alone or in combination" populations. We prefer this classification because it includes everyone identifying with a particular racial group and does not exclude the multiracial. In some instances, the "race alone or in combination" population figures are not available. In these cases, the "race alone" population is shown. The racial classification used is noted at the bottom of each table. Also note that some data sources do not define their racial classifications.

How to use this book

Racial and Ethnic Diversity is designed for easy use. It is divided into five sections devoted to the major racial and ethnic groups: American Indians, Asians, Blacks, Hispanics, and Non-Hispanic Whites. A sixth section provides comparative information for the Total Population. Also included is a seventh section on Attitudes and Behavior by race and Hispanic origin.

In all but the Attitudes and Behavior section, nine chapters are arranged alphabetically: Education, Health, Housing, Income, Labor Force, Living Arrangements, Population, Spending, and Wealth. Each chapter includes introductory text describing the most important trends for the particular racial or ethnic group. For some racial groups, chapters may be absent because data are not available. For example, there are no spending data for American Indians or wealth data for Asians. Within chapters, identically structured tables appear for each racial group. If a table is structured differently, it is because equivalent data are not available.

The Total Population section allows readers to compare a group's numbers with those for the nation as a whole. If total population statistics appear within an individual racial or ethnic table, however, a table of the same statistics is usually omitted from the Total Population chapter.

Most of the tables in *Racial and Ethnic Diversity* are based on data collected by the federal government, in particular the Census Bureau, the Bureau of Labor Statistics, the National Center for Education Statistics, the National Center for Health Statistics, and the Federal Reserve Board. The federal government continues to be the best source of up-to-date, reliable information on the changing characteristics of Americans. A few tables in *Racial and Ethnic Diversity* are based on proprietary data. Proprietary data are used when government data are not available. Examples are the tables on religion and attitudes toward retirement.

Several government surveys are of particular importance to *Racial and Ethnic Diversity*. One is the Census Bureau's Current Population Survey. The CPS is a nationally representative survey of the civilian noninstitutional population aged 15 or older. The Census Bureau takes it monthly, collecting information from 50,000 households on employment and unemployment. Each year, the March survey includes a demographic supplement that is the source of most national data on the characteristics of Americans, such as their educational attainment, living arrangements, and incomes. CPS data appear in many tables of this book.

The American Community Survey is another important source of data for *Racial and Ethnic Diversity*. The ACS is an ongoing nationwide survey of 250,000 households per month, providing detailed demographic data at the community level. Designed to replace the census long-form questionnaire, the ACS includes more than 60 questions that formerly appeared on the long form, such as queries about language spoken at home, income, and education. ACS data are available for the nation, regions, states, counties, metropolitan areas, and many places. Many of the tables in the American Indian section are from the ACS, as are the tables showing population by race and Hispanic origin for states and metropolitan areas.

The Consumer Expenditure Survey is the data source for the Spending chapters. Sponsored by the Bureau of Labor Statistics, the CEX is an ongoing study of the day-to-day spending of American households. The data collected by the survey are used to update prices for the Consumer Price Index. The CEX includes an interview survey and a diary survey administered to two separate, nationally representative samples. The average spending figures shown in the Spending chapters of this book are the integrated data from both the diary and interview components of the survey. For the interview survey, about 7,500 consumer units are interviewed on a rotating panel basis each quarter for five consecutive quarters. For the diary survey, another 7,500 consumer units keep weekly diaries of spending for two consecutive weeks. Spending data for American Indians are not available.

The data in the Wealth chapters come from the Survey of Consumer Finances, a triennial survey taken by the Federal Reserve Board. The SCF collects data on the assets, debt, and net worth of American households. The latest data available are from the 2001 survey, for which the Federal Reserve Board interviewed a representative sample of 4,449 households. The SCF provides wealth data for only two racial and ethnic groups: "non-Hispanic whites" and "non-whites and Hispanics."

Since we published the first edition of *Racial and Ethnic Diversity*, dramatic technological change has reshaped the reference industry. The government's detailed demographic data, once widely available to all in printed reports, is now accessible only to Internet users. The government's web sites, which house enormous spreadsheets of data, are of great value to skilled researchers with the time to search for information. But the shift from printed reports to web sites is a technological barrier that must be crossed before the average student, library patron, or market researcher can access demographic statistics. It can be more time-consuming than ever to get answers to questions about the American population and how changing demographics are remaking our society.

While the government collected most of the data in *Racial and Ethnic Diversity*, the tables published here are not simple reprints of the government's spreadsheets—as is the case in many reference books. Instead, New Strategist's editors spent hundreds of hours scouring web sites, compiling numbers into meaningful statistics, and creating tables with calculations that reveal the trends. Researchers who want more information can use the source listed at the bottom of each table to locate the original data. The book contains a comprehensive table list to help readers locate the information they need. For a more detailed search, use the index at the back of the book. Also in the back of the book is the glossary, which defines most of the terms commonly used in the tables and text.

Racial and Ethnic Diversity gives you the opportunity to discover the many ways Americans are the same—and different. With such knowledge, you will be closer to understanding where the future will take us.

1

American Indians and Alaska Natives

■ Numbering 4.4 million, American Indians and Alaska Natives are one of the smallest minorities in the United States, accounting for just 1.5 percent of the population.

■ Forty-five percent of American Indians aged 25 or older have at least some college experience, and 14 percent are college graduates.

■ Fewer than half of American Indians say their health is very good or excellent, far below the 62 percent of all Americans who rate their health highly.

■ The 56 percent majority of American Indian households own their home, a homeownership rate that exceeds that of blacks or Hispanics.

■ The median annual income of American Indian households stood at $31,121 in 2003, well below the $43,564 median for all households.

■ American Indians are less likely than the average worker to be managers or professionals and more likely to be service workers.

■ Married couples head only 43 percent of American Indian households.

■ American Indians and Alaska Natives account for 19 percent of Alaska's population. In New Mexico and Oklahoma, they are 11 percent of the population.

■ Note: There are no spending or wealth data for American Indians.

American Indians account for less than 2 percent of the U.S. population

(percent distribution of people by race and Hispanic origin, 2004)

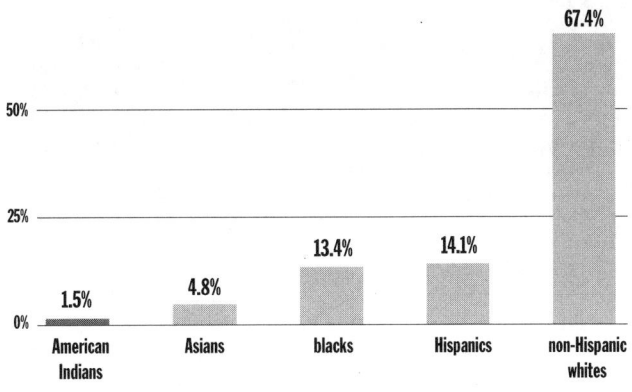

Nearly Half of American Indians Have Attended College For One or More Years

Forty-five percent of American Indians aged 25 or older have at least some college experience, and 14 percent are college graduates. While these figures are lower than those for Asians and non-Hispanic whites, they are almost equal to the black proportions and far above those for Hispanics. Seventy-six percent of American Indians are high school graduates.

American Indians account for fewer than 1 percent of the nation's college students. Among American Indians enrolled in college, 60 percent are women, 84 percent are in public institutions, and slightly more than half are in two-year programs. More than 9,000 American Indians earned a bachelor's degree in 2001–02.

■ The educational attainment of American Indians would rise if college was more afford-able.

Seventy-six percent of American Indians are high school graduates

(percent of American Indians aged 25 or older who are high school graduates or more, have some college or more, or are college graduates, 2003)

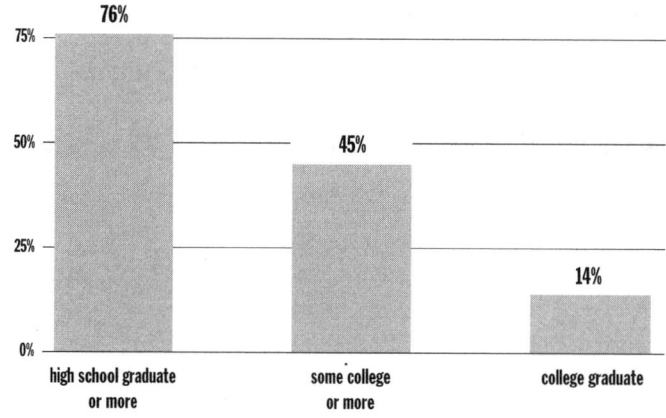

Table 1.1 Educational Attainment of American Indians by Sex, 2003

(number and percent distribution of American Indians aged 25 or older by educational attainment and sex, 2003)

	total	men	women
Total American Indians	**1,288,943**	**630,650**	**658,293**
Less than 9th grade	113,722	58,389	55,333
9th to 12th grade, no diploma	196,946	97,008	99,938
High school graduate	399,799	200,865	198,934
Some college, no degree	301,721	135,742	165,979
Associate's degree	97,942	50,176	47,766
Bachelor's degree	121,901	59,390	62,511
Graduate degree	56,912	29,080	27,832
High school graduate or more	978,275	475,253	503,022
Some college or more	578,476	274,388	304,088
Bachelor's degree or more	178,813	88,470	90,343
PERCENT DISTRIBUTION			
Total American Indians	**100.0%**	**100.0%**	**100.0%**
Less than 9th grade	8.8	9.3	8.4
9th to 12th grade, no diploma	15.3	15.4	15.2
High school graduate	31.0	31.9	30.2
Some college, no degree	23.4	21.5	25.2
Associate's degree	7.6	8.0	7.3
Bachelor's degree	9.5	9.4	9.5
Graduate degree	4.4	4.6	4.2
High school graduate or more	75.9	75.4	76.4
Some college or more	44.9	43.5	46.2
Bachelor's degree or more	13.9	14.0	13.7

Note: American Indians include Alaska Natives. The American Indian and Alaska Native population includes only those identifying themselves as being American Indian or Alaska Native alone and no other race.
Source: Bureau of the Census, 2003 American Community Survey, Internet site http://factfinder.census.gov/servlet/ DatasetMainPageServlet?_program=ACS&_lang=en&_ts=; calculations by New Strategist

Table 1.2 School Enrollment of American Indians, 2003

(total number of people aged 3 or older enrolled in school, number of American Indians enrolled, and American Indian share of total, by level of enrollment, 2003)

		American Indian	
	total	number	share of total
Total enrolled in school	**75,128,957**	**670,930**	**0.9%**
Nursery school, kindergarten	8,604,479	74,355	0.9
Grades 1 to 8	32,706,140	296,042	0.9
Grades 9 to 12	16,599,058	172,035	1.0
College or graduate school	17,219,280	128,498	0.7

Note: American Indians include Alaska Natives. The American Indian and Alaska Native population includes only those identifying themselves as being American Indian or Alaska Native alone and no other race.
Source: Bureau of the Census, 2003 American Community Survey, Internet site http://factfinder.census.gov/servlet/ DatasetMainPageServlet?_program=ACS&_lang=en&_ts=; calculations by New Strategist

Table 1.3 College Enrollment of American Indians, 2001

(number and percent distribution of American Indians enrolled in degree-granting institutions by sex, type of institution, and level of study, 2001)

	number	percent distribution
Total American Indians enrolled	**158,151**	**100.0%**
Men	63,630	40.2
Women	94,521	59.8
Public institutions	133,576	84.5
Private institutions	24,575	15.5
Two-year institutions	79,960	50.6
Four-year institutions	78,191	49.4
Full-time students	89,541	56.6
Part-time students	68,610	43.4
Undergraduate	144,774	91.5
Graduate	11,233	7.1
First-professional	2,144	1.4

Note: American Indians include Alaska Natives. College enrollment figures in this table differ from those in the above table because they are from different years and the figures in this table are based on institutional data, while the figures in the above table are from a household survey.
Source: National Center for Education Statistics, Digest of Education Statistics 2003, Internet site http://nces.ed.gov//programs/

Table 1.4 Associate's Degrees Earned by American Indians by Field of Study, 2001–02

(total number of associate's degrees conferred and number and percent earned by American Indians, by field of study, 2001–02)

	total	earned by American Indians	
		number	percent
Total associate's degrees	**595,133**	**6,830**	**1.1%**
Agriculture and natural resources	6,494	89	1.4
Architecture and related programs	443	3	0.7
Area, ethnic, and cultural studies	319	32	10.0
Biological and life sciences	1,517	44	2.9
Business	108,911	1,244	1.1
Communications	2,819	26	0.9
Communications technologies	2,021	19	0.9
Computer and information sciences	30,965	301	1.0
Construction trades	2,639	62	2.3
Education	9,267	316	3.4
Engineering	1,724	18	1.0
Engineering-related technologies	32,895	263	0.8
English language and literature, letters	864	6	0.7
Foreign languages and literatures	517	16	3.1
Health professions and related sciences	79,888	862	1.1
Home economics	9,480	154	1.6
Law and legal studies	6,825	73	1.1
Liberal arts and sciences, general studies, humanities	207,163	2,170	1.0
Library science	96	1	1.0
Mathematics	685	7	1.0
Mechanics and repairers	12,086	175	1.4
Multi- and interdisciplinary studies	13,204	101	0.8
Parks, recreation, leisure, and fitness	830	10	1.2
Philosophy and religion	134	0	0.0
Physical sciences	2,308	22	1.0
Precision production trades	10,818	109	1.0
Protective services	16,689	200	1.2
Psychology	1,705	33	1.9
Public administration and services	3,323	73	2.2
R.O.T.C. and military technologies	62	0	0.0
Social sciences and history	5,593	172	3.1
Theological studies, religious vocations	414	1	0.2
Transportation and material moving	1,159	13	1.1
Visual and performing arts	20,911	211	1.0
Not classified	365	4	1.1

Note: American Indians include Alaska Natives.
Source: National Center for Education Statistics, Digest of Education Statistics 2003, *Internet site http://nces.ed.gov//programs/ digest/d03/list_tables.asp; calculations by New Strategist*

Table 1.5 Bachelor's Degrees Earned by American Indians by Field of Study, 2001–02

(total number of bachelor's degrees conferred and number and percent earned by American Indians, by field of study, 2001–02)

		earned by American Indians	
	total	number	percent
Total bachelor's degrees	**1,291,900**	**9,165**	**0.7%**
Agriculture and natural resources	23,353	191	0.8
Architecture and related programs	8,808	58	0.7
Area, ethnic, and cultural studies	6,557	132	2.0
Biological and life sciences	60,256	426	0.7
Business	281,330	1,810	0.6
Communications	62,791	344	0.5
Communications technologies	1,110	5	0.5
Computer and information sciences	47,299	239	0.5
Construction trades	202	0	0.0
Education	106,383	1,018	1.0
Engineering	59,481	320	0.5
Engineering-related technologies	14,117	102	0.7
English language and literature, letters	53,162	308	0.6
Foreign languages and literatures	15,318	73	0.5
Health professions and related sciences	70,517	528	0.7
Home economics	18,153	123	0.7
Law and legal studies	1,971	15	0.8
Liberal arts and sciences, general studies, humanities	39,333	442	1.1
Library science	74	0	0.0
Mathematics	12,395	59	0.5
Mechanics and repairers	164	0	0.0
Multi- and interdisciplinary studies	27,629	194	0.7
Parks, recreation, leisure, and fitness	20,554	157	0.8
Philosophy and religion	9,306	56	0.6
Physical sciences	17,851	114	0.6
Precision production trades	468	1	0.2
Protective services	25,536	306	1.2
Psychology	76,671	567	0.7
Public administration and services	19,392	178	0.9
R.O.T.C. and military technologies	3	0	0.0
Social sciences and history	132,874	886	0.7
Theological studies, religious vocations	7,785	28	0.4
Transportation and material moving	4,020	29	0.7
Visual and performing arts	66,773	456	0.7
Not classified	264	0	0.0

Note: American Indians include Alaska Natives.
Source: National Center for Education Statistics, Digest of Education Statistics 2003, *Internet site http://nces.ed.gov//programs/digest/d03/list_tables.asp; calculations by New Strategist*

Table 1.6 Master's Degrees Earned by American Indians by Field of Study, 2001–02

(total number of master's degrees conferred and number and percent earned by American Indians, by field of study, 2001–02)

		earned by American Indians	
	total	number	percent
Total master's degrees	**482,118**	**2,626**	**0.5%**
Agriculture and natural resources	4,519	27	0.6
Architecture and related programs	4,566	14	0.3
Area, ethnic, and cultural studies	1,578	23	1.5
Biological and life sciences	6,205	35	0.6
Business	120,785	510	0.4
Communications	5,510	19	0.3
Communications technologies	549	2	0.4
Computer and information sciences	16,113	36	0.2
Construction trades	9	0	0.0
Education	136,579	955	0.7
Engineering	26,015	61	0.2
Engineering-related technologies	896	4	0.4
English language and literature, letters	7,268	43	0.6
Foreign languages and literatures	2,861	7	0.2
Health professions and related sciences	43,644	227	0.5
Home economics	2,616	22	0.8
Law and legal studies	4,053	11	0.3
Liberal arts and sciences, general studies, humanities	2,754	20	0.7
Library science	5,113	31	0.6
Mathematics	3,487	10	0.3
Multi- and interdisciplinary studies	3,211	24	0.7
Parks, recreation, leisure, and fitness	2,754	9	0.3
Philosophy and religion	1,334	4	0.3
Physical sciences	5,034	21	0.4
Precision production trades	2	0	0.0
Protective services	2,935	25	0.9
Psychology	14,888	111	0.7
Public administration and services	25,448	228	0.9
Social sciences and history	14,112	80	0.6
Theological studies, religious vocations	4,952	10	0.2
Transportation and material moving	709	3	0.4
Visual and performing arts	11,595	54	0.5
Not classified	24	0	0.0

Note: American Indians include Alaska Natives.
Source: National Center for Education Statistics, Digest of Education Statistics 2003, *Internet site http://nces.ed.gov//programs/digest/d03/list_tables.asp; calculations by New Strategist*

Table 1.7 Doctoral Degrees Earned by American Indians by Field of Study, 2001–02

(total number of doctoral degrees conferred and number and percent earned by American Indians, by field of study, 2001–02)

	total	earned by American Indians	
		number	percent
Total doctoral degrees	**44,160**	**180**	**0.4%**
Agriculture and natural resources	1,166	0	0.0
Architecture and related programs	183	0	0.0
Area, ethnic, and cultural studies	216	3	1.4
Biological and life sciences	4,489	14	0.3
Business	1,158	4	0.3
Communications	374	1	0.3
Communications technologies	9	0	0.0
Computer and information sciences	750	1	0.1
Education	6,967	54	0.8
Engineering	5,195	6	0.1
Engineering-related technologies	15	0	0.0
English language and literature, letters	1,446	10	0.7
Foreign languages and literatures	843	1	0.1
Health professions and related sciences	3,523	11	0.3
Home economics	355	0	0.0
Law and legal studies	79	1	1.3
Liberal arts and sciences, general studies, humanities	113	1	0.9
Library science	45	0	0.0
Mathematics	958	2	0.2
Multi- and interdisciplinary studies	384	3	0.8
Parks, recreation, leisure, and fitness	151	0	0.0
Philosophy and religion	606	1	0.2
Physical sciences	3,803	9	0.2
Protective services	49	0	0.0
Psychology	4,341	28	0.6
Public administration and services	571	2	0.4
Social sciences and history	3,902	19	0.5
Theological studies, religious vocations	1,355	4	0.3
Visual and performing arts	1,114	5	0.4

Note: American Indians include Alaska Natives.
Source: National Center for Education Statistics, Digest of Education Statistics 2003, *Internet site http://nces.ed.gov//programs/ digest/d03/list_tables.asp; calculations by New Strategist*

Table 1.8 First-Professional Degrees Earned by American Indians by Field of Study, 2001–02

(total number of first-professional degrees conferred and number and percent earned by American Indians, by field of study, 2001–02)

		earned by American Indians	
	total	number	percent
Total first-professional degrees	**80,698**	**581**	**0.7%**
Dentistry (D.D.S. or D.M.D.)	4,239	26	0.6
Medicine (M.D.)	15,237	123	0.8
Optometry (O.D.)	1,280	8	0.6
Osteopathic medicine (D.O.)	2,416	10	0.4
Pharmacy (Pharm.D.)	7,076	57	0.8
Podiatry (Pod.D., D.P., or D.P.M.)	474	7	1.5
Veterinary medicine (D.V.M.)	2,289	22	1.0
Chiropractic (D.C. or D.C.M.)	3,284	20	0.6
Naturopathic medicine	227	1	0.4
Law (LL.B. or J.D.)	38,981	299	0.8
Theology (M.Div., M.H.L., B.D., or Ord.)	5,195	8	0.2

Note: American Indians include Alaska Natives.
Source: National Center for Education Statistics, Digest of Education Statistics 2003, *Internet site http://nces.ed.gov//programs/ digest/d03/list_tables.asp; calculations by New Strategist*

The Health of American Indians Is below Average

Fewer than half of American Indians say their health is very good or excellent, far below the 62 percent of all Americans who rate their health highly. Twenty-three percent of American Indians say their health is only fair or poor, nearly double the 12 percent share among the population as a whole. Smoking may be one factor behind the poor health of American Indians. One in three smokes cigarettes. Most American Indians are overweight as well, with the proportion reaching 77 percent among men.

The 43,052 births to American Indian women in 2003 accounted for only 1 percent of all U.S. births. But American Indians, including Aleuts and Eskimos, account for 25 percent of births in Alaska, 17 percent in South Dakota, 13 percent in New Mexico, and 12 percent in Montana.

Twenty-four percent of American Indian adults have hypertension. Twenty-three percent have difficulties in physical functioning, with 13 percent saying they would find it very difficult or impossible to walk a quarter of a mile. Heart disease and cancer are the two leading causes of death among American Indians, but they account for only 37 percent of Indian deaths versus the 51 percent majority of deaths among all Americans. Accidents and diabetes are much more likely causes of death among American Indians than among the U.S. population as a whole.

■ Many of the health problems of American Indians are common in populations where poverty is widespread.

Fewer than half of American Indians say their health is very good or excellent

(percent distribution of American Indians aged 18 or older by self-reported health status, 2003)

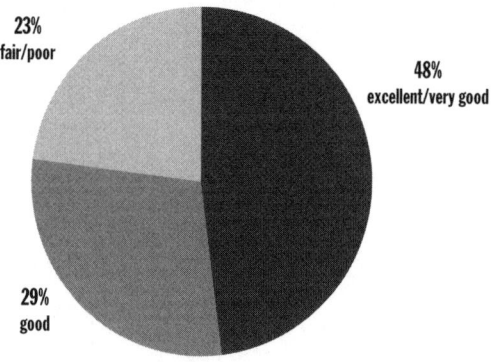

23%
fair/poor

48%
excellent/very good

29%
good

Table 1.9 American Indian Health Status, 2003

(percent distribution of total people and American Indians aged 18 or older by self-reported health status, and index of American Indian to total, 2003)

	total	American Indian	index of American Indian to total
Total people	**100.0%**	**100.0%**	–
Excellent/very good	62.3	47.7	77
Good	25.5	29.5	116
Fair/poor	12.2	22.8	187

Note: American Indians are those identifying themselves as being American Indian or Alaskan Native alone. (–) means not applicable. The index is calculated by dividing the American Indian figure by the total figure and multiplying by 100.
Source: National Center for Health Statistics, Summary Health Statistics for U.S. Adults: National Health Interview Survey, 2003, *Series 10, No. 225, 2005; Internet site http://www.cdc.gov/nchs/nhis.htm; calculations by New Strategist*

Table 1.10 Smoking and Drinking Status of American Indians by Sex, 1999–2003

(percent distribution of American Indians aged 18 or older by smoking and drinking status and sex, 1999–2003)

	total	men	women
SMOKING STATUS			
Total American Indians	100.0%	100.0%	100.0%
Never smoked	44.1	40.9	47.6
Former smoker	22.4	26.9	17.8
Current smoker	33.5	32.3	34.7
DRINKING STATUS			
Total American Indians	100.0	100.0	100.0
Lifetime abstainer	24.7	16.7	32.6
Former drinker	24.6	25.6	23.6
Current light or infrequent drinker	33.0	29.9	35.9
Current moderate or heavier drinker	17.6	27.8	8.0

Note: Never smoked means having had fewer than 100 cigarettes in lifetime. Former smokers have had 100 or more cigarettes in lifetime but did not smoke at time of interview. Current smokers have had at least 100 cigarettes in lifetime and currently smoke. Lifetime abstainers have had fewer than 12 drinks in lifetime. Former drinkers have had 12 or more drinks in lifetime, none in past year. Current light or infrequent drinkers have had 12 or more drinks in lifetime, drank alcohol in past year, and have 3 or fewer drinks per week on average. Current moderate or heavier drinkers drank 12 or more drinks in lifetime, drank alcohol in past year, and drank more than 3 drinks per week on average. American Indians are those identifying themselves as being American Indian or Alaskan Native alone.
Source: National Center for Health Statistics, Health Characteristics of the American Indian and Alaska Native Adult Population: United States, 1999–2003, *Advance Data, No. 356, 2005; Internet site http://www.cdc.gov/nchs/nhis.htm*

Table 1.11 Weight of American Indians by Sex, 1999–2003

(percent distribution of American Indians aged 18 or older by body weight status and sex, 1999–2003)

	total	men	women
Total American Indians	100.0%	100.0%	100.0%
Underweight	2.5	1.5	3.4
Healthy weight	30.4	21.5	39.1
Overweight, total	67.2	77.1	57.5
Overweight, but not obese	33.2	38.6	28.1
Obese	34.0	38.5	29.4

Note: Being overweight is defined as having a body mass index of 25 or higher. Being obese is defined as having a body mass index of 30 or higher. Body mass index is calculated by dividing weight in kilograms by height in meters squared. Data are based on measured height and weight of a sample of the civilian noninstitutionalized population. American Indians are those identifying themselves as being American Indian or Alaskan Native alone.
Source: National Center for Health Statistics, Health Characteristics of the American Indian and Alaska Native Adult Population: United States, 1999–2003, *Advance Data, No. 356, 2005; Internet site http://www.cdc.gov/nchs/nhis.htm*

Table 1.12 Births to American Indian Women by Age, 2003

(total number of births, number and percent distribution of births to American Indians, and American Indian share of total, by age, 2003)

		American Indian		
	total	number	percent distribution	share of total
Total births	**4,089,950**	**43,052**	**100.0%**	**1.1%**
Under age 15	6,661	154	0.4	2.3
Aged 15 to 19	414,580	7,690	17.9	1.9
Aged 20 to 24	1,032,305	14,645	34.0	1.4
Aged 25 to 29	1,086,366	10,524	24.4	1.0
Aged 30 to 34	975,546	6,423	14.9	0.7
Aged 35 to 39	467,642	2,906	6.7	0.6
Aged 40 to 44	101,005	666	1.5	0.7
Aged 45 to 54	5,845	44	0.1	0.8

Note: American Indians include Alaska Natives.
Source: National Center for Health Statistics, Births: Final Data for 2003, *National Vital Statistics Reports, Vol. 54, No. 2, 2005; Internet site http://www.cdc.gov/nchs/products/pubs/pubd/nvsr/54/54-pre.htm; calculations by New Strategist*

Table 1.13 Births to American Indian Women by Age and Marital Status, 2003

(total number of births to American Indians, number of births to unmarried American Indians, and unmarried share of total, by age, 2003)

		unmarried American Indians	
	total	number	share of total
Births to American Indians	**43,052**	**26,401**	**61.3%**
Under age 15	154	152	98.7
Aged 15 to 19	7,690	6,778	88.1
Aged 20 to 24	14,645	10,002	68.3
Aged 25 to 29	10,524	5,293	50.3
Aged 30 to 34	6,423	2,668	41.5
Aged 35 to 39	2,906	1,193	41.1
Aged 40 or older	710	315	44.4

Note: American Indians include Alaska Natives.
Source: National Center for Health Statistics, Births: Final Data for 2003, *National Vital Statistics Reports, Vol. 54, No. 2, 2005; Internet site http://www.cdc.gov/nchs/products/pubs/pubd/nvsr/54/54-pre.htm; calculations by New Strategist*

Table 1.14 Births to American Indian Women by Birth Order, 2003

(total number of births, number and percent distribution of births to American Indians, and American Indian share of total, by birth order, 2003)

		American Indian		
	total	number	percent distribution	share of total
Total births	**4,089,950**	**43,052**	**100.0%**	**1.1%**
First child	1,633,987	15,237	35.4	0.9
Second child	1,320,477	11,788	27.4	0.9
Third child	684,296	7,738	18.0	1.1
Fourth or later child	439,235	8,129	18.9	1.9

Note: American Indians include Alaska Natives. Numbers will not add to total because "not stated" is not shown.
Source: National Center for Health Statistics, Births: Final Data for 2003, National Vital Statistics Reports, Vol. 54, No. 2, 2005; Internet site http://www.cdc.gov/nchs/products/pubs/pubd/nvsr/54/54-pre.htm; calculations by New Strategist

Table 1.15 Births to American Indian Women by State, 2003

(total number of births, number and percent distribution of births to American Indians, and American Indian share of total, by state, 2003)

| | | American Indian births | | |
	total	number	percent distribution	share of total
Total births	**4,089,950**	**43,052**	**100.0%**	**1.1%**
Alabama	59,552	146	0.3	0.2
Alaska	10,086	2,477	5.8	24.6
Arizona	90,967	6,068	14.1	6.7
Arkansas	37,784	259	0.6	0.7
California	540,997	2,916	6.8	0.5
Colorado	69,339	564	1.3	0.8
Connecticut	42,873	262	0.6	0.6
Delaware	11,329	32	0.1	0.3
District of Columbia	7,619	5	0.0	0.1
Florida	212,250	1,088	2.5	0.5
Georgia	135,979	319	0.7	0.2
Hawaii	18,100	71	0.2	0.4
Idaho	21,800	369	0.9	1.7
Illinois	182,495	260	0.6	0.1
Indiana	86,434	136	0.3	0.2
Iowa	38,174	260	0.6	0.7
Kansas	39,476	480	1.1	1.2
Kentucky	55,236	101	0.2	0.2
Louisiana	65,040	403	0.9	0.6
Maine	13,855	99	0.2	0.7
Maryland	74,930	188	0.4	0.3
Massachusetts	80,184	184	0.4	0.2
Michigan	131,094	639	1.5	0.5
Minnesota	70,050	1,416	3.3	2.0
Mississippi	42,380	284	0.7	0.7
Missouri	77,045	366	0.9	0.5
Montana	11,422	1,400	3.3	12.3
Nebraska	25,917	470	1.1	1.8
Nevada	33,647	520	1.2	1.5
New Hampshire	14,393	35	0.1	0.2
New Jersey	116,983	188	0.4	0.2
New Mexico	27,821	3,603	8.4	13.0
New York	253,714	637	1.5	0.3
North Carolina	118,323	1,637	3.8	1.4
North Dakota	7,972	858	2.0	10.8
Ohio	149,679	298	0.7	0.2
Oklahoma	50,981	5,320	12.4	10.4
Oregon	45,953	867	2.0	1.9

(continued)

	total	American Indian		
		number	percent distribution	share of total
Pennsylvania	145,959	333	0.8%	0.2%
Rhode Island	13,209	163	0.4	1.2
South Carolina	55,649	152	0.4	0.3
South Dakota	11,027	1,875	4.4	17.0
Tennessee	78,890	180	0.4	0.2
Texas	377,476	902	2.1	0.2
Utah	49,860	617	1.4	1.2
Vermont	6,589	7	0.0	0.1
Virginia	101,254	178	0.4	0.2
Washington	80,489	2,051	4.8	2.5
West Virginia	20,935	25	0.1	0.1
Wisconsin	70,040	1,054	2.4	1.5
Wyoming	6,700	290	0.7	4.3

Note: American Indians include Alaska Natives.
Source: National Center for Health Statistics, Births: Final Data for 2003, National Vital Statistics Reports, Vol. 54, No. 2, 2005; Internet site http://www.cdc.gov/nchs/products/pubs/pubd/nvsr/54/54-pre.htm; calculations by New Strategist

Table 1.16 Health Conditions among American Indians Aged 18 or Older, 2003

(number of total people and American Indians aged 18 or older with selected health conditions, percent of American Indians with condition, and American Indian share of total with condition, 2003; numbers in thousands)

	total	American Indian number	American Indian percent with condition	American Indian share of total
Total people	**213,042**	**1,285**	–	**0.6%**
Selected circulatory diseases				
Heart disease, all types	23,536	171	13.8%	0.7
Coronary	12,254	89	8.2	0.7
Hypertension	45,927	271	23.9	0.6
Stroke	5,070	21	3.1	0.4
Selected respiratory conditions				
Emphysema	3,115	14	1.1	0.4
Asthma				
Ever	20,697	161	12.4	0.8
Still	13,623	109	8.0	0.8
Hay fever	18,356	112	9.4	0.6
Sinusitis	29,673	177	15.1	0.6
Chronic bronchitis	8,560	72	5.2	0.8
Cancer				
Any cancer	13,973	49	5.7	0.4
Breast cancer (all adults)	2,426	14	1.1	0.6
Cervical cancer (women only)	1,082	3	0.4	0.3
Prostate cancer (men only)	1,332	–	–	–
Other selected diseases and conditions				
Diabetes	14,012	146	12.2	1.0
Ulcers	14,456	144	12.0	1.0
Kidney disease	3,017	38	2.7	1.3
Liver disease	2,511	38	2.4	1.5
Arthritis	45,793	332	30.8	0.7
Chronic joint symptoms	57,242	453	38.1	0.8
Migraines or severe headaches	32,268	380	29.2	1.2
Pain in neck	31,368	226	17.8	0.7
Pain in lower back	58,430	415	32.4	0.7
Pain in face or jaw	9,464	94	7.3	1.0
Selected sensory problems				
Hearing	32,533	137	14.2	0.4
Vision	18,628	190	18.5	1.0
Absence of all natural teeth	15,927	80	10.1	0.5

Note: The conditions shown are those that have ever been diagnosed by a doctor, except as noted. Hay fever, sinusitis, and chronic bronchitis have been diagnosed in the past twelve months. Kidney and liver disease have been diagnosed in the past twelve months and exclude kidney stones, bladder infections, and incontinence. Chronic joint symptoms are shown if respondent had pain, aching, or stiffness in or around a joint (excluding back and neck) and the condition began more than three months ago. Migraines, pain in neck, lower back, face, or jaw are shown only if pain lasted a whole day or more. American Indians are those identifying themselves as being American Indian or Alaskan Native alone. (–) means not applicable or sample is too small to make a reliable estimate.
Source: National Center for Health Statistics, Summary Health Statistics for U.S. Adults: National Health Interview Survey, 2003, *Series 10, No. 225, 2005; Internet site http://www.cdc.gov/nchs/nhis.htm; calculations by New Strategist*

Table 1.17 Health Conditions among American Indian Children, 2003

(number of total people and American Indians under age 18 with selected health conditions, percent of American Indians with condition, and American Indian share of total, 2003; numbers in thousands)

| | total | American Indian | | |
		number	percent with condition	share of total
Total children	**72,973**	**734**	–	**1.0%**
Diagnosed with asthma	9,071	148	20.7%	1.6
Experienced in last 12 months				
Asthma attack	3,975	64	8.9	1.6
Hay fever	7,059	52	7.8	0.7
Respiratory allergies	8,347	94	13.7	1.1
Other allergies	8,407	118	14.8	1.4
Ever told had*				
Learning disability	4,561	51	8.1	1.1
Attention deficit hyperactivity disorder	3,881	83	11.8	2.1
Prescription medication taken regularly for at least 3 months	9,287	103	14.2	1.1

* "Ever told" by a school representative or health professional. Data exclude children under age 3.
Note: Other allergies include food or digestive allergies, eczema, and other skin allergies. American Indians are those identifying themselves as being American Indian or Alaskan Native alone. (–) means not applicable.
Source: National Center for Health Statistics, Summary Health Statistics for U.S. Children: National Health Interview Survey, *2003, Series 10, No. 223, 2005; Internet site http://www.cdc.gov/nchs/nhis.htm; calculations by New Strategist*

Table 1.18 Physician Office Visits by American Indians, 2002

(number of total physician office visits and number of visits by American Indians, American Indian share of total, and average number of visits by American Indians per person per year, 2002)

| | total (000s) | visits by American Indians | | |
		number (000s)	share of total	per person per year
Total visits	889,980	2,237	0.3%	0.8

Source: National Center for Health Statistics, National Ambulatory Medical Care Survey: 2002 Summary, Advance Data No. 346, *2004; Internet site http://www.cdc.gov/nchs/about/major/ahcd/adata.htm; calculations by New Strategist*

Table 1.19 Difficulties in Physical Functioning among American Indians, 2003

(number of total people and American Indians aged 18 or older with difficulties in physical functioning, percent of American Indians with difficulty, and American Indian share of total, by type of difficulty, 2003; numbers in thousands)

		American Indian		
	total	number	percent with difficulty	share of total
TOTAL PEOPLE	**213,042**	**1,285**	–	**0.6%**
Total with any physical difficulty	**31,322**	**244**	**23.4%**	**0.8**
Walk quarter of a mile	14,910	130	13.0	0.9
Climb up ten steps without resting	11,107	105	13.1	0.9
Stand for two hours	18,663	153	16.6	0.8
Sit for two hours	7,211	62	5.6	0.9
Stoop, bend, or kneel	18,250	175	16.8	1.0
Reach over head	6,264	40	4.4	0.6
Grasp or handle small objects	3,943	45	3.6	1.1
Lift or carry ten pounds	9,194	42	3.7	0.5
Push or pull large objects	13,463	79	8.1	0.6

Note: Respondents were classified as having difficulties if they responded "very difficult" or "can't do at all." American Indians are those identifying themselves as being American Indian or Alaskan Native alone.
Source: National Center for Health Statistics, Summary Health Statistics for U.S. Adults: National Health Interview Survey, 2003, Series 10, No. 225, 2005; Internet site http://www.cdc.gov/nchs/nhis.htm; calculations by New Strategist

Table 1.20 AIDS Cases among American Indians, through December 2003

(total number of AIDS cases diagnosed, number and percent distribution of AIDS cases diagnosed among American Indians, and American Indian share of total, by sex and age at diagnosis, through December 2003)

		American Indian		
	total	number	percent distribution	share of total
Total AIDS cases	**874,230**	**2,946**	**100.0%**	**0.3%**
Males aged 13 or older	708,452	2,353	79.9	0.3
Females aged 13 or older	156,837	562	19.1	0.4
Children under age 13	8,939	31	1.1	0.3

Source: National Center for Health Statistics, Health, United States, 2004; Internet site http://www.cdc.gov/nchs/hus.htm; calculations by New Strategist

Table 1.21 Leading Causes of Death among American Indians, 2002

(number and percent distribution of deaths to American Indians accounted for by the ten leading causes of death among American Indians, 2002)

	number	percent distribution
Total American Indian deaths	**12,415**	**100.0%**
1. Diseases of the heart (1)	2,467	19.9
2. Malignant neoplasms (cancer) (2)	2,175	17.5
3. Accidents (unintentional injuries) (5)	1,488	12.0
4. Diabetes mellitus (6)	744	6.0
5. Cerebrovascular diseases (3)	567	4.6
6. Chronic liver disease and cirrhosis (12)	547	4.4
7. Chronic lower respiratory disease (4)	452	3.6
8. Suicide (11)	324	2.6
9. Influenza and pneumonia (7)	293	2.4
10. Homicide (14)	267	2.2
All other causes	3,091	24.9

Note: Number in parentheses shows rank for all Americans if the cause of death is among top fifteen. American Indians include Alaska Natives.
Source: National Center for Health Statistics, Health, United States, 2004; Internet site http://www.cdc.gov/nchs/hus.htm; calculations by New Strategist

Most American Indian Households in the South and West Own Their Home

The 56 percent majority of American Indian households were homeowners in 2004. Although the homeownership rate among American Indians is well below the 69 percent for all households, it is higher than the homeownership rate of blacks or Hispanics. By region, the homeownership rate is highest for American Indians in the South and West, at 59 percent.

Sixty-four percent of American Indian households live in single-family houses, a slightly smaller share than the 68 percent of all households in such housing. Fourteen percent of American Indians live in mobile homes, double the 7 percent share among all households.

■ The low income of American Indian households makes it difficult for many to afford a home.

American Indian homeownership is lowest in the Midwest

(percent of American Indian households that own their home, by region, 2003)

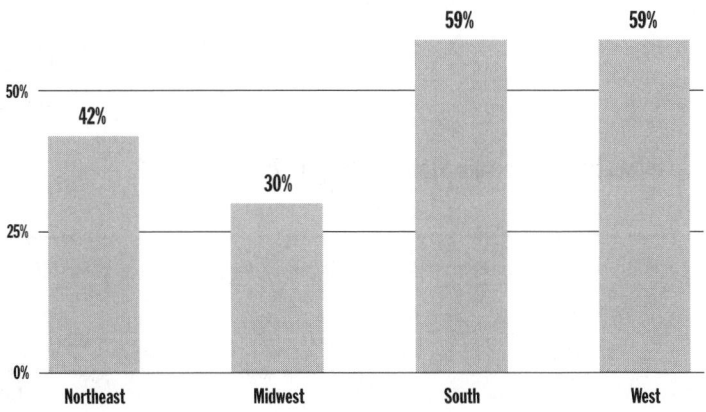

Table 1.22 American Indian Homeownership Rate, 1994 to 2004

(homeownership rate of total and American Indian households and index of American Indian to total, 1994 to 2004; percentage point change in homeownership rate, 1994–2004)

	total households	American Indian households	index
2004	69.0%	55.6%	81
2003	68.3	54.3	80
2002	67.9	54.6	80
2001	67.8	55.4	82
2000	67.4	56.2	83
1999	66.8	56.1	84
1998	66.3	54.3	82
1997	65.7	51.7	79
1996	65.4	51.6	79
1995	64.7	55.8	86
1994	64.0	51.7	81
Percentage point change			
1994 to 2004	5.0	3.9	–

Note: American Indians are those identifying themselves as being of the race alone. The index is calculated by dividing the American Indian homeownership rate by the total rate and multiplying by 100. (–) means not applicable.
Source: Bureau of the Census, American Housing Survey for the United States: 2003, Current Housing Reports, *Internet site http://www.census.gov/hhes/www/ahs.html; calculations by New Strategist*

Table 1.23 American Indian Homeownership Status by Region, 2003

(number and percent of American Indian households by homeownership status and region, 2003; numbers in thousands)

	total	owners		renters	
		number	share of total	number	share of total
Total American Indian households	**664**	**341**	**51.4%**	**322**	**48.5%**
Northeast	65	27	41.5	38	58.5
Midwest	128	38	29.7	90	70.3
South	145	85	58.6	59	40.7
West	326	191	58.6	135	41.4

Note: American Indians include only those identifying themselves as being American Indian alone.
Source: Bureau of the Census, American Housing Survey for the United States: 2003, Current Housing Reports, *Internet site http://www.census.gov/hhes/www/ahs.html; calculations by New Strategist*

Table 1.24 American Indian Homeowners by Region, 2003

(number of total homeowners, number and percent distribution of American Indian homeowners, and American Indian share of total, by region, 2003; numbers in thousands)

| | | American Indian | | |
	total	number	percent distribution	share of total
Total homeowners	**72,238**	**341**	**100.0%**	**0.5%**
Northeast	12,964	27	7.9	0.2
Midwest	17,889	38	11.1	0.2
South	26,699	85	24.9	0.3
West	14,686	191	56.0	1.3

Note: American Indians include only those identifying themselves as being American Indian alone.
Source: Bureau of the Census, American Housing Survey for the United States: 2003, *Current Housing Reports, Internet site http://www.census.gov/hhes/www/ahs.html; calculations by New Strategist*

Table 1.25 Housing Units Occupied by American Indians by Type, 2003

(number of total occupied housing units, number and percent distribution of housing units occupied by American Indians, and American Indian share of total, by number of units in structure, 2003)

| | | American Indians | | |
	total	number	percent distribution	share of total
Total occupied housing units	**108,419,506**	**784,088**	**100.0%**	**0.7%**
One unit, detached or attached	73,740,642	501,147	63.9	0.7
Two to four units	9,374,261	64,644	8.2	0.7
Five or more units	18,089,052	107,303	13.7	0.6
Mobile home	7,128,265	109,573	14.0	1.5
Boat, RV, van, etc.	87,286	1,421	0.2	1.6

Note: American Indians include only those identifying themselves as being American Indian alone.
Source: Bureau of the Census, 2003 American Community Survey, Internet site http://factfinder.census.gov/servlet/ DatasetMainPageServlet?_program=ACS&_lang=en&_ts=; calculations by New Strategist

American Indians Have Below-Average Incomes

The median annual income of the nation's 784,088 American Indian households stood at $31,121 in 2003, according to the American Community Survey. This figure is well below the $43,564 median income of all households, but higher than the median income of black households and only slightly below the median income of Hispanic households.

American Indian household income peaks among householders aged 45 to 64, at $37,947. American Indian men who work full-time had median earnings of $31,102 in 2003—23 percent below the median of all men who work full-time. American Indian women who work full-time had median earnings of $25,773, an amount 16 percent below the median for all women who work full-time.

The 11 percent poverty rate for American Indian married couples is greater than the rate among black couples but below the rate among Hispanic couples. American Indian female-headed families are more likely to be poor (41 percent) than black or Hispanic female-headed families.

■ American Indian households have below-average incomes because a relatively small share are headed by married couples, the most affluent household type.

The median income of American Indian households is only 71 percent as high as the national median

(median income of total and American Indian households, 2003)

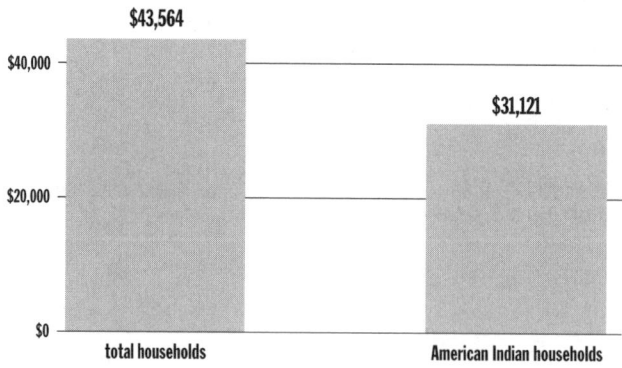

Table 1.26 American Indian Household Income, 2003

(number of total households, number and percent distribution of American Indian households, and American Indian share of total, by household income, 2003)

		American Indian		
	total	number	percent distribution	share of total
Total households	108,419,506	784,088	100.0%	0.7%
Under $10,000	9,764,122	127,600	16.3	1.3
$10,000 to $19,999	13,680,405	126,094	16.1	0.9
$20,000 to $29,999	13,656,404	120,803	15.4	0.9
$30,000 to $39,999	12,617,755	105,190	13.4	0.8
$40,000 to $49,999	11,034,151	83,984	10.7	0.8
$50,000 to $59,999	9,413,849	54,427	6.9	0.6
$60,000 to $74,999	11,291,267	62,610	8.0	0.6
$75,000 to $99,999	11,784,523	51,191	6.5	0.4
$100,000 or more	15,177,030	52,189	6.7	0.3
Median income	$43,564	$31,121	–	–

Note: American Indians include Alaska Natives. The American Indian and Alaska Native population includes only those identifying themselves as being American Indian or Alaska Native alone and no other race. (–) means not applicable.
Source: Bureau of the Census, 2003 American Community Survey, Internet site http://factfinder.census.gov/servlet/ DatasetMainPageServlet?_program=ACS&_lang=en&_ts=; calculations by New Strategist

Table 1.27 High-Income American Indian Households, 2003

(number and percent distribution of American Indian households with incomes of $100,000 or more, 2003)

	number	percent distribution
TOTAL AMERICAN INDIAN HOUSEHOLDS	**784,088**	**100.0%**
$100,000 or more	**52,189**	**6.7**
$100,000 to $149,999	39,647	5.1
$150,000 to $199,999	7,545	1.0
$200,000 or more	4,997	0.6

Note: American Indians include Alaska Natives. The American Indian and Alaska Native population includes only those identifying themselves as being American Indian or Alaska Native alone and no other race.
Source: Bureau of the Census, 2003 American Community Survey, Internet site http://factfinder.census.gov/servlet/ DatasetMainPageServlet?_program=ACS&_lang=en&_ts=; calculations by New Strategist

Table 1.28 American Indian Household Income by Age of Householder, 2003

(number and percent distribution of American Indian households by household income and age of householder, 2003)

	total	under 25	25 to 44	45 to 64	65 or older
Total American Indian households	**784,088**	**56,977**	**340,312**	**289,911**	**96,888**
Under $10,000	127,600	13,857	46,846	45,000	21,897
$10,000 to $19,999	126,094	13,390	51,269	33,650	27,785
$20,000 to $29,999	120,803	12,050	56,138	37,005	15,610
$30,000 to $39,999	105,190	7,252	50,396	36,868	10,674
$40,000 to $49,999	83,984	5,921	37,443	33,232	7,388
$50,000 to $59,999	54,427	2,034	26,002	23,530	2,861
$60,000 to $74,999	62,610	1,526	27,814	29,311	3,959
$75,000 to $99,999	51,191	709	21,694	24,901	3,887
$100,000 or more	52,189	238	22,710	26,414	2,827
Median income	$31,121	$21,030	$33,156	$37,947	$19,554

PERCENT DISTRIBUTION BY INCOME

	total	under 25	25 to 44	45 to 64	65 or older
Total American Indian households	100.0%	100.0%	100.0%	100.0%	100.0%
Under $10,000	16.3	24.3	13.8	15.5	22.6
$10,000 to $19,999	16.1	23.5	15.1	11.6	28.7
$20,000 to $29,999	15.4	21.1	16.5	12.8	16.1
$30,000 to $39,999	13.4	12.7	14.8	12.7	11.0
$40,000 to $49,999	10.7	10.4	11.0	11.5	7.6
$50,000 to $59,999	6.9	3.6	7.6	8.1	3.0
$60,000 to $74,999	8.0	2.7	8.2	10.1	4.1
$75,000 to $99,999	6.5	1.2	6.4	8.6	4.0
$100,000 or more	6.7	0.4	6.7	9.1	2.9

Note: American Indians include Alaska Natives. The American Indian and Alaska Native population includes only those identifying themselves as being American Indian or Alaska Native alone and no other race.
Source: Bureau of the Census, 2003 American Community Survey, Internet site http://factfinder.census.gov/servlet/DatasetMainPageServlet?_program=ACS&_lang=en&_ts=; calculations by New Strategist

Table 1.29 Earnings of American Indians Working Full-Time by Sex, 2003

(number and percent distribution of American Indians aged 16 or older working full-time, year-round by earnings, median earnings, and percent working full-time, by sex, 2003)

	men	women
Total American Indians working full-time	**323,998**	**239,656**
Under $10,000	9,868	8,239
$10,000 to $19,999	58,106	63,989
$20,000 to $29,999	80,661	72,141
$30,000 to $39,999	63,721	42,455
$40,000 to $49,999	42,270	25,903
$50,000 to $64,999	30,255	15,218
$65,000 to $74,999	10,846	6,205
$75,000 to $99,999	18,296	3,974
$100,000 or more	9,975	1,532
Median earnings	$31,102	$25,773
Percent working full-time	41.3%	29.2%
Total American Indians working full-time	**100.0%**	**100.0%**
Under $10,000	3.0	3.4
$10,000 to $19,999	17.9	26.7
$20,000 to $29,999	24.9	30.1
$30,000 to $39,999	19.7	17.7
$40,000 to $49,999	13.0	10.8
$50,000 to $64,999	9.3	6.3
$65,000 to $74,999	3.3	2.6
$75,000 to $99,999	5.6	1.7
$100,000 or more	3.1	0.6

Note: American Indians include Alaska Natives. The American Indian and Alaska Native population includes only those identifying themselves as being American Indian or Alaska Native alone and no other race.
Source: Bureau of the Census, 2003 American Community Survey, Internet site http://factfinder.census.gov/servlet/ DatasetMainPageServlet?_program=ACS&_lang=en&_ts=; calculations by New Strategist

Table 1.30 Earnings of Total People and American Indians, 2003

(median earnings of total people and American Indians aged 16 or older by sex and work status, and index of American Indian earnings to total, 2003)

	total	American Indian	index of American Indian earnings to total
Total people aged 16 or older	**$26,236**	**$20,418**	**78**
Men	31,570	23,615	75
Worked full-time, year-round	40,556	31,102	77
Women	21,139	16,738	79
Worked full-time, year-round	30,599	25,773	84

Note: American Indians include Alaska Natives. The American Indian and Alaska Native population includes only those identifying themselves as being American Indian or Alaska Native alone and no other race.
Source: Bureau of the Census, 2003 American Community Survey, Internet site http://factfinder.census.gov/servlet/ DatasetMainPageServlet?_program=ACS&_lang=en&_ts=; calculations by New Strategist

Table 1.31 American Indian Families in Poverty, 2003

(number and percent of American Indian families in poverty by family type and presence of children under age 18 at home, 2003)

	total	with children	without children
Number in poverty			
Married couples	36,455	25,124	11,331
Female householder, no spouse present	64,798	59,465	5,333
Male householder, no spouse present	10,760	8,743	2,017
Percent in poverty			
Married couples	10.9%	13.7%	7.5%
Female householder, no spouse present	40.8	48.0	15.3
Male householder, no spouse present	19.4	21.8	13.2

Note: American Indians include Alaska Natives. The American Indian and Alaska Native population includes only those identifying themselves as being American Indian or Alaska Native alone and no other race.
Source: Bureau of the Census, 2003 American Community Survey, Internet site http://factfinder.census.gov/servlet/ DatasetMainPageServlet?_program=ACS&_lang=en&_ts=

Table 1.32 Poverty Status of American Indians by Sex and Age, 2003

(total number of American Indians, and number and percent below poverty level by sex and age, 2003)

	total	in poverty number	in poverty percent
Total American Indians	**2,160,974**	**529,701**	**24.5%**
Under age 18	636,836	200,705	31.5
Aged 18 to 24	235,195	67,187	28.6
Aged 25 to 34	306,876	75,944	24.7
Aged 35 to 44	349,774	67,751	19.4
Aged 45 to 54	304,800	49,922	16.4
Aged 55 to 64	174,933	34,299	19.6
Aged 65 or older	152,560	33,893	22.2
American Indian females	**1,099,555**	**286,941**	**26.1**
Under age 18	323,077	100,392	31.1
Aged 18 to 24	118,185	38,149	32.3
Aged 25 to 34	145,048	42,395	29.2
Aged 35 to 44	185,205	40,584	21.9
Aged 45 to 54	153,468	27,291	17.8
Aged 55 to 64	90,581	17,454	19.3
Aged 65 or older	83,991	20,676	24.6
American Indian males	**1,061,419**	**242,760**	**22.9**
Under age 18	313,759	100,313	32.0
Aged 18 to 24	117,010	29,038	24.8
Aged 25 to 34	161,828	33,549	20.7
Aged 35 to 44	164,569	27,167	16.5
Aged 45 to 54	151,332	22,631	15.0
Aged 55 to 64	84,352	16,845	20.0
Aged 65 or older	68,569	13,217	19.3

Note: American Indians include Alaska Natives. The American Indian and Alaska Native population includes only those identifying themselves as being American Indian or Alaska Native alone and no other race.
Source: Bureau of the Census, 2003 American Community Survey, Internet site http://factfinder.census.gov/servlet/ DatasetMainPageServlet?_program=ACS&_lang=en&_ts=

Twenty-Six Percent of American Indian Workers Are Managers or Professionals

The 1 million American Indians in the labor force account for fewer than 1 percent of the nation's workers. American Indians are less likely than the average worker to be employed as managers or professionals (26 versus 35 percent) and more likely to be employed as service workers (21 versus 16 percent).

Overall, 66 percent of American Indian men were in the labor force in 2003, less than the labor force participation rate for all men. Fifty-nine percent of American Indian women are in the labor force, about the same rate as among all women.

■ American Indians are less educated than the average American and more likely to be employed in service occupations, accounting for their below-average incomes.

The labor force participation rate of American Indian men and women is nearly equal

(percent of American Indians aged 16 or older in the labor force, by sex, 2003)

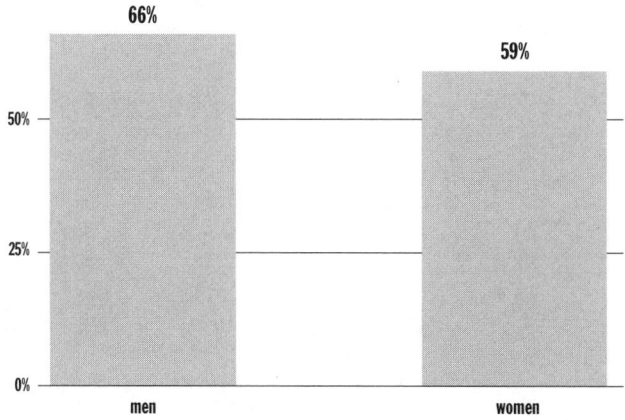

Table 1.33 Employment Status of American Indians by Sex and Age, 2003

(total number of American Indians aged 16 or older, and number in the armed forces and civilian labor force by sex, age, and employment status, 2003)

	total	armed forces	civilian labor force total	percent of population	employed	unemployed number	unemployed percent of labor force
Total American Indians	**1,604,668**	**3,187**	**1,001,742**	**62.4%**	**859,420**	**142,322**	**14.2%**
Aged 16 to 19	151,146	0	58,161	38.5	36,694	21,467	36.9
Aged 20 to 24	164,579	1,598	109,818	66.7	88,114	21,704	19.8
Aged 25 to 54	961,450	1,589	724,130	75.3	634,917	89,213	12.3
Aged 55 to 64	174,933	0	88,840	50.8	81,779	7,061	7.9
Aged 65 or older	152,560	0	20,793	13.6	17,916	2,877	13.8
Aged 65 to 69	56,286	0	15,257	27.1	13,388	1,869	12.3
Aged 70 or older	96,274	0	5,536	5.8	4,528	1,008	18.2
Total American Indian men	**784,930**	**2,876**	**520,644**	**66.3**	**449,936**	**70,708**	**13.6**
Aged 16 to 19	73,936	0	29,596	40.0	19,164	10,432	35.2
Aged 20 to 24	80,344	1,287	56,359	70.1	45,734	10,625	18.9
Aged 25 to 54	477,729	1,589	376,291	78.8	332,463	43,828	11.6
Aged 55 to 64	84,352	0	47,260	56.0	43,059	4,201	8.9
Aged 65 or older	68,569	0	11,138	16.2	9,516	1,622	14.6
Aged 65 to 69	26,922	0	7,464	27.7	6,620	844	11.3
Aged 70 or older	41,647	0	3,674	8.8	2,896	778	21.2
Total American Indian women	**819,738**	**311**	**481,098**	**58.7**	**409,484**	**71,614**	**14.9**
Aged 16 to 19	77,210	0	28,565	37.0	17,530	11,035	38.6
Aged 20 to 24	84,235	311	53,459	63.5	42,380	11,079	20.7
Aged 25 to 54	483,721	0	347,839	71.9	302,454	45,385	13.0
Aged 55 to 64	90,581	0	41,580	45.9	38,720	2,860	6.9
Aged 65 or older	83,991	0	9,655	11.5	8,400	1,255	13.0
Aged 65 to 69	29,364	0	7,793	26.5	6,768	1,025	13.2
Aged 70 or older	54,627	0	1,862	3.4	1,632	230	12.4

Note: American Indians include Alaska Natives. The American Indian and Alaska Native population includes only those identifying themselves as being American Indian or Alaska Native alone and no other race. The civilian labor force equals the number employed plus the number unemployed.
Source: Bureau of the Census, 2003 American Community Survey, Internet site http://factfinder.census.gov/servlet/DatasetMainPageServlet?_program=ACS&_lang=en&_ts=

Table 1.34 American Indian Workers by Occupation, 2003

(total number of employed persons aged 16 or older in the civilian labor force, number and percent distribution of employed American Indians, and American Indian share of total, by occupation, 2003)

	total	American Indian		
		number	percent distribution	share of total
TOTAL EMPLOYED	**132,422,387**	**859,420**	**100.0%**	**0.6%**
Management, professional and related occupations	**45,215,214**	**224,807**	**26.2**	**0.5**
Management, business, and financial operations	18,194,723	82,386	9.6	0.5
Management occupations	12,595,206	58,712	6.8	0.5
Business and financial operations occupations	5,599,517	23,674	2.8	0.4
Professional and related occupations	27,020,491	142,421	16.6	0.5
Computer and mathematical occupations	3,091,652	9,519	1.1	0.3
Architecture and engineering occupations	2,664,636	11,084	1.3	0.4
Life, physical, and social science occupations	1,242,804	6,815	0.8	0.5
Community and social services occupations	2,059,877	18,261	2.1	0.9
Legal occupations	1,495,941	6,077	0.7	0.4
Education, training, and library occupations	7,517,709	47,415	5.5	0.6
Arts, design, entertainment, sports, media occupations	2,444,564	11,658	1.4	0.5
Health care practitioner and technical occupations	6,503,308	31,592	3.7	0.5
Service occupations	**21,351,389**	**181,346**	**21.1**	**0.8**
Health care support occupations	2,909,926	25,103	2.9	0.9
Protective service occupations	2,823,344	23,447	2.7	0.8
Food preparation and serving-related occupations	6,754,655	54,679	6.4	0.8
Building and grounds cleaning and maintenance occupations	4,886,978	42,987	5.0	0.9
Personal care and service occupations	3,976,486	35,130	4.1	0.9
Sales and office occupations	**34,752,972**	**195,594**	**22.8**	**0.6**
Sales and related occupations	15,052,168	78,395	9.1	0.5
Office and administrative support occupations	19,700,804	117,199	13.6	0.6
Natural resources, construction, maintenance occupations	**13,548,558**	**120,169**	**14.0**	**0.9**
Farming, fishing, and forestry occupations	935,847	9,330	1.1	1.0
Construction and extraction occupations	7,827,872	72,848	8.5	0.9
Installation, maintenance, and repair occupations	4,784,839	37,991	4.4	0.8
Production, transportation, material-moving occupations	**17,554,254**	**137,504**	**16.0**	**0.8**
Production occupations	9,513,007	71,486	8.3	0.8
Transportation and material moving occupations	8,041,247	66,018	7.7	0.8

Note: American Indians include Alaska Natives. The American Indian and Alaska Native population includes only those identifying themselves as being American Indian or Alaska Native alone and no other race.
Source: Bureau of the Census, 2003 American Community Survey, Internet site http://factfinder.census.gov/servlet/ DatasetMainPageServlet?_program=ACS&_lang=en&_ts=; calculations by New Strategist

Married Couples Head Fewer than Half of American Indian Households

Married couples account for only 43 percent of households headed by American Indians, according to the Census Bureau's 2003 American Community Survey. Among all households, married couples account for a larger 52 percent share.

Female-headed families are a substantial 20 percent of American Indian households, a much larger share than the 13 percent of households nationwide. Single-person households account for a smaller share of American Indian households (23 percent) than nationally (27 percent).

Thirty-nine percent of American Indian households include children under age 18. Among American Indian married couples, a 49 percent minority includes children. The majority of female- and male-headed families have children at home.

Forty-three percent of American Indian men are currently married and living with their spouse. Among American Indian women, the figure is 40 percent. Twelve percent of American Indian men and 15 percent of American Indian women are currently divorced.

■ The large share of families headed by women without a spouse results in lower incomes and higher poverty rates for American Indians.

One in five American Indian households is headed by a woman without a spouse

(percent distribution of American Indian households, by household type, 2003)

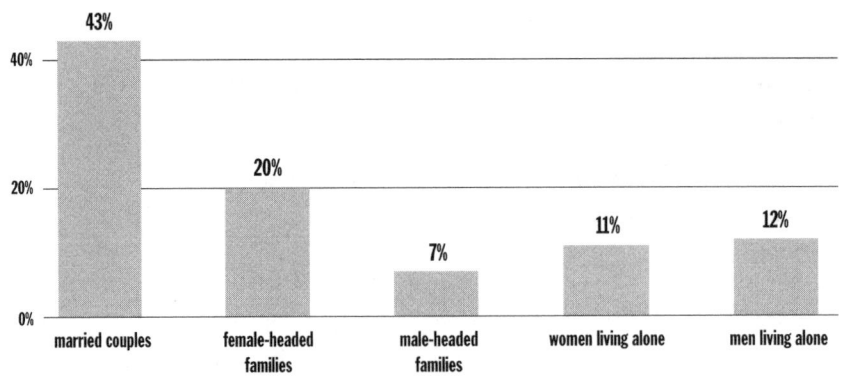

Table 1.35 American Indian Households by Age of Householder, 2003

(number of total households, number and percent distribution of American Indian households, and American Indian share of total, by age of householder, 2003)

		American Indian		
	total	number	percent distribution	share of total
Total households	**108,419,506**	**784,088**	**100.0%**	**0.7%**
Under age 25	6,123,495	56,977	7.3	0.9
Aged 25 to 34	18,543,279	146,653	18.7	0.8
Aged 35 to 44	23,330,304	193,659	24.7	0.8
Aged 45 to 54	22,627,454	173,533	22.1	0.8
Aged 55 to 64	15,926,480	116,378	14.8	0.7
Aged 65 or older	21,868,494	96,888	12.4	0.4
Average household size	2.61	2.93	–	–

Note: American Indians include Alaska Natives. The American Indian and Alaska Native population includes only those identifying themselves as being American Indian or Alaska Native alone and no other race. (–) means not applicable.
Source: Bureau of the Census, 2003 American Community Survey, Internet site http://factfinder.census.gov/servlet/ DatasetMainPageServlet?_program=ACS&_lang=en&_ts=; calculations by New Strategist

Table 1.36 American Indian Households by Household Type, 2004

(number of total households, number and percent distribution of American Indian households, and American Indian share of total, by type, 2003)

		American Indian		
	total	number	percent distribution	share of total
TOTAL HOUSEHOLDS	**108,419,506**	**784,088**	**100.0%**	**0.7%**
Family households	**73,057,960**	**549,299**	**70.1**	**0.8**
Married couples	54,688,008	335,320	42.8	0.6
Female householder, no spouse present	13,632,172	158,640	20.2	1.2
Male householder, no spouse present	4,737,780	55,339	7.1	1.2
Nonfamily households	**35,361,546**	**234,789**	**29.9**	**0.7**
Female householder	19,081,048	101,621	13.0	0.5
Living alone	16,405,202	83,731	10.7	0.5
Male householder	16,280,498	133,168	17.0	0.8
Living alone	12,684,814	97,774	12.5	0.8

Note: American Indians include Alaska Natives. The American Indian and Alaska Native population includes only those identifying themselves as being American Indian or Alaska Native alone and no other race.
Source: Bureau of the Census, 2003 American Community Survey, Internet site http://factfinder.census.gov/servlet/ DatasetMainPageServlet?_program=ACS&_lang=en&_ts=; calculations by New Strategist

Table 1.37 American Indian Households by Type of Household and Presence of Children, 2003

(number and percent distribution of American Indian households by type of household and presence of own children under age 18, 2003)

	number	percent distribution
TOTAL AMERICAN INDIAN HOUSEHOLDS	**784,088**	**100.0%**
American Indian households with children	**302,249**	**38.5**
Married couples	**335,320**	**100.0**
With children under age 18	164,728	49.1
Without children under age 18	170,592	50.9
Female householder, no spouse present	**158,640**	**100.0**
With children under age 18	105,025	66.2
Without children under age 18	53,615	33.8
Male householder, no spouse present	**55,339**	**100.0**
With children under age 18	32,496	58.7
Without children under age 18	22,843	41.3

Note: American Indians include Alaska Natives. The American Indian and Alaska Native population includes only those identifying themselves as being American Indian or Alaska Native alone and no other race.
Source: Bureau of the Census, 2003 American Community Survey, Internet site http://factfinder.census.gov/servlet/ DatasetMainPageServlet?_program=ACS&_lang=en&_ts=; calculations by New Strategist

Table 1.38 **American Indians by Living Arrangement, 2003**

(number and percent distribution of American Indians by living arrangement, 2003)

	number	percent distribution
Total American Indians	**2,173,834**	**100.0%**
In family household	**1,864,634**	**85.8**
Householder	570,440	26.2
Female	285,713	13.1
Male	284,727	13.1
Spouse	321,508	14.8
Child	698,846	32.1
Grandchild	88,158	4.1
Brother or sister	30,655	1.4
Parent	14,188	0.7
Other relative	63,710	2.9
Nonrelative	77,129	3.5
In nonfamily household	**309,200**	**14.2**
Householder	241,178	11.1
Living alone	186,123	8.6
Female	85,971	4.0
Male	100,152	4.6
Not living alone	55,055	2.5
Female	18,497	0.9
Male	36,558	1.7
Nonrelatives	68,022	3.1

Note: American Indians include Alaska Natives. The American Indian and Alaska Native population includes only those identifying themselves as being American Indian or Alaska Native alone and no other race.
Source: Bureau of the Census, 2003 American Community Survey, Internet site http://factfinder.census.gov/servlet/ DatasetMainPageServlet?_program=ACS&_lang=en&_ts=; calculations by New Strategist

Table 1.39 Marital Status of American Indians by Sex, 2003

(number and percent distribution of American Indians aged 15 or older by current marital status and sex, 2003)

	men		women	
	number	percent distribution	number	percent distribution
Total American Indians	**807,599**	**100.0%**	**837,688**	**100.0%**
Never married	298,221	36.9	261,904	31.3
Currently married	391,503	48.5	388,463	46.4
Spouse present	349,618	43.3	334,055	39.9
Spouse absent	41,885	5.2	54,408	6.5
Divorced	97,977	12.1	122,869	14.7
Widowed	19,898	2.5	64,452	7.7

Note: American Indians include Alaska Natives. The American Indian and Alaska Native population includes only those identifying themselves as being American Indian or Alaska Native alone and no other race.
Source: Bureau of the Census, 2003 American Community Survey, Internet site http://factfinder.census.gov/servlet/ DatasetMainPageServlet?_program=ACS&_lang=en&_ts=; calculations by New Strategist

More than 4 Million People Identify Themselves as American Indians

Many American Indians are of mixed race. While 2.8 million people identify their race as American Indian alone, another 1.6 million say they are American Indian and some other race—in most cases white. Nineteen percent of American Indians are also Hispanic. The largest American Indian tribe is the Cherokee, accounting for 19 percent of the 1.7 million American Indians who identify themselves as being of a single tribe and American Indian alone.

Forty-three percent of American Indians live in the West, and another 31 percent live in the South. California is home to 16 percent of American Indians. American Indians account for 19 percent of Alaska's population, the largest share among the 50 states. In New Mexico and Oklahoma, American Indians are a substantial 11 percent of the population.

■ American Indians are a tiny minority of the U.S. population, increasingly dwarfed by Hispanics, blacks, and Asians.

American Indians are a tiny share of the population in every region

(American Indian share of population by region, 2004)

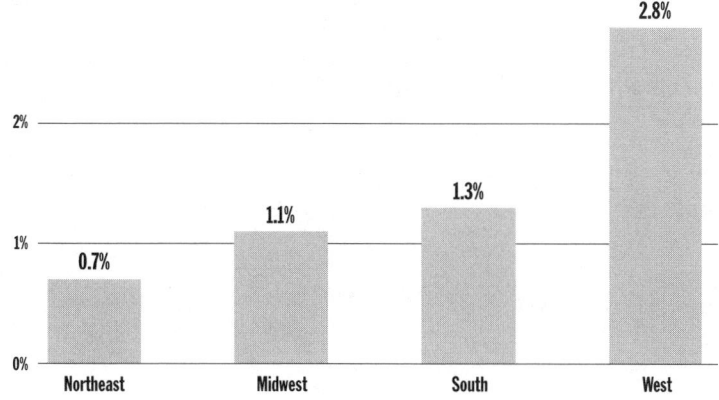

Table 1.40 American Indians by Racial Identification, 2000 and 2004

(total number of people, and number and percent distribution of American Indians by racial identification, 2000 and 2004; percent change, 2000–04)

	2004 number	2004 percent distribution	2000 number	2000 percent distribution	percent change 2000–04
Total people	**293,655,404**	**100.0%**	**282,192,162**	**100.0%**	**4.1%**
American Indian alone or in combination with one or more other races	4,409,446	1.5	4,236,378	1.5	4.1
American Indian alone	2,824,751	1.0	2,673,462	0.9	5.7
American Indian in combination	1,584,695	0.5	1,562,916	0.6	1.4

Source: Bureau of the Census, National Population Estimates, Internet site http://www.census.gov/popest/national/asrh/ NC-EST2004-srh.html; calculations by New Strategist

Table 1.41 American Indians by Hispanic Origin, 2004

(number and percent distribution of American Indians by Hispanic origin and racial identification, 2004)

	American Indian alone or in combination number	American Indian alone or in combination percent distribution	American Indian alone number	American Indian alone percent distribution
Total American Indians	**4,409,446**	**100.0%**	**2,824,751**	**100.0%**
Not Hispanic	3,573,949	81.1	2,206,748	78.1
Hispanic	835,497	18.9	618,003	21.9

Source: Bureau of the Census, National Population Estimates, Internet site http://www.census.gov/popest/national/asrh/ NC-EST2004-asrh.html; calculations by New Strategist

Table 1.42 American Indians by Tribe, 2004

(number and percent distribution of people identifying themselves as American Indian alone by tribe-alone identification, 2004; for the ten largest tribes)

	number	percent distribution
Total American Indians alone specifying one tribe	**1,729,574**	**100.0%**
Cherokee	331,491	19.2
Navajo	230,401	13.3
Chippewa	92,041	5.3
Pueblo	69,203	4.0
Sioux	67,666	3.9
Apache	66,048	3.8
Lumbee	59,433	3.4
Choctaw	55,107	3.2
Iroquois	50,982	2.9
Pima	48,709	2.8
All other tribes	658,493	38.1

Note: American Indians include Alaska Natives. American Indians are those identifying themselves as being of the race alone. Tribes shown are for those identifying themselves as being of the tribe alone.
Source: Bureau of the Census, 2004 American Community Survey, Internet site http://factfinder.census.gov/servlet/ DatasetMainPageServlet?_lang=en&_ts=143469461584&_ds_name=ACS_2004_EST_G00_&_program=ACS; calculations by New Strategist

Table 1.43 American Indians in the Armed Forces, 2003

(number and percent distribution of American Indians aged 18 or older who are in the armed forces or who are veterans, by sex and age, 2003)

	total	in armed forces	veteran
Total American Indians aged 18 or older	**1,524,138**	**3,187**	**184,566**
Men	747,660	2,876	171,902
Aged 18 to 64	679,091	2,876	133,501
Aged 65 or older	68,569	0	38,401
Women	776,478	311	12,664
Aged 18 to 64	692,487	311	11,179
Aged 65 or older	83,991	0	1,485
Total American Indians aged 18 or older	**100.0%**	**0.2%**	**12.1%**
Men	100.0	0.4	23.0
Aged 18 to 64	100.0	0.4	19.7
Aged 65 or older	100.0	0.0	56.0
Women	100.0	0.0	1.6
Aged 18 to 64	100.0	0.0	1.6
Aged 65 or older	100.0	0.0	1.8

Note: American Indians include Alaska Natives. American Indians are those identifying themselves as being of the race alone.
Source: Bureau of the Census, 2003 American Community Survey, Internet site http://factfinder.census.gov/servlet/Dataset MainPageServlet?_program=ACS&_lang=en&_ts=; calculations by New Strategist

Table 1.44 American Indians by Age, 2000 and 2004

(number of American Indians by age, 2000 and 2004; percent change, 2000–04)

	2004	2000	percent change 2000–04
Total American Indians	**4,409,446**	**4,236,378**	**4.1%**
Under age 5	270,587	364,375	−25.7
Aged 5 to 9	372,933	398,770	−6.5
Aged 10 to 14	412,676	413,350	−0.2
Aged 15 to 19	412,187	393,812	4.7
Aged 20 to 24	393,543	331,117	18.9
Aged 25 to 29	325,539	302,589	7.6
Aged 30 to 34	309,645	304,094	1.8
Aged 35 to 39	308,193	334,383	−7.8
Aged 40 to 44	336,936	325,561	3.5
Aged 45 to 49	315,414	280,972	12.3
Aged 50 to 54	267,157	233,762	14.3
Aged 55 to 59	213,617	165,935	28.7
Aged 60 to 64	151,020	121,764	24.0
Aged 65 to 69	108,505	90,424	20.0
Aged 70 to 74	79,288	69,725	13.7
Aged 75 to 79	58,760	50,353	16.7
Aged 80 to 84	39,328	30,181	30.3
Aged 85 or older	34,118	25,211	35.3
Aged 18 or older	3,105,213	2,819,149	10.1
Aged 18 to 24	557,693	484,195	15.2
Aged 65 or older	319,999	265,894	20.3

Note: American Indians are those identifying themselves as being of the race alone and those identifying themselves as being of the race in combination with one or more other races.
Source: Bureau of the Census, National Population Estimates, Internet site http://www.census.gov/popest/national/asrh/ NC-EST2004-asrh.html; calculations by New Strategist

Table 1.45 American Indian Share of Total Population by Age, 2004

(total number of people, number and percent distribution of American Indians, and American Indian share of total, by age, 2004)

		American Indian		
	total	number	percent distribution	share of total
Total people	**293,655,404**	**4,409,446**	**100.0%**	**1.5%**
Under age 5	20,071,268	270,587	6.1	1.3
Aged 5 to 9	19,605,572	372,933	8.5	1.9
Aged 10 to 14	21,145,156	412,676	9.4	2.0
Aged 15 to 19	20,729,802	412,187	9.3	2.0
Aged 20 to 24	20,971,302	393,543	8.9	1.9
Aged 25 to 29	19,560,906	325,539	7.4	1.7
Aged 30 to 34	20,471,032	309,645	7.0	1.5
Aged 35 to 39	21,052,318	308,193	7.0	1.5
Aged 40 to 44	23,056,334	336,936	7.6	1.5
Aged 45 to 49	22,122,629	315,414	7.2	1.4
Aged 50 to 54	19,496,176	267,157	6.1	1.4
Aged 55 to 59	16,489,501	213,617	4.8	1.3
Aged 60 to 64	12,589,423	151,020	3.4	1.2
Aged 65 to 69	9,956,467	108,505	2.5	1.1
Aged 70 to 74	8,507,005	79,288	1.8	0.9
Aged 75 to 79	7,410,757	58,760	1.3	0.8
Aged 80 to 84	5,560,125	39,328	0.9	0.7
Aged 85 or older	4,859,631	34,118	0.8	0.7
Aged 18 or older	220,377,406	3,105,213	70.4	1.4
Aged 18 to 24	29,245,102	557,693	12.6	1.9
Aged 65 or older	36,293,985	319,999	7.3	0.9

Note: American Indians are those identifying themselves as being of the race alone and those identifying themselves as being of the race in combination with one or more other races.
Source: Bureau of the Census, National Population Estimates, Internet site http://www.census.gov/popest/national/asrh/ NC-EST2004-sa.html; calculations by New Strategist

Table 1.46 American Indians by Age and Sex, 2004

(number of American Indians by age and sex, and sex ratio by age, 2004)

	total	females	males	sex ratio
Total American Indians	**4,409,446**	**2,227,310**	**2,182,136**	**98**
Under age 5	270,587	133,353	137,234	103
Aged 5 to 9	372,933	182,870	190,063	104
Aged 10 to 14	412,676	204,052	208,624	102
Aged 15 to 19	412,187	203,099	209,088	103
Aged 20 to 24	393,543	191,825	201,718	105
Aged 25 to 29	325,539	157,353	168,186	107
Aged 30 to 34	309,645	152,027	157,618	104
Aged 35 to 39	308,193	153,875	154,318	100
Aged 40 to 44	336,936	172,069	164,867	96
Aged 45 to 49	315,414	163,712	151,702	93
Aged 50 to 54	267,157	139,514	127,643	91
Aged 55 to 59	213,617	111,683	101,934	91
Aged 60 to 64	151,020	79,481	71,539	90
Aged 65 to 69	108,505	57,644	50,861	88
Aged 70 to 74	79,288	43,636	35,652	82
Aged 75 to 79	58,760	33,659	25,101	75
Aged 80 to 84	39,328	24,100	15,228	63
Aged 85 or older	34,118	23,358	10,760	46
Aged 18 or older	3,105,213	1,584,649	1,520,564	96
Aged 18 to 24	557,693	272,538	285,155	105
Aged 65 or older	319,999	182,397	137,602	75

Note: American Indians are those identifying themselves as being of the race alone and those identifying themselves as being of the race in combination with one or more other races. The sex ratio is the number of males divided by the number of females multiplied by 100.
Source: Bureau of the Census, National Population Estimates, Internet site http://www.census.gov/popest/national/asrh/ NC-EST2004-sa.html; calculations by New Strategist

Table 1.47 American Indians by Region, 2000 and 2004

(number of American Indians by region, 2000 and 2004; percent change, 2000–04)

	2004	2000	percent change 2000–04
Total American Indians	**4,409,446**	**4,119,301**	**7.0%**
Northeast	401,439	374,035	7.3
Midwest	739,673	714,792	3.5
South	1,355,488	1,259,230	7.6
West	1,912,846	1,771,244	8.0

Note: American Indians are those identifying themselves as being of the race alone and those identifying themselves as being of the race in combination with one or more other races. Total number of American Indians in 2000 differs from the total in previous tables of this chapter because these are census counts from April 1, 2000, whereas the others are population estimates.
Source: Bureau of the Census, 2000 Census, Internet site http://factfinder.census.gov/servlet/DatasetMainPageServlet?_program=DEC&_lang=en&_ts=; and State Population Estimates, Internet site http://www.census.gov/popest/states/asrh/SC-EST2004-04.html; calculations by New Strategist

Table 1.48 American Indian Share of the Total Population by Region, 2004

(total number of people, number and percent distribution of American Indians, and American Indian share of total, by region, 2004)

		American Indian		
	total	number	percent distribution	share of total
Total people	**293,655,404**	**4,409,446**	**100.0%**	**1.5%**
Northeast	54,571,147	401,439	9.1	0.7
Midwest	65,729,852	739,673	16.8	1.1
South	105,944,965	1,355,488	30.7	1.3
West	67,409,440	1,912,846	43.4	2.8

Note: American Indians are those identifying themselves as being of the race alone and those identifying themselves as being of the race in combination with one or more other races.
Source: Bureau of the Census, State Population Estimates, Internet site http://www.census.gov/popest/states/asrh/SC-EST2004-04.html; calculations by New Strategist

Table 1.49 American Indians by State, 2000 and 2004

(number of American Indians by state, 2000 and 2004; percent change, 2000–04)

	2004	2000	percent change 2000–04
Total American Indians	**4,409,446**	**4,119,301**	**7.0%**
Alabama	44,892	44,449	1.0
Alaska	123,690	119,241	3.7
Arizona	322,235	292,552	10.1
Arkansas	39,132	37,002	5.8
California	687,366	627,562	9.5
Colorado	85,980	79,689	7.9
Connecticut	26,300	24,488	7.4
Delaware	6,557	6,069	8.0
District of Columbia	4,692	4,775	–1.7
Florida	140,558	117,880	19.2
Georgia	59,844	53,197	12.5
Hawaii	25,981	24,882	4.4
Idaho	29,431	27,237	8.1
Illinois	79,608	73,161	8.8
Indiana	40,912	39,263	4.2
Iowa	19,441	18,246	6.5
Kansas	47,481	47,363	0.2
Kentucky	25,298	24,552	3.0
Louisiana	44,395	42,878	3.5
Maine	13,519	13,156	2.8
Maryland	41,749	39,437	5.9
Massachusetts	40,590	38,050	6.7
Michigan	124,092	124,412	–0.3
Minnesota	84,807	81,074	4.6
Mississippi	21,633	19,555	10.6
Missouri	61,244	60,099	1.9
Montana	69,374	66,320	4.6
Nebraska	23,545	22,204	6.0
Nevada	49,640	42,222	17.6
New Hampshire	8,269	7,885	4.9
New Jersey	55,246	49,104	12.5
New Mexico	207,374	191,475	8.3
New York	183,442	171,581	6.9
North Carolina	141,953	131,736	7.8
North Dakota	36,552	35,228	3.8
Ohio	76,709	76,075	0.8
Oklahoma	398,242	391,949	1.6
Oregon	88,524	85,667	3.3

(continued)

	2004	2000	percent change 2000–04
Pennsylvania	56,155	52,650	6.7%
Rhode Island	11,706	10,725	9.1
South Carolina	29,558	27,456	7.7
South Dakota	72,214	68,281	5.8
Tennessee	41,598	39,188	6.1
Texas	248,339	215,599	15.2
Utah	41,979	40,445	3.8
Vermont	6,212	6,396	−2.9
Virginia	56,256	52,864	6.4
Washington	165,373	158,940	4.0
West Virginia	10,792	10,644	1.4
Wisconsin	73,068	69,386	5.3
Wyoming	15,899	15,012	5.9

Note: American Indians are those identifying themselves as being of the race alone and those identifying themselves as being of the race in combination with one or more other races. Total number of American Indians in 2000 differs from the total in previous tables of this chapter because these are census counts from April 1, 2000, whereas the others are population estimates.
Source: Bureau of the Census, 2000 Census, Internet site http://factfinder.census.gov/servlet/DatasetMainPageServlet?_program=DEC&_lang=en&_ts=; and State Population Estimates, Internet site http://www.census.gov/popest/states/asrh/SC-EST2004-04.html; calculations by New Strategist

Table 1.50 American Indian Share of Total Population by State, 2004

(total number of people, number and percent distribution of American Indians, and American Indian share of total, by state, 2004)

| | | American Indian | | |
	total	number	percent distribution	share of total
Total people	**293,655,404**	**4,409,446**	**100.0%**	**1.5%**
Alabama	4,530,182	44,892	1.0	1.0
Alaska	655,435	123,690	2.8	18.9
Arizona	5,743,834	322,235	7.3	5.6
Arkansas	2,752,629	39,132	0.9	1.4
California	35,893,799	687,366	15.6	1.9
Colorado	4,601,403	85,980	1.9	1.9
Connecticut	3,503,604	26,300	0.6	0.8
Delaware	830,364	6,557	0.1	0.8
District of Columbia	553,523	4,692	0.1	0.8
Florida	17,397,161	140,558	3.2	0.8
Georgia	8,829,383	59,844	1.4	0.7
Hawaii	1,262,840	25,981	0.6	2.1
Idaho	1,393,262	29,431	0.7	2.1
Illinois	12,713,634	79,608	1.8	0.6
Indiana	6,237,569	40,912	0.9	0.7
Iowa	2,954,451	19,441	0.4	0.7
Kansas	2,735,502	47,481	1.1	1.7
Kentucky	4,145,922	25,298	0.6	0.6
Louisiana	4,515,770	44,395	1.0	1.0
Maine	1,317,253	13,519	0.3	1.0
Maryland	5,558,058	41,749	0.9	0.8
Massachusetts	6,416,505	40,590	0.9	0.6
Michigan	10,112,620	124,092	2.8	1.2
Minnesota	5,100,958	84,807	1.9	1.7
Mississippi	2,902,966	21,633	0.5	0.7
Missouri	5,754,618	61,244	1.4	1.1
Montana	926,865	69,374	1.6	7.5
Nebraska	1,747,214	23,545	0.5	1.3
Nevada	2,334,771	49,640	1.1	2.1
New Hampshire	1,299,500	8,269	0.2	0.6
New Jersey	8,698,879	55,246	1.3	0.6
New Mexico	1,903,289	207,374	4.7	10.9
New York	19,227,088	183,442	4.2	1.0
North Carolina	8,541,221	141,953	3.2	1.7
North Dakota	634,366	36,552	0.8	5.8
Ohio	11,459,011	76,709	1.7	0.7
Oklahoma	3,523,553	398,242	9.0	11.3
Oregon	3,594,586	88,524	2.0	2.5

(continued)

	total	American Indian		
		number	percent distribution	share of total
Pennsylvania	12,406,292	56,155	1.3%	0.5%
Rhode Island	1,080,632	11,706	0.3	1.1
South Carolina	4,198,068	29,558	0.7	0.7
South Dakota	770,883	72,214	1.6	9.4
Tennessee	5,900,962	41,598	0.9	0.7
Texas	22,490,022	248,339	5.6	1.1
Utah	2,389,039	41,979	1.0	1.8
Vermont	621,394	6,212	0.1	1.0
Virginia	7,459,827	56,256	1.3	0.8
Washington	6,203,788	165,373	3.8	2.7
West Virginia	1,815,354	10,792	0.2	0.6
Wisconsin	5,509,026	73,068	1.7	1.3
Wyoming	506,529	15,899	0.4	3.1

Note: American Indians are those identifying themselves as being of the race alone and those identifying themselves as being of the race in combination with one or more other races.
Source: Bureau of the Census, State Population Estimates, Internet site http://www.census.gov/popest/states/asrh/ SC-EST2004-04.html; calculations by New Strategist

Table 1.51 American Indians by Metropolitan Area, 2004

(total number of people, number of American Indians, and American Indian share of total, for selected metropolitan areas, 2004)

	total population	American Indian number	American Indian share of total
Albany–Schenectady–Troy, NY MSA	860,976	562	0.1%
Allentown–Bethlehem–Easton, PA MSA	650,230	742	0.1
Anchorage, AK MSA	265,176	15,855	6.0
Appleton–Oshkosh–Neenah, WI MSA	359,711	2,973	0.8
Atlanta, GA MSA	4,477,579	8,960	0.2
Augusta–Aiken, GA–SC MSA	476,167	502	0.1
Austin–San Marcos, TX MSA	1,373,125	6,823	0.5
Bakersfield, CA MSA	702,855	5,216	0.7
Baton Rouge, LA MSA	610,743	243	0.0
Beaumont–Port Arthur, TX MSA	366,244	1,287	0.4
Biloxi–Gulfport–Pascagoula, MS MSA	363,966	0	0.0
Binghamton, NY MSA	239,012	0	0.0
Birmingham, AL MSA	929,694	3,119	0.3
Boise City, ID MSA	479,284	6,567	1.4
Boston–Worcester–Lawrence, MA–NH–ME–CT CMSA	5,749,197	14,904	0.3
Brownsville–Harlingen–San Benito, TX MSA	367,603	360	0.1
Buffalo–Niagara Falls, NY MSA	1,119,037	5,155	0.5
Canton–Massillon, OH MSA	400,919	586	0.1
Charleston–North Charleston, SC MSA	563,828	960	0.2
Chicago, IL PMSA	8,388,723	14,124	0.2
Cleveland–Akron, OH CMSA	2,878,475	5,113	0.2
Colorado Springs, CO MSA	539,225	3,719	0.7
Columbia, SC MSA	543,126	1,554	0.3
Corpus Christi, TX MSA	381,422	1,740	0.5
Dallas–Fort Worth, TX CMSA	5,676,651	26,057	0.5
Davenport–Moline–Rock Island, IA–IL MSA	350,022	2,113	0.6
Dayton–Springfield, OH MSA	916,635	1,874	0.2
Daytona Beach, FL MSA	530,553	1,448	0.3
Denver–Boulder–Greeley, CO CMSA*	2,514,628	16,808	0.7
Des Moines, IA MSA	476,699	1,295	0.3
Detroit–Ann Arbor–Flint, MI CMSA	5,437,277	15,301	0.3
El Paso, TX MSA	700,225	3,662	0.5
Erie, PA MSA	267,426	470	0.2
Eugene–Springfield, OR MSA	324,176	5,609	1.7
Fayetteville, NC MSA	287,220	3,154	1.1
Fayetteville–Springdale–Rogers, AR MSA	345,308	8,022	2.3
Fort Myers–Cape Coral, FL MSA	508,634	287	0.1
Fort Pierce–Port St. Lucie, FL MSA	358,578	544	0.2
Fort Wayne, IN MSA	506,545	391	0.1

(continued)

	total population	American Indian	
		number	share of total
Fresno, CA MSA	978,274	12,839	1.3%
Grand Rapids–Muskegon–Holland, MI MSA	1,102,729	5,640	0.5
Greensboro–Winston-Salem–High Point, NC MSA	1,283,261	4,250	0.3
Greenville–Spartanburg–Anderson, SC MSA	976,678	1,389	0.1
Harrisburg–Lebanon–Carlisle, PA MSA	617,676	594	0.1
Hartford, CT MSA	1,163,367	850	0.1
Hickory–Morganton–Lenoir, NC MSA	345,590	158	0.0
Honolulu, HI MSA	868,751	1,254	0.1
Houston–Galveston–Brazoria, TX CMSA*	4,794,384	12,329	0.3
Huntsville, AL MSA	354,936	3,192	0.9
Indianapolis, IN MSA	1,664,412	2,365	0.1
Jackson, MS MSA	443,275	977	0.2
Jacksonville, FL MSA	1,182,453	3,842	0.3
Johnson City–Kingsport–Bristol, TN–VA MSA	482,047	2,720	0.6
Kalamazoo–Battle Creek, MI MSA	441,059	2,045	0.5
Kansas City, MO–KS MSA	1,823,092	7,510	0.4
Killeen–Temple, TX MSA	298,933	2,731	0.9
Knoxville, TN MSA	707,617	903	0.1
Lafayette, LA MSA	386,812	729	0.2
Lakeland–Winter Haven, FL MSA	511,565	0	0.0
Lancaster, PA MSA	473,104	0	0.0
Lansing–East Lansing, MI MSA	436,485	1,828	0.4
Lexington, KY MSA	478,625	500	0.1
Lincoln, NE MSA	249,670	1,705	0.7
Little Rock–North Little Rock, AR MSA	593,032	1,595	0.3
Los Angeles–Riverside–Orange County, CA CMSA	17,199,115	100,093	0.6
Lubbock, TX MSA	240,721	497	0.2
Macon, GA MSA	329,432	1,115	0.3
Madison, WI MSA	437,843	2,740	0.6
McAllen–Edinburg–Mission, TX MSA	651,974	3,293	0.5
Melbourne–Titusville–Palm Bay, FL MSA	509,248	1,137	0.2
Miami–Fort Lauderdale, FL CMSA	4,051,442	8,236	0.2
Milwaukee–Waukesha, WI PMSA	1,483,023	6,515	0.4
Mobile, AL MSA	547,153	6,933	1.3
Modesto, CA MSA	490,860	3,871	0.8
Montgomery, AL MSA	323,220	1,671	0.5
Nashville, TN MSA	1,275,212	3,339	0.3
New Orleans, LA MSA	1,313,694	5,716	0.4
New York–Northern New Jersey–Long Island, NY–NJ–CT–PA CMSA*	20,345,959	43,857	0.2
Oklahoma City, OK MSA	1,095,252	40,585	3.7
Orlando, FL MSA	1,831,212	11,710	0.6
Pensacola, FL MSA	410,542	1,562	0.4
Peoria–Pekin, IL MSA	337,020	0	0.0
Philadelphia–Wilmington–Atlantic City, PA–NJ–DE–MD CMSA*	5,383,262	8,843	0.2

(continued)

| | | American Indian | |
	total population	number	share of total
Pittsburgh, PA MSA	2,260,551	827	0.0%
Portland, ME MSA	248,827	0	0.0
Providence–Fall River–Warwick, RI–MA MSA	1,165,549	3,944	0.3
Provo–Orem, UT MSA	395,173	1,126	0.3
Raleigh–Durham–Chapel Hill, NC MSA	1,278,372	4,031	0.3
Reading, PA MSA	378,456	0	0.0
Reno, NV MSA	375,344	6,807	1.8
Richmond–Petersburg, VA MSA	1,013,399	3,289	0.3
Rochester, NY MSA	1,057,917	1,089	0.1
Rockford, IL MSA	382,901	758	0.2
Sacramento, CA PMSA	1,803,160	23,481	1.3
Saginaw–Bay City–Midland, MI MSA	393,837	2,279	0.6
St. Louis, MO–IL MSA	2,620,334	3,927	0.1
Salinas, CA MSA	392,192	4,545	1.2
Salt Lake City–Ogden, UT MSA	1,384,041	7,220	0.5
San Antonio, TX MSA	1,683,872	7,839	0.5
San Diego, CA MSA	2,833,275	18,392	0.6
San Francisco–Oakland–San Jose, CA CMSA	6,951,260	41,344	0.6
San Luis Obispo–Atascadero–Paso Robles, CA MSA	238,502	1,442	0.6
Santa Barbara–Santa Maria–Lompoc, CA MSA	385,238	3,687	1.0
Sarasota–Bradenton, FL MSA	639,438	1,273	0.2
Savannah, GA MSA	299,920	262	0.1
Scranton–Wilkes-Barre–Hazleton, PA MSA	587,557	0	0.0
Seattle–Tacoma–Bremerton, WA CMSA*	3,184,924	29,205	0.9
Shreveport–Bossier City, LA MSA	387,312	867	0.2
South Bend, IN MSA	252,944	427	0.2
Spokane, WA MSA	420,592	7,819	1.9
Springfield, MA MSA	560,472	846	0.2
Springfield, MO MSA	332,918	2,800	0.8
Stockton–Lodi, CA MSA	632,143	4,881	0.8
Syracuse, NY MSA	707,901	2,856	0.4
Tallahassee, FL MSA	274,945	717	0.3
Tampa–St. Petersburg–Clearwater, FL MSA	2,537,586	7,158	0.3
Toledo, OH MSA	598,283	414	0.1
Tucson, AZ MSA	885,025	26,701	3.0
Tulsa, OK MSA	810,062	56,487	7.0
Utica–Rome, NY MSA	282,844	849	0.3
Visalia–Tulare–Porterville, CA MSA	395,493	4,876	1.2
West Palm Beach–Boca Raton, FL MSA	1,223,206	3,270	0.3
Wichita, KS MSA	546,308	4,428	0.8
York, PA MSA	393,426	808	0.2
Youngstown–Warren, OH MSA	566,597	180	0.0

Population figures are for only part of the metropolitan area.
Note: Some metropolitan areas are not shown because data are not available. American Indians are those identifying themselves as being of the race alone. For the definition of CMSA, MSA, and PMSA, see the glossary.
Source: Bureau of the Census, 2004 American Community Survey, Internet site http://factfinder.census.gov/servlet/ DatasetMainPageServlet?_program=ACS&_lang=en&_ts=; calculations by New Strategist

2

Asians

■ The Asian population of the United States numbered nearly 14 million in 2004, having grown 15 percent since 2000. Despite the rapid growth, fewer than 5 percent of Americans are Asian.

■ Asians are far better educated than the population as a whole. Nearly half (49 percent) are college graduates versus 28 percent of the total population.

■ Asians are the only racial or ethnic group in which the majority are at a healthy weight. Only 31 percent of Asians are overweight.

■ The $55,262 median income of Asian households in 2003 was 28 percent greater than the all-household average and higher than that of any other racial or ethnic group.

■ Fully 45 percent of Asian workers are employed in managerial or professional occupations—the largest share among all racial and ethnic groups.

■ Asian households are much more likely to be headed by married couples than the average household—61 versus 52 percent.

■ Forty-eight percent of Asians live in the West, where they account for 10 percent of the population. California is home to 34 percent of the nation's Asian population.

■ Asian households spent an average of $44,923 in 2003, 10 percent more than average.

■ Note: There are no wealth data for Asians.

Asians account for 4.8 percent of the U.S. population

(percent distribution of people by race and Hispanic origin, 2004)

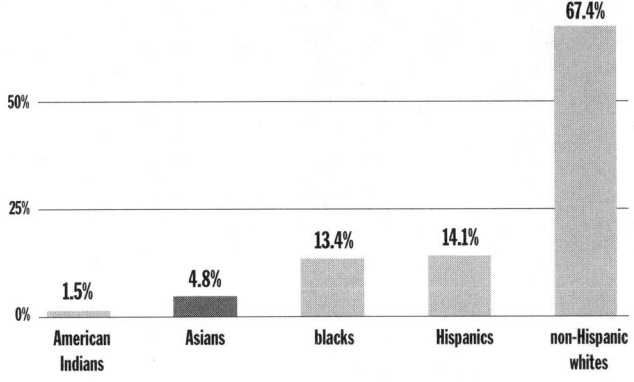

Asians Are Far Better Educated than the Average American

Asians are much more likely to be college graduates than the population as a whole. In 2004, 49 percent of Asians aged 25 or older were college graduates versus 28 percent of the total population. Nineteen percent of Asians have an advanced degree compared with a smaller 10 percent of the total population.

Not only are Asians better educated than the average person, they are more likely to be enrolled in school. While 48 percent of all Americans aged 20 to 21 are students, for example, the figure is 77 percent among Asians in the age group. Nearly half (48 percent) of Asians aged 22 to 24 are still in school versus 28 percent of all Americans in the age group. More than 1 million Asians were enrolled in college in 2003—not far below the number of Hispanic college students, although the Hispanic population is much larger.

Asians earned 6 percent of bachelor's degrees in 2001–02 and 5 percent of master's and doctoral degrees. Asians earned more than 20 percent of first-professional degrees awarded in the fields of dentistry, optometry, and pharmacy in 2001–02.

■ The educational level of Asians is much higher than that of the average American in part because many are immigrants with professional jobs.

Nearly half of Asians are college graduates

(percent of Asians aged 25 or older who are high school graduates or more, have some college or more, or are college graduates, 2004)

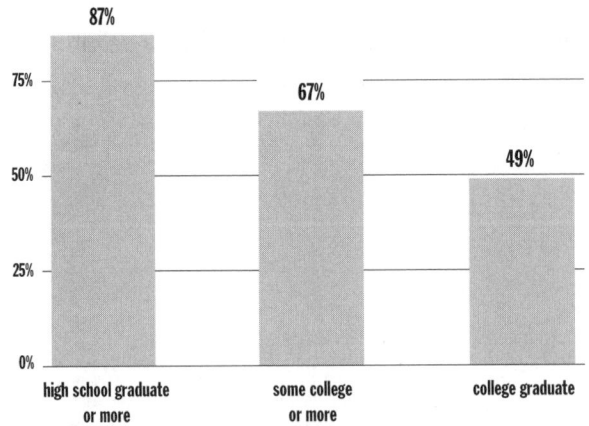

Table 2.1 Educational Attainment of Asians by Age, 2004

(number and percent distribution of Asians aged 25 or older by educational attainment and age, 2004; numbers in thousands)

	total	25 to 34	35 to 44	45 to 54	55 to 64	65 or older
Total Asians	**8,312**	**2,345**	**2,132**	**1,711**	**1,059**	**1,065**
Not a high school graduate	1,089	133	226	217	138	374
High school graduate only	1,657	342	433	403	249	230
Some college, no degree	894	317	211	179	96	92
Associate's degree	610	171	182	123	83	51
Bachelor's degree	2,455	848	631	477	310	189
Master's degree	1,003	371	283	189	97	63
Professional degree	312	105	75	57	42	33
Doctoral degree	293	58	90	67	45	33
High school graduate or more	7,224	2,212	1,905	1,495	922	691
Some college or more	5,567	1,870	1,472	1,092	673	461
Bachelor's degree or more	4,063	1,382	1,079	790	494	318

PERCENT DISTRIBUTION

	total	25 to 34	35 to 44	45 to 54	55 to 64	65 or older
Total Asians	**100.0%**	**100.0%**	**100.0%**	**100.0%**	**100.0%**	**100.0%**
Not a high school graduate	13.1	5.7	10.6	12.7	13.0	35.1
High school graduate only	19.9	14.6	20.3	23.6	23.5	21.6
Some college, no degree	10.8	13.5	9.9	10.5	9.1	8.6
Associate's degree	7.3	7.3	8.5	7.2	7.8	4.8
Bachelor's degree	29.5	36.2	29.6	27.9	29.3	17.7
Master's degree	12.1	15.8	13.3	11.0	9.2	5.9
Professional degree	3.8	4.5	3.5	3.3	4.0	3.1
Doctoral degree	3.5	2.5	4.2	3.9	4.2	3.1
High school graduate or more	86.9	94.3	89.4	87.4	87.1	64.9
Some college or more	67.0	79.7	69.0	63.8	63.6	43.3
Bachelor's degree or more	48.9	58.9	50.6	46.2	46.6	29.9

Note: Asians include those identifying themselves as being Asian alone and those identifying themselves as being Asian in combination with one or more other races.
Source: Bureau of the Census, 2004 Current Population Survey Annual Social and Economic Supplement, Educational Attainment in the United States: 2004, Detailed Tables, Internet site http://www.census.gov/population/www/socdemo/education/cps2004.html; calculations by New Strategist

Table 2.2 Educational Attainment of Asian Men by Age, 2004

(number and percent distribution of Asian men aged 25 or older by educational attainment and age, 2004; numbers in thousands)

	total	25 to 34	35 to 44	45 to 54	55 to 64	65 or older
Total Asian men	**3,942**	**1,147**	**1,033**	**783**	**497**	**483**
Not a high school graduate	441	62	103	93	49	132
High school graduate only	708	155	207	149	100	95
Some college, no degree	439	167	95	92	47	38
Associate's degree	273	84	75	45	45	24
Bachelor's degree	1,132	394	283	217	139	98
Master's degree	579	204	175	102	55	43
Professional degree	166	46	44	31	23	23
Doctoral degree	204	36	53	51	35	28
High school grad. or more	3,501	1,086	932	687	444	349
Some college or more	2,793	931	725	538	344	254
Bachelor's degree or more	2,081	680	555	401	252	192

PERCENT DISTRIBUTION

	total	25 to 34	35 to 44	45 to 54	55 to 64	65 or older
Total Asian men	**100.0%**	**100.0%**	**100.0%**	**100.0%**	**100.0%**	**100.0%**
Not a high school graduate	11.2	5.4	10.0	11.9	9.9	27.3
High school graduate only	18.0	13.5	20.0	19.0	20.1	19.7
Some college, no degree	11.1	14.6	9.2	11.7	9.5	7.9
Associate's degree	6.9	7.3	7.3	5.7	9.1	5.0
Bachelor's degree	28.7	34.4	27.4	27.7	28.0	20.3
Master's degree	14.7	17.8	16.9	13.0	11.1	8.9
Professional degree	4.2	4.0	4.3	4.0	4.6	4.8
Doctoral degree	5.2	3.1	5.1	6.5	7.0	5.8
High school grad. or more	88.8	94.7	90.2	87.7	89.3	72.3
Some college or more	70.9	81.2	70.2	68.7	69.2	52.6
Bachelor's degree or more	52.8	59.3	53.7	51.2	50.7	39.8

Note: Asians include those identifying themselves as being Asian alone and those identifying themselves as being Asian in combination with one or more other races.
Source: Bureau of the Census, 2004 Current Population Survey Annual Social and Economic Supplement, Educational Attainment in the United States: 2004, Detailed Tables, Internet site http://www.census.gov/population/www/socdemo/education/cps2004.html; calculations by New Strategist

Table 2.3 Educational Attainment of Asian Women by Age, 2004

(number and percent distribution of Asian women aged 25 or older by educational attainment and age, 2004; numbers in thousands)

	total	25 to 34	35 to 44	45 to 54	55 to 64	65 or older
Total Asian women	**4,370**	**1,198**	**1,099**	**928**	**562**	**583**
Not a high school graduate	647	72	124	123	87	240
High school graduate only	949	186	226	254	148	135
Some college, no degree	455	150	116	88	49	54
Associate's degree	336	88	108	78	38	27
Bachelor's degree	1,323	453	348	259	171	91
Master's degree	424	167	108	86	42	21
Professional degree	145	59	32	25	19	10
Doctoral degree	89	22	38	16	10	4
High school grad. or more	3,721	1,125	976	806	477	342
Some college or more	2,772	939	750	552	329	207
Bachelor's degree or more	1,981	701	526	386	242	126
PERCENT DISTRIBUTION						
Total Asian women	**100.0%**	**100.0%**	**100.0%**	**100.0%**	**100.0%**	**100.0%**
Not a high school graduate	14.8	6.0	11.3	13.3	15.5	41.2
High school graduate only	21.7	15.5	20.6	27.4	26.3	23.2
Some college, no degree	10.4	12.5	10.6	9.5	8.7	9.3
Associate's degree	7.7	7.3	9.8	8.4	6.8	4.6
Bachelor's degree	30.3	37.8	31.7	27.9	30.4	15.6
Master's degree	9.7	13.9	9.8	9.3	7.5	3.6
Professional degree	3.3	4.9	2.9	2.7	3.4	1.7
Doctoral degree	2.0	1.8	3.5	1.7	1.8	0.7
High school grad. or more	85.1	93.9	88.8	86.9	84.9	58.7
Some college or more	63.4	78.4	68.2	59.5	58.5	35.5
Bachelor's degree or more	45.3	58.5	47.9	41.6	43.1	21.6

Note: Asians include those identifying themselves as being Asian alone and those identifying themselves as being Asian in combination with one or more other races.
Source: Bureau of the Census, 2004 Current Population Survey Annual Social and Economic Supplement, Educational Attainment in the United States: 2004, Detailed Tables, Internet site http://www.census.gov/population/www/socdemo/education/cps2004.html; calculations by New Strategist

Table 2.4 Educational Attainment of Asians by Age and Region, 2004

(percent of Asians aged 25 or older by selected educational attainment, age, and region, 2004)

	Northeast	Midwest	South	West
HIGH SCHOOL GRADUATE OR MORE				
Total Asians	**84.8%**	**89.1%**	**90.9%**	**85.5%**
Aged 25 to 34	90.9	95.6	94.6	95.6
Aged 35 to 44	84.9	90.9	93.0	89.4
Aged 45 to 54	87.0	91.7	90.1	85.4
Aged 55 to 64	83.2	88.0	89.2	86.8
Aged 65 or older	63.7	55.6	67.7	66.0
SOME COLLEGE OR MORE				
Total Asians	**61.4**	**71.6**	**68.3**	**67.5**
Aged 25 to 34	71.2	81.9	81.6	82.4
Aged 35 to 44	58.4	72.5	70.9	72.1
Aged 45 to 54	61.2	68.9	57.4	66.1
Aged 55 to 64	57.0	72.2	52.4	66.3
Aged 65 or older	45.9	35.8	38.7	44.5
BACHELOR'S DEGREE OR MORE				
Total Asians	**50.2**	**57.2**	**51.5**	**45.2**
Aged 25 to 34	58.6	63.2	61.1	56.0
Aged 35 to 44	46.7	61.6	56.6	46.7
Aged 45 to 54	50.3	52.2	40.8	45.2
Aged 55 to 64	46.9	59.4	36.1	46.4
Aged 65 or older	38.2	27.2	31.5	28.0

Note: Asians include those identifying themselves as being Asian alone and those identifying themselves as being Asian in combination with one or more other races.
Source: Bureau of the Census, 2004 Current Population Survey Annual Social and Economic Supplement, Educational Attainment in the United States: 2004, Detailed Tables, Internet site http://www.census.gov/population/www/socdemo/education/cps2004.html; calculations by New Strategist

Table 2.5   Educational Attainment of Asians by State, 2004

(percent of Asians aged 25 or older who are high school or college graduates, for the 25 largest states, 2004)

	high school graduate or more	college graduate
Total Asians	**86.9%**	**48.9%**
Alabama	–	–
Arizona	100.0	51.3
California	85.3	49.9
Colorado	–	–
Florida	86.5	46.2
Georgia	93.0	54.5
Illinois	93.0	59.3
Indiana	–	–
Kentucky	–	–
Louisiana	–	–
Maryland	89.9	51.0
Massachusetts	80.4	54.8
Michigan	90.7	61.0
Minnesota	86.1	47.3
Missouri	77.6	51.3
New Jersey	95.0	67.3
New York	80.6	41.1
North Carolina	87.9	40.8
Ohio	95.7	72.2
Pennsylvania	88.3	54.7
Tennessee	–	–
Texas	93.1	53.1
Virginia	91.2	57.8
Washington	85.1	38.8
Wisconsin	–	–

Note: Asians include those identifying themselves as being Asian alone and those identifying themselves as being Asian in combination with one or more other races. (–) means sample is too small to make a reliable estimate.
Source: Bureau of the Census, 2004 Current Population Survey Annual Social and Economic Supplement, Educational Attainment in the United States: 2004, Detailed Tables, Internet site http://www.census.gov/population/www/socdemo/education/cps2004. html; calculations by New Strategist

Table 2.6 School Enrollment of Asians, 2003

(total number of people aged 3 or older enrolled in school, number of Asians enrolled, and Asian share of total, by age, October 2003; numbers in thousands)

	total	Asian	
		number	share of total
Total aged 3 or older	**74,911**	**3,817**	**5.1%**
Aged 3 to 4	4,590	179	3.9
Aged 5 to 6	7,309	295	4.0
Aged 7 to 9	11,706	577	4.9
Aged 10 to 13	16,478	767	4.7
Aged 14 to 15	8,329	328	3.9
Aged 16 to 17	8,177	356	4.4
Aged 18 to 19	4,856	279	5.7
Aged 20 to 21	3,684	252	6.8
Aged 22 to 24	3,397	304	8.9
Aged 25 to 29	2,212	232	10.5
Aged 30 to 34	1,378	117	8.5
Aged 35 to 44	1,635	87	5.3
Aged 45 to 54	879	30	3.4
Aged 55 or older	283	15	5.3

Note: Asians include those identifying themselves as being Asian alone and those identifying themselves as being Asian in combination with one or more other races.
Source: Bureau of the Census, School Enrollment—Social and Economic Characteristics of Students: October 2003, Detailed Tables, Internet site http://www.census.gov/population/www/socdemo/school/cps2003.html; calculations by New Strategist

Table 2.7 School Enrollment of Asians by Age and Sex, 2003

(number and percent of Asians aged 3 or older enrolled in school, by age and sex, October 2003; numbers in thousands)

	total		female		male	
	number	percent	number	percent	number	percent
Total Asians enrolled	**3,817**	**31.3%**	**1,872**	**29.3%**	**1,946**	**33.4%**
Aged 3 to 4	179	51.4	83	54.2	96	49.3
Aged 5 to 6	295	89.3	126	86.0	169	91.9
Aged 7 to 9	577	99.2	322	100.0	256	98.2
Aged 10 to 13	767	99.4	352	98.7	415	99.9
Aged 14 to 15	328	99.1	177	100.0	151	98.2
Aged 16 to 17	356	95.7	167	95.4	190	95.9
Aged 18 to 19	279	87.1	150	85.1	129	89.6
Aged 20 to 21	252	77.0	137	79.7	115	74.0
Aged 22 to 24	304	48.1	158	48.8	146	47.3
Aged 25 to 29	232	21.6	89	15.8	142	27.9
Aged 30 to 34	117	9.4	44	6.9	73	12.1
Aged 35 to 44	87	4.1	40	3.6	47	4.7
Aged 45 to 54	30	1.7	15	1.7	14	1.8
Aged 55 or older	15	0.7	12	1.1	3	0.3

Note: Asians include those identifying themselves as being Asian alone and those identifying themselves as being Asian in combination with one or more other races.
Source: Bureau of the Census, School Enrollment—Social and Economic Characteristics of Students: October 2003, Detailed Tables, Internet site http://www.census.gov/population/www/socdemo/school/cps2003.html

Table 2.8 Asian Families with Children in College, 2003

(total number of Asian families, number with dependent children aged 5 to 24, and number and percent with children enrolled in college by household income, 2003; numbers in thousands)

| | total | with children aged 5–24 | with one or more children enrolled in college | | |
			number	percent of total Asian families	percent of Asian families with children 5–24
Total Asian families	**3,094**	**1,733**	**424**	**13.7%**	**24.5%**
Less than $10,000	114	55	8	7.0	14.5
$10,000 to $14,999	128	70	23	18.0	32.9
$15,000 to $19,999	82	48	5	6.1	10.4
$20,000 to $24,999	280	177	33	11.8	18.6
$25,000 to $29,999	269	157	29	10.8	18.5
$30,000 to $34,999	179	87	29	16.2	33.3
$35,000 to $39,999	486	267	74	15.2	27.7
$40,000 to $49,999	357	183	34	9.5	18.6
$50,000 to $74,999	325	209	57	17.5	27.3
$75,000 and over	233	135	41	17.6	30.4

Note: Asians include those identifying themselves as being Asian alone and those identifying themselves as being Asian in combination with one or more other races. Numbers will not add to total because not reported is not shown.
Source: Bureau of the Census, School Enrollment—Social and Economic Characteristics of Students: October 2003, Detailed Tables, Internet site http://www.census.gov/population/www/socdemo/school/cps2003.html; calculations by New Strategist

Table 2.9 College Enrollment of Asians, 2003

(total number of people aged 15 or older enrolled in college, number of Asians enrolled, and Asian share of total, by age, October 2003; numbers in thousands)

	total	Asian number	Asian share of total
Total enrolled in college	**16,638**	**1,263**	**7.6%**
Under age 20	3,661	254	6.9
Aged 20 to 21	3,534	248	7.0
Aged 22 to 24	3,320	290	8.7
Aged 25 to 29	2,164	231	10.7
Aged 30 to 34	1,330	117	8.8
Aged 35 to 39	769	42	5.5
Aged 40 to 44	757	42	5.5
Aged 45 to 49	479	15	3.1
Aged 50 to 54	357	12	3.4
Aged 55 or older	268	11	4.1

Note: Asians include those identifying themselves as being Asian alone and those identifying themselves as being Asian in combination with one or more other races.
Source: Bureau of the Census, School Enrollment—Social and Economic Characteristics of Students: October 2003, Detailed Tables, Internet site http://www.census.gov/population/www/socdemo/school/cps2003.html; calculations by New Strategist

Table 2.10 College Enrollment of Asians by Age and Type of School, 2003

(number and percent distribution of Asians aged 15 or older enrolled in college by age and type of school, October 2003; numbers in thousands)

	total	two-year college	four-year college	graduate school
Total Asians enrolled	**1,263**	**256**	**585**	**420**
Under age 20	254	95	160	0
Aged 20 to 21	248	56	187	5
Aged 22 to 24	290	43	159	88
Aged 25 to 29	231	34	40	158
Aged 30 to 34	117	19	20	77
Aged 35 to 39	42	0	12	29
Aged 40 to 44	42	8	6	26
Aged 45 to 49	15	0	0	15
Aged 50 to 54	12	3	0	9
Aged 55 or older	11	0	0	11

PERCENT DISTRIBUTION BY TYPE OF SCHOOL

	total	two-year college	four-year college	graduate school
Total Asians enrolled	**100.0%**	**20.3%**	**46.3%**	**33.3%**
Under age 20	100.0	37.4	63.0	0.0
Aged 20 to 21	100.0	22.6	75.4	2.0
Aged 22 to 24	100.0	14.8	54.8	30.3
Aged 25 to 29	100.0	14.7	17.3	68.4
Aged 30 to 34	100.0	16.2	17.1	65.8
Aged 35 to 39	100.0	0.0	28.6	69.0
Aged 40 to 44	100.0	19.0	14.3	61.9
Aged 45 to 49	100.0	0.0	0.0	100.0
Aged 50 to 54	100.0	25.0	0.0	75.0
Aged 55 or older	100.0	0.0	0.0	100.0

PERCENT DISTRIBUTION BY AGE

	total	two-year college	four-year college	graduate school
Total Asians enrolled	**100.0%**	**100.0%**	**100.0%**	**100.0%**
Under age 20	20.1	37.1	27.4	0.0
Aged 20 to 21	19.6	21.9	32.0	1.2
Aged 22 to 24	23.0	16.8	27.2	21.0
Aged 25 to 29	18.3	13.3	6.8	37.6
Aged 30 to 34	9.3	7.4	3.4	18.3
Aged 35 to 39	3.3	0.0	2.1	6.9
Aged 40 to 44	3.3	3.1	1.0	6.2
Aged 45 to 49	1.2	0.0	0.0	3.6
Aged 50 to 54	1.0	1.2	0.0	2.1
Aged 55 or older	0.9	0.0	0.0	2.6

Note: Asians include those identifying themselves as being Asian alone and those identifying themselves as being Asian in combination with one or more other races.
Source: Bureau of the Census, School Enrollment—Social and Economic Characteristics of Students: October 2003, Detailed Tables, Internet site http://www.census.gov/population/www/socdemo/school/cps2003.html; calculations by New Strategist

Table 2.11 Associate's Degrees Earned by Asians by Field of Study, 2001–02

(total number of associate's degrees conferred and number and percent earned by Asians, by field of study, 2001–02)

	total	earned by Asians	
		number	percent
Total associate's degrees	**595,133**	**30,947**	**5.2%**
Agriculture and natural resources	6,494	39	0.6
Architecture and related programs	443	30	6.8
Area, ethnic, and cultural studies	319	2	0.6
Biological and life sciences	1,517	91	6.0
Business	108,911	5,505	5.1
Communications	2,819	89	3.2
Communications technologies	2,021	55	2.7
Computer and information sciences	30,965	2,392	7.7
Construction trades	2,639	63	2.4
Education	9,267	98	1.1
Engineering	1,724	101	5.9
Engineering-related technologies	32,895	2,154	6.5
English language and literature, letters	864	44	5.1
Foreign languages and literatures	517	26	5.0
Health professions and related sciences	79,888	2,922	3.7
Home economics	9,480	466	4.9
Law and legal studies	6,825	133	1.9
Liberal arts and sciences, general studies, humanities	207,163	11,944	5.8
Library science	96	2	2.1
Mathematics	685	95	13.9
Mechanics and repairers	12,086	613	5.1
Multi- and interdisciplinary studies	13,204	1,137	8.6
Parks, recreation, leisure, and fitness	830	16	1.9
Philosophy and religion	134	17	12.7
Physical sciences	2,308	118	5.1
Precision production trades	10,818	452	4.2
Protective services	16,689	376	2.3
Psychology	1,705	53	3.1
Public administration and services	3,323	87	2.6
R.O.T.C. and military technologies	62	0	0.0
Social sciences and history	5,593	382	6.8
Theological studies, religious vocations	414	4	1.0
Transportation and material moving	1,159	41	3.5
Visual and performing arts	20,911	1,388	6.6
Not classified	365	12	3.3

Source: National Center for Education Statistics, Digest of Education Statistics 2003, *Internet site http://nces.ed.gov//programs/ digest/d03/list_tables.asp; calculations by New Strategist*

Table 2.12 Bachelor's Degrees Earned by Asians by Field of Study, 2001–02

(total number of bachelor's degrees conferred and number and percent earned by Asians, by field of study, 2001–02)

	total	earned by Asians	
		number	percent
Total bachelor's degrees	**1,291,900**	**83,101**	**6.4%**
Agriculture and natural resources	23,353	760	3.3
Architecture and related programs	8,808	729	8.3
Area, ethnic, and cultural studies	6,557	758	11.6
Biological and life sciences	60,256	7,485	12.4
Business	281,330	20,083	7.1
Communications	62,791	2,368	3.8
Communications technologies	1,110	62	5.6
Computer and information sciences	47,299	7,408	15.7
Construction trades	202	1	0.5
Education	106,383	1,916	1.8
Engineering	59,481	7,400	12.4
Engineering-related technologies	14,117	739	5.2
English language and literature, letters	53,162	2,233	4.2
Foreign languages and literatures	15,318	726	4.7
Health professions and related sciences	70,517	3,961	5.6
Home economics	18,153	653	3.6
Law and legal studies	1,971	136	6.9
Liberal arts and sciences, general studies, humanities	39,333	1,572	4.0
Library science	74	4	5.4
Mathematics	12,395	1,057	8.5
Mechanics and repairers	164	13	7.9
Multi- and interdisciplinary studies	27,629	1,474	5.3
Parks, recreation, leisure, and fitness	20,554	447	2.2
Philosophy and religion	9,306	474	5.1
Physical sciences	17,851	1,379	7.7
Precision production trades	468	16	3.4
Protective services	25,536	715	2.8
Psychology	76,671	4,426	5.8
Public administration and services	19,392	595	3.1
R.O.T.C. and military technologies	3	0	0.0
Social sciences and history	132,874	9,258	7.0
Theological studies, religious vocations	7,785	161	2.1
Transportation and material moving	4,020	101	2.5
Visual and performing arts	66,773	3,983	6.0
Not classified	264	8	3.0

Source: National Center for Education Statistics, Digest of Education Statistics 2003, *Internet site http://nces.ed.gov//programs/digest/d03/list_tables.asp; calculations by New Strategist*

Table 2.13 Master's Degrees Earned by Asians by Field of Study, 2001–02

(total number of master's degrees conferred and number and percent earned by Asians, by field of study, 2001–02)

	total	earned by Asians number	earned by Asians percent
Total master's degrees	**482,118**	**25,414**	**5.3%**
Agriculture and natural resources	4,519	139	3.1
Architecture and related programs	4,566	267	5.8
Area, ethnic, and cultural studies	1,578	106	6.7
Biological and life sciences	6,205	552	8.9
Business	120,785	8,352	6.9
Communications	5,510	251	4.6
Communications technologies	549	22	4.0
Computer and information sciences	16,113	2,264	14.1
Construction trades	9	0	0.0
Education	136,579	3,095	2.3
Engineering	26,015	2,378	9.1
Engineering-related technologies	896	36	4.0
English language and literature, letters	7,268	250	3.4
Foreign languages and literatures	2,861	115	4.0
Health professions and related sciences	43,644	3,304	7.6
Home economics	2,616	104	4.0
Law and legal studies	4,053	211	5.2
Liberal arts and sciences, general studies, humanities	2,754	72	2.6
Library science	5,113	152	3.0
Mathematics	3,487	239	6.9
Multi- and interdisciplinary studies	3,211	150	4.7
Parks, recreation, leisure, and fitness	2,754	56	2.0
Philosophy and religion	1,334	64	4.8
Physical sciences	5,034	267	5.3
Precision production trades	2	1	50.0
Protective services	2,935	59	2.0
Psychology	14,888	592	4.0
Public administration and services	25,448	882	3.5
Social sciences and history	14,112	570	4.0
Theological studies, religious vocations	4,952	276	5.6
Transportation and material moving	709	11	1.6
Visual and performing arts	11,595	577	5.0
Not classified	24	0	0.0

Source: National Center for Education Statistics, Digest of Education Statistics 2003, *Internet site http://nces.ed.gov//programs/digest/d03/list_tables.asp; calculations by New Strategist*

Table 2.14   Doctoral Degrees Earned by Asians by Field of Study, 2001–02

(total number of doctoral degrees conferred and number and percent earned by Asians, by field of study, 2001–02)

	total	earned by Asians number	earned by Asians percent
Total doctoral degrees	**44,160**	**2,317**	**5.2%**
Agriculture and natural resources	1,166	24	2.1
Architecture and related programs	183	11	6.0
Area, ethnic, and cultural studies	216	15	6.9
Biological and life sciences	4,489	401	8.9
Business	1,158	53	4.6
Communications	374	14	3.7
Communications technologies	9	0	0.0
Computer and information sciences	750	78	10.4
Education	6,967	180	2.6
Engineering	5,195	380	7.3
Engineering-related technologies	15	1	6.7
English language and literature, letters	1,446	56	3.9
Foreign languages and literatures	843	34	4.0
Health professions and related sciences	3,523	258	7.3
Home economics	355	12	3.4
Law and legal studies	79	0	0.0
Liberal arts and sciences, general studies, humanities	113	1	0.9
Library science	45	0	0.0
Mathematics	958	27	2.8
Multi- and interdisciplinary studies	384	19	4.9
Parks, recreation, leisure, and fitness	151	3	2.0
Philosophy and religion	606	23	3.8
Physical sciences	3,803	196	5.2
Protective services	49	0	0.0
Psychology	4,341	192	4.4
Public administration and services	571	29	5.1
Social sciences and history	3,902	149	3.8
Theological studies, religious vocations	1,355	105	7.7
Visual and performing arts	1,114	56	5.0

Source: National Center for Education Statistics, Digest of Education Statistics 2003, *Internet site http://nces.ed.gov//programs/digest/d03/list_tables.asp; calculations by New Strategist*

Table 2.15 First-Professional Degrees Earned by Asians by Field of Study, 2001–02

(total number of first-professional degrees conferred and number and percent earned by Asians, by field of study, 2001–02)

		earned by Asians	
	total	number	percent
Total first-professional degrees	**80,698**	**9,584**	**11.9%**
Dentistry (D.D.S. or D.M.D.)	4,239	974	23.0
Medicine (M.D.)	15,237	2,959	19.4
Optometry (O.D.)	1,280	344	26.9
Osteopathic medicine (D.O.)	2,416	414	17.1
Pharmacy (Pharm.D.)	7,076	1,501	21.2
Podiatry (Pod.D., D.P., or D.P.M.)	474	71	15.0
Veterinary medicine (D.V.M.)	2,289	65	2.8
Chiropractic (D.C. or D.C.M.)	3,284	354	10.8
Naturopathic medicine	227	11	4.8
Law (LL.B. or J.D.)	38,981	2,621	6.7
Theology (M.Div., M.H.L., B.D., or Ord.)	5,195	270	5.2

Source: National Center for Education Statistics, Digest of Education Statistics 2003, *Internet site http://nces.ed.gov//programs/ digest/d03/list_tables.asp; calculations by New Strategist*

Table 2.16 Asian Participation in Adult Education, 2001

(percent of total people and Asians aged 16 or older participating in adult education activities, by type of adult education activity, 2001)

	percent participating	
	total	Asians
Any adult education course	**47.4%**	**52.3%**
College or university credential programs	7.3	–
Work-related courses	29.7	34.3
Personal interest courses	21.3	18.2
Other educational activities	3.6	–

Note: Adult education activities include apprenticeships, courses for basic skills, English as a second language, work-related courses, and personal development. For those aged 25 or older, credential programs in postsecondary institutions are counted as adult education activities. For those aged 16 to 24, full-time participation (full-year or part-year) in college or university credential programs or vocational or technical diploma programs are excluded. (–) means sample is too small to make a reliable estimate.
Source: National Center for Education Statistics, Adult Education and Lifelong Learning Survey of the National Household Education Surveys Program; Internet site http://nces.ed.gov/programs/coe/2003/section1/tables/t08_2.asp

Few Asians Are Overweight

Asians are the only racial or ethnic group in which those with a healthy weight (neither over-nor underweight) are in the majority. Sixty-two percent of Asians are at a healthy weight, while only 31 percent are overweight. Among all Americans, 59 percent are overweight. Sixty-six percent of Asians report being in very good or excellent health. Just 13 percent smoke cigarettes, and only 44 percent drink alcohol.

More than 221,000 babies were born to Asian women in 2003, or 5 percent of all babies born that year. In Hawaii, 68 percent of births were to Asians in 2003. In California, the figure was 12 percent.

Eighty-one percent of Asians are covered by some type of health insurance, most having employment-based coverage. Only 8 percent of Asian adults have difficulties in physical functioning, far below the 15 percent rate for the total population. The leading causes of death among Asians are cancer and heart disease, which accounted for 52 percent of Asian deaths in 2002.

■ The Asian health advantage could diminish if poorly educated immigrants become a larger share of the Asian population.

Nineteen percent of Asians do not have health insurance

(percent distribution of Asians by health insurance coverage status, 2003; shares do not add to 100 percent because some people have more than one type of health insurance.)

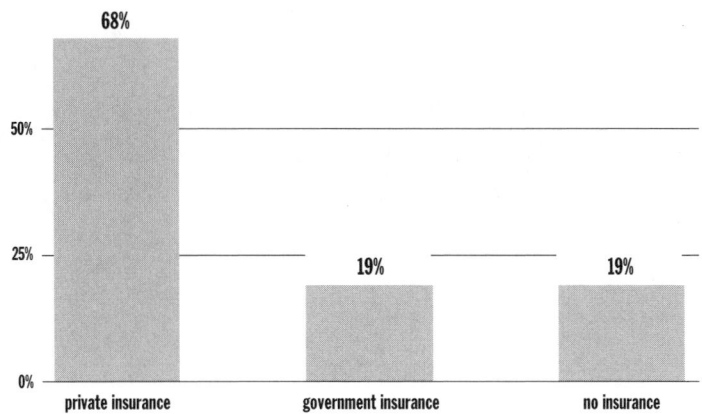

Table 2.17 Asian Health Status, 2003

(percent distribution of total people and Asians aged 18 or older by self-reported health status, and index of Asian to total, 2003)

	total	Asian	index of Asian to total
Total people	**100.0%**	**100.0%**	–
Excellent/very good	62.3	65.9	106
Good	25.5	23.8	93
Fair/poor	12.2	10.3	84

Note: Asians are those identifying themselves as being Asian alone. (–) means not applicable. The index is calculated by dividing the Asian figure by the total figure and multiplying by 100.
Source: National Center for Health Statistics, Summary Health Statistics for U.S. Adults: National Health Interview Survey, 2003, *Series 10, No. 225, 2005; Internet site http://www.cdc.gov/nchs/nhis.htm; calculations by New Strategist*

Table 2.18 Smoking and Drinking Status of Asians by Sex, 1999–2003

(percent distribution of Asians aged 18 or older by smoking and drinking status and sex, 1999–2003)

	total	men	women
SMOKING STATUS			
Total Asians	**100.0%**	**100.0%**	**100.0%**
Never smoked	73.8	60.4	87.0
Former smoker	13.5	20.7	6.4
Current smoker	12.7	18.9	6.5
DRINKING STATUS			
Total Asians	**100.0**	**100.0**	**100.0**
Lifetime abstainer	47.1	32.6	61.2
Former drinker	9.3	10.9	7.9
Current light or infrequent drinker	34.6	41.6	27.9
Current moderate or heavier drinker	8.9	14.9	3.0

Note: Never smoked means having had fewer than 100 cigarettes in lifetime. Former smokers have had 100 or more cigarettes in lifetime but did not smoke at time of interview. Current smokers have had at least 100 cigarettes in lifetime and currently smoke. Lifetime abstainers have had fewer than 12 drinks in lifetime. Former drinkers have had 12 or more drinks in lifetime, none in past year. Current light or infrequent drinkers have had 12 or more drinks in lifetime, drank alcohol in past year, and have 3 or fewer drinks per week on average. Current moderate or heavier drinkers drank 12 or more drinks in lifetime, drank alcohol in past year, and drank more than 3 drinks per week on average. Asians are those identifying themselves as being Asian alone.
Source: National Center for Health Statistics, Health Characteristics of the American Indian and Alaska Native Adult Population: United States, 1999–2003, *Advance Data, No. 356, 2005; Internet site http://www.cdc.gov/nchs/nhis.htm*

Table 2.19 Weight of Asians by Sex, 1999–2003

(percent distribution of Asians aged 18 or older by body weight status and sex, 1999–2003)

	total	men	women
Total Asians	**100.0%**	**100.0%**	**100.0%**
Underweight	5.9	3.0	8.8
Healthy weight	62.8	59.6	66.0
Overweight, total	31.3	37.4	25.2
Overweight, but not obese	25.3	31.2	19.4
Obese	6.0	6.2	5.8

Note: Being overweight is defined as having a body mass index of 25 or higher. Being obese is defined as having a body mass index of 30 or higher. Body mass index is calculated by dividing weight in kilograms by height in meters squared. Data are based on measured height and weight of a sample of the civilian noninstitutionalized population. Asians are those identifying themselves as being Asian alone.
Source: National Center for Health Statistics, Health Characteristics of the American Indian and Alaska Native Adult Population: United States, 1999–2003, *Advance Data, No. 356, 2005; Internet site http://www.cdc.gov/nchs/nhis.htm*

Table 2.20 Births to Asian Women by Age, 2003

(total number of births, number and percent distribution of births to Asians, and Asian share of total, by age, 2003)

		Asian		
	total	number	percent distribution	share of total
Total births	**4,089,950**	**221,203**	**100.0%**	**5.4%**
Under age 15	6,661	104	0.0	1.6
Aged 15 to 19	414,580	7,592	3.4	1.8
Aged 20 to 24	1,032,305	30,482	13.8	3.0
Aged 25 to 29	1,086,366	64,399	29.1	5.9
Aged 30 to 34	975,546	75,692	34.2	7.8
Aged 35 to 39	467,642	35,074	15.9	7.5
Aged 40 to 44	101,005	7,413	3.4	7.3
Aged 45 to 54	5,845	447	0.2	7.6

Note: Asians include Pacific Islanders.
Source: National Center for Health Statistics, Births: Final Data for 2003, *National Vital Statistics Reports, Vol. 54, No. 2, 2005; Internet site http://www.cdc.gov/nchs/products/pubs/pubd/nvsr/54/54-pre.htm; calculations by New Strategist*

Table 2.21 Births to Asian Women by Age and Marital Status, 2003

(total number of births to Asians, number of births to unmarried Asians, and unmarried share of total, by age, 2003)

		unmarried Asians	
	total	number	share of total
Births to Asians	**221,203**	**33,249**	**15.0%**
Under age 15	104	103	99.0
Aged 15 to 19	7,592	5,544	73.0
Aged 20 to 24	30,482	11,115	36.5
Aged 25 to 29	64,399	7,886	12.2
Aged 30 to 34	75,692	5,238	6.9
Aged 35 to 39	35,074	2,580	7.4
Aged 40 or older	7,860	783	10.0

Note: Asians include Pacific Islanders.
Source: National Center for Health Statistics, Births: Final Data for 2003, *National Vital Statistics Reports, Vol. 54, No. 2, 2005; Internet site http://www.cdc.gov/nchs/products/pubs/pubd/nvsr/54/54-pre.htm; calculations by New Strategist*

Table 2.22 Births to Asian Women by Birth Order, 2003

(total number of births, number and percent distribution of births to Asians, and Asian share of total, by birth order, 2003)

	total	Asian number	Asian percent distribution	Asian share of total
Total births	**4,089,950**	**221,203**	**100.0%**	**5.4%**
First child	1,633,987	103,590	46.8	6.3
Second child	1,320,477	76,246	34.5	5.8
Third child	684,296	26,505	12.0	3.9
Fourth or later child	439,235	14,086	6.4	3.2

Note: Asians include Pacific Islanders. Numbers will not add to total because "not stated" is not shown.
Source: National Center for Health Statistics, Births: Final Data for 2003, National Vital Statistics Reports, Vol. 54, No. 2, 2005; Internet site http://www.cdc.gov/nchs/products/pubs/pubd/nvsr/54/54-pre.htm; calculations by New Strategist

Table 2.23 Births to Asian Women by State, 2003

(total number of births, number and percent distribution of births to Asians, and Asian share of total, by state, 2003)

	total	Asian births number	Asian births percent distribution	Asian births share of total
Total births	**4,089,950**	**221,203**	**100.0%**	**5.4%**
Alabama	59,552	607	0.3	1.0
Alaska	10,086	712	0.3	7.1
Arizona	90,967	2,698	1.2	3.0
Arkansas	37,784	539	0.2	1.4
California	540,997	67,358	30.5	12.5
Colorado	69,339	2,672	1.2	3.9
Connecticut	42,873	2,036	0.9	4.7
Delaware	11,329	449	0.2	4.0
District of Columbia	7,619	256	0.1	3.4
Florida	212,250	5,795	2.6	2.7
Georgia	135,979	4,436	2.0	3.3
Hawaii	18,100	12,360	5.6	68.3
Idaho	21,800	351	0.2	1.6
Illinois	182,495	8,850	4.0	4.8
Indiana	86,434	1,382	0.6	1.6
Iowa	38,174	939	0.4	2.5
Kansas	39,476	1,226	0.6	3.1
Kentucky	55,236	868	0.4	1.6
Louisiana	65,040	1,101	0.5	1.7
Maine	13,855	208	0.1	1.5
Maryland	74,930	4,523	2.0	6.0
Massachusetts	80,184	5,395	2.4	6.7
Michigan	131,094	4,722	2.1	3.6
Minnesota	70,050	3,868	1.7	5.5
Mississippi	42,380	292	0.1	0.7
Missouri	77,045	1,697	0.8	2.2
Montana	11,422	124	0.1	1.1
Nebraska	25,917	603	0.3	2.3
Nevada	33,647	2,527	1.1	7.5
New Hampshire	14,393	469	0.2	3.3
New Jersey	116,983	10,737	4.9	9.2
New Mexico	27,821	402	0.2	1.4
New York	253,714	21,223	9.6	8.4
North Carolina	118,323	3,108	1.4	2.6
North Dakota	7,972	115	0.1	1.4
Ohio	149,679	3,086	1.4	2.1
Oklahoma	50,981	1,077	0.5	2.1
Oregon	45,953	2,494	1.1	5.4

(continued)

	total	Asian births		
		number	percent distribution	share of total
Pennsylvania	145,959	5,176	2.3%	3.5%
Rhode Island	13,209	563	0.3	4.3
South Carolina	55,649	893	0.4	1.6
South Dakota	11,027	127	0.1	1.2
Tennessee	78,890	1,489	0.7	1.9
Texas	377,476	13,147	5.9	3.5
Utah	49,860	1,532	0.7	3.1
Vermont	6,589	118	0.1	1.8
Virginia	101,254	6,551	3.0	6.5
Washington	80,489	7,842	3.5	9.7
West Virginia	20,935	146	0.1	0.7
Wisconsin	70,040	2,248	1.0	3.2
Wyoming	6,700	66	0.0	1.0

Note: Asians include Pacific Islanders.
Source: National Center for Health Statistics, Births: Final Data for 2003, *National Vital Statistics Reports, Vol. 54, No. 2, 2005; Internet site http://www.cdc.gov/nchs/products/pubs/pubd/nvsr/54/54-pre.htm; calculations by New Strategist*

Table 2.24 Health Insurance Coverage of Asians by Age, 2003

(number and percent distribution of Asians by age and health insurance coverage status, 2003; numbers in thousands)

	total	with health insurance coverage during year			not covered at any time during the year
		total	private	government	
Total Asians	**12,905**	**10,504**	**8,826**	**2,478**	**2,401**
Under age 18	3,330	2,938	2,371	756	393
Aged 18 to 24	1,263	848	735	158	415
Aged 25 to 34	2,344	1,768	1,644	164	576
Aged 35 to 44	2,132	1,720	1,603	170	412
Aged 45 to 54	1,711	1,349	1,253	125	362
Aged 55 to 64	1,059	851	762	134	208
Aged 65 or older	1,065	1,029	459	970	36
PERCENT DISTRIBUTION BY COVERAGE STATUS					
Total Asians	**100.0%**	**81.4%**	**68.4%**	**19.2%**	**18.6%**
Under age 18	100.0	88.2	71.2	22.7	11.8
Aged 18 to 24	100.0	67.1	58.2	12.5	32.9
Aged 25 to 34	100.0	75.4	70.1	7.0	24.6
Aged 35 to 44	100.0	80.7	75.2	8.0	19.3
Aged 45 to 54	100.0	78.8	73.2	7.3	21.2
Aged 55 to 64	100.0	80.4	72.0	12.7	19.6
Aged 65 or older	100.0	96.6	43.1	91.1	3.4

Note: Asians are those identifying themselves as being of the race alone and those identifying themselves as being of the race in combination with one or more other races. Numbers may not add to total because some people have more than one type of health insurance.
Source: Bureau of the Census, 2004 Current Population Survey, Annual Social and Economic Supplement, detailed tables, Internet site http://pubdb3.census.gov/macro/032004/health/h01_000.htm; calculations by New Strategist

Table 2.25 Asians with Private Health Insurance Coverage by Age, 2003

(number and percent distribution of Asians by age and private health insurance coverage status, 2003; numbers in thousands)

	total	with private health insurance total	employment-based total	own	direct purchase
Total Asians	**12,905**	**8,826**	**7,829**	**3,848**	**1,159**
Under age 18	3,330	2,371	2,157	4	256
Aged 18 to 24	1,263	735	560	185	107
Aged 25 to 34	2,344	1,644	1,505	1,108	173
Aged 35 to 44	2,132	1,603	1,463	1,002	193
Aged 45 to 54	1,711	1,253	1,153	802	139
Aged 55 to 64	1,059	762	666	498	118
Aged 65 or older	1,065	459	323	248	173
PERCENT DISTRIBUTION BY COVERAGE STATUS					
Total Asians	**100.0%**	**68.4%**	**60.7%**	**29.8%**	**9.0%**
Under age 18	100.0	71.2	64.8	0.1	7.7
Aged 18 to 24	100.0	58.2	44.3	14.6	8.5
Aged 25 to 34	100.0	70.1	64.2	47.3	7.4
Aged 35 to 44	100.0	75.2	68.6	47.0	9.1
Aged 45 to 54	100.0	73.2	67.4	46.9	8.1
Aged 55 to 64	100.0	72.0	62.9	47.0	11.1
Aged 65 or older	100.0	43.1	30.3	23.3	16.2

Note: Asians are those identifying themselves as being of the race alone and those identifying themselves as being of the race in combination with one or more other races. Numbers will not add to total because some people have more than one type of health insurance.

Source: Bureau of the Census, 2004 Current Population Survey, Annual Social and Economic Supplement, detailed tables, Internet site http://pubdb3.census.gov/macro/032004/health/h01_000.htm; calculations by New Strategist

Table 2.26 Asians with Government Health Insurance Coverage by Age, 2003

(number and percent distribution of Asians by age and government health insurance coverage status, 2003; numbers in thousands)

	total	with government health insurance			
		total	Medicaid	Medicare	military
Total Asians	**12,905**	**2,478**	**1,385**	**1,096**	**355**
Under age 18	3,330	756	653	32	92
Aged 18 to 24	1,263	158	111	0	50
Aged 25 to 34	2,344	164	120	17	34
Aged 35 to 44	2,132	170	124	12	42
Aged 45 to 54	1,711	125	66	12	48
Aged 55 to 64	1,059	134	61	61	31
Aged 65 or older	1,065	970	252	962	56

PERCENT DISTRIBUTION BY COVERAGE STATUS

Total Asians	**100.0%**	**19.2%**	**10.7%**	**8.5%**	**2.8%**
Under age 18	100.0	22.7	19.6	1.0	2.8
Aged 18 to 24	100.0	12.5	8.8	0.0	4.0
Aged 25 to 34	100.0	7.0	5.1	0.7	1.5
Aged 35 to 44	100.0	8.0	5.8	0.6	2.0
Aged 45 to 54	100.0	7.3	3.9	0.7	2.8
Aged 55 to 64	100.0	12.7	5.8	5.8	2.9
Aged 65 or older	100.0	91.1	23.7	90.3	5.3

Note: Asians are those identifying themselves as being of the race alone and those identifying themselves as being of the race in combination with one or more other races. Numbers will not add to total because some people have more than one type of health insurance.

Source: Bureau of the Census, 2004 Current Population Survey, Annual Social and Economic Supplement, detailed tables, Internet site http://pubdb3.census.gov/macro/032004/health/h01_000.htm; calculations by New Strategist

Table 2.27 Health Conditions among Asians Aged 18 or Older, 2003

(number of total people and Asians aged 18 or older with selected health conditions, percent of Asians with condition, and Asian share of total with condition, 2003; numbers in thousands)

	total	Asian number	Asian percent with condition	Asian share of total
Total people	213,042	7,361	–	3.5%
Selected circulatory diseases				
Heart disease, all types	23,536	280	5.6%	1.2
Coronary	12,254	179	3.8	1.5
Hypertension	45,927	888	16.1	1.9
Stroke	5,070	81	1.8	1.6
Selected respiratory conditions				
Emphysema	3,115	24	0.5	0.8
Asthma				
Ever	20,697	436	6.4	2.1
Still	13,623	172	2.7	1.3
Hay fever	18,356	469	6.5	2.6
Sinusitis	29,673	427	5.5	1.4
Chronic bronchitis	8,560	77	1.4	0.9
Cancer				
Any cancer	13,973	206	3.7	1.5
Breast cancer (all adults)	2,426	49	1.0	2.0
Cervical cancer (women only)	1,082	–	–	–
Prostate cancer (men only)	1,332	5	0.3	0.4
Other selected diseases and conditions				
Diabetes	14,012	355	6.5	2.5
Ulcers	14,456	256	4.6	1.8
Kidney disease	3,017	72	1.2	2.4
Liver disease	2,511	78	1.1	3.1
Arthritis	45,793	633	11.9	1.4
Chronic joint symptoms	57,242	1,004	16.2	1.8
Migraines or severe headaches	32,268	887	12.0	2.7
Pain in neck	31,368	616	9.0	2.0
Pain in lower back	58,430	1,364	19.9	2.3
Pain in face or jaw	9,464	187	2.7	2.0
Selected sensory problems				
Hearing	32,533	520	9.5	1.6
Vision	18,628	374	6.2	2.0
Absence of all natural teeth	15,927	376	6.8	2.4

Note: The conditions shown are those that have ever been diagnosed by a doctor, except as noted. Hay fever, sinusitis, and chronic bronchitis have been diagnosed in the past twelve months. Kidney and liver disease have been diagnosed in the past twelve months and exclude kidney stones, bladder infections, and incontinence. Chronic joint symptoms are shown if respondent had pain, aching, or stiffness in or around a joint (excluding back and neck) and the condition began more than three months ago. Migraines, pain in neck, lower back, face, or jaw are shown only if pain lasted a whole day or more. Asians are those identifying themselves as being Asian alone. (–) means not applicable or sample is too small to make a reliable estimate.
Source: National Center for Health Statistics, Summary Health Statistics for U.S. Adults: National Health Interview Survey, 2003, Series 10, No. 225, 2005; Internet site http://www.cdc.gov/nchs/nhis.htm; calculations by New Strategist

Table 2.28 Health Conditions among Asian Children, 2003

(number of total people and Asians under age 18 with selected health conditions, percent of Asians with condition, and Asian share of total, 2003; numbers in thousands)

	total	Asian number	Asian percent with condition	Asian share of total
Total children	**72,973**	**2,343**	–	**3.2%**
Diagnosed with asthma	9,071	153	6.8%	1.7
Experienced in last 12 months				
Asthma attack	3,975	87	4.0	2.2
Hay fever	7,059	177	7.8	2.5
Respiratory allergies	8,347	173	7.6	2.1
Other allergies	8,407	222	9.2	2.6
Ever told had*				
Learning disability	4,561	73	3.8	1.6
Attention deficit hyperactivity disorder	3,881	11	0.6	0.3
Prescription medication taken regularly for at least 3 months	9,287	120	5.2	1.3

* "Ever told" by a school representative or health professional. Data exclude children under age 3.
Note: Other allergies include food or digestive allergies, eczema, and other skin allergies. Asians are those identifying themselves as being Asian alone. (–) means not applicable.
Source: National Center for Health Statistics, Summary Health Statistics for U.S. Children: National Health Interview Survey, 2003, Series 10, No. 223, 2005; Internet site http://www.cdc.gov/nchs/nhis.htm; calculations by New Strategist

Table 2.29 Physician Office Visits by Asians, 2002

(number of total physician office visits, number of visits by Asians, Asian share of total, and average number of visits by Asians per person per year, 2002)

	total (000s)	visits by Asians number (000s)	visits by Asians share of total	visits by Asians per person per year
Total visits	889,980	26,341	3.0%	2.3

Source: National Center for Health Statistics, National Ambulatory Medical Care Survey: 2002 Summary, Advance Data No. 346, 2004; Internet site http://www.cdc.gov/nchs/about/major/ahcd/adata.htm; calculations by New Strategist

Table 2.30 Difficulties in Physical Functioning among Asians, 2003

(number of total people and Asians aged 18 or older, number with difficulties in physical functioning, percent of Asians with difficulty, and Asian share of total, by type of difficulty, 2003; numbers in thousands)

	total	Asian number	Asian percent with difficulty	Asian share of total
TOTAL PEOPLE	**213,042**	**7,361**	–	**3.5%**
Total with any physical difficulty	**31,322**	**449**	**8.3%**	**1.4**
Walk quarter of a mile	14,910	192	3.8	1.3
Climb up ten steps without resting	11,107	207	3.8	1.9
Stand for two hours	18,663	286	5.4	1.5
Sit for two hours	7,211	165	3.2	2.3
Stoop, bend, or kneel	18,250	268	5.1	1.5
Reach over head	6,264	102	2.0	1.6
Grasp or handle small objects	3,943	56	1.1	1.4
Lift or carry ten pounds	9,194	209	4.0	2.3
Push or pull large objects	13,463	268	5.2	2.0

Note: Respondents were classified as having difficulties if they responded "very difficult" or "can't do at all." Asians are those identifying themselves as being Asian alone. (–) means not applicable.
Source: National Center for Health Statistics, Summary Health Statistics for U.S. Adults: National Health Interview Survey, 2003, Series 10, No. 225, 2005; *Internet site http://www.cdc.gov/nchs/nhis.htm; calculations by New Strategist*

Table 2.31 AIDS Cases among Asians, through December 2003

(total number of AIDS cases diagnosed, number and percent distribution of AIDS cases diagnosed among Asians, and Asian share of total, by sex and age at diagnosis, through December 2003)

	total	Asian number	Asian percent distribution	Asian share of total
Total AIDS cases	**874,230**	**6,837**	**100.0%**	**0.8%**
Males aged 13 or older	708,452	5,875	85.9	0.8
Females aged 13 or older	156,837	905	13.2	0.6
Children under age 13	8,939	57	0.8	0.6

Source: National Center for Health Statistics, Health, United States, 2004; *Internet site http://www.cdc.gov/nchs/hus.htm; calculations by New Strategist*

Table 2.32 Leading Causes of Death among Asians, 2002

(number and percent distribution of deaths to Asians accounted for by the ten leading causes of death among Asians, 2002)

	number	percent distribution
Total Asian deaths	**38,332**	**100.0%**
1. Malignant neoplasms (cancer) (2)	9,998	26.1
2. Diseases of the heart (1)	9,983	26.0
3. Cerebrovascular diseases (3)	3,530	9.2
4. Accidents (unintentional injuries) (5)	1,875	4.9
5. Diabetes mellitus (6)	1,359	3.5
6. Influenza and pneumonia (7)	1,171	3.1
7. Chronic lower respiratory disease (4)	1,138	3.0
8. Suicide (11)	661	1.7
9. Nephritis, nephrotic syndrome, nephrosis (9)	649	1.7
10. Septicemia (10)	423	1.1
All other causes	7,545	19.7

Note: Number in parentheses shows rank for all Americans if the cause of death is among top fifteen.
Source: National Center for Health Statistics, Health, United States, 2004; *Internet site http://www.cdc.gov/nchs/hus.htm; calculations by New Strategist*

More than Half of Asian Householders Own Their Home

Asian households are less likely than the average household to own a home. In 2004, 60 percent of Asian households owned their home versus 69 percent of all households. Although Asians are less likely than average to own a home, they are more likely to be homeowners than blacks, Hispanics, and American Indians. At least 50 percent of Asian households own their home in every region.

Among Asian married couples, the 69 percent majority are homeowners. Homeownership among Asian female- and male-headed families is above 50 percent. But only 31 percent of Asians heading nonfamily households are homeowners.

Asians are less likely to live in single-family homes and more likely to live in apartments than the average American. Only 57 percent of Asian households are in single-family homes, a proportion well below the 68 percent national share. Thirty-two percent of Asians live in apartment buildings with five or more units compared with just 17 percent of households nationally. Sixteen percent of Asians moved between March 2003 and March 2004, a higher rate of mobility than for the population as a whole.

■ Asians are more likely to be homeowners than blacks and Hispanics because they are better educated and earn higher incomes.

Asian homeownership is highest in the South

(percent of Asian households that own their home, by region, 2003)

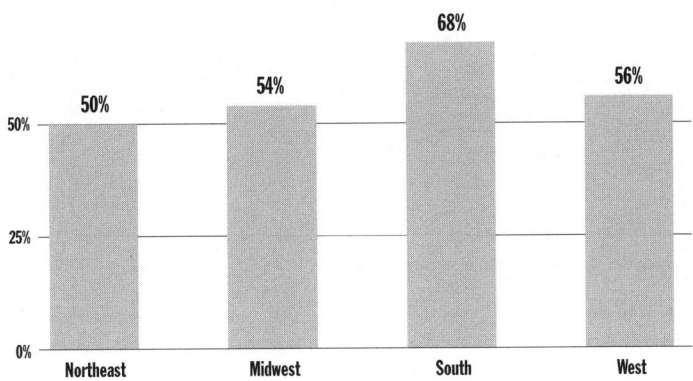

Table 2.33 Asian Homeownership Rate, 1994 to 2004

(homeownership rate of total and Asian households and index of Asian to total, 1994 to 2004; percentage point change in homeownership rate, 1994–2004)

	total households	Asian households	index
2004	69.0%	59.8%	87
2003	68.3	56.3	82
2002	67.9	54.7	81
2001	67.8	53.9	79
2000	67.4	52.8	78
1999	66.8	53.1	79
1998	66.3	52.6	79
1997	65.7	52.8	80
1996	65.4	50.8	78
1995	64.7	50.8	79
1994	64.0	51.3	80
Percentage point change			
1994 to 2004	5.0	8.5	–

Note: Asians are those identifying themselves as being of the race alone. The index is calculated by dividing the Asian homeownership rate by the total rate and multiplying by 100. (–) means not applicable.
Source: Bureau of the Census, American Housing Survey for the United States: 2003, *Current Housing Reports, Internet site http://www.census.gov/hhes/www/ahs.html; calculations by New Strategist*

Table 2.34 Asian Homeownership Status by Household Type, 2003

(number and percent of Asian households by household type and homeownership status, 2003; numbers in thousands)

	total	owner		renter	
		number	percent	number	percent
TOTAL ASIAN HOUSEHOLDS	**4,079**	**2,289**	**56.1%**	**1,790**	**43.9%**
Family households	**2,939**	**1,932**	**65.7**	**1,006**	**34.2**
Married couples	2,344	1,615	68.9	728	31.1
Female householder, no spouse present	354	195	55.1	160	45.2
Male householder, no spouse present	241	123	51.0	118	49.0
Nonfamily households	**1,140**	**356**	**31.2**	**784**	**68.8**
Female householder	567	213	37.6	355	62.6
Male householder	573	143	25.0	430	75.0

Note: Asians include those identifying themselves as being of the race alone and those identifying themselves as being of the race in combination with one or more other races.
Source: Bureau of the Census, America's Families and Living Arrangements, 2003 Current Population Survey Annual Social and Economic Supplement; Internet site http://www.census.gov/population/www/socdemo/hh-fam/cps2003.html; calculations by New Strategist

Table 2.35 Asian Homeowners by Type of Household, 2003

(number of total homeowners, number and percent distribution of Asian homeowners, and Asian share of total, by type of household, 2003; numbers in thousands)

	total	Asian number	Asian percent distribution	Asian share of total
TOTAL HOMEOWNERS	**75,909**	**2,289**	**100.0%**	**3.0%**
Family households	**57,092**	**1,932**	**84.4**	**3.4**
Married couples	47,676	1,615	70.6	3.4
Female householder, no spouse present	6,695	195	8.5	2.9
Male householder, no spouse present	2,721	123	5.4	4.5
Nonfamily households	**18,817**	**356**	**15.6**	**1.9**
Female householder	11,075	213	9.3	1.9
Male householder	7,742	143	6.2	1.8

Note: Asians include those identifying themselves as being of the race alone and those identifying themselves as being of the race in combination with one or more other races.
Source: Bureau of the Census, America's Families and Living Arrangements, 2003 Current Population Survey Annual Social and Economic Supplement; Internet site http://www.census.gov/population/www/socdemo/hh-fam/cps2003.html; calculations by New Strategist

Table 2.36 Asian Homeownership Status by Region, 2003

(number and percent of Asian households by homeownership status and region, 2003; numbers in thousands)

	total	owners number	owners share of total	renters number	renters share of total
Total Asian households	**3,183**	**1,811**	**56.9%**	**1,371**	**43.1%**
Northeast	610	308	50.5	302	49.5
Midwest	342	186	54.4	156	45.6
South	573	389	67.9	184	32.1
West	1,658	928	56.0	730	44.0

Note: Asians include only those identifying themselves as being Asian alone.
Source: Bureau of the Census, American Housing Survey for the United States: 2003, Current Housing Reports, Internet site http://www.census.gov/hhes/www/ahs.html; calculations by New Strategist

Table 2.37 Asian Homeowners by Region, 2003

(number of total homeowners, number and percent distribution of Asian homeowners, and Asian share of total, by region, 2003; numbers in thousands)

| | total | Asian | | |
		number	percent distribution	share of total
Total homeowners	**72,238**	**1,811**	**100.0%**	**2.5%**
Northeast	12,964	308	17.0	2.4
Midwest	17,889	186	10.3	1.0
South	26,699	389	21.5	1.5
West	14,686	928	51.2	6.3

Note: Asians include only those identifying themselves as being Asian alone.
Source: Bureau of the Census, American Housing Survey for the United States: 2003, *Current Housing Reports, Internet site http://www.census.gov/hhes/www/ahs.html; calculations by New Strategist*

Table 2.38 Housing Units Occupied by Asians by Type, 2003

(number of total occupied housing units, number and percent distribution of housing units occupied by Asians, and Asian share of total, by number of units in structure, 2003)

| | total | Asians | | |
		number	percent distribution	share of total
Total occupied housing units	**108,419,506**	**3,767,952**	**100.0%**	**3.5%**
One unit, detached or attached	73,740,642	2,142,940	56.9	2.9
Two to four units	9,374,261	371,656	9.9	4.0
Five or more units	18,089,052	1,215,255	32.3	6.7
Mobile home	7,128,265	37,169	1.0	0.5
Boat, RV, van, etc.	87,286	932	0.0	1.1

Note: Asians include only those identifying themselves as being Asian alone.
Source: Bureau of the Census, 2003 American Community Survey, Internet site http://factfinder.census.gov/servlet/DatasetMainPageServlet?_program=ACS&_lang=en&_ts=; calculations by New Strategist

Table 2.39 Geographical Mobility of Asians by Age, 2003–04

(total number of Asians aged 1 or older, and number and percent who moved between March 2003 and March 2004, by age and type of move; numbers in thousands)

	total	movers total	same county	different county, same state	different state	abroad
Total Asians	**12,727**	**2,002**	**1,000**	**393**	**326**	**283**
Aged 1 to 4	753	157	87	27	28	15
Aged 5 to 9	927	123	57	50	7	9
Aged 10 to 14	909	112	74	20	13	5
Aged 15 to 17	563	86	44	21	13	8
Aged 18 to 19	283	52	35	10	2	5
Aged 20 to 24	980	245	109	51	35	50
Aged 25 to 29	1,093	356	152	46	74	84
Aged 30 to 34	1,252	251	138	38	37	38
Aged 35 to 39	1,128	178	78	49	42	9
Aged 40 to 44	1,004	137	82	26	12	17
Aged 45 to 49	941	96	55	22	9	10
Aged 50 to 54	770	82	38	10	21	13
Aged 55 to 59	629	35	18	0	12	5
Aged 60 to 61	180	12	3	0	5	4
Aged 62 to 64	250	19	6	2	3	8
Aged 65 or older	1,064	63	23	21	16	3

PERCENT DISTRIBUTION BY MOBILITY STATUS

	total	movers total	same county	different county, same state	different state	abroad
Total Asians	**100.0%**	**15.7%**	**7.9%**	**3.1%**	**2.6%**	**2.2%**
Aged 1 to 4	100.0	20.8	11.6	3.6	3.7	2.0
Aged 5 to 9	100.0	13.3	6.1	5.4	0.8	1.0
Aged 10 to 14	100.0	12.3	8.1	2.2	1.4	0.6
Aged 15 to 17	100.0	15.3	7.8	3.7	2.3	1.4
Aged 18 to 19	100.0	18.4	12.4	3.5	0.7	1.8
Aged 20 to 24	100.0	25.0	11.1	5.2	3.6	5.1
Aged 25 to 29	100.0	32.6	13.9	4.2	6.8	7.7
Aged 30 to 34	100.0	20.0	11.0	3.0	3.0	3.0
Aged 35 to 39	100.0	15.8	6.9	4.3	3.7	0.8
Aged 40 to 44	100.0	13.6	8.2	2.6	1.2	1.7
Aged 45 to 49	100.0	10.2	5.8	2.3	1.0	1.1
Aged 50 to 54	100.0	10.6	4.9	1.3	2.7	1.7
Aged 55 to 59	100.0	5.6	2.9	0.0	1.9	0.8
Aged 60 to 61	100.0	6.7	1.7	0.0	2.8	2.2
Aged 62 to 64	100.0	7.6	2.4	0.8	1.2	3.2
Aged 65 or older	100.0	5.9	2.2	2.0	1.5	0.3

Note: Asians include those identifying themselves as being of the race alone and those identifying themselves as being Asian in combination with one or more other races.
Source: Bureau of the Census, Geographic Mobility: 2004, Detailed Tables, Internet site http://www.census.gov/population/www/ socdemo/migrate/cps2004.html; calculations by New Strategist

Asians Have the Highest Incomes

The $55,262 median income of Asian households in 2003 was 28 percent greater than the all-household average and higher than that of any other racial or ethnic group. Asian household income exceeds that of blacks, Hispanics, and non-Hispanic whites although it has been growing more slowly than average. Between 1990 and 2003, the median income of Asian households grew only 5 percent—less than the 6 percent gain for all households during those years, after adjusting for inflation.

Among Asian households, median income peaks at $67,011 for householders aged 35 to 44. By household type, Asian married couples have the highest median income—$70,548 in 2003. Fully 23 percent of Asian households have incomes of $100,000 or more.

Among full-time workers, the median income of Asian men rose 23 percent between 1990 and 2003, after adjusting for inflation, while their female counterparts saw a 15 percent increase. Even during the 2000-to-2003 time period, when many workers lost ground, Asians with full-time jobs saw their incomes grow.

Asians are less likely to be poor than blacks or Hispanics, but more likely to be poor than non-Hispanic whites. The poverty rate of Asian married couples stood at 8 percent in 2003. Among Asian female-headed families, the poverty rate was 24 percent, double the 12 percent poverty rate among Asian male-headed families.

■ Asian households have higher incomes than black, Hispanic, and non-Hispanic white households because Asians are much better educated and have more earners in the home.

Asian household income grew more slowly than average between 1990 and 2003

(percent change in total and Asian median household income, 1990 to 2003; in 2003 dollars)

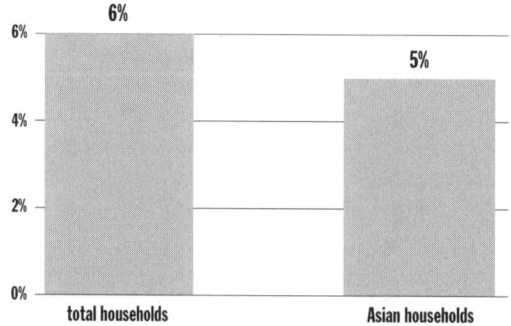

Table 2.40 Median Income of Asian Households, 1990 to 2003

(median income of total and Asian households, and index of Asian to total, 1990 to 2003; percent change in incomes, 2000–03 and 1990–2003; in 2003 dollars)

	total households	Asian households	index
2003	$43,318	$55,262	128
2002	43,381	53,483	123
2001	43,882	55,736	127
2000	44,853	59,559	133
1999	44,922	56,251	125
1998	43,825	52,562	120
1997	42,294	51,716	122
1996	41,431	50,517	122
1995	40,845	48,682	119
1994	39,613	49,703	125
1993	39,165	48,073	123
1992	39,364	48,570	123
1991	39,679	48,007	121
1990	40,865	52,475	128
Percent change			
2000 to 2003	–3.4%	–7.2%	–
1990 to 2003	6.0	5.3	–

Note: Data for Asians in 2002 and 2003 are for those identifying themselves as being of the race alone and those identifying themselves as being of the race in combination with other races. (–) means not applicable.
Source: Bureau of the Census, Current Population Surveys, Internet site http://www.census.gov/hhes/income/histinc/h05.html; calculations by New Strategist

Table 2.41 High-Income Asian Households, 2003

(number and percent distribution of Asian households with incomes of $100,000 or more, 2003; households in thousands as of 2004)

	total	percent
TOTAL ASIAN HOUSEHOLDS	**4,235**	**100.0%**
$100,000 or more	**973**	**23.0**
$100,000 to $149,999	594	14.0
$150,000 to $199,999	238	5.6
$200,000 to $249,999	70	1.7
$250,000 or more	71	1.7

Note: Asians include those identifying themselves as being of the race alone and those identifying themselves as being of the race in combination with other races.
Source: Bureau of the Census, 2004 Current Population Survey, Internet site http://pubdb3.census.gov/macro/032004/hhinc/new06_000.htm; calculations by New Strategist

Table 2.42 Asian Household Income by Age of Householder, 2003

(number and percent distribution of Asian households by household income and age of householder, 2003; households in thousands as of 2004)

	total	15 to 24	25 to 34	35 to 44	45 to 54	55 to 64	aged 65 or older total	65 to 74	75 or older
Asian households	4,235	286	1,012	1,026	824	547	540	307	233
Under $10,000	447	61	102	56	43	57	128	58	68
$10,000 to $19,999	431	45	73	81	62	26	144	72	72
$20,000 to $29,999	309	43	67	56	54	34	56	33	21
$30,000 to $39,999	359	31	88	82	73	49	38	27	14
$40,000 to $49,999	401	30	110	90	80	46	45	28	16
$50,000 to $59,999	309	25	68	80	73	49	15	5	9
$60,000 to $69,999	293	10	90	98	42	30	23	15	10
$70,000 to $79,999	302	10	94	86	60	40	11	7	4
$80,000 to $89,999	218	11	58	60	48	32	8	7	1
$90,000 to $99,999	192	9	42	54	44	25	17	12	4
$100,000 or more	974	11	221	286	244	157	55	44	12
Median income	$55,262	$27,427	$59,199	$67,011	$64,658	$62,086	$19,734	$27,161	$15,707

PERCENT DISTRIBUTION BY INCOME

	total	15 to 24	25 to 34	35 to 44	45 to 54	55 to 64	aged 65 or older total	65 to 74	75 or older
Asian households	100.0%	100.0%	100.0%	100.0%	100.0%	100.0%	100.0%	100.0%	100.0%
Under $10,000	10.6	21.3	10.1	5.5	5.2	10.4	23.7	18.9	29.2
$10,000 to $19,999	10.2	15.7	7.2	7.9	7.5	4.8	26.7	23.5	30.9
$20,000 to $29,999	7.3	15.0	6.6	5.5	6.6	6.2	10.4	10.7	9.0
$30,000 to $39,999	8.5	10.8	8.7	8.0	8.9	9.0	7.0	8.8	6.0
$40,000 to $49,999	9.5	10.5	10.9	8.8	9.7	8.4	8.3	9.1	6.9
$50,000 to $59,999	7.3	8.7	6.7	7.8	8.9	9.0	2.8	1.6	3.9
$60,000 to $69,999	6.9	3.5	8.9	9.6	5.1	5.5	4.3	4.9	4.3
$70,000 to $79,999	7.1	3.5	9.3	8.4	7.3	7.3	2.0	2.3	1.7
$80,000 to $89,999	5.1	3.8	5.7	5.8	5.8	5.9	1.5	2.3	0.4
$90,000 to $99,999	4.5	3.1	4.2	5.3	5.3	4.6	3.1	3.9	1.7
$100,000 or more	23.0	3.8	21.8	27.9	29.6	28.7	10.2	14.3	5.2

Note: Asians include those identifying themselves as being of the race alone and those identifying themselves as being of the race in combination with other races.
Source: Bureau of the Census, 2004 Current Population Survey, Internet site http://pubdb3.census.gov/macro/032004/hhinc/new02_001.htm; calculations by New Strategist

Table 2.43 Asian Household Income by Household Type, 2003

(number and percent distribution of households headed by Asians by household income and household type, 2003; households in thousands as of 2004)

| | | family households | | | nonfamily households | | | |
| | | | female hh, no spouse present | male hh, no spouse present | female householder | | male householder | |
	total	married couples			total	living alone	total	living alone
Asian households	**4,235**	**2,574**	**378**	**241**	**548**	**447**	**495**	**374**
Under $10,000	447	127	52	16	153	148	97	87
$10,000 to $19,999	431	174	57	23	106	91	72	55
$20,000 to $29,999	309	152	38	34	44	40	44	37
$30,000 to $39,999	359	199	41	19	47	33	55	36
$40,000 to $49,999	401	230	48	29	32	24	63	44
$50,000 to $59,999	309	203	36	15	33	26	20	16
$60,000 to $69,999	293	186	26	26	30	26	26	18
$70,000 to $79,999	302	223	20	12	23	19	24	20
$80,000 to $89,999	218	144	16	20	20	12	17	12
$90,000 to $99,999	192	138	13	11	13	5	12	5
$100,000 or more	974	801	26	35	47	23	65	44
Median income	$55,262	$70,548	$39,877	$52,768	$22,369	$17,248	$36,311	$32,059

PERCENT DISTRIBUTION BY INCOME

Asian households	**100.0%**	**100.0%**	**100.0%**	**100.0%**	**100.0%**	**100.0%**	**100.0%**	**100.0%**
Under $10,000	10.6	4.9	13.8	6.6	27.9	33.1	19.6	23.3
$10,000 to $19,999	10.2	6.8	15.1	9.5	19.3	20.4	14.5	14.7
$20,000 to $29,999	7.3	5.9	10.1	14.1	8.0	8.9	8.9	9.9
$30,000 to $39,999	8.5	7.7	10.8	7.9	8.6	7.4	11.1	9.6
$40,000 to $49,999	9.5	8.9	12.7	12.0	5.8	5.4	12.7	11.8
$50,000 to $59,999	7.3	7.9	9.5	6.2	6.0	5.8	4.0	4.3
$60,000 to $69,999	6.9	7.2	6.9	10.8	5.5	5.8	5.3	4.8
$70,000 to $79,999	7.1	8.7	5.3	5.0	4.2	4.3	4.8	5.3
$80,000 to $89,999	5.1	5.6	4.2	8.3	3.6	2.7	3.4	3.2
$90,000 to $99,999	4.5	5.4	3.4	4.6	2.4	1.1	2.4	1.3
$100,000 or more	23.0	31.1	6.9	14.5	8.6	5.1	13.1	11.8

Note: Asians include those identifying themselves as being of the race alone and those identifying themselves as being of the race in combination with other races.
Source: Bureau of the Census, 2004 Current Population Survey, Internet site http://pubdb3.census.gov/macro/032004/hhinc/ new02_000.htm; calculations by New Strategist

Table 2.44 Income Distribution of Households Headed by the Asian Foreign-Born, 2003

(number and percent distribution of foreign-born householders from Asia by household income, 2003; households in thousands as of 2004)

	number	percent distribution
Total foreign-born Asian householders	**3,626**	**100.0%**
Less than $10,000	393	10.8
$10,000 to $14,999	145	4.0
$15,000 to $19,999	209	5.8
$20,000 to $24,999	138	3.8
$25,000 to $34,999	261	7.2
$35,000 to $49,999	514	14.2
$50,000 to $74,999	673	18.6
$75,000 or more	1,293	35.7
Median income	$55,684	–

Note: (–) means not applicable.
Source: Bureau of the Census, Foreign-Born Population of the United States, Current Population Survey, March 2004, detailed tables (PPL-176), Internet site http://www.census.gov/population/www/socdemo/foreign/ppl-176.html; calculations by New Strategist

Table 2.45 Income of Asian Men by Age, 2003

(number and percent distribution of Asian men aged 15 or older by income and age, median income of men with income and of men working full-time, year-round, and percent working full-time, year-round, 2003; men in thousands as of 2004)

	total	under 25	25 to 34	35 to 44	45 to 54	55 to 64	65 or older
TOTAL ASIAN MEN	**4,889**	**947**	**1,147**	**1,033**	**783**	**497**	**483**
Without income	**623**	**387**	**103**	**41**	**29**	**34**	**31**
With income	**4,266**	**560**	**1,044**	**992**	**754**	**463**	**452**
Under $10,000	779	331	110	76	74	35	154
$10,000 to $19,999	678	129	139	111	96	72	132
$20,000 to $29,999	557	56	167	110	99	69	56
$30,000 to $39,999	473	19	132	142	83	58	41
$40,000 to $49,999	409	15	140	111	69	50	24
$50,000 to $59,999	272	4	62	80	70	39	15
$60,000 to $69,999	239	3	89	80	45	21	3
$70,000 to $79,999	197	1	55	59	58	23	–
$80,000 to $89,999	150	1	38	45	31	27	6
$90,000 to $99,999	84	1	31	38	10	3	1
$100,000 or more	425	–	81	140	120	67	17
Median income of men with income	$31,737	$6,859	$36,645	$44,080	$41,797	$39,936	$14,150
Median income of men working full-time	45,822	20,697	44,248	50,193	50,553	46,443	–
Percent of men working full-time	55.0%	12.1%	67.2%	79.5%	75.2%	68.4%	11.0%
TOTAL ASIAN MEN	**100.0%**	**100.0%**	**100.0%**	**100.0%**	**100.0%**	**100.0%**	**100.0%**
Without income	**12.7**	**40.9**	**9.0**	**4.0**	**3.7**	**6.8**	**6.4**
With income	**87.3**	**59.1**	**91.0**	**96.0**	**96.3**	**93.2**	**93.6**
Under $10,000	15.9	35.0	9.6	7.4	9.5	7.0	31.9
$10,000 to $19,999	13.9	13.6	12.1	10.7	12.3	14.5	27.3
$20,000 to $29,999	11.4	5.9	14.6	10.6	12.6	13.9	11.6
$30,000 to $39,999	9.7	2.0	11.5	13.7	10.6	11.7	8.5
$40,000 to $49,999	8.4	1.6	12.2	10.7	8.8	10.1	5.0
$50,000 to $59,999	5.6	0.4	5.4	7.7	8.9	7.8	3.1
$60,000 to $69,999	4.9	0.3	7.8	7.7	5.7	4.2	0.6
$70,000 to $79,999	4.0	0.1	4.8	5.7	7.4	4.6	–
$80,000 to $89,999	3.1	0.1	3.3	4.4	4.0	5.4	1.2
$90,000 to $99,999	1.7	0.1	2.7	3.7	1.3	0.6	0.2
$100,000 or more	8.7	–	7.1	13.6	15.3	13.5	3.5

Note: Asians include those identifying themselves as being of the race alone and those identifying themselves as being of the race in combination with one or more other races. (–) means sample is too small to make a reliable estimate.
Source: Bureau of the Census, 2004 Current Population Survey, Internet site http://pubdb3.census.gov/macro/032004/perinc/ new01_000.htm; calculations by New Strategist

Table 2.46 Income of Asian Women by Age, 2003

(number and percent distribution of Asian women aged 15 or older by income and age, median income of women with income and of women working full-time, year-round, and percent working full-time, year-round, 2003; women in thousands as of 2004)

	total	under 25	25 to 34	35 to 44	45 to 54	55 to 64	65 or older
TOTAL ASIAN WOMEN	**5,256**	**886**	**1,197**	**1,099**	**928**	**562**	**583**
Without income	**1,004**	**357**	**218**	**137**	**146**	**76**	**69**
With income	**4,252**	**529**	**979**	**962**	**782**	**486**	**514**
Under $10,000	1,409	268	257	256	170	155	302
$10,000 to $19,999	829	118	155	167	167	86	136
$20,000 to $29,999	602	83	136	137	136	75	36
$30,000 to $39,999	431	40	134	120	78	42	19
$40,000 to $49,999	284	6	81	97	62	38	1
$50,000 to $59,999	207	7	63	49	50	36	3
$60,000 to $69,999	159	3	52	36	40	22	5
$70,000 to $79,999	94	1	33	21	30	8	1
$80,000 to $89,999	77	1	23	19	23	6	5
$90,000 to $99,999	37	2	10	15	8	1	1
$100,000 or more	122	–	36	47	19	15	5
Median income of women with income	$17,879	$9,747	$25,578	$23,505	$22,710	$20,172	$9,131
Median income of women working full-time	34,457	21,860	36,574	37,135	31,555	34,265	–
Percent of women working full-time	37.8%	15.2%	45.4%	49.0%	55.0%	43.4%	2.9%
TOTAL ASIAN WOMEN	**100.0%**	**100.0%**	**100.0%**	**100.0%**	**100.0%**	**100.0%**	**100.0%**
Without income	**19.1**	**40.3**	**18.2**	**12.5**	**15.7**	**13.5**	**11.8**
With income	**80.9**	**59.7**	**81.8**	**87.5**	**84.3**	**86.5**	**88.2**
Under $10,000	26.8	30.2	21.5	23.3	18.3	27.6	51.8
$10,000 to $19,999	15.8	13.3	12.9	15.2	18.0	15.3	23.3
$20,000 to $29,999	11.5	9.4	11.4	12.5	14.7	13.3	6.2
$30,000 to $39,999	8.2	4.5	11.2	10.9	8.4	7.5	3.3
$40,000 to $49,999	5.4	0.7	6.8	8.8	6.7	6.8	0.2
$50,000 to $59,999	3.9	0.8	5.3	4.5	5.4	6.4	0.5
$60,000 to $69,999	3.0	0.3	4.3	3.3	4.3	3.9	0.9
$70,000 to $79,999	1.8	0.1	2.8	1.9	3.2	1.4	0.2
$80,000 to $89,999	1.5	0.1	1.9	1.7	2.5	1.1	0.9
$90,000 to $99,999	0.7	0.2	0.8	1.4	0.9	0.2	0.2
$100,000 or more	2.3	–	3.0	4.3	2.0	2.7	0.9

Note: Asians include those identifying themselves as being of the race alone and those identifying themselves as being of the race in combination with one or more other races. (–) means sample is too small to make a reliable estimate.
Source: Bureau of the Census, 2004 Current Population Survey, Internet site http://pubdb3.census.gov/macro/032004/perinc/new01_000.htm; calculations by New Strategist

Table 2.47 Median Income of Asians Working Full-Time by Sex, 1990 to 2003

(median income of Asians working full-time, year-round by sex; index of Asian to total population median income, and Asian women's income as a percent of Asian men's income, 1990 to 2003; percent change in income, 2000–03 and 1990–2003; in 2003 dollars)

| | Asian men | | Asian women | | Asian women's income as a percent of Asian men's income |
	median income	index Asian/total	median income	index Asian/total	
2003	$45,822	110	$34,457	109	75.2%
2002	43,420	105	32,765	103	75.5
2001	44,368	106	32,510	103	73.3
2000	44,148	106	33,034	106	74.8
1999	42,399	103	33,370	110	78.7
1998	40,138	98	31,492	104	78.5
1997	40,337	100	33,273	112	82.5
1996	41,776	107	30,716	106	73.5
1995	38,412	100	30,572	107	79.6
1994	39,890	103	30,689	107	76.9
1993	39,222	101	31,390	111	80.0
1992	39,730	100	31,017	109	78.1
1991	41,073	103	28,442	102	69.2
1990	37,255	94	30,068	107	80.7
Percent change					
2000 to 2003	3.8%	–	4.3%	–	–
1990 to 2003	23.0	–	14.6	–	–

Note: Data for Asians in 2002 and 2003 are for those identifying themselves as being of the race alone and those identifying themselves as being of the race in combination with other races. The Asian/total indexes are calculated by dividing the median income of Asian men and women by the median income of total men and women and multiplying by 100. (–) means not applicable.
Source: Bureau of the Census, Current Population Surveys, Internet site http://www.census.gov/hhes/income/histinc/p36b.html; calculations by New Strategist

Table 2.48 Earnings Distribution of Foreign-Born Men from Asia Working Full-Time, 2003

(number and percent distribution of foreign-born men aged 15 or older from Asia working full-time, year-round, by earnings, 2003; men in thousands as of 2004)

	number	percent distribution
Total foreign-born men from Asia working full-time	**2,321**	**100.0%**
Less than $10,000	52	2.2
$10,000 to $14,999	73	3.1
$15,000 to $19,999	181	7.8
$20,000 to $24,999	177	7.6
$25,000 to $34,999	312	13.4
$35,000 to $49,999	456	19.6
$50,000 to $74,999	483	20.8
$75,000 or more	588	25.3
Median income	$46,304	–

Note: (–) means not applicable.
Source: Bureau of the Census, Foreign-born Population of the United States, Current Population Survey, March 2004, detailed tables (PPL-176), Internet site http://www.census.gov/population/www/socdemo/foreign/ppl-176.html; calculations by New Strategist

Table 2.49 Earnings Distribution of Foreign-Born Women from Asia Working Full-Time, 2003

(number and percent distribution of foreign-born women aged 15 or older from Asia working full-time, year-round, by earnings, 2003; women in thousands as of 2004)

	number	percent distribution
Total foreign-born women from Asia working full-time	**1,626**	**100.0%**
Less than $10,000	53	3.3
$10,000 to $14,999	138	8.5
$15,000 to $19,999	185	11.4
$20,000 to $24,999	187	11.5
$25,000 to $34,999	317	19.5
$35,000 to $49,999	300	18.5
$50,000 to $74,999	272	16.7
$75,000 or more	174	10.7
Median income	$31,644	–

Note: (–) means not applicable.
Source: Bureau of the Census, Foreign-born Population of the United States, Current Population Survey, March 2004, detailed tables (PPL-176), Internet site http://www.census.gov/population/www/socdemo/foreign/ppl-176.html; calculations by New Strategist

Table 2.50 Median Earnings of Asians Working Full-Time by Education and Sex, 2003

(median earnings of Asians aged 25 or older working full-time, year-round, by educational attainment and sex, and Asian women's earnings as a percent of Asian men's earnings, 2003)

	men	women	Asian women's earnings as a percent of Asian men's earnings
Total Asians	**$46,207**	**$35,138**	**76.0%**
Less than 9th grade	19,964	17,935	89.8
9th to 12th grade, no diploma	27,315	–	–
High school graduate	30,084	23,425	77.9
Some college, no degree	35,459	28,929	81.6
Associate's degree	40,755	31,581	77.5
Bachelor's degree or more	62,314	50,425	80.9

Note: (–) means sample is too small to make a reliable estimate.
Source: Bureau of the Census, 2004 Current Population Survey, Internet site http://pubdb3.census.gov/macro/032004/perinc/new03_000.htm; calculations by New Strategist

Table 2.51 Poverty Status of Asian Families, 2003

(total number of Asian families, and number and percent below poverty level by type of family and presence of children under age 18 at home, 2003; families in thousands as of 2004)

	total	in poverty	
		number	percent
Total Asian families	**3,194**	**320**	**10.0%**
Married couples	2,576	203	7.9
Female householder, no spouse present	378	89	23.5
Male householder, no spouse present	241	28	11.8
Asian families with children	**1,830**	**199**	**10.9**
Married couples	1,514	121	8.0
Female householder, no spouse present	235	66	28.2
Male householder, no spouse present	82	12	15.2

Note: Asians include those identifying themselves as being of the race alone and those identifying themselves as being of the race in combination with other races.
Source: Bureau of the Census, 2004 Current Population Survey, Internet site http://www.census.gov/hhes/www/poverty/histpov/hstpov4.html; calculations by New Strategist

Table 2.52 Poverty Status of Asians by Sex and Age, 2003

(total number of Asians, and number and percent below poverty level by sex and age, 2003; people in thousands as of 2004)

	total	in poverty	
		number	percent
Total Asians	**12,891**	**1,527**	**11.8%**
Under age 18	3,316	420	12.7
Aged 18 to 24	1,263	202	16.0
Aged 25 to 34	2,344	308	13.1
Aged 35 to 44	2,132	175	8.2
Aged 45 to 54	1,711	167	9.8
Aged 55 to 59	629	51	8.1
Aged 60 to 64	430	52	12.1
Aged 65 or older	1,065	152	14.2
Asian females	**6,618**	**802**	**12.1**
Under age 18	1,644	203	12.4
Aged 18 to 24	604	78	13.0
Aged 25 to 34	1,197	168	14.0
Aged 35 to 44	1,099	103	9.4
Aged 45 to 54	928	94	10.1
Aged 55 to 59	341	25	7.4
Aged 60 to 64	221	38	17.3
Aged 65 or older	583	92	15.8
Asian males	**6,273**	**725**	**11.6**
Under age 18	1,673	217	13.0
Aged 18 to 24	659	124	18.8
Aged 25 to 34	1,147	140	12.2
Aged 35 to 44	1,033	72	7.0
Aged 45 to 54	783	73	9.3
Aged 55 to 59	288	26	8.9
Aged 60 to 64	209	14	6.7
Aged 65 or older	483	60	12.3

Note: Asians include those identifying themselves as being of the race alone and those identifying themselves as being of the race in combination with other races.
Source: Bureau of the Census, 2004 Current Population Survey, Internet site http://pubdb3.census.gov/macro/032004/pov/new01_100.htm

Table 2.53 Poverty Status of the Foreign-Born from Asia, 2003

(number and percent of the foreign-born from Asia living below poverty level by age, 2003; people in thousands as of 2004)

	total	in poverty	
		number	percent
Foreign-born from Asia	**8,684**	**1,045**	**12.0%**
Under age 18	648	112	17.3
Aged 18 to 64	7,095	789	11.1
Aged 65 or older	941	143	15.2

Note: Asians include those identifying themselves as being of the race alone and those identifying themselves as being of the race in combination with other races.
Source: Bureau of the Census, Foreign-Born Population of the United States, Current Population Survey, March 2004, detailed tables (PPL-176), Internet site http://www.census.gov/population/www/socdemo/foreign/ppl-176.html; calculations by New Strategist

Nearly Half of Asian Workers Are Managers or Professionals

More than 6 million Asians aged 16 or older were in the civilian labor force in 2004. Seventy-five percent of Asian men and 58 percent of Asian women are in the labor force.

Fully 45 percent of Asian workers are employed in managerial or professional occupations—the largest share among all racial and ethnic groups. Although Asians account for only 4 percent of the nation's employed, they account for 24 percent of computer software engineers, 18 percent of medical scientists, and 17 percent of physicians and surgeons.

Forty-seven percent of Asian households have two or more earners. Among Asian couples, the 54 percent majority are dual earners.

Between 2002 and 2012, the number of Asian workers will expand by an enormous 51 percent. Despite the rapid growth, the Asian share of the labor force will rise from only 4.1 to 5.5 percent between 2002 and 2012.

■ Asian incomes are well above average because so many Asian households are headed by two-earner couples.

Most Asian women are in the labor force

(percent of Asians aged 16 or older in the labor force, by sex, 2004)

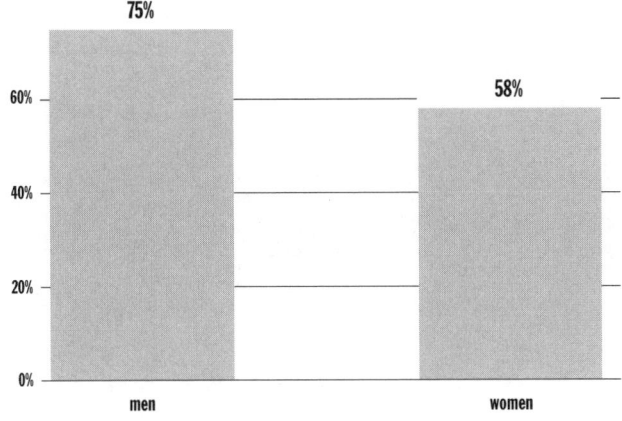

Table 2.54 Labor Force Participation Rate of Asians by Age and Sex, 2004

(percent of Asians aged 16 or older in the civilian labor force, by age and sex, 2004)

	total	men	women
Total Asians	**65.9%**	**75.0%**	**57.6%**
Aged 16 to 19	28.4	29.0	27.7
Aged 20 to 24	61.5	63.8	59.3
Aged 25 to 29	72.9	83.9	62.4
Aged 30 to 34	80.0	91.2	69.4
Aged 35 to 39	80.1	92.9	68.4
Aged 40 to 44	83.5	93.0	74.4
Aged 45 to 49	84.2	94.4	75.4
Aged 50 to 54	79.1	89.2	70.4
Aged 55 to 59	74.9	83.0	67.7
Aged 60 to 64	49.4	60.6	39.9
Aged 65 or older	13.1	18.9	8.8
Aged 65 to 69	26.9	38.7	16.5
Aged 70 to 74	9.6	12.4	7.5
Aged 75 or older	5.2	6.3	4.5

Note: The civilian labor force equals the number of employed plus the number of unemployed.
Source: Bureau of Labor Statistics, 2004 Current Population Survey, http://www.bls.gov/cps/home.htm

Table 2.55 Employment Status of Asians by Sex and Age, 2004

(number and percent of Asians aged 16 or older in the civilian labor force by sex, age, and employment status, 2004; numbers in thousands)

	civilian non-institutional population	civilian labor force			unemployed	
		total	percent of population	employed	number	percent of labor force
Total Asians	**9,519**	**6,271**	**65.9%**	**5,994**	**277**	**4.4%**
Aged 16 to 19	606	172	28.4	152	20	11.5
Aged 20 to 24	876	539	61.5	493	46	8.6
Aged 25 to 34	2,234	1,714	76.7	1,646	68	4.0
Aged 35 to 44	2,044	1,671	81.7	1,613	58	3.5
Aged 45 to 54	1,665	1,363	81.8	1,312	51	3.8
Aged 55 to 64	1,052	676	64.2	649	27	4.0
Aged 65 or older	1,041	137	13.1	130	6	4.7
Total Asian men	**4,529**	**3,396**	**75.0**	**3,243**	**153**	**4.5**
Aged 16 to 19	313	91	29.0	78	13	14.0
Aged 20 to 24	434	277	63.8	255	23	8.2
Aged 25 to 34	1,089	957	87.8	918	39	4.1
Aged 35 to 44	986	917	93.0	883	34	3.7
Aged 45 to 54	770	709	92.0	683	26	3.6
Aged 55 to 64	490	361	73.8	347	14	3.9
Aged 65 or older	445	84	18.9	79	5	5.9
Total Asian women	**4,990**	**2,876**	**57.6**	**2,751**	**124**	**4.3**
Aged 16 to 19	293	81	27.7	74	7	8.7
Aged 20 to 24	442	262	59.3	238	24	9.0
Aged 25 to 34	1,144	757	66.2	728	29	3.9
Aged 35 to 44	1,058	754	71.2	730	24	3.2
Aged 45 to 54	895	654	73.1	629	25	3.9
Aged 55 to 64	562	315	55.9	302	13	4.1
Aged 65 or older	596	53	8.8	51	1	2.7

Note: The civilian labor force equals the number of the employed plus the number of the unemployed. The civilian population equals the number in the labor force plus the number not in the labor force.
Source: Bureau of Labor Statistics, 2004 Current Population Survey, Internet site http://www.bls.gov/cps/home.htm

Table 2.56 Asian Workers by Occupation, 2004

(total number of employed persons aged 16 or older in the civilian labor force, number and percent distribution of employed Asians, and Asian share of total, by occupation, 2004; numbers in thousands)

		Asian		
	total	number	percent distribution	share of total
TOTAL EMPLOYED	**139,252**	**5,994**	**100.0%**	**4.3%**
Management, professional and related occupations	**48,532**	**2,707**	**45.2**	**5.6**
Management, business, and financial operations	20,235	906	15.1	4.5
Management occupations	14,555	584	9.7	4.0
Business and financial operations occupations	5,860	322	5.4	5.5
Professional and related occupations	28,297	1,801	30.0	6.4
Computer and mathematical occupations	3,140	439	7.3	14.0
Architecture and engineering occupations	2,760	231	3.9	8.4
Life, physical, and social science occupations	1,365	126	2.1	9.2
Community and social services occupations	2,170	62	1.0	2.9
Legal occupations	1,554	47	0.8	3.0
Education, training, and library occupations	7,900	271	4.5	3.4
Arts, design, entertainment, sports, and media occupations	2,687	128	2.1	4.8
Health care practitioner and technical occupations	6,721	497	8.3	7.4
Service occupations	**22,720**	**972**	**16.2**	**4.3**
Health care support occupations	2,921	102	1.7	3.5
Protective service occupations	2,847	54	0.9	1.9
Food preparation and serving-related occupations	7,279	377	6.3	5.2
Building and grounds cleaning and maintenance occupations	5,185	159	2.7	3.1
Personal care and service occupations	4,488	281	4.7	6.3
Sales and office occupations	**35,464**	**1,380**	**23.0**	**3.9**
Sales and related occupations	15,983	676	11.3	4.2
Office and administrative support occupations	19,481	705	11.8	3.6
Natural resources, construction, maintenance occupations	**14,582**	**261**	**4.4**	**1.8**
Farming, fishing, and forestry occupations	991	21	0.4	2.1
Construction and extraction occupations	8,522	87	1.5	1.0
Installation, maintenance, and repair occupations	5,069	153	2.6	3.0
Production, transportation, material-moving occupations	**17,954**	**674**	**11.2**	**3.8**
Production occupations	9,462	501	8.4	5.3
Transportation and material moving occupations	8,491	173	2.9	2.0

Source: Bureau of Labor Statistics, 2004 Current Population Survey, Internet site http://www.bls.gov/cps/home.htm; calculations by New Strategist

Table 2.57 Asian Workers by Detailed Occupation, 2004

(total number of employed workers aged 16 or older and percent Asian, by detailed occupation, 2004; numbers in thousands)

	total	percent Asian
TOTAL EMPLOYED	**139,252**	**4.3%**
Management, professional and related occupations	**48,532**	**5.6**
Management, business, and financial operations occupations	20,235	4.5
Management occupations	14,555	4.0
Chief executives	1,680	3.4
General and operations managers	795	3.5
Advertising and promotions managers	70	0.9
Marketing and sales managers	806	3.7
Administrative services managers	87	2.5
Computer and information systems managers	337	7.3
Financial managers	1,045	4.8
Human resources managers	262	1.3
Industrial production managers	280	1.2
Purchasing managers	170	2.9
Transportation, storage, and distribution managers	241	2.0
Farm, ranch, and other agricultural managers	199	0.2
Farmers and ranchers	817	0.5
Construction managers	851	1.7
Education administrators	757	2.1
Engineering managers	106	7.0
Food service managers	916	12.1
Lodging managers	152	11.7
Medical and health services managers	508	4.3
Property, real estate, and community association managers	604	1.9
Social and community service managers	280	2.2
Business and financial operations occupations	5,680	5.7
Wholesale and retail buyers, except farm products	212	3.1
Purchasing agents, except wholesale, retail, and farm products	285	2.5
Claims adjusters, appraisers, examiners, and investigators	281	2.4
Compliance officers, excluding agriculture, construction, health and safety, and transportation	126	1.3
Cost estimators	98	0.7
Human resources, training, and labor relations specialists	694	3.9
Management analysts	554	4.7
Accountants and auditors	1,723	9.5
Appraisers and assessors of real estate	138	2.1
Personal financial advisors	331	4.1
Insurance underwriters	98	4.2
Loan counselors and officers	425	4.4
Tax examiners, collectors, and revenue agents	81	4.5
Tax preparers	88	9.9
Professional and related occupations	28,297	6.4
Computer and mathematical occupations	3,140	14.0
Computer scientists and systems analysts	700	10.1
Computer programmers	564	14.1

(continued)

	total	percent Asian
Computer software engineers	813	24.2%
Computer support specialists	325	7.9
Database administrators	94	16.5
Network and computer systems administrators	190	6.9
Network systems and data communications analysts	312	7.7
Operations research analysts	90	10.6
Architecture and engineering occupations	2,760	8.4
Architects, except naval	207	5.8
Aerospace engineers	113	9.2
Chemical engineers	63	14.1
Civil engineers	293	11.7
Computer hardware engineers	96	19.0
Electrical and electronics engineers	343	12.3
Industrial engineers, including health and safety	177	6.1
Mechanical engineers	311	6.5
Drafters	206	4.8
Engineering technicians, except drafters	416	5.8
Surveying and mapping technicians	80	0.8
Life, physical, and social science occupations	1,365	9.2
Biological scientists	123	12.7
Medical scientists	93	17.6
Chemists and materials scientists	141	14.8
Environmental scientists and geoscientists	86	1.5
Market and survey researchers	124	7.6
Psychologists	185	1.4
Chemical technicians	84	7.8
Community and social services occupations	2,170	2.8
Counselors	643	2.0
Social workers	687	2.9
Miscellaneous community and social service specialists	283	1.7
Clergy	403	5.1
Directors, religious activities and education	55	1.5
Religious workers, all other	99	2.4
Legal occupations	1,554	3.0
Lawyers	954	2.9
Judges, magistrates, and other judicial workers	64	2.2
Paralegals and legal assistants	322	2.8
Miscellaneous legal support workers	215	4.1
Education, training, and library occupations	7,900	3.4
Postsecondary teachers	1,176	11.0
Preschool and kindergarten teachers	656	2.5
Elementary and middle school teachers	2,580	1.7
Secondary school teachers	1,151	1.5
Special education teachers	384	1.3
Other teachers and instructors	667	4.8
Librarians	217	4.5
Teacher assistants	920	1.8
Arts, design, entertainment, sports, and media occupations	2,687	4.8
Artists and related workers	222	3.9
Designers	792	7.1
Producers and directors	137	3.4

(continued)

	total	percent Asian
Athletes, coaches, umpires, and related workers	239	2.2%
Musicians, singers, and related workers	179	3.4
Announcers	54	1.9
News analysts, reporters, and correspondents	81	4.7
Public relations specialists	133	3.3
Editors	164	3.3
Writers and authors	194	2.2
Miscellaneous media and communication workers	74	12.8
Broadcast and sound engineering technicians and radio operators	92	2.7
Photographers	158	6.6
Health care practitioner and technical occupations	6,721	7.4
Chiropractors	73	2.8
Dentists	167	11.7
Dietitians and nutritionists	84	3.3
Pharmacists	233	11.0
Physicians and surgeons	830	16.5
Physician assistants	70	7.6
Registered nurses	2,464	6.8
Occupational therapists	84	8.8
Physical therapists	173	10.3
Respiratory therapists	103	3.8
Speech-language pathologists	93	0.5
Veterinarians	58	1.9
Clinical laboratory technologists and technicians	333	10.2
Dental hygienists	130	1.1
Diagnostic related technologists and technicians	284	3.4
Emergency medical technicians and paramedics	139	1.5
Health diagnosing and treating practitioner support technicians	397	4.2
Licensed practical and licensed vocational nurses	517	3.4
Medical records and health information technicians	91	4.4
Service occupations	**22,720**	**4.3**
Health care support occupations	2,921	3.5
Nursing, psychiatric, and home health aides	1,806	3.7
Physical therapist assistants and aides	61	7.5
Massage therapists	106	2.9
Dental assistants	242	2.5
Protective service occupations	2,847	1.9
First-line supervisors and managers of police and detectives	133	1.4
Firefighters	268	1.3
Bailiffs, correctional officers, and jailers	373	1.4
Detectives and criminal investigators	121	1.6
Police and sheriff's patrol officers	664	1.6
Private detectives and investigators	81	2.2
Security guards and gaming surveillance officers	798	2.7
Food preparation and serving related occupations	7,279	5.2
Chefs and head cooks	299	10.7
First-line supervisors/managers of food preparation and serving workers	644	3.9
Cooks	1,791	5.8
Food preparation workers	621	6.3

(continued)

	total	percent Asian
Bartenders	360	1.9%
Combined food preparation and serving workers, including fast food	296	4.1
Counter attendants, cafeteria, food concession, and coffee shop	327	4.2
Waiters and waitresses	1,892	4.8
Food servers, nonrestaurant	165	8.3
Dining room and cafeteria attendants and bartender helpers	379	5.5
Dishwashers	267	3.4
Hosts and hostesses, restaurant, lounge, and coffee shop	237	4.3
Building and grounds cleaning and maintenance occupations	5,185	3.1
First-line supervisors and managers of housekeeping and janitorial workers	191	0.9
First-line supervisors/managers of landscaping, lawn service, and groundskeeping workers	227	1.1
Janitors and building cleaners	2,047	3.3
Maids and housekeeping cleaners	1,365	4.9
Pest control workers	75	1.7
Grounds maintenance workers	1,280	1.5
Personal care and service occupations	4,488	6.3
First-line supervisors and managers of gaming workers	140	1.5
First-line supervisors and managers of personal service workers	174	16.6
Nonfarm animal caretakers	128	0.2
Gaming services workers	95	19.1
Barbers	101	3.9
Hairdressers, hair stylists, and cosmetologists	722	3.3
Miscellaneous personal appearance workers	200	47.5
Baggage porters, bellhops, and concierges	70	5.6
Transportation attendants	116	4.3
Child care workers	1,332	2.1
Personal and home care aides	630	6.1
Recreation and fitness workers	314	3.2
Sales and office occupations	**35,464**	**3.9**
Sales and related occupations	15,983	4.2
First-line supervisors and managers of retail sales workers	3,299	4.6
First-line supervisors and managers of nonretail sales workers	1,390	5.7
Cashiers	2,971	5.6
Counter and rental clerks	186	4.1
Parts salespersons	147	3.6
Retail salespersons	3,130	3.8
Advertising sales agents	211	1.3
Insurance sales agents	508	2.8
Securities, commodities, and financial services sales agents	382	3.9
Travel agents	95	7.9
Sales representatives, services, all other	476	1.9
Sales representatives, wholesale and manufacturing	1,416	2.9
Models, demonstrators, and product promoters	68	0.4
Real estate brokers and sales agents	912	3.6
Telemarketers	180	2.7
Door-to-door sales workers, news and street vendors, related workers	312	3.1
Sales and related workers, all other	260	2.0
Office and administrative support occupations	19,481	3.6
First-line supervisors/managers of office, administrative support workers	1,631	3.0
Switchboard operators, including answering service	66	2.2

(continued)

	total	percent Asian
Telephone operators	56	1.0%
Bill and account collectors	229	2.9
Billing and posting clerks and machine operators	441	5.2
Bookkeeping, accounting, and auditing clerks	1,567	3.9
Payroll and timekeeping clerks	153	4.8
Tellers	424	5.0
Court, municipal, and license clerks	102	1.8
Credit authorizers, checkers, and clerks	65	2.4
Customer service representatives	1,749	2.9
Eligibility interviewers, government programs	66	4.7
File clerks	387	7.6
Hotel, motel, and resort desk clerks	106	2.9
Interviewers, except eligibility and loan	143	2.8
Library assistants, clerical	117	5.0
Loan interviewers and clerks	186	5.2
Order clerks	114	4.6
Human resources assistants, except payroll and timekeeping	64	5.0
Receptionists and information clerks	1,373	2.5
Reservation and transportation ticket agents and travel clerks	161	5.9
Couriers and messengers	293	4.2
Dispatchers	257	2.5
Postal service clerks	167	9.4
Postal service mail carriers	336	5.0
Postal service mail sorters, processors, and processing machine operators	116	15.2
Production, planning, and expediting clerks	288	3.7
Shipping, receiving, and traffic clerks	584	3.1
Stock clerks and order fillers	1,350	3.8
Weighers, measurers, checkers, and samplers, recordkeeping	64	0.2
Secretaries and administrative assistants	3,522	2.0
Computer operators	191	5.6
Data entry keyers	504	3.7
Word processors and typists	319	4.4
Insurance claims and policy processing clerks	277	1.0
Mail clerks and mail machine operators, except postal service	154	5.1
Office clerks, general	982	6.1
Office machine operators, except computer	61	7.5
Natural resources, constructions, maintenance occupations	**14,582**	**1.8**
Farming, fishing, and forestry occupations	991	2.1
First-line supervisors and managers of farming, fishing, forestry workers	59	0.3
Graders and sorters, agricultural products	68	5.4
Logging workers	92	–
Construction and extraction occupations	8,522	1.0
First-line supervisors/managers of construction trades, extraction workers	887	1.5
Brickmasons, blockmasons, and stonemasons	239	0.7
Carpenters	1,764	0.8
Carpet, floor, and tile installers and finishers	268	1.1
Cement masons, concrete finishers, and terrazzo workers	115	0.3
Construction laborers	1,234	1.0
Operating engineers and other construction equipment operators	367	0.5

(continued)

	total	percent Asian
Drywall installers, ceiling tile installers, and tapers	213	0.4%
Electricians	781	1.2
Painters, construction and maintenance	719	2.1
Pipe layers, plumbers, pipe fitters, and steam fitters	635	1.0
Roofers	269	0.2
Sheet metal workers	152	0.9
Structural iron and steel workers	66	3.9
Helpers, construction trades	121	0.7
Construction and building inspectors	104	2.7
Highway maintenance workers	96	0.3
Installation, maintenance, and repair occupations	5,069	3.0
First-line supervisors/managers of mechanics, installers, and repairers	327	0.4
Computer, automated teller, and office machine repairers	369	6.7
Radio and telecommunications equipment installers and repairers	235	4.1
Electric motor, power tool, and related repairers	56	3.1
Security and fire alarm systems installers	65	2.4
Aircraft mechanics and service technicians	135	2.6
Automotive body and related repairers	169	2.1
Automotive service technicians and mechanics	936	5.0
Bus and truck mechanics and diesel engine specialists	325	1.0
Heavy vehicle and mobile equipment service technicians and mechanics	205	2.7
Small-engine mechanics	58	0.5
Heating, air conditioning, and refrigeration mechanics and installers	351	2.1
Industrial and refractory machinery mechanics	434	2.6
Maintenance and repair workers, general	300	2.1
Millwrights	59	0.5
Electrical power line installers and repairers	120	1.4
Telecommunications line installers and repairers	142	4.2
Precision instrument and equipment repairers	53	5.2
Coin, vending, and amusement machine servicers and repairers	54	0.6
Production, transportation, material-moving occupations	**17,954**	**3.8**
Production occupations	9,462	5.3
First-line supervisors and managers of production and operating workers	921	4.4
Electrical, electronics, and electromechanical assemblers	226	17.6
Bakers	188	6.6
Butchers and other meat, poultry, and fish processing workers	304	4.1
Food batchmakers	85	6.3
Cutting, punching, press machine setters, operators, tenders, metal/plastic	139	1.5
Grinding, lapping, polishing, and buffing machine tool setters, operators, and tenders, metal and plastic	74	1.1
Machinists	445	3.8
Molders, molding machine setters, operators, tenders, metal and plastic	70	1.5
Tool and die makers	86	0.8
Welding, soldering, and brazing workers	572	1.5
Job printers	65	6.2
Prepress technicians and workers	55	3.5
Printing machine operators	195	2.5
Laundry and dry-cleaning workers	195	8.3
Pressers, textile, garment, and related materials	76	7.3

(continued)

	total	percent Asian
Sewing machine operators	281	15.2%
Tailors, dressmakers, and sewers	101	19.7
Cabinetmakers and bench carpenters	86	0.8
Stationary engineers and boiler operators	105	2.4
Water and liquid waste treatment plant and system operators	56	–
Chemical processing machine setters, operators, and tenders	63	0.3
Crushing, grinding, polishing, mixing, and blending workers	111	1.6
Cutting workers	83	2.9
Inspectors, testers, sorters, samplers, and weighers	690	5.7
Jewelers and precious stone and metal workers	59	14.0
Medical, dental, and ophthalmic laboratory technicians	92	12.7
Packaging and filling machine operators and tenders	318	3.5
Painting workers	191	2.3
Photographic process workers and processing machine operators	59	2.1
Paper goods machine setters, operators, and tenders	53	7.6
Helpers—production workers	64	7.8
Transportation and material-moving occupations	8,491	2.0
Supervisors, transportation and material-moving workers	220	4.0
Aircraft pilots and flight engineers	118	1.5
Bus drivers	602	2.0
Driver sales workers and truck drivers	3,276	1.4
Taxi drivers and chauffeurs	277	10.5
Railroad conductors and yardmasters	58	–
Parking lot attendants	77	5.5
Service station attendants	120	1.7
Crane and tower operators	65	1.3
Dredge, excavating, and loading machine operators	80	–
Industrial truck and tractor operators	530	0.5
Cleaners of vehicles and equipment	316	2.2
Laborers and freight, stock, and material movers, hand	1,797	2.2
Machine feeders and offbearers	55	2.4
Packers and packagers, hand	432	3.5
Refuse and recyclable material collectors	81	0.5

Note: (–) means percentage is less than 0.05.
Source: Bureau of Labor Statistics, 2004 Current Population Survey, Internet site http://www.bls.gov/cps/home.htm

Tabnle 2.58 Asian Workers by Industry, 2004

(total number of employed people aged 16 or older in the civilian labor force, number and percent distribution of employed Asians, and Asian share of total, by industry, 2004; numbers in thousands)

			Asian	
	total	number	percent distribution	share of total
Total employed	**139,252**	**5,995**	**100.0%**	**4.3%**
Agriculture, forestry, fishing, hunting	2,232	23	0.4	1.0
Mining	539	4	0.1	0.7
Construction	10,768	139	2.3	1.3
Manufacturing	16,484	835	13.9	5.1
Durable goods	10,329	553	9.2	5.4
Nondurable goods	6,155	282	4.7	4.6
Wholesale and retail trade	20,869	887	14.8	4.3
Wholesale trade	4,600	199	3.3	4.3
Retail trade	16,269	688	11.5	4.2
Transportation and utilities	7,013	237	4.0	3.4
Information	3,463	154	2.6	4.4
Financial activities	9,969	432	7.2	4.3
Professional and business services	14,108	726	12.1	5.1
Educational and health services	28,719	1,253	20.9	4.4
Leisure and hospitality	11,820	704	11.7	6.0
Other services	6,903	385	6.4	5.6
Other services, except private households	6,124	362	6.0	5.9
Private households	779	23	0.4	3.0
Public administration	6,365	216	3.6	3.4

Source: Bureau of Labor Statistics, 2004 Current Population Survey, Internet site http://www.bls.gov/cps/home.htm; calculations by New Strategist

Table 2.59 Asian Full-Time and Part-Time Workers by Age and Sex, 2004

(number and percent distribution of employed Asians aged 16 or older by age, employment status, and sex, 2004; numbers in thousands)

	men			women		
	total	full-time	part-time	total	full-time	part-time
Total employed Asians	**3,243**	**2,905**	**338**	**2,752**	**2,180**	**572**
Aged 16 to 19	78	24	54	74	16	58
Aged 20 to 24	254	151	103	239	146	93
Aged 25 to 54	2,484	2,343	141	2,086	1,745	341
Aged 55 or older	427	387	40	353	274	79
PERCENT DISTRIBUTION BY EMPLOYMENT STATUS						
Total employed Asians	**100.0%**	**89.6%**	**10.4%**	**100.0%**	**79.2%**	**20.8%**
Aged 16 to 19	100.0	30.8	69.2	100.0	21.6	78.4
Aged 20 to 24	100.0	59.4	40.6	100.0	61.1	38.9
Aged 25 to 54	100.0	94.3	5.7	100.0	83.7	16.3
Aged 55 or older	100.0	90.6	9.4	100.0	77.6	22.4
PERCENT DISTRIBUTION BY AGE						
Total employed Asians	**100.0%**	**100.0%**	**100.0%**	**100.0%**	**100.0%**	**100.0%**
Aged 16 to 19	2.4	0.8	16.0	2.7	0.7	10.1
Aged 20 to 24	7.8	5.2	30.5	8.7	6.7	16.3
Aged 25 to 54	76.6	80.7	41.7	75.8	80.0	59.6
Aged 55 or older	13.2	13.3	11.8	12.8	12.6	13.8

Source: Bureau of Labor Statistics, 2004 Current Population Survey, Internet site http://www.bls.gov/cps/home.htm; calculations by New Strategist

Table 2.60 Asian Labor Force by Educational Attainment, 2004

(number of total people and Asians aged 25 or older in the civilian labor force, Asian labor force participation rate, distribution of Asian labor force, and Asian share of total labor force, by educational attainment, 2004; numbers in thousands)

		Asian labor force			
	total labor force	number	participation rate	percent distribution	share of total
Total aged 25 or older	**125,133**	**5,561**	**69.2%**	**100.0%**	**4.4%**
Not a high school graduate	12,470	456	44.2	8.2	3.7
High school graduate only	37,834	1,052	64.5	18.9	2.8
Some college	22,298	587	70.8	10.6	2.6
Associate's degree	12,141	417	74.7	7.5	3.4
Bachelor's degree or more	40,390	3,049	76.4	54.8	7.5

Source: Bureau of Labor Statistics, 2004 Current Population Survey, Internet site http://www.bls.gov/cps/home.htm; calculations by New Strategist

Table 2.61 Asian Workers by Job Tenure and Sex, 2004

(total number of employed Asian wage and salary workers aged 16 or older and percent distribution by tenure with current employer, by sex, 2004; numbers in thousands)

	total	men	women
Total Asian workers, number	**5,131**	**2,678**	**2,453**
Total Asian workers, percent	**100.0%**	**100.0%**	**100.0%**
12 months or less	22.3	20.3	24.3
13 to 23 months	7.2	7.2	7.2
2 years	7.5	6.8	8.2
3 to 4 years	21.5	22.4	20.6
5 to 9 years	22.8	23.5	21.9
10 to 14 years	8.6	9.5	7.6
15 to 19 years	5.3	4.8	5.8
20 or more years	4.9	5.4	4.3

Note: The Asian population includes only those identifying themselves as being Asian alone.
Source: Bureau of Labor Statistics, 2004 Current Population Survey, Internet site http://www.bls.gov/cps/home.htm; calculations by New Strategist

Table 2.62 Asian Households by Number of Earners, 2004

(number of total households, number and percent distribution of Asian households and Asian share of total, by number of earners per household, 2004; numbers in thousands)

		Asian		
	total	number	percent distribution	share of total
Total households	**112,000**	**4,235**	**100.0%**	**3.8%**
No earners	23,932	630	14.9	2.6
One earner	40,769	1,600	37.8	3.9
Two or more earners	47,299	2,004	47.3	4.2
Two earners	37,917	1,541	36.4	4.1
Three earners	6,998	311	7.3	4.4
Four or more earners	2,384	152	3.6	6.4
Average number of earners per household	1.36	1.52	–	–

Note: Asians include those identifying themselves as being Asian alone and those identifying themselves as Asian in combination with another race. (–) means not applicable.

_Source: Bureau of the Census, 2004 Current Population Survey, Annual Social and Economic Supplement, Internet site http://pubdb3.census.gov/macro/032004/hhinc/new01_000.htm; calculations by New Strategist_

Table 2.63 Labor Force Status of Asian Married Couples, 2003

(number and percent distribution of Asian married couples aged 20 or older by age of householder and labor force status of husband and wife, 2003; numbers in thousands)

| | total | husband and/or wife in labor force | | | neither husband nor wife in labor force |
		husband and wife	husband only	wife only	
Total Asian couples	**2,344**	**1,275**	**687**	**138**	**245**
Aged 20 to 24	36	19	8	10	0
Aged 25 to 29	147	64	69	8	5
Aged 30 to 34	335	186	137	7	6
Aged 35 to 39	359	199	141	12	9
Aged 40 to 44	343	227	96	15	5
Aged 45 to 54	558	387	113	40	19
Aged 55 to 64	320	160	90	25	45
Aged 65 or older	244	33	33	22	156
Total Asian couples	**100.0%**	**54.4%**	**29.3%**	**5.9%**	**10.5%**
Aged 20 to 24	100.0	52.8	22.2	27.8	0.0
Aged 25 to 29	100.0	43.5	46.9	5.4	3.4
Aged 30 to 34	100.0	55.5	40.9	2.1	1.8
Aged 35 to 39	100.0	55.4	39.3	3.3	2.5
Aged 40 to 44	100.0	66.2	28.0	4.4	1.5
Aged 45 to 54	100.0	69.4	20.3	7.2	3.4
Aged 55 to 64	100.0	50.0	28.1	7.8	14.1
Aged 65 or older	100.0	13.5	13.5	9.0	63.9

Note: Asians include those identifying themselves as being Asian alone and those identifying themselves as being Asian in combination with another race.
Source: Bureau of the Census, America's Families and Living Arrangements: 2003, detailed tables, Internet site http://www.census .gov/population/www/socdemo/hh-fam/cps2003.html; calculations by New Strategist

Table 2.64 Asian Minimum Wage Workers, 2004

(number and percent distribution of total and Asian wage and salary workers aged 16 or older paid hourly rates and those paid at or below minimum wage, by sex, 2004; numbers in thousands)

	total paid hourly rates	at or below minimum wage		
		total	at $5.15/hour	below $5.15/hour
NUMBER				
Total workers aged 16 or older	**73,939**	**2,003**	**520**	**1,483**
Asian workers aged 16 or older	2,672	38	8	30
Asian men	1,295	15	3	12
Asian women	1,378	23	5	18
PERCENT DISTRIBUTION BY RACE/SEX				
Total workers aged 16 or older	100.0%	100.0%	100.0%	100.0%
Asian workers aged 16 or older	3.6	1.9	1.5	2.0
Asian men	1.8	0.7	0.6	0.8
Asian women	1.9	1.1	1.0	1.2
PERCENT DISTRIBUTION BY WAGE STATUS				
Total workers aged 16 or older	**100.0%**	**2.7%**	**0.7%**	**2.0%**
Asian workers aged 16 or older	100.0	1.4	0.3	1.1
Asian men	100.0	1.2	0.2	0.9
Asian women	100.0	1.7	0.4	1.3

Source: Bureau of Labor Statistics, 2004 Current Population Survey, Internet site http://www.bls.gov/cps/home.htm

Table 2.65 Asian Multiple Job Holders, 2004

(total number of employed people aged 16 or older holding more than one job, number and percent of Asians holding more than one job, and Asian share of total, by sex, 2004; numbers in thousands)

		Asian multiple job holders		
	total	number	percent	share of total
Total multiple job holders	**7,473**	**226**	**3.8%**	**3.0%**
Men	3,835	118	3.6	3.1
Women	3,638	108	3.9	3.0

Source: Bureau of Labor Statistics, 2004 Current Population Survey, Internet site http://www.bls.gov/cps/home.htm

Table 2.66   Union Representation of Asian Workers by Sex, 2004

(number of employed Asian wage and salary workers aged 16 or older, number and percent represented by unions, and median weekly earnings of those working full-time by union representation status, by sex, 2004; numbers in thousands)

	total	men	women
Total employed Asians	**5,280**	**2,815**	**2,465**
Number represented by unions	670	371	299
Percent represented by unions	12.7%	13.2%	12.1%
Median weekly earnings of Asian full-time workers	**$708**	**$802**	**$613**
Asian workers represented by unions	774	786	762
Asian workers not represented by unions	691	809	594

Note: Workers represented by unions are either members of a labor union or similar employee association or workers who report no union affiliation but whose jobs are covered by a union or an employee association contract.
Source: Bureau of Labor Statistics, 2004 Current Population Survey, Internet site http://www.bls.gov/cps/home.htm

Table 2.67 Asian Labor Force Projections, 2002 and 2012

(number and percent of total people and Asians aged 16 or older in the civilian labor force by sex, 2002 and 2012; percent change in number and percentage point change in rate, 2002–12; numbers in thousands)

	2002	2012	percent change
NUMBER			
Total labor force	**144,863**	**162,269**	**12.0%**
Asian labor force	5,949	8,971	50.8
Total men in labor force	**77,500**	**85,252**	**10.0**
Asian men in labor force	3,215	4,941	53.7
Total women in labor force	**67,363**	**77,017**	**14.3**
Asian women in labor force	2,734	4,030	47.4

	2002	2012	percentage point change
PARTICIPATION RATE			
Total people	**66.6%**	**67.2%**	**0.6**
Total Asians	66.3	68.7	2.4
Total men	**74.1**	**73.1**	**–1.0**
Asian men	75.6	77.3	1.7
Total women	**59.6**	**61.6**	**2.0**
Asian women	57.9	61.3	3.4

Note: Asians include only those who identified their race as Asian alone.
Source: Bureau of Labor Statistics, "Labor Force Projections to 2012: The graying of the U.S. workforce," Monthly Labor Review, February 2004, Internet site http://www.bls.gov/opub/mlr/2004/02/art3exc.htm; calculations by New Strategist

Table 2.68 Asian Labor Force Entrants and Leavers, 2002 to 2012

(number and percent distribution of total people and Asians aged 16 or older in the civilian labor force in 2002 and 2012, and number and percent distribution of entrants, leavers, and stayers, 2002–12; numbers in thousands)

	2002 labor force	2002 to 2012 entrants	2002 to 2012 leavers	2002 to 2012 stayers	2012 labor force
NUMBER					
Total labor force	**144,863**	**40,461**	**23,055**	**121,808**	**162,269**
Asian labor force	5,949	1,783	1,771	4,178	8,971
PERCENT DISTRIBUTION					
Total labor force	**100.0%**	**100.0%**	**100.0%**	**100.0%**	**100.0%**
Asian labor force	4.1	4.4	7.7	3.4	5.5

Note: Asians include only those identifying their race as Asian alone.
Source: Bureau of Labor Statistics, "Labor Force Projections to 2012: The graying of the U.S. workforce," Monthly Labor Review, February 2004, Internet site http://www.bls.gov/opub/mlr/2004/02/art3exc.htm; calculations by New Strategist

Married Couples Head Most Asian Households

Asians head 4 million of the nation's 112 million households—or 3.8 percent in 2004. Asian households are much more likely to be headed by married couples than the average household—61 versus 52 percent, according to the Census Bureau's 2004 Current Population Survey. Among households headed by the foreign-born from Asian countries, married couples head an even larger 65 percent.

Asian children are much more likely to live with both parents than the average American child. Eighty-three percent of Asian children under age 18 live with both parents. In comparison, a much smaller 68 percent of children nationwide live with both mom and dad. Thirty-seven percent of Asian households include children under age 18. Among Asian married couples, 56 percent have children living with them.

Many Asians are immigrants trying to establish themselves in the United States, which explains why more than one in ten Asian men and women live in the households of relatives. Among all men and women, the proportion is just 5 percent. It also helps to explain why Asian households are larger than average.

Divorce is relatively uncommon among Asian men and women. Only 9 percent of Asian men have ever divorced, with the proportion peaking at 16 percent among men in their forties. Among Asian women, only 10 percent have ever divorced, with a peak of 21 percent among women aged 50 to 59.

■ Because many Asians are immigrants from countries with traditional family values, married couples are more common in Asian households than in the average household.

Few Asian households are female-headed families

(percent distribution of Asian households by household type, 2004)

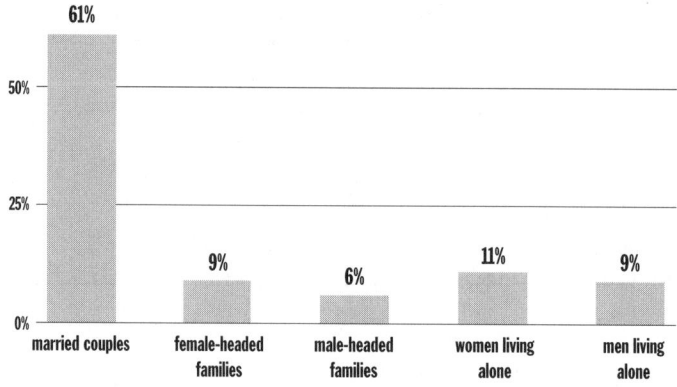

Table 2.69 Asian Households by Age of Householder, 2004

(number of total households, number and percent distribution of Asian households, and Asian share of total, by age of householder, 2004, numbers in thousands)

	total	Asian number	Asian percent distribution	Asian share of total
Total households	**112,000**	**4,235**	**100.0%**	**3.8%**
Under age 25	6,610	286	6.8	4.3
Aged 25 to 29	8,737	410	9.7	4.7
Aged 30 to 34	10,421	602	14.2	5.8
Aged 35 to 39	10,997	548	12.9	5.0
Aged 40 to 44	12,225	478	11.3	3.9
Aged 45 to 49	12,360	485	11.5	3.9
Aged 50 to 54	10,777	339	8.0	3.1
Aged 55 to 59	9,504	326	7.7	3.4
Aged 60 to 64	7,320	221	5.2	3.0
Aged 65 or older	23,048	540	12.8	2.3

Note: Asians include those identifying themselves as being of the race alone and those identifying themselves as being of the race in combination with other races.
Source: Bureau of the Census, 2004 Current Population Survey Annual Social and Economic Supplement, Internet site http://pubdb3.census.gov/macro/032004/hhinc/toc.htm; calculations by New Strategist

Table 2.70 Asian Households by Household Type, 2004

(number of total households, number and percent distribution of Asian households, and Asian share of total, by type, 2004; numbers in thousands)

	total	Asian		
		number	percent distribution	share of total
TOTAL HOUSEHOLDS	**112,000**	**4,235**	**100.0%**	**3.8%**
Family households	**76,217**	**3,192**	**75.4**	**4.2**
Married couples	57,719	2,574	60.8	4.5
Female householder, no spouse present	13,781	378	8.9	2.7
Male householder, no spouse present	4,717	241	5.7	5.1
Nonfamily households	**35,783**	**1,043**	**24.6**	**2.9**
Female householder	19,647	548	12.9	2.8
Living alone	17,024	447	10.6	2.6
Male householder	16,136	495	11.7	3.1
Living alone	12,562	374	8.8	3.0

Note: Asians include those identifying themselves as being of the race alone and those identifying themselves as being of the race in combination with other races.
Source: Bureau of the Census, 2004 Current Population Survey Annual Social and Economic Supplement, Internet site http:// pubdb3.census.gov/macro/032004/hhinc/toc.htm; calculations by New Strategist

Table 2.71 Households Headed by the Foreign-born from Asia by Household Type, 2004

(number and percent distribution of households headed by foreign-born householders from Asia, by household type, 2004; numbers in thousands)

	number	percent distribution
FOREIGN-BORN HOUSEHOLDERS FROM ASIA	**3,626**	**100.0%**
Family households	**2,860**	**78.9**
Married couples	2,351	64.8
Female householder, no spouse present	329	9.1
Male householder, no spouse present	180	5.0
Nonfamily households	**766**	**21.1**
Female householder	400	11.0
Male householder	366	10.1

Source: Bureau of the Census, Foreign-Born Population of the United States, Current Population Survey, March 2004, detailed tables (PPL-176), Internet site http://www.census.gov/population/www/socdemo/foreign/ppl-176.html; calculations by New Strategist

Table 2.72 Asian Households by Age of Householder and Household Type, 2004

(number and percent distribution of Asian households by age of householder and household type, 2004; numbers in thousands)

| | | family households | | | nonfamily households | | | |
| | | | | | female-headed | | male-headed | |
	total	married couples	female hh, no spouse present	male hh, no spouse present	total	living alone	total	living alone
Total Asian households	**4,235**	**2,574**	**378**	**241**	**548**	**447**	**495**	**374**
Under age 25	286	38	51	69	52	27	77	45
Aged 25 to 34	1,012	539	80	70	138	101	186	138
Aged 35 to 44	1,026	713	108	36	76	64	94	71
Aged 45 to 54	824	624	82	28	52	44	38	31
Aged 55 to 64	547	374	37	20	68	57	48	40
Aged 65 or older	540	287	21	18	163	155	52	49
PERCENT DISTRIBUTION BY HOUSEHOLD TYPE								
Total Asian households	**100.0%**	**60.8%**	**8.9%**	**5.7%**	**12.9%**	**10.6%**	**11.7%**	**8.8%**
Under age 25	100.0	13.3	17.8	24.1	18.2	9.4	26.9	15.7
Aged 25 to 34	100.0	53.3	7.9	6.9	13.6	10.0	18.4	13.6
Aged 35 to 44	100.0	69.5	10.5	3.5	7.4	6.2	9.2	6.9
Aged 45 to 54	100.0	75.7	10.0	3.4	6.3	5.3	4.6	3.8
Aged 55 to 64	100.0	68.4	6.8	3.7	12.4	10.4	8.8	7.3
Aged 65 or older	100.0	53.1	3.9	3.3	30.2	28.7	9.6	9.1
PERCENT DISTRIBUTION BY AGE								
Total Asian households	**100.0%**	**100.0%**	**100.0%**	**100.0%**	**100.0%**	**100.0%**	**100.0%**	**100.0%**
Under age 25	6.8	1.5	13.5	28.6	9.5	6.0	15.6	12.0
Aged 25 to 34	23.9	20.9	21.2	29.0	25.2	22.6	37.6	36.9
Aged 35 to 44	24.2	27.7	28.6	14.9	13.9	14.3	19.0	19.0
Aged 45 to 54	19.5	24.2	21.7	11.6	9.5	9.8	7.7	8.3
Aged 55 to 64	12.9	14.5	9.8	8.3	12.4	12.8	9.7	10.7
Aged 65 or older	12.8	11.1	5.6	7.5	29.7	34.7	10.5	13.1

Note: Asians include those identifying themselves as being of the race alone and those identifying themselves as being of the race in combination with other races.
Source: Bureau of the Census, 2004 Current Population Survey Annual Social and Economic Supplement, Internet site http:// pubdb3.census.gov/macro/032004/hhinc/toc.htm; calculations by New Strategist

Table 2.73 Asian Households by Size, 2004

(number of total households, number and percent distribution of Asian households, and Asian share of total, by size, 2004; numbers in thousands)

	total	Asian number	Asian percent distribution	Asian share of total
Total households	**112,000**	**4,235**	**100.0%**	**3.8%**
One person	29,586	821	19.4	2.8
Two people	37,366	1,147	27.1	3.1
Three people	17,968	868	20.5	4.8
Four people	16,065	821	19.4	5.1
Five people	7,150	343	8.1	4.8
Six people	2,476	136	3.2	5.5
Seven or more people	1,388	99	2.3	7.1
Average number of persons per household	2.57	2.90	–	–

Note: Asians include those identifying themselves as being of the race alone and those identifying themselves as being of the race in combination with other races. (–) means not applicable.
Source: Bureau of the Census, 2004 Current Population Survey Annual Social and Economic Supplement, Internet site http://pubdb3.census.gov/macro/032004/hhinc/toc.htm; calculations by New Strategist

Table 2.74 Asians Living Alone by Sex and Age, 2004

(total number of Asian households, number and percent distribution of Asian single-person households, and single-person household share of total, by age of householder, 2004; numbers in thousands)

| | | living alone | | |
	total	number	percent distribution	share of total
Total Asians	**10,145**	**821**	**100.0%**	**8.1%**
Under age 25	1,833	72	8.8	3.9
Aged 25 to 34	2,344	239	29.1	10.2
Aged 35 to 44	2,132	135	16.4	6.3
Aged 45 to 54	1,711	75	9.1	4.4
Aged 55 to 64	1,059	97	11.8	9.2
Aged 65 to 74	650	79	9.6	12.2
Aged 75 or older	416	125	15.2	30.0
Asian men	**4,889**	**374**	**100.0**	**7.6**
Under age 25	947	45	12.0	4.8
Aged 25 to 34	1,147	138	36.9	12.0
Aged 35 to 44	1,033	71	19.0	6.9
Aged 45 to 54	783	31	8.3	4.0
Aged 55 to 64	497	40	10.7	8.0
Aged 65 to 74	308	23	6.1	7.5
Aged 75 or older	175	26	7.0	14.9
Asian women	**5,256**	**447**	**100.0**	**8.5**
Under age 25	886	27	6.0	3.0
Aged 25 to 34	1,197	101	22.6	8.4
Aged 35 to 44	1,099	64	14.3	5.8
Aged 45 to 54	928	44	9.8	4.7
Aged 55 to 64	562	57	12.8	10.1
Aged 65 to 74	342	56	12.5	16.4
Aged 75 or older	241	99	22.1	41.1

Note: Asians include those identifying themselves as being of the race alone and those identifying themselves as being of the race in combination with other races.
Source: Bureau of the Census, 2004 Current Population Survey Annual Social and Economic Supplement, Internet site http://pubdb3.census.gov/macro/032004/hhinc/toc.htm; calculations by New Strategist

Table 2.75 Asian Households by Age of Householder, Type of Household, And Presence of Children, 2003

(number and percent distribution of Asian households by age of householder, type of household, and presence of own children under age 18, and average age of householder, 2003; numbers in thousands)

	all households		married couples		female-headed families		male-headed families	
	total	with children	total	with children	total	with children	total	with children
Total Asian households	**4,079**	**1,514**	**2,344**	**1,323**	**354**	**142**	**241**	**49**
Under age 25	313	27	36	17	37	3	63	7
Aged 25 to 29	420	76	147	59	29	11	35	6
Aged 30 to 34	578	267	335	233	34	28	28	7
Aged 35 to 39	546	355	359	314	45	32	30	9
Aged 40 to 44	483	327	343	296	32	23	35	8
Aged 45 to 49	444	279	317	240	42	29	17	10
Aged 50 to 54	368	117	241	108	43	9	7	1
Aged 55 to 64	482	54	320	49	53	4	18	1
Aged 65 or older	447	11	244	7	39	3	9	–
Average age of householder	43.7	40.4	45.7	40.6	44.9	40.3	35.9	36.8

PERCENT OF HOUSEHOLDS WITH CHILDREN BY TYPE

	all households		married couples		female-headed families		male-headed families	
Total Asian households	**100.0%**	**37.1%**	**100.0%**	**56.4%**	**100.0%**	**40.1%**	**100.0%**	**20.3%**
Under age 25	100.0	8.6	100.0	47.2	100.0	8.1	100.0	11.1
Aged 25 to 29	100.0	18.1	100.0	40.1	100.0	37.9	100.0	17.1
Aged 30 to 34	100.0	46.2	100.0	69.6	100.0	82.4	100.0	25.0
Aged 35 to 39	100.0	65.0	100.0	87.5	100.0	71.1	100.0	30.0
Aged 40 to 44	100.0	67.7	100.0	86.3	100.0	71.9	100.0	22.9
Aged 45 to 49	100.0	62.8	100.0	75.7	100.0	69.0	100.0	58.8
Aged 50 to 54	100.0	31.8	100.0	44.8	100.0	20.9	100.0	14.3
Aged 55 to 64	100.0	11.2	100.0	15.3	100.0	7.5	100.0	5.6
Aged 65 or older	100.0	2.5	100.0	2.9	100.0	7.7	100.0	–

Note: Asians include those identifying themselves as being of the race alone and those identifying themselves as being of the race in combination with other races. (–) means number is less than 500.
Source: Bureau of the Census, America's Families and Living Arrangements, 2003 Current Population Survey Annual Social and Economic Supplement; Internet site http://www.census.gov/population/www/socdemo/hh-fam/cps2003.html; calculations by New Strategist

Table 2.76 Living Arrangements of Asian Children, 2003

(number of total children under age 18, number and percent distribution of Asian children, and Asian share of total, by living arrangement, 2003; numbers in thousands)

	total	Asian		
		number	percent distribution	share of total
Total children	**73,001**	**2,681**	**100.0%**	**3.7%**
Living with both parents	49,903	2,227	83.1	4.5
Living with mother only	16,771	291	10.9	1.7
Never married	7,006	95	3.5	1.4
Divorced or separated	9,102	166	6.2	1.8
Widowed	663	30	1.1	4.5
Living with father only	3,324	76	2.8	2.3
Never married	1,172	27	1.0	2.3
Divorced or separated	1,979	46	1.7	2.3
Widowed	173	3	0.1	1.7
Living with neither parent	3,004	87	3.2	2.9

Note: Asians include those identifying themselves as being of the race alone and those identifying themselves as being of the race in combination with one or more other races.
Source: Bureau of the Census, America's Families and Living Arrangements, 2003 Current Population Survey Annual Social and Economic Supplement; Internet site http://www.census.gov/population/www/socdemo/hh-fam/cps2003.html; calculations by New Strategist

Table 2.77 Asian Men by Living Arrangement and Age, 2003

(number and percent distribution of Asian men aged 15 or older by living arrangement and age, 2003; numbers in thousands)

	total	under 25	25 to 29	30 to 34	35 to 44	45 to 54	55 to 64	65 or older
Total Asian men	**4,685**	**914**	**543**	**572**	**1,010**	**752**	**452**	**443**
Married couple householder or spouse	2,280	20	132	296	681	566	327	258
Other householder	814	157	152	131	180	98	52	46
Male family householder	241	63	35	28	65	24	18	9
Living alone	411	53	72	79	85	58	28	37
Living with nonrelatives	162	41	45	24	30	16	6	–
Nonhouseholder	1,592	738	259	146	150	88	73	139
Child of householder	785	538	117	60	48	18	1	4
Other relative of householder	535	119	72	36	54	57	65	133
Living with nonrelatives	272	81	70	50	48	13	7	2
Total Asian men	**100.0%**	**100.0%**	**100.0%**	**100.0%**	**100.0%**	**100.0%**	**100.0%**	**100.0%**
Married-couple householder or spouse	48.7	2.2	24.3	51.7	67.4	75.3	72.3	58.2
Other householder	17.4	17.2	28.0	22.9	17.8	13.0	11.5	10.4
Male family householder	5.1	6.9	6.4	4.9	6.4	3.2	4.0	2.0
Living alone	8.8	5.8	13.3	13.8	8.4	7.7	6.2	8.4
Living with nonrelatives	3.5	4.5	8.3	4.2	3.0	2.1	1.3	–
Nonhouseholder	34.0	80.7	47.7	25.5	14.9	11.7	16.2	31.4
Child of householder	16.8	58.9	21.5	10.5	4.8	2.4	0.2	0.9
Other relative of householder	11.4	13.0	13.3	6.3	5.3	7.6	14.4	30.0
Living with nonrelatives	5.8	8.9	12.9	8.7	4.8	1.7	1.5	0.5

Note: Asians include those identifying themselves as being of the race alone and those identifying themselves as being of the race in combination with other races. (–) means sample is too small to make a reliable estimate.
Source: Bureau of the Census, America's Families and Living Arrangements, 2003 Current Population Survey Annual Social and Economic Supplement; Internet site http://www.census.gov/population/www/socdemo/hh-fam/cps2003.html; calculations by New Strategist

Table 2.78 Asian Women by Living Arrangement and Age, 2003

(number and percent distribution of Asian women aged 15 or older by living arrangement and age, 2003; numbers in thousands)

	total	under 25	25 to 29	30 to 34	35 to 44	45 to 54	55 to 64	65 or older
Total Asian women	**5,114**	**909**	**559**	**622**	**1,057**	**895**	**521**	**551**
Married couple householder or spouse	2,645	76	284	413	749	603	325	195
Other householder	922	120	122	112	147	155	110	156
Female family householder	354	37	29	34	77	85	53	39
Living alone	435	47	54	58	61	57	53	105
Living with nonrelatives	133	36	39	20	9	13	4	12
Nonhouseholder	1,548	713	154	97	161	136	87	198
Child of householder	644	513	54	22	41	13	–	–
Other relative of householder	608	100	47	27	73	91	70	198
Living with nonrelatives	296	100	53	48	47	32	17	–
Total Asian women	**100.0%**	**100.0%**	**100.0%**	**100.0%**	**100.0%**	**100.0%**	**100.0%**	**100.0%**
Married-couple householder or spouse	51.7	8.4	50.8	66.4	70.9	67.4	62.4	35.4
Other householder	18.0	13.2	21.8	18.0	13.9	17.3	21.1	28.3
Female family householder	6.9	4.1	5.2	5.5	7.3	9.5	10.2	7.1
Living alone	8.5	5.2	9.7	9.3	5.8	6.4	10.2	19.1
Living with nonrelatives	2.6	4.0	7.0	3.2	0.9	1.5	0.8	2.2
Nonhouseholder	30.3	78.4	27.5	15.6	15.2	15.2	16.7	35.9
Child of householder	12.6	56.4	9.7	3.5	3.9	1.5	–	–
Other relative of householder	11.9	11.0	8.4	4.3	6.9	10.2	13.4	35.9
Living with nonrelatives	5.8	11.0	9.5	7.7	4.4	3.6	3.3	–

Note: Asians include those identifying themselves as being of the race alone and those identifying themselves as being of the race in combination with other races. (–) means sample is too small to make a reliable estimate.
Source: Bureau of the Census, America's Families and Living Arrangements, 2003 Current Population Survey Annual Social and Economic Supplement; Internet site http://www.census.gov/population/www/socdemo/hh-fam/cps2003.html; calculations by New Strategist

Table 2.79 Marital Status of Asian Men by Age, 2003

(number and percent distribution of Asian men aged 18 or older by age and current marital status, 2003; numbers in thousands)

	total	never married	married, spouse present	married, spouse absent	separated	divorced	widowed
Total Asian men	**4,414**	**1,482**	**2,459**	**188**	**61**	**153**	**70**
Aged 18 to 19	161	157	1	3	0	0	0
Aged 20 to 24	482	449	24	3	4	1	0
Aged 25 to 29	543	369	141	19	2	12	0
Aged 30 to 34	572	233	310	17	2	10	0
Aged 35 to 39	534	116	356	29	13	19	0
Aged 40 to 44	476	72	354	16	6	26	1
Aged 45 to 49	401	34	313	30	3	17	4
Aged 50 to 54	351	29	283	10	3	24	2
Aged 55 to 64	452	13	372	24	12	27	4
Aged 65 to 74	290	8	203	26	10	15	28
Aged 75 to 84	132	1	93	11	5	0	21
Aged 85 or older	21	0	9	1	0	1	10
Total Asian men	**100.0%**	**33.6%**	**55.7%**	**4.3%**	**1.4%**	**3.5%**	**1.6%**
Aged 18 to 19	100.0	97.5	0.6	1.9	0.0	0.0	0.0
Aged 20 to 24	100.0	93.2	5.0	0.6	0.8	0.2	0.0
Aged 25 to 29	100.0	68.0	26.0	3.5	0.4	2.2	0.0
Aged 30 to 34	100.0	40.7	54.2	3.0	0.3	1.7	0.0
Aged 35 to 39	100.0	21.7	66.7	5.4	2.4	3.6	0.0
Aged 40 to 44	100.0	15.1	74.4	3.4	1.3	5.5	0.2
Aged 45 to 49	100.0	8.5	78.1	7.5	0.7	4.2	1.0
Aged 50 to 54	100.0	8.3	80.6	2.8	0.9	6.8	0.6
Aged 55 to 64	100.0	2.9	82.3	5.3	2.7	6.0	0.9
Aged 65 to 74	100.0	2.8	70.0	9.0	3.4	5.2	9.7
Aged 75 to 84	100.0	0.8	70.5	8.3	3.8	0.0	15.9
Aged 85 or older	100.0	0.0	42.9	4.8	0.0	4.8	47.6

Note: Asians include those who identified themselves as being Asian alone and those who identified themselves as being Asian in combination with other races.
Source: Bureau of the Census, America's Families and Living Arrangements, 2003 Current Population Survey Annual Social and Economic Supplement; Internet site http://www.census.gov/population/www/socdemo/hh-fam/cps2003.html

Table 2.80 Marital Status of Asian Women by Age, 2003

(number and percent distribution of Asian women aged 18 or older by age and current marital status, 2003; numbers in thousands)

	total	never married	married, spouse present	married, spouse absent	separated	divorced	widowed
Total Asian women	**4,853**	**1,173**	**2,818**	**127**	**108**	**282**	**347**
Aged 18 to 19	168	158	7	3	0	0	0
Aged 20 to 24	480	398	76	4	1	2	0
Aged 25 to 29	559	226	297	14	5	14	2
Aged 30 to 34	622	135	426	16	15	25	5
Aged 35 to 39	560	94	393	18	8	40	6
Aged 40 to 44	497	40	387	14	13	41	2
Aged 45 to 49	487	35	357	14	26	40	15
Aged 50 to 54	408	34	284	10	17	42	21
Aged 55 to 64	521	22	357	14	5	44	79
Aged 65 to 74	340	21	175	12	11	30	91
Aged 75 to 84	152	5	53	4	6	3	82
Aged 85 or older	59	5	6	3	0	0	45
Total Asian women	**100.0%**	**24.2%**	**58.1%**	**2.6%**	**2.2%**	**5.8%**	**7.2%**
Aged 18 to 19	100.0	94.0	4.2	1.8	0.0	0.0	0.0
Aged 20 to 24	100.0	82.9	15.8	0.8	0.2	0.4	0.0
Aged 25 to 29	100.0	40.4	53.1	2.5	0.9	2.5	0.4
Aged 30 to 34	100.0	21.7	68.5	2.6	2.4	4.0	0.8
Aged 35 to 39	100.0	16.8	70.2	3.2	1.4	7.1	1.1
Aged 40 to 44	100.0	8.0	77.9	2.8	2.6	8.2	0.4
Aged 45 to 49	100.0	7.2	73.3	2.9	5.3	8.2	3.1
Aged 50 to 54	100.0	8.3	69.6	2.5	4.2	10.3	5.1
Aged 55 to 64	100.0	4.2	68.5	2.7	1.0	8.4	15.2
Aged 65 to 74	100.0	6.2	51.5	3.5	3.2	8.8	26.8
Aged 75 to 84	100.0	3.3	34.9	2.6	3.9	2.0	53.9
Aged 85 or older	100.0	8.5	10.2	5.1	0.0	0.0	76.3

Note: Asians include those who identified themselves as being Asian alone and those who identified themselves as being Asian in combination with other races.
Source: Bureau of the Census, America's Families and Living Arrangements, 2003 Current Population Survey Annual Social and Economic Supplement; Internet site http://www.census.gov/population/www/socdemo/hh-fam/cps2003.html

Table 2.81 Marital History of Asian Men by Age, 2001

(number of Asian men aged 15 or older and percent distribution by marital history and age, 2001; numbers in thousands)

	total	15 to 19	20 to 24	25 to 29	30 to 34	35 to 39	40 to 49	50 to 59	60 to 69	70 or older
Total Asian men, number	4,311	393	429	514	538	473	834	556	259	315
Total Asian men, percent	100.0%	100.0%	100.0%	100.0%	100.0%	100.0%	100.0%	100.0%	100.0%	100.0%
Never married	33.4	99.3	82.6	66.7	24.9	23.1	7.9	5.0	3.7	2.1
Ever married	66.6	0.7	17.4	33.3	75.1	76.9	92.1	95.0	96.3	97.9
Married once	59.7	0.7	16.4	32.4	70.8	71.5	80.5	84.2	81.8	83.9
Still married	54.4	0.7	15.8	30.7	65.4	66.4	75.7	74.6	76.0	65.8
Married twice	6.1	0.0	1.0	0.8	3.8	5.4	10.2	9.6	13.0	11.3
Still married	4.8	0.0	1.0	0.8	3.8	3.6	8.8	5.7	8.3	10.7
Married three or more times	0.8	0.0	0.0	0.0	0.5	0.0	1.4	1.3	1.5	2.7
Still married	0.5	0.0	0.0	0.0	0.5	0.0	0.8	0.5	1.5	1.7
Ever divorced	8.8	0.0	1.7	1.5	9.0	9.6	15.5	13.9	12.7	10.6
Currently divorced	3.9	0.0	0.7	0.6	4.7	6.3	4.9	9.1	3.2	1.8
Ever widowed	3.1	0.0	0.0	0.0	0.0	0.9	0.4	5.8	9.3	22.1
Currently widowed	2.3	0.0	0.0	0.0	0.0	0.0	0.0	4.5	6.2	17.9

Source: Bureau of the Census, Number, Timing, and Duration of Marriages and Divorces: 2001, *Current Population Report P70-97, 2005; Internet site http://www.census.gov/population/www/socdemo/marr-div.html*

Table 2.82 Marital History of Asian Women by Age, 2001

(number of Asian women aged 15 or older and percent distribution by marital history and age, 2001; numbers in thousands)

	total	15 to 19	20 to 24	25 to 29	30 to 34	35 to 39	40 to 49	50 to 59	60 to 69	70 or older
Total Asian women, number	4,645	339	511	501	558	527	1,007	562	334	306
Total Asian women, percent	100.0%	100.0%	100.0%	100.0%	100.0%	100.0%	100.0%	100.0%	100.0%	100.0%
Never married	25.3	96.3	75.2	38.6	17.4	7.9	8.0	7.9	0.4	2.3
Ever married	74.7	3.7	24.8	61.4	82.6	92.1	92.0	92.1	99.6	97.7
Married once	67.9	2.7	23.9	61.4	76.7	85.7	80.6	80.0	92.2	87.1
Still married	56.3	2.7	21.8	57.4	73.0	72.2	71.6	58.9	64.7	49.5
Married twice	5.9	1.0	0.8	0.0	6.0	6.4	10.6	8.1	4.8	10.6
Still married	4.6	1.0	0.8	0.0	6.0	5.5	8.7	4.6	4.8	5.0
Married three or more times	0.8	0.0	0.0	0.0	0.0	0.0	0.8	3.9	2.6	0.0
Still married	0.6	0.0	0.0	0.0	0.0	0.0	0.8	1.6	2.6	0.0
Ever divorced	10.4	1.0	0.8	2.5	8.9	16.6	16.1	20.9	9.9	4.9
Currently divorced	5.8	0.0	0.0	2.5	2.9	11.1	7.0	14.8	5.9	2.3
Ever widowed	6.7	0.0	0.0	0.6	0.0	0.0	3.5	10.3	26.5	42.1
Currently widowed	5.4	0.0	0.0	0.6	0.0	0.0	2.0	7.8	20.3	38.3

Source: Bureau of the Census, Number, Timing, and Duration of Marriages and Divorces: 2001, *Current Population Report P70-97, 2005; Internet site http://www.census.gov/population/www/socdemo/marr-div.html*

The Asian Population Numbers Nearly 14 Million

The number of Asians grew 15 percent between 2000 and 2004, increasing from 12 million to nearly 14 million—a figure that includes Asians identifying themselves as being Asian alone and those identifying themselves as being Asian in combination with one or more other races. Despite the rapid growth of the Asian population, Asians account for just 4.8 percent of the total U.S. population and are greatly outnumbered by Hispanics and blacks.

Behind the growth of the Asian population is immigration. Asian immigrants accounted for 35 percent of all immigrants to the United States in 2004, the largest numbers coming from India, the Philippines, and China. One-fourth of the nation's foreign-born are from Asian countries. Two million U.S. residents speak Chinese at home, and more than 1 million speak Tagalog and Vietnamese, respectively.

Forty-eight percent of Asians live in the West, where they account for 10 percent of the population. California is home to 34 percent of the nation's Asian population, where they account for 13 percent of the state's population. Los Angeles has more Asians (1.9 million) than any other metropolitan area, but Asians account for a larger share of the San Francisco metropolitan area population—21 percent in San Francisco versus 11 percent in Los Angeles.

■ The Asian population is much larger in some areas than others, but the Asian influence on American culture can be felt throughout the nation.

Asians are a substantial share of the population only in the West

(Asian share of population by region, 2004)

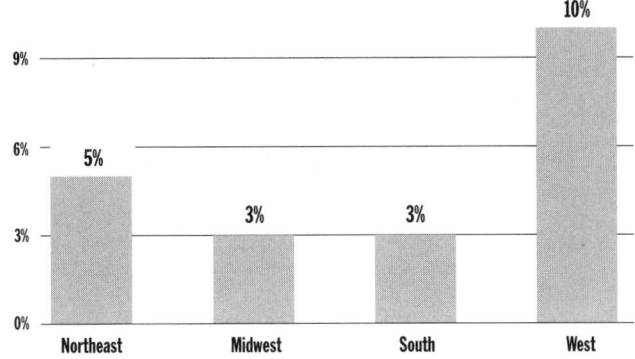

Table 2.83 Asians by Racial Identification, 2000 and 2004

(total number of people, and number and percent distribution of Asians by racial identification, 2000 and 2004; percent change, 2000–04)

	2004		2000		
	number	percent distribution	number	percent distribution	percent change 2000–04
Total people	**293,655,404**	**100.0%**	**282,192,162**	**100.0%**	**4.1%**
Asian alone or in combination with one or more other races	13,956,612	4.8	12,121,816	4.3	15.1
Asian alone	12,326,216	4.2	10,691,993	3.8	15.3
Asian in combination	1,630,396	0.6	1,429,823	0.5	14.0

Source: Bureau of the Census, National Population Estimates, Internet site http://www.census.gov/popest/national/asrh/ NC-EST2004-srh.html; calculations by New Strategist

Table 2.84 Asians by Hispanic Origin, 2004

(number and percent distribution of Asians by Hispanic origin and racial identification, 2004)

	Asian alone or in combination		Asian alone	
	number	percent distribution	number	percent distribution
Total Asians	**13,956,612**	**100.0%**	**12,326,216**	**100.0%**
Not Hispanic	13,529,769	96.9	12,068,424	97.9
Hispanic	426,843	3.1	257,792	2.1

Source: Bureau of the Census, National Population Estimates, Internet site http://www.census.gov/popest/national/asrh/ NC-EST2004-asrh.html; calculations by New Strategist

Table 2.85 Asians Ranked by Ethnic Group, 2004

(number and percent distribution of people identifying themselves as Asian alone by ethnic group alone identification, 2004)

	number	percent
Total Asians alone specifying one ethnic origin	**12,097,281**	**100.0%**
Chinese (except Taiwanese)	2,829,627	23.4
Asian Indian	2,245,239	18.6
Filipino	2,148,227	17.8
Vietnamese	1,267,510	10.5
Korean	1,251,092	10.3
Japanese	832,039	6.9
Laotian	226,661	1.9
Pakistani	208,852	1.7
Cambodian	195,208	1.6
Hmong	163,733	1.4
Thai	130,548	1.1
Taiwanese	70,771	0.6
Indonesian	52,267	0.4
Bangladeshi	50,473	0.4
Sri Lankan	22,339	0.2
Malaysian	11,458	0.1
Other Asian	391,237	3.2

Source: Bureau of the Census, 2004 American Community Survey, Internet site http://factfinder.census.gov/servlet/ DatasetMainPageServlet?_lang=en&_ts=143469461584&_ds_name=ACS_2004_EST_G00_&_program=ACS; calculations by New Strategist

Table 2.86 Asians in the Armed Forces, 2003

(number and percent distribution of Asians aged 18 or older who are in the armed forces or who are veterans, by sex and age, 2003)

	total	in armed forces	veteran
Total Asians aged 18 or older	**9,035,699**	**21,393**	**276,066**
Men	4,275,265	17,731	256,042
Aged 18 to 64	3,872,314	17,731	165,623
Aged 65 or older	402,951	0	90,419
Women	4,760,434	3,662	20,024
Aged 18 to 64	4,214,989	3,662	17,391
Aged 65 or older	545,445	0	2,633
Total Asians aged 18 or older	**100.0%**	**0.2%**	**3.1%**
Men	100.0	0.4	6.0
Aged 18 to 64	100.0	0.5	4.3
Aged 65 or older	100.0	0.0	22.4
Women	100.0	0.1	0.4
Aged 18 to 64	100.0	0.1	0.4
Aged 65 or older	100.0	0.0	0.5

Note: Asians are those identifying themselves as being Asian alone.
Source: Bureau of the Census, 2003 American Community Survey, Internet site http://factfinder.census.gov/servlet/ DatasetMainPageServlet?_program=ACS&_lang=en&_ts=; calculations by New Strategist

Table 2.87 Asian Share of Total Population by Age, 2004

(total number of people, number and percent distribution of Asians, and Asian share of total, by age, 2004)

| | | Asian | | |
	total	number	percent distribution	share of total
Total people	**293,655,404**	**13,956,612**	**100.0%**	**4.8%**
Under age 5	20,071,268	1,050,541	7.5	5.2
Aged 5 to 9	19,605,572	993,477	7.1	5.1
Aged 10 to 14	21,145,156	975,203	7.0	4.6
Aged 15 to 19	20,729,802	955,252	6.8	4.6
Aged 20 to 24	20,971,302	1,068,011	7.7	5.1
Aged 25 to 29	19,560,906	1,192,279	8.5	6.1
Aged 30 to 34	20,471,032	1,348,348	9.7	6.6
Aged 35 to 39	21,052,318	1,187,125	8.5	5.6
Aged 40 to 44	23,056,334	1,105,655	7.9	4.8
Aged 45 to 49	22,122,629	992,266	7.1	4.5
Aged 50 to 54	19,496,176	850,403	6.1	4.4
Aged 55 to 59	16,489,501	659,966	4.7	4.0
Aged 60 to 64	12,589,423	469,581	3.4	3.7
Aged 65 to 69	9,956,467	366,349	2.6	3.7
Aged 70 to 74	8,507,005	286,040	2.0	3.4
Aged 75 to 79	7,410,757	213,874	1.5	2.9
Aged 80 to 84	5,560,125	138,637	1.0	2.5
Aged 85 or older	4,859,631	103,605	0.7	2.1
Aged 18 to 24	29,245,102	1,452,446	10.4	5.0
Aged 18 or older	220,377,406	10,366,574	74.3	4.7
Aged 65 or older	36,293,985	1,108,505	7.9	3.1

Note: Asians are those identifying themselves as being of the race alone and those identifying themselves as being of the race in combination with one or more other races.
Source: Bureau of the Census, National Population Estimates, Internet site http://www.census.gov/popest/national/asrh/NC-EST2004-sa.html; calculations by New Strategist

Table 2.88 Asians by Age and Sex, 2004

(number of Asians by age and sex, and sex ratio by age, 2004)

	total	females	males	sex ratio
Total Asians	**13,956,612**	**7,167,636**	**6,788,976**	**95**
Under age 5	1,050,541	512,266	538,275	105
Aged 5 to 9	993,477	494,028	499,449	101
Aged 10 to 14	975,203	473,718	501,485	106
Aged 15 to 19	955,252	464,508	490,744	106
Aged 20 to 24	1,068,011	528,445	539,566	102
Aged 25 to 29	1,192,279	607,233	585,046	96
Aged 30 to 34	1,348,348	688,581	659,767	96
Aged 35 to 39	1,187,125	608,611	578,514	95
Aged 40 to 44	1,105,655	572,510	533,145	93
Aged 45 to 49	992,266	523,743	468,523	89
Aged 50 to 54	850,403	455,664	394,739	87
Aged 55 to 59	659,966	354,179	305,787	86
Aged 60 to 64	469,581	250,057	219,524	88
Aged 65 to 69	366,349	198,400	167,949	85
Aged 70 to 74	286,040	164,018	122,022	74
Aged 75 to 79	213,874	126,041	87,833	70
Aged 80 to 84	138,637	81,384	57,253	70
Aged 85 or older	103,605	64,250	39,355	61
Aged 18 or older	10,366,574	5,410,328	4,956,246	92
Aged 18 to 24	1,452,446	715,657	736,789	103
Aged 65 or older	1,108,505	634,093	474,412	75

Note: Asians are those identifying themselves as being of the race alone and those identifying themselves as being of the race in combination with one or more other races. The sex ratio is the number of males divided by the number of females multiplied by 100.
Source: Bureau of the Census, National Population Estimates, Internet site http://www.census.gov/popest/national/asrh/ NC-EST2004-sa.html; calculations by New Strategist

Table 2.89 Asians by Age, 2000 and 2004

(number of Asians by age, 2000 and 2004; percent change, 2000–04)

	2004	2000	percent change 2000–04
Total Asians	**13,956,612**	**12,121,816**	**15.1%**
Under age 5	1,050,541	935,623	12.3
Aged 5 to 9	993,477	913,580	8.7
Aged 10 to 14	975,203	890,030	9.6
Aged 15 to 19	955,252	926,918	3.1
Aged 20 to 24	1,068,011	977,901	9.2
Aged 25 to 29	1,192,279	1,134,729	5.1
Aged 30 to 34	1,348,348	1,089,416	23.8
Aged 35 to 39	1,187,125	1,032,840	14.9
Aged 40 to 44	1,105,655	956,127	15.6
Aged 45 to 49	992,266	835,005	18.8
Aged 50 to 54	850,403	696,103	22.2
Aged 55 to 59	659,966	478,922	37.8
Aged 60 to 64	469,581	376,716	24.7
Aged 65 to 69	366,349	299,292	22.4
Aged 70 to 74	286,040	240,487	18.9
Aged 75 to 79	213,874	170,991	25.1
Aged 80 to 84	138,637	97,372	42.4
Aged 85 or older	103,605	69,764	48.5
Aged 18 or older	10,366,574	8,843,891	17.2
Aged 18 to 24	1,452,446	1,366,127	6.3
Aged 65 or older	1,108,505	877,906	26.3

Note: Asians are those identifying themselves as being of the race alone and those identifying themselves as being of the race in combination with one or more other races.
Source: Bureau of the Census, National Population Estimates, Internet site http://www.census.gov/popest/national/asrh/ NC-EST2004-asrh.html; calculations by New Strategist

Table 2.90 Asians by Age, 2000 to 2020

(number and percent distribution of Asians and Pacific Islanders by age, 2000 to 2020, percent change, 2000–10 and 2010–20; numbers in thousands)

	2000	2010	2020	percent change 2000–10	percent change 2010–20
Total Asians	**10,684**	**14,241**	**17,988**	**33.3%**	**26.3%**
Under age 5	712	919	1,063	29.0	15.7
Aged 5 to 9	719	888	1,047	23.4	17.9
Aged 10 to 14	720	834	1,054	15.8	26.4
Aged 15 to 19	777	886	1,071	14.1	20.9
Aged 20 to 24	850	943	1,076	10.9	14.0
Aged 25 to 29	1,021	1,041	1,177	1.9	13.1
Aged 30 to 34	995	1,166	1,293	17.2	10.9
Aged 35 to 39	945	1,319	1,375	39.5	4.3
Aged 40 to 44	878	1,208	1,403	37.6	16.1
Aged 45 to 49	779	1,105	1,490	41.8	34.8
Aged 50 to 54	654	997	1,332	52.5	33.6
Aged 55 to 59	451	857	1,178	89.9	37.4
Aged 60 to 64	356	706	1,034	98.4	46.4
Aged 65 or older	826	1,371	2,395	65.9	74.7

Note: Asians are those identifying themselves as being Asian alone.
Source: Bureau of the Census, Internet site http://www.census.gov/ipc/www/usinterimproj/; calculations by New Strategist

Table 2.91 Asians by Region, 2000 and 2004

(number of Asians by region, 2000 and 2004; percent change, 2000–04)

	2004	2000	percent change 2000–04
Total Asians	**13,956,612**	**11,898,828**	**17.3%**
Northeast	2,808,763	2,368,297	18.6
Midwest	1,643,980	1,392,938	18.0
South	2,795,854	2,267,094	23.3
West	6,708,015	5,870,499	14.3

Note: Asians are those identifying themselves as being of the race alone and those identifying themselves as being of the race in combination with one or more other races. Total number of Asians in 2000 differs from the total in previous tables of this chapter because these are census counts from April 1, 2000, whereas the others are population estimates.
Source: Bureau of the Census, 2000 Census, Internet site http://factfinder.census.gov/servlet/DatasetMainPageServlet?_program=DEC&_lang=en&_ts=; and State Population Estimates, Internet site http://www.census.gov/popest/states/asrh/SC-EST2004-04.html; calculations by New Strategist

Table 2.92 Asian Share of the Total Population by Region, 2004

(total number of people, number and percent distribution of Asians, and Asian share of total, by region, 2004)

		Asian		
	total	number	percent distribution	share of total
Total people	**293,655,404**	**13,956,612**	**100.0%**	**4.8%**
Northeast	54,571,147	2,808,763	20.1	5.1
Midwest	65,729,852	1,643,980	11.8	2.5
South	105,944,965	2,795,854	20.0	2.6
West	67,409,440	6,708,015	48.1	10.0

Note: Asians are those identifying themselves as being of the race alone and those identifying themselves as being of the race in combination with one or more other races.
Source: Bureau of the Census, State Population Estimates, Internet site http://www.census.gov/popest/states/asrh/SC-EST2004-04.html; calculations by New Strategist

Table 2.93 Asians by State, 2000 and 2004

(number of Asians by state, 2000 and 2004; percent change, 2000–04)

	2004	2000	percent change 2000–04
Total Asians	**13,956,612**	**11,898,828**	**17.3%**
Alabama	45,415	39,458	15.1
Alaska	37,920	32,686	16.0
Arizona	152,112	118,672	28.2
Arkansas	31,581	25,401	24.3
California	4,756,181	4,155,685	14.4
Colorado	144,323	120,779	19.5
Connecticut	120,206	95,368	26.0
Delaware	24,366	18,944	28.6
District of Columbia	19,477	17,956	8.5
Florida	424,951	333,013	27.6
Georgia	258,372	199,812	29.3
Hawaii	727,650	703,232	3.5
Idaho	20,242	17,390	16.4
Illinois	552,638	473,649	16.7
Indiana	87,873	72,839	20.6
Iowa	48,824	43,119	13.2
Kansas	66,238	56,049	18.2
Kentucky	45,055	37,062	21.6
Louisiana	71,542	64,350	11.2
Maine	13,790	11,827	16.6
Maryland	286,136	238,408	20.0
Massachusetts	319,618	264,814	20.7
Michigan	253,661	208,329	21.8
Minnesota	192,536	162,414	18.5
Mississippi	26,292	23,281	12.9
Missouri	90,301	76,210	18.5
Montana	7,593	7,101	6.9
Nebraska	31,920	26,809	19.1
Nevada	154,843	112,456	37.7
New Hampshire	25,629	19,219	33.4
New Jersey	647,906	524,356	23.6
New Mexico	31,189	26,619	17.2
New York	1,346,049	1,169,200	15.1
North Carolina	171,600	136,212	26.0
North Dakota	5,586	4,967	12.5
Ohio	187,784	159,776	17.5
Oklahoma	66,215	58,723	12.8
Oregon	149,746	127,339	17.6

(continued)

	2004	2000	percent change 2000–04
Pennsylvania	295,266	248,601	18.8%
Rhode Island	32,556	28,290	15.1
South Carolina	53,954	44,931	20.1
South Dakota	6,986	6,009	16.3
Tennessee	84,404	68,918	22.5
Texas	797,325	644,193	23.8
Utah	56,692	48,692	16.4
Vermont	7,743	6,622	16.9
Virginia	376,428	304,559	23.6
Washington	464,856	395,741	17.5
West Virginia	12,741	11,873	7.3
Wisconsin	119,633	102,768	16.4
Wyoming	4,668	4,107	13.7

Note: Asians are those identifying themselves as being of the race alone and those identifying themselves as being of the race in combination with one or more other races. Total number of Asians in 2000 differs from the total in previous tables of this chapter because these are census counts from April 1, 2000, whereas the others are population estimates.
Source: Bureau of the Census, 2000 Census, Internet site http://factfinder.census.gov/servlet/DatasetMainPageServlet?_program=DEC&_lang=en&_ts=; and State Population Estimates, Internet site http://www.census.gov/popest/states/asrh/SC-EST2004-04.html; calculations by New Strategist

Table 2.94 Asian Share of Total Population by State, 2004

(total number of people, number and percent distribution of Asians, and Asian share of total, by state, 2004)

	total	Asian number	percent distribution	share of total
Total people	**293,655,404**	**13,956,612**	**100.0%**	**4.8%**
Alabama	4,530,182	45,415	0.3	1.0
Alaska	655,435	37,920	0.3	5.8
Arizona	5,743,834	152,112	1.1	2.6
Arkansas	2,752,629	31,581	0.2	1.1
California	35,893,799	4,756,181	34.1	13.3
Colorado	4,601,403	144,323	1.0	3.1
Connecticut	3,503,604	120,206	0.9	3.4
Delaware	830,364	24,366	0.2	2.9
District of Columbia	553,523	19,477	0.1	3.5
Florida	17,397,161	424,951	3.0	2.4
Georgia	8,829,383	258,372	1.9	2.9
Hawaii	1,262,840	727,650	5.2	57.6
Idaho	1,393,262	20,242	0.1	1.5
Illinois	12,713,634	552,638	4.0	4.3
Indiana	6,237,569	87,873	0.6	1.4
Iowa	2,954,451	48,824	0.3	1.7
Kansas	2,735,502	66,238	0.5	2.4
Kentucky	4,145,922	45,055	0.3	1.1
Louisiana	4,515,770	71,542	0.5	1.6
Maine	1,317,253	13,790	0.1	1.0
Maryland	5,558,058	286,136	2.1	5.1
Massachusetts	6,416,505	319,618	2.3	5.0
Michigan	10,112,620	253,661	1.8	2.5
Minnesota	5,100,958	192,536	1.4	3.8
Mississippi	2,902,966	26,292	0.2	0.9
Missouri	5,754,618	90,301	0.6	1.6
Montana	926,865	7,593	0.1	0.8
Nebraska	1,747,214	31,920	0.2	1.8
Nevada	2,334,771	154,843	1.1	6.6
New Hampshire	1,299,500	25,629	0.2	2.0
New Jersey	8,698,879	647,906	4.6	7.4
New Mexico	1,903,289	31,189	0.2	1.6
New York	19,227,088	1,346,049	9.6	7.0
North Carolina	8,541,221	171,600	1.2	2.0
North Dakota	634,366	5,586	0.0	0.9
Ohio	11,459,011	187,784	1.3	1.6
Oklahoma	3,523,553	66,215	0.5	1.9
Oregon	3,594,586	149,746	1.1	4.2

(continued)

	total	Asian		
		number	percent distribution	share of total
Pennsylvania	12,406,292	295,266	2.1%	2.4%
Rhode Island	1,080,632	32,556	0.2	3.0
South Carolina	4,198,068	53,954	0.4	1.3
South Dakota	770,883	6,986	0.1	0.9
Tennessee	5,900,962	84,404	0.6	1.4
Texas	22,490,022	797,325	5.7	3.5
Utah	2,389,039	56,692	0.4	2.4
Vermont	621,394	7,743	0.1	1.2
Virginia	7,459,827	376,428	2.7	5.0
Washington	6,203,788	464,856	3.3	7.5
West Virginia	1,815,354	12,741	0.1	0.7
Wisconsin	5,509,026	119,633	0.9	2.2
Wyoming	506,529	4,668	0.0	0.9

Note: Asians are those identifying themselves as being of the race alone and those identifying themselves as being of the race in combination with one or more other races.
Source: Bureau of the Census, State Population Estimates, Internet site http://www.census.gov/popest/states/asrh/SC-EST2004-04.html; calculations by New Strategist

Table 2.95 Asians by State and Ethnicity, 2004

(total number of Asians and percent distribution by state and ethnicity, 2004)

	total number	total percent	Chinese	Filipino	Asian Indian	Vietnamese	Korean	Japanese	other Asian
Total Asians	**12,097,281**	**100.0%**	**23.4%**	**18.6%**	**17.8%**	**10.5%**	**10.3%**	**6.9%**	**12.6%**
Alabama	33,570	100.0	15.5	13.6	5.7	39.0	15.6	7.3	3.3
Alaska	27,970	100.0	4.3	1.5	45.2	0.8	14.0	8.8	25.3
Arizona	123,766	100.0	15.6	26.5	16.3	15.5	6.9	6.4	12.8
Arkansas	25,294	100.0	15.5	22.2	4.7	23.6	5.0	1.4	27.7
California	4,256,198	100.0	25.8	9.5	24.9	11.6	9.7	7.4	11.1
Colorado	113,570	100.0	15.7	13.4	5.5	15.4	22.0	12.2	15.8
Connecticut	102,377	100.0	22.6	28.4	9.8	6.4	10.9	7.5	14.4
Delaware	22,264	100.0	18.5	28.0	22.1	8.0	8.0	1.4	14.0
District of Columbia	15,244	100.0	18.5	27.8	13.6	8.3	9.0	11.5	11.2
Florida	348,112	100.0	15.9	32.0	17.7	9.9	6.2	4.7	13.6
Georgia	238,281	100.0	16.9	22.0	7.3	12.5	16.9	5.2	19.3
Hawaii	524,613	100.0	9.7	0.2	36.0	1.9	4.8	39.3	8.0
Idaho	15,656	100.0	22.9	16.3	6.6	8.1	19.3	15.8	11.1
Illinois	502,263	100.0	16.4	30.4	21.3	2.9	14.6	4.3	10.1
Indiana	65,891	100.0	23.9	26.7	11.9	9.9	14.2	7.2	6.1
Iowa	35,056	100.0	25.9	11.2	9.2	11.4	6.9	0.9	34.3
Kansas	56,701	100.0	14.8	11.7	12.5	23.7	9.0	4.0	24.3
Kentucky	35,164	100.0	22.6	17.4	8.9	17.3	15.6	8.1	10.2
Louisiana	58,035	100.0	19.7	14.5	5.1	35.9	6.0	2.4	16.5
Maine	9,182	100.0	11.7	15.8	23.5	5.7	4.9	12.0	26.3
Maryland	254,393	100.0	24.4	27.4	10.0	6.3	15.5	3.0	13.4
Massachusetts	283,635	100.0	39.0	22.1	3.8	14.4	5.2	4.2	11.4
Michigan	219,855	100.0	14.2	42.6	9.8	5.4	12.1	4.5	11.5
Minnesota	176,182	100.0	13.7	11.1	3.9	8.9	12.8	3.2	46.4
Mississippi	10,811	100.0	14.4	37.8	24.6	3.5	11.7	3.7	4.3
Missouri	67,518	100.0	25.3	19.2	13.1	11.5	14.7	2.7	13.5
Montana	3,395	100.0	16.0	10.7	36.7	–	12.7	14.6	9.3
Nebraska	24,707	100.0	18.8	10.0	12.9	27.7	14.4	2.7	13.5
Nevada	130,681	100.0	13.4	4.4	44.9	7.7	9.3	9.4	11.0
New Hampshire	21,973	100.0	21.6	24.0	12.7	10.8	11.9	1.4	17.7
New Jersey	601,939	100.0	22.0	38.2	15.3	4.9	11.8	1.6	6.3
New Mexico	24,705	100.0	19.3	14.9	15.1	4.1	14.5	12.8	19.3
New York	1,215,205	100.0	41.4	26.1	8.1	2.1	10.6	2.8	8.9
North Carolina	139,422	100.0	17.3	25.9	9.8	10.9	16.6	2.2	17.4
North Dakota	4,147	100.0	14.3	27.9	22.8	12.4	6.9	3.7	12.0
Ohio	159,146	100.0	22.8	28.8	11.5	8.8	10.3	6.0	11.9
Oklahoma	52,311	100.0	9.2	22.0	11.8	27.4	10.7	9.0	10.0
Oregon	123,018	100.0	19.3	7.1	12.5	23.1	10.1	10.2	17.7

(continued)

	total		Chinese	Filipino	Asian Indian	Vietnamese	Korean	Japanese	other Asian
	number	percent							
Pennsylvania	258,591	100.0%	26.6%	29.8%	5.8%	15.9%	8.2%	2.4%	11.2%
Rhode Island	27,930	100.0	13.3	18.9	7.6	9.0	5.4	2.5	43.4
South Carolina	43,842	100.0	17.2	18.4	19.3	11.7	13.9	4.6	15.0
South Dakota	5,371	100.0	15.2	14.1	22.0	26.2	6.8	6.8	8.8
Tennessee	72,931	100.0	14.8	23.7	10.0	11.2	12.6	4.6	23.2
Texas	701,483	100.0	18.0	26.0	10.3	21.9	7.7	2.8	13.3
Utah	46,132	100.0	16.9	21.5	10.8	11.2	5.2	8.8	25.5
Vermont	5,671	100.0	9.6	30.9	0.3	21.6	18.6	10.9	8.1
Virginia	326,563	100.0	15.4	24.7	15.5	13.9	13.9	2.0	14.7
Washington	381,867	100.0	19.1	10.8	17.6	14.7	12.5	8.9	16.3
West Virginia	7,128	100.0	20.1	27.7	18.9	5.0	4.4	5.6	18.4
Wisconsin	94,414	100.0	12.9	20.6	5.2	5.3	8.8	2.6	44.6
Wyoming	3,108	100.0	17.1	5.8	25.2	6.1	14.5	13.1	18.2

Note: Asians include only those identifying themselves as being Asian alone. Other Asian includes other Asian alone and two or more Asian ethnic categories. (–) means sample is too small to make a reliable estimate.
Source: Bureau of the Census, 2004 American Community Survey, Internet site http://factfinder.census.gov/servlet/ DatasetMainPageServlet?_lang=en&_ts=143469461584&_ds_name=ACS_2004_EST_G00_&_program=ACS; calculations by New Strategist

Table 2.96 Asians by Metropolitan Area, 2004

(total number of people, number of Asians, and Asian share of total, for selected metropolitan areas, 2004)

	total population	Asian number	Asian share of total
Albany–Schenectady–Troy, NY MSA	860,976	20,657	2.4%
Allentown–Bethlehem–Easton, PA MSA	650,230	13,537	2.1
Anchorage, AK MSA	265,176	17,899	6.7
Appleton–Oshkosh–Neenah, WI MSA	359,711	8,509	2.4
Atlanta, GA MSA	4,477,579	177,876	4.0
Augusta–Aiken, GA–SC MSA	476,167	7,261	1.5
Austin–San Marcos, TX MSA	1,373,125	56,489	4.1
Bakersfield, CA MSA	702,855	27,508	3.9
Baton Rouge, LA MSA	610,743	10,620	1.7
Beaumont–Port Arthur, TX MSA	366,244	8,811	2.4
Biloxi–Gulfport–Pascagoula, MS MSA	363,966	1,472	0.4
Binghamton, NY MSA	239,012	2,104	0.9
Birmingham, AL MSA	929,694	7,360	0.8
Boise City, ID MSA	479,284	7,708	1.6
Boston–Worcester–Lawrence, MA–NH–ME–CT CMSA	5,749,197	280,111	4.9
Brownsville–Harlingen–San Benito, TX MSA	367,603	2,909	0.8
Buffalo–Niagara Falls, NY MSA	1,119,037	16,569	1.5
Canton–Massillon, OH MSA	400,919	1,504	0.4
Charleston–North Charleston, SC MSA	563,828	8,202	1.5
Chicago, IL PMSA	8,388,723	456,188	5.4
Cleveland–Akron, OH CMSA	2,878,475	46,870	1.6
Colorado Springs, CO MSA	539,225	13,784	2.6
Columbia, SC MSA	543,126	9,322	1.7
Corpus Christi, TX MSA	381,422	4,997	1.3
Dallas–Fort Worth, TX CMSA	5,676,651	252,658	4.5
Davenport–Moline–Rock Island, IA–IL MSA	350,022	627	0.2
Dayton–Springfield, OH MSA	916,635	14,055	1.5
Daytona Beach, FL MSA	530,553	5,247	1.0
Denver–Boulder–Greeley, CO CMSA*	2,514,628	85,929	3.4
Des Moines, IA MSA	476,699	14,243	3.0
Detroit–Ann Arbor–Flint, MI CMSA	5,437,277	168,400	3.1
El Paso, TX MSA	700,225	7,522	1.1
Erie, PA MSA	267,426	1,423	0.5
Eugene–Springfield, OR MSA	324,176	8,992	2.8
Fayetteville, NC MSA	287,220	5,796	2.0
Fayetteville–Springdale–Rogers, AR MSA	345,308	6,860	2.0
Fort Myers–Cape Coral, FL MSA	508,634	5,980	1.2
Fort Pierce–Port St. Lucie, FL MSA	358,578	4,036	1.1
Fort Wayne, IN MSA	506,545	7,183	1.4

(continued)

	total population	Asian	
		number	share of total
Fresno, CA MSA	978,274	77,601	7.9%
Grand Rapids–Muskegon–Holland, MI MSA	1,102,729	19,944	1.8
Greensboro–Winston-Salem–High Point, NC MSA	1,283,261	23,811	1.9
Greenville–Spartanburg–Anderson, SC MSA	976,678	14,441	1.5
Harrisburg–Lebanon–Carlisle, PA MSA	617,676	12,520	2.0
Hartford, CT MSA	1,163,367	31,476	2.7
Hickory–Morganton–Lenoir, NC MSA	345,590	9,362	2.7
Honolulu, HI MSA	868,751	425,930	49.0
Houston–Galveston–Brazoria, TX CMSA*	4,794,384	274,649	5.7
Huntsville, AL MSA	354,936	7,347	2.1
Indianapolis, IN MSA	1,664,412	26,541	1.6
Jackson, MS MSA	443,275	2,894	0.7
Jacksonville, FL MSA	1,182,453	34,020	2.9
Johnson City–Kingsport–Bristol, TN–VA MSA	482,047	3,346	0.7
Kalamazoo–Battle Creek, MI MSA	441,059	5,946	1.3
Kansas City, MO–KS MSA	1,823,092	35,353	1.9
Killeen–Temple, TX MSA	298,933	9,394	3.1
Knoxville, TN MSA	707,617	8,367	1.2
Lafayette, LA MSA	386,812	928	0.2
Lakeland–Winter Haven, FL MSA	511,565	6,755	1.3
Lancaster, PA MSA	473,104	8,292	1.8
Lansing–East Lansing, MI MSA	436,485	12,658	2.9
Lexington, KY MSA	478,625	8,696	1.8
Lincoln, NE MSA	249,670	8,029	3.2
Little Rock–North Little Rock, AR MSA	593,032	6,192	1.0
Los Angeles–Riverside–Orange County, CA CMSA	17,199,115	1,946,192	11.3
Lubbock, TX MSA	240,721	1,515	0.6
Macon, GA MSA	329,432	4,946	1.5
Madison, WI MSA	437,843	18,827	4.3
McAllen–Edinburg–Mission, TX MSA	651,974	3,696	0.6
Melbourne–Titusville–Palm Bay, FL MSA	509,248	8,592	1.7
Miami–Fort Lauderdale, FL CMSA	4,051,442	84,766	2.1
Milwaukee–Waukesha, WI PMSA	1,483,023	37,926	2.6
Mobile, AL MSA	547,153	7,060	1.3
Modesto, CA MSA	490,860	24,712	5.0
Montgomery, AL MSA	323,220	3,614	1.1
Nashville, TN MSA	1,275,212	25,700	2.0
New Orleans, LA MSA	1,313,694	31,727	2.4
New York–Northern New Jersey–Long Island, NY–NJ–CT–PA CMSA*	20,345,959	1,697,426	8.3
Oklahoma City, OK MSA	1,095,252	30,175	2.8
Orlando, FL MSA	1,831,212	61,706	3.4
Pensacola, FL MSA	410,542	8,660	2.1
Peoria–Pekin, IL MSA	337,020	4,768	1.4
Philadelphia–Wilmington–Atlantic City, PA–NJ–DE–MD CMSA*	5,383,262	223,646	4.2

(continued)

	total population	Asian number	share of total
Pittsburgh, PA MSA	2,260,551	31,507	1.4%
Portland, ME MSA	248,827	4,768	1.9
Providence–Fall River–Warwick, RI–MA MSA	1,165,549	31,092	2.7
Provo–Orem, UT MSA	395,173	7,824	2.0
Raleigh–Durham–Chapel Hill, NC MSA	1,278,372	46,166	3.6
Reading, PA MSA	378,456	2,659	0.7
Reno, NV MSA	375,344	19,321	5.1
Richmond–Petersburg, VA MSA	1,013,399	24,318	2.4
Rochester, NY MSA	1,057,917	23,012	2.2
Rockford, IL MSA	382,901	6,141	1.6
Sacramento, CA PMSA	1,803,160	194,516	10.8
Saginaw–Bay City–Midland, MI MSA	393,837	3,637	0.9
St. Louis, MO–IL MSA	2,620,334	43,915	1.7
Salinas, CA MSA	392,192	26,680	6.8
Salt Lake City–Ogden, UT MSA	1,384,041	33,050	2.4
San Antonio, TX MSA	1,683,872	28,980	1.7
San Diego, CA MSA	2,833,275	292,751	10.3
San Francisco–Oakland–San Jose, CA CMSA	6,951,260	1,463,092	21.0
San Luis Obispo–Atascadero–Paso Robles, CA MSA	238,502	7,562	3.2
Santa Barbara–Santa Maria–Lompoc, CA MSA	385,238	17,349	4.5
Sarasota–Bradenton, FL MSA	639,438	7,205	1.1
Savannah, GA MSA	299,920	5,730	1.9
Scranton–Wilkes-Barre–Hazleton, PA MSA	587,557	5,323	0.9
Seattle–Tacoma–Bremerton, WA CMSA*	3,184,924	312,679	9.8
Shreveport–Bossier City, LA MSA	387,312	3,941	1.0
South Bend, IN MSA	252,944	1,556	0.6
Spokane, WA MSA	420,592	7,774	1.8
Springfield, MA MSA	560,472	13,252	2.4
Springfield, MO MSA	332,918	3,704	1.1
Stockton–Lodi, CA MSA	632,143	89,915	14.2
Syracuse, NY MSA	707,901	11,996	1.7
Tallahassee, FL MSA	274,945	6,063	2.2
Tampa–St. Petersburg–Clearwater, FL MSA	2,537,586	59,558	2.3
Toledo, OH MSA	598,283	7,486	1.3
Tucson, AZ MSA	885,025	22,151	2.5
Tulsa, OK MSA	810,062	11,670	1.4
Utica–Rome, NY MSA	282,844	2,090	0.7
Visalia–Tulare–Porterville, CA MSA	395,493	13,989	3.5
West Palm Beach–Boca Raton, FL MSA	1,223,206	23,524	1.9
Wichita, KS MSA	546,308	19,136	3.5
York, PA MSA	393,426	4,403	1.1
Youngstown–Warren, OH MSA	566,597	3,296	0.6

* Population figures are for only part of the metropolitan area.
Note: Some metropolitan areas are not shown because data are not available. Asians are those identifying themselves as being of the race alone. For the definition of CMSA, MSA, and PMSA, see the glossary.
Source: Bureau of the Census, 2004 American Community Survey, Internet site http://factfinder.census.gov/servlet/ DatasetMainPageServlet?_program=ACS&_lang=en&_ts=; calculations by New Strategist

Table 2.97 Immigrants from Asia, 2004

(total number of immigrants admitted for legal permanent residence, and number and percent distribution of immigrants from Asia, by country of birth, 2004)

	number	percent distribution
TOTAL IMMIGRANTS	**946,142**	**100.0%**
Immigrants from Asia	**330,004**	**34.9**
IMMIGRANTS FROM ASIA	**330,004**	**100.0%**
India	70,116	21.2
Philippines	57,827	17.5
China, People's Republic	51,156	15.5
Vietnam	31,514	9.5
Korea	19,766	6.0
Pakistan	12,086	3.7
Iran	10,434	3.2
Taiwan	8,961	2.7
Bangladesh	8,061	2.4
Japan	7,694	2.3
Thailand	4,314	1.3
Israel	4,160	1.3
Hong Kong	3,951	1.2
Turkey	3,833	1.2
Lebanon	3,811	1.2
Cambodia	3,534	1.1
Iraq	3,494	1.1
Jordan	3,431	1.0
Nepal	2,842	0.9
Indonesia	2,418	0.7
Syria	2,256	0.7
Afghanistan	2,137	0.6
Malaysia	1,987	0.6
Yemen	1,760	0.5
Sri Lanka	1,431	0.4
Burma	1,379	0.4
Laos	1,147	0.3
Kuwait	1,091	0.3
Singapore	966	0.3
Saudi Arabia	906	0.3
United Arab Emirates	586	0.2
Mongolia	211	0.1
Macau	192	0.1
Cyprus	143	0.0
Qatar	125	0.0
Oman	122	0.0
Bahrain	116	0.0
Brunei	22	0.0
Bhutan	17	0.0
Maldives	7	0.0

Source: Office of Immigration Statistics, 2004 Yearbook of Immigration Statistics, Internet site http://uscis.gov/graphics/shared/statistics/yearbook/YrBk04Im.htm; calculations by New Strategist

Table 2.98 Total and Asian Foreign-Born by Age, 2004

(number of total foreign-born, number and percent distribution of Asian foreign-born, and Asian share of total, by age, 2004; numbers in thousands)

	total	Asian foreign-born number	percent distribution	share of total
Total foreign-born	**34,244**	**8,685**	**100.0%**	**25.4%**
Under age 5	334	86	1.0	25.7
Aged 5 to 9	709	123	1.4	17.3
Aged 10 to 14	1,113	216	2.5	19.4
Aged 15 to 19	1,677	355	4.1	21.2
Aged 20 to 24	2,884	539	6.2	18.7
Aged 25 to 29	3,751	804	9.3	21.4
Aged 30 to 34	4,033	1,039	12.0	25.8
Aged 35 to 39	3,873	1,057	12.2	27.3
Aged 40 to 44	3,686	950	10.9	25.8
Aged 45 to 49	3,049	879	10.1	28.8
Aged 50 to 54	2,267	708	8.2	31.2
Aged 55 to 59	1,811	600	6.9	33.1
Aged 60 to 64	1,360	389	4.5	28.6
Aged 65 or older	3,697	940	10.8	25.4

Source: Bureau of the Census, Foreign-born Population of the United States, Current Population Survey, March 2004, detailed tables (PPL-176), Internet site http://www.census.gov/population/www/socdemo/foreign/ppl-176.html; calculations by New Strategist

Table 2.99 Asian Foreign-Born by U.S. Region of Residence, 2004

(number of total people, number and percent distribution of Asian foreign-born, and Asian foreign-born share of total, by U.S. region of residence, 2004; numbers in thousands)

	total	Asian foreign-born number	percent distribution	share of total
Total people	**288,280**	**8,685**	**100.0%**	**3.0%**
Northeast	53,703	1,693	19.5	3.2
Midwest	64,784	1,183	13.6	1.8
South	103,545	1,882	21.7	1.8
West	66,247	3,927	45.2	5.9

Source: Bureau of the Census, Foreign-Born Population of the United States, Current Population Survey, March 2004, detailed tables (PPL-176), Internet site http://www.census.gov/population/www/socdemo/foreign/ppl-176.html; calculations by New Strategist

Table 2.100 People Who Speak Selected Asian Languages at Home, by State, 2003

(total number of people aged 5 or older, and number and percent who speak selected Asian languages at home, by state, 2003; Asian languages shown are those with at least 1 million at-home speakers)

	total aged 5 or older	speak Chinese at home		speak Tagalog at home		speak Vietnamese at home	
		number	percent	number	percent	number	percent
United States	**263,230,104**	**2,193,370**	**0.8%**	**1,261,746**	**0.5%**	**1,104,248**	**0.4%**
Alabama	4,087,909	13,130	0.3	198	0.0	805	0.0
Alaska	581,706	1,250	0.2	11,077	1.9	387	0.1
Arizona	5,031,761	18,773	0.4	13,114	0.3	17,142	0.3
Arkansas	2,460,507	560	0.0	837	0.0	6,115	0.2
California	32,115,612	856,896	2.7	611,652	1.9	450,024	1.4
Colorado	4,123,589	19,907	0.5	6,395	0.2	16,645	0.4
Connecticut	3,157,963	17,838	0.6	8,678	0.3	5,957	0.2
Delaware	738,327	2,557	0.3	1,402	0.2	350	0.0
District of Columbia	495,397	2,380	0.5	1,939	0.4	1,806	0.4
Florida	15,572,360	42,557	0.3	40,324	0.3	45,460	0.3
Georgia	7,779,928	26,624	0.3	9,200	0.1	37,406	0.5
Hawaii	1,136,645	26,478	2.3	52,848	4.6	3,550	0.3
Idaho	1,229,675	3,443	0.3	1,252	0.1	803	0.1
Illinois	11,442,014	76,240	0.7	61,283	0.5	27,554	0.2
Indiana	5,595,593	6,114	0.1	6,521	0.1	2,952	0.1
Iowa	2,660,537	6,279	0.2	2,300	0.1	8,083	0.3
Kansas	2,450,103	11,638	0.5	1,279	0.1	9,144	0.4
Kentucky	3,732,957	1,739	0.0	1,675	0.0	837	0.0
Louisiana	4,038,853	9,454	0.2	2,494	0.1	26,681	0.7
Maine	1,203,618	1,569	0.1	1,355	0.1	1,651	0.1
Maryland	5,006,754	55,066	1.1	18,979	0.4	15,426	0.3
Massachusetts	5,822,123	71,560	1.2	9,673	0.2	40,057	0.7
Michigan	9,178,031	28,777	0.3	18,622	0.2	11,811	0.1
Minnesota	4,591,314	14,181	0.3	3,738	0.1	15,240	0.3
Mississippi	2,577,551	2,799	0.1	1,856	0.1	7,235	0.3
Missouri	5,159,771	13,908	0.3	6,464	0.1	10,855	0.2
Montana	840,297	553	0.1	452	0.1	420	0.0
Nebraska	1,568,543	4,892	0.3	1,023	0.1	7,995	0.5
Nevada	2,045,157	12,098	0.6	35,498	1.7	2,162	0.1
New Hampshire	1,179,322	3,251	0.3	907	0.1	847	0.1
New Jersey	7,887,106	100,359	1.3	65,016	0.8	8,906	0.1
New Mexico	1,708,107	4,052	0.2	2,079	0.1	390	0.0
New York	17,394,711	415,929	2.4	66,405	0.4	15,783	0.1
North Carolina	7,557,056	19,766	0.3	5,979	0.1	15,689	0.2
North Dakota	572,574	1,286	0.2	129	0.0	0	0.0
Ohio	10,396,176	25,413	0.2	4,893	0.0	5,849	0.1
Oklahoma	3,162,666	4,759	0.2	2,198	0.1	18,639	0.6
Oregon	3,256,681	19,732	0.6	5,719	0.2	15,249	0.5

(continued)

	total aged 5 or older	speak Chinese at home		speak Tagalog at home		speak Vietnamese at home	
		number	percent	number	percent	number	percent
Pennsylvania	11,218,258	34,258	0.3%	13,047	0.1%	29,452	0.3%
Rhode Island	976,471	3,464	0.4	726	0.1	847	0.1
South Carolina	3,736,487	5,817	0.2	3,290	0.1	5,208	0.1
South Dakota	683,219	545	0.1	445	0.1	755	0.1
Tennessee	5,309,621	6,649	0.1	1,756	0.0	3,719	0.1
Texas	19,751,381	104,588	0.5	49,674	0.3	115,686	0.6
Utah	2,082,635	4,042	0.2	2,519	0.1	11,503	0.6
Vermont	567,271	1,078	0.2	66	0.0	1,616	0.3
Virginia	6,667,441	34,616	0.5	35,486	0.5	35,115	0.5
Washington	5,600,233	45,589	0.8	62,940	1.1	40,181	0.7
West Virginia	1,663,592	367	0.0	1,149	0.1	822	0.0
Wisconsin	4,978,150	7,483	0.2	5,081	0.1	3,393	0.1
Wyoming	456,351	1,067	0.2	114	0.0	46	0.0

Source: Bureau of the Census, 2003 American Community Survey, Internet site http://factfinder.census.gov/servlet/ DatasetMainPageServlet?_lang=en&_ts=143386397087&_ds_name=ACS_2003_EST_G00_&_program=; calculations by New Strategist

Asian Households Spend the Most

In 2003, for the first time, the Consumer Expenditure Survey collected data on the spending of Asian households (called consumer units by the Bureau of Labor Statistics). The results show that households headed by Asians spend more than those headed by blacks, Hispanics, or whites. The nation's 3.6 million Asian households spent an average of $44,923 in 2003, 10 percent more than the $40,817 spent by the average household.

Reasons for the higher spending of Asians include their larger household size (2.8 people per household versus an average of 2.5) and their high level of education. The Asian investment in education is revealed in these statistics. Asian households spend more than twice the average on education, accounting for a disproportionate 7 percent of the market. Asians also spend more than twice the average on fish and seafood and twice the average on public transportation. They spend more than five times the average on gifts of transportation.

■ Asian spending is above average because many Asians households have two or more earners, boosting incomes.

Asian households spend 10 percent more than the average household

(average annual spending of total and Asian consumer units, 2003)

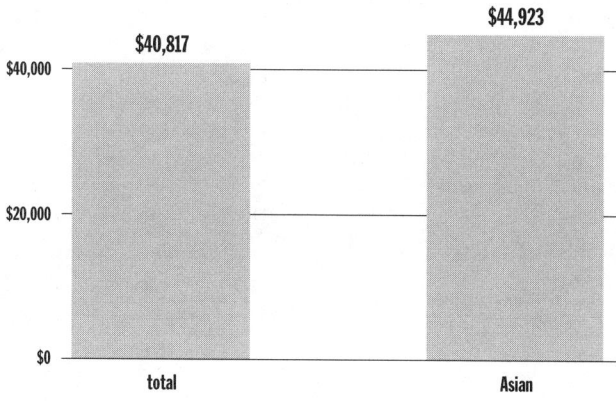

Table 2.101 Spending of Households Headed by Asians, 2003

(average annual spending of total consumer units (CU), and average annual, indexed, and market share of spending of consumer units headed by Asians, by product and service category, 2003)

	total consumer units	Asian consumer units		
		average spending	indexed spending	market share
Number of consumer units (000s)	115,356	3,573	–	3.1%
Persons per consumer unit	2.5	2.8	–	–
Average income before taxes	$51,128	$60,393	118	3.7
Average annual spending	40,817	44,923	110	3.4
FOOD	5,340	6,285	118	3.6
Food at home	3,129	3,302	106	3.3
Cereals and bakery products	442	437	99	3.1
Cereals and cereal products	150	180	120	3.7
Bakery products	292	257	88	2.7
Meats, poultry, fish, and eggs	825	978	119	3.7
Beef	246	193	78	2.4
Pork	171	174	102	3.2
Other meats	102	81	79	2.5
Poultry	145	182	126	3.9
Fish and seafood	124	304	245	7.6
Eggs	37	43	116	3.6
Dairy products	328	247	75	2.3
Fresh milk and cream	127	112	88	2.7
Other dairy products	201	136	68	2.1
Fruits and vegetables	535	788	147	4.6
Fresh fruits	171	275	161	5.0
Fresh vegetables	172	322	187	5.8
Processed fruits	108	123	114	3.5
Processed vegetables	84	68	81	2.5
Other food at home	999	852	85	2.6
Sugar and other sweets	119	102	86	2.7
Fats and oils	86	63	73	2.3
Miscellaneous foods	490	400	82	2.5
Nonalcoholic beverages	268	248	93	2.9
Food prepared by CU on trips	36	40	111	3.4
Food away from home	2,211	2,983	135	4.2
ALCOHOLIC BEVERAGES	391	308	79	2.4
HOUSING	13,432	16,326	122	3.8
Shelter	7,887	10,902	138	4.3
Owned dwellings	5,263	6,835	130	4.0
Mortgage interest and charges	2,954	4,348	147	4.6
Property taxes	1,344	1,713	127	3.9
Maintenance, repair, insurance, other expenses	965	774	80	2.5
Rented dwellings	2,179	3,661	168	5.2
Other lodging	445	406	91	2.8
Utilities, fuels, and public services	2,811	2,536	90	2.8
Natural gas	392	385	98	3.0
Electricity	1,028	780	76	2.4

(continued)

	total consumer units	Asian consumer units		
		average spending	indexed spending	market share
Fuel oil and other fuels	$110	$27	25	0.8%
Telephone	956	1,026	107	3.3
Water and other public services	326	318	98	3.0
Household services	**707**	**783**	**111**	**3.4**
Personal services	294	381	130	4.0
Other household services	414	403	97	3.0
Housekeeping supplies	**529**	**471**	**89**	**2.8**
Laundry and cleaning supplies	132	96	73	2.3
Other household products	263	228	87	2.7
Postage and stationery	133	146	110	3.4
Household furnishings and equipment	**1,497**	**1,634**	**109**	**3.4**
Household textiles	113	67	59	1.8
Furniture	401	334	83	2.6
Floor coverings	52	21	40	1.3
Major appliances	196	283	144	4.5
Small appliances, misc. housewares	88	128	145	4.5
Miscellaneous household equipment	648	802	124	3.8
APPAREL AND RELATED SERVICES	**1,640**	**1,736**	**106**	**3.3**
Men and boys	**372**	**342**	**92**	**2.8**
Men, aged 16 or older	282	290	103	3.2
Boys, aged 2 to 15	89	52	58	1.8
Women and girls	**634**	**609**	**96**	**3.0**
Women, aged 16 or older	529	538	102	3.2
Girls, aged 2 to 15	106	71	67	2.1
Children under age 2	**81**	**125**	**154**	**4.8**
Footwear	**294**	**292**	**99**	**3.1**
Other apparel products and services	**258**	**368**	**143**	**4.4**
TRANSPORTATION	**7,781**	**7,454**	**96**	**3.0**
Vehicle purchases	**3,732**	**2,992**	**80**	**2.5**
Cars and trucks, new	2,052	2,156	105	3.3
Cars and trucks, used	1,611	836	52	1.6
Other vehicles	68	–	–	–
Gasoline and motor oil	**1,333**	**1,313**	**98**	**3.1**
Other vehicle expenses	**2,331**	**2,383**	**102**	**3.2**
Vehicle finance charges	371	282	76	2.4
Maintenance and repairs	619	546	88	2.7
Vehicle insurance	905	989	109	3.4
Vehicle rentals, leases, licenses, other charges	436	565	130	4.0
Public transportation	**385**	**766**	**199**	**6.2**
HEALTH CARE	**2,416**	**1,955**	**81**	**2.5**
Health insurance	1,252	1,071	86	2.6
Medical services	591	476	81	2.5
Drugs	467	340	73	2.3
Medical supplies	107	69	64	2.0
ENTERTAINMENT	**2,060**	**1,713**	**83**	**2.6**
Fees and admissions	494	516	104	3.2
Television, radio, sound equipment	730	621	85	2.6
Pets, toys, and playground equipment	378	197	52	1.6
Other entertainment products and services	457	378	83	2.6

(continued)

	total consumer units	Asian consumer units		
		average spending	indexed spending	market share
PERSONAL CARE PRODUCTS, SERVICES	$527	$520	99	3.1%
READING	127	111	87	2.7
EDUCATION	783	1,890	241	7.5
TOBACCO PRODUCTS, SMOKING SUPPLIES	290	119	41	1.3
MISCELLANEOUS	606	432	71	2.2
CASH CONTRIBUTIONS	1,370	1,311	96	3.0
PERSONAL INSURANCE AND PENSIONS	4,055	4,762	117	3.6
Life and other personal insurance	397	414	104	3.2
Pensions and Social Security	3,658	4,348	119	3.7
PERSONAL TAXES	2,532	2,882	114	3.5
Federal income taxes	1,843	1,993	108	3.3
State and local income taxes	502	650	129	4.0
Other taxes	187	240	128	4.0
GIFTS FOR NONHOUSEHOLD MEMBERS	1,007	1,342	133	4.1
Food	78	116	149	4.6
Alcoholic beverages	16	12	75	2.3
Housing	220	139	63	2.0
Housekeeping supplies	42	20	48	1.5
Household textiles	13	1	8	0.2
Appliances and misc. housewares	25	20	80	2.5
Major appliances	7	5	71	2.2
Small appliances and misc. housewares	18	15	83	2.6
Miscellaneous household equipment	57	50	88	2.7
Other housing	85	47	55	1.7
Apparel and services	225	179	80	2.5
Males, aged 2 or older	56	57	102	3.2
Females, aged 2 or older	80	53	66	2.1
Children under age 2	39	46	118	3.7
Other apparel products and services	50	24	48	1.5
Jewelry and watches	26	20	77	2.4
All other apparel products and services	25	4	16	0.5
Transportation	60	324	540	16.7
Health care	48	34	71	2.2
Entertainment	69	55	80	2.5
Toys, games, hobbies, and tricycles	26	13	50	1.5
Other entertainment	43	43	100	3.1
Personal care products and services	16	23	144	4.5
Reading	1	1	100	3.1
Education	200	388	194	6.0
All other gifts	74	71	96	3.0

Definitions: The index compares the spending of the average Asian consumer unit with the spending of the average consumer unit by dividing Asian spending by average spending in each category and multiplying by 100. An index of 100 means Asian spending in the category equals average spending. An index of 125 means Asian spending is 25 percent above average, while an index of 75 means Asian spending is 25 percent below average. The market share is the percentage of total spending on a product or service category that is accounted for by consumer units headed by Asians.

Note: The Bureau of Labor Statistics uses consumer unit rather than household as the sampling unit in the Consumer Expenditure Survey. For the definition of consumer unit, see the glossary. Spending by category will not add to total spending because gift spending is also included in the preceding product and service categories and personal taxes are not included in the total. (–) means sample is too small to make a reliable estimate or not applicable.

Source: Bureau of Labor Statistics, 2003 Consumer Expenditure Survey, Internet site http://www.bls.gov/cex/; calculations by New Strategist

3

Blacks

■ The black population numbered 39 million in 2004, accounting for a substantial 13 percent of the U.S. population.

■ The 55 percent majority of black high school graduates go to college within one year of graduating from high school.

■ Only 51 percent of blacks say they are in very good or excellent health, less than the 62 percent share among the total population.

■ Forty-nine percent of the nation's black households owned their home in 2004.

■ The $29,689 median income of black households in 2003 was 16 percent greater than in 1990, after adjusting for inflation.

■ The 26 percent of blacks employed as managers or professionals account for 8 percent of Americans working in those occupations.

■ Black households are diverse. Married couples head 30 percent of black households, while female-headed families account for 29 percent.

■ More than half of blacks (54 percent) live in the South, where they account for 20 percent of the population.

■ The average black household spent $28,708 in 2003. Blacks spend more than average on telephone services, footwear, and children's clothes.

■ Only 19 percent of black workers are "very confident" they will have enough money to live comfortably throughout their retirement years.

Blacks account for 13.4 percent of the U.S. population

(percent distribution of people by race and Hispanic origin, 2004)

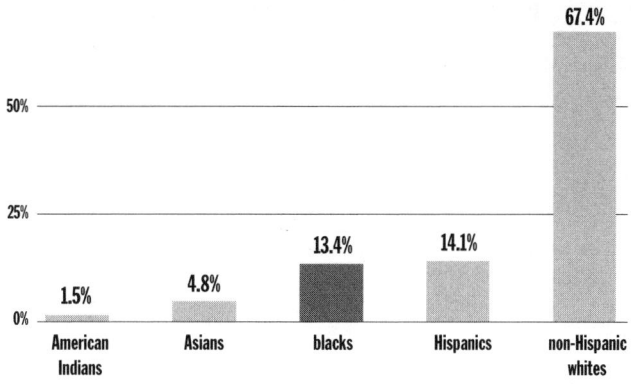

Nearly Half of Blacks Have Attended College for One or More Years

Forty-five percent of blacks aged 25 or older have at least some college experience, and 18 percent are college graduates. While these figures are lower than the shares among Asians and non-Hispanic whites, they are far above the figures for Hispanics. The educational attainment of blacks is rising as younger generations with more schooling replace the older, less-educated population. Among blacks aged 25 to 34, the 52 percent majority has college experience and 19 percent are college graduates.

A growing proportion of blacks are enrolling in college. The 55 percent majority of black high school graduates go to college within one year of graduating from high school, up from only 47 percent who went on to college in 1990. Twelve percent of black families with children aged 5 to 24 have at least one child enrolled in college. More than 2 million blacks were in college in 2003, accounting for 13 percent of the nation's college students. Fifty-four percent of black college students attend four-year undergraduate schools, 31 percent are in two-year schools, and 15 percent are in graduate school.

Blacks earned 11 percent of associate's degrees awarded in 2001–02. They earned 9 percent of bachelor's degrees, 8 percent of master's degrees, and 5 percent of doctorates. Twelve percent of first-professional degrees in theology were awarded to blacks.

■ The proportion of blacks with a college education will continue to climb, but only if college remains affordable for the middle class.

Nearly one in five blacks is a college graduate

(percent of blacks aged 25 or older who are high school graduates or more, have some college or more, or are college graduates, 2004)

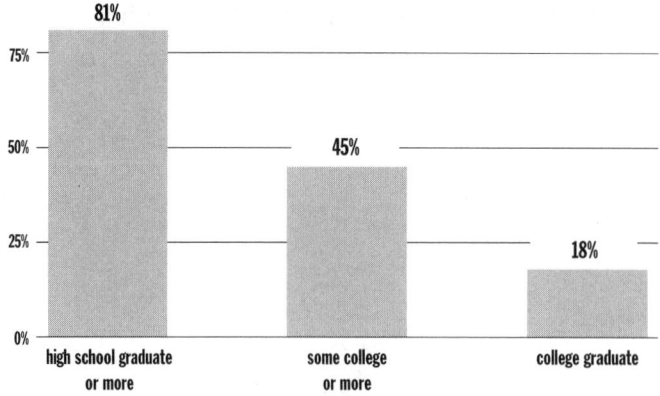

Table 3.1 Educational Attainment of Blacks by Age, 2004

(number and percent distribution of blacks aged 25 or older by educational attainment and age, 2004; numbers in thousands)

	total	25 to 34	35 to 44	45 to 54	55 to 64	65 or older
Total blacks	**21,290**	**5,190**	**5,530**	**4,812**	**2,825**	**2,933**
Not a high school graduate	4,122	580	753	739	660	1,387
High school graduate only	7,624	1,893	2,081	1,786	1,059	805
Some college, no degree	4,117	1,318	1,115	912	466	306
Associate's degree	1,667	414	498	439	194	122
Bachelor's degree	2,622	757	809	627	262	167
Master's degree	875	175	211	238	136	114
Professional degree	163	43	38	36	27	18
Doctoral degree	101	7	27	36	20	12
High school graduate or more	17,169	4,607	4,779	4,074	2,164	1,544
Some college or more	9,545	2,714	2,698	2,288	1,105	739
Bachelor's degree or more	3,761	982	1,085	937	445	311
PERCENT DISTRIBUTION						
Total blacks	**100.0%**	**100.0%**	**100.0%**	**100.0%**	**100.0%**	**100.0%**
Not a high school graduate	19.4	11.2	13.6	15.4	23.4	47.3
High school graduate only	35.8	36.5	37.6	37.1	37.5	27.4
Some college, no degree	19.3	25.4	20.2	19.0	16.5	10.4
Associate's degree	7.8	8.0	9.0	9.1	6.9	4.2
Bachelor's degree	12.3	14.6	14.6	13.0	9.3	5.7
Master's degree	4.1	3.4	3.8	4.9	4.8	3.9
Professional degree	0.8	0.8	0.7	0.7	1.0	0.6
Doctoral degree	0.5	0.1	0.5	0.7	0.7	0.4
High school graduate or more	80.6	88.8	86.4	84.7	76.6	52.6
Some college or more	44.8	52.3	48.8	47.5	39.1	25.2
Bachelor's degree or more	17.7	18.9	19.6	19.5	15.8	10.6

Note: Blacks include those identifying themselves as being black alone and those identifying themselves as being black in combination with one or more other races.
Source: Bureau of the Census, 2004 Current Population Survey Annual Social and Economic Supplement, Educational Attainment in the United States: 2004, Detailed Tables, Internet site http://www.census.gov/population/www/socdemo/education/cps2004.html; calculations by New Strategist

Table 3.2 Educational Attainment of Black Men by Age, 2004

(number and percent distribution of black men aged 25 or older by educational attainment and age, 2004; numbers in thousands)

	total	25 to 34	35 to 44	45 to 54	55 to 64	65 or older
Total black men	**9,366**	**2,324**	**2,496**	**2,178**	**1,245**	**1,123**
Not a high school graduate	1,842	231	371	369	305	569
High school graduate only	3,572	946	1,014	865	483	265
Some college, no degree	1,765	599	468	385	190	123
Associate's degree	639	165	181	169	74	49
Bachelor's degree	1,066	301	345	252	114	55
Master's degree	338	63	83	99	49	42
Professional degree	90	15	21	27	14	13
Doctoral degree	54	3	14	13	16	8
High school grad. or more	7,524	2,092	2,126	1,810	940	555
Some college or more	3,952	1,146	1,112	945	457	290
Bachelor's degree or more	1,548	382	463	391	193	118
PERCENT DISTRIBUTION						
Total black men	**100.0%**	**100.0%**	**100.0%**	**100.0%**	**100.0%**	**100.0%**
Not a high school graduate	19.7	9.9	14.9	16.9	24.5	50.7
High school graduate only	38.1	40.7	40.6	39.7	38.8	23.6
Some college, no degree	18.8	25.8	18.8	17.7	15.3	11.0
Associate's degree	6.8	7.1	7.3	7.8	5.9	4.4
Bachelor's degree	11.4	13.0	13.8	11.6	9.2	4.9
Master's degree	3.6	2.7	3.3	4.5	3.9	3.7
Professional degree	1.0	0.6	0.8	1.2	1.1	1.2
Doctoral degree	0.6	0.1	0.6	0.6	1.3	0.7
High school grad. or more	80.3	90.0	85.2	83.1	75.5	49.4
Some college or more	42.2	49.3	44.6	43.4	36.7	25.8
Bachelor's degree or more	16.5	16.4	18.5	18.0	15.5	10.5

Note: Blacks include those identifying themselves as being black alone and those identifying themselves as being black in combination with one or more other races.
Source: Bureau of the Census, 2004 Current Population Survey Annual Social and Economic Supplement, Educational Attainment in the United States: 2004, Detailed Tables, Internet site http://www.census.gov/population/www/socdemo/education/cps2004.html; calculations by New Strategist

Table 3.3 Educational Attainment of Black Women by Age, 2004

(number and percent distribution of black women aged 25 or older by educational attainment and age, 2004; numbers in thousands)

	total	25 to 34	35 to 44	45 to 54	55 to 64	65 or older
Total black women	**11,925**	**2,866**	**3,034**	**2,634**	**1,580**	**1,810**
Not a high school graduate	2,279	349	382	371	354	819
High school graduate only	4,052	946	1,067	920	578	541
Some college, no degree	2,352	719	647	527	277	183
Associate's degree	1,028	251	317	270	118	73
Bachelor's degree	1,556	456	465	375	149	113
Master's degree	537	112	128	139	86	72
Professional degree	73	28	17	10	12	5
Doctoral degree	47	4	12	22	4	4
High school grad. or more	9,645	2,516	2,653	2,263	1,224	991
Some college or more	5,593	1,570	1,586	1,343	646	450
Bachelor's degree or more	2,213	600	622	546	251	194
PERCENT DISTRIBUTION						
Total black women	**100.0%**	**100.0%**	**100.0%**	**100.0%**	**100.0%**	**100.0%**
Not a high school graduate	19.1	12.2	12.6	14.1	22.4	45.2
High school graduate only	34.0	33.0	35.2	34.9	36.6	29.9
Some college, no degree	19.7	25.1	21.3	20.0	17.5	10.1
Associate's degree	8.6	8.8	10.4	10.3	7.5	4.0
Bachelor's degree	13.0	15.9	15.3	14.2	9.4	6.2
Master's degree	4.5	3.9	4.2	5.3	5.4	4.0
Professional degree	0.6	1.0	0.6	0.4	0.8	0.3
Doctoral degree	0.4	0.1	0.4	0.8	0.3	0.2
High school grad. or more	80.9	87.8	87.4	85.9	77.5	54.8
Some college or more	46.9	54.8	52.3	51.0	40.9	24.9
Bachelor's degree or more	18.6	20.9	20.5	20.7	15.9	10.7

Note: Blacks include those identifying themselves as being black alone and those identifying themselves as being black in combination with one or more other races.
Source: Bureau of the Census, 2004 Current Population Survey Annual Social and Economic Supplement, Educational Attainment in the United States: 2004, Detailed Tables, Internet site http://www.census.gov/population/www/socdemo/education/cps2004.html; calculations by New Strategist

Table 3.4 Educational Attainment of Blacks by Age and Region, 2004

(percent of blacks aged 25 or older by selected educational attainment, age, and region, 2004)

	Northeast	Midwest	South	West
HIGH SCHOOL GRADUATE OR MORE				
Total blacks	**79.2%**	**81.6%**	**79.9%**	**85.6%**
Aged 25 to 34	87.3	86.4	90.1	88.9
Aged 35 to 44	84.3	89.6	85.9	87.2
Aged 45 to 54	79.5	87.7	84.6	87.7
Aged 55 to 64	79.8	76.5	73.9	87.2
Aged 65 or older	57.6	53.2	47.5	69.3
SOME COLLEGE OR MORE				
Total blacks	**40.9**	**45.7**	**43.0**	**61.6**
Aged 25 to 34	50.3	49.6	52.3	61.2
Aged 35 to 44	46.5	51.0	45.9	65.2
Aged 45 to 54	40.1	50.1	45.8	64.5
Aged 55 to 64	35.7	39.1	36.8	62.0
Aged 65 or older	23.1	27.7	21.1	48.7
BACHELOR'S DEGREE OR MORE				
Total blacks	**18.8**	**16.1**	**17.0**	**22.0**
Aged 25 to 34	21.6	16.4	19.1	18.0
Aged 35 to 44	20.7	16.3	18.7	28.0
Aged 45 to 54	19.0	20.1	18.2	25.5
Aged 55 to 64	17.0	13.1	15.0	23.1
Aged 65 or older	12.2	10.8	10.0	9.6

Note: Blacks include those identifying themselves as being black alone and those identifying themselves as being black in combination with one or more other races.
Source: Bureau of the Census, 2004 Current Population Survey Annual Social and Economic Supplement, Educational Attainment in the United States: 2004, Detailed Tables, Internet site http://www.census.gov/population/www/socdemo/education/cps2004.html; calculations by New Strategist

Table 3.5 Educational Attainment of Blacks by State, 2004

(percent of blacks aged 25 or older who are high school or college graduates, for the 25 largest states, 2004)

	high school graduate or more	college graduate
Total blacks	**80.6%**	**17.7%**
Alabama	76.6	11.7
Arizona	90.4	16.6
California	84.9	22.9
Colorado	81.4	21.5
Florida	76.7	14.2
Georgia	83.0	19.7
Illinois	78.8	15.9
Indiana	85.0	12.7
Kentucky	84.8	11.5
Louisiana	69.6	12.0
Maryland	89.0	27.8
Massachusetts	70.8	18.9
Michigan	82.8	15.4
Minnesota	90.7	25.8
Missouri	83.9	20.5
New Jersey	82.2	21.8
New York	79.3	19.5
North Carolina	76.6	18.7
Ohio	82.7	16.1
Pennsylvania	79.3	14.6
Tennessee	83.3	16.8
Texas	85.5	20.5
Virginia	81.1	16.8
Washington	90.2	21.5
Wisconsin	67.5	10.6

Note: Blacks include those identifying themselves as being black alone and those identifying themselves as being black in combination with one or more other races.
Source: Bureau of the Census, 2004 Current Population Survey Annual Social and Economic Supplement, Educational Attainment in the United States: 2004, Detailed Tables, Internet site http://www.census.gov/population/www/socdemo/education/cps2004. html; calculations by New Strategist

Table 3.6 School Enrollment of Blacks, 2003

(total number of people aged 3 or older enrolled in school, number of blacks enrolled, and black share of total, by age, October 2003; numbers in thousands)

	total	black number	black share of total
Total aged 3 or older	**74,911**	**12,144**	**16.2%**
Aged 3 to 4	4,590	798	17.4
Aged 5 to 6	7,309	1,204	16.5
Aged 7 to 9	11,706	2,015	17.2
Aged 10 to 13	16,478	2,804	17.0
Aged 14 to 15	8,329	1,379	16.6
Aged 16 to 17	8,177	1,321	16.2
Aged 18 to 19	4,856	688	14.2
Aged 20 to 21	3,684	490	13.3
Aged 22 to 24	3,397	469	13.8
Aged 25 to 29	2,212	311	14.1
Aged 30 to 34	1,378	220	16.0
Aged 35 to 44	1,635	255	15.6
Aged 45 to 54	879	150	17.1
Aged 55 or older	283	40	14.1

Note: Blacks include those identifying themselves as being black alone and those identifying themselves as being black in combination with one or more other races.
Source: Bureau of the Census, School Enrollment—Social and Economic Characteristics of Students: October 2003, Detailed Tables, Internet site http://www.census.gov/population/www/socdemo/school/cps2003.html

Table 3.7 School Enrollment of Blacks by Age and Sex, 2003

(number and percent of blacks aged 3 or older enrolled in school, by age and sex, October 2003; numbers in thousands)

	total		female		male	
	number	percent	number	percent	number	percent
Total blacks enrolled	**12,144**	**34.2%**	**6,290**	**32.9%**	**5,854**	**35.7%**
Aged 3 to 4	798	56.5	370	55.3	429	57.6
Aged 5 to 6	1,204	94.6	626	95.9	578	93.2
Aged 7 to 9	2,015	98.1	954	97.3	1,061	98.8
Aged 10 to 13	2,804	98.3	1,451	98.4	1,353	98.2
Aged 14 to 15	1,379	98.0	629	97.6	751	98.3
Aged 16 to 17	1,321	94.2	660	94.5	661	93.8
Aged 18 to 19	688	60.9	367	60.7	321	61.1
Aged 20 to 21	490	42.1	302	47.5	187	35.6
Aged 22 to 24	469	27.2	278	30.7	191	23.4
Aged 25 to 29	311	12.4	206	14.7	105	9.4
Aged 30 to 34	220	8.4	136	9.4	84	7.2
Aged 35 to 44	255	4.7	191	6.3	64	2.6
Aged 45 to 54	150	3.1	94	3.6	56	2.6
Aged 55 or older	40	0.7	26	0.8	14	0.6

Note: Blacks include those identifying themselves as being black alone and those identifying themselves as being black in combination with one or more other races.
Source: Bureau of the Census, School Enrollment—Social and Economic Characteristics of Students: October 2003, Detailed Tables, Internet site http://www.census.gov/population/www/socdemo/school/cps2003.html

Table 3.8 Black Families with Children in College, 2003

(total number of black families, number with dependent children aged 5 to 24, and number and percent with children enrolled in college by household income, 2003; numbers in thousands)

			with one or more children enrolled in college		
	total	with children aged 5–24	number	percent of total black families	percent of black families with children 5–24
Total black families	**9,309**	**5,797**	**675**	**7.3%**	**11.6%**
Less than $10,000	1,192	828	40	3.4	4.8
$10,000 to $14,999	710	450	36	5.1	8.0
$15,000 to $19,999	557	343	32	5.7	9.3
$20,000 to $24,999	1,126	727	53	4.7	7.3
$25,000 to $29,999	1,022	685	99	9.7	14.5
$30,000 to $34,999	583	352	48	8.2	13.6
$35,000 to $39,999	1,132	723	97	8.6	13.4
$40,000 to $49,999	550	310	42	7.6	13.5
$50,000 to $74,999	330	183	25	7.6	13.7
$75,000 and over	118	67	17	14.4	25.4

Note: Blacks include those identifying themselves as being black alone and those identifying themselves as being black in combination with one or more other races. Numbers will not add to total because not reported is not shown.
Source: Bureau of the Census, School Enrollment—Social and Economic Characteristics of Students: October 2003, Detailed Tables, Internet site http://www.census.gov/population/www/socdemo/school/cps2003.html; calculations by New Strategist

Table 3.9 Black College Enrollment Rate, 1990 to 2001

(percent of total people and blacks aged 16 to 24 graduating from high school in the previous 12 months who were enrolled in college as of October of each year, percentage point change in enrollment rate, 1990–2001)

	total	black
2001	61.7%	54.6%
2000	63.3	54.9
1999	62.9	58.9
1998	65.6	61.9
1997	67.0	58.5
1996	65.0	56.0
1995	61.9	51.2
1994	61.9	50.8
1993	62.6	55.6
1992	61.9	48.2
1991	62.5	46.4
1990	60.1	46.8

Percentage point change

1990–2001	1.5	7.8

Source: National Center for Education Statistics, Digest of Education Statistics 2003; Internet site http://nces.ed.gov/programs/ digest/d03/list_tables3.asp#c3; calculations by New Strategist

Table 3.10 College Enrollment of Blacks, 2003

(total number of people aged 15 or older enrolled in college, number of blacks enrolled, and black share of total, by age, October 2003; numbers in thousands)

	total	black number	black share of total
Total enrolled in college	**16,638**	**2,227**	**13.4%**
Under age 20	3,661	430	11.7
Aged 20 to 21	3,534	441	12.5
Aged 22 to 24	3,320	445	13.4
Aged 25 to 29	2,164	303	14.0
Aged 30 to 34	1,330	214	16.1
Aged 35 to 39	769	129	16.8
Aged 40 to 44	757	95	12.5
Aged 45 to 49	479	81	16.9
Aged 50 to 54	357	58	16.2
Aged 55 or older	268	34	12.7

Note: Blacks include those identifying themselves as being black alone and those identifying themselves as being black in combination with one or more other races.
Source: Bureau of the Census, School Enrollment—Social and Economic Characteristics of Students: October 2003, Detailed Tables, Internet site http://www.census.gov/population/www/socdemo/school/cps2003.html; calculations by New Strategist

Table 3.11 College Enrollment of Blacks by Age and Type of School, 2003

(number and percent distribution of blacks aged 15 or older enrolled in college by age and type of school, October 2003; numbers in thousands)

	total	two-year college	four-year college	graduate school
Total blacks enrolled	**2,227**	**694**	**1,195**	**338**
Under age 20	430	160	260	9
Aged 20 to 21	441	109	319	12
Aged 22 to 24	445	142	243	60
Aged 25 to 29	303	96	141	66
Aged 30 to 34	214	53	105	58
Aged 35 to 39	129	55	38	37
Aged 40 to 44	95	26	42	29
Aged 45 to 49	81	34	23	23
Aged 50 to 54	58	18	15	26
Aged 55 or older	34	2	12	19

PERCENT DISTRIBUTION BY TYPE OF SCHOOL

	total	two-year college	four-year college	graduate school
Total blacks enrolled	**100.0%**	**31.2%**	**53.7%**	**15.2%**
Under age 20	100.0	37.2	60.5	2.1
Aged 20 to 21	100.0	24.7	72.3	2.7
Aged 22 to 24	100.0	31.9	54.6	13.5
Aged 25 to 29	100.0	31.7	46.5	21.8
Aged 30 to 34	100.0	24.8	49.1	27.1
Aged 35 to 39	100.0	42.6	29.5	28.7
Aged 40 to 44	100.0	27.4	44.2	30.5
Aged 45 to 49	100.0	42.0	28.4	28.4
Aged 50 to 54	100.0	31.0	25.9	44.8
Aged 55 or older	100.0	5.9	35.3	55.9

PERCENT DISTRIBUTION BY AGE

	total	two-year college	four-year college	graduate school
Total blacks enrolled	**100.0%**	**100.0%**	**100.0%**	**100.0%**
Under age 20	19.3	23.1	21.8	2.7
Aged 20 to 21	19.8	15.7	26.7	3.6
Aged 22 to 24	20.0	20.5	20.3	17.8
Aged 25 to 29	13.6	13.8	11.8	19.5
Aged 30 to 34	9.6	7.6	8.8	17.2
Aged 35 to 39	5.8	7.9	3.2	10.9
Aged 40 to 44	4.3	3.7	3.5	8.6
Aged 45 to 49	3.6	4.9	1.9	6.8
Aged 50 to 54	2.6	2.6	1.3	7.7
Aged 55 or older	1.5	0.3	1.0	5.6

Note: Blacks include those identifying themselves as being black alone and those identifying themselves as being black in combination with one or more other races.
Source: Bureau of the Census, School Enrollment—Social and Economic Characteristics of Students: October 2003, Detailed Tables, Internet site http://www.census.gov/population/www/socdemo/school/cps2003.html; calculations by New Strategist

Table 3.12 Associate's Degrees Earned by Non-Hispanic Blacks by Field of Study, 2001–02

(total number of associate's degrees conferred and number and percent earned by non-Hispanic blacks, by field of study, 2001–02)

	total	earned by blacks	
		number	percent
Total associate's degrees	**595,133**	**67,337**	**11.3%**
Agriculture and natural resources	6,494	51	0.8
Architecture and related programs	443	23	5.2
Area, ethnic, and cultural studies	319	13	4.1
Biological and life sciences	1,517	141	9.3
Business	108,911	16,052	14.7
Communications	2,819	240	8.5
Communications technologies	2,021	166	8.2
Computer and information sciences	30,965	4,328	14.0
Construction trades	2,639	172	6.5
Education	9,267	1,397	15.1
Engineering	1,724	140	8.1
Engineering-related technologies	32,895	3,743	11.4
English language and literature, letters	864	69	8.0
Foreign languages and literatures	517	13	2.5
Health professions and related sciences	79,888	9,381	11.7
Home economics	9,480	1,792	18.9
Law and legal studies	6,825	1,174	17.2
Liberal arts and sciences, general studies, humanities	207,163	19,935	9.6
Library science	96	3	3.1
Mathematics	685	28	4.1
Mechanics and repairers	12,086	824	6.8
Multi- and interdisciplinary studies	13,204	1,379	10.4
Parks, recreation, leisure, and fitness	830	88	10.6
Philosophy and religion	134	21	15.7
Physical sciences	2,308	205	8.9
Precision production trades	10,818	673	6.2
Protective services	16,689	1,941	11.6
Psychology	1,705	147	8.6
Public administration and services	3,323	817	24.6
R.O.T.C. and military technologies	62	27	43.5
Social sciences and history	5,593	650	11.6
Theological studies, religious vocations	414	68	16.4
Transportation and material moving	1,159	61	5.3
Visual and performing arts	20,911	1,521	7.3
Not classified	365	54	14.8

Source: National Center for Education Statistics, Digest of Education Statistics 2003, *Internet site http://nces.ed.gov//programs/digest/d03/list_tables.asp; calculations by New Strategist*

Table 3.13 Bachelor's Degrees Earned by Non-Hispanic Blacks by Field of Study, 2001–02

(total number of bachelor's degrees conferred and number and percent earned by non-Hispanic blacks, by field of study, 2001–02)

	total	earned by blacks	
		number	percent
Total bachelor's degrees	**1,291,900**	**116,624**	**9.0%**
Agriculture and natural resources	23,353	653	2.8
Architecture and related programs	8,808	348	4.0
Area, ethnic, and cultural studies	6,557	881	13.4
Biological and life sciences	60,256	4,807	8.0
Business	281,330	28,153	10.0
Communications	62,791	5,540	8.8
Communications technologies	1,110	149	13.4
Computer and information sciences	47,299	5,030	10.6
Construction trades	202	6	3.0
Education	106,383	6,976	6.6
Engineering	59,481	3,099	5.2
Engineering-related technologies	14,117	1,387	9.8
English language and literature, letters	53,162	4,049	7.6
Foreign languages and literatures	15,318	622	4.1
Health professions and related sciences	70,517	8,011	11.4
Home economics	18,153	1,659	9.1
Law and legal studies	1,971	303	15.4
Liberal arts and sciences, general studies, humanities	39,333	4,688	11.9
Library science	74	0	0.0
Mathematics	12,395	935	7.5
Mechanics and repairers	164	18	11.0
Multi- and interdisciplinary studies	27,629	2,739	9.9
Parks, recreation, leisure, and fitness	20,554	1,751	8.5
Philosophy and religion	9,306	481	5.2
Physical sciences	17,851	1,142	6.4
Precision production trades	468	25	5.3
Protective services	25,536	4,484	17.6
Psychology	76,671	8,107	10.6
Public administration and services	19,392	4,036	20.8
R.O.T.C. and military technologies	3	0	0.0
Social sciences and history	132,874	12,530	9.4
Theological studies, religious vocations	7,785	411	5.3
Transportation and material moving	4,020	220	5.5
Visual and performing arts	66,773	3,373	5.1
Not classified	264	11	4.2

Source: National Center for Education Statistics, Digest of Education Statistics 2003, *Internet site http://nces.ed.gov//programs/ digest/d03/list_tables.asp; calculations by New Strategist*

Table 3.14 Master's Degrees Earned by Non-Hispanic Blacks by Field of Study, 2001–02

(total number of master's degrees conferred and number and percent earned by non-Hispanic blacks, by field of study, 2001–02)

	total	earned by blacks number	earned by blacks percent
Total master's degrees	**482,118**	**40,373**	**8.4%**
Agriculture and natural resources	4,519	122	2.7
Architecture and related programs	4,566	164	3.6
Area, ethnic, and cultural studies	1,578	130	8.2
Biological and life sciences	6,205	303	4.9
Business	120,785	10,434	8.6
Communications	5,510	532	9.7
Communications technologies	549	36	6.6
Computer and information sciences	16,113	745	4.6
Construction trades	9	1	11.1
Education	136,579	13,069	9.6
Engineering	26,015	794	3.1
Engineering-related technologies	896	75	8.4
English language and literature, letters	7,268	349	4.8
Foreign languages and literatures	2,861	55	1.9
Health professions and related sciences	43,644	3,249	7.4
Home economics	2,616	270	10.3
Law and legal studies	4,053	176	4.3
Liberal arts and sciences, general studies, humanities	2,754	214	7.8
Library science	5,113	259	5.1
Mathematics	3,487	126	3.6
Multi- and interdisciplinary studies	3,211	250	7.8
Parks, recreation, leisure, and fitness	2,754	210	7.6
Philosophy and religion	1,334	60	4.5
Physical sciences	5,034	149	3.0
Precision production trades	2	0	0.0
Protective services	2,935	482	16.4
Psychology	14,888	1,837	12.3
Public administration and services	25,448	4,386	17.2
Social sciences and history	14,112	1,022	7.2
Theological studies, religious vocations	4,952	334	6.7
Transportation and material moving	709	32	4.5
Visual and performing arts	11,595	508	4.4
Not classified	24	0	0.0

Source: National Center for Education Statistics, Digest of Education Statistics 2003, *Internet site http://nces.ed.gov//programs/ digest/d03/list_tables.asp; calculations by New Strategist*

Table 3.15 Doctoral Degrees Earned by Non-Hispanic Blacks by Field of Study, 2001–02

(total number of doctoral degrees conferred and number and percent earned by non-Hispanic blacks, by field of study, 2001–02)

		earned by blacks	
	total	number	percent
Total doctoral degrees	**44,160**	**2,397**	**5.4%**
Agriculture and natural resources	1,166	19	1.6
Architecture and related programs	183	8	4.4
Area, ethnic, and cultural studies	216	33	15.3
Biological life sciences	4,489	117	2.6
Business	1,158	71	6.1
Communications	374	33	8.8
Communications technologies	9	0	0.0
Computer and information sciences	750	22	2.9
Education	6,967	900	12.9
Engineering	5,195	86	1.7
Engineering-related technologies	15	0	0.0
English language and literature, letters	1,446	74	5.1
Foreign languages and literatures	843	17	2.0
Health professions and related sciences	3,523	124	3.5
Home economics	355	32	9.0
Law and legal studies	79	1	1.3
Liberal arts and sciences, general studies, humanities	113	6	5.3
Library science	45	5	11.1
Mathematics	958	16	1.7
Multi- and interdisciplinary studies	384	18	4.7
Parks, recreation, leisure, and fitness	151	5	3.3
Philosophy and religion	606	17	2.8
Physical sciences	3,803	77	2.0
Protective services	49	3	6.1
Psychology	4,341	257	5.9
Public administration and services	571	75	13.1
Social sciences and history	3,902	206	5.3
Theological studies, religious vocations	1,355	150	11.1
Visual and performing arts	1,114	25	2.2

Source: National Center for Education Statistics, Digest of Education Statistics 2003, *Internet site http://nces.ed.gov//programs/ digest/d03/list_tables.asp; calculations by New Strategist*

Table 3.16 First-Professional Degrees Earned by Non-Hispanic Blacks by Field of Study, 2001–02

(total number of first-professional degrees conferred and number and percent earned by non-Hispanic blacks, by field of study, 2001–02)

		earned by blacks	
	total	number	percent
Total first-professional degrees	**80,698**	**5,811**	**7.2%**
Dentistry (D.D.S. or D.M.D.)	4,239	155	3.7
Medicine (M.D.)	15,237	1,104	7.2
Optometry (O.D.)	1,280	22	1.7
Osteopathic medicine (D.O.)	2,416	97	4.0
Pharmacy (Pharm.D.)	7,076	570	8.1
Podiatry (Pod.D., D.P., or D.P.M.)	474	38	8.0
Veterinary medicine (D.V.M.)	2,289	67	2.9
Chiropractic (D.C. or D.C.M.)	3,284	116	3.5
Naturopathic medicine	227	4	1.8
Law (LL.B. or J.D.)	38,981	3,002	7.7
Theology (M.Div., M.H.L., B.D., or Ord.)	5,195	636	12.2

Source: National Center for Education Statistics, Digest of Education Statistics 2003, *Internet site http://nces.ed.gov//programs/ digest/d03/list_tables.asp; calculations by New Strategist*

Table 3.17 Black Participation in Adult Education, 2001

(percent of total people and blacks aged 16 or older participating in adult education activities, by type of adult education activity, 2001)

	percent participating	
	total	blacks
Any adult education course	**47.4%**	**43.9%**
College or university credential programs	7.3	7.5
Work-related courses	29.7	23.4
Personal interest courses	21.3	25.7
Other educational activities	3.6	4.5

Note: Adult education activities include apprenticeships, courses for basic skills, English as a second language, work-related courses, and personal development. For those aged 25 or older, credential programs in postsecondary institutions are counted as adult education activities. For those aged 16 to 24, full-time participation (full-year or part-year) in college or university credential programs or vocational or technical diploma programs are excluded.
Source: National Center for Education Statistics, Adult Education and Lifelong Learning Survey of the National Household Education Surveys Program; Internet site http://nces.ed.gov/programs/coe/2003/section1/tables/t08_2.asp

About Half of Blacks Say Their Health Is Very Good or Excellent

Slightly more than 50 percent of blacks say they are in very good or excellent health, according to the National Center for Health Statistics. For comparison, a larger 62 percent of the total population rates its health so highly. Nineteen percent of blacks say they are in fair or poor health, far above the 12 percent of the total population that feels that way.

Two-thirds of black men and women are overweight. About one in five blacks are current smokers, and one in three drink regularly.

Black women gave birth to nearly 600,000 babies in 2003, accounting for 15 percent of all babies born that year. Sixty-eight percent of black babies are born to unmarried women, the highest proportion among all racial and ethnic groups. Blacks account for 44 percent of all births in Mississippi and at least 30 percent of births in Alabama, Georgia, Louisiana, Maryland, and South Carolina.

Only 50 percent of blacks are covered by employment-based health insurance, a much lower proportion than the 60 percent share among the total population. Twenty-five percent of blacks have Medicaid coverage. Blacks visit a doctor an average of 2.5 times a year, less often than the 3.1 times the average American goes to the doctor. Eighteen percent of blacks aged 18 or older have physical difficulties, a slightly greater share than the 15 percent among all American adults.

Heart disease, cancer, and cerebrovascular disease are the leading causes of death among blacks, just as they are for the population as a whole. But AIDS ranks seventh as a cause of death among blacks, while it is not among the top ten for the total population. Blacks account for 41 percent of all AIDS cases diagnosed through 2003, and for an even larger 61 percent of cases diagnosed among women and 62 percent among children under age 13.

■ While blacks have made substantial gains in income and education over the past few decades, their health status is lagging.

Nearly one in five blacks do not have health insurance

(percent distribution of blacks by health insurance coverage status, 2003; shares do not add to 100 percent because some people have more than one kind of health insurance.)

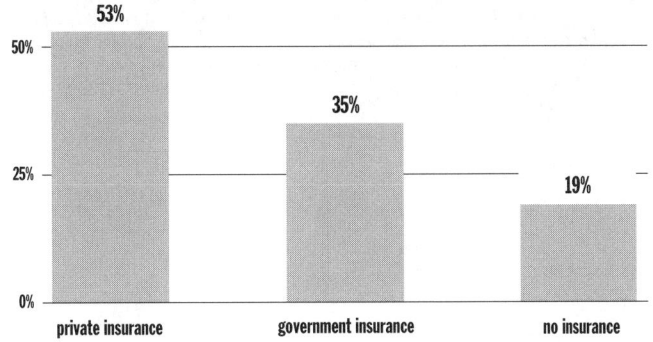

Table 3.18 Black Health Status, 2003

(percent distribution of total people and blacks aged 18 or older by self-reported health status, and index of black to total, 2003)

	total	black	index of black to total
Total people	100.0%	100.0%	–
Excellent/very good	62.3	50.8	82
Good	25.5	30.0	118
Fair/poor	12.2	19.2	157

Note: Blacks are those identifying themselves as being black alone. (–) means not applicable. The index is calculated by dividing the black figure by the total figure and multiplying by 100.
Source: National Center for Health Statistics, Summary Health Statistics for U.S. Adults: National Health Interview Survey, 2003, *Series 10, No. 225, 2005; Internet site http://www.cdc.gov/nchs/nhis.htm; calculations by New Strategist*

Table 3.19 Smoking and Drinking Status of Blacks by Sex, 2003

(percent distribution of blacks aged 18 or older by smoking and drinking status and sex, 2003)

	total	men	women
SMOKING STATUS			
Total blacks	100.0%	100.0%	100.0%
Never smoked	63.6	54.5	70.3
Former smoker	15.5	20.6	11.9
Current smoker	20.9	24.8	17.9
DRINKING STATUS			
Total blacks	100.0	100.0	100.0
Lifetime abstainer	35.6	26.3	42.5
Former drinker	16.7	19.6	15.0
Current infrequent drinker	13.6	11.4	15.3
Current regular drinker	33.2	41.8	26.1

Note: Never smoked means having had fewer than 100 cigarettes in lifetime. Former smokers have had 100 or more cigarettes in lifetime but did not smoke at time of interview. Current smokers have had at least 100 cigarettes in lifetime and currently smoke. Lifetime abstainers have had fewer than 12 drinks in lifetime. Former drinkers have had 12 or more drinks in lifetime, none in past year. Current infrequent drinkers have had 12 or more drinks in lifetime and fewer than 12 drinks in past year. Current regular drinkers have had at least 12 drinks in past year. Blacks are those identifying themselves as being black alone.
Source: National Center for Health Statistics, Summary Health Statistics for U.S. Adults: National Health Interview Survey, 2003, *Series 10, No. 225, 2005; Internet site http://www.cdc.gov/nchs/nhis.htm*

Table 3.20 Weight in Pounds of Blacks by Age and Sex, 1999–2002

(average weight in pounds of non-Hispanic blacks aged 20 or older by age and sex, 1999–2002)

	men	women
WEIGHT IN POUNDS		
Total blacks	**189.2**	**182.4**
Aged 20 to 39	189.1	179.2
Aged 40 to 59	191.1	189.3
Aged 60 or older	186.5	176.6

Note: Data are based on measured weight of a sample of the civilian noninstitutionalized population.
Source: National Center for Health Statistics, Mean Body Weight, Height, and Body Mass Index, United States 1960–2002; *Advance Data, No. 347, 2004; Internet site http://www.cdc.gov/nchs/products/pubs/pubd/ad/341-350/341-350.htm*

Table 3.21 Weight Status of Blacks by Sex, 2003

(percent distribution of blacks aged 18 or older by weight status and sex, 2003)

	total	men	women
Total blacks	**100.0%**	**100.0%**	**100.0%**
Underweight	1.1	0.9	1.2
Healthy weight	30.2	31.1	30.2
Overweight, total	68.7	68.1	68.6
Overweight, but not obese	35.1	40.7	30.4
Obese	33.6	27.4	38.2

Note: Being overweight is defined as having a body mass index of 25 or higher. Being obese is defined as having a body mass index of 30 or higher. Body mass index is calculated by dividing weight in kilograms by height in meters squared. Data are based on measured height and weight of a sample of the civilian noninstitutionalized population. Blacks are those identifying themselves as being black alone.
Source: National Center for Health Statistics, Summary Health Statistics for U.S. Adults: National Health Interview Survey, 2003, *Series 10, No. 225, 2005; Internet site http://www.cdc.gov/nchs/nhis.htm*

Table 3.22 Births to Black Women by Age, 2003

(total number of births, number and percent distribution of births to blacks, and black share of total, by age, 2003)

	total	black number	black percent distribution	black share of total
Total births	**4,089,950**	**599,847**	**100.0%**	**14.7%**
Under age 15	6,661	2,726	0.5	40.9
Aged 15 to 19	414,580	100,951	16.8	24.4
Aged 20 to 24	1,032,305	196,268	32.7	19.0
Aged 25 to 29	1,086,366	139,947	23.3	12.9
Aged 30 to 34	975,546	97,529	16.3	10.0
Aged 35 to 39	467,642	49,889	8.3	10.7
Aged 40 to 44	101,005	11,895	2.0	11.8
Aged 45 to 54	5,845	642	0.1	11.0

Source: National Center for Health Statistics, Births: Final Data for 2003, *National Vital Statistics Reports, Vol. 54, No. 2, 2005; Internet site http://www.cdc.gov/nchs/products/pubs/pubd/nvsr/54/54-pre.htm; calculations by New Strategist*

Table 3.23 Births to Black Women by Age and Marital Status, 2003

(total number of births to blacks, number of births to unmarried blacks, and unmarried share of total, by age, 2003)

	total	unmarried blacks number	unmarried blacks share of total
Births to blacks	**599,847**	**409,333**	**68.2%**
Under age 15	2,726	2,715	99.6
Aged 15 to 19	100,951	97,000	96.1
Aged 20 to 24	196,268	160,312	81.7
Aged 25 to 29	139,947	83,421	59.6
Aged 30 to 34	97,529	41,692	42.7
Aged 35 to 39	49,889	19,260	38.6
Aged 40 or older	12,537	4,933	39.3

Source: National Center for Health Statistics, Births: Final Data for 2003, *National Vital Statistics Reports, Vol. 54, No. 2, 2005; Internet site http://www.cdc.gov/nchs/products/pubs/pubd/nvsr/54/54-pre.htm; calculations by New Strategist*

Table 3.24 Births to Black Women by Birth Order, 2003

(total number of births, number and percent distribution of births to blacks, and black share of total, by birth order, 2003)

		black		
	total	number	percent distribution	share of total
Total births	**4,089,950**	**599,847**	**100.0%**	**14.7%**
First child	1,633,987	226,476	37.8	13.9
Second child	1,320,477	174,614	29.1	13.2
Third child	684,296	105,788	17.6	15.5
Fourth or later child	439,235	90,638	15.1	20.6

Note: Numbers will not add to total because "not stated" is not shown.
Source: National Center for Health Statistics, Births: Final Data for 2003, National Vital Statistics Reports, Vol. 54, No. 2, 2005; Internet site http://www.cdc.gov/nchs/products/pubs/pubd/nvsr/54/54-pre.htm; calculations by New Strategist

Table 3.25 Births to Black Women by State, 2003

(total number of births, number and percent distribution of births to blacks, and black share of total, by state, 2003)

	total	black births number	black births percent distribution	black births share of total
Total births	**4,089,950**	**599,847**	**100.0%**	**14.7%**
Alabama	59,552	17,931	3.0	30.1
Alaska	10,086	404	0.1	4.0
Arizona	90,967	3,261	0.5	3.6
Arkansas	37,784	7,236	1.2	19.2
California	540,997	32,349	5.4	6.0
Colorado	69,339	2,937	0.5	4.2
Connecticut	42,873	5,187	0.9	12.1
Delaware	11,329	2,907	0.5	25.7
District of Columbia	7,619	5,250	0.9	68.9
Florida	212,250	47,341	7.9	22.3
Georgia	135,979	43,099	7.2	31.7
Hawaii	18,100	583	0.1	3.2
Idaho	21,800	106	0.0	0.5
Illinois	182,495	31,565	5.3	17.3
Indiana	86,434	9,375	1.6	10.8
Iowa	38,174	1,287	0.2	3.4
Kansas	39,476	2,763	0.5	7.0
Kentucky	55,236	4,851	0.8	8.8
Louisiana	65,040	26,224	4.4	40.3
Maine	13,855	183	0.0	1.3
Maryland	74,930	25,515	4.3	34.1
Massachusetts	80,184	8,596	1.4	10.7
Michigan	131,094	22,567	3.8	17.2
Minnesota	70,050	5,362	0.9	7.7
Mississippi	42,380	18,553	3.1	43.8
Missouri	77,045	11,166	1.9	14.5
Montana	11,422	50	0.0	0.4
Nebraska	25,917	1,468	0.2	5.7
Nevada	33,647	2,900	0.5	8.6
New Hampshire	14,393	243	0.0	1.7
New Jersey	116,983	20,200	3.4	17.3
New Mexico	27,821	532	0.1	1.9
New York	253,714	48,025	8.0	18.9
North Carolina	118,323	27,171	4.5	23.0
North Dakota	7,972	109	0.0	1.4
Ohio	149,679	22,678	3.8	15.2
Oklahoma	50,981	4,625	0.8	9.1
Oregon	45,953	1,018	0.2	2.2

(continued)

	total	black births		
		number	percent distribution	share of total
Pennsylvania	145,959	22,056	3.7%	15.1%
Rhode Island	13,209	1,258	0.2	9.5
South Carolina	55,649	18,334	3.1	32.9
South Dakota	11,027	122	0.0	1.1
Tennessee	78,890	16,249	2.7	20.6
Texas	377,476	41,885	7.0	11.1
Utah	49,860	383	0.1	0.8
Vermont	6,589	53	0.0	0.8
Virginia	101,254	22,607	3.8	22.3
Washington	80,489	4,015	0.7	5.0
West Virginia	20,935	721	0.1	3.4
Wisconsin	70,040	6,494	1.1	9.3
Wyoming	6,700	53	0.0	0.8

Source: National Center for Health Statistics, Births: Final Data for 2003, *National Vital Statistics Reports, Vol. 54, No. 2, 2005; Internet site http://www.cdc.gov/nchs/products/pubs/pubd/nvsr/54/54-pre.htm; calculations by New Strategist*

Table 3.26 Health Insurance Coverage of Blacks by Age, 2003

(number and percent distribution of blacks by age and health insurance coverage status, 2003; numbers in thousands)

	total	with health insurance coverage during year			not covered at any time during the year
		total	private	government	
Total blacks	**37,651**	**30,344**	**20,136**	**13,195**	**7,307**
Under age 18	12,363	10,636	5,879	5,775	1,727
Aged 18 to 24	3,998	2,600	1,782	972	1,397
Aged 25 to 34	5,190	3,678	2,848	990	1,512
Aged 35 to 44	5,530	4,265	3,561	911	1,265
Aged 45 to 54	4,812	3,875	3,126	949	937
Aged 55 to 64	2,825	2,393	1,772	827	432
Aged 65 or older	2,933	2,897	1,168	2,771	36
PERCENT DISTRIBUTION BY COVERAGE STATUS					
Total blacks	**100.0%**	**80.6%**	**53.5%**	**35.0%**	**19.4%**
Under age 18	100.0	86.0	47.6	46.7	14.0
Aged 18 to 24	100.0	65.0	44.6	24.3	34.9
Aged 25 to 34	100.0	70.9	54.9	19.1	29.1
Aged 35 to 44	100.0	77.1	64.4	16.5	22.9
Aged 45 to 54	100.0	80.5	65.0	19.7	19.5
Aged 55 to 64	100.0	84.7	62.7	29.3	15.3
Aged 65 or older	100.0	98.8	39.8	94.5	1.2

Note: Blacks are those identifying themselves as being of the race alone and those identifying themselves as being of the race in combination with one or more other races. Numbers may not add to total because some people have more than one type of health insurance.

Source: Bureau of the Census, 2004 Current Population Survey, Annual Social and Economic Supplement, detailed tables, Internet site http://pubdb3.census.gov/macro/032004/health/h01_000.htm; calculations by New Strategist

Table 3.27 Blacks with Private Health Insurance Coverage by Age, 2003

(number and percent distribution of blacks by age and private health insurance coverage status, 2003; numbers in thousands)

| | | with private health insurance | | | |
| | | total | employment-based | | |
	total	total	total	own	direct purchase
Total blacks	**37,651**	**20,136**	**18,669**	**10,282**	**1,732**
Under age 18	12,363	5,879	5,550	29	359
Aged 18 to 24	3,998	1,782	1,543	627	164
Aged 25 to 34	5,190	2,848	2,694	2,257	183
Aged 35 to 44	5,530	3,561	3,413	2,781	206
Aged 45 to 54	4,812	3,126	3,000	2,523	234
Aged 55 to 64	2,825	1,772	1,645	1,356	180
Aged 65 or older	2,933	1,168	823	709	406
PERCENT DISTRIBUTION BY COVERAGE STATUS					
Total blacks	**100.0%**	**53.5%**	**49.6%**	**27.3%**	**4.6%**
Under age 18	100.0	47.6	44.9	0.2	2.9
Aged 18 to 24	100.0	44.6	38.6	15.7	4.1
Aged 25 to 34	100.0	54.9	51.9	43.5	3.5
Aged 35 to 44	100.0	64.4	61.7	50.3	3.7
Aged 45 to 54	100.0	65.0	62.3	52.4	4.9
Aged 55 to 64	100.0	62.7	58.2	48.0	6.4
Aged 65 or older	100.0	39.8	28.1	24.2	13.8

Note: Blacks are those identifying themselves as being of the race alone and those identifying themselves as being of the race in combination with one or more other races. Numbers will not add to total because some people have more than one type of health insurance.
Source: Bureau of the Census, 2004 Current Population Survey, Annual Social and Economic Supplement, detailed tables, Internet site http://pubdb3.census.gov/macro/032004/health/h01_000.htm; calculations by New Strategist

Table 3.28 Blacks with Government Health Insurance Coverage by Age, 2003

(number and percent distribution of blacks by age and government health insurance coverage status, 2003; numbers in thousands)

	total	with government health insurance total	Medicaid	Medicare	military
Total blacks	**37,651**	**13,195**	**9,292**	**4,080**	**1,283**
Under age 18	12,363	5,775	5,417	167	362
Aged 18 to 24	3,998	972	858	47	108
Aged 25 to 34	5,190	990	831	131	134
Aged 35 to 44	5,530	911	630	204	203
Aged 45 to 54	4,812	949	584	337	197
Aged 55 to 64	2,825	827	416	439	149
Aged 65 or older	2,933	2,771	555	2,755	130

PERCENT DISTRIBUTION BY COVERAGE STATUS

	total	with government health insurance total	Medicaid	Medicare	military
Total blacks	**100.0%**	**35.0%**	**24.7%**	**10.8%**	**3.4%**
Under age 18	100.0	46.7	43.8	1.4	2.9
Aged 18 to 24	100.0	24.3	21.5	1.2	2.7
Aged 25 to 34	100.0	19.1	16.0	2.5	2.6
Aged 35 to 44	100.0	16.5	11.4	3.7	3.7
Aged 45 to 54	100.0	19.7	12.1	7.0	4.1
Aged 55 to 64	100.0	29.3	14.7	15.5	5.3
Aged 65 or older	100.0	94.5	18.9	93.9	4.4

Note: Blacks are those identifying themselves as being of the race alone and those identifying themselves as being of the race in combination with one or more other races. Numbers will not add to total because some people have more than one type of health insurance.

Source: Bureau of the Census, 2004 Current Population Survey, Annual Social and Economic Supplement, detailed tables, Internet site http://pubdb3.census.gov/macro/032004/health/h01_000.htm; calculations by New Strategist

Table 3.29 Health Conditions among Blacks Aged 18 or Older, 2003

(number of total people and blacks aged 18 or older with selected health conditions, percent of blacks with condition, and black share of total with condition, 2003; numbers in thousands)

	total	black number	black percent with condition	black share of total
Total people	**213,042**	**24,111**	–	**11.3%**
Selected circulatory diseases				
Heart disease, all types	23,536	2,091	9.9%	8.9
Coronary	12,254	1,053	5.3	8.6
Hypertension	45,927	6,822	31.6	14.9
Stroke	5,070	707	3.5	13.9
Selected respiratory conditions				
Emphysema	3,115	194	1.0	6.2
Asthma				
Ever	20,697	2,610	10.7	12.6
Still	13,623	1,765	7.2	13.0
Hay fever	18,356	1,654	6.8	9.0
Sinusitis	29,673	3,421	14.3	11.5
Chronic bronchitis	8,560	910	3.9	10.6
Cancer				
Any cancer	13,973	772	3.8	5.5
Breast cancer (all adults)	2,426	132	0.6	5.4
Cervical cancer (women only)	1,082	70	0.5	6.5
Prostate cancer (men only)	1,332	187	2.4	14.0
Other selected diseases and conditions				
Diabetes	14,012	2,120	10.1	15.1
Ulcers	14,456	1,319	5.8	9.1
Kidney disease	3,017	427	2.1	14.2
Liver disease	2,511	306	1.4	12.2
Arthritis	45,793	4,679	22.2	10.2
Chronic joint symptoms	57,242	5,567	25.1	9.7
Migraines or severe headaches	32,268	3,752	15.2	11.6
Pain in neck	31,368	2,833	12.1	9.0
Pain in lower back	58,430	5,902	25.0	10.1
Pain in face or jaw	9,464	706	3.0	7.5
Selected sensory problems				
Hearing	32,533	1,932	9.2	5.9
Vision	18,628	2,385	10.8	12.8
Absence of all natural teeth	15,927	1,710	8.9	10.7

Note: The conditions shown are those that have ever been diagnosed by a doctor, except as noted. Hay fever, sinusitis, and chronic bronchitis have been diagnosed in the past twelve months. Kidney and liver disease have been diagnosed in the past twelve months and exclude kidney stones, bladder infections, and incontinence. Chronic joint symptoms are shown if respondent had pain, aching, or stiffness in or around a joint (excluding back and neck) and the condition began more than three months ago. Migraines, pain in neck, lower back, face, or jaw are shown only if pain lasted a whole day or more. Blacks are those identifying themselves as being black alone. (–) means not applicable.

Source: National Center for Health Statistics, Summary Health Statistics for U.S. Adults: National Health Interview Survey, *2003, Series 10, No. 225, 2005; Internet site http://www.cdc.gov/nchs/nhis.htm; calculations by New Strategist*

Table 3.30 Health Conditions among Black Children, 2003

(number of total people and blacks under age 18 with selected health conditions, percent of blacks with condition, and black share of total, 2003; numbers in thousands)

	total	black number	black percent with condition	black share of total
Total children	**72,973**	**11,061**	–	**15.2%**
Diagnosed with asthma	9,071	1,893	17.2%	20.9
Experienced in last 12 months				
Asthma attack	3,975	877	8.0	22.1
Hay fever	7,059	954	8.7	13.5
Respiratory allergies	8,347	1,154	10.5	13.8
Other allergies	8,407	1,568	14.2	18.7
Ever told had*				
Learning disability	4,561	678	7.3	14.9
Attention deficit hyperactivity disorder	3,881	545	5.9	14.0
Prescription medication taken regularly for at least 3 months	9,287	1,316	11.9	14.2

* *"Ever told" by a school representative or health professional. Data exclude children under age 3.*
Note: Other allergies include food or digestive allergies, eczema, and other skin allergies. Blacks are those identifying themselves as being black alone. (–) means not applicable.
Source: National Center for Health Statistics, Summary Health Statistics for U.S. Children: National Health Interview Survey, 2003, *Series 10, No. 223, 2005; Internet site http://www.cdc.gov/nchs/nhis.htm; calculations by New Strategist*

Table 3.31 Physician Office Visits by Blacks by Age, 2002

(number of total physician office visits, number and percent distribution of visits by blacks, black share of total, and average number of visits by blacks per person per year, by age, 2002)

	total (000s)	visits by blacks number (000s)	visits by blacks percent distribution	visits by blacks share of total	visits by blacks per person per year
Total visits	**889,980**	**89,455**	**100.0%**	**10.1%**	**2.5**
Under age 15	159,235	19,867	22.2	12.5	2.1
Aged 15 to 24	71,865	8,071	9.0	11.2	1.4
Aged 25 to 44	192,359	18,750	21.0	9.7	1.8
Aged 45 to 64	242,142	22,496	25.1	9.3	3.2
Aged 65 to 74	109,331	10,733	12.0	9.8	6.6
Aged 75 or older	115,049	9,538	10.7	8.3	8.1

Source: National Center for Health Statistics, National Ambulatory Medical Care Survey: 2002 Summary, *Advance Data No. 346, 2004; Internet site http://www.cdc.gov/nchs/about/major/ahcd/adata.htm; calculations by New Strategist*

Table 3.32 Difficulties in Physical Functioning among Blacks, 2003

(number of total people and blacks aged 18 or older, number with difficulties in physical functioning, percent of blacks with difficulty, and black share of total, by type of difficulty, 2003; numbers in thousands)

		black		
	total	number	percent with difficulty	share of total
TOTAL PEOPLE	**213,042**	**24,111**	–	**11.3%**
Total with any physical difficulty	**31,322**	**3,876**	**18.2%**	**12.4**
Walk quarter of a mile	14,910	2,097	10.2	14.1
Climb up ten steps without resting	11,107	1,753	8.7	15.8
Stand for two hours	18,663	2,431	11.5	13.0
Sit for two hours	7,211	947	4.4	13.1
Stoop, bend, or kneel	18,250	2,350	11.2	12.9
Reach over head	6,264	915	4.6	14.6
Grasp or handle small objects	3,943	544	2.7	13.8
Lift or carry ten pounds	9,194	1,329	6.5	14.5
Push or pull large objects	13,463	1,685	8.1	12.5

Note: Respondents were classified as having difficulties if they responded "very difficult" or "can't do at all." Blacks are those identifying themselves as being black alone. (–) means not applicable.
Source: National Center for Health Statistics, Summary Health Statistics for U.S. Adults: National Health Interview Survey, 2003, Series 10, No. 225, 2005; Internet site http://www.cdc.gov/nchs/nhis.htm; calculations by New Strategist

Table 3.33 AIDS Cases among Blacks, through December 2003

(total number of AIDS cases diagnosed, number and percent distribution of AIDS cases diagnosed among blacks, and black share of total, by sex and age at diagnosis, through December 2003)

		black		
	total	number	percent distribution	share of total
Total AIDS cases	**874,230**	**354,920**	**100.0%**	**40.6%**
Males aged 13 or older	708,452	253,078	71.3	35.7
Females aged 13 or older	156,837	96,338	27.1	61.4
Children under age 13	8,939	5,504	1.6	61.6

Source: National Center for Health Statistics, Health, United States, 2004; Internet site http://www.cdc.gov/nchs/hus.htm; calculations by New Strategist

Table 3.34 Leading Causes of Death among Blacks, 2002

(number and percent distribution of deaths to blacks accounted for by the ten leading causes of death among blacks, 2002)

		number	percent distribution
Total black deaths		**290,051**	**100.0%**
1.	Diseases of the heart (1)	77,621	26.8
2.	Malignant neoplasms (cancer) (2)	62,617	21.6
3.	Cerebrovascular diseases (3)	18,856	6.5
4.	Diabetes mellitus (6)	12,687	4.4
5.	Accidents (unintentional injuries) (5)	12,513	4.3
6.	Homicide (14)	8,287	2.9
7.	Human immunodeficiency virus infection	7,835	2.7
8.	Chronic lower respiratory disease (4)	7,831	2.7
9.	Nephritis, nephrotic syndrome, nephrosis (9)	7,488	2.6
10.	Septicemia (10)	6,137	2.1
	All other causes	68,179	23.5

Note: Number in parentheses shows rank for all Americans if the cause of death is among top fifteen.
Source: National Center for Health Statistics, Health, United States, 2004; Internet site http://www.cdc.gov/nchs/hus.htm; calculations by New Strategist

Table 3.35 Life Expectancy of Blacks at Birth and Age 65 by Sex, 1990 to 2002

(number of years of life remaining for blacks at birth and age 65, by sex, 1990 to 2002; change in years, 1990 to 2002)

	total blacks	black females	black males
Birth			
2002	72.3	75.6	68.8
2000	71.9	75.2	68.3
1990	69.1	73.6	64.5
Change, 1990 to 2002	3.2	2.0	4.3
Age 65			
2002	16.6	18.0	14.6
2000	16.2	17.7	14.2
1990	15.4	17.2	13.2
Change, 1990 to 2002	1.2	0.8	1.4

Source: National Center for Health Statistics, Health, United States, 2004; Internet site http://www.cdc.gov/nchs/hus.htm; calculations by New Strategist

Most Black Households in the South Own Their Home

Forty-nine percent of the nation's black households owned their home in 2004 compared with a much higher homeownership rate of 69 percent for all households. According to an analysis of homeownership in 2003, homeownership among black married couples stood at an impressive 70 percent. By age, black homeownership surpasses 60 percent in the 55-or-older age group. Fifty-three percent of black households in the South own their home, the only region in which the majority of black households are homeowners. In the Northeast, only 35 percent of black households own their home.

The 76 percent majority of black homeowners live in single-family, detached homes. Black homeowners estimate the value of their home at a median of $97,176.

Most black householders are satisfied with their home and neighborhood. On a scale of one to ten, 72 percent of black homeowners rate their home an eight or higher. Among black renters, however, barely more than half rate their home at least an eight. Only 12 percent of black homeowners and 18 percent of renters report that crime is a bothersome problem in their neighborhood.

Seventeen percent of blacks moved between 2003 and 2004, a higher mobility rate than for the population as a whole. Among black homeowners who moved in the past year, the main reason was to establish their own household.

■ Because so many black households are female-headed families—one of the household types least likely to own a home—black homeownership is well below average.

Black homeownership is lowest in the Northeast

(percent of black households that own their home, by region, 2004)

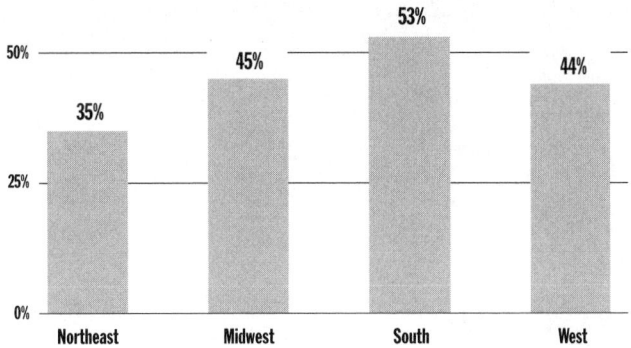

Table 3.36 Black Homeownership Rate, 1994 to 2004

(homeownership rate of total and black households and index of black to total, 1994 to 2004; percentage point change in homeownership rate, 1994–2004)

	total households	black households	index
2004	69.0%	49.1%	71
2003	68.3	48.1	70
2002	67.9	47.3	70
2001	67.8	47.7	70
2000	67.4	47.2	70
1999	66.8	46.3	69
1998	66.3	45.6	69
1997	65.7	44.8	68
1996	65.4	44.1	67
1995	64.7	42.7	66
1994	64.0	42.3	66
Percentage point change			
1994 to 2004	5.0	6.8	–

Note: Blacks are those identifying themselves as being of the race alone. The index is calculated by dividing the black homeownership rate by the total rate and multiplying by 100. (–) means not applicable.
Source: Bureau of the Census, American Housing Survey for the United States: 2003, Current Housing Reports, *Internet site http://www.census.gov/hhes/www/ahs.html; calculations by New Strategist*

Table 3.37　Black Homeownership Status by Age of Householder, 2003

(number and percent of black households by age of householder and homeownership status, 2003; numbers in thousands)

	total	owner		renter	
		number	percent	number	percent
Total black households	**13,004**	**6,193**	**47.6%**	**6,811**	**52.4%**
Under age 25	983	119	12.1	864	87.9
Aged 25 to 29	1,017	234	23.0	783	77.0
Aged 30 to 34	1,492	492	33.0	1,000	67.0
Aged 35 to 44	2,906	1,318	45.4	1,589	54.7
Aged 45 to 54	2,904	1,615	55.6	1,289	44.4
Aged 55 to 64	1,657	1,059	63.9	598	36.1
Aged 65 to 74	1,172	775	66.1	397	33.9
Aged 75 or older	873	581	66.6	292	33.4
Median age	45	50	–	39	–

Note: Blacks include only those identifying themselves as being black alone. (–) means not applicable.
Source: Bureau of the Census, American Housing Survey for the United States: 2003, *Current Housing Reports, Internet site http://www.census.gov/hhes/www/ahs.html; calculations by New Strategist*

Table 3.38　Black Homeowners by Age of Householder, 2003

(number of total homeowners, number and percent distribution of black homeowners, and black share of total, by age, 2003; numbers in thousands)

	total	black		
		number	percent distribution	share of total
Total homeowners	**72,238**	**6,193**	**100.0%**	**8.6%**
Under age 25	1,272	119	1.9	9.4
Aged 25 to 29	3,207	234	3.8	7.3
Aged 30 to 34	5,845	492	7.9	8.4
Aged 35 to 44	15,406	1,318	21.3	8.6
Aged 45 to 54	16,661	1,615	26.1	9.7
Aged 55 to 64	12,497	1,059	17.1	8.5
Aged 65 to 74	8,876	775	12.5	8.7
Aged 75 or older	8,474	581	9.4	6.9

Note: Blacks include only those identifying themselves as being black alone.
Source: Bureau of the Census, American Housing Survey for the United States: 2003, *Current Housing Reports, Internet site http://www.census.gov/hhes/www/ahs.html; calculations by New Strategist*

Table 3.39 Black Homeownership Status by Household Type, 2003

(number and percent of black households by household type and homeownership status, 2003; numbers in thousands)

	total	owner number	owner percent	renter number	renter percent
TOTAL BLACK HOUSEHOLDS	**13,778**	**6,549**	**47.5%**	**7,229**	**52.5%**
Family households	**9,128**	**4,791**	**52.5**	**4,337**	**47.5**
Married couples	4,268	3,007	70.5	1,262	29.6
Female householder, no spouse present	4,069	1,404	34.5	2,665	65.5
Male householder, no spouse present	791	381	48.2	410	51.8
Nonfamily households	**4,650**	**1,758**	**37.8**	**2,892**	**62.2**
Female householder	2,550	1,101	43.2	1,449	56.8
Male householder	2,100	657	31.3	1,443	68.7

Note: Blacks include those identifying themselves as being of the race alone and those identifying themselves as being of the race in combination with one or more other races.
Source: Bureau of the Census, America's Families and Living Arrangements, 2003 Current Population Survey Annual Social and Economic Supplement; Internet site http://www.census.gov/population/www/socdemo/hh-fam/cps2003.html; calculations by New Strategist

Table 3.40 Black Homeowners by Type of Household, 2003

(number of total homeowners, number and percent distribution of black homeowners, and black share of total, by type of household, 2003; numbers in thousands)

	total	black number	black percent distribution	share of total
TOTAL HOMEOWNERS	**75,909**	**6,549**	**100.0%**	**8.6%**
Family households	**57,092**	**4,791**	**73.2**	**8.4**
Married couples	47,676	3,007	45.9	6.3
Female householder, no spouse present	6,695	1,404	21.4	21.0
Male householder, no spouse present	2,721	381	5.8	14.0
Nonfamily households	**18,817**	**1,758**	**26.8**	**9.3**
Female householder	11,075	1,101	16.8	9.9
Male householder	7,742	657	10.0	8.5

Note: Blacks include those identifying themselves as being of the race alone and those identifying themselves as being of the race in combination with one or more other races.
Source: Bureau of the Census, America's Families and Living Arrangements, 2003 Current Population Survey Annual Social and Economic Supplement; Internet site http://www.census.gov/population/www/socdemo/hh-fam/cps2003.html; calculations by New Strategist

Table 3.41 Black Homeownership Status by Region, 2003

(number and percent of black households by homeownership status and region, 2003; numbers in thousands)

	total	owners		renters	
		number	percent	number	percent
Total black households	**13,004**	**6,193**	**47.6%**	**6,811**	**52.4%**
Northeast	2,361	833	35.3	1,528	64.7
Midwest	2,424	1,100	45.4	1,324	54.6
South	7,050	3,743	53.1	3,307	46.9
West	1,168	516	44.2	652	55.8

Note: Blacks include only those identifying themselves as being black alone.
Source: Bureau of the Census, American Housing Survey for the United States: 2003, *Current Housing Reports, Internet site http://www.census.gov/hhes/www/ahs.html; calculations by New Strategist*

Table 3.42 Black Homeowners by Region, 2003

(number of total homeowners, number and percent distribution of black homeowners, and black share of total, by region, 2003; numbers in thousands)

	total	black		
		number	percent distribution	share of total
Total homeowners	**72,238**	**6,193**	**100.0%**	**8.6%**
Northeast	12,964	833	13.5	6.4
Midwest	17,889	1,100	17.8	6.1
South	26,699	3,743	60.4	14.0
West	14,686	516	8.3	3.5

Note: Blacks include only those identifying themselves as being black alone.
Source: Bureau of the Census, American Housing Survey for the United States: 2003, *Current Housing Reports, Internet site http://www.census.gov/hhes/www/ahs.html; calculations by New Strategist*

Table 3.43 Characteristics of Housing Units Occupied by Blacks, 2003

(number and percent distribution of housing units occupied by blacks by selected housing characteristics and homeownership status, 2003; numbers in thousands)

	total	owner-occupied		renter-occupied	
		number	percent distribution	number	percent distribution
UNITS IN STRUCTURE					
Total black households	**13,004**	**6,193**	**100.0%**	**6,811**	**100.0%**
One, detached	6,104	4,718	76.2	1,386	20.3
One, attached	1,220	610	9.8	610	9.0
Two to four	1,705	180	2.9	1,525	22.4
Five to nine	1,154	28	0.5	1,126	16.5
10 to 19	869	46	0.7	823	12.1
20 to 49	549	22	0.4	527	7.7
50 or more	736	51	0.8	684	10.0
Mobile home or trailer	667	537	8.7	130	1.9
Median square footage of unit*	1,565	1,655	–	1,278	–
NUMBER OF BEDROOMS					
Total black households	**13,004**	**6,193**	**100.0**	**6,811**	**100.0**
None	145	0	0.0	145	2.1
One	1,942	115	1.9	1,828	26.8
Two	3,905	1,040	16.8	2,865	42.1
Three	5,129	3,497	56.5	1,632	24.0
Four or more	1,883	1,541	24.9	342	5.0
NUMBER OF BATHROOMS					
Total black households	**13,004**	**6,193**	**100.0**	**6,811**	**100.0**
None	125	45	0.7	79	1.2
One	6,767	1,888	30.5	4,880	71.6
One-and-one-half	2,178	1,370	22.1	808	11.9
Two or more	3,934	2,890	46.7	1,045	15.3
ROOM USED FOR BUSINESS					
Total black households	**13,004**	**6,193**	**100.0**	**6,811**	**100.0**
With room(s) used for business	2,271	1,359	21.9	913	13.4
SELECTED AMENITIES					
Porch, deck, balcony, or patio	9,858	5,318	85.9	4540	66.7
Telephone available	12,496	6,010	97.0	6,486	95.2
Usable fireplace	2,400	1,859	30.0	541	7.9
Separate dining room	5,788	3,758	60.7	2,030	29.8
Two or more living or recreation rooms	2,333	1,990	32.1	344	5.1
Garage or carport	4,793	3,500	56.5	1,293	19.0
No cars, trucks, vans available	2,578	495	8.0	2,083	30.6

* Single-family detached and mobile/manufactured homes only.
Note: Blacks include only those identifying themselves as being black alone. (–) means not applicable.
Source: Bureau of the Census, American Housing Survey for the United States: 2003, Current Housing Reports, Internet site http://www.census.gov/hhes/www/ahs.html; calculations by New Strategist

Table 3.44 Housing Value for Black Homeowners, 2003

(number and percent distribution of black homeowners by value of home, 2003; numbers in thousands)

	number	percent distribution
Total black homeowners	**6,193**	**100.0%**
Under $10,000	168	2.7
$10,000 to $19,999	153	2.5
$20,000 to $29,999	212	3.4
$30,000 to $39,999	275	4.4
$40,000 to $49,999	301	4.9
$50,000 to $59,999	357	5.8
$60,000 to $69,999	361	5.8
$70,000 to $79,999	510	8.2
$80,000 to $99,999	884	14.3
$100,000 to $119,999	511	8.3
$120,000 to $149,999	691	11.2
$150,000 to $199,999	682	11.0
$200,000 to $249,999	311	5.0
$250,000 to $299,999	246	4.0
$300,000 or more	531	8.6
Median home value	$97,176	–

Note: (–) means not applicable.
Note: Blacks include only those identifying themselves as being black alone.
Source: Bureau of the Census, American Housing Survey for the United States: 2003, Current Housing Reports, Internet site http://www.census.gov/hhes/www/ahs.html; calculations by New Strategist

Table 3.45 Neighborhood Characteristics of Housing Units Occupied by Blacks, 2003

(number and percent distribution of housing units occupied by blacks by selected neighborhood characteristics and homeownership status, 2003; numbers in thousands)

	total	owner-occupied		renter-occupied	
		number	percent distribution	number	percent distribution
DESCRIPTION OF AREA WITHIN 300 FEET OF HOME					
Total black households	**13,004**	**6,193**	**100.0%**	**6,811**	**100.0%**
Single-family detached homes	9,673	5,338	86.2	4,335	63.6
Single-family attached homes	2,359	886	14.3	1,473	21.6
One-to-three-story multiunit	4,478	941	15.2	3,537	51.9
Four-to-six-story multiunit	1,286	217	3.5	1,069	15.7
Seven-or-more-story multiunit	624	101	1.6	523	7.7
Manufactured/mobile homes	1,161	851	13.7	310	4.6
Commercial or institutional	4,787	1,502	24.3	3,285	48.2
Industrial or factories	776	244	3.9	532	7.8
Open space, park, woods, farm, or ranch	3,596	1,752	28.3	1,844	27.1
Four-or-more-lane highway, railroad, or airport	2,342	796	12.9	1,546	22.7
Waterfront property	99	41	0.7	58	0.9
NEIGHBORHOOD PROBLEMS					
Total black households	**13,004**	**6,193**	**100.0**	**6,811**	**100.0**
Bothersome street noise problem	1,703	713	11.5	990	14.5
Bothersome neighborhood crime problem	2,012	762	12.3	1,250	18.4
Bothersome odor problem	725	254	4.1	471	6.9
Noise problem	378	149	2.4	229	3.4
Litter or housing deterioration	403	210	3.4	193	2.8
Poor city or county services	221	120	1.9	102	1.5
Undesirable commercial, institutional, industrial	113	60	1.0	53	0.8
People problem	683	293	4.7	390	5.7
Other problems	1,135	544	8.8	591	8.7
PUBLIC SCHOOLS					
Total black households with children under 14	**4,571**	**1,999**	**100.0**	**2,572**	**100.0**
Satisfactory public elementary school	3,371	1,547	77.4	1,824	70.9
PUBLIC SERVICES					
Total black households	**13,004**	**6,193**	**100.0**	**6,811**	**100.0**
With public transportation	9,257	3,805	61.4	5,451	80.0
Satisfactory neighborhood shopping	10,438	4,745	76.6	5,692	83.6
Satisfactory police protection	10,985	5,266	85.0	5,720	84.0

Note: Blacks include only those identifying themselves as being black alone.
Source: Bureau of the Census, American Housing Survey for the United States: 2003, *Current Housing Reports, Internet site http://www.census.gov/hhes/www/ahs.html; calculations by New Strategist*

Table 3.46 Opinion of Blacks toward Housing Unit and Neighborhood, 2003

(number and percent distribution of black households by opinion of housing unit and neighborhood, by homeownership status, 2003; numbers in thousands)

	total	owner-occupied		renter-occupied	
		number	percent distribution	number	percent distribution
OPINION OF HOUSING UNIT					
Total black households	**13,004**	**6,193**	**100.0%**	**6,811**	**100.0%**
1 (worst)	136	27	0.4	109	1.6
2	92	7	0.1	85	1.2
3	170	26	0.4	144	2.1
4	204	40	0.6	164	2.4
5	1,051	348	5.6	703	10.3
6	902	289	4.7	614	9.0
7	1,806	711	11.5	1,095	16.1
8	3,113	1,512	24.4	1,601	23.5
9	1,622	976	15.8	646	9.5
10 (best)	3,215	1,958	31.6	1,257	18.5
Not reported	695	300	4.8	395	5.8
OPINION OF NEIGHBORHOOD					
Total black households	**13,004**	**6,193**	**100.0**	**6,811**	**100.0**
1 (worst)	314	91	1.5	223	3.3
2	125	32	0.5	93	1.4
3	267	78	1.3	189	2.8
4	310	104	1.7	206	3.0
5	1,275	460	7.4	814	12.0
6	981	364	5.9	618	9.1
7	1,855	847	13.7	1,008	14.8
8	3,024	1,589	25.7	1,434	21.1
9	1,466	810	13.1	656	9.6
10 (best)	2,658	1,502	24.3	1,156	17.0
No neighborhood	30	13	0.2	16	0.2
Not reported	700	302	4.9	398	5.8

Note: Blacks include only those identifying themselves as being black alone.
Source: Bureau of the Census, American Housing Survey for the United States: 2003, *Current Housing Reports, Internet site http://www.census.gov/hhes/www/ahs.html; calculations by New Strategist*

Table 3.47 Geographical Mobility of Blacks by Age, 2003–04

(total number of blacks aged 1 or older, and number and percent who moved between March 2003 and March 2004, by age and type of move; numbers in thousands)

	total	movers total	same county	different county, same state	different state	abroad
Total blacks	**37,050**	**6,232**	**3,920**	**1,051**	**1,158**	**103**
Aged 1 to 4	2,717	768	532	126	110	0
Aged 5 to 9	3,239	707	463	125	116	3
Aged 10 to 14	3,625	642	394	104	132	12
Aged 15 to 17	2,181	322	204	55	56	7
Aged 18 to 19	1,047	175	125	21	26	3
Aged 20 to 24	2,951	741	465	149	119	8
Aged 25 to 29	2,571	659	413	119	118	9
Aged 30 to 34	2,619	536	338	82	105	11
Aged 35 to 39	2,674	448	257	80	98	13
Aged 40 to 44	2,856	419	262	58	77	22
Aged 45 to 49	2,632	269	148	52	62	7
Aged 50 to 54	2,180	201	117	33	46	5
Aged 55 to 59	1,566	142	87	22	32	1
Aged 60 to 61	547	27	9	2	16	0
Aged 62 to 64	712	56	25	7	21	3
Aged 65 or older	2,933	122	78	19	25	0

PERCENT DISTRIBUTION BY MOBILITY STATUS

Total blacks	**100.0%**	**16.8%**	**10.6%**	**2.8%**	**3.1%**	**0.3%**
Aged 1 to 4	100.0	28.3	19.6	4.6	4.0	0.0
Aged 5 to 9	100.0	21.8	14.3	3.9	3.6	0.1
Aged 10 to 14	100.0	17.7	10.9	2.9	3.6	0.3
Aged 15 to 17	100.0	14.8	9.4	2.5	2.6	0.3
Aged 18 to 19	100.0	16.7	11.9	2.0	2.5	0.3
Aged 20 to 24	100.0	25.1	15.8	5.0	4.0	0.3
Aged 25 to 29	100.0	25.6	16.1	4.6	4.6	0.4
Aged 30 to 34	100.0	20.5	12.9	3.1	4.0	0.4
Aged 35 to 39	100.0	16.8	9.6	3.0	3.7	0.5
Aged 40 to 44	100.0	14.7	9.2	2.0	2.7	0.8
Aged 45 to 49	100.0	10.2	5.6	2.0	2.4	0.3
Aged 50 to 54	100.0	9.2	5.4	1.5	2.1	0.2
Aged 55 to 59	100.0	9.1	5.6	1.4	2.0	0.1
Aged 60 to 61	100.0	4.9	1.6	0.4	2.9	0.0
Aged 62 to 64	100.0	7.9	3.5	1.0	2.9	0.4
Aged 65 or older	100.0	4.2	2.7	0.6	0.9	0.0

Note: Blacks include those identifying themselves as being of the race alone and those identifying themselves as being black in combination with one or more other races.
Source: Bureau of the Census, Geographic Mobility: 2004, Detailed Tables, Internet site http://www.census.gov/population/www/ socdemo/migrate/cps2004.html; calculations by New Strategist

Table 3.48 Reasons for Moving among Black Movers by Homeownership Status, 2003

(number and percent distribution of black households with respondents who moved in the past 12 months by main reason for move and for choosing new neighborhood and house, by homeownership status, 2003; numbers in thousands)

		owners		renters	
	total	number	percent distribution	number	percent distribution
MAIN REASON FOR LEAVING PREVIOUS HOUSING UNIT					
Total black movers	**2,659**	**421**	**100.0%**	**2,238**	**100.0%**
All reported reasons equal	29	2	0.5	27	1.2
Private displacement	17	0	0.0	17	0.8
Government displacement	10	0	0.0	10	0.4
Disaster loss (fire, flood, etc.)	31	0	0.0	31	1.4
New job or job transfer	165	25	5.9	139	6.2
To be closer to work/school/other	129	15	3.6	114	5.1
Other financial/employment reason	115	8	1.9	107	4.8
To establish own household	416	76	18.1	339	15.1
Needed larger house or apartment	318	51	12.1	268	12.0
Married, widowed, divorced, separated	111	20	4.8	91	4.1
Other family/personal reason	199	35	8.3	164	7.3
Wanted better home	276	55	13.1	222	9.9
Change from owner to renter/renter to owner	81	64	15.2	17	0.8
Wanted lower rent or maintenance	122	5	1.2	117	5.2
Other housing related reasons	149	8	1.9	141	6.3
Other	333	36	8.6	297	13.3
Not reported	157	21	5.0	136	6.1
MAIN REASON FOR CHOOSING PRESENT NEIGHBORHOOD					
Total black movers	**2,659**	**421**	**100.0**	**2,238**	**100.0**
All reported reasons equal	59	11	2.6	48	2.1
Convenient to job	461	35	8.3	426	19.0
Convenient to friends or relatives	393	51	12.1	343	15.3
Convenient to leisure activities	36	10	2.4	26	1.2
Convenient to public transportation	63	2	0.5	62	2.8
Good schools	118	16	3.8	102	4.6
Other public services	49	4	1.0	45	2.0
Looks/design of neighborhood	368	70	16.6	298	13.3
House was most important consideration	371	108	25.7	263	11.8
Other	614	92	21.9	522	23.3
Not reported	126	23	5.5	104	4.6

(continued)

MAIN REASON FOR CHOOSING PRESENT HOME	total	owners		renters	
		number	percent distribution	number	percent distribution
Total black movers	**2,659**	**421**	**100.0%**	**2,238**	**100.0%**
All reported reasons equal	56	11	2.6	45	2.0
Financial reasons	780	88	20.9	692	30.9
Room layout/design	437	117	27.8	320	14.3
Kitchen	19	3	0.7	16	0.7
Size	425	54	12.8	371	16.6
Exterior appearance	78	8	1.9	70	3.1
Yard/trees/view	50	18	4.3	32	1.4
Quality of construction	64	16	3.8	47	2.1
Only one available	191	8	1.9	183	8.2
Other	438	79	18.8	359	16.0
Not reported	122	20	4.8	102	4.6

Note: Blacks include only those identifying themselves as being black alone.
Source: Bureau of the Census, American Housing Survey for the United States: 2003, *Current Housing Reports, Internet site http://www.census.gov/hhes/www/ahs.html; calculations by New Strategist*

Black Incomes Have Been Growing as Blacks Make Gains in Education and Jobs

The median income of black households fell 6 percent between 2000 and 2003. Despite the decline, the $29,689 median of black households in 2003 was still 16 percent higher than in 1990, after adjusting for inflation.

The median income of black households was only 69 percent as high as that of the average household in 2003. Black household income is below average because married couples—typically the most affluent household type—head only 30 percent of black households. Female-headed families account for fully 29 percent of black households. Black couples had a median income of $52,671 in 2003, while female-headed families had a much lower median of $22,739.

For black men and women, incomes peak in the 35-to-54 age group. Black men working full-time had a median income of $33,464 in 2003, while their female counterparts had a median income of $27,675. Both men and women have seen their incomes grow substantially since 1990. The earnings of blacks rise steadily with education. Black men with at least a bachelor's degree who work full-time earned a median of $50,006 in 2003.

Black families are more likely to be poor than the average American family, but the percentage of black married couples and female-headed families in poverty fell between 1990 and 2003. Among married couples, the poverty rate declined from 13 to 8 percent. Among female-headed families, the rate fell from 48 to 37 percent. Black male-headed families saw their poverty rate increase during those years, however, rising from 21 to 24 percent.

■ Black household income will remain below average as long as female-headed families account for such a large share of black households.

Black household income grew faster than average between 1990 and 2003

(percent change in median household income for total and black households, 1990 to 2003; in 2003 dollars)

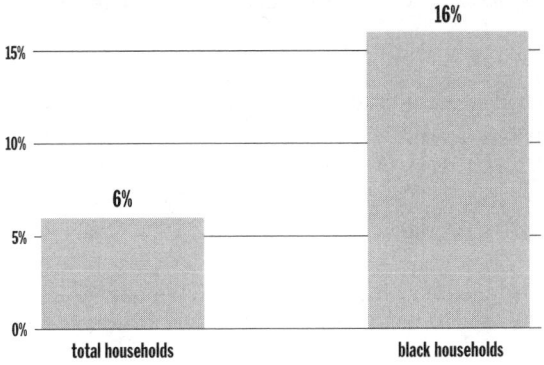

Table 3.49 Median Income of Black Households, 1990 to 2003

(median income of total and black households, and index of black to total, 1990 to 2003; percent change in incomes, 2000–03 and 1990–2003; in 2003 dollars)

	total households	black households	index
2003	$43,318	$29,689	69
2002	43,381	29,845	69
2001	43,882	30,625	70
2000	44,853	31,690	71
1999	44,922	30,808	69
1998	43,825	28,572	65
1997	42,294	28,630	68
1996	41,431	27,411	66
1995	40,845	26,842	66
1994	39,613	25,816	65
1993	39,165	24,487	63
1992	39,364	24,098	61
1991	39,679	24,771	62
1990	40,865	25,488	62
Percent change			
2000 to 2003	–3.4%	–6.3%	–
1990 to 2003	6.0	16.5	–

Note: Data for blacks in 2002 and 2003 are for those identifying themselves as being of the race alone and those identifying themselves as being of the race in combination with other races. (–) means not applicable.
Source: Bureau of the Census, Current Population Surveys, Internet site http://www.census.gov/hhes/income/histinc/h05.html; calculations by New Strategist

Table 3.50 High-Income Black Households, 2003

(number and percent distribution of black households with incomes of $100,000 or more, 2003; households in thousands as of 2004)

	total	percent
TOTAL BLACK HOUSEHOLDS	**13,969**	**100.0%**
$100,000 or more	**946**	**6.8**
$100,000 to $149,999	679	4.9
$150,000 to $199,999	160	1.1
$200,000 to $249,999	61	0.4
$250,000 or more	46	0.3

Note: Blacks are those identifying themselves as being of the race alone and those identifying themselves as being of the race in combination with other races.
Source: Bureau of the Census, 2004 Current Population Survey, Internet site http://pubdb3.census.gov/macro/032004/hhinc/new06_000.htm; calculations by New Strategist

Table 3.51 Black Household Income by Age of Householder, 2003

(number and percent distribution of black households by household income and age of householder, 2003; house-holds in thousands as of 2004)

	total	15 to 24	25 to 34	35 to 44	45 to 54	55 to 64	aged 65 or older total	65 to 74	75 or older
Black households	**13,969**	**1,133**	**2,824**	**3,146**	**2,953**	**1,827**	**2,085**	**1,144**	**942**
Under $10,000	2,450	360	447	366	370	334	576	259	318
$10,000 to $19,999	2,497	278	456	454	381	298	629	328	300
$20,000 to $29,999	2,091	204	442	456	434	265	290	170	122
$30,000 to $39,999	1,649	108	363	435	339	211	197	125	73
$40,000 to $49,999	1,299	59	329	346	330	122	112	84	28
$50,000 to $59,999	1,011	40	228	273	244	145	79	51	29
$60,000 to $69,999	743	19	159	197	231	82	56	28	27
$70,000 to $79,999	574	15	122	156	153	92	37	26	10
$80,000 to $89,999	410	18	61	127	107	70	26	22	5
$90,000 to $99,999	299	10	58	83	94	37	17	8	10
$100,000 or more	945	21	161	254	270	176	65	44	21
Median income	$29,689	$16,967	$31,218	$37,024	$38,470	$30,636	$16,736	$19,510	$14,004

PERCENT DISTRIBUTION BY INCOME

Black households	**100.0%**	**100.0%**	**100.0%**	**100.0%**	**100.0%**	**100.0%**	**100.0%**	**100.0%**	**100.0%**
Under $10,000	17.5	31.8	15.8	11.6	12.5	18.3	27.6	22.6	33.8
$10,000 to $19,999	17.9	24.5	16.1	14.4	12.9	16.3	30.2	28.7	31.8
$20,000 to $29,999	15.0	18.0	15.7	14.5	14.7	14.5	13.9	14.9	13.0
$30,000 to $39,999	11.8	9.5	12.9	13.8	11.5	11.5	9.4	10.9	7.7
$40,000 to $49,999	9.3	5.2	11.7	11.0	11.2	6.7	5.4	7.3	3.0
$50,000 to $59,999	7.2	3.5	8.1	8.7	8.3	7.9	3.8	4.5	3.1
$60,000 to $69,999	5.3	1.7	5.6	6.3	7.8	4.5	2.7	2.4	2.9
$70,000 to $79,999	4.1	1.3	4.3	5.0	5.2	5.0	1.8	2.3	1.1
$80,000 to $89,999	2.9	1.6	2.2	4.0	3.6	3.8	1.2	1.9	0.5
$90,000 to $99,999	2.1	0.9	2.1	2.6	3.2	2.0	0.8	0.7	1.1
$100,000 or more	6.8	1.9	5.7	8.1	9.1	9.6	3.1	3.8	2.2

Note: Blacks are those identifying themselves as being black alone and those identifying themselves as being black in combina-tion with other races.
Source: Bureau of the Census, 2004 Current Population Survey, Internet site http://pubdb3.census.gov/macro/032004/hhinc/ new02_001.htm; calculations by New Strategist

Table 3.52 Black Household Income by Household Type, 2003

(number and percent distribution of households headed by blacks by household income and household type, 2003; households in thousands as of 2004)

| | total | family households | | | nonfamily households | | | |
| | | married couples | female hh, no spouse present | male hh, no spouse present | female householder | | male householder | |
					total	living alone	total	living alone
Black households	**13,969**	**4,259**	**4,067**	**804**	**2,768**	**2,505**	**2,072**	**1,733**
Under $10,000	2,450	157	878	99	834	811	483	467
$10,000 to $19,999	2,497	337	950	131	676	646	403	363
$20,000 to $29,999	2,091	464	736	116	450	389	323	267
$30,000 to $39,999	1,649	493	518	109	265	236	266	224
$40,000 to $49,999	1,299	522	321	84	199	170	172	140
$50,000 to $59,999	1,011	467	215	66	126	94	138	99
$60,000 to $69,999	743	379	157	54	76	64	77	52
$70,000 to $79,999	574	327	104	27	39	24	74	46
$80,000 to $89,999	410	235	57	34	28	21	55	36
$90,000 to $99,999	299	208	36	33	13	7	11	9
$100,000 or more	945	670	94	53	62	44	67	32
Median income	$29,689	$52,671	$22,739	$35,660	$17,001	$15,542	$24,495	$21,304

PERCENT DISTRIBUTION BY INCOME

	total	married couples	female hh, no spouse present	male hh, no spouse present	female total	living alone	male total	living alone
Black households	**100.0%**	**100.0%**	**100.0%**	**100.0%**	**100.0%**	**100.0%**	**100.0%**	**100.0%**
Under $10,000	17.5	3.7	21.6	12.3	30.1	32.4	23.3	26.9
$10,000 to $19,999	17.9	7.9	23.4	16.3	24.4	25.8	19.4	20.9
$20,000 to $29,999	15.0	10.9	18.1	14.4	16.3	15.5	15.6	15.4
$30,000 to $39,999	11.8	11.6	12.7	13.6	9.6	9.4	12.8	12.9
$40,000 to $49,999	9.3	12.3	7.9	10.4	7.2	6.8	8.3	8.1
$50,000 to $59,999	7.2	11.0	5.3	8.2	4.6	3.8	6.7	5.7
$60,000 to $69,999	5.3	8.9	3.9	6.7	2.7	2.6	3.7	3.0
$70,000 to $79,999	4.1	7.7	2.6	3.4	1.4	1.0	3.6	2.7
$80,000 to $89,999	2.9	5.5	1.4	4.2	1.0	0.8	2.7	2.1
$90,000 to $99,999	2.1	4.9	0.9	4.1	0.5	0.3	0.5	0.5
$100,000 or more	6.8	15.7	2.3	6.6	2.2	1.8	3.2	1.8

Note: Blacks are those identifying themselves as being black alone and those identifying themselves as being black in combination with other races.
Source: Bureau of the Census, 2004 Current Population Survey, Internet site http://pubdb3.census.gov/macro/032004/hhinc/new02_000.htm; calculations by New Strategist

Table 3.53 Income of Black Men by Age, 2003

(number and percent distribution of black men aged 15 or older by income and age, median income of men with income and of men working full-time, year-round, and percent working full-time, year-round, 2003; men in thousands as of 2004)

	total	under 25	25 to 34	35 to 44	45 to 54	55 to 64	65 or older
TOTAL BLACK MEN	**12,354**	**2,989**	**2,324**	**2,496**	**2,177**	**1,245**	**1,123**
Without income	**2,063**	**1,312**	**256**	**191**	**169**	**94**	**41**
With income	**10,291**	**1,677**	**2,068**	**2,305**	**2,008**	**1,151**	**1,082**
Under $10,000	2,537	937	387	312	342	231	326
$10,000 to $19,999	2,129	345	425	405	334	220	399
$20,000 to $29,999	1,814	269	450	427	324	196	151
$30,000 to $39,999	1,271	75	334	385	284	131	60
$40,000 to $49,999	947	29	228	293	242	97	59
$50,000 to $59,999	580	8	77	192	186	85	33
$60,000 to $69,999	339	6	71	98	90	55	19
$70,000 to $79,999	201	–	34	66	58	38	4
$80,000 to $89,999	146	–	18	44	52	20	12
$90,000 to $99,999	102	5	14	23	27	30	–
$100,000 or more	227	4	28	62	71	45	18
Median income of men with income	$21,935	$8,060	$24,647	$30,153	$30,073	$26,031	$14,374
Median income of men working full-time	33,464	22,058	30,982	35,990	38,441	41,784	40,180
Percent of men working full-time	44.8%	14.6%	59.6%	67.1%	62.5%	43.9%	11.3%
TOTAL BLACK MEN	**100.0%**	**100.0%**	**100.0%**	**100.0%**	**100.0%**	**100.0%**	**100.0%**
Without income	**16.7**	**43.9**	**11.0**	**7.7**	**7.8**	**7.6**	**3.7**
With income	**83.3**	**56.1**	**89.0**	**92.3**	**92.2**	**92.4**	**96.3**
Under $10,000	20.5	31.3	16.7	12.5	15.7	18.6	29.0
$10,000 to $19,999	17.2	11.5	18.3	16.2	15.3	17.7	35.5
$20,000 to $29,999	14.7	9.0	19.4	17.1	14.9	15.7	13.4
$30,000 to $39,999	10.3	2.5	14.4	15.4	13.0	10.5	5.3
$40,000 to $49,999	7.7	1.0	9.8	11.7	11.1	7.8	5.3
$50,000 to $59,999	4.7	0.3	3.3	7.7	8.5	6.8	2.9
$60,000 to $69,999	2.7	0.2	3.1	3.9	4.1	4.4	1.7
$70,000 to $79,999	1.6	–	1.5	2.6	2.7	3.1	0.4
$80,000 to $89,999	1.2	–	0.8	1.8	2.4	1.6	1.1
$90,000 to $99,999	0.8	0.2	0.6	0.9	1.2	2.4	–
$100,000 or more	1.8	0.1	1.2	2.5	3.3	3.6	1.6

Note: Blacks are those identifying themselves as being black alone and those identifying themselves as being black in combination with other races. (–) means sample is too small to make a reliable estimate.
Source: Bureau of the Census, 2004 Current Population Survey, Internet site http://pubdb3.census.gov/macro/032004/perinc/new01_000.htm; calculations by New Strategist

Table 3.54 Income of Black Women by Age, 2003

(number and percent distribution of black women aged 15 or older by income and age, median income of women with income and of women working full-time, year-round, and percent working full-time, year-round, 2003; women in thousands as of 2004)

	total	under 25	25 to 34	35 to 44	45 to 54	55 to 64	65 or older
TOTAL BLACK WOMEN	**15,103**	**3,178**	**2,866**	**3,034**	**2,634**	**1,581**	**1,810**
Without income	**2,179**	**1,227**	**262**	**244**	**213**	**151**	**81**
With income	**12,924**	**1,951**	**2,604**	**2,790**	**2,421**	**1,430**	**1,729**
Under $10,000	4,160	1,179	645	523	503	419	891
$10,000 to $19,999	3,191	500	628	638	538	330	554
$20,000 to $29,999	2,317	191	586	643	504	248	147
$30,000 to $39,999	1,406	51	362	390	354	182	65
$40,000 to $49,999	791	18	172	273	210	90	25
$50,000 to $59,999	408	3	92	138	107	50	18
$60,000 to $69,999	265	4	37	80	85	43	17
$70,000 to $79,999	147	–	26	52	44	24	2
$80,000 to $89,999	66	4	9	9	21	19	1
$90,000 to $99,999	46	–	16	17	11	4	–
$100,000 or more	127	–	29	28	42	21	7
Median income of women with income	$16,540	$6,896	$20,366	$23,078	$23,090	$18,374	$9,807
Median income of women working full-time	27,675	18,206	27,455	28,787	30,131	30,547	30,732
Percent of women working full-time	40.3%	14.5%	53.8%	60.5%	58.2%	39.8%	4.5%
TOTAL BLACK WOMEN	**100.0%**	**100.0%**	**100.0%**	**100.0%**	**100.0%**	**100.0%**	**100.0%**
Without income	**14.4**	**38.6**	**9.1**	**8.0**	**8.1**	**9.6**	**4.5**
With income	**85.6**	**61.4**	**90.9**	**92.0**	**91.9**	**90.4**	**95.5**
Under $10,000	27.5	37.1	22.5	17.2	19.1	26.5	49.2
$10,000 to $19,999	21.1	15.7	21.9	21.0	20.4	20.9	30.6
$20,000 to $29,999	15.3	6.0	20.4	21.2	19.1	15.7	8.1
$30,000 to $39,999	9.3	1.6	12.6	12.9	13.4	11.5	3.6
$40,000 to $49,999	5.2	0.6	6.0	9.0	8.0	5.7	1.4
$50,000 to $59,999	2.7	0.1	3.2	4.5	4.1	3.2	1.0
$60,000 to $69,999	1.8	0.1	1.3	2.6	3.2	2.7	0.9
$70,000 to $79,999	1.0	–	0.9	1.7	1.7	1.5	0.1
$80,000 to $89,999	0.4	0.1	0.3	0.3	0.8	1.2	0.1
$90,000 to $99,999	0.3	–	0.6	0.6	0.4	0.3	–
$100,000 or more	0.8	–	1.0	0.9	1.6	1.3	0.4

Note: Blacks are those identifying themselves as being black alone and those identifying themselves as being black in combination with other races. (–) means sample is too small to make a reliable estimate.
Source: Bureau of the Census, 2004 Current Population Survey, Internet site http://pubdb3.census.gov/macro/032004/perinc/new01_000.htm; calculations by New Strategist

Table 3.55 Median Income of Blacks Working Full-Time by Sex, 1990 to 2003

(median income of blacks working full-time, year-round by sex; index of black to total population median income, and black women's income as a percent of black men's income, 1990 to 2003; percent change in income, 2000–03 and 1990–2003; in 2003 dollars)

	black men		black women		black women's income as a percent of black men's income
	median income	index black/total	median income	index black/total	
2003	$33,464	81	$27,675	87	82.7%
2002	32,698	79	28,338	89	86.7
2001	33,172	80	28,366	90	85.5
2000	32,568	78	27,506	88	84.5
1999	33,285	81	27,751	92	83.4
1998	30,962	76	26,896	89	86.9
1997	30,741	76	26,017	87	84.6
1996	31,676	81	25,669	88	81.0
1995	29,724	77	25,267	89	85.0
1994	29,964	77	25,326	89	84.5
1993	29,543	76	25,467	90	86.2
1992	29,541	75	26,029	92	88.1
1991	29,804	75	25,202	90	84.6
1990	29,316	74	25,308	90	86.3
Percent change					
2000 to 2003	2.8%	–	0.6%	–	–
1990 to 2003	14.1	–	9.4	–	–

Note: Data for blacks in 2002 and 2003 are for those identifying themselves as being of the race alone and those identifying themselves as being of the race in combination with other races. The black/total indexes are calculated by dividing the median income of black men and women by the median income of total men and women and multiplying by 100. (–) means not applicable.
Source: Bureau of the Census, Current Population Surveys, Internet site http://www.census.gov/hhes/income/histinc/p36b.html; calculations by New Strategist

Table 3.56 Median Earnings of Blacks Working Full-Time by Education and Sex, 2003

(median earnings of blacks aged 25 or older working full-time, year-round, by educational attainment and sex, and black women's earnings as a percent of black men's earnings, 2003)

	men	women	black women's earnings as a percent of black men's earnings
Total blacks	**$35,024**	**$27,910**	**79.7%**
Less than 9th grade	21,338	19,855	93.0
9th to 12th grade, no diploma	21,669	18,674	86.2
High school graduate	30,409	23,956	78.8
Some college, no degree	35,746	28,017	78.4
Associate's degree	38,344	28,022	73.1
Bachelor's degree or more	50,006	41,335	82.7

Note: Blacks are those identifying themselves as being black alone and those identifying themselves as being black in combination with other races. (–) means sample is too small to make a reliable estimate.
Source: Bureau of the Census, 2004 Current Population Survey, Internet site http://pubdb3.census.gov/macro/032004/perinc/new03_000.htm; calculations by New Strategist

Table 3.57 Poverty Status of Black Married Couples, 1990 to 2003

(total number of black married couples, and number and percent below poverty level by presence of children under age 18 at home, 1990 to 2003; percent change in numbers and percentage point change in rates, 2000–03 and 1990–2003; married couples in thousands as of March the following year)

		in poverty	
	total	number	percent
Total black married couples			
2003	4,259	331	7.8%
2002	4,268	340	8.0
2001	4,234	328	7.8
2000	4,214	266	6.3
1999	4,150	295	7.1
1998	3,979	290	7.3
1997	3,921	312	8.0
1996	3,851	352	9.1
1995	3,713	314	8.5
1994	3,842	336	8.7
1993	3,715	458	12.3
1992	3,777	490	13.0
1991	3,631	399	11.0
1990	3,569	448	12.6

	percent change		percentage point change
2000 to 2003	1.1%	24.4%	1.5
1990 to 2003	19.3	−26.1	−4.8

Black married couples with children			
2003	2,323	210	9.1%
2002	2,340	199	8.5
2001	2,342	205	8.7
2000	2,343	157	6.7
1999	2,301	199	8.7
1998	2,198	189	8.6
1997	2,275	205	9.0
1996	2,174	239	11.0
1995	2,119	209	9.9
1994	2,147	245	11.4
1993	2,147	298	13.9
1992	2,229	343	15.4
1991	2,129	263	12.4
1990	2,104	301	14.3

	percent change		percentage point change
2000 to 2003	−0.9%	33.8%	2.4
1990 to 2003	10.4	−30.2	−5.2

Note: Data for blacks in 2002 and 2003 are for those identifying themselves as being of the race alone and those identifying themselves as being of the race in combination with other races.
Source: Bureau of the Census, Current Population Surveys, Internet site http://www.census.gov/hhes/www/poverty/histpov/hstpov4.html; calculations by New Strategist

Table 3.58 Poverty Status of Black Female-Headed Families, 1990 to 2003

(total number of black female-headed families, and number and percent below poverty level by presence of children under age 18 at home, 1990 to 2003; percent change in numbers and percentage point change in rates, 2000–03 and 1990–2003; families in thousands as of March the following year)

| | | in poverty | |
	total	number	percent
Total black female-headed families			
2003	4,068	1,496	36.8%
2002	4,072	1,454	35.7
2001	3,838	1,351	35.2
2000	3,785	1,300	34.3
1999	3,797	1,487	39.2
1998	3,813	1,557	40.8
1997	3,926	1,563	39.8
1996	3,947	1,724	43.7
1995	3,769	1,701	45.1
1994	3,716	1,715	46.2
1993	3,828	1,908	49.9
1992	3,738	1,878	50.2
1991	3,582	1,834	51.2
1990	3,430	1,648	48.1

	percent change		percentage point change
2000 to 2003	7.5%	15.1%	2.5
1990 to 2003	18.6	−9.2	−11.3

Black female-headed families with children			
2003	3,144	1,341	42.7%
2002	3,120	1,288	41.3
2001	2,994	1,220	40.8
2000	2,873	1,177	41.0
1999	2,869	1,320	46.0
1998	2,940	1,397	47.5
1997	3,060	1,436	46.9
1996	3,120	1,593	51.0
1995	2,884	1,533	53.2
1994	2,951	1,591	53.9
1993	3,084	1,780	57.7
1992	2,971	1,706	57.4
1991	2,771	1,676	60.5
1990	2,698	1,513	56.1

	percent change		percentage point change
2000 to 2003	9.4	13.9%	1.7
1990 to 2003	16.5	−11.4	−13.4

Note: Data for blacks in 2002 and 2003 are for those identifying themselves as being of the race alone and those identifying themselves as being of the race in combination with other races.
Source: Bureau of the Census, Current Population Surveys, Internet site http://www.census.gov/hhes/www/poverty/histpov/ hstpov4.html; calculations by New Strategist

Table 3.59 Poverty Status of Black Male-Headed Families, 1990 to 2003

(total number of black male-headed families, and number and percent below poverty level by presence of children under age 18 at home, 1990 to 2003; percent change in numbers and percentage point change in rates, 2000–03 and 1990–2003; families in thousands as of March the following year)

		in poverty	
	total	number	percent
Total black male-headed families			
2003	804	194	24.1%
2002	793	165	20.8
2001	775	150	19.4
2000	732	120	16.3
1999	706	105	14.8
1998	660	134	20.3
1997	562	111	19.7
1996	657	130	19.8
1995	573	112	19.5
1994	535	161	30.1
1993	450	133	29.6
1992	467	116	24.8
1991	503	110	21.9
1990	472	97	20.6

	percent change		percentage point change
2000 to 2003	9.8%	61.7%	7.8
1990 to 2003	70.3	100.0	3.5

	total	number	percent
Black male-headed families with children			
2003	476	146	30.7%
2002	420	110	26.3
2001	404	99	24.6
2000	352	76	21.7
1999	386	84	21.7
1998	353	88	24.8
1997	312	81	25.8
1996	401	109	27.2
1995	337	79	23.4
1994	341	118	34.6
1993	294	93	31.6
1992	248	83	33.5
1991	243	77	31.7
1990	267	73	27.3

	percent change		percentage point change
2000 to 2003	35.2%	92.1%	9.0
1990 to 2003	78.3	100.0	3.4

Note: Data for blacks in 2002 and 2003 are for those identifying themselves as being of the race alone and those identifying themselves as being of the race in combination with other races.
Source: Bureau of the Census, Current Population Surveys, Internet site http://www.census.gov/hhes/www/poverty/histpov/hstpov4.html; calculations by New Strategist

Table 3.60 Poverty Status of Blacks by Sex and Age, 2003

(total number of blacks, and number and percent below poverty level by sex and age, 2003; people in thousands as of 2004)

	total	in poverty	
		number	percent
Total blacks	**37,503**	**9,108**	**24.3%**
Under age 18	12,215	4,108	33.6
Aged 18 to 24	3,998	1,062	26.6
Aged 25 to 34	5,190	1,133	21.8
Aged 35 to 44	5,530	914	16.5
Aged 45 to 54	4,812	722	15.0
Aged 55 to 59	1,566	247	15.8
Aged 60 to 64	1,259	233	18.5
Aged 65 or older	2,933	688	23.5
Black females	**20,079**	**5,300**	**26.4**
Under age 18	6,076	2,047	33.7
Aged 18 to 24	2,078	678	32.6
Aged 25 to 34	2,866	769	26.8
Aged 35 to 44	3,034	596	19.7
Aged 45 to 54	2,634	423	16.1
Aged 55 to 59	862	151	17.5
Aged 60 to 64	718	148	20.5
Aged 65 or older	1,810	490	27.1
Black males	**17,424**	**3,808**	**21.9**
Under age 18	6,138	2,061	33.6
Aged 18 to 24	1,920	385	20.0
Aged 25 to 34	2,324	365	15.7
Aged 35 to 44	2,496	318	12.7
Aged 45 to 54	2,177	299	13.7
Aged 55 to 59	704	97	13.7
Aged 60 to 64	541	86	15.8
Aged 65 or older	1,123	198	17.7

Note: Blacks are those identifying themselves as being of the race alone and those identifying themselves as being of the race in combination with other races.
Source: Bureau of the Census, 2004 Current Population Survey, Internet site http://pubdb3.census.gov/macro/032004/pov/new01_100.htm

Twenty-Six Percent of Black Workers Are Managers or Professionals

The 26 percent of blacks employed as managers or professionals account for 8 percent of Americans working in those occupations. Another 26 percent of employed blacks work in sales and office jobs, while 24 percent are in service occupations. Blacks account for 11 percent of all workers, but for 20 percent of social workers, 21 percent of dietitians, and 35 percent of home health aides and barbers.

Overall, 67 percent of black men were in the labor force in 2004, a smaller share than the 73 percent level among all men. Sixty-two percent of black women are in the labor force, a higher rate than the 59 percent for all women. Among black couples, 59 percent have both husband and wife in the labor force. Nevertheless, only 33 percent of black households have two or more earners—well below the 42 percent among all households—because married couples head a relatively small share of black households.

Black workers spent a median of 23 minutes getting to work in 2003, traveling a median distance of 11 miles. Seventy-three percent of black workers get to work by car, driving alone.

Between 2002 and 2012, the number of black workers will grow 19 percent. The black share of the labor force will rise from 11 to 12 percent during the decade.

■ Black incomes have been rising because younger, better-educated blacks are entering managerial and professional occupations.

The labor force participation rate of black women almost matches that of black men

(percent of blacks aged 16 or older in the labor force, by sex, 2004)

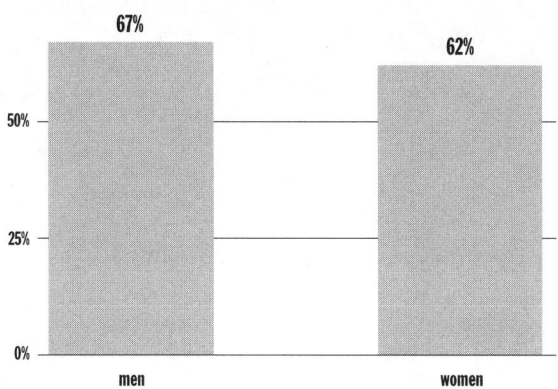

Table 3.61 Labor Force Participation Rate of Blacks by Age and Sex, 2004

(percent of blacks aged 16 or older in the civilian labor force, by age and sex, 2004)

	total	men	women
Total blacks	**63.8%**	**66.7%**	**61.5%**
Aged 16 to 19	31.4	30.0	32.8
Aged 20 to 24	68.3	69.9	66.8
Aged 25 to 29	79.0	83.6	75.2
Aged 30 to 34	83.4	88.7	79.1
Aged 35 to 39	83.3	86.5	80.8
Aged 40 to 44	80.9	81.7	80.3
Aged 45 to 49	78.0	79.1	77.0
Aged 50 to 54	72.5	74.3	71.0
Aged 55 to 59	63.1	66.7	60.1
Aged 60 to 64	43.6	44.6	42.9
Aged 65 or older	13.1	17.0	10.7
Aged 65 to 69	22.5	25.1	20.5
Aged 70 to 74	13.4	18.0	10.6
Aged 75 or older	5.7	8.3	4.4

Note: The civilian labor force equals the number of employed plus the number of unemployed.
Source: Bureau of Labor Statistics, 2004 Current Population Survey, http://www.bls.gov/cps/home.htm

Table 3.62 Employment Status of Blacks by Sex and Age, 2004

(number and percent of blacks aged 16 or older in the civilian labor force by sex, age, and employment status, 2004; numbers in thousands)

| | civilian non-institutional population | civilian labor force | | | unemployed | |
		total	percent of population	employed	number	percent of labor force
Total blacks	**26,065**	**16,638**	**63.8%**	**14,909**	**1,729**	**10.4%**
Aged 16 to 19	2,423	762	31.4	520	241	31.7
Aged 20 to 24	2,821	1,926	68.3	1,572	353	18.4
Aged 25 to 34	5,020	4,076	81.2	3,635	441	10.8
Aged 35 to 44	5,335	4,380	82.1	4,039	341	7.8
Aged 45 to 54	4,739	3,578	75.5	3,332	245	6.9
Aged 55 to 64	2,827	1,538	54.4	1,452	86	5.6
Aged 65 or older	2,899	380	13.1	359	21	5.5
Total black men	**11,656**	**7,773**	**66.7**	**6,912**	**860**	**11.1**
Aged 16 to 19	1,195	359	30.0	231	128	35.6
Aged 20 to 24	1,326	927	69.9	739	188	20.3
Aged 25 to 34	2,242	1,931	86.1	1,720	211	10.9
Aged 35 to 44	2,382	2,000	84.0	1,840	160	8.0
Aged 45 to 54	2,150	1,654	76.9	1,534	120	7.2
Aged 55 to 64	1,250	714	57.1	668	46	6.4
Aged 65 or older	1,111	188	17.0	180	8	4.2
Total black women	**14,409**	**8,865**	**61.5**	**7,997**	**868**	**9.8**
Aged 16 to 19	1,227	403	32.8	289	114	28.2
Aged 20 to 24	1,495	999	66.8	833	166	16.6
Aged 25 to 34	2,778	2,144	77.2	1,914	230	10.7
Aged 35 to 44	2,954	2,380	80.6	2,199	180	7.6
Aged 45 to 54	2,590	1,924	74.3	1,798	126	6.5
Aged 55 to 64	1,577	824	52.3	784	40	4.8
Aged 65 or older	1,789	192	10.7	179	13	6.8

Note: The civilian labor force equals the number of the employed plus the number of the unemployed. The civilian population equals the number in the labor force plus the number not in the labor force.
Source: Bureau of Labor Statistics, 2004 Current Population Survey, Internet site http://www.bls.gov/cps/home.htm

Table 3.63 Black Workers by Occupation, 2004

(total number of employed persons aged 16 or older in the civilian labor force, number and percent distribution of employed blacks, and black share of total, by occupation, 2004; numbers in thousands)

		black		
	total	number	percent distribution	share of total
TOTAL EMPLOYED	**139,252**	**14,909**	**100.0%**	**10.7%**
Management, professional and related occupations	**48,532**	**3,949**	**26.5**	**8.1**
Management, business, and financial operations	20,235	1,408	9.4	7.0
Management occupations	14,555	864	5.8	5.9
Business and financial operations occupations	5,860	544	3.6	9.3
Professional and related occupations	28,297	2,541	17.0	9.0
Computer and mathematical occupations	3,140	236	1.6	7.5
Architecture and engineering occupations	2,760	135	0.9	4.9
Life, physical, and social science occupations	1,365	76	0.5	5.6
Community and social services occupations	2,170	415	2.8	19.1
Legal occupations	1,554	100	0.7	6.4
Education, training, and library occupations	7,900	742	5.0	9.4
Arts, design, entertainment, sports, and media occupations	2,687	164	1.1	6.1
Health care practitioner and technical occupations	6,721	673	4.5	10.0
Service occupations	**22,720**	**3,543**	**23.8**	**15.6**
Health care support occupations	2,921	758	5.1	26.0
Protective service occupations	2,847	510	3.4	17.9
Food preparation and serving-related occupations	7,279	835	5.6	11.5
Building and grounds cleaning and maintenance occupations	5,185	773	5.2	14.9
Personal care and service occupations	4,488	667	4.5	14.9
Sales and office occupations	**35,464**	**3,918**	**26.3**	**11.0**
Sales and related occupations	15,983	1,430	9.6	8.9
Office and administrative support occupations	19,481	2,487	16.7	12.8
Natural resources, construction, maintenance occupations	**14,582**	**1,012**	**6.8**	**6.9**
Farming, fishing, and forestry occupations	991	53	0.4	5.3
Construction and extraction occupations	8,522	572	3.8	6.7
Installation, maintenance, and repair occupations	5,069	387	2.6	7.6
Production, transportation, material moving occupations	**17,954**	**2,488**	**16.7**	**13.9**
Production occupations	9,462	1,124	7.5	11.9
Transportation and material moving occupations	8,491	1,364	9.1	16.1

Source: Bureau of Labor Statistics, 2004 Current Population Survey, Internet site http://www.bls.gov/cps/home.htm; calculations by New Strategist

Table 3.64 Black Workers by Detailed Occupation, 2004

(total number of employed workers aged 16 or older and percent black, by detailed occupation, 2004; numbers in thousands)

	total	percent black
TOTAL EMPLOYED	**139,252**	**10.7%**
Management, professional, and related occupations	**48,532**	**8.1**
Management, business, and financial operations occupations	20,235	7.0
Management occupations	14,555	5.9
Chief executives	1,680	3.2
General and operations managers	795	5.8
Advertising and promotions managers	70	5.2
Marketing and sales managers	806	3.4
Administrative services managers	87	7.6
Computer and information systems managers	337	4.9
Financial managers	1,045	7.8
Human resources managers	262	7.3
Industrial production managers	280	4.7
Purchasing managers	170	5.6
Transportation, storage, and distribution managers	241	7.1
Farm, ranch, and other agricultural managers	199	0.1
Farmers and ranchers	817	0.4
Construction managers	851	2.4
Education administrators	757	12.8
Engineering managers	106	1.7
Food service managers	916	8.2
Lodging managers	152	4.1
Medical and health services managers	508	8.8
Property, real estate, and community association managers	604	6.8
Social and community service managers	280	13.6
Business and financial operations occupations	5,680	9.6
Wholesale and retail buyers, except farm products	212	5.0
Purchasing agents, except wholesale, retail, and farm products	285	11.6
Claims adjusters, appraisers, examiners, and investigators	281	16.2
Compliance officers, excluding agriculture, construction, health and safety, and transportation	126	14.4
Cost estimators	98	2.5
Human resources, training, and labor relations specialists	694	13.2
Management analysts	554	6.9
Accountants and auditors	1,723	8.6
Appraisers and assessors of real estate	138	2.4
Personal financial advisors	331	5.8
Insurance underwriters	98	8.4
Loan counselors and officers	425	10.0
Tax examiners, collectors, and revenue agents	81	19.1
Tax preparers	88	6.1
Professional and related occupations	28,297	9.0
Computer and mathematical occupations	3,140	7.5
Computer scientists and systems analysts	700	9.8
Computer programmers	564	6.9

(continued)

	total	percent black
Computer software engineers	813	5.3%
Computer support specialists	325	9.2
Database administrators	94	5.5
Network and computer systems administrators	190	8.5
Network systems and data communications analysts	312	8.0
Operations research analysts	90	9.4
Architecture and engineering occupations	2,760	4.9
Architects, except naval	207	2.6
Aerospace engineers	113	4.4
Chemical engineers	63	4.4
Civil engineers	293	7.7
Computer hardware engineers	96	7.4
Electrical and electronics engineers	343	4.8
Industrial engineers, including health and safety	177	4.9
Mechanical engineers	311	4.2
Drafters	206	5.0
Engineering technicians, except drafters	416	5.9
Surveying and mapping technicians	80	1.0
Life, physical, and social science occupations	1,365	5.6
Biological scientists	123	3.1
Medical scientists	93	5.1
Chemists and materials scientists	141	7.0
Environmental scientists and geoscientists	86	5.1
Market and survey researchers	124	6.6
Psychologists	185	3.3
Chemical technicians	84	10.6
Community and social services occupations	2,170	19.1
Counselors	643	21.9
Social workers	687	20.4
Miscellaneous community and social service specialists	283	24.7
Clergy	403	11.6
Directors, religious activities and education	55	11.6
Religious workers, all other	99	11.0
Legal occupations	1,554	6.4
Lawyers	954	4.7
Judges, magistrates, and other judicial workers	64	12.8
Paralegals and legal assistants	322	10.4
Miscellaneous legal support workers	215	6.0
Education, training, and library occupations	7,900	9.4
Postsecondary teachers	1,176	5.9
Preschool and kindergarten teachers	656	15.2
Elementary and middle school teachers	2,580	9.5
Secondary school teachers	1,151	6.6
Special education teachers	384	9.7
Other teachers and instructors	667	8.6
Librarians	217	5.6
Teacher assistants	920	14.6
Arts, design, entertainment, sports, and media occupations	2,687	6.1
Artists and related workers	222	2.2
Designers	792	5.0
Producers and directors	137	8.4

(continued)

	total	percent black
Athletes, coaches, umpires, and related workers	239	7.8%
Musicians, singers, and related workers	179	8.6
Announcers	54	9.3
News analysts, reporters, and correspondents	81	7.4
Public relations specialists	133	7.6
Editors	164	4.1
Writers and authors	194	3.6
Miscellaneous media and communication workers	74	7.7
Broadcast and sound engineering technicians and radio operators	92	12.2
Photographers	158	8.0
Health care practitioner and technical occupations	6,721	10.0
Chiropractors	73	0.3
Dentists	167	5.0
Dietitians and nutritionists	84	21.1
Pharmacists	233	3.1
Physicians and surgeons	830	6.1
Physician assistants	70	6.8
Registered nurses	2,464	10.1
Occupational therapists	84	5.1
Physical therapists	173	7.1
Respiratory therapists	103	11.9
Speech-language pathologists	93	6.0
Veterinarians	58	–
Clinical laboratory technologists and technicians	333	14.6
Dental hygienists	130	2.6
Diagnostic related technologists and technicians	284	7.3
Emergency medical technicians and paramedics	139	9.0
Health diagnosing and treating practitioner support technicians	397	10.8
Licensed practical and licensed vocational nurses	517	20.8
Medical records and health information technicians	91	16.0
Service occupations	**22,720**	**15.6**
Health care support occupations	2,921	25.9
Nursing, psychiatric, and home health aides	1,806	34.6
Physical therapist assistants and aides	61	10.7
Massage therapists	106	4.4
Dental assistants	242	5.1
Protective service occupations	2,847	17.9
First-line supervisors and managers of police and detectives	133	10.2
Firefighters	268	8.4
Bailiffs, correctional officers, and jailers	373	20.2
Detectives and criminal investigators	121	17.1
Police and sheriff's patrol officers	664	15.7
Private detectives and investigators	81	7.8
Security guards and gaming surveillance officers	798	28.4
Food preparation and serving related occupations	7,279	11.5
Chefs and head cooks	299	11.5
First-line supervisors/managers of food preparation and serving workers	644	12.7
Cooks	1,791	16.2
Food preparation workers	621	15.1

(continued)

	total	percent black
Bartenders	360	2.6%
Combined food preparation and serving workers, including fast food	296	12.8
Counter attendants, cafeteria, food concession, and coffee shop	327	12.2
Waiters and waitresses	1,892	7.0
Food servers, nonrestaurant	165	19.4
Dining room and cafeteria attendants and bartender helpers	379	8.8
Dishwashers	267	14.5
Hosts and hostesses, restaurant, lounge, and coffee shop	237	4.1
Building and grounds cleaning and maintenance occupations	5,185	14.9
First-line supervisors and managers of housekeeping and janitorial workers	191	19.6
First-line supervisors and managers of landscaping, lawn service, and groundskeeping workers	227	3.3
Janitors and building cleaners	2,047	17.8
Maids and housekeeping cleaners	1,365	18.0
Pest control workers	75	11.6
Grounds maintenance workers	1,280	8.5
Personal care and service occupations	4,488	14.9
First-line supervisors and managers of gaming workers	140	8.2
First-line supervisors and managers of personal service workers	174	9.1
Nonfarm animal caretakers	128	2.8
Gaming services workers	95	7.8
Barbers	101	34.9
Hairdressers, hair stylists, and cosmetologists	722	12.1
Miscellaneous personal appearance workers	200	3.7
Baggage porters, bellhops, and concierges	70	11.1
Transportation attendants	116	15.2
Child care workers	1,332	17.8
Personal and home care aides	630	21.8
Recreation and fitness workers	314	12.6
Sales and office occupations	**35,464**	**11.0**
Sales and related occupations	15,983	9.0
First-line supervisors and managers of retail sales workers	3,299	7.1
First-line supervisors and managers of nonretail sales workers	1,390	5.4
Cashiers	2,971	15.6
Counter and rental clerks	186	10.5
Parts salespersons	147	7.2
Retail salespersons	3,130	10.9
Advertising sales agents	211	5.3
Insurance sales agents	508	6.3
Securities, commodities, and financial services sales agents	382	7.0
Travel agents	95	7.1
Sales representatives, services, all other	476	7.1
Sales representatives, wholesale and manufacturing	1,416	3.5
Models, demonstrators, and product promoters	68	8.5
Real estate brokers and sales agents	912	5.7
Telemarketers	180	18.6
Door-to-door sales workers, news and street vendors, related workers	312	5.6
Sales and related workers, all other	260	6.6
Office and administrative support occupations	19,481	12.8
First-line supervisors/managers of office, administrative support workers	1,631	11.1
Switchboard operators, including answering service	66	18.2

(continued)

	total	percent black
Telephone operators	56	39.8%
Bill and account collectors	229	20.1
Billing and posting clerks and machine operators	441	13.2
Bookkeeping, accounting, and auditing clerks	1,567	7.4
Payroll and timekeeping clerks	153	5.8
Tellers	424	10.9
Court, municipal, and license clerks	102	12.0
Credit authorizers, checkers, and clerks	65	9.9
Customer service representatives	1,749	16.4
Eligibility interviewers, government programs	66	22.4
File clerks	387	14.1
Hotel, motel, and resort desk clerks	106	14.1
Interviewers, except eligibility and loan	143	19.7
Library assistants, clerical	117	6.8
Loan interviewers and clerks	186	11.5
Order clerks	114	7.9
Human resources assistants, except payroll and timekeeping	64	15.3
Receptionists and information clerks	1,373	10.6
Reservation and transportation ticket agents and travel clerks	161	16.8
Couriers and messengers	293	14.4
Dispatchers	257	12.2
Postal service clerks	167	30.4
Postal service mail carriers	336	14.6
Postal service mail sorters, processors, and processing machine operators	116	29.8
Production, planning, and expediting clerks	288	7.6
Shipping, receiving, and traffic clerks	584	15.9
Stock clerks and order fillers	1,350	14.8
Weighers, measurers, checkers, and samplers, recordkeeping	64	6.2
Secretaries and administrative assistants	3,522	9.4
Computer operators	191	14.6
Data entry keyers	504	15.7
Word processors and typists	319	19.5
Insurance claims and policy processing clerks	277	16.8
Mail clerks and mail machine operators, except postal service	154	28.4
Office clerks, general	982	12.7
Office machine operators, except computer	61	13.1
Natural resources, construction, maintenance occupations	**14,582**	**6.9**
Farming, fishing, and forestry occupations	991	5.4
First-line supervisors/managers of farming, fishing, and forestry workers	59	3.9
Graders and sorters, agricultural products	68	10.0
Logging workers	92	12.1
Construction and extraction occupations	8,522	6.7
First-line supervisors/managers of construction trades, extraction workers	887	3.9
Brickmasons, blockmasons, and stonemasons	239	12.7
Carpenters	1,764	5.2
Carpet, floor, and tile installers and finishers	268	3.9
Cement masons, concrete finishers, and terrazzo workers	115	9.6
Construction laborers	1,234	8.9
Operating engineers and other construction equipment operators	367	5.2

(continued)

	total	percent black
Drywall installers, ceiling tile installers, and tapers	213	6.9%
Electricians	781	6.5
Painters, construction and maintenance	719	7.6
Pipe layers, plumbers, pipe fitters, and steam fitters	635	8.7
Roofers	269	8.2
Sheet metal workers	152	4.0
Structural iron and steel workers	66	3.4
Helpers, construction trades	121	8.9
Construction and building inspectors	104	8.5
Highway maintenance workers	96	10.6
Installation, maintenance, and repair occupations	5,069	7.6
First-line supervisors and managers of mechanics, installers, and repairers	327	7.6
Computer, automated teller, and office machine repairers	369	11.8
Radio and telecommunications equipment installers and repairers	235	14.7
Electric motor, power tool, and related repairers	56	5.0
Security and fire alarm systems installers	65	5.6
Aircraft mechanics and service technicians	135	6.2
Automotive body and related repairers	169	4.7
Automotive service technicians and mechanics	936	6.1
Bus and truck mechanics and diesel engine specialists	325	6.2
Heavy vehicle and mobile equipment service technicians and mechanics	205	6.5
Small-engine mechanics	58	0.9
Heating, air conditioning, and refrigeration mechanics and installers	351	5.3
Industrial and refractory machinery mechanics	434	7.3
Maintenance and repair workers, general	300	8.6
Millwrights	59	4.5
Electrical power line installers and repairers	120	13.2
Telecommunications line installers and repairers	142	12.4
Precision instrument and equipment repairers	53	6.5
Coin, vending, and amusement machine servicers and repairers	54	5.7
Production, transportation, material moving occupations	**17,954**	**13.9**
Production occupations	9,462	11.9
First-line supervisors and managers of production and operating workers	921	9.6
Electrical, electronics, and electromechanical assemblers	226	12.0
Bakers	188	13.0
Butchers and other meat, poultry, and fish processing workers	304	12.1
Food batchmakers	85	8.7
Cutting, punching, press machine setters, operators, tenders, metal/plastic	139	8.9
Grinding, lapping, polishing, and buffing machine tool setters, operators, and tenders, metal and plastic	74	15.5
Machinists	445	6.0
Molders, molding machine setters, operators, tenders, metal and plastic	70	4.2
Tool and die makers	86	2.8
Welding, soldering, and brazing workers	572	7.9
Job printers	65	11.2
Prepress technicians and workers	55	14.8
Printing machine operators	195	8.7
Laundry and dry-cleaning workers	195	18.5
Pressers, textile, garment, and related materials	76	21.8

(continued)

	total	percent black
Sewing machine operators	281	13.5%
Tailors, dressmakers, and sewers	101	7.8
Cabinetmakers and bench carpenters	86	1.5
Stationary engineers and boiler operators	105	11.4
Water and liquid waste treatment plant and system operators	56	10.7
Chemical processing machine setters, operators, and tenders	63	19.9
Crushing, grinding, polishing, mixing, and blending workers	111	14.1
Cutting workers	83	9.9
Inspectors, testers, sorters, samplers, and weighers	690	11.0
Jewelers and precious stone and metal workers	59	1.6
Medical, dental, and ophthalmic laboratory technicians	92	8.4
Packaging and filling machine operators and tenders	318	20.4
Painting workers	191	6.1
Photographic process workers and processing machine operators	59	14.8
Paper goods machine setters, operators, and tenders	53	15.4
Helpers—production workers	64	12.4
Transportation and material-moving occupations	8,491	16.1
Supervisors, transportation and material-moving workers	220	15.4
Aircraft pilots and flight engineers	118	1.7
Bus drivers	602	24.4
Driver sales workers and truck drivers	3,276	13.4
Taxi drivers and chauffeurs	277	28.7
Railroad conductors and yardmasters	58	15.5
Parking lot attendants	77	15.5
Service station attendants	120	8.7
Crane and tower operators	65	18.3
Dredge, excavating, and loading machine operators	80	5.4
Industrial truck and tractor operators	530	22.2
Cleaners of vehicles and equipment	316	16.2
Laborers and freight, stock, and material movers, hand	1,797	17.0
Machine feeders and offbearers	55	22.6
Packers and packagers, hand	432	14.1
Refuse and recyclable material collectors	81	29.5

Note: (–) means percentage is less than 0.05.
Source: Bureau of Labor Statistics, 2004 Current Population Survey, Internet site http://www.bls.gov/cps/home.htm

Table 3.65 Black Workers by Industry, 2004

(total number of employed people aged 16 or older in the civilian labor force, number and percent distribution of employed blacks, and black share of total, by industry, 2004; numbers in thousands)

	total	black number	black percent distribution	black share of total
Total employed	**139,252**	**14,909**	**100.0%**	**10.7%**
Agriculture, forestry, fishing, hunting	2,232	53	0.4	2.4
Mining	539	26	0.2	4.8
Construction	10,768	630	4.2	5.9
Manufacturing	16,484	1,556	10.4	9.4
Durable goods	10,329	844	5.7	8.2
Nondurable goods	6,155	712	4.8	11.6
Wholesale and retail trade	20,869	1,965	13.2	9.4
Wholesale trade	4,600	341	2.3	7.4
Retail trade	16,269	1,623	10.9	10.0
Transportation and utilities	7,013	1,087	7.3	15.5
Information	3,463	375	2.5	10.8
Financial activities	9,969	982	6.6	9.9
Professional and business services	14,108	1,239	8.3	8.8
Educational and health services	28,719	3,973	26.6	13.8
Leisure and hospitality	11,820	1,256	8.4	10.6
Other services	6,903	732	4.9	10.6
Other services, except private households	6,124	628	4.2	10.3
Private households	779	103	0.7	13.2
Public administration	6,365	1,035	6.9	16.3

Source: Bureau of Labor Statistics, 2004 Current Population Survey, Internet site http://www.bls.gov/cps/home.htm; calculations by New Strategist

Table 3.66 Black Workers by Full-Time and Part-Time Status, Age, and Sex, 2004

(number and percent distribution of employed blacks aged 16 or older by age, employment status, and sex, 2004; numbers in thousands)

	men			women		
	total	full-time	part-time	total	full-time	part-time
Total employed blacks	**6,913**	**6,177**	**736**	**7,996**	**6,597**	**1,399**
Aged 16 to 19	231	87	144	289	85	204
Aged 20 to 24	739	567	172	833	561	272
Aged 25 to 54	5,094	4,794	300	5,912	5,199	713
Aged 55 or older	848	729	119	963	753	210
PERCENT DISTRIBUTION BY EMPLOYMENT STATUS						
Total employed blacks	**100.0%**	**89.4%**	**10.6%**	**100.0%**	**82.5%**	**17.5%**
Aged 16 to 19	100.0	37.7	62.3	100.0	29.4	70.6
Aged 20 to 24	100.0	76.7	23.3	100.0	67.3	32.7
Aged 25 to 54	100.0	94.1	5.9	100.0	87.9	12.1
Aged 55 or older	100.0	86.0	14.0	100.0	78.2	21.8
PERCENT DISTRIBUTION BY AGE						
Total employed blacks	**100.0%**	**100.0%**	**100.0%**	**100.0%**	**100.0%**	**100.0%**
Aged 16 to 19	3.3	1.4	19.6	3.6	1.3	14.6
Aged 20 to 24	10.7	9.2	23.4	10.4	8.5	19.4
Aged 25 to 54	73.7	77.6	40.8	73.9	78.8	51.0
Aged 55 or older	12.3	11.8	16.2	12.0	11.4	15.0

Source: Bureau of Labor Statistics, 2004 Current Population Survey, Internet site http://www.bls.gov/cps/home.htm; calculations by New Strategist

Table 3.67 Black Workers by Educational Attainment, 2004

(number of total people and blacks aged 25 or older in the civilian labor force, black labor force participation rate, distribution of blacks in labor force, and black share of total labor force, by educational attainment, 2004; numbers in thousands)

		black labor force			
	total labor force	number	participation rate	percent distribution	share of total
Total aged 25 or older	**125,133**	**13,950**	**67.0%**	**100.0%**	**11.1%**
Not a high school graduate	12,470	1,568	39.6	11.2	12.6
High school graduate only	37,834	5,044	67.6	36.2	13.3
Some college	22,298	2,964	73.9	21.2	13.3
Associate's degree	12,141	1,268	77.4	9.1	10.4
Bachelor's degree or more	40,390	3,106	82.9	22.3	7.7

Source: Bureau of Labor Statistics, 2004 Current Population Survey, Internet site http://www.bls.gov/cps/home.htm; calculations by New Strategist

Table 3.68 Black Workers by Job Tenure and Sex, 2004

(total number of employed black wage and salary workers aged 16 or older and percent distribution by tenure with current employer, by sex, 2004; numbers in thousands)

	total	men	women
Total black workers, number	**13,401**	**6,097**	**7,304**
Total black workers, percent	**100.0%**	**100.0%**	**100.0%**
12 months or less	24.5	23.4	25.4
13 to 23 months	5.8	5.4	6.1
2 years	6.6	7.0	6.2
3 to 4 years	19.2	18.7	19.6
5 to 9 years	20.5	20.6	20.4
10 to 14 years	8.4	9.3	7.6
15 to 19 years	5.9	5.8	6.1
20 or more years	9.1	9.8	8.5

Note: The black population includes only those identifying themselves as black alone.
Source: Bureau of Labor Statistics, 2004 Current Population Survey, Internet site http://www.bls.gov/cps/home.htm; calculations by New Strategist

Table 3.69 Black Households by Number of Earners, 2004

(number of total households, number and percent distribution of black households and black share of total, by number of earners per household, 2004; numbers in thousands)

	total	black number	black percent distribution	black share of total
Total households	**112,000**	**13,969**	**100.0%**	**12.5%**
No earners	23,932	3,167	22.7	13.2
One earner	40,769	6,254	44.8	15.3
Two or more earners	47,299	4,548	32.6	9.6
Two earners	37,917	3,773	27.0	10.0
Three earners	6,998	653	4.7	9.3
Four or more earners	2,384	122	0.9	5.1
Average number of earners per household	1.36	1.22	–	–

Note: Blacks include those identifying themselves as being black alone and those identifying themselves as being black in combination with another race. (–) means not applicable.
Source: Bureau of the Census, 2004 Current Population Survey, Annual Social and Economic Supplement, Internet site http://pubdb3.census.gov/macro/032004/hhinc/new01_000.htm; calculations by New Strategist

Table 3.70   **Black Married Couples by Labor Force Status of Husband and Wife, 2003**

(number and percent distribution of black married couples aged 20 or older by age of householder and labor force status of husband and wife, 2003; numbers in thousands)

	total	husband and/or wife in labor force			neither husband nor wife in labor force
		husband and wife	husband only	wife only	
Total black couples	**4,261**	**2,514**	**690**	**427**	**630**
Aged 20 to 24	113	62	43	4	4
Aged 25 to 29	275	199	60	10	6
Aged 30 to 34	483	357	99	15	13
Aged 35 to 39	527	404	80	33	10
Aged 40 to 44	598	473	76	35	15
Aged 45 to 54	1,052	728	167	98	57
Aged 55 to 64	636	248	118	144	127
Aged 65 or older	577	41	47	89	399
Total black couples	**100.0%**	**59.0%**	**16.2%**	**10.0%**	**14.8%**
Aged 20 to 24	100.0	54.9	38.1	3.5	3.5
Aged 25 to 29	100.0	72.4	21.8	3.6	2.2
Aged 30 to 34	100.0	73.9	20.5	3.1	2.7
Aged 35 to 39	100.0	76.7	15.2	6.3	1.9
Aged 40 to 44	100.0	79.1	12.7	5.9	2.5
Aged 45 to 54	100.0	69.2	15.9	9.3	5.4
Aged 55 to 64	100.0	39.0	18.6	22.6	20.0
Aged 65 or older	100.0	7.1	8.1	15.4	69.2

Note: Blacks include those identifying themselves as being black alone and those identifying themselves as being black in combination with another race.
Source: Bureau of the Census, America's Families and Living Arrangements: 2003, detailed tables, Internet site http://www .censusgov/population/www/socdemo/hh-fam/cps2003.html; calculations by New Strategist

Table 3.71 Black Minimum Wage Workers by Sex, 2004

(number and percent distribution of total and black wage and salary workers aged 16 or older paid hourly rates and those paid at or below minimum wage, by sex, 2004; numbers in thousands)

	total paid hourly rates	at or below minimum wage		
		total	at $5.15/hour	below $5.15/hour
Total workers aged 16 or older	**73,939**	**2,003**	**520**	**1,483**
Black workers aged 16 or older	9,417	228	99	128
Black men	4,243	89	40	49
Black women	5,174	138	59	79
PERCENT DISTRIBUTION BY RACE/SEX				
Total workers aged 16 or older	**100.0%**	**100.0%**	**100.0%**	**100.0%**
Black workers aged 16 or older	12.7	11.4	19.0	8.6
Black men	5.7	4.4	7.7	3.3
Black women	7.0	6.9	11.3	5.3
PERCENT DISTRIBUTION BY WAGE STATUS				
Total workers aged 16 or older	**100.0%**	**2.7%**	**0.7%**	**2.0%**
Black workers aged 16 or older	100.0	2.4	1.1	1.4
Black men	100.0	2.1	0.9	1.2
Black women	100.0	2.7	1.1	1.5

Source: Bureau of Labor Statistics, 2004 Current Population Survey, Internet site http://www.bls.gov/cps/home.htm

Table 3.72 Black Multiple Job Holders by Sex, 2004

(total number of employed people aged 16 or older who hold more than one job, number and percent of blacks holding more than one job, and black share of total, by sex, 2004; numbers in thousands)

	total	black multiple job holders		
		number	percent	share of total
Total multiple job holders	**7,473**	**705**	**4.7%**	**9.4%**
Men	3,835	360	5.2	9.4
Women	3,638	345	4.3	9.5

Source: Bureau of Labor Statistics, 2004 Current Population Survey, Internet site http://www.bls.gov/cps/home.htm

Table 3.73 Union Representation of Black Workers by Sex, 2004

(number of employed black wage and salary workers aged 16 or older, number and percent represented by unions, and median weekly earnings of those working full-time by union representation status, by sex, 2004; number in thousands)

	total	men	women
Total employed blacks	**14,090**	**6,409**	**7,681**
Number represented by unions	2,355	1,185	1,170
Percent represented by unions	16.7%	18.5%	15.2%
Median weekly earnings of black full-time workers	**$525**	**$569**	**$505**
Black workers represented by unions	651	679	621
Black workers not represented by unions	507	534	490

Note: Workers represented by unions are either members of a labor union or similar employee association or workers who report no union affiliation but whose jobs are covered by a union or an employee association contract.
Source: Bureau of Labor Statistics, 2004 Current Population Survey, Internet site http://www.bls.gov/cps/home.htm

Table 3.74 Journey to Work by Black Workers, 2003

(number and percent distribution of black workers aged 16 or older by principal means of transportation to work, travel time from home to work, distance from home to work, and departure time to work, 2003; numbers in thousands)

	number	percent distribution
Total black workers	**12,209**	**100.0%**
Principal means of transportation to work		
Drives self	8,908	73.0
Carpool	1,237	10.1
Mass transportation	1,364	11.2
Taxicab	29	0.2
Bicycle or motorcycle	22	0.2
Walks only	381	3.1
Other means	96	0.8
Works at home	172	1.4
Travel time from home to work		
Less than 15 minutes	3,338	27.3
15 to 29 minutes	4,359	35.7
30 to 44 minutes	2,118	17.3
45 to 59 minutes	922	7.6
1 hour or more	655	5.4
Works at home	172	1.4
No fixed place of work	645	5.3
Median travel time (minutes)	23	–
Distance from home to work		
Less than 1 mile	447	3.7
1 to 4 miles	2,460	20.1
5 to 9 miles	2,610	21.4
10 to 19 miles	3,412	27.9
20 to 29 miles	1,454	11.9
30 miles or more	1,010	8.3
Works at home	172	1.4
No fixed place of work	645	5.3
Median distance (miles)	11	–
Departure time to work		
12:00 a.m. to 2:59 a.m.	91	0.7
3:00 a.m. to 5:59 a.m.	1,246	10.2
6:00 a.m. to 6:59 a.m.	2,009	16.5
7:00 a.m. to 7:29 a.m.	1,585	13.0
7:30 a.m. to 7:59 a.m.	1,390	11.4
8:00 a.m. to 8:29 a.m.	1,187	9.7
8:30 a.m. to 8:59 a.m.	479	3.9
9:00 a.m. to 9:59 a.m.	549	4.5
10:00 a.m. to 3:59 p.m.	1,429	11.7
4:00 p.m. to 11:59 p.m.	992	8.1

Note: Departure time numbers may not add to total because not reported is not shown and those who work at home are not included. (–) means not applicable.
Source: Bureau of the Census, American Housing Survey for the United States: 2003, *Current Housing Reports, Internet site http://www.census.gov/hhes/www/ahs.html; calculations by New Strategist*

Table 3.75 Black Labor Force Projections, 2002 and 2012

(number and percent of total people and blacks aged 16 or older in the civilian labor force by sex, 2002 and 2012; percent change in number and percentage point change in rate, 2002–12; numbers in thousands)

	2002	2012	percent change
NUMBER			
Total labor force	**144,863**	**162,269**	**12.0%**
Black labor force	16,564	19,765	19.3
Total men in labor force	**77,500**	**85,252**	**10.0**
Black men in labor force	7,793	9,318	19.6
Total women in labor force	**67,363**	**77,017**	**14.3**
Black women in labor force	8,771	10,447	19.1

	2002	2012	percentage point change
PARTICIPATION RATE			
Total people	**66.6%**	**67.2%**	**0.6**
Total blacks	64.8	66.3	1.5
Total men	**74.1**	**73.1**	**–1.0**
Black men	68.4	69.1	0.7
Total women	**59.6**	**61.6**	**2.0**
Black women	61.8	64.0	2.2

Note: Blacks include only those who identified their race as black alone.
Source: Bureau of Labor Statistics, "Labor Force Projections to 2012: The graying of the U.S. workforce," Monthly Labor Review, February 2004, Internet site http://www.bls.gov/opub/mlr/2004/02/art3exc.htm; calculations by New Strategist

Table 3.76 Black Labor Force Entrants and Leavers, 2002 to 2012

(number and percent distribution of total people and blacks aged 16 or older in the civilian labor force in 2002 and 2012, and number and percent distribution of entrants, leavers, and stayers, 2002–12; numbers in thousands)

	2002 labor force	2002 to 2012 entrants	2002 to 2012 leavers	2002 to 2012 stayers	2012 labor force
NUMBER					
Total labor force	**144,863**	**40,461**	**23,055**	**121,808**	**162,269**
Black labor force	16,564	5,538	2,338	14,226	19,765
PERCENT DISTRIBUTION					
Total labor force	**100.0%**	**100.0%**	**100.0%**	**100.0%**	**100.0%**
Black labor force	11.4	13.7	10.1	11.7	12.2

Source: Bureau of Labor Statistics, "Labor Force Projections to 2012: The graying of the U.S. workforce," Monthly Labor Review, February 2004, Internet site http://www.bls.gov/opub/mlr/2004/02/art3exc.htm; calculations by New Strategist

Black Married Couples Only Slightly Outnumber Female-Headed Families

The 14 million households headed by blacks in 2004 accounted for 12 percent of the nation's 112 million households. Black households are more diverse than those of other racial and ethnic groups. Married couples head 30 percent of black households, while female-headed families account for 29 percent.

The average black household is home to 2.64 people versus 2.57 people in the average household. Thirty-seven percent of black households include children under age 18. Fifty percent of black married couples have children at home, as do 65 percent of black female-headed families. A 37 percent minority of black children live with both parents, while 50 percent live with their mother only. Only 5 percent of black children live with only their father.

Nine percent of black men are currently divorced, but a larger 19 percent have ever divorced. The proportion of black men who have ever divorced peaks at 40 percent among those in their fifties. Among black women, 14 percent are currently divorced and 20 percent have ever divorced. The percentage of black women who have ever divorced peaks at 38 percent in the 50-to-59 age group.

■ Because so many black households are female-headed families, the poorest household type, the income of black households is well below average.

Black households are diverse

(percent distribution of black households by household type, 2004)

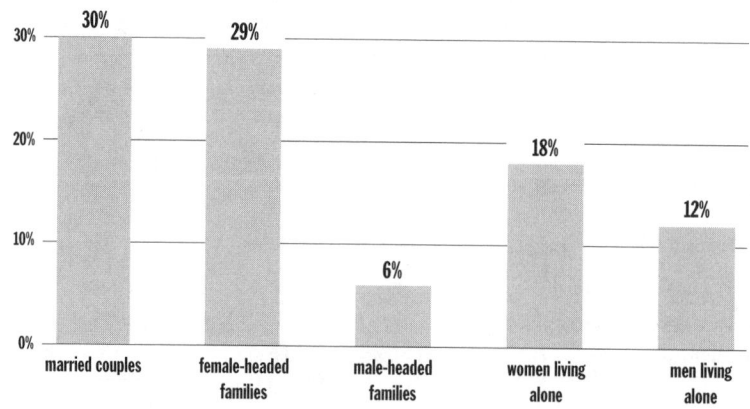

Table 3.77 Black Households by Age of Householder, 2004

(number of total households, number and percent distribution of black households, and black share of total, by age of householder, 2004, numbers in thousands)

		black		
	total	number	percent distribution	share of total
Total households	**112,000**	**13,969**	**100.0%**	**12.5%**
Under age 25	6,610	1,133	8.1	17.1
Aged 25 to 29	8,737	1,299	9.3	14.9
Aged 30 to 34	10,421	1,526	10.9	14.6
Aged 35 to 39	10,997	1,485	10.6	13.5
Aged 40 to 44	12,225	1,661	11.9	13.6
Aged 45 to 49	12,360	1,607	11.5	13.0
Aged 50 to 54	10,777	1,346	9.6	12.5
Aged 55 to 59	9,504	1,003	7.2	10.6
Aged 60 to 64	7,320	824	5.9	11.3
Aged 65 or older	23,048	2,085	14.9	9.0

Note: Blacks include those identifying themselves as being of the race alone and those identifying themselves as being of the race in combination with other races.
Source: Bureau of the Census, 2004 Current Population Survey Annual Social and Economic Supplement, Internet site http:// pubdb3.census.gov/macro/032004/hhinc/toc.htm; calculations by New Strategist

Table 3.78 Black Households by Household Type, 2004

(number of total households, number and percent distribution of black households, and black share of total, by type, 2004; numbers in thousands)

		black		
	total	number	percent distribution	share of total
TOTAL HOUSEHOLDS	**112,000**	**13,969**	**100.0%**	**12.5%**
Family households	**76,217**	**9,129**	**65.4**	**12.0**
Married couples	57,719	4,259	30.5	7.4
Female householder, no spouse present	13,781	4,067	29.1	29.5
Male householder, no spouse present	4,717	804	5.8	17.0
Nonfamily households	**35,783**	**4,840**	**34.6**	**13.5**
Female householder	19,647	2,768	19.8	14.1
Living alone	17,024	2,505	17.9	14.7
Male householder	16,136	2,072	14.8	12.8
Living alone	12,562	1,733	12.4	13.8

Note: Blacks include those identifying themselves as being of the race alone and those identifying themselves as being of the race in combination with other races.
Source: Bureau of the Census, 2004 Current Population Survey Annual Social and Economic Supplement, Internet site http:// pubdb3.census.gov/macro/032004/hhinc/toc.htm; calculations by New Strategist

Table 3.79　Black Households by Age of Householder and Household Type, 2004

(number and percent distribution of black households by age of householder and household type, 2004; numbers in thousands)

| | total | family households | | | nonfamily households | | | |
| | | | | | female-headed | | male-headed | |
		married couples	female hh, no spouse present	male hh, no spouse present	total	living alone	total	living alone
Total black households	**13,969**	**4,259**	**4,067**	**804**	**2,768**	**2,505**	**2,072**	**1,733**
Under age 25	1,133	120	491	139	233	170	151	101
Aged 25 to 34	2,824	770	1,059	188	394	350	413	311
Aged 35 to 44	3,146	1,107	1,068	172	342	300	456	393
Aged 45 to 54	2,953	1,044	741	161	569	503	438	374
Aged 55 to 64	1,827	670	330	84	454	430	289	258
Aged 65 or older	2,085	548	378	60	776	752	324	297

PERCENT DISTRIBUTION BY HOUSEHOLD TYPE

Total black households	**100.0%**	**30.5%**	**29.1%**	**5.8%**	**19.8%**	**17.9%**	**14.8%**	**12.4%**
Under age 25	100.0	10.6	43.3	12.3	20.6	15.0	13.3	8.9
Aged 25 to 34	100.0	27.3	37.5	6.7	14.0	12.4	14.6	11.0
Aged 35 to 44	100.0	35.2	33.9	5.5	10.9	9.5	14.5	12.5
Aged 45 to 54	100.0	35.4	25.1	5.5	19.3	17.0	14.8	12.7
Aged 55 to 64	100.0	36.7	18.1	4.6	24.8	23.5	15.8	14.1
Aged 65 or older	100.0	26.3	18.1	2.9	37.2	36.1	15.5	14.2

PERCENT DISTRIBUTION BY AGE

Total black households	**100.0%**	**100.0%**	**100.0%**	**100.0%**	**100.0%**	**100.0%**	**100.0%**	**100.0%**
Under age 25	8.1	2.8	12.1	17.3	8.4	6.8	7.3	5.8
Aged 25 to 34	20.2	18.1	26.0	23.4	14.2	14.0	19.9	17.9
Aged 35 to 44	22.5	26.0	26.3	21.4	12.4	12.0	22.0	22.7
Aged 45 to 54	21.1	24.5	18.2	20.0	20.6	20.1	21.1	21.6
Aged 55 to 64	13.1	15.7	8.1	10.4	16.4	17.2	13.9	14.9
Aged 65 or older	14.9	12.9	9.3	7.5	28.0	30.0	15.6	17.1

Note: Blacks include those identifying themselves as being of the race alone and those identifying themselves as being of the race in combination with other races.
Source: Bureau of the Census, 2004 Current Population Survey Annual Social and Economic Supplement, Internet site http:// pubdb3.census.gov/macro/032004/hhinc/toc.htm; calculations by New Strategist

Table 3.80 Black Households by Size, 2004

(number of total households, number and percent distribution of black households, and black share of total, by size, 2004; numbers in thousands)

		black		
	total	number	percent distribution	share of total
Total households	**112,000**	**13,969**	**100.0%**	**12.5%**
One person	29,586	4,238	30.3	14.3
Two people	37,366	3,771	27.0	10.1
Three people	17,968	2,505	17.9	13.9
Four people	16,065	1,954	14.0	12.2
Five people	7,150	901	6.4	12.6
Six people	2,476	360	2.6	14.5
Seven or more people	1,388	241	1.7	17.4
Average number of persons per household	2.57	2.64	–	–

Note: Blacks include those identifying themselves as being of the race alone and those identifying themselves as being of the race in combination with other races. (–) means not applicable.
Source: Bureau of the Census, 2004 Current Population Survey Annual Social and Economic Supplement, Internet site http:// pubdb3.census.gov/macro/032004/hhinc/toc.htm; calculations by New Strategist

Table 3.81 Blacks Living Alone by Sex and Age, 2004

(total number of blacks aged 15 or older, number and percent living alone, and percent distribution of blacks living alone, by sex and age, 2004; numbers in thousands)

| | total | living alone | | |
		number	percent distribution	share of total
Total blacks	**27,457**	**4,238**	**100.0%**	**15.4%**
Under age 25	6,167	271	6.4	4.4
Aged 25 to 34	5,190	661	15.6	12.7
Aged 35 to 44	5,530	693	16.4	12.5
Aged 45 to 54	4,812	877	20.7	18.2
Aged 55 to 64	2,825	688	16.2	24.4
Aged 65 to 74	1,631	501	11.8	30.7
Aged 75 or older	1,302	548	12.9	42.1
Black men	**12,354**	**1,733**	**100.0**	**14.0**
Under age 25	2,989	101	5.8	3.4
Aged 25 to 34	2,324	311	17.9	13.4
Aged 35 to 44	2,496	393	22.7	15.7
Aged 45 to 54	2,177	374	21.6	17.2
Aged 55 to 64	1,245	258	14.9	20.7
Aged 65 to 74	665	161	9.3	24.2
Aged 75 or older	459	136	7.8	29.6
Black women	**15,103**	**2,505**	**100.0**	**16.6**
Under age 25	3,178	170	6.8	5.3
Aged 25 to 34	2,866	350	14.0	12.2
Aged 35 to 44	3,034	300	12.0	9.9
Aged 45 to 54	2,634	503	20.1	19.1
Aged 55 to 64	1,581	430	17.2	27.2
Aged 65 to 74	966	340	13.6	35.2
Aged 75 or older	843	412	16.4	48.9

Note: Blacks include those identifying themselves as being of the race alone and those identifying themselves as being of the race in combination with other races.
Source: Bureau of the Census, 2004 Current Population Survey Annual Social and Economic Supplement, Internet site http:// pubdb3.census.gov/macro/032004/hhinc/toc.htm; calculations by New Strategist

Table 3.82 Black Households by Age of Householder, Type of Household, And Presence of Children, 2003

(number and percent distribution of black households by age of householder, type of household, and presence of own children under age 18, and average age of householder, 2003; numbers in thousands)

	all households		married couples		female-headed families		male-headed families	
	total	with children	total	with children	total	with children	total	with children
Total black households	**13,778**	**5,069**	**4,268**	**2,139**	**4,069**	**2,630**	**791**	**299**
Under age 25	1,193	494	120	90	486	367	194	37
Aged 25 to 29	1,214	739	275	214	528	500	77	24
Aged 30 to 34	1,481	919	483	392	526	480	82	47
Aged 35 to 39	1,524	976	527	430	550	495	77	51
Aged 40 to 44	1,663	887	598	432	555	394	92	62
Aged 45 to 49	1,541	616	581	338	427	238	78	40
Aged 50 to 54	1,295	240	471	133	289	89	65	18
Aged 55 to 64	1,794	166	636	94	340	54	69	18
Aged 65 or older	2,073	31	577	16	367	12	58	4
Average age of householder	45.9	36.8	47.2	39.2	41.2	34.8	38.9	38.5

PERCENT OF HOUSEHOLDS WITH CHILDREN BY TYPE

	all households		married couples		female-headed families		male-headed families	
Total black households	**100.0%**	**36.8%**	**100.0%**	**50.1%**	**100.0%**	**64.6%**	**100.0%**	**37.8%**
Under age 25	100.0	41.4	100.0	75.0	100.0	75.5	100.0	19.1
Aged 25 to 29	100.0	60.9	100.0	77.8	100.0	94.7	100.0	31.2
Aged 30 to 34	100.0	62.1	100.0	81.2	100.0	91.3	100.0	57.3
Aged 35 to 39	100.0	64.0	100.0	81.6	100.0	90.0	100.0	66.2
Aged 40 to 44	100.0	53.3	100.0	72.2	100.0	71.0	100.0	67.4
Aged 45 to 49	100.0	40.0	100.0	58.2	100.0	55.7	100.0	51.3
Aged 50 to 54	100.0	18.5	100.0	28.2	100.0	30.8	100.0	27.7
Aged 55 to 64	100.0	9.3	100.0	14.8	100.0	15.9	100.0	26.1
Aged 65 or older	100.0	1.5	100.0	2.8	100.0	3.3	100.0	6.9

Note: Blacks include those identifying themselves as being of the race alone and those identifying themselves as being of the race in combination with other races.
Source: Bureau of the Census, America's Families and Living Arrangements, 2003 Current Population Survey Annual Social and Economic Supplement; Internet site http://www.census.gov/population/www/socdemo/hh-fam/cps2003.html; calculations by New Strategist

Table 3.83 Living Arrangements of Black Children, 2003

(number of total children under age 18, number and percent distribution of black children, and black share of total, by living arrangement, 2003; numbers in thousands)

	total	black number	black percent distribution	black share of total
Total children	**73,001**	**12,187**	**100.0%**	**16.7%**
Living with both parents	49,903	4,468	36.7	9.0
Living with mother only	16,771	6,129	50.3	36.5
Never married	7,006	3,672	30.1	52.4
Divorced or separated	9,102	2,297	18.8	25.2
Widowed	663	160	1.3	24.1
Living with father only	3,324	565	4.6	17.0
Never married	1,172	274	2.2	23.4
Divorced or separated	1,979	259	2.1	13.1
Widowed	173	32	0.3	18.5
Living with neither parent	3,004	1,024	8.4	34.1

Note: Blacks include those identifying themselves as being of the race alone and those identifying themselves as being of the race in combination with one or more other races.
Source: Bureau of the Census, America's Families and Living Arrangements, 2003 Current Population Survey Annual Social and Economic Supplement; Internet site http://www.census.gov/population/www/socdemo/hh-fam/cps2003.html; calculations by New Strategist

Table 3.84 Black Men by Living Arrangement and Age, 2003

(number and percent distribution of black men aged 15 or older by living arrangement and age, 2003; numbers in thousands)

	total	under 25	25 to 29	30 to 34	35 to 44	45 to 54	55 to 64	65 or older
Total black men	**12,159**	**2,930**	**1,104**	**1,217**	**2,489**	**2,111**	**1,166**	**1,140**
Married-couple householder or spouse	4,362	96	259	490	1,133	1,055	700	628
Other householder	2,891	372	260	288	639	567	344	420
Male family householder	791	194	77	82	169	143	69	58
Living alone	1,753	114	136	162	393	371	241	335
Living with nonrelatives	347	64	47	44	77	53	34	27
Nonhouseholder	4,907	2,462	585	439	717	489	122	92
Child of householder	2,994	1,889	324	206	355	184	34	2
Other relative of householder	1,025	378	143	71	165	149	50	69
Living with nonrelatives	888	195	118	162	197	156	38	21
Total black men	**100.0%**	**100.0%**	**100.0%**	**100.0%**	**100.0%**	**100.0%**	**100.0%**	**100.0%**
Married-couple householder or spouse	35.9	3.3	23.5	40.3	45.5	50.0	60.0	55.1
Other householder	23.8	12.7	23.6	23.7	25.7	26.9	29.5	36.8
Male family householder	6.5	6.6	7.0	6.7	6.8	6.8	5.9	5.1
Living alone	14.4	3.9	12.3	13.3	15.8	17.6	20.7	29.4
Living with nonrelatives	2.9	2.2	4.3	3.6	3.1	2.5	2.9	2.4
Nonhouseholder	40.4	84.0	53.0	36.1	28.8	23.2	10.5	8.1
Child of householder	24.6	64.5	29.3	16.9	14.3	8.7	2.9	0.2
Other relative of householder	8.4	12.9	13.0	5.8	6.6	7.1	4.3	6.1
Living with nonrelatives	7.3	6.7	10.7	13.3	7.9	7.4	3.3	1.8

Note: Blacks include those identifying themselves as being of the race alone and those identifying themselves as being of the race in combination with other races.
Source: Bureau of the Census, America's Families and Living Arrangements, 2003 Current Population Survey Annual Social and Economic Supplement; Internet site http://www.census.gov/population/www/socdemo/hh-fam/cps2003.html; calculations by New Strategist

Table 3.85 Black Women by Living Arrangement and Age, 2003

(number and percent distribution of black women aged 15 or older by living arrangement and age, 2003; numbers in thousands)

	total	under 25	25 to 29	30 to 34	35 to 44	45 to 54	55 to 64	65 or older
Total black women	**14,884**	**3,112**	**1,372**	**1,473**	**3,062**	**2,560**	**1,522**	**1,781**
Married-couple householder or spouse	4,179	168	323	527	1,187	1,005	529	439
Other householder	6,619	701	679	709	1,422	1,217	815	1,075
Female family householder	4,069	486	528	526	1,105	716	340	367
Living alone	2,318	156	126	161	286	444	454	692
Living with nonrelatives	232	59	25	22	31	57	21	16
Nonhouseholder	4,086	2,244	370	237	452	336	178	269
Child of householder	2,281	1,701	201	106	155	83	30	3
Other relative of householder	1,249	381	82	57	191	177	120	244
Living with nonrelatives	556	162	87	74	106	76	28	22
Total black women	**100.0%**	**100.0%**	**100.0%**	**100.0%**	**100.0%**	**100.0%**	**100.0%**	**100.0%**
Married-couple householder or spouse	28.1	5.4	23.5	35.8	38.8	39.3	34.8	24.6
Other householder	44.5	22.5	49.5	48.1	46.4	47.5	53.5	60.4
Female family householder	27.3	15.6	38.5	35.7	36.1	28.0	22.3	20.6
Living alone	15.6	5.0	9.2	10.9	9.3	17.3	29.8	38.9
Living with nonrelatives	1.6	1.9	1.8	1.5	1.0	2.2	1.4	0.9
Nonhouseholder	27.5	72.1	27.0	16.1	14.8	13.1	11.7	15.1
Child of householder	15.3	54.7	14.7	7.2	5.1	3.2	2.0	0.2
Other relative of householder	8.4	12.2	6.0	3.9	6.2	6.9	7.9	13.7
Living with nonrelatives	3.7	5.2	6.3	5.0	3.5	3.0	1.8	1.2

Note: Blacks include those identifying themselves as being of the race alone and those identifying themselves as being of the race in combination with other races.
Source: Bureau of the Census, America's Families and Living Arrangements, 2003 Current Population Survey Annual Social and Economic Supplement; Internet site http://www.census.gov/population/www/socdemo/hh-fam/cps2003.html; calculations by New Strategist

Table 3.86 Marital Status of Black Men by Age, 2003

(number and percent distribution of black men aged 18 or older by age and current marital status, 2003; numbers in thousands)

	total	never married	married, spouse present	married, spouse absent	separated	divorced	widowed
Total black men	**11,150**	**4,619**	**4,472**	**206**	**469**	**1,054**	**329**
Aged 18 to 19	561	559	1	0	2	0	0
Aged 20 to 24	1,361	1,239	105	5	8	4	0
Aged 25 to 29	1,104	745	273	17	29	38	2
Aged 30 to 34	1,217	591	503	9	43	69	2
Aged 35 to 39	1,211	461	526	27	75	120	3
Aged 40 to 44	1,278	396	633	36	57	146	9
Aged 45 to 49	1,159	267	589	33	63	180	27
Aged 50 to 54	952	174	488	25	65	186	14
Aged 55 to 64	1,166	108	710	28	80	188	52
Aged 65 to 74	717	50	421	12	36	94	104
Aged 75 to 84	348	26	193	13	11	25	80
Aged 85 or older	75	4	30	3	0	3	36
Total black men	**100.0%**	**41.4%**	**40.1%**	**1.8%**	**4.2%**	**9.5%**	**3.0%**
Aged 18 to 19	100.0	99.6	0.2	0.0	0.4	0.0	0.0
Aged 20 to 24	100.0	91.0	7.7	0.4	0.6	0.3	0.0
Aged 25 to 29	100.0	67.5	24.7	1.5	2.6	3.4	0.2
Aged 30 to 34	100.0	48.6	41.3	0.7	3.5	5.7	0.2
Aged 35 to 39	100.0	38.1	43.4	2.2	6.2	9.9	0.2
Aged 40 to 44	100.0	31.0	49.5	2.8	4.5	11.4	0.7
Aged 45 to 49	100.0	23.0	50.8	2.8	5.4	15.5	2.3
Aged 50 to 54	100.0	18.3	51.3	2.6	6.8	19.5	1.5
Aged 55 to 64	100.0	9.3	60.9	2.4	6.9	16.1	4.5
Aged 65 to 74	100.0	7.0	58.7	1.7	5.0	13.1	14.5
Aged 75 to 84	100.0	7.5	55.5	3.7	3.2	7.2	23.0
Aged 85 or older	100.0	5.3	40.0	4.0	0.0	4.0	48.0

Note: Blacks include those who identified themselves as being black alone and those who identified themselves as being black in combination with other races.
Source: Bureau of the Census, America's Families and Living Arrangements, 2003 Current Population Survey Annual Social and Economic Supplement; Internet site http://www.census.gov/population/www/socdemo/hh-fam/cps2003.html

Table 3.87   Marital Status of Black Women by Age, 2003

(number and percent distribution of black women aged 18 or older by age and current marital status, 2003; numbers in thousands)

	total	never married	married, spouse present	married, spouse absent	separated	divorced	widowed
Total black women	**13,909**	**5,201**	**4,289**	**310**	**807**	**1,902**	**1,400**
Aged 18 to 19	596	581	10	5	0	0	0
Aged 20 to 24	1,542	1,328	169	13	20	8	4
Aged 25 to 29	1,372	867	341	27	85	42	9
Aged 30 to 34	1,473	655	538	46	89	132	12
Aged 35 to 39	1,510	477	610	42	118	243	22
Aged 40 to 44	1,552	417	607	53	140	287	48
Aged 45 to 49	1,392	326	558	34	124	303	48
Aged 50 to 54	1,168	188	463	36	72	316	93
Aged 55 to 64	1,522	225	545	28	95	372	257
Aged 65 to 74	972	87	324	19	52	141	350
Aged 75 to 84	618	41	116	7	9	53	391
Aged 85 or older	191	8	9	1	2	5	166
Total black women	**100.0%**	**37.4%**	**30.8%**	**2.2%**	**5.8%**	**13.7%**	**10.1%**
Aged 18 to 19	100.0	97.5	1.7	0.8	0.0	0.0	0.0
Aged 20 to 24	100.0	86.1	11.0	0.8	1.3	0.5	0.3
Aged 25 to 29	100.0	63.2	24.9	2.0	6.2	3.1	0.7
Aged 30 to 34	100.0	44.5	36.5	3.1	6.0	9.0	0.8
Aged 35 to 39	100.0	31.6	40.4	2.8	7.8	16.1	1.5
Aged 40 to 44	100.0	26.9	39.1	3.4	9.0	18.5	3.1
Aged 45 to 49	100.0	23.4	40.1	2.4	8.9	21.8	3.4
Aged 50 to 54	100.0	16.1	39.6	3.1	6.2	27.1	8.0
Aged 55 to 64	100.0	14.8	35.8	1.8	6.2	24.4	16.9
Aged 65 to 74	100.0	9.0	33.3	2.0	5.3	14.5	36.0
Aged 75 to 84	100.0	6.6	18.8	1.1	1.5	8.6	63.3
Aged 85 or older	100.0	4.2	4.7	0.5	1.0	2.6	86.9

Note: Blacks include those who identified themselves as being black alone and those who identified themselves as being black in combination with other races.
Source: Bureau of the Census, America's Families and Living Arrangements, 2003 Current Population Survey Annual Social and Economic Supplement; Internet site http://www.census.gov/population/www/socdemo/hh-fam/cps2003.html

Table 3.88 Marital History of Black Men by Age, 2001

(number of black men aged 15 or older and percent distribution by marital history and age, 2001; numbers in thousands)

	total	15 to 19	20 to 24	25 to 29	30 to 34	35 to 39	40 to 49	50 to 59	60 to 69	70 or older
Total black men, number	**11,554**	**1,507**	**1,223**	**1,088**	**1,149**	**1,229**	**2,314**	**1,505**	**844**	**695**
Total black men, percent	**100.0%**	**100.0%**	**100.0%**	**100.0%**	**100.0%**	**100.0%**	**100.0%**	**100.0%**	**100.0%**	**100.0%**
Never married	43.3	99.2	89.2	60.6	41.5	34.0	25.1	11.6	10.2	3.1
Ever married	56.7	0.8	10.8	39.4	58.5	66.0	74.9	88.4	89.8	96.9
Married once	44.3	0.8	10.8	38.0	51.6	56.3	57.5	62.0	60.8	72.3
Still married	31.4	0.3	9.9	31.2	39.3	42.5	38.2	41.9	43.6	43.8
Married twice	10.0	0.0	0.0	1.4	6.7	8.1	13.6	21.9	21.7	20.0
Still married	7.3	0.0	0.0	1.4	5.9	7.0	11.0	13.4	16.5	10.8
Married three or more times	2.3	0.0	0.0	0.0	0.1	1.6	3.8	4.5	7.2	4.7
Still married	1.5	0.0	0.0	0.0	0.1	1.3	3.2	2.2	3.5	3.1
Ever divorced	18.8	0.2	0.0	4.2	13.7	18.2	28.1	40.2	35.1	26.9
Currently divorced	9.2	0.2	0.0	2.8	7.6	9.5	14.0	21.1	12.9	10.3
Ever widowed	3.7	0.0	0.3	0.0	0.2	1.0	1.9	4.2	10.9	30.4
Currently widowed	2.9	0.0	0.3	0.0	0.0	0.6	1.0	3.2	8.6	25.2

Source: Bureau of the Census, Number, Timing, and Duration of Marriages and Divorces: 2001, *Current Population Report P70-97, 2005; Internet site http://www.census.gov/population/www/socdemo/marr-div.html*

Table 3.89 Marital History of Black Women by Age, 2001

(number of black women aged 15 or older and percent distribution by marital history and age, 2001; numbers in thousands)

	total	15 to 19	20 to 24	25 to 29	30 to 34	35 to 39	40 to 49	50 to 59	60 to 69	70 or older
Total black women, number	**14,284**	**1,520**	**1,465**	**1,358**	**1,437**	**1,526**	**2,804**	**1,842**	**1,215**	**1,117**
Total black women, percent	**100.0%**	**100.0%**	**100.0%**	**100.0%**	**100.0%**	**100.0%**	**100.0%**	**100.0%**	**100.0%**	**100.0%**
Never married	41.9	97.9	82.6	59.4	49.5	34.0	27.9	14.4	10.4	6.8
Ever married	58.1	2.1	17.4	40.6	50.5	66.0	72.1	85.6	89.6	93.2
Married once	46.9	1.8	17.4	37.7	44.3	55.5	56.0	66.1	67.5	72.4
Still married	25.1	0.9	14.7	26.7	32.2	35.0	31.1	32.1	27.7	17.3
Married twice	9.8	0.3	0.0	2.8	6.3	9.2	13.7	16.3	19.3	18.1
Still married	5.0	0.3	0.0	2.3	5.1	5.4	8.1	9.6	7.5	2.7
Married three or more times	1.5	0.0	0.0	0.2	0.0	1.2	2.5	3.2	2.8	2.8
Still married	0.8	0.0	0.0	0.0	0.0	0.6	1.9	1.6	0.9	0.5
Ever divorced	20.1	0.3	0.6	8.4	12.4	24.6	30.4	38.2	30.3	23.7
Currently divorced	11.9	0.0	0.6	6.1	6.4	16.3	18.5	24.1	15.7	10.4
Ever widowed	10.5	0.0	0.3	0.8	1.1	0.9	5.1	13.1	32.0	60.7
Currently widowed	9.7	0.0	0.3	0.5	0.8	0.9	4.1	11.1	30.2	59.1

Source: Bureau of the Census, Number, Timing, and Duration of Marriages and Divorces: 2001, *Current Population Report P70-97, 2005; Internet site http://www.census.gov/population/www/socdemo/marr-div.html*

The Black Population Numbers Nearly 40 Million

The number of blacks in the U.S. population grew 5 percent between 2000 and 2004, from 37 million to 39 million—a figure that includes blacks identifying themselves as being black alone and those identifying themselves as being black in combination with one or more other races. Blacks account for 13 percent of the U.S. population, slightly less than the 14 percent share held by Hispanics. Hispanics will increasingly outnumber blacks because the Hispanic population is growing much faster.

More than half of blacks (54 percent) live in the South, where they account for 20 percent of the population. In Mississippi, 37 percent of the population is black, as are 33 percent of the residents of Louisiana and 30 percent of those in South Carolina. No single state is home to more than 10 percent of the black population.

Among metropolitan areas, blacks account for the largest share of the population in Jackson, Mississippi (47 percent). Blacks account for more than one-third of the populations of eight other metropolitan areas: Augusta, GA; Fayetteville, NC; Macon, GA; Montgomery, AL; New Orleans, LA; Savannah, GA; Shreveport, LA; and Tallahassee, FL.

■ Unlike Hispanics or Asians, most of whom live in only a few states, blacks are an important segment of the population throughout the country. This relatively even distribution adds to their cultural influence and political power.

Blacks are a substantial share of the population in every region

(black share of population by region, 2004)

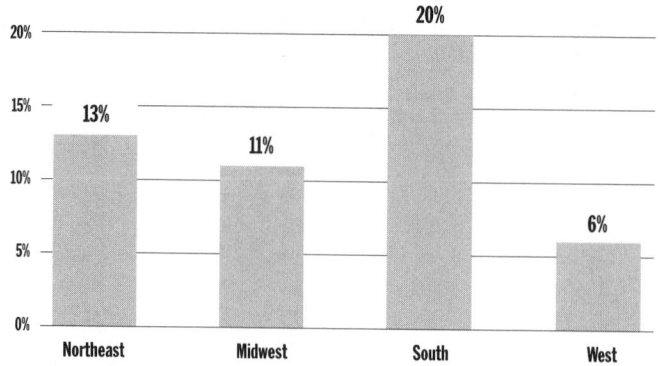

Table 3.90 Blacks by Racial Identification, 2000 and 2004

(total number of people, and number and percent distribution of blacks by racial identification, 2000 and 2004; percent change, 2000–04)

	2004		2000		
	number	percent distribution	number	percent distribution	percent change 2000–04
Total people	**293,655,404**	**100.0%**	**282,192,162**	**100.0%**	**4.1%**
Black alone or in combination with one or more other races	39,232,489	13.4	37,231,182	13.2	5.4
Black alone	37,502,320	12.8	35,812,716	12.7	4.7
Black in combination	1,730,169	0.6	1,418,466	0.5	22.0

Source: Bureau of the Census, National Population Estimates, Internet site http://www.census.gov/popest/national/asrh/ NC-EST2004-srh.html; calculations by New Strategist

Table 3.91 Blacks by Hispanic Origin, 2004

(number and percent distribution of blacks by Hispanic origin and racial identification, 2004)

	black alone or in combination		black alone	
	number	percent distribution	number	percent distribution
Total blacks	**39,232,489**	**100.0%**	**37,502,320**	**100.0%**
Not Hispanic	37,426,144	95.4	35,963,702	95.9
Hispanic	1,806,345	4.6	1,538,618	4.1

Source: Bureau of the Census, National Population Estimates, Internet site http://www.census.gov/popest/national/asrh/ NC-EST2004-asrh.html; calculations by New Strategist

Table 3.92 Blacks in the Armed Forces, 2003

(number and percent distribution of blacks aged 18 or older who are in the armed forces or who are veterans, by sex and age, 2003)

	total	in armed forces	veteran
Total blacks aged 18 or older	**23,471,387**	**99,495**	**2,320,561**
Men	10,423,618	78,124	2,040,667
Aged 18 to 64	9,355,822	78,124	1,557,366
Aged 65 or older	1,067,796	0	483,301
Women	13,047,769	21,371	279,894
Aged 18 to 64	11,319,744	21,371	266,338
Aged 65 or older	1,728,025	0	13,556
Total blacks aged 18 or older	**100.0%**	**0.4%**	**9.9%**
Men	100.0	0.7	19.6
Aged 18 to 64	100.0	0.8	16.6
Aged 65 or older	100.0	0.0	45.3
Women	100.0	0.2	2.1
Aged 18 to 64	100.0	0.2	2.4
Aged 65 or older	100.0	0.0	0.8

Note: Blacks are those identifying themselves as being black alone.
Source: Bureau of the Census, 2003 American Community Survey, Internet site http://factfinder.census.gov/servlet/ DatasetMainPageServlet?_program=ACS&_lang=en&_ts=; calculations by New Strategist

Table 3.93 Blacks by Age, 2000 and 2004

(number of blacks by age, 2000 and 2004; percent change, 2000–04)

	2004	2000	percent change 2000–04
Total blacks	**39,232,489**	**37,231,182**	**5.4%**
Under age 5	3,404,107	3,242,091	5.0
Aged 5 to 9	3,282,706	3,549,175	−7.5
Aged 10 to 14	3,641,535	3,422,857	6.4
Aged 15 to 19	3,353,557	3,163,098	6.0
Aged 20 to 24	3,195,719	2,860,217	11.7
Aged 25 to 29	2,797,467	2,720,688	2.8
Aged 30 to 34	2,804,522	2,777,344	1.0
Aged 35 to 39	2,813,882	2,970,657	−5.3
Aged 40 to 44	2,963,780	2,842,102	4.3
Aged 45 to 49	2,717,696	2,390,713	13.7
Aged 50 to 54	2,242,845	1,908,275	17.5
Aged 55 to 59	1,688,751	1,363,018	23.9
Aged 60 to 64	1,228,417	1,104,070	11.3
Aged 65 to 69	973,482	911,822	6.8
Aged 70 to 74	767,856	752,919	2.0
Aged 75 to 79	593,674	569,457	4.3
Aged 80 to 84	405,895	358,417	13.2
Aged 85 or older	356,598	324,262	10.0
Aged 18 or older	26,854,689	25,119,146	6.9
Aged 18 to 24	4,499,824	4,125,402	9.1
Aged 65 or older	3,097,505	2,916,877	6.2

Note: Blacks are those identifying themselves as being of the race alone and those identifying themselves as being of the race in combination with one or more other races.
Source: Bureau of the Census, National Population Estimates, Internet site http://www.census.gov/popest/national/asrh/ NC-EST2004-asrh.html; calculations by New Strategist

Table 3.94   Black Share of Total Population by Age, 2004

(total number of people, number and percent distribution of blacks, and black share of total, by age, 2004)

	total	black number	black percent distribution	black share of total
Total people	**293,655,404**	**39,232,489**	**100.0%**	**13.4%**
Under age 5	20,071,268	3,404,107	8.7	17.0
Aged 5 to 9	19,605,572	3,282,706	8.4	16.7
Aged 10 to 14	21,145,156	3,641,535	9.3	17.2
Aged 15 to 19	20,729,802	3,353,557	8.5	16.2
Aged 20 to 24	20,971,302	3,195,719	8.1	15.2
Aged 25 to 29	19,560,906	2,797,467	7.1	14.3
Aged 30 to 34	20,471,032	2,804,522	7.1	13.7
Aged 35 to 39	21,052,318	2,813,882	7.2	13.4
Aged 40 to 44	23,056,334	2,963,780	7.6	12.9
Aged 45 to 49	22,122,629	2,717,696	6.9	12.3
Aged 50 to 54	19,496,176	2,242,845	5.7	11.5
Aged 55 to 59	16,489,501	1,688,751	4.3	10.2
Aged 60 to 64	12,589,423	1,228,417	3.1	9.8
Aged 65 to 69	9,956,467	973,482	2.5	9.8
Aged 70 to 74	8,507,005	767,856	2.0	9.0
Aged 75 to 79	7,410,757	593,674	1.5	8.0
Aged 80 to 84	5,560,125	405,895	1.0	7.3
Aged 85 or older	4,859,631	356,598	0.9	7.3
Aged 18 or older	220,377,406	26,854,689	68.5	12.2
Aged 18 to 24	29,245,102	4,499,824	11.5	15.4
Aged 65 or older	36,293,985	3,097,505	7.9	8.5

Note: Blacks are those identifying themselves as being of the race alone and those identifying themselves as being of the race in combination with one or more other races.
Source: Bureau of the Census, National Population Estimates, Internet site http://www.census.gov/popest/national/asrh/ NC-EST2004-sa.html; calculations by New Strategist

Table 3.95 Blacks by Age and Sex, 2004

(number of blacks by age and sex, and sex ratio by age, 2004)

	total	females	males	sex ratio
Total blacks	**39,232,489**	**20,519,704**	**18,712,785**	**91**
Under age 5	3,404,107	1,676,707	1,727,400	103
Aged 5 to 9	3,282,706	1,617,017	1,665,689	103
Aged 10 to 14	3,641,535	1,794,905	1,846,630	103
Aged 15 to 19	3,353,557	1,655,549	1,698,008	103
Aged 20 to 24	3,195,719	1,594,805	1,600,914	100
Aged 25 to 29	2,797,467	1,447,489	1,349,978	93
Aged 30 to 34	2,804,522	1,475,268	1,329,254	90
Aged 35 to 39	2,813,882	1,485,974	1,327,908	89
Aged 40 to 44	2,963,780	1,576,211	1,387,569	88
Aged 45 to 49	2,717,696	1,452,763	1,264,933	87
Aged 50 to 54	2,242,845	1,215,805	1,027,040	84
Aged 55 to 59	1,688,751	926,641	762,110	82
Aged 60 to 64	1,228,417	690,425	537,992	78
Aged 65 to 69	973,482	558,703	414,779	74
Aged 70 to 74	767,856	457,462	310,394	68
Aged 75 to 79	593,674	372,846	220,828	59
Aged 80 to 84	405,895	265,834	140,061	53
Aged 85 or older	356,598	255,300	101,298	40
Aged 18 or older	26,854,689	14,419,069	12,435,620	86
Aged 18 to 24	4,499,824	2,238,348	2,261,476	101
Aged 65 or older	3,097,505	1,910,145	1,187,360	62

Note: Blacks are those identifying themselves as being of the race alone and those identifying themselves as being of the race in combination with one or more other races. The sex ratio is the number of males divided by the number of females multiplied by 100.
Source: Bureau of the Census, National Population Estimates, Internet site http://www.census.gov/popest/national/asrh/NC-EST2004-sa.html; calculations by New Strategist

Table 3.96 Blacks by Age, 2000 to 2020

(number and percent distribution of blacks by age, 2000 to 2020, percent change, 2000–10 and 2010–20; numbers in thousands)

	2000	2010	2020	percent change 2000–10	percent change 2010–20
Total blacks	**35,818**	**40,454**	**45,365**	**12.9%**	**12.1%**
Under age 5	2,927	3,332	3,540	13.8	6.2
Aged 5 to 9	3,299	3,127	3,515	–5.2	12.4
Aged 10 to 14	3,243	2,976	3,386	–8.2	13.8
Aged 15 to 19	3,029	3,396	3,235	12.1	–4.7
Aged 20 to 24	2,757	3,357	3,109	21.7	–7.4
Aged 25 to 29	2,632	3,130	3,516	18.9	12.3
Aged 30 to 34	2,713	2,856	3,469	5.3	21.5
Aged 35 to 39	2,907	2,701	3,207	–7.1	18.8
Aged 40 to 44	2,785	2,724	2,879	–2.2	5.7
Aged 45 to 49	2,349	2,844	2,663	21.1	–6.4
Aged 50 to 54	1,876	2,657	2,620	41.6	–1.4
Aged 55 to 59	1,342	2,176	2,661	62.2	22.3
Aged 60 to 64	1,087	1,674	2,401	54.0	43.5
Aged 65 or older	2,873	3,505	5,164	22.0	47.3

Note: Blacks are those identifying themselves as being black alone.
Source: Bureau of the Census, Internet site http://www.census.gov/ipc/www/usinterimproj/; calculations by New Strategist

Table 3.97 Blacks by Region, 2000 and 2004

(number of blacks by region, 2000 and 2004; percent change, 2000–04)

	2004	2000	percent change 2000–04
Total blacks	**39,232,489**	**36,419,434**	**7.7%**
Northeast	7,192,004	6,556,909	9.7
Midwest	7,177,716	6,838,669	5.0
South	21,000,623	19,528,231	7.5
West	3,862,146	3,495,625	10.5

Note: Blacks are those identifying themselves as being of the race alone and those identifying themselves as being of the race in combination with one or more other races. Total number of blacks in 2000 differs from the total in previous tables of this chapter because these are census counts from April 1, 2000, whereas the others are population estimates.
Source: Bureau of the Census, 2000 Census, Internet site http://factfinder.census.gov/servlet/DatasetMainPageServlet?_program=DEC&_lang=en&_ts=; and State Population Estimates, Internet site http://www.census.gov/popest/states/asrh/SC-EST2004-04.html; calculations by New Strategist

Table 3.98 Black Share of the Total Population by Region, 2004

(total number of people, number and percent distribution of blacks, and black share of total, by region, 2004)

		black		
	total	number	percent distribution	share of total
Total people	**293,655,404**	**39,232,489**	**100.0%**	**13.4%**
Northeast	54,571,147	7,192,004	18.3	13.2
Midwest	65,729,852	7,177,716	18.3	10.9
South	105,944,965	21,000,623	53.5	19.8
West	67,409,440	3,862,146	9.8	5.7

Note: Blacks are those identifying themselves as being of the race alone and those identifying themselves as being of the race in combination with one or more other races.
Source: Bureau of the Census, State Population Estimates, Internet site http://www.census.gov/popest/states/asrh/SC-EST2004-04.html; calculations by New Strategist

Table 3.99 Blacks by State, 2000 and 2004

(number of blacks by state, 2000 and 2004; percent change, 2000–04)

	2004	2000	percent change 2000–04
Total blacks	**39,232,489**	**36,419,434**	**7.7%**
Alabama	1,208,591	1,168,998	3.4
Alaska	29,611	27,147	9.1
Arizona	234,244	185,599	26.2
Arkansas	443,869	427,152	3.9
California	2,684,307	2,513,041	6.8
Colorado	217,919	190,717	14.3
Connecticut	378,936	339,078	11.8
Delaware	175,936	157,152	12.0
District of Columbia	324,626	350,455	−7.4
Florida	2,823,769	2,471,730	14.2
Georgia	2,658,068	2,393,425	11.1
Hawaii	41,327	33,343	23.9
Idaho	11,304	8,127	39.1
Illinois	1,989,954	1,937,671	2.7
Indiana	581,896	538,015	8.2
Iowa	80,053	72,512	10.4
Kansas	179,432	170,610	5.2
Kentucky	329,778	311,878	5.7
Louisiana	1,508,792	1,468,317	2.8
Maine	13,058	9,553	36.7
Maryland	1,661,509	1,525,036	8.9
Massachusetts	479,798	398,479	20.4
Michigan	1,518,585	1,474,613	3.0
Minnesota	245,143	202,972	20.8
Mississippi	1,077,480	1,041,708	3.4
Missouri	690,392	655,377	5.3
Montana	5,635	4,441	26.9
Nebraska	83,251	75,833	9.8
Nevada	195,028	150,508	29.6
New Hampshire	16,329	12,218	33.6
New Jersey	1,319,953	1,211,750	8.9
New Mexico	52,840	42,412	24.6
New York	3,529,241	3,234,165	9.1
North Carolina	1,903,862	1,776,283	7.2
North Dakota	6,076	5,372	13.1
Ohio	1,441,383	1,372,501	5.0
Oklahoma	297,799	284,766	4.6
Oregon	83,868	72,647	15.4

(continued)

	2004	2000	percent change 2000–04
Pennsylvania	1,373,946	1,289,123	6.6%
Rhode Island	75,352	58,051	29.8
South Carolina	1,250,132	1,200,901	4.1
South Dakota	8,283	6,687	23.9
Tennessee	1,014,565	953,349	6.4
Texas	2,720,123	2,493,057	9.1
Utah	30,387	24,382	24.6
Vermont	5,391	4,492	20.0
Virginia	1,537,156	1,441,207	6.7
Washington	269,915	238,398	13.2
West Virginia	64,568	62,817	2.8
Wisconsin	353,268	326,506	8.2
Wyoming	5,761	4,863	18.5

Note: Blacks are those identifying themselves as being of the race alone and those identifying themselves as being of the race in combination with one or more other races. Total number of blacks in 2000 differs from the total in previous tables of this chapter because these are census counts from April 1, 2000, whereas the others are population estimates.
Source: Bureau of the Census, 2000 Census, Internet site http://factfinder.census.gov/servlet/DatasetMainPageServlet?_ program=DEC&_lang=en&_ts=; and State Population Estimates, Internet site http://www.census.gov/popest/states/asrh/ SC-EST2004-04.html; calculations by New Strategist

Table 3.100 Black Share of Total Population by State, 2004

(total number of people, number and percent distribution of blacks, and black share of total, by state, 2004)

	total	black number	black percent distribution	black share of total
Total people	**293,655,404**	**39,232,489**	**100.0%**	**13.4%**
Alabama	4,530,182	1,208,591	3.1	26.7
Alaska	655,435	29,611	0.1	4.5
Arizona	5,743,834	234,244	0.6	4.1
Arkansas	2,752,629	443,869	1.1	16.1
California	35,893,799	2,684,307	6.8	7.5
Colorado	4,601,403	217,919	0.6	4.7
Connecticut	3,503,604	378,936	1.0	10.8
Delaware	830,364	175,936	0.4	21.2
District of Columbia	553,523	324,626	0.8	58.6
Florida	17,397,161	2,823,769	7.2	16.2
Georgia	8,829,383	2,658,068	6.8	30.1
Hawaii	1,262,840	41,327	0.1	3.3
Idaho	1,393,262	11,304	0.0	0.8
Illinois	12,713,634	1,989,954	5.1	15.7
Indiana	6,237,569	581,896	1.5	9.3
Iowa	2,954,451	80,053	0.2	2.7
Kansas	2,735,502	179,432	0.5	6.6
Kentucky	4,145,922	329,778	0.8	8.0
Louisiana	4,515,770	1,508,792	3.8	33.4
Maine	1,317,253	13,058	0.0	1.0
Maryland	5,558,058	1,661,509	4.2	29.9
Massachusetts	6,416,505	479,798	1.2	7.5
Michigan	10,112,620	1,518,585	3.9	15.0
Minnesota	5,100,958	245,143	0.6	4.8
Mississippi	2,902,966	1,077,480	2.7	37.1
Missouri	5,754,618	690,392	1.8	12.0
Montana	926,865	5,635	0.0	0.6
Nebraska	1,747,214	83,251	0.2	4.8
Nevada	2,334,771	195,028	0.5	8.4
New Hampshire	1,299,500	16,329	0.0	1.3
New Jersey	8,698,879	1,319,953	3.4	15.2
New Mexico	1,903,289	52,840	0.1	2.8
New York	19,227,088	3,529,241	9.0	18.4
North Carolina	8,541,221	1,903,862	4.9	22.3
North Dakota	634,366	6,076	0.0	1.0
Ohio	11,459,011	1,441,383	3.7	12.6
Oklahoma	3,523,553	297,799	0.8	8.5
Oregon	3,594,586	83,868	0.2	2.3

(continued)

	total	black		
		number	percent distribution	share of total
Pennsylvania	12,406,292	1,373,946	3.5%	11.1%
Rhode Island	1,080,632	75,352	0.2	7.0
South Carolina	4,198,068	1,250,132	3.2	29.8
South Dakota	770,883	8,283	0.0	1.1
Tennessee	5,900,962	1,014,565	2.6	17.2
Texas	22,490,022	2,720,123	6.9	12.1
Utah	2,389,039	30,387	0.1	1.3
Vermont	621,394	5,391	0.0	0.9
Virginia	7,459,827	1,537,156	3.9	20.6
Washington	6,203,788	269,915	0.7	4.4
West Virginia	1,815,354	64,568	0.2	3.6
Wisconsin	5,509,026	353,268	0.9	6.4
Wyoming	506,529	5,761	0.0	1.1

Note: Blacks are those identifying themselves as being of the race alone and those identifying themselves as being of the race in combination with one or more other races.
Source: Bureau of the Census, State Population Estimates, Internet site http://www.census.gov/popest/states/asrh/ SC-EST2004-04.html; calculations by New Strategist

Table 3.101   Blacks by Metropolitan Area, 2004

(total number of people, number of blacks, and black share of total, for selected metropolitan areas, 2004)

	total population	black number	black share of total
Albany–Schenectady–Troy, NY MSA	860,976	52,886	6.1%
Allentown–Bethlehem–Easton, PA MSA	650,230	26,138	4.0
Anchorage, AK MSA	265,176	15,246	5.7
Appleton–Oshkosh–Neenah, WI MSA	359,711	94	0.0
Atlanta, GA MSA	4,477,579	1,344,191	30.0
Augusta–Aiken, GA–SC MSA	476,167	166,379	34.9
Austin–San Marcos, TX MSA	1,373,125	101,352	7.4
Bakersfield, CA MSA	702,855	35,781	5.1
Baton Rouge, LA MSA	610,743	198,141	32.4
Beaumont–Port Arthur, TX MSA	366,244	89,383	24.4
Biloxi–Gulfport–Pascagoula, MS MSA	363,966	83,390	22.9
Binghamton, NY MSA	239,012	7,650	3.2
Birmingham, AL MSA	929,694	284,359	30.6
Boise City, ID MSA	479,284	2,571	0.5
Boston–Worcester–Lawrence, MA–NH–ME–CT CMSA	5,749,197	324,914	5.7
Brownsville–Harlingen–San Benito, TX MSA	367,603	641	0.2
Buffalo–Niagara Falls, NY MSA	1,119,037	132,998	11.9
Canton–Massillon, OH MSA	400,919	30,870	7.7
Charleston–North Charleston, SC MSA	563,828	169,389	30.0
Chicago, IL PMSA	8,388,723	1,522,241	18.1
Cleveland–Akron, OH CMSA	2,878,475	492,171	17.1
Colorado Springs, CO MSA	539,225	36,427	6.8
Columbia, SC MSA	543,126	179,733	33.1
Corpus Christi, TX MSA	381,422	12,664	3.3
Dallas–Fort Worth, TX CMSA	5,676,651	773,715	13.6
Davenport–Moline–Rock Island, IA–IL MSA	350,022	25,285	7.2
Dayton–Springfield, OH MSA	916,635	131,756	14.4
Daytona Beach, FL MSA	530,553	50,477	9.5
Denver–Boulder–Greeley, CO CMSA*	2,514,628	135,812	5.4
Des Moines, IA MSA	476,699	17,837	3.7
Detroit–Ann Arbor–Flint, MI CMSA	5,437,277	1,141,028	21.0
El Paso, TX MSA	700,225	18,111	2.6
Erie, PA MSA	267,426	17,664	6.6
Eugene–Springfield, OR MSA	324,176	3,982	1.2
Fayetteville, NC MSA	287,220	105,364	36.7
Fayetteville–Springdale–Rogers, AR MSA	345,308	3,677	1.1
Fort Myers–Cape Coral, FL MSA	508,634	36,522	7.2
Fort Pierce–Port St. Lucie, FL MSA	358,578	41,642	11.6
Fort Wayne, IN MSA	506,545	36,428	7.2

(continued)

	total population	black number	black share of total
Fresno, CA MSA	978,274	42,440	4.3%
Grand Rapids–Muskegon–Holland, MI MSA	1,102,729	74,923	6.8
Greensboro–Winston-Salem–High Point, NC MSA	1,283,261	256,641	20.0
Greenville–Spartanburg–Anderson, SC MSA	976,678	164,892	16.9
Harrisburg–Lebanon–Carlisle, PA MSA	617,676	45,872	7.4
Hartford, CT MSA	1,163,367	112,746	9.7
Hickory–Morganton–Lenoir, NC MSA	345,590	22,968	6.6
Honolulu, HI MSA	868,751	19,324	2.2
Houston–Galveston–Brazoria, TX CMSA*	4,794,384	791,877	16.5
Huntsville, AL MSA	354,936	74,160	20.9
Indianapolis, IN MSA	1,664,412	224,554	13.5
Jackson, MS MSA	443,275	207,040	46.7
Jacksonville, FL MSA	1,182,453	258,543	21.9
Johnson City–Kingsport–Bristol, TN–VA MSA	482,047	5,354	1.1
Kalamazoo–Battle Creek, MI MSA	441,059	38,441	8.7
Kansas City, MO–KS MSA	1,823,092	226,670	12.4
Killeen–Temple, TX MSA	298,933	55,951	18.7
Knoxville, TN MSA	707,617	43,492	6.1
Lafayette, LA MSA	386,812	113,022	29.2
Lakeland–Winter Haven, FL MSA	511,565	71,699	14.0
Lancaster, PA MSA	473,104	11,138	2.4
Lansing–East Lansing, MI MSA	436,485	38,769	8.9
Lexington, KY MSA	478,625	45,317	9.5
Lincoln, NE MSA	249,670	5,681	2.3
Little Rock–North Little Rock, AR MSA	593,032	133,249	22.5
Los Angeles–Riverside–Orange County, CA CMSA	17,199,115	1,209,778	7.0
Lubbock, TX MSA	240,721	16,698	6.9
Macon, GA MSA	329,432	126,421	38.4
Madison, WI MSA	437,843	19,732	4.5
McAllen–Edinburg–Mission, TX MSA	651,974	0	0.0
Melbourne–Titusville–Palm Bay, FL MSA	509,248	46,084	9.0
Miami–Fort Lauderdale, FL CMSA	4,051,442	879,532	21.7
Milwaukee–Waukesha, WI PMSA	1,483,023	238,751	16.1
Mobile, AL MSA	547,153	152,187	27.8
Modesto, CA MSA	490,860	15,775	3.2
Montgomery, AL MSA	323,220	127,424	39.4
Nashville, TN MSA	1,275,212	198,373	15.6
New Orleans, LA MSA	1,313,694	500,357	38.1
New York–Northern New Jersey–Long Island, NY–NJ–CT–PA CMSA*	20,345,959	3,564,702	17.5
Oklahoma City, OK MSA	1,095,252	109,394	10.0
Orlando, FL MSA	1,831,212	269,704	14.7
Pensacola, FL MSA	410,542	68,739	16.7
Peoria–Pekin, IL MSA	337,020	31,503	9.3
Philadelphia–Wilmington–Atlantic City, PA–NJ–DE–MD CMSA*	5,383,262	1,048,248	19.5

(continued)

		black	
	total population	number	share of total
Pittsburgh, PA MSA	2,260,551	190,341	8.4%
Portland, ME MSA	248,827	3,739	1.5
Providence–Fall River–Warwick, RI–MA MSA	1,165,549	60,570	5.2
Provo–Orem, UT MSA	395,173	1,832	0.5
Raleigh–Durham–Chapel Hill, NC MSA	1,278,372	287,097	22.5
Reading, PA MSA	378,456	10,840	2.9
Reno, NV MSA	375,344	8,331	2.2
Richmond–Petersburg, VA MSA	1,013,399	302,950	29.9
Rochester, NY MSA	1,057,917	107,949	10.2
Rockford, IL MSA	382,901	27,813	7.3
Sacramento, CA PMSA	1,803,160	144,767	8.0
Saginaw–Bay City–Midland, MI MSA	393,837	36,575	9.3
St. Louis, MO–IL MSA	2,620,334	486,142	18.6
Salinas, CA MSA	392,192	8,953	2.3
Salt Lake City–Ogden, UT MSA	1,384,041	16,328	1.2
San Antonio, TX MSA	1,683,872	108,448	6.4
San Diego, CA MSA	2,833,275	149,657	5.3
San Francisco–Oakland–San Jose, CA CMSA	6,951,260	457,505	6.6
San Luis Obispo–Atascadero–Paso Robles, CA MSA	238,502	1,934	0.8
Santa Barbara–Santa Maria–Lompoc, CA MSA	385,238	6,754	1.8
Sarasota–Bradenton, FL MSA	639,438	38,557	6.0
Savannah, GA MSA	299,920	105,276	35.1
Scranton–Wilkes-Barre–Hazleton, PA MSA	587,557	8,437	1.4
Seattle–Tacoma–Bremerton, WA CMSA*	3,184,924	163,072	5.1
Shreveport–Bossier City, LA MSA	387,312	142,614	36.8
South Bend, IN MSA	252,944	34,085	13.5
Spokane, WA MSA	420,592	6,651	1.6
Springfield, MA MSA	560,472	38,919	6.9
Springfield, MO MSA	332,918	4,137	1.2
Stockton–Lodi, CA MSA	632,143	47,534	7.5
Syracuse, NY MSA	707,901	45,257	6.4
Tallahassee, FL MSA	274,945	93,034	33.8
Tampa–St. Petersburg–Clearwater, FL MSA	2,537,586	274,994	10.8
Toledo, OH MSA	598,283	77,966	13.0
Tucson, AZ MSA	885,025	26,073	2.9
Tulsa, OK MSA	810,062	73,084	9.0
Utica–Rome, NY MSA	282,844	6,517	2.3
Visalia–Tulare–Porterville, CA MSA	395,493	6,581	1.7
West Palm Beach–Boca Raton, FL MSA	1,223,206	186,340	15.2
Wichita, KS MSA	546,308	38,785	7.1
York, PA MSA	393,426	13,937	3.5
Youngstown–Warren, OH MSA	566,597	57,854	10.2

Population figures are for only part of the metropolitan area.
Note: Some metropolitan areas are not shown because data are not available. Blacks are those identifying themselves as being black alone. For the definition of CMSA, MSA, and PMSA, see the glossary.
Source: Bureau of the Census, 2004 American Community Survey, Internet site http://factfinder.census.gov/servlet/ DatasetMainPageServlet?_program=ACS&_lang=en&_ts=; calculations by New Strategist

Black Households Spend 70 Percent as Much as the Average Household

The nation's 14 million black households spent an average of $28,708 in 2003, according to the Consumer Expenditure Survey. While the annual spending of black households (called consumer units by the Bureau of Labor Statistics) is less than the $40,817 spent by the average household, on some items blacks spend more.

One reason for the lower spending of blacks is that married couples head relatively few black households, and married couples are the most affluent household type. Nevertheless, blacks spend more than average on items such as pork, poultry, and fish. They are also big spenders on footwear, accounting for 18 percent of consumer spending on shoes. Telephone spending by blacks is 7 percent above average. Black households spend 11 to 28 percent more than average on children's clothes.

■ Because the incomes of blacks are rising faster than those of other racial and ethnic groups, black spending should approach or exceed the average on many more items in the years ahead.

Black households spend less than the average household

(average annual spending of total and black consumer units, 2003)

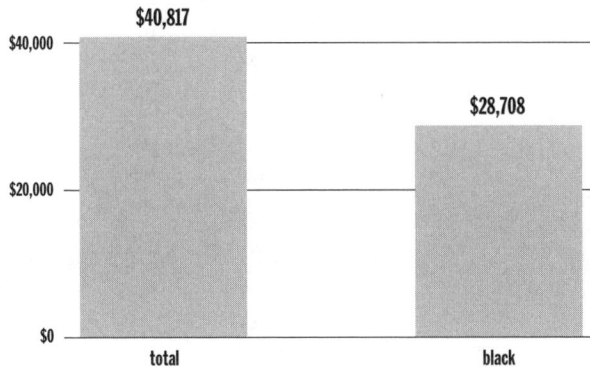

Table 3.102 Spending of Households Headed by Blacks, 2003

(average annual spending of total consumer units (CU), and average annual, indexed, and market share of spending of consumer units headed by blacks, by product and service category, 2003)

	total consumer units	black consumer units average spending	black consumer units indexed spending	black consumer units market share
Number of consumer units (000s)	115,356	13,743	–	11.9%
Persons per consumer unit	2.5	2.6	–	–
Average income before taxes	$51,128	$34,485	67	8.0
Average annual spending	**40,817**	**28,708**	**70**	**8.4**
FOOD	**5,340**	**4,007**	**75**	**8.9**
Food at home	**3,129**	**2,664**	**85**	**10.1**
Cereals and bakery products	442	370	84	10.0
Cereals and cereal products	150	139	93	11.0
Bakery products	292	231	79	9.4
Meats, poultry, fish, and eggs	825	882	107	12.7
Beef	246	232	94	11.2
Pork	171	206	120	14.4
Other meats	102	90	88	10.5
Poultry	145	177	122	14.5
Fish and seafood	124	140	113	13.5
Eggs	37	36	97	11.6
Dairy products	328	227	69	8.2
Fresh milk and cream	127	94	74	8.8
Other dairy products	201	133	66	7.9
Fruits and vegetables	535	438	82	9.8
Fresh fruits	171	128	75	8.9
Fresh vegetables	172	133	77	9.2
Processed fruits	108	100	93	11.0
Processed vegetables	84	77	92	10.9
Other food at home	999	747	75	8.9
Sugar and other sweets	119	93	78	9.3
Fats and oils	86	80	93	11.1
Miscellaneous foods	490	360	73	8.8
Nonalcoholic beverages	268	202	75	9.0
Food prepared by CU on trips	36	12	33	4.0
Food away from home	**2,211**	**1,343**	**61**	**7.2**
ALCOHOLIC BEVERAGES	**391**	**169**	**43**	**5.1**
HOUSING	**13,432**	**10,622**	**79**	**9.4**
Shelter	**7,887**	**6,117**	**78**	**9.2**
Owned dwellings	5,263	3,042	58	6.9
Mortgage interest and charges	2,954	1,848	63	7.5
Property taxes	1,344	748	56	6.6
Maintenance, repair, insurance, other expenses	965	446	46	5.5
Rented dwellings	2,179	2,946	135	16.1
Other lodging	445	129	29	3.5
Utilities, fuels, and public services	**2,811**	**2,910**	**104**	**12.3**
Natural gas	392	465	119	14.1
Electricity	1,028	1,094	106	12.7

(continued)

	total consumer units	black consumer units		
		average spending	indexed spending	market share
Fuel oil and other fuels	$110	$46	42	5.0%
Telephone	956	1,027	107	12.8
Water and other public services	326	278	85	10.2
Household services	**707**	**453**	**64**	**7.6**
Personal services	294	247	84	10.0
Other household services	414	206	50	5.9
Housekeeping supplies	**529**	**357**	**67**	**8.0**
Laundry and cleaning supplies	132	137	104	12.4
Other household products	263	168	64	7.6
Postage and stationery	133	53	40	4.7
Household furnishings and equipment	**1,497**	**785**	**52**	**6.2**
Household textiles	113	61	54	6.4
Furniture	401	234	58	7.0
Floor coverings	52	11	21	2.5
Major appliances	196	118	60	7.2
Small appliances, misc. housewares	88	43	49	5.8
Miscellaneous household equipment	648	318	49	5.8
APPAREL AND RELATED SERVICES	**1,640**	**1,601**	**98**	**11.6**
Men and boys	**372**	**292**	**78**	**9.4**
Men, aged 16 or older	282	181	64	7.6
Boys, aged 2 to 15	89	112	126	15.0
Women and girls	**634**	**565**	**89**	**10.6**
Women, aged 16 or older	529	446	84	10.0
Girls, aged 2 to 15	106	118	111	13.3
Children under age 2	**81**	**104**	**128**	**15.3**
Footwear	**294**	**440**	**150**	**17.8**
Other apparel products and services	**258**	**201**	**78**	**9.3**
TRANSPORTATION	**7,781**	**5,074**	**65**	**7.8**
Vehicle purchases	**3,732**	**2,097**	**56**	**6.7**
Cars and trucks, new	2,052	929	45	5.4
Cars and trucks, used	1,611	1,164	72	8.6
Other vehicles	68	4	6	0.7
Gasoline and motor oil	**1,333**	**1,016**	**76**	**9.1**
Other vehicle expenses	**2,331**	**1,728**	**74**	**8.8**
Vehicle finance charges	371	308	83	9.9
Maintenance and repairs	619	413	67	7.9
Vehicle insurance	905	730	81	9.6
Vehicle rentals, leases, licenses, other charges	436	278	64	7.6
Public transportation	**385**	**233**	**61**	**7.2**
HEALTH CARE	**2,416**	**1,309**	**54**	**6.5**
Health insurance	1,252	774	62	7.4
Medical services	591	229	39	4.6
Drugs	467	263	56	6.7
Medical supplies	107	43	40	4.8
ENTERTAINMENT	**2,060**	**1,007**	**49**	**5.8**
Fees and admissions	494	163	33	3.9
Television, radio, sound equipment	730	616	84	10.1
Pets, toys, and playground equipment	378	123	33	3.9
Other entertainment products and services	457	105	23	2.7

(continued)

	total consumer units	black consumer units		
		average spending	indexed spending	market share
PERSONAL CARE PRODUCTS, SERVICES	$527	$461	87	10.4%
READING	127	52	41	4.9
EDUCATION	783	442	56	6.7
TOBACCO PRODUCTS, SMOKING SUPPLIES	290	180	62	7.4
MISCELLANEOUS	606	447	74	8.8
CASH CONTRIBUTIONS	1,370	832	61	7.2
PERSONAL INSURANCE AND PENSIONS	4,055	2,504	62	7.4
Life and other personal insurance	397	295	74	8.9
Pensions and Social Security	3,658	2,209	60	7.2
PERSONAL TAXES	2,532	966	38	4.5
Federal income taxes	1,843	592	32	3.8
State and local income taxes	502	317	63	7.5
Other taxes	187	57	30	3.6
GIFTS FOR NONHOUSEHOLD MEMBERS	1,007	524	52	6.2
Food	78	32	41	4.9
Alcoholic beverages	16	4	25	3.0
Housing	220	96	44	5.2
Housekeeping supplies	42	13	31	3.7
Household textiles	13	2	15	1.8
Appliances and misc. housewares	25	15	60	7.1
Major appliances	7	8	114	13.6
Small appliances and misc. housewares	18	7	39	4.6
Miscellaneous household equipment	57	15	26	3.1
Other housing	85	50	59	7.0
Apparel and services	225	222	99	11.8
Males, aged 2 or older	56	30	54	6.4
Females, aged 2 or older	80	93	116	13.8
Children under age 2	39	44	113	13.4
Other apparel products and services	50	54	108	12.9
Jewelry and watches	26	21	81	9.6
All other apparel products and services	25	33	132	15.7
Transportation	60	38	63	7.5
Health care	48	22	46	5.5
Entertainment	69	26	38	4.5
Toys, games, hobbies, and tricycles	26	13	50	6.0
Other entertainment	43	14	33	3.9
Personal care products and services	16	8	50	6.0
Reading	1	–	–	–
Education	200	45	23	2.7
All other gifts	74	30	41	4.8

Definitions: The index compares the spending of the average black consumer unit with the spending of the average consumer unit by dividing black spending by average spending in each category and multiplying by 100. An index of 100 means black spending in the category equals average spending. An index of 125 means black spending is 25 percent above average, while an index of 75 means black spending is 25 percent below average. The market share is the percentage of total spending on a product or service category that is accounted for by consumer units headed by blacks.

Note: The Bureau of Labor Statistics uses consumer unit rather than household as the sampling unit in the Consumer Expenditure Survey. For the definition of consumer unit, see the glossary. Spending by category will not add to total spending because gift spending is also included in the preceding product and service categories and personal taxes are not included in the total. (–) means sample is too small to make a reliable estimate or not applicable.

Source: Bureau of Labor Statistics, 2003 Consumer Expenditure Survey, Internet site http://www.bls.gov/cex/; calculations by New Strategist

Nonwhite Households Have Little Wealth

The median net worth (assets minus debts) of nonwhite and Hispanic households amounted to just $17,100 in 2001 (the latest data available), far below the $86,100 net worth of the average American household. On every measure of wealth, nonwhites and Hispanics have less than the average household. Their financial assets are just 26 percent as high as the average, and their nonfinancial assets are only 51 percent of the average. (Note: The Federal Reserve collects wealth data for only two racial and ethnic categories: non-Hispanic whites, and nonwhites and Hispanics. The nonwhite-and-Hispanic category includes primarily blacks and Hispanics, but also Asians and American Indians.)

The net worth of nonwhite and Hispanic households is below average in large part because blacks and Hispanics are less likely to own a home than the average householder. Home equity accounts for the largest share of Americans' net worth. In 2001, just 47 percent of nonwhite and Hispanic householders owned their home.

Nonwhite and Hispanic householders have a median of only $7,200 in financial assets. The median debt of nonwhite and Hispanic householders stood at $20,000 in 2001, much lower than average in part because fewer have mortgage debt.

Blacks not only have little wealth, but they are short on retirement savings as well. Only 26 percent of black workers have an IRA or participate in a 401(k)-type retirement plan. Among the 24 percent who participate in a retirement plan, the median balance is just $10,000. This may explain why only 19 percent of black workers are "very confident" they will have enough money to live comfortably throughout their retirement years.

■ Among blacks aged 65 or older, 88 percent receive Social Security benefits. Only 32 percent receive retirement income from pensions or IRAs.

The net worth of nonwhite and Hispanic households is well below average

(median net worth of total and nonwhite and Hispanic households, 2001)

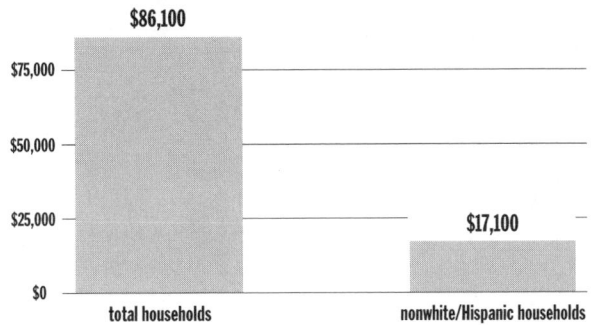

Table 3.103 Net Worth, Assets, and Debt of Nonwhite and Hispanic Households, 2001

(median net worth, median value of assets for owners, and median amount of debt for debtors, for total and non-white/Hispanic households, and index of nonwhite/Hispanic to total, 2001)

		nonwhite/Hispanic households	
	total households	median	index
Median net worth	**$86,100**	**$17,100**	**20**
Median value of financial assets	28,000	7,200	26
Median value of nonfinancial assets	113,500	58,200	51
Median amount of debt	38,775	20,000	52

Note: The index is calculated by dividing the nonwhite/Hispanic figure by the total figure and multiplying by 100.
Source: Federal Reserve Board, "Recent Changes in U.S. Family Finances: Evidence from the 1998 and 2001 Survey of Consumer Finances," Federal Reserve Bulletin, January 2003; calculations by New Strategist

Table 3.104 Financial Assets of Nonwhite and Hispanic Households, 2001

(percent of nonwhite/Hispanic households owning financial assets, and median value of assets for owners, 2001)

	percent owning asset	median value
Any financial asset	**82.4%**	**$7,200**
Transaction accounts	78.2	1,700
Certificates of deposit	6.7	9,000
Savings bonds	7.8	700
Bonds	0.4	7,600
Stocks	11.0	8,000
Mutual funds	7.2	17,500
Retirement accounts	37.3	10,000
Life insurance	22.3	8,100
Other managed assets	1.8	45,000
Other financial assets	9.7	1,700

Source: Federal Reserve Board, "Recent Changes in U.S. Family Finances: Evidence from the 1998 and 2001 Survey of Consumer Finances," Federal Reserve Bulletin, January 2003; calculations by New Strategist

Table 3.105 Nonfinancial Assets of Nonwhite and Hispanic Households, 2001

(percent of nonwhite/Hispanic households owning nonfinancial assets, and median value of assets for owners, 2001)

	percent owning asset	median value
Any nonfinancial asset	**77.9%**	**$58,200**
Vehicles	70.9	10,000
Primary residence	47.0	92,000
Other residential property	6.4	60,000
Nonresidential property	4.1	22,500
Business	5.1	50,000
Other nonfinancial asset	2.9	5,000

Source: Federal Reserve Board, "Recent Changes in U.S. Family Finances: Evidence from the 1998 and 2001 Survey of Consumer Finances," Federal Reserve Bulletin, *January 2003*

Table 3.106 Debt of Nonwhite and Hispanic Households, 2001

(percent of nonwhite/Hispanic households with debt, and median amount of debt for those with debt, 2001)

	percent with debt	median amount
Any debt	**72.9%**	**$20,000**
Home-secured	35.1	60,958
Other residential property	2.5	40,000
Installment loans	44.6	8,133
Other lines of credit	47.7	1,527
Credit card	1.1	1,000
Other debt	6.5	2,000

Source: Federal Reserve Board, "Recent Changes in U.S. Family Finances: Evidence from the 1998 and 2001 Survey of Consumer Finances," Federal Reserve Bulletin, *January 2003*

Table 3.107 Black Ownership of IRAs and 401(k)-Type Plans, 2002

(percent of total and black workers aged 21 to 64 owning IRAs and 401(k)-type plans, 2002)

	total workers	black workers
IRA or 401(k)-type plan	**40.4%**	**25.9%**
IRA only	9.6	2.5
401(k)-type plan only	21.7	20.5
Both IRA and 401(k)-type plan	9.2	2.9
Neither IRA nor 401(k)-type plan	**59.6**	**74.1**

Source: Employee Benefit Research Institute, "401(k)-Type Plan and IRA Ownership," by Craig Copeland, EBRI Notes, Vol. 26, No. 1, January 2005; Internet site http://www.ebri.org/

Table 3.108 Black Participation and Savings in IRAs and 401(k)s, 2002

(percent of total and black workers aged 21 to 64 owning an IRA or participating in 401(k)-type plan, and average and median balance of IRA and 401(k), 2002)

	percent owning IRA	IRA balance		percent participating in 401(k)	401(k) balance	
		average	median		average	median
Total workers	**18.7%**	**$26,951**	**$10,000**	**30.9%**	**$33,647**	**$14,000**
Black workers	5.4	20,688	9,000	23.5	20,338	10,000

Source: Employee Benefit Research Institute, "401(k)-Type Plan and IRA Ownership," by Craig Copeland, EBRI Notes, Vol. 26, No. 1, January 2005; Internet site http://www.ebri.org/

Table 3.109 Retirement Confidence among Black Workers, 2003

(percent distribution of black workers aged 25 or older by degree of confidence in retirement savings and planning, 2003)

	very confident	somewhat confident	not too confident	not at all confident
Having enough money to live comfortably throughout retirement years	19%	34%	22%	20%
Having enough money to take care of basic expenses	29	36	21	12
Doing a good job of preparing financially for retirement	22	39	22	16
Not outliving retirement savings	21	32	20	20
Having enough money to take care of medical expenses	19	34	27	19
Having enough money to pay for long-term care	11	30	29	28

Source: The 2003 Minority Retirement Confidence Survey Summary of Findings, *Employee Benefit Research Institute, American Savings Education Council, and Mathew Greenwald & Associates; Internet site http://www.ebri.org/surveys/rcs/2003/*

Table 3.110 Sources of Income for Blacks Aged 65 or Older, 2003

(number and percent of blacks aged 65 or older with income from selected sources and average income for those with income, ranked by number receiving income, 2003; people in thousands as of 2004)

	number with income	percent with income	average amount received by those with income
Blacks aged 65 or older with income	**2,811**	**100.0%**	**$11,352**
Social Security	2,482	88.3	8,491
Retirement income, including pensions	909	32.3	8,273
Interest	772	27.5	1,470
Earnings	460	16.4	14,518
SSI (Supplemental Security Income)	277	9.9	2,309
Dividends	147	5.2	1,513
Survivor's benefits	116	4.1	6,457
Rents, royalties, estates, or trusts	92	3.3	2,117
Veteran's benefits	76	2.7	4,118

Note: Blacks include those identifying themselves as being black alone and those identifying themselves as being black in combination with one or more other races.
Source: Bureau of the Census, 2004 Current Population Survey, Internet site http://pubdb3.census.gov/macro/032004/perinc/ new09_001.htm; calculations by New Strategist

CHAPTER

4

Hispanics

■ Hispanics are the largest minority in the United States, numbering 41 million in 2004 and accounting for 14 percent of the U.S. population.

■ Only 58 percent of Hispanics have a high school diploma.

■ Hispanics are more likely to be without health insurance than any other racial or ethnic group. In 2003, a substantial 33 percent did not have health insurance.

■ Forty-eight percent of the nation's Hispanic households owned their home in 2004.

■ The $32,997 median income of Hispanic households in 2003 was 8 percent higher than in 1990, after adjusting for inflation.

■ Seventeen percent of Hispanic workers are in managerial or professional jobs, the figure ranging from a low of 14 percent among Mexican Americans to a high of 30 percent among Cuban Americans.

■ Married couples head more than half of Hispanic households. Sixty-five percent of Hispanic couples have children under age 18 at home.

■ Thirty percent of Hispanics live in California, where they account for 35 percent of the state's population.

■ Hispanic households spent an average of $34,575 in 2003. They spend 15 percent more than the average household on groceries.

■ Only 13 percent of Hispanic workers are "very confident" they will have enough money to live comfortably throughout their retirement years.

Hispanics account for 14.1 percent of the U.S. population

(percent distribution of people by race and Hispanic origin, 2004)

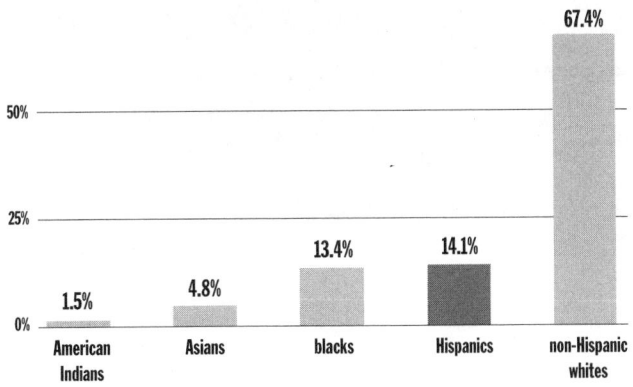

Hispanic Educational Attainment Lags behind That of Asians, Non-Hispanic Whites, and Blacks

Hispanics are much less educated than the average American because many are immigrants who came to the United States as adults with few years of schooling. Only 58 percent of Hispanics have a high school diploma versus 85 percent of the total population. Among Hispanics born in the United States, 75 percent are high school graduates. Among those born outside the United States, the figure is just 46 percent.

Only 12 percent of Hispanics have a college degree, versus 28 percent of the total population. In 2003, 1.7 million Hispanics were enrolled in college, accounting for 10 percent of the nation's college students. Among college students, blacks outnumber Hispanics by more than one-half million.

Hispanics earned 10 percent of associate's degrees awarded in 2001–02, 6 percent of bachelor's degrees, 5 percent of master's degrees, and 3 percent of doctoral degrees. They earned 6 percent of law degrees awarded in 2001–02.

■ The educational attainment of Hispanics will remain below average as long as poorly educated immigrants make up a large proportion of the Hispanic population.

Many Hispanics have not graduated from high school

(percent distribution of Hispanics aged 25 or older by high school graduation status, 2004)

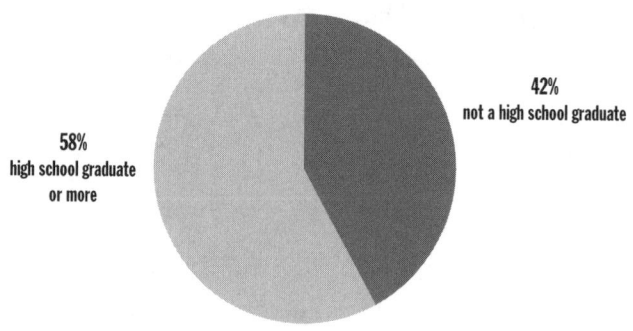

42%
not a high school graduate

58%
high school graduate
or more

Table 4.1 Educational Attainment of Hispanics by Age, 2004

(number and percent distribution of Hispanics aged 25 or older by educational attainment and age, 2004; numbers in thousands)

	total	25 to 34	35 to 44	45 to 54	55 to 64	65 or older
Total Hispanics	**21,596**	**7,422**	**6,007**	**3,926**	**2,162**	**2,080**
Not a high school graduate	8,986	2,881	2,325	1,540	940	1,297
High school graduate only	5,977	2,169	1,752	1,090	555	412
Some college, no degree	2,861	1,128	762	522	301	148
Associate's degree	1,166	408	380	224	104	49
Bachelor's degree	1,892	675	567	378	167	105
Master's degree	478	102	165	109	64	38
Professional degree	142	47	35	38	12	10
Doctoral degree	94	12	19	24	18	20
High school graduate or more	12,610	4,541	3,680	2,385	1,221	782
Some college or more	6,633	2,372	1,928	1,295	666	370
Bachelor's degree or more	2,606	836	786	549	261	173

PERCENT DISTRIBUTION

	total	25 to 34	35 to 44	45 to 54	55 to 64	65 or older
Total Hispanics	**100.0%**	**100.0%**	**100.0%**	**100.0%**	**100.0%**	**100.0%**
Not a high school graduate	41.6	38.8	38.7	39.2	43.5	62.4
High school graduate only	27.7	29.2	29.2	27.8	25.7	19.8
Some college, no degree	13.2	15.2	12.7	13.3	13.9	7.1
Associate's degree	5.4	5.5	6.3	5.7	4.8	2.4
Bachelor's degree	8.8	9.1	9.4	9.6	7.7	5.0
Master's degree	2.2	1.4	2.7	2.8	3.0	1.8
Professional degree	0.7	0.6	0.6	1.0	0.6	0.5
Doctoral degree	0.4	0.2	0.3	0.6	0.8	1.0
High school graduate or more	58.4	61.2	61.3	60.7	56.5	37.6
Some college or more	30.7	32.0	32.1	33.0	30.8	17.8
Bachelor's degree or more	12.1	11.3	13.1	14.0	12.1	8.3

Source: Bureau of the Census, 2004 Current Population Survey Annual Social and Economic Supplement, Educational Attainment in the United States: 2004, Detailed Tables, Internet site http://www.census.gov/population/www/socdemo/education/cps2004.html; calculations by New Strategist

Table 4.2 Educational Attainment of Hispanic Men by Age, 2004

(number and percent distribution of Hispanic men aged 25 or older by educational attainment and age, 2004; numbers in thousands)

	total	25 to 34	35 to 44	45 to 54	55 to 64	65 or older
Total Hispanic men	**10,986**	**4,001**	**3,126**	**1,955**	**1,023**	**881**
Not a high school graduate	4,691	1,648	1,268	807	446	517
High school graduate only	3,009	1,203	886	505	247	167
Some college, no degree	1,464	560	424	258	145	78
Associate's degree	527	184	176	101	42	23
Bachelor's degree	926	328	267	189	86	56
Master's degree	240	56	72	56	36	21
Professional degree	79	16	21	27	7	9
Doctoral degree	52	6	12	13	12	9
High school grad. or more	6,297	2,353	1,858	1,149	575	363
Some college or more	3,288	1,150	972	644	328	196
Bachelor's degree or more	1,297	406	372	285	141	95
PERCENT DISTRIBUTION						
Total Hispanic men	**100.0%**	**100.0%**	**100.0%**	**100.0%**	**100.0%**	**100.0%**
Not a high school graduate	42.7	41.2	40.6	41.3	43.6	58.7
High school graduate only	27.4	30.1	28.3	25.8	24.1	19.0
Some college, no degree	13.3	14.0	13.6	13.2	14.2	8.9
Associate's degree	4.8	4.6	5.6	5.2	4.1	2.6
Bachelor's degree	8.4	8.2	8.5	9.7	8.4	6.4
Master's degree	2.2	1.4	2.3	2.9	3.5	2.4
Professional degree	0.7	0.4	0.7	1.4	0.7	1.0
Doctoral degree	0.5	0.1	0.4	0.7	1.2	1.0
High school grad. or more	57.3	58.8	59.4	58.8	56.2	41.2
Some college or more	29.9	28.7	31.1	32.9	32.1	22.2
Bachelor's degree or more	11.8	10.1	11.9	14.6	13.8	10.8

Source: Bureau of the Census, 2004 Current Population Survey Annual Social and Economic Supplement, Educational Attainment in the United States: 2004, Detailed Tables, Internet site http://www.census.gov/population/www/socdemo/education/cps2004.html; calculations by New Strategist

Table 4.3 Educational Attainment of Hispanic Women by Age, 2004

*(number and percent distribution of Hispanic women aged 25 or older by educational attainment and age, 2004;
numbers in thousands)*

	total	25 to 34	35 to 44	45 to 54	55 to 64	65 or older
Total Hispanic women	**10,610**	**3,422**	**2,880**	**1,970**	**1,138**	**1,199**
Not a high school graduate	4,296	1,235	1,057	732	495	778
High school graduate only	2,968	966	865	586	308	244
Some college, no degree	1,397	568	338	264	156	71
Associate's degree	640	224	203	124	62	25
Bachelor's degree	966	347	300	190	80	50
Master's degree	238	46	93	53	28	18
Professional degree	63	30	16	12	4	2
Doctoral degree	41	6	7	11	6	11
High school grad. or more	6,313	2,187	1,822	1,240	644	421
Some college or more	3,345	1,221	957	654	336	177
Bachelor's degree or more	1,308	429	416	266	118	81

PERCENT DISTRIBUTION

	total	25 to 34	35 to 44	45 to 54	55 to 64	65 or older
Total Hispanic women	**100.0%**	**100.0%**	**100.0%**	**100.0%**	**100.0%**	**100.0%**
Not a high school graduate	40.5	36.1	36.7	37.2	43.5	64.9
High school graduate only	28.0	28.2	30.0	29.7	27.1	20.4
Some college, no degree	13.2	16.6	11.7	13.4	13.7	5.9
Associate's degree	6.0	6.5	7.0	6.3	5.4	2.1
Bachelor's degree	9.1	10.1	10.4	9.6	7.0	4.2
Master's degree	2.2	1.3	3.2	2.7	2.5	1.5
Professional degree	0.6	0.9	0.6	0.6	0.4	0.2
Doctoral degree	0.4	0.2	0.2	0.6	0.5	0.9
High school grad. or more	59.5	63.9	63.3	62.9	56.6	35.1
Some college or more	31.5	35.7	33.2	33.2	29.5	14.8
Bachelor's degree or more	12.3	12.5	14.4	13.5	10.4	6.8

*Source: Bureau of the Census, 2004 Current Population Survey Annual Social and Economic Supplement, Educational Attainment
in the United States: 2004, Detailed Tables, Internet site http://www.census.gov/population/www/socdemo/education/cps2004.html;
calculations by New Strategist*

Table 4.4 Educational Attainment of Hispanics by Foreign-Born Status, 2004

(number and percent distribution of Hispanics aged 25 or older by educational attainment and foreign-born status, 2004; numbers in thousands)

	total	native-born	foreign-born
Total Hispanics	**21,596**	**9,143**	**12,453**
Not a high school graduate	8,985	2,255	6,732
High school graduate only	5,977	2,981	2,995
Some college, no degree	2,861	1,808	1,053
Associate's degree	1,166	745	421
Bachelor's degree	1,892	985	907
Master's degree	478	263	215
Professional degree	142	63	79
Doctoral degree	94	43	50
High school graduate or more	12,610	6,888	5,720
Some college or more	6,633	3,907	2,725
Bachelor's degree or more	2,606	1,354	1,251
PERCENT DISTRIBUTION			
Total Hispanics	**100.0%**	**100.0%**	**100.0%**
Not a high school graduate	41.6	24.7	54.1
High school graduate only	27.7	32.6	24.1
Some college, no degree	13.2	19.8	8.5
Associate's degree	5.4	8.1	3.4
Bachelor's degree	8.8	10.8	7.3
Master's degree	2.2	2.9	1.7
Professional degree	0.7	0.7	0.6
Doctoral degree	0.4	0.5	0.4
High school graduate or more	58.4	75.3	45.9
Some college or more	30.7	42.7	21.9
Bachelor's degree or more	12.1	14.8	10.0

Source: Bureau of the Census, 2004 Current Population Survey Annual Social and Economic Supplement, Educational Attainment in the United States: 2004, Detailed Tables, Internet site http://www.census.gov/population/www/socdemo/education/cps2004.html; calculations by New Strategist

Table 4.5 Educational Attainment of Hispanics by Age and Region, 2004

(percent of Hispanics aged 25 or older by selected educational attainment, age, and region, 2004)

	Northeast	Midwest	South	West
HIGH SCHOOL GRADUATE OR MORE				
Total Hispanics	**64.3%**	**61.6%**	**57.9%**	**56.2%**
Aged 25 to 34	71.4	62.1	58.4	59.9
Aged 35 to 44	70.1	65.4	63.7	56.0
Aged 45 to 54	59.1	64.5	65.3	56.8
Aged 55 to 64	57.1	58.5	56.3	56.0
Aged 65 or older	44.4	38.3	33.2	40.7
SOME COLLEGE OR MORE				
Total Hispanics	**31.1**	**31.7**	**30.5**	**30.6**
Aged 25 to 34	34.9	32.7	30.9	31.7
Aged 35 to 44	36.1	33.3	32.6	30.3
Aged 45 to 54	30.5	31.9	36.2	31.3
Aged 55 to 64	22.1	29.2	32.3	33.1
Aged 65 or older	17.3	20.0	14.0	22.8
BACHELOR'S DEGREE OR MORE				
Total Hispanics	**13.8**	**11.7**	**13.5**	**10.3**
Aged 25 to 34	13.4	12.3	12.1	9.5
Aged 35 to 44	15.5	13.6	14.9	10.9
Aged 45 to 54	15.7	10.6	17.6	10.8
Aged 55 to 64	10.9	7.7	12.9	12.5
Aged 65 or older	10.2	6.7	8.8	7.5

Source: Bureau of the Census, 2004 Current Population Survey Annual Social and Economic Supplement, Educational Attainment in the United States: 2004, Detailed Tables, Internet site http://www.census.gov/population/www/socdemo/education/cps2004.html; calculations by New Strategist

Table 4.6 Educational Attainment of Hispanics by State, 2004

(percent of Hispanics aged 25 or older who are high school or college graduates, for the 25 largest states, 2004)

	high school graduate or more	college graduate
Total Hispanics	**58.4%**	**12.1%**
Alabama	–	–
Arizona	57.4	10.8
California	54.2	9.8
Colorado	61.2	11.1
Florida	70.8	21.8
Georgia	62.1	15.9
Illinois	62.0	9.9
Indiana	58.5	5.9
Kentucky	–	–
Louisiana	–	–
Maryland	48.8	15.5
Massachusetts	62.3	8.8
Michigan	57.1	15.4
Minnesota	69.5	19.2
Missouri	72.2	20.3
New Jersey	65.2	15.6
New York	62.5	13.8
North Carolina	46.8	8.0
Ohio	65.1	11.7
Pennsylvania	70.8	13.2
Tennessee	46.2	12.4
Texas	52.4	9.2
Virginia	65.8	19.8
Washington	55.8	13.4
Wisconsin	55.8	7.1

Note: (–) means sample is too small to make a reliable estimate.
Source: Bureau of the Census, 2004 Current Population Survey Annual Social and Economic Supplement, Educational Attainment in the United States: 2004, Detailed Tables, Internet site http://www.census.gov/population/www/socdemo/education/cps2004 .html; calculations by New Strategist

Table 4.7 School Enrollment of Hispanics, 2003

(total number of people aged 3 or older enrolled in school, number of Hispanics enrolled, and Hispanic share of total, by age, October 2003; numbers in thousands)

	total	Hispanic number	Hispanic share of total
Total aged 3 or older	**74,911**	**11,929**	**15.9%**
Aged 3 to 4	4,590	728	15.9
Aged 5 to 6	7,309	1,386	19.0
Aged 7 to 9	11,706	2,230	19.1
Aged 10 to 13	16,478	2,843	17.3
Aged 14 to 15	8,329	1,415	17.0
Aged 16 to 17	8,177	1,242	15.2
Aged 18 to 19	4,856	614	12.6
Aged 20 to 21	3,684	454	12.3
Aged 22 to 24	3,397	353	10.4
Aged 25 to 29	2,212	240	10.8
Aged 30 to 34	1,378	174	12.6
Aged 35 to 44	1,635	185	11.3
Aged 45 to 54	879	42	4.8
Aged 55 or older	283	23	8.1

Source: Bureau of the Census, School Enrollment—Social and Economic Characteristics of Students: October 2003, Detailed Tables, Internet site http://www.census.gov/population/www/socdemo/school/cps2003.html; calculations by New Strategist

Table 4.8 School Enrollment of Hispanics by Age and Sex, 2003

(number and percent of Hispanics aged 3 or older enrolled in school, by age and sex, October 2003; numbers in thousands)

	total		female		male	
	number	percent	number	percent	number	percent
Total Hispanics enrolled	**11,929**	**31.6%**	**5,967**	**32.5%**	**5,962**	**30.8%**
Aged 3 to 4	728	43.7	335	44.7	393	42.9
Aged 5 to 6	1,386	91.6	696	92.0	690	91.3
Aged 7 to 9	2,230	97.5	1,076	97.5	1,154	97.5
Aged 10 to 13	2,843	98.3	1,331	98.2	1,512	98.4
Aged 14 to 15	1,415	96.7	732	96.8	683	96.7
Aged 16 to 17	1,242	92.1	633	93.8	609	90.4
Aged 18 to 19	614	50.5	315	54.4	298	47.0
Aged 20 to 21	454	33.7	257	41.1	197	27.2
Aged 22 to 24	353	16.1	195	19.4	157	13.3
Aged 25 to 29	240	6.2	138	7.9	102	4.9
Aged 30 to 34	174	4.6	99	5.6	75	3.8
Aged 35 to 44	185	3.0	118	4.0	67	2.1
Aged 45 to 54	42	1.1	26	1.3	16	0.8
Aged 55 or older	23	0.5	14	0.6	8	0.4

Source: Bureau of the Census, School Enrollment—Social and Economic Characteristics of Students: October 2003, Detailed Tables, Internet site http://www.census.gov/population/www/socdemo/school/cps2003.html

Table 4.9 Hispanic Families with Children in College, 2003

(total number of Hispanic families, number with dependent children aged 5 to 24, and number and percent with children enrolled in college by household income, 2003; numbers in thousands)

	total	with children aged 5–24	with one or more children enrolled in college		
			number	percent of total Hispanic families	percent of Hispanic families with children 5–24
Total Hispanic families	**9,765**	**6,265**	**706**	**7.2%**	**11.3%**
Less than $10,000	851	543	33	3.9	6.1
$10,000 to $14,999	992	584	45	4.5	7.7
$15,000 to $19,999	658	416	15	2.3	3.6
$20,000 to $24,999	1,688	1,099	115	6.8	10.5
$25,000 to $29,999	1,368	919	74	5.4	8.1
$30,000 to $34,999	721	504	62	8.6	12.3
$35,000 to $39,999	1,124	693	116	10.3	16.7
$40,000 to $49,999	458	301	71	15.5	23.6
$50,000 to $74,999	258	148	24	9.3	16.2
$75,000 and over	119	87	24	20.2	27.6

Note: Numbers will not add to total because not reported is not shown.
Source: Bureau of the Census, School Enrollment—Social and Economic Characteristics of Students: October 2003, Detailed Tables, Internet site http://www.census.gov/population/www/socdemo/school/cps2003.html; calculations by New Strategist

Table 4.10 Hispanic College Enrollment Rate, 1990 to 2000

(percent of total people and Hispanics aged 16 to 24 graduating from high school in the previous 12 months who were enrolled in college as of October of each year, percentage point change in enrollment rate, 1990–2000)

	total	Hispanic
2000	63.3%	49.0%
1999	62.9	47.5
1998	65.6	51.8
1997	67.0	54.6
1996	65.0	56.7
1995	61.9	51.2
1994	61.9	55.0
1993	62.6	55.4
1992	61.9	58.1
1991	62.5	51.6
1990	60.1	51.7

Percentage point change

1990–2000	3.2	–2.7

Note: Hispanic enrollment rates are a three-year moving average.
Source: National Center for Education Statistics, Digest of Education Statistics 2003; *Internet site http://nces.ed.gov/programs/digest/d03/list_tables3.asp#c3; calculations by New Strategist*

Table 4.11 College Enrollment of Hispanics, 2003

(total number of people aged 15 or older enrolled in college, number of Hispanics enrolled, and Hispanic share of total, by age, October 2003; numbers in thousands)

	total	Hispanic number	Hispanic share of total
Total enrolled in college	**16,638**	**1,715**	**10.3%**
Under age 20	3,661	390	10.7
Aged 20 to 21	3,534	408	11.5
Aged 22 to 24	3,320	330	9.9
Aged 25 to 29	2,164	224	10.4
Aged 30 to 34	1,330	155	11.7
Aged 35 to 39	769	84	10.9
Aged 40 to 44	757	68	9.0
Aged 45 to 49	479	19	4.0
Aged 50 to 54	357	17	4.8
Aged 55 or older	268	19	7.1

Source: Bureau of the Census, School Enrollment—Social and Economic Characteristics of Students: October 2003, Detailed Tables, Internet site http://www.census.gov/population/www/socdemo/school/cps2003.html; calculations by New Strategist

Table 4.12 College Enrollment of Hispanics by Age and Type of School, 2003

(number and percent distribution of Hispanics aged 15 or older enrolled in college by age and type of school, October 2003; numbers in thousands)

	total	two-year college	four-year college	graduate school
Total Hispanics enrolled	**1,715**	**627**	**918**	**170**
Under age 20	390	171	216	3
Aged 20 to 21	408	124	277	7
Aged 22 to 24	330	121	185	24
Aged 25 to 29	224	72	109	43
Aged 30 to 34	155	52	71	32
Aged 35 to 39	84	26	23	35
Aged 40 to 44	68	39	16	13
Aged 45 to 49	19	5	8	6
Aged 50 to 54	17	7	4	6
Aged 55 or older	19	9	9	1

PERCENT DISTRIBUTION BY TYPE OF SCHOOL

Total Hispanics enrolled	**100.0%**	**36.6%**	**53.5%**	**9.9%**
Under age 20	100.0	43.8	55.4	0.8
Aged 20 to 21	100.0	30.4	67.9	1.7
Aged 22 to 24	100.0	36.7	56.1	7.3
Aged 25 to 29	100.0	32.1	48.7	19.2
Aged 30 to 34	100.0	33.5	45.8	20.6
Aged 35 to 39	100.0	31.0	27.4	41.7
Aged 40 to 44	100.0	57.4	23.5	19.1
Aged 45 to 49	100.0	26.3	42.1	31.6
Aged 50 to 54	100.0	41.2	23.5	35.3
Aged 55 or older	100.0	47.4	47.4	5.3

PERCENT DISTRIBUTION BY AGE

Total Hispanics enrolled	**100.0%**	**100.0%**	**100.0%**	**100.0%**
Under age 20	22.7	27.3	23.5	1.8
Aged 20 to 21	23.8	19.8	30.2	4.1
Aged 22 to 24	19.2	19.3	20.2	14.1
Aged 25 to 29	13.1	11.5	11.9	25.3
Aged 30 to 34	9.0	8.3	7.7	18.8
Aged 35 to 39	4.9	4.1	2.5	20.6
Aged 40 to 44	4.0	6.2	1.7	7.6
Aged 45 to 49	1.1	0.8	0.9	3.5
Aged 50 to 54	1.0	1.1	0.4	3.5
Aged 55 or older	1.1	1.4	1.0	0.6

Source: Bureau of the Census, School Enrollment—Social and Economic Characteristics of Students: October 2003, Detailed Tables, Internet site http://www.census.gov/population/www/socdemo/school/cps2003.html; calculations by New Strategist

Table 4.13 Associate's Degrees Earned by Hispanics by Field of Study, 2001–02

(total number of associate's degrees conferred and number and percent earned by Hispanics, by field of study, 2001–02)

	total	earned by Hispanics number	earned by Hispanics percent
Total associate's degrees	**595,133**	**60,003**	**10.1%**
Agriculture and natural resources	6,494	120	1.8
Architecture and related programs	443	28	6.3
Area, ethnic, and cultural studies	319	17	5.3
Biological and life sciences	1,517	137	9.0
Business	108,911	9,823	9.0
Communications	2,819	167	5.9
Communications technologies	2,021	185	9.2
Computer and information sciences	30,965	3,024	9.8
Construction trades	2,639	117	4.4
Education	9,267	1,050	11.3
Engineering	1,724	124	7.2
Engineering-related technologies	32,895	3,468	10.5
English language and literature, letters	864	101	11.7
Foreign languages and literatures	517	143	27.7
Health professions and related sciences	79,888	5,903	7.4
Home economics	9,480	1,252	13.2
Law and legal studies	6,825	626	9.2
Liberal arts and sciences, general studies, humanities	207,163	23,275	11.2
Library science	96	5	5.2
Mathematics	685	112	16.4
Mechanics and repairers	12,086	1,343	11.1
Multi- and interdisciplinary studies	13,204	1,476	11.2
Parks, recreation, leisure, and fitness	830	68	8.2
Philosophy and religion	134	27	20.1
Physical sciences	2,308	200	8.7
Precision production trades	10,818	1,033	9.5
Protective services	16,689	1,832	11.0
Psychology	1,705	270	15.8
Public administration and services	3,323	460	13.8
R.O.T.C. and military technologies	62	3	4.8
Social sciences and history	5,593	946	16.9
Theological studies, religious vocations	414	16	3.9
Transportation and material moving	1,159	96	8.3
Visual and performing arts	20,911	2,545	12.2
Not classified	365	11	3.0

Source: National Center for Education Statistics, Digest of Education Statistics 2003, *Internet site http://nces.ed.gov//programs/ digest/d03/list_tables.asp; calculations by New Strategist*

Table 4.14 Bachelor's Degrees Earned by Hispanics by Field of Study, 2001–02

(total number of bachelor's degrees conferred and number and percent earned by Hispanics, by field of study, 2001–02)

	total	earned by Hispanics number	earned by Hispanics percent
Total bachelor's degrees	**1,291,900**	**82,969**	**6.4%**
Agriculture and natural resources	23,353	744	3.2
Architecture and related programs	8,808	640	7.3
Area, ethnic, and cultural studies	6,557	775	11.8
Biological and life sciences	60,256	3,256	5.4
Business	281,330	17,557	6.2
Communications	62,791	3,510	5.6
Communications technologies	1,110	94	8.5
Computer and information sciences	47,299	2,442	5.2
Construction trades	202	10	5.0
Education	106,383	4,893	4.6
Engineering	59,481	3,208	5.4
Engineering-related technologies	14,117	875	6.2
English language and literature, letters	53,162	2,908	5.5
Foreign languages and literatures	15,318	2,558	16.7
Health professions and related sciences	70,517	3,700	5.2
Home economics	18,153	724	4.0
Law and legal studies	1,971	146	7.4
Liberal arts and sciences, general studies, humanities	39,333	4,106	10.4
Library science	74	1	1.4
Mathematics	12,395	695	5.6
Mechanics and repairers	164	21	12.8
Multi- and interdisciplinary studies	27,629	2,793	10.1
Parks, recreation, leisure, and fitness	20,554	1,068	5.2
Philosophy and religion	9,306	472	5.1
Physical sciences	17,851	709	4.0
Precision production trades	468	24	5.1
Protective services	25,536	2,659	10.4
Psychology	76,671	6,381	8.3
Public administration and services	19,392	1,847	9.5
R.O.T.C. and military technologies	3	0	0.0
Social sciences and history	132,874	9,917	7.5
Theological studies, religious vocations	7,785	258	3.3
Transportation and material moving	4,020	181	4.5
Visual and performing arts	66,773	3,787	5.7
Not classified	264	10	3.8

Source: National Center for Education Statistics, Digest of Education Statistics 2003, *Internet site http://nces.ed.gov//programs/ digest/d03/list_tables.asp; calculations by New Strategist*

Table 4.15 Master's Degrees Earned by Hispanics by Field of Study, 2001–02

(total number of master's degrees conferred and number and percent earned by Hispanics, by field of study, 2001–02)

	total	earned by Hispanics	
		number	percent
Total master's degrees	**482,118**	**22,387**	**4.6%**
Agriculture and natural resources	4,519	117	2.6
Architecture and related programs	4,566	220	4.8
Area, ethnic, and cultural studies	1,578	125	7.9
Biological and life sciences	6,205	261	4.2
Business	120,785	5,024	4.2
Communications	5,510	189	3.4
Communications technologies	549	11	2.0
Computer and information sciences	16,113	307	1.9
Construction trades	9	2	22.2
Education	136,579	7,751	5.7
Engineering	26,015	775	3.0
Engineering-related technologies	896	21	2.3
English language and literature, letters	7,268	243	3.3
Foreign languages and literatures	2,861	351	12.3
Health professions and related sciences	43,644	1,740	4.0
Home economics	2,616	130	5.0
Law and legal studies	4,053	167	4.1
Liberal arts and sciences, general studies, humanities	2,754	119	4.3
Library science	5,113	212	4.1
Mathematics	3,487	85	2.4
Multi- and interdisciplinary studies	3,211	156	4.9
Parks, recreation, leisure, and fitness	2,754	71	2.6
Philosophy and religion	1,334	36	2.7
Physical sciences	5,034	148	2.9
Precision production trades	2	1	50.0
Protective services	2,935	159	5.4
Psychology	14,888	921	6.2
Public administration and services	25,448	1,743	6.8
Social sciences and history	14,112	670	4.7
Theological studies, religious vocations	4,952	164	3.3
Transportation and material moving	709	31	4.4
Visual and performing arts	11,595	437	3.8
Not classified	24	0	0.0

Source: National Center for Education Statistics, Digest of Education Statistics 2003, *Internet site http://nces.ed.gov//programs/ digest/d03/list_tables.asp; calculations by New Strategist*

Table 4.16 Doctoral Degrees Earned by Hispanics by Field of Study, 2001–02

(total number of doctoral degrees conferred and number and percent earned by Hispanics, by field of study, 2001–02)

	total	earned by Hispanics number	earned by Hispanics percent
Total doctoral degrees	**44,160**	**1,432**	**3.2%**
Agriculture and natural resources	1,166	25	2.1
Architecture and related programs	183	8	4.4
Area, ethnic, and cultural studies	216	11	5.1
Biological, life sciences	4,489	127	2.8
Business	1,158	22	1.9
Communications	374	8	2.1
Communications technologies	9	0	0.0
Computer and information sciences	750	21	2.8
Education	6,967	312	4.5
Engineering	5,195	93	1.8
Engineering-related technologies	15	0	0.0
English language and literature, letters	1,446	49	3.4
Foreign languages and literatures	843	96	11.4
Health professions and related sciences	3,523	82	2.3
Home economics	355	10	2.8
Law and legal studies	79	1	1.3
Liberal arts and sciences, general studies, humanities	113	2	1.8
Library science	45	1	2.2
Mathematics	958	9	0.9
Multi/interdisciplinary studies	384	14	3.6
Parks, recreation, leisure, and fitness	151	4	2.6
Philosophy and religion	606	13	2.1
Physical sciences	3,803	68	1.8
Protective services	49	1	2.0
Psychology	4,341	263	6.1
Public administration and services	571	13	2.3
Social sciences and history	3,902	120	3.1
Theological studies, religious vocations	1,355	22	1.6
Visual and performing arts	1,114	37	3.3

Source: National Center for Education Statistics, Digest of Education Statistics 2003, *Internet site http://nces.ed.gov//programs/ digest/d03/list_tables.asp; calculations by New Strategist*

Table 4.17 First-Professional Degrees Earned by Hispanics by Field of Study, 2001–02

(total number of first-professional degrees conferred and number and percent earned by Hispanics, by field of study, 2001–02)

	total	earned by Hispanics number	earned by Hispanics percent
Total first-professional degrees	**80,698**	**3,965**	**4.9%**
Dentistry (D.D.S. or D.M.D.)	4,239	173	4.1
Medicine (M.D.)	15,237	757	5.0
Optometry (O.D.)	1,280	40	3.1
Osteopathic medicine (D.O.)	2,416	67	2.8
Pharmacy (Pharm.D.)	7,076	229	3.2
Podiatry (Pod.D., D.P., or D.P.M.)	474	15	3.2
Veterinary medicine (D.V.M.)	2,289	61	2.7
Chiropractic (D.C. or D.C.M.)	3,284	121	3.7
Naturopathic medicine	227	2	0.9
Law (LL.B. or J.D.)	38,981	2,368	6.1
Theology (M.Div., M.H.L., B.D., or Ord.)	5,195	132	2.5

Source: National Center for Education Statistics, Digest of Education Statistics 2003, *Internet site http://nces.ed.gov//programs/ digest/d03/list_tables.asp; calculations by New Strategist*

Table 4.18 Hispanic Participation in Adult Education, 2001

(percent of total people and Hispanics aged 16 or older participating in adult education activities, by type of adult education activity, 2001)

	percent participating total	percent participating Hispanics
Any adult education course	**47.4%**	**42.9%**
College or university credential programs	7.3	7.1
Work-related courses	29.7	21.6
Personal interest courses	21.3	16.3
Other educational activities	3.6	12.2

Note: Adult education activities include apprenticeships, courses for basic skills, English as a second language, work-related courses, and personal development. For those aged 25 or older, credential programs in postsecondary institutions are counted as adult education activities. For those aged 16 to 24, full-time participation (full-year or part-year) in college or university credential programs or vocational or technical diploma programs are excluded.
Source: National Center for Education Statistics, Adult Education and Lifelong Learning Survey of the National Household Education Surveys Program; Internet site http://nces.ed.gov/programs/coe/2003/section1/tables/t08_2.asp

Millions of Hispanics Lack Health Insurance

Fifty-two percent of Hispanics rate their health as very good or excellent, well below the 62 percent share among the total population. One reason for the relatively poor health of Hispanics may be their limited access to health care because so many lack health insurance. Only 16 percent of Hispanics are cigarette smokers, while a larger 37 percent drink alcohol regularly. Two out of three Hispanics are overweight, and one in four is obese.

More than 912,000 babies were born to Hispanic women in 2003, accounting for a substantial 22 percent of all births that year. Mexican Americans account for 72 percent of Hispanic births. In California, 50 percent of births are to Hispanics. The figure is 49 percent in Texas and 44 percent in Arizona.

Hispanics are more likely to be without health insurance than any other racial or ethnic group. In 2003, a substantial 33 percent did not have health insurance, more than double the 16 percent among the total population. More than one in four Hispanics have experienced lower back pain for at least one day in the past 12 months.

The leading causes of death among Hispanics are heart disease and cancer, followed by accidents. Among the population as a whole, cerebrovascular disease ranks third. Accidents are a more important cause of death among Hispanics because the population is younger than average, and accidents account for a large share of deaths among children and young adults.

■ The health status of Hispanics is greatly influenced by immigration. Not only do immigrants boost the Hispanic birth rate, but many do not have health insurance.

One-third of Hispanics do not have health insurance

(percent distribution of Hispanics by health insurance coverage status, 2003; shares do not add to 100 percent because some people have more than one kind of health insurance)

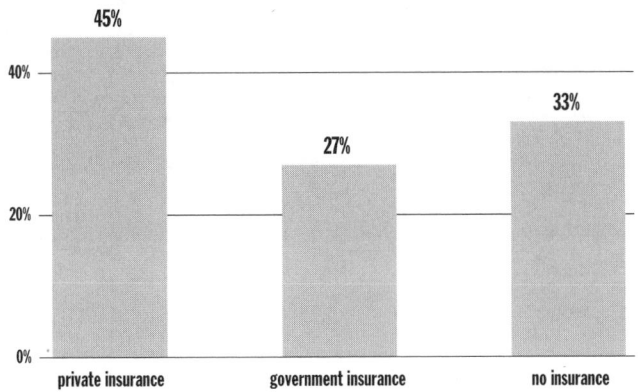

Table 4.19 Hispanic Health Status, 2003

(percent distribution of total people and Hispanics aged 18 or older by self-reported health status, and index of Hispanic to total, 2003)

	total	Hispanic	index of Hispanic to total
Total people	**100.0%**	**100.0%**	—
Excellent/very good	62.3	51.7	83
Good	25.5	29.4	115
Fair/poor	12.2	19.0	156

Note: (–) means not applicable. The index is calculated by dividing the Hispanic figure by the total figure and multiplying by 100.
Source: National Center for Health Statistics, Summary Health Statistics for U.S. Adults: National Health Interview Survey, 2003, *Series 10, No. 225, 2005; Internet site http://www.cdc.gov/nchs/nhis.htm; calculations by New Strategist*

Table 4.20 Smoking and Drinking Status of Hispanics by Sex, 2003

(percent distribution of Hispanics aged 18 or older by smoking and drinking status and sex, 2003)

	total	men	women
SMOKING STATUS			
Total Hispanics	**100.0%**	**100.0%**	**100.0%**
Never smoked	69.6	59.4	79.7
Former smoker	14.8	19.7	10.1
Current smoker	15.6	20.9	10.2
DRINKING STATUS			
Total Hispanics	**100.0**	**100.0**	**100.0**
Lifetime abstainer	37.1	23.0	50.9
Former drinker	13.3	15.2	11.7
Current infrequent drinker	11.7	9.3	14.2
Current regular drinker	37.1	51.3	22.6

Note: Never smoked means having had fewer than 100 cigarettes in lifetime. Former smokers have had 100 or more cigarettes in lifetime but did not smoke at time of interview. Current smokers have had at least 100 cigarettes in lifetime and currently smoke. Lifetime abstainers have had fewer than 12 drinks in lifetime. Former drinkers have had 12 or more drinks in lifetime, none in past year. Current infrequent drinkers have had 12 or more drinks in lifetime and fewer than 12 drinks in past year. Current regular drinkers have had at least 12 drinks in past year.
Source: National Center for Health Statistics, Summary Health Statistics for U.S. Adults: National Health Interview Survey, 2003, *Series 10, No. 225, 2005; Internet site http://www.cdc.gov/nchs/nhis.htm*

Table 4.21 Weight in Pounds of Hispanics by Age and Sex, 1999–2002

(average weight in pounds of Hispanics of Mexican origin aged 20 or older by age and sex, 1999–2002)

	men	women
WEIGHT IN POUNDS		
Total aged 20 or older	**177.3**	**157.1**
Aged 20 to 39	172.5	152.9
Aged 40 to 59	183.6	165.5
Aged 60 or older	175.7	150.7

Note: Data are based on measured weight of a sample of the civilian noninstitutionalized population.
Source: National Center for Health Statistics, Mean Body Weight, Height, and Body Mass Index, United States 1960–2002; *Advance Data, No. 347, 2004; Internet site http://www.cdc.gov/nchs/products/pubs/pubd/ad/341-350/341-350.htm*

Table 4.22 Weight Status of Hispanics by Sex, 2003

(percent distribution of Hispanics aged 18 or older by weight status and sex, 2003))

	total	men	women
Total Hispanics	**100.0%**	**100.0%**	**100.0%**
Underweight	1.1	0.9	1.3
Healthy weight	33.9	30.4	38.1
Overweight, total	65.0	68.7	60.6
Overweight, but not obese	39.8	45.8	33.3
Obese	25.2	22.9	27.3

Note: Being overweight is defined as having a body mass index of 25 or higher. Being obese is defined as having a body mass index of 30 or higher. Body mass index is calculated by dividing weight in kilograms by height in meters squared. Data are based on measured height and weight of a sample of the civilian noninstitutionalized population.
Source: National Center for Health Statistics, Summary Health Statistics for U.S. Adults: National Health Interview Survey, 2003, *Series 10, No. 225, 2005; Internet site http://www.cdc.gov/nchs/nhis.htm*

Table 4.23 Births to Hispanic Women by Age, 2003

(total number of births, number and percent distribution of births to Hispanics, and Hispanic share of total, by age, 2003)

	total	Hispanic number	Hispanic percent distribution	Hispanic share of total
Total births	**4,089,950**	**912,329**	**100.0%**	**22.3%**
Under age 15	6,661	2,356	0.3	35.4
Aged 15 to 19	414,580	128,524	14.1	31.0
Aged 20 to 24	1,032,305	273,311	30.0	26.5
Aged 25 to 29	1,086,366	246,361	27.0	22.7
Aged 30 to 34	975,546	169,054	18.5	17.3
Aged 35 to 39	467,642	75,801	8.3	16.2
Aged 40 to 44	101,005	16,172	1.8	16.0
Aged 45 to 54	5,845	750	0.1	12.8

Source: National Center for Health Statistics, Births: Final Data for 2003, National Vital Statistics Reports, Vol. 54, No. 2, 2005; Internet site http://www.cdc.gov/nchs/products/pubs/pubd/nvsr/54/54-pre.htm; calculations by New Strategist

Table 4.24 Births to Hispanics by Age and Ethnic Origin, 2003

(number and percent distribution of births to Hispanics by age and ethnic origin, 2003)

	total	Mexican	Puerto Rican	Cuban	Central and South American	other Hispanic
Total Hispanic births	**912,329**	**654,504**	**58,400**	**14,867**	**135,586**	**48,972**
Under age 20	130,880	100,238	10,430	1,177	11,271	7764
Aged 20 to 24	273,311	203,314	19,004	2,608	33,588	14,797
Aged 25 to 29	246,361	177,499	14,169	3,966	38,505	12,222
Aged 30 to 34	169,054	115,033	9,301	4,298	31,448	8,974
Aged 35 to 39	75,801	48,120	4,515	2,283	16,629	4,254
Aged 40 to 44	16,172	9,858	934	511	3,960	909
Aged 45 or older	750	442	47	24	185	52

PERCENT DISTRIBUTION BY ETHNIC ORIGIN

	total	Mexican	Puerto Rican	Cuban	Central and South American	other Hispanic
Total Hispanic births	**100.0%**	**71.7%**	**6.4%**	**1.6%**	**14.9%**	**5.4%**
Under age 20	100.0	76.6	8.0	0.9	8.6	5.9
Aged 20 to 24	100.0	74.4	7.0	1.0	12.3	5.4
Aged 25 to 29	100.0	72.0	5.8	1.6	15.6	5.0
Aged 30 to 34	100.0	68.0	5.5	2.5	18.6	5.3
Aged 35 to 39	100.0	63.5	6.0	3.0	21.9	5.6
Aged 40 to 44	100.0	61.0	5.8	3.2	24.5	5.6
Aged 45 or older	100.0	58.9	6.3	3.2	24.7	6.9

PERCENT DISTRIBUTION BY AGE

	total	Mexican	Puerto Rican	Cuban	Central and South American	other Hispanic
Total Hispanic births	**100.0%**	**100.0%**	**100.0%**	**100.0%**	**100.0%**	**100.0%**
Under age 20	14.3	15.3	17.9	7.9	8.3	15.9
Aged 20 to 24	30.0	31.1	32.5	17.5	24.8	30.2
Aged 25 to 29	27.0	27.1	24.3	26.7	28.4	25.0
Aged 30 to 34	18.5	17.6	15.9	28.9	23.2	18.3
Aged 35 to 39	8.3	7.4	7.7	15.4	12.3	8.7
Aged 40 to 44	1.8	1.5	1.6	3.4	2.9	1.9
Aged 45 or older	0.1	0.1	0.1	0.2	0.1	0.1

Source: National Center for Health Statistics, Births: Final Data for 2003, *National Vital Statistics Reports, Vol. 54, No. 2, 2005; Internet site http://www.cdc.gov/nchs/products/pubs/pubd/nvsr/54/54-pre.htm; calculations by New Strategist*

Table 4.25   Births to Hispanic Women by Age and Marital Status, 2003

(total number of births to Hispanics, number of births to unmarried Hispanics, and unmarried share of total, by age, 2003)

		unmarried Hispanics	
	total	number	share of total
Births to Hispanics	**912,329**	**410,620**	**45.0%**
Under age 15	2,356	2,224	94.4
Aged 15 to 19	128,524	97,925	76.2
Aged 20 to 24	273,311	146,729	53.7
Aged 25 to 29	246,361	91,644	37.2
Aged 30 to 34	169,054	46,995	27.8
Aged 35 to 39	75,801	20,158	26.6
Aged 40 or older	16,922	4,945	29.2

Source: National Center for Health Statistics, Births: Final Data for 2003, *National Vital Statistics Reports, Vol. 54, No. 2, 2005; Internet site http://www.cdc.gov/nchs/products/pubs/pubd/nvsr/54/54-pre.htm; calculations by New Strategist*

Table 4.26   Births to Hispanic Women by Birth Order, 2003

(total number of births, number and percent distribution of births to Hispanics, and Hispanic share of total, by birth order, 2003)

		Hispanic		
	total	number	percent distribution	share of total
Total births	**4,089,950**	**912,329**	**100.0%**	**22.3%**
First child	1,633,987	330,032	36.2	20.2
Second child	1,320,477	280,462	30.7	21.2
Third child	684,296	175,225	19.2	25.6
Fourth or later child	439,235	124,238	13.6	28.3

Note: Numbers will not add to total because "not stated" is not shown.
Source: National Center for Health Statistics, Births: Final Data for 2003, *National Vital Statistics Reports, Vol. 54, No. 2, 2005; Internet site http://www.cdc.gov/nchs/products/pubs/pubd/nvsr/54/54-pre.htm; calculations by New Strategist*

Table 4.27 Births to Hispanic Women by State, 2003

(total number of births, number and percent distribution of births to Hispanics, and Hispanic share of total, by state, 2003)

	total	Hispanic births number	percent distribution	share of total
Total births	**4,089,950**	**912,329**	**100.0%**	**22.3%**
Alabama	59,552	2,904	0.3	4.9
Alaska	10,086	770	0.1	7.6
Arizona	90,967	39,780	4.4	43.7
Arkansas	37,784	3,278	0.4	8.7
California	540,997	269,705	29.6	49.9
Colorado	69,339	21,387	2.3	30.8
Connecticut	42,873	7,547	0.8	17.6
Delaware	11,329	1,380	0.2	12.2
District of Columbia	7,619	962	0.1	12.6
Florida	212,250	54,857	6.0	25.8
Georgia	135,979	18,262	2.0	13.4
Hawaii	18,100	2,617	0.3	14.5
Idaho	21,800	2,939	0.3	13.5
Illinois	182,495	42,460	4.7	23.3
Indiana	86,434	6,779	0.7	7.8
Iowa	38,174	2,519	0.3	6.6
Kansas	39,476	5,442	0.6	13.8
Kentucky	55,236	1,959	0.2	3.5
Louisiana	65,040	1,675	0.2	2.6
Maine	13,855	166	0.0	1.2
Maryland	74,930	6,976	0.8	9.3
Massachusetts	80,184	9,800	1.1	12.2
Michigan	131,094	7,670	0.8	5.9
Minnesota	70,050	4,932	0.5	7.0
Mississippi	42,380	543	0.1	1.3
Missouri	77,045	3,483	0.4	4.5
Montana	11,422	379	0.0	3.3
Nebraska	25,917	3,453	0.4	13.3
Nevada	33,647	12,198	1.3	36.3
New Hampshire	14,393	528	0.1	3.7
New Jersey	116,983	26,534	2.9	22.7
New Mexico	27,821	14,843	1.6	53.4
New York	253,714	55,281	6.1	21.8
North Carolina	118,323	16,080	1.8	13.6
North Dakota	7,972	168	0.0	2.1
Ohio	149,679	5,352	0.6	3.6
Oklahoma	50,981	5,733	0.6	11.2
Oregon	45,953	8,439	0.9	18.4

(continued)

	total	Hispanic births		
		number	percent distribution	share of total
Pennsylvania	145,959	10,832	1.2%	7.4%
Rhode Island	13,209	2,483	0.3	18.8
South Carolina	55,649	3,662	0.4	6.6
South Dakota	11,027	340	0.0	3.1
Tennessee	78,890	4,934	0.5	6.3
Texas	377,476	183,139	20.1	48.5
Utah	49,860	7,069	0.8	14.2
Vermont	6,589	59	0.0	0.9
Virginia	101,254	10,401	1.1	10.3
Washington	80,489	13,320	1.5	16.5
West Virginia	20,935	104	0.0	0.5
Wisconsin	70,040	5,539	0.6	7.9
Wyoming	6,700	667	0.1	10.0

Source: National Center for Health Statistics, Births: Final Data for 2003, *National Vital Statistics Reports, Vol. 54, No. 2, 2005; Internet site http://www.cdc.gov/nchs/products/pubs/pubd/nvsr/54/54-pre.htm; calculations by New Strategist*

Table 4.28 Health Insurance Coverage of Hispanics by Age, 2003

(number and percent distribution of Hispanics by age and health insurance coverage status, 2003; numbers in thousands)

	total	with health insurance coverage during year			not covered at any time during the year
		total	private	government	
Total Hispanics	**40,425**	**27,188**	**18,183**	**10,716**	**13,237**
Under age 18	13,854	10,944	5,824	5,817	2,911
Aged 18 to 24	4,974	2,429	1,848	712	2,545
Aged 25 to 34	7,423	3,832	3,205	725	3,591
Aged 35 to 44	6,007	3,754	3,223	646	2,253
Aged 45 to 54	3,925	2,742	2,281	556	1,184
Aged 55 to 64	2,161	1,526	1,168	422	635
Aged 65 or older	2,080	1,962	633	1,838	118
PERCENT DISTRIBUTION BY COVERAGE STATUS					
Total Hispanics	**100.0%**	**67.3%**	**45.0%**	**26.5%**	**32.7%**
Under age 18	100.0	79.0	42.0	42.0	21.0
Aged 18 to 24	100.0	48.8	37.2	14.3	51.2
Aged 25 to 34	100.0	51.6	43.2	9.8	48.4
Aged 35 to 44	100.0	62.5	53.7	10.8	37.5
Aged 45 to 54	100.0	69.9	58.1	14.2	30.2
Aged 55 to 64	100.0	70.6	54.0	19.5	29.4
Aged 65 or older	100.0	94.3	30.4	88.4	5.7

Note: Numbers may not add to total because some people have more than one type of health insurance.
Source: Bureau of the Census, 2004 Current Population Survey, Annual Social and Economic Supplement, detailed tables, Internet site http://pubdb3.census.gov/macro/032004/health/h01_000.htm; calculations by New Strategist

Table 4.29 Hispanics with Private Health Insurance Coverage by Age, 2003

(number and percent distribution of Hispanics by age and private health insurance coverage status, 2003; numbers in thousands)

| | | with private health insurance | | | |
| | | total | employment-based | | |
	total	total	total	own	direct purchase
Total Hispanics	**40,425**	**18,183**	**16,788**	**8,046**	**1,551**
Under age 18	13,854	5,824	5,483	29	389
Aged 18 to 24	4,974	1,848	1,590	722	153
Aged 25 to 34	7,423	3,205	3,034	2,311	218
Aged 35 to 44	6,007	3,223	3,042	2,241	238
Aged 45 to 54	3,925	2,281	2,123	1,600	201
Aged 55 to 64	2,161	1,168	1,070	797	131
Aged 65 or older	2,080	633	446	345	221
PERCENT DISTRIBUTION BY COVERAGE STATUS					
Total Hispanics	**100.0%**	**45.0%**	**41.5%**	**19.9%**	**3.8%**
Under age 18	100.0	42.0	39.6	0.2	2.8
Aged 18 to 24	100.0	37.2	32.0	14.5	3.1
Aged 25 to 34	100.0	43.2	40.9	31.1	2.9
Aged 35 to 44	100.0	53.7	50.6	37.3	4.0
Aged 45 to 54	100.0	58.1	54.1	40.8	5.1
Aged 55 to 64	100.0	54.0	49.5	36.9	6.1
Aged 65 or older	100.0	30.4	21.4	16.6	10.6

Note: Numbers will not add to total because some people have more than one type of health insurance.
Source: Bureau of the Census, 2004 Current Population Survey, Annual Social and Economic Supplement, detailed tables, Internet site http://pubdb3.census.gov/macro/032004/health/h01_000.htm; calculations by New Strategist

Table 4.30　Hispanics with Government Health Insurance Coverage by Age, 2003

(number and percent distribution of Hispanics by age and government health insurance coverage status, 2003;
numbers in thousands)

	total	with government health insurance			
		total	Medicaid	Medicare	military
Total Hispanics	**40,425**	**10,716**	**8,505**	**2,462**	**639**
Under age 18	13,854	5,817	5,585	120	190
Aged 18 to 24	4,974	712	606	20	113
Aged 25 to 34	7,423	725	630	49	75
Aged 35 to 44	6,007	646	535	80	77
Aged 45 to 54	3,925	556	410	148	71
Aged 55 to 64	2,161	422	251	213	47
Aged 65 or older	2,080	1,838	488	1,833	67
PERCENT DISTRIBUTION BY COVERAGE STATUS					
Total Hispanics	**100.0%**	**26.5%**	**21.0%**	**6.1%**	**1.6%**
Under age 18	100.0	42.0	40.3	0.9	1.4
Aged 18 to 24	100.0	14.3	12.2	0.4	2.3
Aged 25 to 34	100.0	9.8	8.5	0.7	1.0
Aged 35 to 44	100.0	10.8	8.9	1.3	1.3
Aged 45 to 54	100.0	14.2	10.4	3.8	1.8
Aged 55 to 64	100.0	19.5	11.6	9.9	2.2
Aged 65 or older	100.0	88.4	23.5	88.1	3.2

Note: Numbers will not add to total because some people have more than one type of health insurance.
Source: Bureau of the Census, 2004 Current Population Survey, Annual Social and Economic Supplement, detailed tables, Internet
site http://pubdb3.census.gov/macro/032004/health/h01_000.htm; calculations by New Strategist

Table 4.31 Health Conditions among Hispanics Aged 18 or Older, 2003

(number of total people and Hispanics aged 18 or older with selected health conditions, percent of Hispanics with condition, and Hispanic share of total with condition, 2003; numbers in thousands)

		Hispanic		
	total	number	percent with condition	share of total
Total people	**213,042**	**26,272**	–	**12.3%**
Selected circulatory diseases				
Heart disease, all types	23,536	1,470	7.7%	6.2
Coronary	12,254	761	4.5	6.2
Hypertension	45,927	3,497	19.0	7.6
Stroke	5,070	316	2.2	6.2
Selected respiratory conditions				
Emphysema	3,115	80	0.6	2.6
Asthma				
Ever	20,697	1,904	7.5	9.2
Still	13,623	1,207	4.8	8.9
Hay fever	18,356	1,529	6.3	8.3
Sinusitis	29,673	2,030	8.5	6.8
Chronic bronchitis	8,560	604	2.8	7.1
Cancer				
Any cancer	13,973	530	2.9	3.8
Breast cancer (all adults)	2,426	95	0.6	3.9
Cervical cancer (women only)	1,082	67	0.5	6.2
Prostate cancer (men only)	1,332	50	0.9	3.8
Other selected diseases and conditions				
Diabetes	14,012	1,556	8.6	11.1
Ulcers	14,456	1,285	5.7	8.9
Kidney disease	3,017	402	1.9	13.3
Liver disease	2,511	310	1.4	12.3
Arthritis	45,793	2,896	16.4	6.3
Chronic joint symptoms	57,242	4,218	20.2	7.4
Migraines or severe headaches	32,268	4,179	15.9	13.0
Pain in neck	31,368	3,329	14.5	10.6
Pain in lower back	58,430	6,465	26.5	11.1
Pain in face or jaw	9,464	926	3.8	9.8
Selected sensory problems				
Hearing	32,533	1,811	9.8	5.6
Vision	18,628	1,899	9.1	10.2
Absence of all natural teeth	15,927	1,161	7.4	7.3

Note: The conditions shown are those that have ever been diagnosed by a doctor, except as noted. Hay fever, sinusitis, and chronic bronchitis have been diagnosed in the past twelve months. Kidney and liver disease have been diagnosed in the past twelve months and exclude kidney stones, bladder infections, and incontinence. Chronic joint symptoms are shown if respondent had pain, aching, or stiffness in or around a joint (excluding back and neck) and the condition began more than three months ago. Migraines, pain in neck, lower back, face, or jaw are shown only if pain lasted a whole day or more. (–) means not applicable.
Source: National Center for Health Statistics, Summary Health Statistics for U.S. Adults: National Health Interview Survey, 2003, Series 10, No. 225, 2005; Internet site http://www.cdc.gov/nchs/nhis.htm; calculations by New Strategist

Table 4.32 Health Conditions among Hispanic Children, 2003

(number of total people and Hispanics under age 18 with selected health conditions, percent of Hispanics with condition, and Hispanic share of total, 2003; numbers in thousands)

		Hispanic		
	total	number	percent with condition	share of total
Total children	**72,973**	**13,464**	–	**18.5%**
Diagnosed with asthma	9,071	1,575	12.0%	17.4
Experienced in last 12 months				
Asthma attack	3,975	597	4.5	15.0
Hay fever	7,059	952	7.3	13.5
Respiratory allergies	8,347	1,051	8.0	12.6
Other allergies	8,407	1,074	8.0	12.8
Ever told had*				
Learning disability	4,561	677	6.3	14.8
Attention deficit hyperactivity disorder	3,881	403	3.8	10.4
Prescription medication taken regularly for at least 3 months	9,287	1,032	7.9	11.1

* *"Ever told" by a school representative or health professional. Data exclude children under age 3.*
Note: Other allergies include food or digestive allergies, eczema, and other skin allergies. (–) means not applicable.
Source: National Center for Health Statistics, Summary Health Statistics for U.S. Children: National Health Interview Survey, 2003, *Series 10, No. 223, 2005; Internet site http://www.cdc.gov/nchs/nhis.htm; calculations by New Strategist*

Table 4.33 Difficulties in Physical Functioning among Hispanics, 2003

(number of total people and Hispanics aged 18 or older, number with difficulties in physical functioning, percent of Hispanics with difficulty, and Hispanic share of total, by type of difficulty, 2003; numbers in thousands)

		Hispanic		
	total	number	percent with difficulty	share of total
TOTAL PEOPLE	**213,042**	**26,272**	–	**12.3%**
Total with any physical difficulty	**31,322**	**2,549**	**13.8%**	**8.1**
Walk quarter of a mile	14,910	1,182	7.0	7.9
Climb up ten steps without resting	11,107	1,134	6.8	10.2
Stand for two hours	18,663	1,561	8.8	8.4
Sit for two hours	7,211	882	4.3	12.2
Stoop, bend, or kneel	18,250	1,541	8.6	8.4
Reach over head	6,264	530	3.0	8.5
Grasp or handle small objects	3,943	342	2.1	8.7
Lift or carry ten pounds	9,194	941	5.5	10.2
Push or pull large objects	13,463	1,173	6.7	8.7

Note: Respondents were classified as having difficulties if they responded "very difficult" or "can't do at all." (–) means not applicable.
Source: National Center for Health Statistics, Summary Health Statistics for U.S. Adults: National Health Interview Survey, 2003, *Series 10, No. 225, 2005; Internet site http://www.cdc.gov/nchs/nhis.htm; calculations by New Strategist*

Table 4.34 AIDS Cases among Hispanics, through December 2003

(total number of AIDS cases diagnosed, number and percent distribution of AIDS cases diagnosed among Hispanics, and Hispanic share of total, by sex and age at diagnosis, through December 2003)

		Hispanic		
	total	number	percent distribution	share of total
Total AIDS cases	**874,230**	**138,812**	**100.0%**	**15.9%**
Males aged 13 or older	708,452	112,101	80.8	15.8
Females aged 13 or older	156,837	24,997	18.0	15.9
Children under age 13	8,939	1,714	1.2	19.2

Source: National Center for Health Statistics, Health, United States, 2004; *Internet site http://www.cdc.gov/nchs/hus.htm; calculations by New Strategist*

Table 4.35 Leading Causes of Death among Hispanics, 2002

(number and percent distribution of deaths to Hispanics accounted for by the ten leading causes of death among Hispanics, 2002)

	number	percent distribution
Total Hispanic deaths	**117,135**	**100.0%**
1. Diseases of the heart (1)	27,887	23.8
2. Malignant neoplasms (cancer) (2)	23,141	19.8
3. Accidents (unintentional injuries) (5)	10,106	8.6
4. Cerebrovascular diseases (3)	6,451	5.5
5. Diabetes mellitus (6)	5,912	5.0
6. Chronic liver disease and cirrhosis (12)	3,409	2.9
7. Homicide (14)	3,129	2.7
8. Chronic lower respiratory disease (4)	3,058	2.6
9. Influenza and pneumonia (7)	2,824	2.4
10. Certain conditions originating in perinatal period	2,402	2.1
All other causes	28,816	24.6

Note: Number in parentheses shows rank for all Americans if the cause of death is among top fifteen.
Source: National Center for Health Statistics, Health, United States, 2004; *Internet site http://www.cdc.gov/nchs/hus.htm; calculations by New Strategist*

Hispanics Are Much Less Likely than the Average American to Own a Home

Forty-eight percent of the nation's Hispanic households owned their home in 2004 compared with a much higher homeownership rate of 69 percent for all households. According to an analysis of homeownership in 2003, homeownership among Hispanic married couples stood at 69 percent. By age, Hispanic homeownership surpasses 60 percent in the 55-or-older age group. More than half of Hispanic households in the Midwest and South own their home. In the Northeast, only 26 percent do.

The 83 percent majority of Hispanic homeowners live in single-family, detached homes. Hispanic homeowners estimate the value of their home at a median of $139,068.

Most Hispanic householders are satisfied with their home and neighborhood. On a scale of one to ten, 76 percent of Hispanic homeowners rate their home an eight or higher. Among Hispanic renters, however, a much smaller 55 percent rate their home at least an eight. Only 9 percent of Hispanic homeowners and 16 percent of renters report that crime is a bothersome problem in their neighborhood.

Seventeen percent of Hispanics moved between 2003 and 2004, a higher mobility rate than for the population as a whole. The main reason Hispanic homeowners moved is because their homeownership status changed from renter to owner.

■ Hispanic homeownership will continue to lag behind the national average because many Hispanics are immigrants with low incomes.

Hispanic homeownership is lowest in the Northeast

(percent of Hispanic households that own their home, by region)

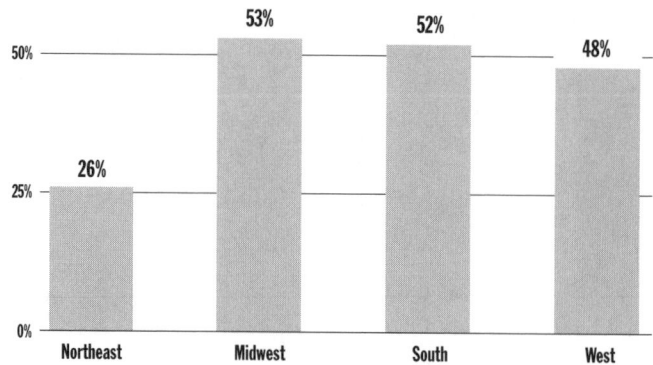

Table 4.36 Hispanic Homeownership Rate, 1994 to 2004

(homeownership rate of total and Hispanic households and index of Hispanic to total, 1994 to 2004; percentage point change in homeownership rate, 1994–2004)

	total households	Hispanic households	index
2004	69.0%	48.1%	70
2003	68.3	46.7	68
2002	67.9	48.2	71
2001	67.8	47.3	70
2000	67.4	46.3	69
1999	66.8	45.5	68
1998	66.3	44.7	67
1997	65.7	43.3	66
1996	65.4	42.8	65
1995	64.7	42.1	65
1994	64.0	41.2	64
Percentage point change			
1994 to 2004	5.0	6.9	–

Note: The index is calculated by dividing the Hispanic homeownership rate by the total rate and multiplying by 100. (–) means not applicable.
Source: Bureau of the Census, American Housing Survey for the United States: 2003, Current Housing Reports, Internet site http://www.census.gov/hhes/www/ahs.html; calculations by New Strategist

Table 4.37 Hispanic Homeownership Status by Age of Householder, 2003

(number and percent of Hispanic households by age of householder and homeownership status, 2003; numbers in thousands)

	total	owner number	owner percent	renter number	renter percent
Total Hispanic households	**11,038**	**5,106**	**46.3%**	**5,931**	**53.7%**
Under age 25	938	127	13.5	811	86.5
Aged 25 to 29	1,311	350	26.7	961	73.3
Aged 30 to 34	1,684	621	36.9	1,063	63.1
Aged 35 to 44	2,785	1,392	50.0	1,394	50.1
Aged 45 to 54	1,966	1,139	57.9	828	42.1
Aged 55 to 64	1,133	719	63.5	414	36.5
Aged 65 to 74	698	422	60.5	276	39.5
Aged 75 or older	522	337	64.6	185	35.4
Median age	40	45	–	35	–

Note: (–) means not applicable.
Source: Bureau of the Census, American Housing Survey for the United States: 2003, Current Housing Reports, Internet site http://www.census.gov/hhes/www/ahs.html; calculations by New Strategist

Table 4.38 Hispanic Homeowners by Age of Householder, 2003

(number of total homeowners, number and percent distribution of Hispanic homeowners, and Hispanic share of total, by age, 2003; numbers in thousands)

	total	Hispanic number	Hispanic percent distribution	share of total
Total homeowners	**72,238**	**5,106**	**100.0%**	**7.1%**
Under age 25	1,272	127	2.5	10.0
Aged 25 to 29	3,207	350	6.9	10.9
Aged 30 to 34	5,845	621	12.2	10.6
Aged 35 to 44	15,406	1,392	27.3	9.0
Aged 45 to 54	16,661	1,139	22.3	6.8
Aged 55 to 64	12,497	719	14.1	5.8
Aged 65 to 74	8,876	422	8.3	4.8
Aged 75 or older	8,474	337	6.6	4.0

Source: Bureau of the Census, American Housing Survey for the United States: 2003, Current Housing Reports, Internet site http://www.census.gov/hhes/www/ahs.html; calculations by New Strategist

Table 4.39 Hispanic Homeownership Status by Household Type, 2003

(number and percent of Hispanic households by household type and homeownership status, 2003; numbers in thousands)

		owner		renter	
	total	number	percent	number	percent
TOTAL HISPANIC HOUSEHOLDS	**11,339**	**5,385**	**47.5%**	**5,955**	**52.5%**
Family households	**9,090**	**4,690**	**51.6**	**4,400**	**48.4**
Married couples	6,189	3,690	59.6	2,499	40.4
Female householder, no spouse present	2,029	674	33.2	1,355	66.8
Male householder, no spouse present	872	325	37.3	547	62.7
Nonfamily households	**2,249**	**694**	**30.9**	**1,555**	**69.1**
Female householder	1,021	376	36.8	646	63.3
Male householder	1,228	319	26.0	909	74.0

Source: Bureau of the Census, America's Families and Living Arrangements, 2003 Current Population Survey Annual Social and Economic Supplement; Internet site http://www.census.gov/population/www/socdemo/hh-fam/cps2003.html; calculations by New Strategist

Table 4.40 Hispanic Homeowners by Type of Household, 2003

(number of total homeowners, number and percent distribution of Hispanic homeowners, and Hispanic share of total, by type of household, 2003; numbers in thousands)

		Hispanic		
	total	number	percent distribution	share of total
TOTAL HOMEOWNERS	**75,909**	**5,385**	**100.0%**	**7.1%**
Family households	**57,092**	**4,690**	**87.1**	**8.2**
Married couples	47,676	3,690	68.5	7.7
Female householder, no spouse present	6,695	674	12.5	10.1
Male householder, no spouse present	2,721	325	6.0	11.9
Nonfamily households	**18,817**	**694**	**12.9**	**3.7**
Female householder	11,075	376	7.0	3.4
Male householder	7,742	319	5.9	4.1

Source: Bureau of the Census, America's Families and Living Arrangements, 2003 Current Population Survey Annual Social and Economic Supplement; Internet site http://www.census.gov/population/www/socdemo/hh-fam/cps2003.html; calculations by New Strategist

Table 4.41 Hispanic Homeownership Status by Region, 2003

(number and percent of Hispanic households by homeownership status and region, 2003; numbers in thousands)

	total	owners		renters	
		number	share of total	number	share of total
Total Hispanic households	**11,038**	**5,106**	**46.3%**	**5,931**	**53.7%**
Northeast	1,739	444	25.5	1,296	74.5
Midwest	946	504	53.3	442	46.7
South	3,881	2,020	52.0	1,861	48.0
West	4,472	2,139	47.8	2,333	52.2

Source: Bureau of the Census, American Housing Survey for the United States: 2003, *Current Housing Reports, Internet site http://www.census.gov/hhes/www/ahs.html; calculations by New Strategist*

Table 4.42 Hispanic Homeowners by Region, 2003

(number of total homeowners, number and percent distribution of Hispanic homeowners, and Hispanic share of total, by region, 2003; numbers in thousands)

	total	Hispanic		
		number	percent distribution	share of total
Total homeowners	**72,238**	**5,106**	**100.0%**	**7.1%**
Northeast	12,964	444	8.7	3.4
Midwest	17,889	504	9.9	2.8
South	26,699	2,020	39.6	7.6
West	14,686	2,139	41.9	14.6

Source: Bureau of the Census, American Housing Survey for the United States: 2003, *Current Housing Reports, Internet site http://www.census.gov/hhes/www/ahs.html; calculations by New Strategist*

Table 4.43 Characteristics of Housing Units Occupied by Hispanics, 2003

(number and percent distribution of housing units occupied by Hispanics by selected housing characteristics and homeownership status, 2003; numbers in thousands)

	total	owner-occupied		renter-occupied	
		number	percent distribution	number	percent distribution
UNITS IN STRUCTURE					
Total Hispanic households	**11,038**	**5,106**	**100.0%**	**5,931**	**100.0%**
One, detached	5,511	4,227	82.8	1,284	21.6
One, attached	717	237	4.6	479	8.1
Two to four	1,357	178	3.5	1,179	19.9
Five to nine	996	41	0.8	955	16.1
10 to 19	774	45	0.9	729	12.3
20 to 49	676	52	1.0	624	10.5
50 or more	560	51	1.0	508	8.6
Mobile home or trailer	447	274	5.4	173	2.9
Median square footage of unit*	1,455	1,552	–	1,203	–
NUMBER OF BEDROOMS					
Total Hispanic households	**11,038**	**5,106**	**100.0**	**5,931**	**100.0**
None	118	3	0.1	116	2.0
One	1,873	137	2.7	1,736	29.3
Two	3,769	1,089	21.3	2,681	45.2
Three	3,826	2,664	52.2	1,162	19.6
Four or more	1,451	1,214	23.8	237	4.0
NUMBER OF BATHROOMS					
Total Hispanic households	**11,038**	**5,106**	**100.0**	**5,931**	**100.0**
None	69	24	0.5	45	0.8
One	5,949	1,598	31.3	4,352	73.4
One-and-one-half	1,197	741	14.5	456	7.7
Two or more	3,823	2,744	53.7	1,078	18.2
ROOM USED FOR BUSINESS					
Total Hispanic households	**11,038**	**5,106**	**100.0**	**5,931**	**100.0**
With room(s) used for business	1,333	822	16.1	510	8.6
SELECTED AMENITIES					
Porch, deck, balcony, or patio	8,445	4,580	89.7	3,865	65.2
Telephone available	10,637	4,953	97.0	5,684	95.8
Usable fireplace	2,193	1,647	32.3	546	9.2
Separate dining room	4,099	2,569	50.3	1,530	25.8
Two or more living or recreation rooms	1,548	1,353	26.5	195	3.3
Garage or carport	5,674	3,799	74.4	1,875	31.6
No cars, trucks, or vans available	1,482	178	3.5	1,304	22.0

* *Single-family detached and mobile/manufactured homes only.*
Note: (–) means not applicable.
Source: Bureau of the Census, American Housing Survey for the United States: 2003, *Current Housing Reports, Internet site http://www.census.gov/hhes/www/ahs.html; calculations by New Strategist*

Table 4.44 Housing Value for Hispanic Homeowners, 2003

(number and percent distribution of Hispanic homeowners by value of home, 2003; numbers in thousands)

	number	percent distribution
Total Hispanic homeowners	**5,106**	**100.0%**
Under $10,000	159	3.1
$10,000 to $19,999	86	1.7
$20,000 to $29,999	103	2.0
$30,000 to $39,999	129	2.5
$40,000 to $49,999	149	2.9
$50,000 to $59,999	206	4.0
$60,000 to $69,999	210	4.1
$70,000 to $79,999	262	5.1
$80,000 to $99,999	496	9.7
$100,000 to $119,999	403	7.9
$120,000 to $149,999	551	10.8
$150,000 to $199,999	655	12.8
$200,000 to $249,999	483	9.5
$250,000 to $299,999	376	7.4
$300,000 or more	839	16.4
Median home value	$139,068	–

Note: (–) means not applicable.
Source: Bureau of the Census, American Housing Survey for the United States: 2003, Current Housing Reports, Internet site http://www.census.gov/hhes/www/ahs.html; calculations by New Strategist

Table 4.45 Neighborhood Characteristics of Housing Units Occupied by Hispanics, 2003

(number and percent distribution of housing units occupied by Hispanics by selected neighborhood characteristics and homeownership status, 2003; numbers in thousands)

	total	owner-occupied number	owner-occupied percent distribution	renter-occupied number	renter-occupied percent distribution
DESCRIPTION OF AREA WITHIN 300 FEET OF HOME					
Total Hispanic households	**11,038**	**5,106**	**100.0%**	**5,931**	**100.0%**
Single-family detached homes	8,399	4,495	88.0	3,904	65.8
Single-family attached homes	1,587	572	11.2	1,016	17.1
One-to-three-story multiunit	4,066	834	16.3	3,232	54.5
Four-to-six-story multiunit	1,036	157	3.1	879	14.8
Seven-or-more-story multiunit	485	82	1.6	403	6.8
Manufactured/mobile homes	969	543	10.6	427	7.2
Commercial or institutional	4,227	1,235	24.2	2,991	50.4
Industrial or factories	679	183	3.6	496	8.4
Open space, park, woods, farm, or ranch	2,796	1,340	26.2	1,455	24.5
Four-or-more-lane highway, railroad, or airport	1,729	574	11.2	1,155	19.5
Waterfront property	108	69	1.4	39	0.7
NEIGHBORHOOD PROBLEMS					
Total Hispanic households	**11,038**	**5,106**	**100.0**	**5,931**	**100.0**
Bothersome street noise problem	1,378	563	11.0	815	13.7
Bothersome neighborhood crime problem	1,358	437	8.6	921	15.5
Bothersome odor problem	565	186	3.6	379	6.4
Noise problem	348	146	2.9	201	3.4
Litter or housing deterioration	248	100	2.0	148	2.5
Poor city or county services	117	51	1.0	66	1.1
Undesirable commercial, institutional, industrial	107	44	0.9	63	1.1
People problem	525	200	3.9	325	5.5
Other problems	901	501	9.8	400	6.7
PUBLIC SCHOOLS					
Total Hispanic households with children under 14	**5,269**	**2,362**	**100.0**	**2,906**	**100.0**
Satisfactory public elementary school	4,093	1,864	78.9	2,229	76.7
PUBLIC SERVICES					
Total Hispanic households	**11,038**	**5,106**	**100.0**	**5,931**	**100.0**
With public transportation	8,012	3,272	64.1	4,739	79.9
Satisfactory neighborhood shopping	9,655	4,323	84.7	5,332	89.9
Satisfactory police protection	9,578	4,475	87.6	5,103	86.0

Source: Bureau of the Census, American Housing Survey for the United States: 2003, *Current Housing Reports, Internet site http://www.census.gov/hhes/www/ahs.html; calculations by New Strategist*

Table 4.46 Opinion of Hispanics toward Housing Unit and Neighborhood, 2003

(number and percent distribution of Hispanic households by opinion of housing unit and neighborhood, by homeownership status, 2003; numbers in thousands)

	total	owner-occupied		renter-occupied	
		number	percent distribution	number	percent distribution
OPINION OF HOUSING UNIT					
Total Hispanic households	**11,038**	**5,106**	**100.0%**	**5,931**	**100.0%**
1 (worst)	72	1	0.0	71	1.2
2	57	0	0.0	57	1.0
3	98	11	0.2	86	1.5
4	153	13	0.3	139	2.3
5	888	223	4.4	665	11.2
6	718	210	4.1	508	8.6
7	1,525	577	11.3	948	16.0
8	2,895	1,449	28.4	1,445	24.4
9	1,505	830	16.3	676	11.4
10 (best)	2,740	1,607	31.5	1,133	19.1
Not reported	387	185	3.6	202	3.4
OPINION OF NEIGHBORHOOD					
Total Hispanic households	**11,038**	**5,106**	**100.0**	**5,931**	**100.0**
1 (worst)	99	17	0.3	82	1.4
2	80	24	0.5	56	0.9
3	162	44	0.9	118	2.0
4	194	40	0.8	154	2.6
5	1,013	332	6.5	681	11.5
6	772	293	5.7	479	8.1
7	1,528	661	12.9	867	14.6
8	2,672	1,354	26.5	1,318	22.2
9	1,522	848	16.6	675	11.4
10 (best)	2,540	1,284	25.1	1,255	21.2
No neighborhood	33	14	0.3	19	0.3
Not reported	422	195	3.8	228	3.8

Source: Bureau of the Census, American Housing Survey for the United States: 2003, *Current Housing Reports, Internet site http://www.census.gov/hhes/www/ahs.html; calculations by New Strategist*

Table 4.47 Geographical Mobility of Hispanics by Age, 2003–04

(total number of Hispanics aged 1 or older, and number and percent who moved between March 2003 and March 2004, by age and type of move; numbers in thousands)

		movers				
	total	total	same county	different county, same state	different state	abroad
Total Hispanics	**39,561**	**6,903**	**4,505**	**1,095**	**822**	**481**
Aged 1 to 4	3,404	771	549	135	64	23
Aged 5 to 9	3,852	710	498	91	79	42
Aged 10 to 14	3,766	583	377	108	74	24
Aged 15 to 17	1,968	312	212	41	38	21
Aged 18 to 19	1,274	239	131	51	34	23
Aged 20 to 24	3,700	1,010	664	119	131	96
Aged 25 to 29	3,823	907	605	139	87	76
Aged 30 to 34	3,599	729	482	114	85	48
Aged 35 to 39	3,197	577	362	100	61	54
Aged 40 to 44	2,810	431	281	70	44	36
Aged 45 to 49	2,211	218	118	48	45	7
Aged 50 to 54	1,715	155	89	26	29	11
Aged 55 to 59	1,287	82	48	13	15	6
Aged 60 to 61	374	30	13	6	8	3
Aged 62 to 64	501	32	15	5	10	2
Aged 65 or older	2,081	119	63	29	18	9
PERCENT DISTRIBUTION BY MOBILITY STATUS						
Total Hispanics	**100.0%**	**17.4%**	**11.4%**	**2.8%**	**2.1%**	**1.2%**
Aged 1 to 4	100.0	22.6	16.1	4.0	1.9	0.7
Aged 5 to 9	100.0	18.4	12.9	2.4	2.1	1.1
Aged 10 to 14	100.0	15.5	10.0	2.9	2.0	0.6
Aged 15 to 17	100.0	15.9	10.8	2.1	1.9	1.1
Aged 18 to 19	100.0	18.8	10.3	4.0	2.7	1.8
Aged 20 to 24	100.0	27.3	17.9	3.2	3.5	2.6
Aged 25 to 29	100.0	23.7	15.8	3.6	2.3	2.0
Aged 30 to 34	100.0	20.3	13.4	3.2	2.4	1.3
Aged 35 to 39	100.0	18.0	11.3	3.1	1.9	1.7
Aged 40 to 44	100.0	15.3	10.0	2.5	1.6	1.3
Aged 45 to 49	100.0	9.9	5.3	2.2	2.0	0.3
Aged 50 to 54	100.0	9.0	5.2	1.5	1.7	0.6
Aged 55 to 59	100.0	6.4	3.7	1.0	1.2	0.5
Aged 60 to 61	100.0	8.0	3.5	1.6	2.1	0.8
Aged 62 to 64	100.0	6.4	3.0	1.0	2.0	0.4
Aged 65 or older	100.0	5.7	3.0	1.4	0.9	0.4

Source: Bureau of the Census, Geographic Mobility: 2004, Detailed Tables, Internet site http://www.census.gov/population/www/ socdemo/migrate/cps2004.html; calculations by New Strategist

Table 4.48 Reasons for Moving among Hispanic Movers by Homeownership Status, 2003

(number and percent distribution of Hispanic households with respondents who moved in the past 12 months by main reason for move and for choosing new neighborhood and house, by homeownership status, 2003; numbers in thousands)

	total	owners		renters	
		number	percent distribution	number	percent distribution
MAIN REASON FOR LEAVING PREVIOUS HOUSING UNIT					
Total Hispanic movers	**2,642**	**591**	**100.0%**	**2,051**	**100.0%**
All reported reasons equal	39	4	0.7	34	1.7
Private displacement	23	4	0.7	19	0.9
Government displacement	8	0	0.0	8	0.4
Disaster loss (fire, flood, etc.)	5	2	0.3	3	0.1
New job or job transfer	230	19	3.2	211	10.3
To be closer to work/school/other	180	20	3.4	160	7.8
Other financial/employment reason	100	18	3.0	82	4.0
To establish own household	385	114	19.3	271	13.2
Needed larger house or apartment	336	52	8.8	284	13.8
Married, widowed, divorced, separated	97	31	5.2	66	3.2
Other family/personal reason	241	35	5.9	206	10.0
Wanted better home	216	58	9.8	158	7.7
Change from owner to renter/renter to owner	164	146	24.7	17	0.8
Wanted lower rent or maintenance	132	4	0.7	128	6.2
Other housing related reasons	143	17	2.9	126	6.1
Other	253	42	7.1	211	10.3
Not reported	90	22	3.7	67	3.3
MAIN REASON FOR CHOOSING PRESENT NEIGHBORHOOD					
Total Hispanic movers	**2,642**	**591**	**100.0**	**2,051**	**100.0**
All reported reasons equal	80	16	2.7	63	3.1
Convenient to job	557	81	13.7	476	23.2
Convenient to friends or relatives	466	71	12.0	395	19.3
Convenient to leisure activities	16	1	0.2	15	0.7
Convenient to public transportation	22	0	0.0	22	1.1
Good schools	170	40	6.8	130	6.3
Other public services	48	8	1.4	40	2.0
Looks/design of neighborhood	348	120	20.3	228	11.1
House was most important consideration	381	137	23.2	244	11.9
Other	482	97	16.4	384	18.7
Not reported	74	19	3.2	55	2.7

(continued)

		owners		renters	
	total	number	percent distribution	number	percent distribution
MAIN REASON FOR CHOOSING PRESENT HOME					
Total Hispanic movers	**2,642**	**591**	**100.0%**	**2,051**	**100.0%**
All reported reasons equal	97	27	4.6	71	3.5
Financial reasons	847	167	28.3	680	33.2
Room layout/design	350	97	16.4	254	12.4
Kitchen	13	3	0.5	10	0.5
Size	408	78	13.2	330	16.1
Exterior appearance	100	34	5.8	66	3.2
Yard/trees/view	107	28	4.7	78	3.8
Quality of construction	84	38	6.4	46	2.2
Only one available	162	14	2.4	149	7.3
Other	409	90	15.2	319	15.6
Not reported	65	15	2.5	49	2.4

Source: Bureau of the Census, American Housing Survey for the United States: 2003, *Current Housing Reports, Internet site http://www.census.gov/hhes/www/ahs.html; calculations by New Strategist*

The Incomes of Hispanics Are Well Below Average

The median income of Hispanic households fell 7 percent between 2000 and 2003, after adjusting for inflation. Despite the decline, the $32,997 median income of Hispanic households in 2003 was 8 percent higher than in 1990, after adjusting for inflation. The median income of Hispanic households is only 76 percent as high as that of the average household.

Hispanic household income peaks among householders aged 45 to 54, at a median of $40,253. By household type, median income is greatest for Hispanic married couples, at $40,675. Hispanic men who work full-time had a median income of $26,414 in 2003, while their female counterparts had a median income of $23,062.

Between 1990 and 2003, the median income of Hispanic men who work full-time did not rise at all, after adjusting for inflation. The median income of their female counterparts rose just 4 percent. Hispanics earn less than the average worker because many are recent immigrants with little education. Among foreign-born men who work full-time, immigrants from Central America (including Mexico) earn the least, a median of just $21,798 in 2003.

Sixteen percent of Hispanic married couples are poor—a higher poverty rate than is found among Asian, black, or non-Hispanic white couples. But poverty among Hispanic families has declined since 1990. Among Hispanic female-headed families, the poverty rate fell from 48 to 37 percent during those years.

■ The economic status of Hispanics will remain below that of the average American as long as immigrants account for a large share of the Hispanic population.

Hispanic incomes are growing only slightly faster than average

(percent change in median income of total and Hispanic households, 1990 to 2003; in 2003 dollars)

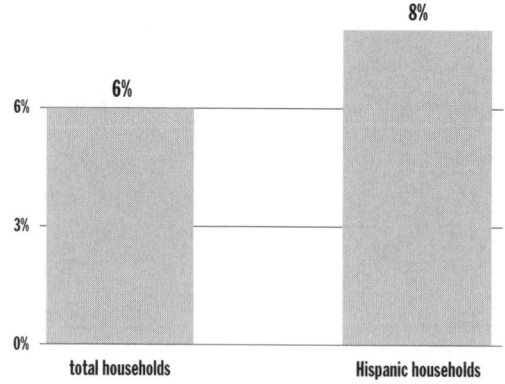

Table 4.49 Median Income of Hispanic Households, 1990 to 2003

(median income of total and Hispanic households, and index of Hispanic to total, 1990 to 2003; percent change in incomes, 2000–03 and 1990–2003; in 2003 dollars)

	total households	Hispanic households	index
2003	$43,318	$32,997	76
2002	43,381	33,861	78
2001	43,882	34,880	79
2000	44,853	35,429	79
1999	44,922	33,938	76
1998	43,825	31,929	73
1997	42,294	30,434	72
1996	41,431	29,073	70
1995	40,845	27,401	67
1994	39,613	28,756	73
1993	39,165	28,690	73
1992	39,364	29,035	74
1991	39,679	29,887	75
1990	40,865	30,475	75
Percent change			
2000 to 2003	–3.4%	–6.9%	–
1990 to 2003	6.0	8.3	–

Source: Bureau of the Census, Current Population Surveys, Internet site http://www.census.gov/hhes/income/histinc/h05.html; calculations by New Strategist

Table 4.50 High-Income Hispanic Households, 2003

(number and percent distribution of Hispanic households with incomes of $100,000 or more, 2003; households in thousands as of 2004)

	total	percent
TOTAL HISPANIC HOUSEHOLDS	**11,693**	**100.0%**
$100,000 or more	**871**	**7.4**
$100,000 to $149,999	572	4.9
$150,000 to $199,999	171	1.5
$200,000 to $249,999	58	0.5
$250,000 or more	70	0.6

Source: Bureau of the Census, 2004 Current Population Survey, Internet site http://pubdb3.census.gov/macro/032004/hhinc/new06_000.htm; calculations by New Strategist

Table 4.51 Hispanic Household Income by Age of Householder, 2003

(number and percent distribution of Hispanic households by household income and age of householder, 2003; households in thousands as of 2004)

	total	15 to 24	25 to 34	35 to 44	45 to 54	55 to 64	aged 65 or older total	65 to 74	75 or older
Hispanic households	**11,693**	**1,163**	**3,181**	**2,986**	**2,022**	**1,229**	**1,113**	**683**	**430**
Under $10,000	1,264	172	278	212	163	157	280	162	119
$10,000 to $19,999	1,984	236	534	409	274	187	342	194	149
$20,000 to $29,999	1,954	225	566	531	292	185	156	97	59
$30,000 to $39,999	1,659	177	549	424	273	141	93	58	34
$40,000 to $49,999	1,200	129	350	323	194	135	67	49	17
$50,000 to $59,999	879	77	239	272	157	91	45	32	12
$60,000 to $69,999	690	50	198	190	143	68	42	27	15
$70,000 to $79,999	537	41	147	152	116	58	25	19	5
$80,000 to $89,999	374	22	78	115	99	48	12	11	1
$90,000 to $99,999	280	5	70	104	69	24	6	3	3
$100,000 or more	872	30	169	255	240	136	42	27	15
Median income	$32,997	$26,912	$32,867	$37,200	$40,253	$34,555	$17,771	$19,199	$15,685

PERCENT DISTRIBUTION BY INCOME

	total	15 to 24	25 to 34	35 to 44	45 to 54	55 to 64	aged 65 or older total	65 to 74	75 or older
Hispanic households	**100.0%**	**100.0%**	**100.0%**	**100.0%**	**100.0%**	**100.0%**	**100.0%**	**100.0%**	**100.0%**
Under $10,000	10.8	14.8	8.7	7.1	8.1	12.8	25.2	23.7	27.7
$10,000 to $19,999	17.0	20.3	16.8	13.7	13.6	15.2	30.7	28.4	34.7
$20,000 to $29,999	16.7	19.3	17.8	17.8	14.4	15.1	14.0	14.2	13.7
$30,000 to $39,999	14.2	15.2	17.3	14.2	13.5	11.5	8.4	8.5	7.9
$40,000 to $49,999	10.3	11.1	11.0	10.8	9.6	11.0	6.0	7.2	4.0
$50,000 to $59,999	7.5	6.6	7.5	9.1	7.8	7.4	4.0	4.7	2.8
$60,000 to $69,999	5.9	4.3	6.2	6.4	7.1	5.5	3.8	4.0	3.5
$70,000 to $79,999	4.6	3.5	4.6	5.1	5.7	4.7	2.2	2.8	1.2
$80,000 to $89,999	3.2	1.9	2.5	3.9	4.9	3.9	1.1	1.6	0.2
$90,000 to $99,999	2.4	0.4	2.2	3.5	3.4	2.0	0.5	0.4	0.7
$100,000 or more	7.5	2.6	5.3	8.5	11.9	11.1	3.8	4.0	3.5

Source: Bureau of the Census, 2004 Current Population Survey, Internet site http://pubdb3.census.gov/macro/032004/hhinc/ new02_001.htm; calculations by New Strategist

Table 4.52 Hispanic Household Income by Household Type, 2003

(number and percent distribution of households headed by Hispanics by household income and household type, 2003; households in thousands as of 2004)

| | | family households | | | nonfamily households | | | |
| | | | female hh, no spouse present | male hh, no spouse present | female householder | | male householder | |
	total	married couples			total	living alone	total	living alone
Hispanic households	**11,693**	**6,227**	**2,138**	**908**	**1,078**	**863**	**1,343**	**891**
Under $10,000	1,264	286	366	56	334	313	223	203
$10,000 to $19,999	1,984	845	508	120	240	211	271	223
$20,000 to $29,999	1,954	1,003	421	144	141	107	245	156
$30,000 to $39,999	1,659	913	294	161	98	78	191	121
$40,000 to $49,999	1,200	736	170	98	92	65	103	55
$50,000 to $59,999	879	546	106	91	48	25	90	48
$60,000 to $69,999	690	444	87	71	34	21	56	23
$70,000 to $79,999	537	371	51	53	24	11	38	12
$80,000 to $89,999	374	253	43	29	18	11	31	11
$90,000 to $99,999	280	210	21	17	11	4	20	7
$100,000 or more	872	622	69	68	36	14	77	30
Median income	$32,997	$40,675	$24,459	$37,834	$18,018	$14,576	$26,450	$20,571

PERCENT DISTRIBUTION BY INCOME

Hispanic households	**100.0%**	**100.0%**	**100.0%**	**100.0%**	**100.0%**	**100.0%**	**100.0%**	**100.0%**
Under $10,000	10.8	4.6	17.1	6.2	31.0	36.3	16.6	22.8
$10,000 to $19,999	17.0	13.6	23.8	13.2	22.3	24.4	20.2	25.0
$20,000 to $29,999	16.7	16.1	19.7	15.9	13.1	12.4	18.2	17.5
$30,000 to $39,999	14.2	14.7	13.8	17.7	9.1	9.0	14.2	13.6
$40,000 to $49,999	10.3	11.8	8.0	10.8	8.5	7.5	7.7	6.2
$50,000 to $59,999	7.5	8.8	5.0	10.0	4.5	2.9	6.7	5.4
$60,000 to $69,999	5.9	7.1	4.1	7.8	3.2	2.4	4.2	2.6
$70,000 to $79,999	4.6	6.0	2.4	5.8	2.2	1.3	2.8	1.3
$80,000 to $89,999	3.2	4.1	2.0	3.2	1.7	1.3	2.3	1.2
$90,000 to $99,999	2.4	3.4	1.0	1.9	1.0	0.5	1.5	0.8
$100,000 or more	7.5	10.0	3.2	7.5	3.3	1.6	5.7	3.4

Source: Bureau of the Census, 2004 Current Population Survey, Internet site http://pubdb3.census.gov/macro/032004/hhinc/ new02_000.htm; calculations by New Strategist

Table 4.53 Income Distribution of Households Headed by the Foreign-Born from Latin America, 2003

(number and percent distribution of foreign-born householders from Latin America by household income and Latin American region, 2003; households in thousands as of 2004)

	total	Caribbean	Central America	South America
Total foreign-born Hispanic householders	**7,097**	**1,497**	**4,758**	**842**
Less than $10,000	744	190	483	71
$10,000 to $14,999	607	137	419	51
$15,000 to $19,999	687	125	504	58
$20,000 to $24,999	674	107	507	61
$25,000 to $34,999	1,210	212	884	113
$35,000 to $49,999	1,156	210	817	129
$50,000 to $74,999	1,060	251	662	147
$75,000 or more	957	263	482	213
Median income	$33,180	$33,939	$30,271	$42,791
Total foreign-born Hispanic householders	**100.0%**	**100.0%**	**100.0%**	**100.0%**
Less than $10,000	10.5	12.7	10.2	8.4
$10,000 to $14,999	8.6	9.2	8.8	6.1
$15,000 to $19,999	9.7	8.4	10.6	6.9
$20,000 to $24,999	9.5	7.1	10.7	7.2
$25,000 to $34,999	17.0	14.2	18.6	13.4
$35,000 to $49,999	16.3	14.0	17.2	15.3
$50,000 to $74,999	14.9	16.8	13.9	17.5
$75,000 or more	13.5	17.6	10.1	25.3

Note: Most of the foreign-born from Central America are from Mexico.
Source: Bureau of the Census, Foreign-Born Population of the United States, Current Population Survey, March 2004, detailed tables (PPL-176), Internet site http://www.census.gov/population/www/socdemo/foreign/ppl-176.html; calculations by New Strategist

Table 4.54 Income of Hispanic Men by Age, 2003

(number and percent distribution of Hispanic men aged 15 or older by income and age, median income of men with income and of men working full-time, year-round, and percent working full-time, year-round, 2003; men in thousands as of 2004)

	total	under 25	25 to 34	35 to 44	45 to 54	55 to 64	65 or older
TOTAL HISPANIC MEN	**14,664**	**3,677**	**4,001**	**3,126**	**1,955**	**1,023**	**545**
Without income	**1,911**	**1,342**	**224**	**149**	**94**	**56**	**26**
With income	**12,753**	**2,335**	**3,777**	**2,977**	**1,861**	**967**	**519**
Under $10,000	2,285	856	436	311	238	140	174
$10,000 to $19,999	3,660	898	1,130	669	434	230	191
$20,000 to $29,999	2,694	378	930	733	362	188	57
$30,000 to $39,999	1,644	125	617	468	267	112	39
$40,000 to $49,999	932	39	317	299	169	93	12
$50,000 to $59,999	542	19	130	185	121	62	20
$60,000 to $69,999	338	5	97	103	73	49	10
$70,000 to $79,999	158	7	34	44	60	12	1
$80,000 to $89,999	129	2	20	57	25	18	5
$90,000 to $99,999	89	1	15	29	29	12	2
$100,000 or more	282	5	52	79	86	49	10
Median income of men with income	$21,053	$12,366	$22,167	$26,217	$26,384	$25,476	$13,409
Median income of men working full-time	26,414	18,388	25,554	30,064	32,008	32,503	29,286
Percent of men working full-time	56.8%	30.1%	71.7%	73.8%	68.7%	57.5%	18.2%
TOTAL HISPANIC MEN	**100.0%**	**100.0%**	**100.0%**	**100.0%**	**100.0%**	**100.0%**	**100.0%**
Without income	**13.0**	**36.5**	**5.6**	**4.8**	**4.8**	**5.5**	**4.8**
With income	**87.0**	**63.5**	**94.4**	**95.2**	**95.2**	**94.5**	**95.2**
Under $10,000	15.6	23.3	10.9	9.9	12.2	13.7	31.9
$10,000 to $19,999	25.0	24.4	28.2	21.4	22.2	22.5	35.0
$20,000 to $29,999	18.4	10.3	23.2	23.4	18.5	18.4	10.5
$30,000 to $39,999	11.2	3.4	15.4	15.0	13.7	10.9	7.2
$40,000 to $49,999	6.4	1.1	7.9	9.6	8.6	9.1	2.2
$50,000 to $59,999	3.7	0.5	3.2	5.9	6.2	6.1	3.7
$60,000 to $69,999	2.3	0.1	2.4	3.3	3.7	4.8	1.8
$70,000 to $79,999	1.1	0.2	0.8	1.4	3.1	1.2	0.2
$80,000 to $89,999	0.9	0.1	0.5	1.8	1.3	1.8	0.9
$90,000 to $99,999	0.6	0.0	0.4	0.9	1.5	1.2	0.4
$100,000 or more	1.9	0.1	1.3	2.5	4.4	4.8	1.8

Source: Bureau of the Census, 2004 Current Population Survey, Internet site http://pubdb3.census.gov/macro/032004/perinc/new01_000.htm; calculations by New Strategist

Table 4.55 Income of Hispanic Women by Age, 2003

(number and percent distribution of Hispanic women aged 15 or older by income and age, median income of women with income and of women working full-time, year-round, and percent working full-time, year-round, 2003; women in thousands as of 2004)

	total	under 25	25 to 34	35 to 44	45 to 54	55 to 64	65 or older
TOTAL HISPANIC WOMEN	**13,902**	**3,292**	**3,422**	**2,880**	**1,970**	**1,138**	**1,199**
Without income	**3,727**	**1,510**	**906**	**584**	**353**	**253**	**119**
With income	**10,175**	**1,782**	**2,516**	**2,296**	**1,617**	**885**	**1,080**
Under $10,000	3,836	963	794	593	431	349	705
$10,000 to $19,999	2,879	506	724	679	476	242	253
$20,000 to $29,999	1,567	213	453	424	290	123	64
$30,000 to $39,999	844	58	291	244	168	68	18
$40,000 to $49,999	460	28	122	159	99	36	18
$50,000 to $59,999	209	6	43	74	49	28	8
$60,000 to $69,999	150	1	41	44	47	14	2
$70,000 to $79,999	69	2	17	21	12	16	–
$80,000 to $89,999	45	1	8	13	17	3	3
$90,000 to $99,999	28	–	4	11	4	3	3
$100,000 or more	92	5	21	33	26	3	4
Median income of women with income	$13,642	$8,679	$15,871	$17,451	$17,265	$12,510	$8,328
Median income of women working full-time	23,062	17,358	24,416	25,023	24,598	24,030	23,092
Percent of women working full-time	33.0%	17.3%	38.5%	45.6%	47.7%	32.9%	6.7%
TOTAL HISPANIC WOMEN	**100.0%**	**100.0%**	**100.0%**	**100.0%**	**100.0%**	**100.0%**	**100.0%**
Without income	26.8	45.9	26.5	20.3	17.9	22.2	9.9
With income	73.2	54.1	73.5	79.7	82.1	77.8	90.1
Under $10,000	27.6	29.3	23.2	20.6	21.9	30.7	58.8
$10,000 to $19,999	20.7	15.4	21.2	23.6	24.2	21.3	21.1
$20,000 to $29,999	11.3	6.5	13.2	14.7	14.7	10.8	5.3
$30,000 to $39,999	6.1	1.8	8.5	8.5	8.5	6.0	1.5
$40,000 to $49,999	3.3	0.9	3.6	5.5	5.0	3.2	1.5
$50,000 to $59,999	1.5	0.2	1.3	2.6	2.5	2.5	0.7
$60,000 to $69,999	1.1	0.0	1.2	1.5	2.4	1.2	0.2
$70,000 to $79,999	0.5	0.1	0.5	0.7	0.6	1.4	–
$80,000 to $89,999	0.3	0.0	0.2	0.5	0.9	0.3	0.3
$90,000 to $99,999	0.2	–	0.1	0.4	0.2	0.3	0.3
$100,000 or more	0.7	0.2	0.6	1.1	1.3	0.3	0.3

Note: (–) means sample is too small to make a reliable estimate.
Source: Bureau of the Census, 2004 Current Population Survey, Internet site http://pubdb3.census.gov/macro/032004/perinc/new01_000.htm; calculations by New Strategist

Table 4.56 Median Income of Hispanics Working Full-Time by Sex, 1990 to 2003

(median income of Hispanics working full-time, year-round by sex; index of Hispanic to total population median income, and Hispanic women's income as a percent of Hispanic men's income, 1990 to 2003; percent change in income, 2000–2003 and 1990–03; in 2003 dollars)

	Hispanic men		Hispanic women		Hispanic women's income as a percent of Hispanic men's income
	median income	index Hispanic/total	median income	index Hispanic/total	
2003	$26,414	64	$23,062	73	87.3%
2002	26,736	65	22,867	72	85.5
2001	26,261	63	22,834	72	87.0
2000	25,823	62	22,641	73	87.7
1999	25,076	61	22,100	73	88.1
1998	25,364	62	22,335	74	88.1
1997	24,914	62	22,488	76	90.3
1996	24,823	63	22,497	77	90.6
1995	24,636	64	21,402	75	86.9
1994	25,200	65	22,613	79	89.7
1993	25,603	66	21,452	76	83.8
1992	25,512	64	22,709	80	89.0
1991	26,378	66	21,796	78	82.6
1990	26,419	67	22,083	79	83.6
Percent change					
2000 to 2003	2.3%	–	1.9%	–	–
1990 to 2003	0.0	–	4.4	–	–

Note: The Hispanic/total indexes are calculated by dividing the median income of Hispanic men and women by the median income of total men and women and multiplying by 100. (–) means not applicable.
Source: Bureau of the Census, Current Population Surveys, Internet site http://www.census.gov/hhes/income/histinc/p36b.html; calculations by New Strategist

Table 4.57 Earnings Distribution of Foreign-Born Men from Latin America Working Full-Time, 2003

(number and percent distribution of foreign-born men aged 15 or older from Latin America working full-time, year-round, by earnings and Latin American region, 2003; men in thousands as of 2004)

	total	Caribbean	Central America	South America
Total foreign-born men from Latin America working full-time	**5,596**	**749**	**4,206**	**641**
Less than $10,000	227	20	184	22
$10,000 to $14,999	777	47	679	51
$15,000 to $19,999	1,054	101	888	65
$20,000 to $24,999	914	102	734	79
$25,000 to $34,999	1,158	153	852	153
$35,000 to $49,999	772	152	507	113
$50,000 to $74,999	443	94	269	79
$75,000 or more	251	80	91	80
Median income	$23,615	$31,206	$21,798	$30,542
Total foreign-born men from Latin America working full-time	**100.0%**	**100.0%**	**100.0%**	**100.0%**
Less than $10,000	4.1	2.7	4.4	3.4
$10,000 to $14,999	13.9	6.3	16.1	8.0
$15,000 to $19,999	18.8	13.5	21.1	10.1
$20,000 to $24,999	16.3	13.6	17.5	12.3
$25,000 to $34,999	20.7	20.4	20.3	23.9
$35,000 to $49,999	13.8	20.3	12.1	17.6
$50,000 to $74,999	7.9	12.6	6.4	12.3
$75,000 or more	4.5	10.7	2.2	12.5

Note: Most of the foreign-born from Central America are from Mexico.
Source: Bureau of the Census, Foreign-born Population of the United States, Current Population Survey, March 2004, detailed tables (PPL-176), Internet site http://www.census.gov/population/www/socdemo/foreign/ppl-176.html; calculations by New Strategist

Table 4.58 Earnings Distribution of Foreign-Born Women from Latin America Working Full-Time, 2003

(number and percent distribution of foreign-born women aged 15 or older from Latin America working full-time, year-round, by earnings and Latin American region, 2003; women in thousands as of 2004)

	total	Caribbean	Central America	South America
Total foreign-born women from Latin America working full-time	**2,670**	**728**	**1,551**	**391**
Less than $10,000	196	39	135	22
$10,000 to $14,999	531	102	376	53
$15,000 to $19,999	541	105	394	42
$20,000 to $24,999	437	105	263	69
$25,000 to $34,999	454	144	218	92
$35,000 to $49,999	260	110	96	54
$50,000 to $74,999	164	81	49	34
$75,000 or more	86	42	21	23
Median income	$20,575	$25,505	$17,369	$25,526
Total foreign-born women from Latin America working full-time	**100.0%**	**100.0%**	**100.0%**	**100.0%**
Less than $10,000	7.3	5.4	8.7	5.6
$10,000 to $14,999	19.9	14.0	24.2	13.6
$15,000 to $19,999	20.3	14.4	25.4	10.7
$20,000 to $24,999	16.4	14.4	17.0	17.6
$25,000 to $34,999	17.0	19.8	14.1	23.5
$35,000 to $49,999	9.7	15.1	6.2	13.8
$50,000 to $74,999	6.1	11.1	3.2	8.7
$75,000 or more	3.2	5.8	1.4	5.9

Note: Most of the foreign-born from Central America are from Mexico.
Source: Bureau of the Census, Foreign-Born Population of the United States, Current Population Survey, March 2004, detailed tables (PPL-176), Internet site http://www.census.gov/population/www/socdemo/foreign/ppl-176.html; calculations by New Strategist

Table 4.59 Median Earnings of Hispanics Working Full-Time by Education and Sex, 2003

(median earnings of Hispanics aged 25 or older working full-time, year-round, by educational attainment and sex, and Hispanic women's earnings as a percent of Hispanic men's earnings, 2003)

	men	women	Hispanic women's earnings as a percent of Hispanic men's earnings
Total Hispanics	**$27,617**	**$23,714**	**85.9%**
Less than 9th grade	20,575	15,916	77.4
9th to 12th grade, no diploma	23,520	16,396	69.7
High school graduate	28,530	22,596	79.2
Some college, no degree	36,639	26,491	72.3
Associate's degree	37,116	30,543	82.3
Bachelor's degree or more	49,228	40,751	82.8

Source: Bureau of the Census, 2004 Current Population Survey, Internet site http://pubdb3.census.gov/macro/032004/perinc/new03_000.htm; calculations by New Strategist

Table 4.60 Poverty Status of Hispanic Married Couples, 1990 to 2003

(total number of Hispanic married couples, and number and percent below poverty level by presence of children under age 18 at home, 1990 to 2003; percent change in numbers and percentage point change in rates, 2000–03 and 1990–2003; married couples in thousands as of March the following year)

		in poverty	
	total	number	percent
Total Hispanic married couples			
2003	6,228	976	15.7%
2002	6,189	927	15.0
2001	5,778	799	13.8
2000	5,426	772	14.2
1999	5,273	758	14.4
1998	4,945	775	15.7
1997	4,804	836	17.4
1996	4,520	815	18.0
1995	4,247	803	18.9
1994	4,236	827	19.5
1993	4,038	770	19.1
1992	3,940	743	18.8
1991	3,532	674	19.1
1990	3,454	605	17.5

	percent change		percentage point change
2000 to 2003	14.8%	26.4%	1.5
1990 to 2003	80.3	61.3	−1.8

	total	number	percent
Hispanic married couples with children			
2003	4,288	789	18.4%
2002	4,242	752	17.7
2001	3,976	646	16.2
2000	3,857	649	16.8
1999	3,762	640	17.0
1998	3,398	656	19.3
1997	3,293	692	21.0
1996	3,124	687	22.0
1995	2,902	657	22.6
1994	2,923	698	23.9
1993	2,747	652	23.7
1992	2,692	615	22.9
1991	2,445	575	23.5
1990	2,405	501	20.8

	percent change		percentage point change
2000 to 2003	11.2%	21.6%	1.6
1990 to 2003	78.3	57.5	−2.4

Source: Bureau of the Census, Current Population Surveys, Internet site http://www.census.gov/hhes/www/poverty/histpov/hstpov4.html; calculations by New Strategist

Table 4.61 Poverty Status of Hispanic Female-Headed Families, 1990 to 2003

(total number of Hispanic female-headed families, and number and percent below poverty level by presence of children under age 18 at home, 1990 to 2003; percent change in numbers and percentage point change in rates, 2000–03 and 1990–2003; families in thousands as of March the following year)

	total	in poverty number	in poverty percent
Total Hispanic female-headed families			
2003	2,138	792	37.0%
2002	2,033	717	35.3
2001	1,922	711	37.0
2000	1,826	664	36.4
1999	1,827	717	39.3
1998	1,728	756	43.7
1997	1,612	767	47.6
1996	1,617	823	50.9
1995	1,604	792	49.4
1994	1,485	773	52.1
1993	1,498	772	51.6
1992	1,348	664	49.3
1991	1,261	627	49.7
1990	1,186	573	48.3

	percent change		percentage point change
2000 to 2003	17.1%	19.3%	0.6
1990 to 2003	80.3	38.2	−11.3

	total	in poverty number	in poverty percent
Hispanic female-headed families with children			
2003	1,657	713	43.0%
2002	1,587	657	41.4
2001	1,493	645	43.2
2000	1,391	597	42.9
1999	1,416	662	46.8
1998	1,355	707	52.2
1997	1,292	701	54.2
1996	1,274	760	59.7
1995	1,283	735	57.3
1994	1,182	700	59.2
1993	1,167	706	60.5
1992	1,037	598	57.7
1991	972	584	60.1
1990	921	536	58.2

	percent change		percentage point change
2000 to 2003	19.1%	19.4%	0.1
1990 to 2003	79.9	33.0	−15.2

Source: Bureau of the Census, Current Population Surveys, Internet site http://www.census.gov/hhes/www/poverty/histpov/ hstpov4.html; calculations by New Strategist

Table 4.62 Poverty Status of Hispanic Male-Headed Families, 1990 to 2003

(total number of Hispanic male-headed families, and number and percent below poverty level by presence of children under age 18 at home, 1990 to 2003; percent change in numbers and percentage point change in rates, 2000–03 and 1990–2003; families in thousands as of March the following year)

		in poverty	
	total	number	percent
Total Hispanic male-headed families			
2003	908	157	17.3%
2002	872	148	17.0
2001	817	139	17.0
2000	765	104	13.6
1999	688	117	17.0
1998	600	117	19.6
1997	545	119	21.7
1996	494	110	22.3
1995	436	100	22.9
1994	481	124	25.8
1993	410	83	20.2
1992	445	122	27.4
1991	383	71	18.5
1990	341	66	19.4
	percent change		percentage point change
2000 to 2003	18.7%	51.0%	3.7
1990 to 2003	166.3	137.9	–2.1
Hispanic male-headed families with children			
2003	508	127	24.9%
2002	500	118	23.6
2001	468	115	24.5
2000	421	77	18.4
1999	377	98	26.1
1998	325	91	28.0
1997	324	99	30.5
1996	291	102	35.1
1995	237	78	32.9
1994	272	99	36.4
1993	239	66	27.6
1992	233	89	38.2
1991	204	60	29.4
1990	171	48	28.1
	percent change		percentage point change
2000 to 2003	20.7%	64.9%	6.5
1990 to 2003	197.1	164.6	–3.2

Source: Bureau of the Census, Current Population Surveys, Internet site http://www.census.gov/hhes/www/poverty/histpov/ hstpov4.html; calculations by New Strategist

Table 4.63 Poverty Status of Hispanics by Sex and Age, 2003

(total number of Hispanics, and number and percent below poverty level by sex and age, 2003; people in thousands as of 2004)

	total	in poverty number	in poverty percent
Total Hispanics	**40,300**	**9,051**	**22.5%**
Under age 18	13,730	4,077	29.7
Aged 18 to 24	4,974	1,043	21.0
Aged 25 to 34	7,423	1,589	21.4
Aged 35 to 44	6,007	1,058	17.6
Aged 45 to 54	3,925	541	13.8
Aged 55 to 59	1,287	168	13.1
Aged 60 to 64	875	169	19.3
Aged 65 or older	2,080	406	19.5
Hispanic females	**19,629**	**4,790**	**24.4**
Under age 18	6,754	1,989	29.4
Aged 18 to 24	2,266	573	25.3
Aged 25 to 34	3,422	901	26.3
Aged 35 to 44	2,880	576	20.0
Aged 45 to 54	1,970	279	14.2
Aged 55 to 59	668	107	16.0
Aged 60 to 64	470	105	22.3
Aged 65 or older	1,199	260	21.7
Hispanic males	**20,670**	**4,262**	**20.6**
Under age 18	6,976	2,088	29.9
Aged 18 to 24	2,708	469	17.3
Aged 25 to 34	4,001	688	17.2
Aged 35 to 44	3,126	483	15.4
Aged 45 to 54	1,955	262	13.4
Aged 55 to 59	619	61	9.9
Aged 60 to 64	404	64	15.9
Aged 65 or older	881	146	16.6

Source: Bureau of the Census, 2004 Current Population Survey, Internet site http://pubdb3.census.gov/macro/032004/pov/new01_100.htm

Table 4.64 Poverty Status of the Foreign-Born from Latin America, 2003

(number and percent of the foreign-born from Latin America living below poverty level by sex, age, and Latin American region of birth, 2003; people in thousands as of 2004)

	total	Caribbean	Central America	South America
Total number of foreign-born from Latin America	**18,294**	**3,320**	**12,909**	**2,066**
Under age 18	1,817	249	1,348	220
Aged 18 to 64	15,250	2,569	10,984	1,697
Aged 65 or older	1,228	502	576	149
Total number of foreign-born from Latin America in poverty	**4,044**	**581**	**3,204**	**259**
Under age 18	666	94	528	45
Aged 18 to 64	3,116	391	2,532	193
Aged 65 or older	261	97	144	21
Percent of foreign-born from Latin America in poverty	**22.1%**	**17.5%**	**24.8%**	**12.5%**
Under age 18	36.7	37.6	39.2	20.4
Aged 18 to 64	20.4	15.2	23.1	11.4
Aged 65 or older	21.3	19.2	25.0	13.9

Note: Most of the foreign-born from Central America are from Mexico.
Source: Bureau of the Census, Foreign-Born Population of the United States, Current Population Survey, March 2004, detailed tables (PPL-176), Internet site http://www.census.gov/population/www/socdemo/foreign/ppl-176.html; calculations by New Strategist

The Labor Force Participation Rate of Hispanic Men Is above Average

The labor force participation rate of Hispanic men, at 80 percent, is well above the 73 percent rate among all men. Only 56 percent of Hispanic women are in the labor force, a rate lower than the 59 percent for all women. Among Hispanic women, those of Cuban origin are least likely to work, with a labor force participation rate of just 52 percent.

Only 17 percent of Hispanic workers are in managerial or professional jobs, accounting for 6 percent of Americans employed in those occupations. The occupational distribution of Hispanics varies by ethnicity, however. Fully 30 percent of Cuban Americans are employed in managerial or professional occupations. In contrast, the figure is just 14 percent among Mexican Americans. Hispanics account for 13 percent of all workers, but they are a larger 38 percent of construction laborers, 40 percent of grounds maintenance workers, and 44 percent of butchers.

Forty-eight percent of Hispanic households have two or more earners, a greater share than the 42 percent of all households with at least two earners. Nevertheless, among Hispanic married couples, only 50 percent are dual earners—a smaller share than the 56 percent among all couples. For 34 percent of Hispanic couples, the husband is the only worker.

Hispanic workers spend a median of 22 minutes commuting to their job each day and travel a median distance of 10 miles. Sixty-seven percent drive their car alone to work.

Between 2002 and 2012, the number of Hispanic workers will grow 33 percent. Hispanics will account for 15 percent of the labor force by 2012.

■ Because a large share of Hispanics are poorly educated immigrants, they are less likely than the average worker to be employed in a managerial or professional occupation.

Hispanic men have a much higher labor force participation rate than Hispanic women

(percent of Hispanics aged 16 or older in the labor force, by sex, 2004)

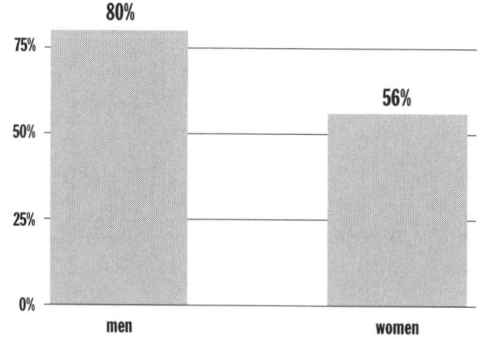

Table 4.65 Labor Force Participation Rate of Hispanics by Age and Sex, 2004

(percent of Hispanics aged 16 or older in the civilian labor force, by age and sex, 2004)

	total	men	women
Total Hispanics	**68.6%**	**80.4%**	**56.1%**
Aged 16 to 19	38.2	80.4	33.7
Aged 20 to 24	74.5	42.4	62.9
Aged 25 to 29	79.0	84.4	62.0
Aged 30 to 34	79.9	93.1	63.7
Aged 35 to 39	81.5	94.1	68.0
Aged 40 to 44	81.4	93.6	69.4
Aged 45 to 49	80.7	92.8	71.9
Aged 50 to 54	73.5	89.3	62.9
Aged 55 to 59	65.8	84.5	55.6
Aged 60 to 64	47.3	77.1	36.7
Aged 65 or older	14.5	59.1	9.8
Aged 65 to 69	25.0	34.0	17.9
Aged 70 to 74	12.5	16.2	9.8
Aged 75 or older	6.6	11.6	3.2

Note: The civilian labor force equals the number of employed plus the number of unemployed.
Source: Bureau of Labor Statistics, 2004 Current Population Survey, http://www.bls.gov/cps/home.htm

Table 4.66 Employment Status of Hispanics by Sex and Age, 2004

(number and percent of Hispanics aged 16 or older in the civilian labor force by sex, age, and employment status, 2004; numbers in thousands)

		civilian labor force				
					unemployed	
	civilian non-institutional population	total	percent of population	employed	number	percent of labor force
Total Hispanics	**28,109**	**19,272**	**68.6%**	**17,930**	**1,342**	**7.0%**
Aged 16 to 19	2,608	995	38.2	792	203	20.4
Aged 20 to 24	3,666	2,732	74.5	2,477	255	9.3
Aged 25 to 34	7,470	5,931	79.4	5,560	371	6.3
Aged 35 to 44	6,055	4,931	81.4	4,671	261	5.3
Aged 45 to 54	3,987	3,093	77.6	2,932	161	5.2
Aged 55 to 64	2,208	1,284	58.1	1,210	74	5.8
Aged 65 or older	2,115	306	14.5	288	18	6.0
Total Hispanic men	**14,417**	**11,587**	**80.4**	**10,832**	**755**	**6.5**
Aged 16 to 19	1,336	567	42.4	446	120	21.2
Aged 20 to 24	1,981	1,671	84.4	1,514	158	9.4
Aged 25 to 34	4,024	3,765	93.6	3,557	207	5.5
Aged 35 to 44	3,147	2,934	93.2	2,801	133	4.5
Aged 45 to 54	1,990	1,736	87.2	1,654	82	4.7
Aged 55 to 64	1,046	728	69.6	687	41	5.7
Aged 65 or older	894	186	20.8	174	13	6.9
Total Hispanic women	**13,692**	**7,685**	**56.1**	**7,098**	**587**	**7.6**
Aged 16 to 19	1,272	429	33.7	346	83	19.3
Aged 20 to 24	1,685	1,060	62.9	964	97	9.1
Aged 25 to 34	3,447	2,166	62.9	2,003	164	7.6
Aged 35 to 44	2,908	1,998	68.7	1,870	128	6.4
Aged 45 to 54	1,997	1,357	67.9	1,279	78	5.8
Aged 55 to 64	1,162	556	47.8	523	32	5.8
Aged 65 or older	1,221	119	9.8	114	5	4.6

Note: The civilian labor force equals the number of the employed plus the number of the unemployed. The civilian population equals the number in the labor force plus the number not in the labor force.
Source: Bureau of Labor Statistics, Current Population Survey, Internet site http://www.bls.gov/cps/home.htm

Table 4.67 Employment Status of Hispanics by Sex and Ethnicity, 2004

(employment status of the civilian noninstitutionalized Hispanic population aged 16 or older, by sex and ethnicity, 2004; numbers in thousands)

| | | civilian labor force | | | | |
| | | | | | unemployed | |
	civilian non-institututional population	total	percent of population	employed	number	percent of labor force
Total Hispanics	**28,109**	**19,272**	**68.6%**	**17,930**	**1,342**	**7.0%**
Mexican	17,900	12,340	68.9	11,449	892	7.2
Puerto Rican	2,547	1,610	63.2	1,481	130	8.1
Cuban	1,264	769	60.9	735	34	4.5
Hispanic men	**14,417**	**11,587**	**80.4**	**10,832**	**755**	**6.5**
Mexican	9,456	7,776	82.2	7,272	504	6.5
Puerto Rican	1,186	824	69.5	756	68	8.2
Cuban	649	450	69.4	428	22	4.9
Hispanic women	**13,692**	**7,685**	**56.1**	**7,098**	**587**	**7.6**
Mexican	8,444	4,564	54.1	4,177	387	8.5
Puerto Rican	1,360	786	57.8	725	62	7.9
Cuban	616	319	51.9	307	12	3.8

Note: The civilian labor force equals the number of employed plus the number of unemployed. The civilian population equals the number in the labor force plus the number not in the labor force. Numbers will not add to total because not all ethnicities are shown.
Source: Bureau of Labor Statistics, 2004 Current Population Survey, http://www.bls.gov/cps/home.htm

Table 4.68 Hispanic Workers by Occupation, 2004

(total number of employed persons aged 16 or older in the civilian labor force, number and percent distribution of employed Hispanics, and Hispanic share of total, by occupation, 2004; numbers in thousands)

	total	Hispanic number	Hispanic percent distribution	Hispanic share of total
TOTAL EMPLOYED	**139,252**	**17,930**	**100.0%**	**12.9%**
Management, professional and related occupations	**48,532**	**3,101**	**17.3**	**6.4**
Management, business, and financial operations	20,235	1,290	7.2	6.4
Management occupations	14,555	920	5.1	6.3
Business and financial operations occupations	5,860	370	2.1	6.3
Professional and related occupations	28,297	1,811	10.1	6.4
Computer and mathematical occupations	3,140	172	1.0	5.5
Architecture and engineering occupations	2,760	158	0.9	5.7
Life, physical, and social science occupations	1,365	69	0.4	5.1
Community and social services occupations	2,170	203	1.1	9.4
Legal occupations	1,554	89	0.5	5.7
Education, training, and library occupations	7,900	549	3.1	6.9
Arts, design, entertainment, sports, and media occupations	2,687	202	1.1	7.5
Health care practitioner and technical occupations	6,721	368	2.1	5.5
Service occupations	**22,720**	**4,336**	**24.2**	**19.1**
Health care support occupations	2,921	384	2.1	13.1
Protective service occupations	2,847	315	1.8	11.1
Food preparation and serving-related occupations	7,279	1,405	7.8	19.3
Building and grounds cleaning and maintenance occupations	5,185	1,661	9.3	32.0
Personal care and service occupations	4,488	571	3.2	12.7
Sales and office occupations	**35,464**	**3,818**	**21.3**	**10.8**
Sales and related occupations	15,983	1,654	9.2	10.3
Office and administrative support occupations	19,481	2,164	12.1	11.1
Natural resources, construction, maintenance occupations	**14,582**	**3,229**	**18.0**	**22.1**
Farming, fishing, and forestry occupations	991	387	2.2	39.1
Construction and extraction occupations	8,522	2,127	11.9	25.0
Installation, maintenance, and repair occupations	5,069	715	4.0	14.1
Production, transportation, material moving occupations	**17,954**	**3,446**	**19.2**	**19.2**
Production occupations	9,462	1,894	10.6	20.0
Transportation and material moving occupations	8,491	1,552	8.7	18.3

Source: Bureau of Labor Statistics, 2004 Current Population Survey, Internet site http://www.bls.gov/cps/home.htm; calculations by New Strategist

Table 4.69 Hispanic Workers by Occupation and Ethnicity, 2004

(number and percent distribution of employed Hispanics aged 16 or older in the civilian labor force, by occupation and ethnicity, 2004; numbers in thousands)

	total	Mexican	Puerto Rican	Cuban
TOTAL EMPLOYED HISPANICS	**17,930**	**11,449**	**1,481**	**735**
Management, professional and related occupations	**3,101**	**1,620**	**352**	**221**
Management, business, and financial operations	1,290	683	131	108
Management occupations	920	491	94	83
Business and financial operations occupations	370	192	37	25
Professional and related occupations	1,811	937	221	113
Computer and mathematical occupations	172	75	24	8
Architecture and engineering occupations	158	79	16	9
Life, physical, and social science occupations	69	34	10	6
Community and social services occupations	203	110	29	7
Legal occupations	89	38	7	11
Education, training, and library occupations	549	313	76	28
Arts, design, entertainment, sports, and media occupations	202	115	16	14
Health care practitioner and technical occupations	368	174	44	30
Service occupations	**4,336**	**2,788**	**334**	**112**
Health care support occupations	384	205	57	16
Protective service occupations	315	186	51	17
Food preparation and serving-related occupations	1,405	975	82	24
Building and grounds cleaning and maintenance occupations	1,661	1,092	81	42
Personal care and service occupations	571	330	63	14
Sales and office occupations	**3,818**	**2,260**	**428**	**203**
Sales and related occupations	1,654	996	158	86
Office and administrative support occupations	2,164	1,264	269	117
Natural resources, construction, maintenance occupations	**3,229**	**2,407**	**142**	**100**
Farming, fishing, and forestry occupations	387	361	8	1
Construction and extraction occupations	2,127	1,588	67	48
Installation, maintenance, and repair occupations	715	459	68	51
Production, transportation, material moving occupations	**3,446**	**2,373**	**224**	**98**
Production occupations	1,894	1,336	110	44
Transportation and material moving occupations	1,552	1,037	114	54

(continued)

	total	Mexican	Puerto Rican	Cuban
PERCENT DISTRIBUTION BY OCCUPATION				
TOTAL EMPLOYED HISPANICS	100.0%	100.0%	100.0%	100.0%
Management, professional and related occupations	**17.3**	**14.1**	**23.8**	**30.1**
Management, business, and financial operations	7.2	6.0	8.8	14.7
Management occupations	5.1	4.3	6.3	11.3
Business and financial operations occupations	2.1	1.7	2.5	3.4
Professional and related occupations	10.1	8.2	14.9	15.4
Computer and mathematical occupations	1.0	0.7	1.6	1.1
Architecture and engineering occupations	0.9	0.7	1.1	1.2
Life, physical, and social science occupations	0.4	0.3	0.7	0.8
Community and social services occupations	1.1	1.0	2.0	1.0
Legal occupations	0.5	0.3	0.5	1.5
Education, training, and library occupations	3.1	2.7	5.1	3.8
Arts, design, entertainment, sports, and media occupations	1.1	1.0	1.1	1.9
Health care practitioner and technical occupations	2.1	1.5	3.0	4.1
Service occupations	**24.2**	**24.4**	**22.6**	**15.2**
Health care support occupations	2.1	1.8	3.8	2.2
Protective service occupations	1.8	1.6	3.4	2.3
Food preparation and serving-related occupations	7.8	8.5	5.5	3.3
Building and grounds cleaning and maintenance occupations	9.3	9.5	5.5	5.7
Personal care and service occupations	3.2	2.9	4.3	1.9
Sales and office occupations	**21.3**	**19.7**	**28.9**	**27.6**
Sales and related occupations	9.2	8.7	10.7	11.7
Office and administrative support occupations	12.1	11.0	18.2	15.9
Natural resources, construction, maintenance occupations	**18.0**	**21.0**	**9.6**	**13.6**
Farming, fishing, and forestry occupations	2.2	3.2	0.5	0.1
Construction and extraction occupations	11.9	13.9	4.5	6.5
Installation, maintenance, and repair occupations	4.0	4.0	4.6	6.9
Production, transportation, material moving occupations	**19.2**	**20.7**	**15.1**	**13.3**
Production occupations	10.6	11.7	7.4	6.0
Transportation and material moving occupations	8.7	9.1	7.7	7.3

(continued)

PERCENT DISTRIBUTION BY ETHNICITY	total	Mexican	Puerto Rican	Cuban
TOTAL EMPLOYED HISPANICS	**100.0%**	**63.9%**	**8.3%**	**4.1%**
Management, professional and related occupations	**100.0**	**52.2**	**11.4**	**7.1**
Management, business, and financial operations	100.0	52.9	10.2	8.4
Management occupations	100.0	53.4	10.2	9.0
Business and financial operations occupations	100.0	51.9	10.0	6.8
Professional and related occupations	100.0	51.7	12.2	6.2
Computer and mathematical occupations	100.0	43.6	14.0	4.7
Architecture and engineering occupations	100.0	50.0	10.1	5.7
Life, physical, and social science occupations	100.0	49.3	14.5	8.7
Community and social services occupations	100.0	54.2	14.3	3.4
Legal occupations	100.0	42.7	7.9	12.4
Education, training, and library occupations	100.0	57.0	13.8	5.1
Arts, design, entertainment, sports, and media occupations	100.0	56.9	7.9	6.9
Health care practitioner and technical occupations	100.0	47.3	12.0	8.2
Service occupations	**100.0**	**64.3**	**7.7**	**2.6**
Health care support occupations	100.0	53.4	14.8	4.2
Protective service occupations	100.0	59.0	16.2	5.4
Food preparation and serving-related occupations	100.0	69.4	5.8	1.7
Building and grounds cleaning and maintenance occupations	100.0	65.7	4.9	2.5
Personal care and service occupations	100.0	57.8	11.0	2.5
Sales and office occupations	**100.0**	**59.2**	**11.2**	**5.3**
Sales and related	100.0	60.2	9.6	5.2
Office and administrative support	100.0	58.4	12.4	5.4
Natural resources, construction, maintenance occupations	**100.0**	**74.5**	**4.4**	**3.1**
Farming, fishing, and forestry occupations	100.0	93.3	2.1	0.3
Construction and extraction occupations	100.0	74.7	3.1	2.3
Installation, maintenance, and repair occupations	100.0	64.2	9.5	7.1
Production, transportation, material moving occupations	**100.0**	**68.9**	**6.5**	**2.8**
Production occupations	100.0	70.5	5.8	2.3
Transportation and material moving occupations	100.0	66.8	7.3	3.5

Note: Numbers will not add to total because not all ethnicities are shown.
Source: Bureau of Labor Statistics, 2004 Current Population Survey, Internet site http://www.bls.gov/cps/home.htm; calculations by New Strategist

Table 4.70 Hispanic Workers by Detailed Occupation, 2004

(total number of employed workers aged 16 or older and percent Hispanic, by detailed occupation, 2004; numbers in thousands)

	total	percent Hispanic
TOTAL EMPLOYED	**139,252**	**12.9%**
Management, professional and related occupations	**48,532**	**6.4**
Management, business, and financial operations occupations	20,235	6.4
Management occupations	14,555	6.3
Chief executives	1,680	3.7
General and operations managers	795	7.1
Advertising and promotions managers	70	4.1
Marketing and sales managers	806	4.8
Administrative services managers	87	9.0
Computer and information systems managers	337	5.2
Financial managers	1,045	6.9
Human resources managers	262	6.6
Industrial production managers	280	6.7
Purchasing managers	170	6.3
Transportation, storage, and distribution managers	241	8.2
Farm, ranch, and other agricultural managers	199	9.9
Farmers and ranchers	817	1.8
Construction managers	851	8.0
Education administrators	757	5.3
Engineering managers	106	2.9
Food service managers	916	11.1
Lodging managers	152	4.2
Medical and health services managers	508	4.7
Property, real estate, and community association managers	604	11.8
Social and community service managers	280	6.1
Business and financial operations occupations	5,680	6.5
Wholesale and retail buyers, except farm products	212	8.0
Purchasing agents, except wholesale, retail, and farm products	285	6.2
Claims adjusters, appraisers, examiners, and investigators	281	6.1
Compliance officers, excluding agriculture, construction, health and safety, and transportation	126	8.3
Cost estimators	98	4.5
Human resources, training, and labor relations specialists	694	7.8
Management analysts	554	4.3
Accountants and auditors	1,723	6.7
Appraisers and assessors of real estate	138	4.0
Personal financial advisors	331	2.9
Insurance underwriters	98	4.9
Loan counselors and officers	425	8.2
Tax examiners, collectors, and revenue agents	81	5.9
Tax preparers	88	8.1
Professional and related occupations	28,297	6.4
Computer and mathematical occupations	3,140	5.5
Computer scientists and systems analysts	700	6.6
Computer programmers	564	3.9

(continued)

	total	percent Hispanic
Computer software engineers	813	4.1%
Computer support specialists	325	8.7
Database administrators	94	3.3
Network and computer systems administrators	190	6.1
Network systems and data communications analysts	312	7.0
Operations research analysts	90	5.9
Architecture and engineering occupations	2,760	5.7
Architects, except naval	207	7.1
Aerospace engineers	113	4.2
Chemical engineers	63	3.4
Civil engineers	293	4.6
Computer hardware engineers	96	5.8
Electrical and electronics engineers	343	4.0
Industrial engineers, including health and safety	177	5.4
Mechanical engineers	311	3.9
Drafters	206	9.9
Engineering technicians, except drafters	416	8.8
Surveying and mapping technicians	80	7.7
Life, physical, and social science occupations	1,365	5.1
Biological scientists	123	2.2
Medical scientists	93	3.1
Chemists and materials scientists	141	4.3
Environmental scientists and geoscientists	86	2.3
Market and survey researchers	124	4.8
Psychologists	185	4.6
Chemical technicians	84	6.3
Community and social services occupations	2,170	9.4
Counselors	643	9.7
Social workers	687	10.9
Miscellaneous community and social service specialists	283	12.3
Clergy	403	6.0
Directors, religious activities and education	55	2.0
Religious workers, all other	99	6.0
Legal occupations	1,554	5.7
Lawyers	954	3.4
Judges, magistrates, and other judicial workers	64	7.4
Paralegals and legal assistants	322	10.7
Miscellaneous legal support workers	215	8.1
Education, training, and library occupations	7,900	6.9
Postsecondary teachers	1,176	3.5
Preschool and kindergarten teachers	656	8.2
Elementary and middle school teachers	2,580	6.4
Secondary school teachers	1,151	5.2
Special education teachers	384	5.0
Other teachers and instructors	667	8.6
Librarians	217	4.6
Teacher assistants	920	14.3
Arts, design, entertainment, sports, and media occupations	2,687	7.5
Artists and related workers	222	6.4
Designers	792	7.4
Producers and directors	137	8.8

(continued)

	total	percent Hispanic
Athletes, coaches, umpires, and related workers	239	5.4%
Musicians, singers, and related workers	179	5.4
Announcers	54	12.6
News analysts, reporters, and correspondents	81	3.4
Public relations specialists	133	4.6
Editors	164	4.1
Writers and authors	194	2.6
Miscellaneous media and communication workers	74	33.8
Broadcast and sound engineering technicians and radio operators	92	12.1
Photographers	158	7.1
Health care practitioner and technical occupations	6,721	5.5
Chiropractors	73	1.9
Dentists	167	4.1
Dietitians and nutritionists	84	11.3
Pharmacists	233	3.7
Physicians and surgeons	830	5.3
Physician assistants	70	9.4
Registered nurses	2,464	4.4
Occupational therapists	84	3.7
Physical therapists	173	3.3
Respiratory therapists	103	6.4
Speech-language pathologists	93	2.1
Veterinarians	58	4.1
Clinical laboratory technologists and technicians	333	6.9
Dental hygienists	130	4.2
Diagnostic related technologists and technicians	284	7.4
Emergency medical technicians and paramedics	139	8.9
Health diagnosing and treating practitioner support technicians	397	7.7
Licensed practical and licensed vocational nurses	517	5.6
Medical records and health information technicians	91	18.6
Service occupations	**22,720**	**19.1**
Health care support occupations	2,921	13.1
Nursing, psychiatric, and home health aides	1,806	13.4
Physical therapist assistants and aides	61	6.2
Massage therapists	106	6.5
Dental assistants	242	15.3
Protective service occupations	2,847	11.1
First-line supervisors and managers of police and detectives	133	6.5
Firefighters	268	8.6
Bailiffs, correctional officers, and jailers	373	10.3
Detectives and criminal investigators	121	7.3
Police and sheriff's patrol officers	664	12.7
Private detectives and investigators	81	8.8
Security guards and gaming surveillance officers	798	14.5
Food preparation and serving related occupations	7,279	19.3
Chefs and head cooks	299	20.9
First-line supervisors/managers of food preparation and serving workers	644	14.6
Cooks	1,791	28.0
Food preparation workers	621	22.8

(continued)

	total	percent Hispanic
Bartenders	360	10.7%
Combined food preparation and serving workers, including fast food	296	13.4
Counter attendants, cafeteria, food concession, and coffee shop	327	12.3
Waiters and waitresses	1,892	12.7
Food servers, nonrestaurant	165	16.1
Dining room and cafeteria attendants and bartender helpers	379	27.6
Dishwashers	267	34.3
Hosts and hostesses, restaurant, lounge, and coffee shop	237	9.6
Building and grounds cleaning and maintenance occupations	5,185	32.0
First-line supervisors and managers of housekeeping and janitorial workers	191	20.2
First-line supervisors and managers of landscaping, lawn service, and groundskeeping workers	227	12.7
Janitors and building cleaners	2,047	26.8
Maids and housekeeping cleaners	1,365	38.2
Pest control workers	75	13.1
Grounds maintenance workers	1,280	40.2
Personal care and service occupations	4,488	12.7
First-line supervisors and managers of gaming workers	140	8.2
First-line supervisors and managers of personal service workers	174	7.7
Nonfarm animal caretakers	128	9.8
Gaming services workers	95	7.7
Barbers	101	6.6
Hairdressers, hair stylists, and cosmetologists	722	11.5
Miscellaneous personal appearance workers	200	8.2
Baggage porters, bellhops, and concierges	70	25.1
Transportation attendants	116	11.2
Child care workers	1,332	16.5
Personal and home care aides	630	16.1
Recreation and fitness workers	314	7.0
Sales and office occupations	**35,464**	**10.8**
Sales and related occupations	15,983	10.3
First-line supervisors and managers of retail sales workers	3,299	9.2
First-line supervisors and managers of nonretail sales workers	1,390	9.6
Cashiers	2,971	15.9
Counter and rental clerks	186	12.6
Parts salespersons	147	9.4
Retail salespersons	3,130	10.9
Advertising sales agents	211	5.7
Insurance sales agents	508	6.1
Securities, commodities, and financial services sales agents	382	6.2
Travel agents	95	10.5
Sales representatives, services, all other	476	7.4
Sales representatives, wholesale and manufacturing	1,416	7.2
Models, demonstrators, and product promoters	68	6.9
Real estate brokers and sales agents	912	6.7
Telemarketers	180	17.0
Door-to-door sales workers, news and street vendors, and related workers	312	11.8
Sales and related workers, all other	260	6.9
Office and administrative support occupations	19,481	11.1
First-line supervisors/managers of office, administrative support workers	1,631	8.4
Switchboard operators, including answering service	66	6.0

(continued)

	total	percent Hispanic
Telephone operators	56	13.1%
Bill and account collectors	229	15.4
Billing and posting clerks and machine operators	441	10.7
Bookkeeping, accounting, and auditing clerks	1,567	6.9
Payroll and timekeeping clerks	153	7.3
Tellers	424	10.0
Court, municipal, and license clerks	102	10.5
Credit authorizers, checkers, and clerks	65	12.0
Customer service representatives	1,749	12.4
Eligibility interviewers, government programs	66	22.4
File clerks	387	11.9
Hotel, motel, and resort desk clerks	106	13.0
Interviewers, except eligibility and loan	143	13.4
Library assistants, clerical	117	9.1
Loan interviewers and clerks	186	10.6
Order clerks	114	12.2
Human resources assistants, except payroll and timekeeping	64	13.5
Receptionists and information clerks	1,373	14.0
Reservation and transportation ticket agents and travel clerks	161	12.2
Couriers and messengers	293	15.0
Dispatchers	257	9.2
Postal service clerks	167	12.0
Postal service mail carriers	336	6.9
Postal service mail sorters, processors, and processing machine operators	116	12.0
Production, planning, and expediting clerks	288	6.1
Shipping, receiving, and traffic clerks	584	22.9
Stock clerks and order fillers	1,350	15.8
Weighers, measurers, checkers, and samplers, recordkeeping	64	17.7
Secretaries and administrative assistants	3,522	8.1
Computer operators	191	9.0
Data entry keyers	504	13.1
Word processors and typists	319	8.6
Insurance claims and policy processing clerks	277	11.0
Mail clerks and mail machine operators, except postal service	154	15.4
Office clerks, general	982	14.8
Office machine operators, except computer	61	14.8
Natural resources, constructions, and maintenance occupations	**14,582**	**22.1**
Farming, fishing, and forestry occupations	991	39.0
First-line supervisors/managers of farming, fishing, and forestry workers	59	31.3
Graders and sorters, agricultural products	68	44.7
Logging workers	92	10.1
Construction and extraction occupations	8,522	25.0
First-line supervisors/managers of construction trades and extraction workers	887	11.7
Brickmasons, blockmasons, and stonemasons	239	34.1
Carpenters	1,764	21.8
Carpet, floor, and tile installers and finishers	268	35.6
Cement masons, concrete finishers, and terrazzo workers	115	44.0
Construction laborers	1,234	38.1
Operating engineers and other construction equipment operators	367	11.1

(continued)

	total	percent Hispanic
Drywall installers, ceiling tile installers, and tapers	213	49.6%
Electricians	781	13.6
Painters, construction and maintenance	719	36.2
Pipe layers, plumbers, pipe fitters, and steam fitters	635	17.3
Roofers	269	39.4
Sheet metal workers	152	12.8
Structural iron and steel workers	66	9.8
Helpers, construction trades	121	36.0
Construction and building inspectors	104	11.8
Highway maintenance workers	96	14.8
Installation, maintenance, and repair occupations	5,069	14.1
First-line supervisors and managers of mechanics, installers, and repairers	327	9.3
Computer, automated teller, and office machine repairers	369	9.5
Radio and telecommunications equipment installers and repairers	235	10.7
Electric motor, power tool, and related repairers	56	17.1
Security and fire alarm systems installers	65	14.8
Aircraft mechanics and service technicians	135	15.5
Automotive body and related repairers	169	20.5
Automotive service technicians and mechanics	936	19.0
Bus and truck mechanics and diesel engine specialists	325	12.2
Heavy vehicle and mobile equipment service technicians and mechanics	205	12.2
Small engine mechanics	58	4.9
Heating, air conditioning, and refrigeration mechanics and installers	351	13.1
Industrial and refractory machinery mechanics	434	10.1
Maintenance and repair workers, general	300	17.0
Millwrights	59	2.6
Electrical power line installers and repairers	120	11.9
Telecommunications line installers and repairers	142	16.7
Precision instrument and equipment repairers	53	4.9
Coin, vending, and amusement machine servicers and repairers	54	7.8
Production, transportation, material-moving occupations	**17,954**	**19.2**
Production occupations	9,462	20.0
First-line supervisors and managers of production and operating workers	921	11.6
Electrical, electronics, and electromechanical assemblers	226	21.1
Bakers	188	28.4
Butchers and other meat, poultry, and fish processing workers	304	44.3
Food batchmakers	85	20.5
Cutting, punching, press machine setters, operators, tenders, metal/plastic	139	16.3
Grinding, lapping, polishing, and buffing machine tool setters, operators, and tenders, metal and plastic	74	26.2
Machinists	445	10.9
Molders, molding machine setters, operators, and tenders, metal and plastic	70	18.8
Tool and die makers	86	3.7
Welding, soldering, and brazing workers	572	23.3
Job printers	65	18.0
Prepress technicians and workers	55	14.0
Printing machine operators	195	15.2
Laundry and dry-cleaning workers	195	27.5
Pressers, textile, garment, and related materials	76	47.1

(continued)

	total	percent Hispanic
Sewing machine operators	281	32.5%
Tailors, dressmakers, and sewers	101	18.3
Cabinetmakers and bench carpenters	86	18.0
Stationary engineers and boiler operators	105	9.6
Water and liquid waste treatment plant and system operators	56	9.1
Chemical processing machine setters, operators, and tenders	63	11.4
Crushing, grinding, polishing, mixing, and blending workers	111	16.6
Cutting workers	83	26.4
Inspectors, testers, sorters, samplers, and weighers	690	13.3
Jewelers and precious stone and metal workers	59	15.0
Medical, dental, and ophthalmic laboratory technicians	92	15.4
Packaging and filling machine operators and tenders	318	42.4
Painting workers	191	24.5
Photographic process workers and processing machine operators	59	9.2
Paper goods machine setters, operators, and tenders	53	9.3
Helpers—production workers	64	33.9
Transportation and material-moving occupations	8,491	18.3
Supervisors, transportation and material-moving workers	220	13.3
Aircraft pilots and flight engineers	118	3.2
Bus drivers	602	12.8
Driver sales workers and truck drivers	3,276	15.8
Taxi drivers and chauffeurs	277	12.4
Railroad conductors and yardmasters	58	10.4
Parking lot attendants	77	23.0
Service station attendants	120	9.4
Crane and tower operators	65	8.2
Dredge, excavating, and loading machine operators	80	11.6
Industrial truck and tractor operators	530	25.0
Cleaners of vehicles and equipment	316	29.5
Laborers and freight, stock, and material movers, hand	1,797	20.6
Machine feeders and offbearers	55	18.1
Packers and packagers, hand	432	44.1
Refuse and recyclable material collectors	81	14.4

Source: Bureau of Labor Statistics, 2004 Current Population Survey, Internet site http://www.bls.gov/cps/home.htm

Table 4.71 Hispanic Workers by Industry, 2004

(total number of employed people aged 16 or older in the civilian labor force, number and percent distribution of employed Hispanics, and Hispanic share of total, by industry, 2004; numbers in thousands)

		Hispanic		
	total	number	percent distribution	share of total
Total employed	**139,252**	**17,930**	**100.0%**	**12.9%**
Agriculture, forestry, fishing, hunting	2,232	441	2.5	19.8
Mining	539	60	0.3	11.1
Construction	10,768	2,303	12.8	21.4
Manufacturing	16,484	2,358	13.2	14.3
Wholesale and retail trade	20,869	2,566	14.3	12.3
Transportation and utilities	7,013	867	4.8	12.4
Information	3,463	319	1.8	9.2
Financial activities	9,969	913	5.1	9.2
Professional and business services	14,108	1,843	10.3	13.1
Educational and health services	28,719	2,619	14.6	9.1
Leisure and hospitality	11,820	2,078	11.6	17.6
Other services	6,903	1,035	5.8	15.0
Public administration	6,365	528	2.9	8.3

Source: Bureau of Labor Statistics, 2004 Current Population Survey, Internet site http://www.bls.gov/cps/home.htm; calculations by New Strategist

Table 4.72 Hispanic Workers by Full-Time and Part-Time Status, Age, and Sex, 2004

(number and percent distribution of employed Hispanics aged 16 or older by age, employment status, and sex, 2004; numbers in thousands)

	men			women		
	total	full-time	part-time	total	full-time	part-time
Total employed Hispanics	**10,832**	**9,896**	**936**	**7,098**	**5,411**	**1,687**
Aged 16 to 19	447	246	201	346	112	234
Aged 20 to 24	1,513	1,261	252	963	639	324
Aged 25 to 54	8,011	7,627	384	5,151	4,179	972
Aged 55 or older	861	762	99	638	481	157
PERCENT DISTRIBUTION BY EMPLOYMENT STATUS						
Total employed Hispanics	**100.0%**	**91.4%**	**8.6%**	**100.0%**	**76.2%**	**23.8%**
Aged 16 to 19	100.0	55.0	45.0	100.0	32.4	67.6
Aged 20 to 24	100.0	83.3	16.7	100.0	66.4	33.6
Aged 25 to 54	100.0	95.2	4.8	100.0	81.1	18.9
Aged 55 or older	100.0	88.5	11.5	100.0	75.4	24.6
PERCENT DISTRIBUTION BY AGE						
Total employed Hispanics	**100.0%**	**100.0%**	**100.0%**	**100.0%**	**100.0%**	**100.0%**
Aged 16 to 19	4.1	2.5	21.5	4.9	2.1	13.9
Aged 20 to 24	14.0	12.7	26.9	13.6	11.8	19.2
Aged 25 to 54	74.0	77.1	41.0	72.6	77.2	57.6
Aged 55 or older	7.9	7.7	10.6	9.0	8.9	9.3

Source: Bureau of Labor Statistics, 2004 Current Population Survey, Internet site http://www.bls.gov/cps/home.htm; calculations by New Strategist

Table 4.73 Hispanic Workers by Educational Attainment, 2004

(number of total people and Hispanics aged 25 or older in the civilian labor force, Hispanic labor force participation rate, distribution of Hispanics in labor force, and Hispanic share of total labor force, by educational attainment, 2004; numbers in thousands)

		Hispanic labor force			
	total labor force	number	participation rate	percent distribution	share of total
Total aged 25 or older	**125,133**	**15,545**	**71.2%**	**100.0%**	**12.4%**
Not a high school graduate	12,470	5,553	62.3	35.7	44.5
High school graduate only	37,834	4,566	74.0	29.4	12.1
Some college	22,298	2,251	79.1	14.5	10.1
Associate's degree	12,141	971	79.8	6.2	8.0
Bachelor's degree or more	40,390	2,204	82.1	14.2	5.5

Source: Bureau of Labor Statistics, 2004 Current Population Survey, Internet site http://www.bls.gov/cps/home.htm; calculations by New Strategist

Table 4.74 Hispanic Workers by Job Tenure and Sex, 2004

(total number of employed Hispanic wage and salary workers aged 16 or older and percent distribution by tenure with current employer, by sex, 2004; numbers in thousands)

	total	men	women
Total Hispanic workers, number	**16,338**	**9,778**	**6,560**
Total Hispanic workers, percent	**100.0%**	**100.0%**	**100.0%**
12 months or less	26.9	26.4	27.6
13 to 23 months	7.4	7.5	7.3
2 years	7.8	7.4	8.5
3 to 4 years	22.8	23.2	22.2
5 to 9 years	18.2	17.9	18.7
10 to 14 years	8.0	8.2	7.7
15 to 19 years	4.4	4.5	4.3
20 or more years	4.4	4.7	3.8

Source: Bureau of Labor Statistics, 2004 Current Population Survey, Internet site http://www.bls.gov/cps/home.htm; calculations by New Strategist

Table 4.75 Hispanic Households by Number of Earners, 2004

(number of total households, number and percent distribution of Hispanic households and Hispanic share of total, by number of earners per household, 2004; numbers in thousands)

	total	Hispanic number	Hispanic percent distribution	Hispanic share of total
Total households	**112,000**	**11,693**	**100.0%**	**10.4%**
No earners	23,932	1,498	12.8	6.3
One earner	40,769	4,591	39.3	11.3
Two or more earners	47,299	5,604	47.9	11.8
Two earners	37,917	4,158	35.6	11.0
Three earners	6,998	1,005	8.6	14.4
Four or more earners	2,384	441	3.8	18.5
Average number of earners per household	1.36	1.60	–	–

Note: (–) means not applicable.
Source: Bureau of the Census, 2004 Current Population Survey, Annual Social and Economic Supplement, Internet site http://pubdb3.census.gov/macro/032004/hhinc/new01_000.htm; calculations by New Strategist

Table 4.76 Hispanic Married Couples by Labor Force Status of Husband and Wife, 2003

(number and percent distribution of Hispanic married couples aged 20 or older by age of householder and labor force status of husband and wife, 2003; numbers in thousands)

	total	husband and/or wife in labor force			neither husband nor wife in labor force
		husband and wife	husband only	wife only	
Total Hispanic couples	**6,169**	**3,107**	**2,086**	**300**	**676**
Aged 20 to 24	341	162	161	9	10
Aged 25 to 29	715	396	290	12	18
Aged 30 to 34	930	512	377	29	11
Aged 35 to 39	994	571	392	20	11
Aged 40 to 44	867	524	291	36	17
Aged 45 to 54	1,099	629	324	72	75
Aged 55 to 64	689	287	181	74	147
Aged 65 or older	532	27	68	48	388
Total Hispanic couples	**100.0%**	**50.4%**	**33.8%**	**4.9%**	**11.0%**
Aged 20 to 24	100.0	47.5	47.2	2.6	2.9
Aged 25 to 29	100.0	55.4	40.6	1.7	2.5
Aged 30 to 34	100.0	55.1	40.5	3.1	1.2
Aged 35 to 39	100.0	57.4	39.4	2.0	1.1
Aged 40 to 44	100.0	60.4	33.6	4.2	2.0
Aged 45 to 54	100.0	57.2	29.5	6.6	6.8
Aged 55 to 64	100.0	41.7	26.3	10.7	21.3
Aged 65 or older	100.0	5.1	12.8	9.0	72.9

Source: Bureau of the Census, America's Families and Living Arrangements: 2003, detailed tables, Internet site http://www.census .gov/population/www/socdemo/hh-fam/cps2003.html; calculations by New Strategist

Table 4.77   Hispanic Minimum Wage Workers by Sex, 2004

(number and percent distribution of total and Hispanic wage and salary workers aged 16 or older paid hourly rates and those paid at or below minimum wage, by sex, 2004; numbers in thousands)

	total paid hourly rates	at or below minimum wage		
		total	at $5.15/hour	below $5.15/hour
Total workers aged 16 or older	**73,939**	**2,003**	**520**	**1,483**
Hispanic workers aged 16 or older	12,073	250	82	168
Hispanic men	7,183	99	32	66
Hispanic women	4,890	151	49	102
PERCENT DISTRIBUTION BY RACE/SEX				
Total workers aged 16 or older	**100.0%**	**100.0%**	**100.0%**	**100.0%**
Hispanic workers aged 16 or older	16.3	12.5	15.8	11.3
Hispanic men	9.7	4.9	6.2	4.5
Hispanic women	6.6	7.5	9.4	6.9
PERCENT DISTRIBUTION BY WAGE STATUS				
Total workers aged 16 or older	**100.0%**	**2.7%**	**0.7%**	**2.0%**
Hispanic workers aged 16 or older	100.0	2.1	0.7	1.4
Hispanic men	100.0	1.4	0.4	0.9
Hispanic women	100.0	3.1	1.0	2.1

Source: Bureau of Labor Statistics, 2004 Current Population Survey, Internet site http://www.bls.gov/cps/home.htm

Table 4.78   Hispanic Multiple Job Holders by Sex, 2004

(total number of employed people aged 16 or older who hold more than one job, number and percent of Hispanics holding more than one job, and Hispanic share of total, by sex, 2004; numbers in thousands)

		Hispanic multiple job holders		
	total	number	percent	share of total
Total multiple job holders	**7,473**	**612**	**3.4%**	**8.2%**
Men	3,835	363	3.4	9.5
Women	3,638	248	3.5	6.8

Source: Bureau of Labor Statistics, 2004 Current Population Survey, Internet site http://www.bls.gov/cps/home.htm

Table 4.79 Union Representation of Hispanic Workers by Sex, 2004

(number of employed Hispanic wage and salary workers aged 16 or older, number and percent represented by unions, and median weekly earnings of those working full-time by union representation status, by sex, 2004; number in thousands)

	total	men	women
Total employed Hispanics	**16,533**	**9,857**	**6,676**
Number represented by unions	1,888	1,130	758
Percent represented by unions	11.4%	11.5%	11.4%
Median weekly earnings of full-time Hispanic workers	**$456**	**$480**	**$419**
Hispanic workers represented by unions	670	690	616
Hispanic workers not represented by unions	428	455	401

Note: Workers represented by unions are either members of a labor union or similar employee association or workers who report no union affiliation but whose jobs are covered by a union or an employee association contract.
Source: Bureau of Labor Statistics, 2004 Current Population Survey, Internet site http://www.bls.gov/cps/home.htm

Table 4.80 Journey to Work by Hispanic Workers, 2003

(number and percent distribution of Hispanic workers aged 16 or older by principal means of transportation to work, travel time from home to work, distance from home to work, and departure time to work, 2003; numbers in thousands)

	number	percent distribution
Total Hispanic workers	**14,518**	**100.0%**
Principal means of transportation to work		
Drives self	9,793	67.5
Carpool	2,630	18.1
Mass transportation	1,119	7.7
Taxicab	20	0.1
Bicycle or motorcycle	84	0.6
Walks only	430	3.0
Other means	215	1.5
Works at home	228	1.6
Travel time from home to work		
Less than 15 minutes	4,154	28.6
15 to 29 minutes	4,807	33.1
30 to 44 minutes	2,277	15.7
45 to 59 minutes	905	6.2
1 hour or more	798	5.5
Works at home	228	1.6
No fixed place of work	1,350	9.3
Median travel time (minutes)	22	–
Distance from home to work		
Less than 1 mile	591	4.1
1 to 4 miles	2,839	19.6
5 to 9 miles	3,013	20.8
10 to 19 miles	3,715	25.6
20 to 29 miles	1,564	10.8
30 miles or more	1,218	8.4
Works at home	228	1.6
No fixed place of work	1,350	9.3
Median distance (miles)	10	–
Departure time to work		
12:00 a.m. to 2:59 a.m.	109	0.8
3:00 a.m. to 5:59 a.m.	2,035	14.0
6:00 a.m. to 6:59 a.m.	2,865	19.7
7:00 a.m. to 7:29 a.m.	1,968	13.6
7:30 a.m. to 7:59 a.m.	1,465	10.1
8:00 a.m. to 8:29 a.m.	1,510	10.4
8:30 a.m. to 8:59 a.m.	561	3.9
9:00 a.m. to 9:59 a.m.	746	5.1
10:00 a.m. to 3:59 p.m.	1,361	9.4
4:00 p.m. to 11:59 p.m.	885	6.1

Note: Departure time numbers may not add to total because not reported is not shown and those who work at home are not included. (–) means not applicable.
Source: Bureau of the Census, American Housing Survey for the United States: 2003, Current Housing Reports, Internet site http://www.census.gov/hhes/www/ahs.html; calculations by New Strategist

Table 4.81 Hispanic Labor Force Projections, 2002 and 2012

(number and percent of total people and Hispanics aged 16 or older in the civilian labor force by sex, 2002 and 2012; percent change in number and percentage point change in rate, 2002–12; numbers in thousands)

	2002	2012	percent change
NUMBER			
Total labor force	**144,863**	**162,269**	**12.0%**
Hispanic labor force	17,941	23,785	32.6
Total men in labor force	**77,500**	**85,252**	**10.0**
Hispanic men in labor force	10,609	13,674	28.9
Total women in labor force	**67,363**	**77,017**	**14.3**
Hispanic women in labor force	7,332	10,111	37.9

	2002	2012	percentage point change
PARTICIPATION RATE			
Total people	**66.6%**	**67.2%**	**0.6**
Total Hispanics	69.1	68.8	−0.3
Total men	**74.1**	**73.1**	**−1.0**
Hispanic men	80.2	79.0	−1.2
Total women	**59.6**	**61.6**	**2.0**
Hispanic women	57.5	58.6	1.1

Source: Bureau of Labor Statistics, "Labor Force Projections to 2012: The graying of the U.S. workforce," Monthly Labor Review, February 2004, Internet site http://www.bls.gov/opub/mlr/2004/02/art3exc.htm; calculations by New Strategist

Table 4.82 Hispanic Labor Force Entrants and Leavers, 2002 to 2012

(number and percent distribution of total people and Hispanics aged 16 or older in the civilian labor force in 2002 and 2012, and number and percent distribution of entrants, leavers, and stayers, 2002–12; numbers in thousands)

	2002 labor force	2002 to 2012			2012 labor force
		entrants	leavers	stayers	
NUMBER					
Total labor force	**144,863**	**40,461**	**23,055**	**121,808**	**162,269**
Hispanic labor force	17,941	7,866	2,022	15,919	23,785
PERCENT DISTRIBUTION					
Total labor force	**100.0%**	**100.0%**	**100.0%**	**100.0%**	**100.0%**
Hispanic labor force	12.4	19.4	8.8	13.1	14.7

Source: Bureau of Labor Statistics, "Labor Force Projections to 2012: The graying of the U.S. workforce," Monthly Labor Review, February 2004, Internet site http://www.bls.gov/opub/mlr/2004/02/art3exc.htm; calculations by New Strategist

Most Hispanic Couples Have Children under Age 18 at Home

Among the nation's 112 million households in 2004, Hispanics headed 12 million, or 10 percent. Hispanic householders are younger than average. Consequently, Hispanics account for a relatively large share of households headed by young adults. Sixteen to 18 percent of householders under age 35 are Hispanic compared with only 5 percent of householders aged 65 or older.

Married couples account for the 53 percent majority of Hispanic households. Among households headed by the foreign-born from Central America (most are from Mexico), fully 61 percent are married couples. Half of Hispanic households include children. Among Hispanic married couples, 65 percent have children under age 18 in their home. Although black households outnumbered Hispanic households in 2003, Hispanic married couples with children outnumbered their black counterparts by 1.9 million. Sixty-five percent of Hispanic children live with both parents.

Many Hispanics are immigrants trying to establish themselves in the United States, which explains why 13 percent of Hispanic men and 10 percent of Hispanic women are living in the households of relatives. Among total men and women, the proportion is just 5 percent. It also explains why Hispanic households are larger than average. Among households with seven or more people, Hispanics head 33 percent.

■ Children are more commonly found in Hispanic households than in black or non-Hispanic white households because many Hispanics are immigrants from countries where traditional family life is common.

Married couples dominate Hispanic households

(percent distribution of Hispanic households, by household type, 2004)

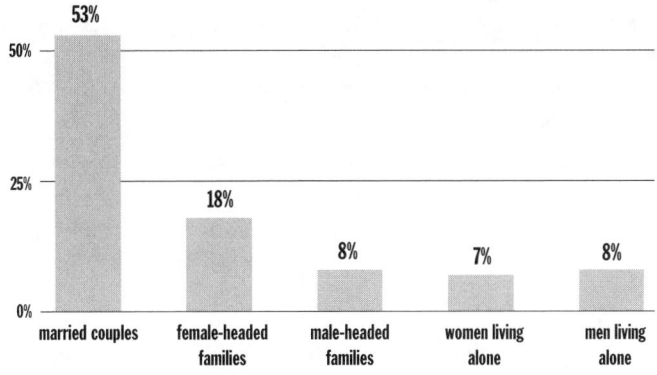

Table 4.83 Hispanic Households by Age of Householder, 2004

(number of total households, number and percent distribution of Hispanic households, and Hispanic share of total, by age of householder, 2004, numbers in thousands)

| | | Hispanic | | |
	total	number	percent distribution	share of total
Total households	**112,000**	**11,693**	**100.0%**	**10.4%**
Under age 25	6,610	1,163	9.9	17.6
Aged 25 to 29	8,737	1,479	12.6	16.9
Aged 30 to 34	10,421	1,702	14.6	16.3
Aged 35 to 39	10,997	1,570	13.4	14.3
Aged 40 to 44	12,225	1,416	12.1	11.6
Aged 45 to 49	12,360	1,191	10.2	9.6
Aged 50 to 54	10,777	831	7.1	7.7
Aged 55 to 59	9,504	706	6.0	7.4
Aged 60 to 64	7,320	522	4.5	7.1
Aged 65 or older	23,048	1,113	9.5	4.8

Source: Bureau of the Census, 2004 Current Population Survey Annual Social and Economic Supplement, Internet site http:// pubdb3.census.gov/macro/032004/hhinc/toc.htm; calculations by New Strategist

Table 4.84 Hispanic Households by Household Type, 2004

(number of total households, number and percent distribution of Hispanic households, and Hispanic share of total, by type, 2004; numbers in thousands)

| | | Hispanic | | |
	total	number	percent distribution	share of total
TOTAL HOUSEHOLDS	**112,000**	**11,693**	**100.0%**	**10.4%**
Family households	**76,217**	**9,273**	**79.3**	**12.2**
Married couples	57,719	6,227	53.3	10.8
Female householder, no spouse present	13,781	2,138	18.3	15.5
Male householder, no spouse present	4,717	908	7.8	19.2
Nonfamily households	**35,783**	**2,420**	**20.7**	**6.8**
Female householder	19,647	1,078	9.2	5.5
Living alone	17,024	863	7.4	5.1
Male householder	16,136	1,343	11.5	8.3
Living alone	12,562	891	7.6	7.1

Source: Bureau of the Census, 2004 Current Population Survey Annual Social and Economic Supplement, Internet site http:// pubdb3.census.gov/macro/032004/hhinc/toc.htm; calculations by New Strategist

Table 4.85 Households Headed by the Foreign-Born from Latin America by Household Type, 2004

(number and percent distribution of households headed by foreign-born householders from Latin America, by household type and Latin American region, 2004; numbers in thousands)

	total	Caribbean	Central America	South America
Foreign-born householders from Latin America	**7,097**	**1,496**	**4,758**	**842**
Family households	5,852	1,132	4,084	636
Married couples	4,057	684	2,923	451
Female householder, no spouse present	1,231	347	753	131
Male householder, no spouse present	563	101	408	55
Nonfamily households	1,245	365	674	206
Male householder	710	141	445	124
Female householder	535	224	229	81
Foreign-born householders from Latin America	**100.0%**	**100.0%**	**100.0%**	**100.0%**
Family households	82.5	75.7	85.8	75.5
Married couples	57.2	45.7	61.4	53.6
Female householder, no spouse present	17.3	23.2	15.8	15.6
Male householder, no spouse present	7.9	6.8	8.6	6.5
Nonfamily households	17.5	24.4	14.2	24.5
Male householder	10.0	9.4	9.4	14.7
Female householder	7.5	15.0	4.8	9.6

Note: Most of the foreign-born from Central America are from Mexico.
Source: Bureau of the Census, Foreign-Born Population of the United States, Current Population Survey, March 2004, detailed tables (PPL-176), Internet site http://www.census.gov/population/www/socdemo/foreign/ppl-176.html; calculations by New Strategist

Table 4.86 Hispanic Households by Age of Householder and Household Type, 2004

(number and percent distribution of Hispanic households by age of householder and household type, 2004; numbers in thousands)

| | | family households | | | nonfamily households | | | |
| | | | | | female-headed | | male-headed | |
	total	married couples	female hh, no spouse present	male hh, no spouse present	total	living alone	total	living alone
Total Hispanic households	**11,693**	**6,227**	**2,138**	**908**	**1,078**	**863**	**1,343**	**891**
Under age 25	1,163	364	264	221	118	56	195	84
Aged 25 to 34	3,181	1,754	572	287	178	131	390	231
Aged 35 to 44	2,986	1,773	599	206	132	93	276	188
Aged 45 to 54	2,022	1,160	382	111	172	132	195	141
Aged 55 to 64	1,228	700	180	41	172	153	136	108
Aged 65 or older	1,113	476	139	43	305	298	150	138

PERCENT DISTRIBUTION BY HOUSEHOLD TYPE

Total Hispanic households	**100.0%**	**53.3%**	**18.3%**	**7.8%**	**9.2%**	**7.4%**	**11.5%**	**7.6%**
Under age 25	100.0	31.3	22.7	19.0	10.1	4.8	16.8	7.2
Aged 25 to 34	100.0	55.1	18.0	9.0	5.6	4.1	12.3	7.3
Aged 35 to 44	100.0	59.4	20.1	6.9	4.4	3.1	9.2	6.3
Aged 45 to 54	100.0	57.4	18.9	5.5	8.5	6.5	9.6	7.0
Aged 55 to 64	100.0	57.0	14.7	3.3	14.0	12.5	11.1	8.8
Aged 65 or older	100.0	42.8	12.5	3.9	27.4	26.8	13.5	12.4

PERCENT DISTRIBUTION BY AGE

Total Hispanic households	**100.0%**	**100.0%**	**100.0%**	**100.0%**	**100.0%**	**100.0%**	**100.0%**	**100.0%**
Under age 25	9.9	5.8	12.3	24.3	10.9	6.5	14.5	9.4
Aged 25 to 34	27.2	28.2	26.8	31.6	16.5	15.2	29.0	25.9
Aged 35 to 44	25.5	28.5	28.0	22.7	12.2	10.8	20.6	21.1
Aged 45 to 54	17.3	18.6	17.9	12.2	16.0	15.3	14.5	15.8
Aged 55 to 64	10.5	11.2	8.4	4.5	16.0	17.7	10.1	12.1
Aged 65 or older	9.5	7.6	6.5	4.7	28.3	34.5	11.2	15.5

Source: Bureau of the Census, 2004 Current Population Survey Annual Social and Economic Supplement, Internet site http://pubdb3.census.gov/macro/032004/hhinc/toc.htm; calculations by New Strategist

Table 4.87 Hispanic Households by Size, 2004

(number of total households, number and percent distribution of Hispanic households, and Hispanic share of total, by size, 2004; numbers in thousands)

| | | Hispanic | | |
	total	number	percent distribution	share of total
Total households	**112,000**	**11,693**	**100.0%**	**10.4%**
One person	29,586	1,753	15.0	5.9
Two people	37,366	2,627	22.5	7.0
Three people	17,968	2,253	19.3	12.5
Four people	16,065	2,387	20.4	14.9
Five people	7,150	1,552	13.3	21.7
Six people	2,476	664	5.7	26.8
Seven or more people	1,388	456	3.9	32.9
Average number of persons per household	2.57	3.34	–	–

Note: (–) means not applicable.
Source: Bureau of the Census, 2004 Current Population Survey Annual Social and Economic Supplement, Internet site http:// pubdb3.census.gov/macro/032004/hhinc/toc.htm; calculations by New Strategist

Table 4.88 Hispanics Living Alone by Sex and Age, 2004

(total number of Hispanic households, number and percent distribution of Hispanic single-person households, and single-person household share of total, by age of householder, 2004; numbers in thousands)

| | | living alone | | |
	total	number	percent distribution	share of total
Total Hispanics	**28,566**	**1,754**	**100.0%**	**6.1%**
Under age 25	6,970	140	8.0	2.0
Aged 25 to 34	7,423	362	20.6	4.9
Aged 35 to 44	6,007	281	16.0	4.7
Aged 45 to 54	3,925	273	15.6	7.0
Aged 55 to 64	2,161	261	14.9	12.1
Aged 65 to 74	1,272	249	14.2	19.6
Aged 75 or older	808	187	10.7	23.1
Hispanic men	**14,664**	**891**	**100.0**	**6.1**
Under age 25	3,677	84	9.4	2.3
Aged 25 to 34	4,001	231	25.9	5.8
Aged 35 to 44	3,126	188	21.1	6.0
Aged 45 to 54	1,955	141	15.8	7.2
Aged 55 to 64	1,023	108	12.1	10.6
Aged 65 to 74	545	87	9.8	16.0
Aged 75 or older	336	51	5.7	15.2
Hispanic women	**13,902**	**863**	**100.0**	**6.2**
Under age 25	3,292	56	6.5	1.7
Aged 25 to 34	3,422	131	15.2	3.8
Aged 35 to 44	2,880	93	10.8	3.2
Aged 45 to 54	1,970	132	15.3	6.7
Aged 55 to 64	1,138	153	17.7	13.4
Aged 65 to 74	727	162	18.8	22.3
Aged 75 or older	473	136	15.8	28.8

Source: Bureau of the Census, 2004 Current Population Survey Annual Social and Economic Supplement, Internet site http:// pubdb3.census.gov/macro/032004/hhinc/toc.htm; calculations by New Strategist

Table 4.89   **Hispanic Households by Age of Householder, Type of Household, And Presence of Children, 2003**

(number and percent distribution of Hispanic households by age of householder, type of household, and presence of own children under age 18, and average age of householder, 2003; numbers in thousands)

	all households		married couples		female-headed families		male-headed families	
	total	with children	total	with children	total	with children	total	with children
Total Hispanic households	**11,339**	**5,704**	**6,189**	**4,001**	**2,029**	**1,357**	**872**	**346**
Under age 25	1,073	479	361	263	272	174	188	42
Aged 25 to 29	1,368	884	715	588	248	223	139	74
Aged 30 to 34	1,612	1,104	930	800	270	246	131	59
Aged 35 to 39	1,625	1,233	994	892	304	284	111	56
Aged 40 to 44	1,478	1,005	867	708	289	238	100	58
Aged 45 to 49	1,092	564	627	421	202	109	70	34
Aged 50 to 54	822	268	472	196	137	55	48	16
Aged 55 to 64	1,150	129	689	111	146	16	47	3
Aged 65 or older	1,119	39	532	24	161	13	38	3
Average age of householder	42.1	36.4	42.5	36.9	40.1	35.3	36.1	35.1

PERCENT OF HOUSEHOLDS WITH CHILDREN BY TYPE

	all households		married couples		female-headed families		male-headed families	
Total Hispanic households	**100.0%**	**50.3%**	**100.0%**	**64.6%**	**100.0%**	**66.9%**	**100.0%**	**39.7%**
Under age 25	100.0	44.6	100.0	72.9	100.0	64.0	100.0	22.3
Aged 25 to 29	100.0	64.6	100.0	82.2	100.0	89.9	100.0	53.2
Aged 30 to 34	100.0	68.5	100.0	86.0	100.0	91.1	100.0	45.0
Aged 35 to 39	100.0	75.9	100.0	89.7	100.0	93.4	100.0	50.5
Aged 40 to 44	100.0	68.0	100.0	81.7	100.0	82.4	100.0	58.0
Aged 45 to 49	100.0	51.6	100.0	67.1	100.0	54.0	100.0	48.6
Aged 50 to 54	100.0	32.6	100.0	41.5	100.0	40.1	100.0	33.3
Aged 55 to 64	100.0	11.2	100.0	16.1	100.0	11.0	100.0	6.4
Aged 65 or older	100.0	3.5	100.0	4.5	100.0	8.1	100.0	7.9

Source: Bureau of the Census, America's Families and Living Arrangements, 2003 Current Population Survey Annual Social and Economic Supplement; Internet site http://www.census.gov/population/www/socdemo/hh-fam/cps2003.html; calculations by New Strategist

Table 4.90 Living Arrangements of Hispanic Children, 2003

(number of total children under age 18, number and percent distribution of Hispanic children, and Hispanic share of total, by living arrangement, 2003; numbers in thousands)

		Hispanic		
	total	number	percent distribution	share of total
Total children	**73,001**	**13,284**	**100.0%**	**18.2%**
Living with both parents	49,903	8,584	64.6	17.2
Living with mother only	16,771	3,262	24.6	19.5
Never married	7,006	1,495	11.3	21.3
Divorced or separated	9,102	1,626	12.2	17.9
Widowed	663	141	1.1	21.3
Living with father only	3,324	737	5.5	22.2
Never married	1,172	421	3.2	35.9
Divorced or separated	1,979	295	2.2	14.9
Widowed	173	21	0.2	12.1
Living with neither parent	3,004	702	5.3	23.4

Source: Bureau of the Census, America's Families and Living Arrangements, 2003 Current Population Survey Annual Social and Economic Supplement; Internet site http://www.census.gov/population/www/socdemo/hh-fam/cps2003.html; calculations by New Strategist

Table 4.91 Hispanic Men by Living Arrangement and Age, 2003

(number and percent distribution of Hispanic men aged 15 or older by living arrangement and age, 2003; numbers in thousands)

	total	under 25	25 to 29	30 to 34	35 to 44	45 to 54	55 to 64	65 or older
Total Hispanic men	**14,336**	**3,602**	**2,107**	**1,884**	**3,061**	**1,759**	**1,018**	**907**
Married-couple householder or spouse	6,196	291	690	948	1,867	1,096	723	580
Other householder	2,100	323	313	334	508	309	151	163
Male family householder	872	188	139	131	211	118	47	38
Living alone	809	52	91	117	213	138	90	109
Living with nonrelatives	419	83	83	86	84	53	14	16
Nonhouseholder	6,041	2,988	1,104	601	687	355	144	163
Child of householder	2,791	2,034	384	146	151	64	13	–
Other relative of householder	1,844	591	391	198	276	152	100	136
Living with nonrelatives	1,406	363	329	257	260	139	31	27
Total Hispanic men	**100.0%**	**100.0%**	**100.0%**	**100.0%**	**100.0%**	**100.0%**	**100.0%**	**100.0%**
Married-couple householder or spouse	43.2	8.1	32.7	50.3	61.0	62.3	71.0	63.9
Other householder	14.6	9.0	14.9	17.7	16.6	17.6	14.8	18.0
Male family householder	6.1	5.2	6.6	7.0	6.9	6.7	4.6	4.2
Living alone	5.6	1.4	4.3	6.2	7.0	7.8	8.8	12.0
Living with nonrelatives	2.9	2.3	3.9	4.6	2.7	3.0	1.4	1.8
Nonhouseholder	42.1	83.0	52.4	31.9	22.4	20.2	14.1	18.0
Child of householder	19.5	56.5	18.2	7.7	4.9	3.6	1.3	–
Other relative of householder	12.9	16.4	18.6	10.5	9.0	8.6	9.8	15.0
Living with nonrelatives	9.8	10.1	15.6	13.6	8.5	7.9	3.0	3.0

Note: (–) means sample is too small to make a reliable estimate.
Source: Bureau of the Census, America's Families and Living Arrangements, 2003 Current Population Survey Annual Social and Economic Supplement; Internet site http://www.census.gov/population/www/socdemo/hh-fam/cps2003.html; calculations by New Strategist

Table 4.92 Hispanic Women by Living Arrangement and Age, 2003

(number and percent distribution of Hispanic women aged 15 or older by living arrangement and age, 2003; numbers in thousands)

	total	under 25	25 to 29	30 to 34	35 to 44	45 to 54	55 to 64	65 or older
Total Hispanic women	**13,599**	**3,168**	**1,722**	**1,711**	**2,865**	**1,903**	**1,084**	**1,146**
Married-couple householder or spouse	6,306	484	855	1,059	1,762	1,116	607	424
Other householder	3,050	388	341	348	735	505	309	425
Female family householder	2,029	272	248	270	593	339	146	161
Living alone	791	57	56	58	103	124	142	251
Living with nonrelatives	230	59	37	20	39	42	21	13
Nonhouseholder	4,244	2,296	527	304	368	282	168	298
Child of householder	2,077	1,666	199	98	72	33	9	1
Other relative of householder	1,352	346	147	99	161	181	131	285
Living with nonrelatives	815	284	181	107	135	68	28	12
Total Hispanic women	**100.0%**	**100.0%**	**100.0%**	**100.0%**	**100.0%**	**100.0%**	**100.0%**	**100.0%**
Married-couple householder or spouse	46.4	15.3	49.7	61.9	61.5	58.6	56.0	37.0
Other householder	22.4	12.2	19.8	20.3	25.7	26.5	28.5	37.1
Female family householder	14.9	8.6	14.4	15.8	20.7	17.8	13.5	14.0
Living alone	5.8	1.8	3.3	3.4	3.6	6.5	13.1	21.9
Living with nonrelatives	1.7	1.9	2.1	1.2	1.4	2.2	1.9	1.1
Nonhouseholder	31.2	72.5	30.6	17.8	12.8	14.8	15.5	26.0
Child of householder	15.3	52.6	11.6	5.7	2.5	1.7	0.8	0.1
Other relative of householder	9.9	10.9	8.5	5.8	5.6	9.5	12.1	24.9
Living with nonrelatives	6.0	9.0	10.5	6.3	4.7	3.6	2.6	1.0

Source: Bureau of the Census, America's Families and Living Arrangements, 2003 Current Population Survey Annual Social and Economic Supplement; Internet site http://www.census.gov/population/www/socdemo/hh-fam/cps2003.html; calculations by New Strategist

Table 4.93 Marital Status of Hispanic Men by Age, 2003

(number and percent distribution of Hispanic men aged 18 or older by age and current marital status, 2003; numbers in thousands)

	total	never married	married, spouse present	married, spouse absent	separated	divorced	widowed
Total Hispanic men	**13,357**	**4,794**	**6,596**	**637**	**346**	**803**	**182**
Aged 18 to 19	673	655	15	0	0	1	2
Aged 20 to 24	1,949	1,537	325	58	15	15	0
Aged 25 to 29	2,107	1,113	752	100	60	73	10
Aged 30 to 34	1,884	612	1,004	113	49	97	9
Aged 35 to 39	1,653	320	1,051	98	48	130	5
Aged 40 to 44	1,408	214	909	88	53	135	9
Aged 45 to 49	985	145	637	48	49	99	7
Aged 50 to 54	774	79	528	42	22	92	12
Aged 55 to 64	1,018	75	750	55	29	91	17
Aged 65 to 74	557	17	403	25	18	51	42
Aged 75 to 84	292	26	191	6	3	16	50
Aged 85 or older	58	4	29	3	0	3	19
Total Hispanic men	**100.0%**	**35.9%**	**49.4%**	**4.8%**	**2.6%**	**6.0%**	**1.4%**
Aged 18 to 19	100.0	97.3	2.2	0.0	0.0	0.1	0.3
Aged 20 to 24	100.0	78.9	16.7	3.0	0.8	0.8	0.0
Aged 25 to 29	100.0	52.8	35.7	4.7	2.8	3.5	0.5
Aged 30 to 34	100.0	32.5	53.3	6.0	2.6	5.1	0.5
Aged 35 to 39	100.0	19.4	63.6	5.9	2.9	7.9	0.3
Aged 40 to 44	100.0	15.2	64.6	6.3	3.8	9.6	0.6
Aged 45 to 49	100.0	14.7	64.7	4.9	5.0	10.1	0.7
Aged 50 to 54	100.0	10.2	68.2	5.4	2.8	11.9	1.6
Aged 55 to 64	100.0	7.4	73.7	5.4	2.8	8.9	1.7
Aged 65 to 74	100.0	3.1	72.4	4.5	3.2	9.2	7.5
Aged 75 to 84	100.0	8.9	65.4	2.1	1.0	5.5	17.1
Aged 85 or older	100.0	6.9	50.0	5.2	0.0	5.2	32.8

Source: Bureau of the Census, America's Families and Living Arrangements, 2003 Current Population Survey Annual Social and Economic Supplement; Internet site http://www.census.gov/population/www/socdemo/hh-fam/cps2003.html

Table 4.94 Marital Status of Hispanic Women by Age, 2003

(number and percent distribution of Hispanic women aged 18 or older by age and current marital status, 2003; numbers in thousands)

	total	never married	married spouse present	married spouse absent	separated	divorced	widowed
Total Hispanic women	**12,624**	**3,150**	**6,693**	**292**	**666**	**1,089**	**735**
Aged 18 to 19	573	491	64	11	6	1	0
Aged 20 to 24	1,620	1,033	486	33	46	19	3
Aged 25 to 29	1,722	597	926	39	86	62	12
Aged 30 to 34	1,711	375	1,099	29	80	120	8
Aged 35 to 39	1,534	216	1,009	36	109	143	21
Aged 40 to 44	1,331	146	836	41	89	188	30
Aged 45 to 49	1,072	95	679	26	90	149	34
Aged 50 to 54	831	68	502	30	51	139	41
Aged 55 to 64	1,084	75	635	34	54	153	133
Aged 65 to 74	666	41	322	8	40	82	172
Aged 75 to 84	367	11	115	3	14	27	196
Aged 85 or older	113	1	20	3	2	4	84
Total Hispanic women	**100.0%**	**25.0%**	**53.0%**	**2.3%**	**5.3%**	**8.6%**	**5.8%**
Aged 18 to 19	100.0	85.7	11.2	1.9	1.0	0.2	0.0
Aged 20 to 24	100.0	63.8	30.0	2.0	2.8	1.2	0.2
Aged 25 to 29	100.0	34.7	53.8	2.3	5.0	3.6	0.7
Aged 30 to 34	100.0	21.9	64.2	1.7	4.7	7.0	0.5
Aged 35 to 39	100.0	14.1	65.8	2.3	7.1	9.3	1.4
Aged 40 to 44	100.0	11.0	62.8	3.1	6.7	14.1	2.3
Aged 45 to 49	100.0	8.9	63.3	2.4	8.4	13.9	3.2
Aged 50 to 54	100.0	8.2	60.4	3.6	6.1	16.7	4.9
Aged 55 to 64	100.0	6.9	58.6	3.1	5.0	14.1	12.3
Aged 65 to 74	100.0	6.2	48.3	1.2	6.0	12.3	25.8
Aged 75 to 84	100.0	3.0	31.3	0.8	3.8	7.4	53.4
Aged 85 or older	100.0	0.9	17.7	2.7	1.8	3.5	74.3

Source: Bureau of the Census, America's Families and Living Arrangements, 2003 Current Population Survey Annual Social and Economic Supplement; Internet site http://www.census.gov/population/www/socdemo/hh-fam/cps2003.html

Table 4.95 Marital History of Hispanic Men by Age, 2001

(number of Hispanic men aged 15 or older and percent distribution by marital history and age, 2001; numbers in thousands)

	total	15 to 19	20 to 24	25 to 29	30 to 34	35 to 39	40 to 49	50 to 59	60 to 69	70 or older
Total Hispanic men, number	**13,007**	**1,603**	**1,913**	**1,832**	**1,751**	**1,330**	**2,247**	**1,210**	**621**	**500**
Total Hispanic men, percent	**100.0%**	**100.0%**	**100.0%**	**100.0%**	**100.0%**	**100.0%**	**100.0%**	**100.0%**	**100.0%**	**100.0%**
Never married	40.0	98.1	81.1	46.9	28.2	22.9	14.3	5.8	2.8	1.3
Ever married	60.0	1.9	18.9	53.1	71.8	77.1	85.7	94.2	97.2	98.7
Married once	51.6	1.9	18.8	51.3	61.9	70.3	72.2	70.8	75.1	83.0
Still married	43.2	1.7	17.0	43.9	54.9	57.9	63.2	53.7	63.1	54.3
Married twice	7.1	0.0	0.1	1.8	8.7	6.3	11.0	18.8	18.9	13.0
Still married	5.8	0.0	0.1	1.6	7.5	6.0	9.1	13.2	16.8	9.4
Married three or more times	1.3	0.0	0.0	0.0	1.1	0.5	2.5	4.6	3.3	2.6
Still married	0.7	0.0	0.0	0.0	0.8	0.2	1.6	1.8	2.5	1.4
Ever divorced	12.7	0.0	0.8	7.1	13.1	16.0	18.4	33.7	23.6	18.8
Currently divorced	6.0	0.0	0.7	5.5	4.3	9.8	7.2	17.7	6.3	10.3
Ever widowed	2.1	0.0	0.0	0.0	0.3	0.4	1.6	4.6	6.9	25.4
Currently widowed	1.6	0.0	0.0	0.0	0.0	0.4	1.4	3.1	4.4	21.8

Source: Bureau of the Census, Number, Timing, and Duration of Marriages and Divorces: 2001, *Current Population Report P70-97, 2005; Internet site http://www.census.gov/population/www/socdemo/marr-div.html*

Table 4.96 Marital History of Hispanic Women by Age, 2001

(number of Hispanic women aged 15 or older and percent distribution by marital history and age, 2001; numbers in thousands)

	total	15 to 19	20 to 24	25 to 29	30 to 34	35 to 39	40 to 49	50 to 59	60 to 69	70 or older
Total Hispanic women, number	**12,545**	**1,539**	**1,527**	**1,577**	**1,513**	**1,457**	**2,213**	**1,260**	**826**	**633**
Total Hispanic women, percent	**100.0%**	**100.0%**	**100.0%**	**100.0%**	**100.0%**	**100.0%**	**100.0%**	**100.0%**	**100.0%**	**100.0%**
Never married	29.7	89.9	66.3	28.0	15.8	15.0	8.6	10.4	8.8	6.1
Ever married	70.3	10.1	33.7	72.0	84.2	85.0	91.4	89.6	91.2	93.9
Married once	61.0	10.1	32.9	67.5	77.2	72.6	76.4	71.0	76.2	76.5
Still married	44.4	9.1	28.4	57.2	63.0	55.6	54.4	46.1	44.3	27.4
Married twice	8.0	0.0	0.8	4.4	5.9	12.0	13.2	15.4	10.2	14.1
Still married	5.6	0.0	0.5	3.8	4.5	8.9	10.5	10.1	6.3	4.5
Married three or more times	1.3	0.0	0.0	0.0	1.0	0.3	1.8	3.2	4.8	3.3
Still married	0.8	0.0	0.0	0.0	0.8	0.1	1.5	1.6	3.3	1.2
Ever divorced	15.9	0.0	2.5	9.0	13.0	22.5	26.1	30.4	24.1	20.2
Currently divorced	8.9	0.0	1.7	4.9	7.2	13.0	14.3	17.4	13.0	11.1
Ever widowed	5.9	0.0	0.7	0.3	0.6	1.3	4.3	11.0	19.4	48.7
Currently widowed	5.3	0.0	0.7	0.3	0.6	0.8	3.3	9.1	16.8	47.3

Source: Bureau of the Census, Number, Timing, and Duration of Marriages and Divorces: 2001, *Current Population Report P70-97, 2005; Internet site http://www.census.gov/population/www/socdemo/marr-div.html*

Hispanics Are the Largest Minority Group in the United States

The Hispanic population grew 16 percent between 2000 and 2004, from 36 million to 41 million. Hispanics account for 14 percent of the U.S. population. The number of Hispanics is growing rapidly because of immigration. Forty-two percent of immigrants to the U.S. in 2004 were from Mexico or other Latin American countries. Nineteen percent were from Mexico alone. The 53 percent majority of the nation's foreign-born are from Latin America.

Hispanic is an ethnic identity, not a race. There are white, black, American Indian, and Asian Hispanics. According to Census Bureau estimates for 2004, whites account for the great majority of Hispanics—92 percent—while blacks account for 4 percent.

Among Hispanics, Mexicans are the largest ethnic group (64 percent). Ten percent of Hispanics are Puerto Rican, 4 percent Cuban, and 3 percent hail from the Dominican Republic. Ten percent of Americans speak Spanish at home, with the proportion peaking at more than 25 percent in California, New Mexico, and Texas.

Hispanics are most likely to live in the West (43 percent) and South (34 percent). Thirty percent of Hispanics live in California, where they account for 35 percent of the state's population. Another 19 percent live in Texas, where they, too, account for 35 percent of the population. Los Angeles is home to more Hispanics than any other U.S. metropolitan area—7.3 million. Hispanics are 43 percent of the population of Los Angeles.

■ Hispanics are growing rapidly in almost every state. Because many are not citizens, however, their political power is limited.

Hispanics account for more than one-quarter of the population in the West

(Hispanic share of population by region, 2004)

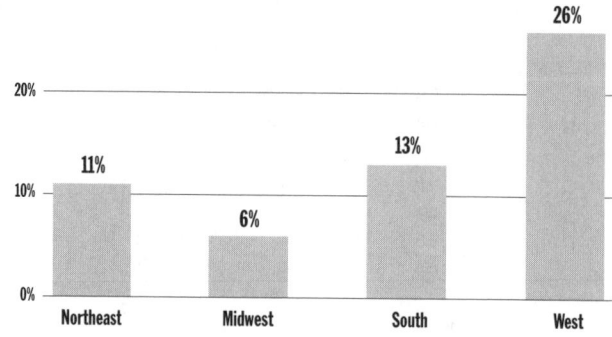

Table 4.97 Hispanics by Race, 2000 and 2004

(total number of people, number and percent Hispanic, and number and percent distribution of Hispanics by race, 2000 and 2004; percent change, 2000–04)

	2004		2000		
	number	percent distribution	number	percent distribution	percent change 2000–04
Total people	**293,655,404**	**100.0%**	**282,192,162**	**100.0%**	**4.1%**
Hispanics	41,322,070	14.1	35,647,334	12.6	15.9
Total Hispanics	**41,322,070**	**100.0**	**35,647,334**	**100.0**	**15.9**
One race	40,738,794	98.6	35,150,635	98.6	15.9
American Indian	618,003	1.5	569,527	1.6	8.5
Asian	257,792	0.6	234,010	0.7	10.2
Black	1,538,618	3.7	1,399,914	3.9	9.9
Native Hawaiian	107,441	0.3	96,154	0.3	11.7
White	38,216,940	92.5	32,851,030	92.2	16.3
Two or more races	583,276	1.4	496,699	1.4	17.4

Note: American Indians include Alaska Natives. Native Hawaiians include other Pacific Islanders.
Source: Bureau of the Census, National Population Estimates, Internet site http://www.census.gov/popest/national/asrh/ NC-EST2004-srh.html; calculations by New Strategist

Table 4.98 Hispanics by Ethnic Origin, 2004

(number and percent distribution of Hispanics by ethnic origin, 2004)

	number	percent distribution
Total Hispanics	**40,459,196**	**100.0%**
Mexican	25,894,763	64.0
Puerto Rican	3,874,322	9.6
Cuban	1,437,828	3.6
Dominican (Dominican Republic)	1,051,032	2.6
Central American	2,901,679	7.2
Costa Rican	120,316	0.3
Guatemalan	698,745	1.7
Honduran	407,994	1.0
Nicaraguan	248,725	0.6
Panamanian	113,053	0.3
Salvadoran	1,201,002	3.0
Other Central American	111,844	0.3
South American	2,215,503	5.5
Argentinean	189,190	0.5
Bolivian	90,401	0.2
Chilean	106,458	0.3
Colombian	686,185	1.7
Ecuadorian	453,360	1.1
Paraguayan	14,123	0.0
Peruvian	399,240	1.0
Uruguayan	41,577	0.1
Venezuelan	164,699	0.4
Other South American	70,270	0.2
Other Hispanic	3,084,069	7.6

Source: Bureau of the Census, 2004 American Community Survey, Internet site http://factfinder.census.gov/servlet/ DatasetMainPageServlet?_lang=en&_ts=143469461584&_ds_name=ACS_2004_EST_G00_&_program=ACS; calculations by New Strategist

Table 4.99 Hispanics in the Armed Forces, 2003

(number and percent distribution of Hispanics aged 18 or older who are in the armed forces or who are veterans, by sex and age, 2003)

	total	in armed forces	veteran
Total Hispanics aged 18 or older	**25,703,972**	**53,266**	**1,112,534**
Men	13,109,895	46,689	1,022,694
Aged 18 to 64	12,271,366	46,689	780,778
Aged 65 or older	838,529	0	241,916
Women	12,594,077	6,577	89,840
Aged 18 to 64	11,432,577	6,577	82,954
Aged 65 or older	1,161,500	0	6,886
Total Hispanics aged 18 or older	**100.0%**	**0.2%**	**4.3%**
Men	100.0	0.4	7.8
Aged 18 to 64	100.0	0.4	6.4
Aged 65 or older	100.0	0.0	28.9
Women	100.0	0.1	0.7
Aged 18 to 64	100.0	0.1	0.7
Aged 65 or older	100.0	0.0	0.6

Source: Bureau of the Census, 2003 American Community Survey, Internet site http://factfinder.census.gov/servlet/ DatasetMainPageServlet?_program=ACS&_lang=en&_ts=; calculations by New Strategist

Table 4.100 Hispanics by Age, 2000 and 2004

(number of Hispanics by age, 2000 and 2004; percent change, 2000–04)

	2004	2000	percent change 2000–04
Total Hispanics	**41,322,070**	**35,647,334**	**15.9%**
Under age 5	4,369,923	3,740,790	16.8
Aged 5 to 9	3,877,702	3,644,417	6.4
Aged 10 to 14	3,784,493	3,203,099	18.2
Aged 15 to 19	3,332,812	3,170,530	5.1
Aged 20 to 24	3,764,765	3,443,996	9.3
Aged 25 to 29	3,915,451	3,415,937	14.6
Aged 30 to 34	3,701,092	3,157,582	17.2
Aged 35 to 39	3,271,988	2,853,576	14.7
Aged 40 to 44	2,888,473	2,339,736	23.5
Aged 45 to 49	2,284,403	1,800,024	26.9
Aged 50 to 54	1,743,889	1,385,732	25.8
Aged 55 to 59	1,300,420	974,083	33.5
Aged 60 to 64	921,672	758,895	21.4
Aged 65 to 69	715,635	604,427	18.4
Aged 70 to 74	554,622	483,508	14.7
Aged 75 to 79	418,058	332,732	25.6
Aged 80 to 84	266,452	184,090	44.7
Aged 85 or older	210,220	154,180	36.3
Aged 18 or older	27,280,450	23,224,316	17.5
Aged 18 to 24	5,088,075	4,779,814	6.4
Aged 65 or older	2,164,987	1,758,937	23.1

Source: Bureau of the Census, National Population Estimates, Internet site http://www.census.gov/popest/national/asrh/ NC-EST2004-asrh.html; calculations by New Strategist

Table 4.101 Hispanic Share of Total Population by Age, 2004

(total number of people, number and percent distribution of Hispanics, and Hispanic share of total, by age, 2004)

	total	Hispanic		
		number	percent distribution	share of total
Total people	**293,655,404**	**41,322,070**	**100.0%**	**14.1%**
Under age 5	20,071,268	4,369,923	10.6	21.8
Aged 5 to 9	19,605,572	3,877,702	9.4	19.8
Aged 10 to 14	21,145,156	3,784,493	9.2	17.9
Aged 15 to 19	20,729,802	3,332,812	8.1	16.1
Aged 20 to 24	20,971,302	3,764,765	9.1	18.0
Aged 25 to 29	19,560,906	3,915,451	9.5	20.0
Aged 30 to 34	20,471,032	3,701,092	9.0	18.1
Aged 35 to 39	21,052,318	3,271,988	7.9	15.5
Aged 40 to 44	23,056,334	2,888,473	7.0	12.5
Aged 45 to 49	22,122,629	2,284,403	5.5	10.3
Aged 50 to 54	19,496,176	1,743,889	4.2	8.9
Aged 55 to 59	16,489,501	1,300,420	3.1	7.9
Aged 60 to 64	12,589,423	921,672	2.2	7.3
Aged 65 to 69	9,956,467	715,635	1.7	7.2
Aged 70 to 74	8,507,005	554,622	1.3	6.5
Aged 75 to 79	7,410,757	418,058	1.0	5.6
Aged 80 to 84	5,560,125	266,452	0.6	4.8
Aged 85 or older	4,859,631	210,220	0.5	4.3
Aged 18 or older	220,377,406	27,280,450	66.0	12.4
Aged 18 to 24	29,245,102	5,088,075	12.3	17.4
Aged 65 or older	36,293,985	2,164,987	5.2	6.0

Source: Bureau of the Census, National Population Estimates, Internet site http://www.census.gov/popest/national/asrh/ NC-EST2004-sa.html; calculations by New Strategist

Table 4.102 Hispanics by Age and Sex, 2004

(number of Hispanics by age and sex, and sex ratio by age, 2004)

	total	females	males	sex ratio
Total Hispanics	**41,322,070**	**19,974,997**	**21,347,073**	**107**
Under age 5	4,369,923	2,137,621	2,232,302	104
Aged 5 to 9	3,877,702	1,894,260	1,983,442	105
Aged 10 to 14	3,784,493	1,849,237	1,935,256	105
Aged 15 to 19	3,332,812	1,610,905	1,721,907	107
Aged 20 to 24	3,764,765	1,692,202	2,072,563	122
Aged 25 to 29	3,915,451	1,746,375	2,169,076	124
Aged 30 to 34	3,701,092	1,707,610	1,993,482	117
Aged 35 to 39	3,271,988	1,531,561	1,740,427	114
Aged 40 to 44	2,888,473	1,387,058	1,501,415	108
Aged 45 to 49	2,284,403	1,124,015	1,160,388	103
Aged 50 to 54	1,743,889	881,520	862,369	98
Aged 55 to 59	1,300,420	672,465	627,955	93
Aged 60 to 64	921,672	491,713	429,959	87
Aged 65 to 69	715,635	391,638	323,997	83
Aged 70 to 74	554,622	313,060	241,562	77
Aged 75 to 79	418,058	244,428	173,630	71
Aged 80 to 84	266,452	160,488	105,964	66
Aged 85 or older	210,220	138,841	71,379	51
Aged 18 or older	27,280,450	13,115,077	14,165,373	108
Aged 18 to 24	5,088,075	2,324,305	2,763,770	119
Aged 65 or older	2,164,987	1,248,455	916,532	73

Note: The sex ratio is the number of males divided by the number of females multiplied by 100.
Source: Bureau of the Census, National Population Estimates, Internet site http://www.census.gov/popest/national/asrh/
NC-EST2004-sa.html; calculations by New Strategist

Table 4.103 Hispanics by Age, 2000 to 2020

(number and percent distribution of Hispanics by age, 2000 to 2020, percent change, 2000–10 and 2010–20; numbers in thousands)

	2000	2010	2020	percent change 2000–10	percent change 2010–20
Total Hispanics	**35,622**	**47,756**	**59,756**	**34.1%**	**25.1%**
Under age 5	3,745	4,824	5,570	28.8	15.5
Aged 5 to 9	3,639	4,515	5,306	24.1	17.5
Aged 10 to 14	3,207	4,057	5,075	26.5	25.1
Aged 15 to 19	3,175	4,162	4,950	31.1	18.9
Aged 20 to 24	3,427	3,927	4,656	14.6	18.6
Aged 25 to 29	3,408	3,878	4,714	13.8	21.6
Aged 30 to 34	3,155	3,973	4,325	25.9	8.9
Aged 35 to 39	2,852	3,769	4,117	32.2	9.3
Aged 40 to 44	2,336	3,343	4,082	43.1	22.1
Aged 45 to 49	1,802	2,939	3,796	63.1	29.2
Aged 50 to 54	1,384	2,371	3,314	71.3	39.8
Aged 55 to 59	976	1,806	2,863	85.0	58.5
Aged 60 to 64	759	1,365	2,262	79.9	65.7
Aged 65 or older	1,757	2,826	4,723	60.8	67.2

Source: Bureau of the Census, Internet site http://www.census.gov/ipc/www/usinterimproj/; calculations by New Strategist

Table 4.104 Hispanics by Region, 2000 and 2004

(number of Hispanics by region, 2000 and 2004; percent change, 2000–04)

	2004	2000	percent change 2000–04
Total Hispanics	**41,322,070**	**35,305,818**	**17.0%**
Northeast	5,870,890	5,254,087	11.7
Midwest	3,705,062	3,124,532	18.6
South	14,025,905	11,586,696	21.1
West	17,720,213	15,340,503	15.5

Note: Total number of Hispanics in 2000 differs from the total in previous tables of this chapter because these are census counts from April 1, 2000, whereas the others are population estimates.
Source: Bureau of the Census, 2000 Census, Internet site http://factfinder.census.gov/servlet/DatasetMainPageServlet?_program=DEC&_lang=en&_ts=; and State Population Estimates, Internet site http://www.census.gov/popest/states/asrh/SC-EST2004-04.html; calculations by New Strategist

Table 4.105 Hispanic Share of the Total Population by Region, 2004

(total number of people, number and percent distribution of Hispanics, and Hispanic share of total, by region, 2004)

	total	Hispanic number	Hispanic percent distribution	Hispanic share of total
Total people	**293,655,404**	**41,322,070**	**100.0%**	**14.1%**
Northeast	54,571,147	5,870,890	14.2	10.8
Midwest	65,729,852	3,705,062	9.0	5.6
South	105,944,965	14,025,905	33.9	13.2
West	67,409,440	17,720,213	42.9	26.3

Source: Bureau of the Census, State Population Estimates, Internet site http://www.census.gov/popest/states/asrh/SC-EST2004-04.html; calculations by New Strategist

Table 4.106 Hispanics by State, 2000 and 2004

(number of Hispanics by state, 2000 and 2004; percent change, 2000–04)

	2004	2000	percent change 2000–04
Total Hispanics	**41,322,070**	**35,305,818**	**17.0%**
Alabama	98,388	75,830	29.7
Alaska	32,386	25,852	25.3
Arizona	1,608,698	1,295,617	24.2
Arkansas	120,820	86,866	39.1
California	12,442,626	10,966,556	13.5
Colorado	878,803	735,601	19.5
Connecticut	371,818	320,323	16.1
Delaware	48,153	37,277	29.2
District of Columbia	47,258	44,953	5.1
Florida	3,304,832	2,682,715	23.2
Georgia	598,322	435,227	37.5
Hawaii	99,830	87,699	13.8
Idaho	123,900	101,690	21.8
Illinois	1,774,551	1,530,262	16.0
Indiana	269,267	214,536	25.5
Iowa	104,119	82,473	26.2
Kansas	220,288	188,252	17.0
Kentucky	77,055	59,939	28.6
Louisiana	124,222	107,738	15.3
Maine	12,476	9,360	33.3
Maryland	297,717	227,916	30.6
Massachusetts	494,188	428,729	15.3
Michigan	375,041	323,877	15.8
Minnesota	179,303	143,382	25.1
Mississippi	49,075	39,569	24.0
Missouri	148,201	118,592	25.0
Montana	21,841	18,081	20.8
Nebraska	119,975	94,425	27.1
Nevada	531,929	393,970	35.0
New Hampshire	27,500	20,489	34.2
New Jersey	1,294,422	1,117,191	15.9
New Mexico	823,352	765,386	7.6
New York	3,076,697	2,867,583	7.3
North Carolina	517,617	378,963	36.6
North Dakota	9,755	7,786	25.3
Ohio	252,269	217,123	16.2
Oklahoma	223,005	179,304	24.4
Oregon	343,278	275,314	24.7

(continued)

	2004	2000	percent change 2000–04
Pennsylvania	475,552	394,088	20.7%
Rhode Island	111,823	90,820	23.1
South Carolina	130,432	95,076	37.2
South Dakota	15,093	10,903	38.4
Tennessee	167,025	123,838	34.9
Texas	7,781,211	6,669,666	16.7
Utah	253,073	201,559	25.6
Vermont	6,414	5,504	16.5
Virginia	426,152	329,540	29.3
Washington	526,667	441,509	19.3
West Virginia	14,621	12,279	19.1
Wisconsin	237,200	192,921	23.0
Wyoming	33,830	31,669	6.8

Note: Total number of Hispanics in 2000 differs from the total in previous tables of this chapter because these are census counts from April 1, 2000, whereas the others are population estimates.
Source: Bureau of the Census, 2000 Census, Internet site http://factfinder.census.gov/servlet/DatasetMainPageServlet?_program=DEC&_lang=en&_ts=; and State Population Estimates, Internet site http://www.census.gov/popest/states/asrh/SC-EST2004-04.html; calculations by New Strategist

Table 4.107 Hispanic Share of Total Population by State, 2004

(total number of people, number and percent distribution of Hispanics, and Hispanic share of total, by state, 2004)

		Hispanic		
	total	number	percent distribution	share of total
Total people	**293,655,404**	**41,322,070**	**100.0%**	**14.1%**
Alabama	4,530,182	98,388	0.2	2.2
Alaska	655,435	32,386	0.1	4.9
Arizona	5,743,834	1,608,698	3.9	28.0
Arkansas	2,752,629	120,820	0.3	4.4
California	35,893,799	12,442,626	30.1	34.7
Colorado	4,601,403	878,803	2.1	19.1
Connecticut	3,503,604	371,818	0.9	10.6
Delaware	830,364	48,153	0.1	5.8
District of Columbia	553,523	47,258	0.1	8.5
Florida	17,397,161	3,304,832	8.0	19.0
Georgia	8,829,383	598,322	1.4	6.8
Hawaii	1,262,840	99,830	0.2	7.9
Idaho	1,393,262	123,900	0.3	8.9
Illinois	12,713,634	1,774,551	4.3	14.0
Indiana	6,237,569	269,267	0.7	4.3
Iowa	2,954,451	104,119	0.3	3.5
Kansas	2,735,502	220,288	0.5	8.1
Kentucky	4,145,922	77,055	0.2	1.9
Louisiana	4,515,770	124,222	0.3	2.8
Maine	1,317,253	12,476	0.0	0.9
Maryland	5,558,058	297,717	0.7	5.4
Massachusetts	6,416,505	494,188	1.2	7.7
Michigan	10,112,620	375,041	0.9	3.7
Minnesota	5,100,958	179,303	0.4	3.5
Mississippi	2,902,966	49,075	0.1	1.7
Missouri	5,754,618	148,201	0.4	2.6
Montana	926,865	21,841	0.1	2.4
Nebraska	1,747,214	119,975	0.3	6.9
Nevada	2,334,771	531,929	1.3	22.8
New Hampshire	1,299,500	27,500	0.1	2.1
New Jersey	8,698,879	1,294,422	3.1	14.9
New Mexico	1,903,289	823,352	2.0	43.3
New York	19,227,088	3,076,697	7.4	16.0
North Carolina	8,541,221	517,617	1.3	6.1
North Dakota	634,366	9,755	0.0	1.5
Ohio	11,459,011	252,269	0.6	2.2
Oklahoma	3,523,553	223,005	0.5	6.3
Oregon	3,594,586	343,278	0.8	9.5

(continued)

	total	Hispanic		
		number	percent distribution	share of total
Pennsylvania	12,406,292	475,552	1.2%	3.8%
Rhode Island	1,080,632	111,823	0.3	10.3
South Carolina	4,198,068	130,432	0.3	3.1
South Dakota	770,883	15,093	0.0	2.0
Tennessee	5,900,962	167,025	0.4	2.8
Texas	22,490,022	7,781,211	18.8	34.6
Utah	2,389,039	253,073	0.6	10.6
Vermont	621,394	6,414	0.0	1.0
Virginia	7,459,827	426,152	1.0	5.7
Washington	6,203,788	526,667	1.3	8.5
West Virginia	1,815,354	14,621	0.0	0.8
Wisconsin	5,509,026	237,200	0.6	4.3
Wyoming	506,529	33,830	0.1	6.7

Source: Bureau of the Census, State Population Estimates, Internet site http://www.census.gov/popest/states/asrh/SC-EST2004-04.html; calculations by New Strategist

Table 4.108 Hispanics by State and Ethnicity, 2004

(total number of Hispanics and percent distribution by state and ethnicity, 2004)

	total number	total percent	Mexican	Puerto Rican	Cuban	Dominican	other Hispanic
Total Hispanics	**40,459,196**	**100.0%**	**64.0%**	**9.6%**	**3.6%**	**2.6%**	**20.3%**
Alabama	86,116	100.0	77.6	5.9	1.5	0.7	14.3
Alaska	30,293	100.0	56.6	12.0	4.5	1.8	25.2
Arizona	1,584,217	100.0	90.5	1.1	0.3	0.1	8.0
Arkansas	117,568	100.0	81.9	4.3	0.0	0.0	13.8
California	12,246,122	100.0	82.2	1.4	0.6	0.0	15.8
Colorado	862,631	100.0	74.6	2.5	0.6	0.1	22.2
Connecticut	359,093	100.0	11.6	55.6	1.6	3.6	27.6
Delaware	47,526	100.0	45.8	35.6	3.3	2.7	12.6
District of Columbia	45,879	100.0	10.9	6.0	3.9	2.6	76.6
Florida	3,250,768	100.0	14.3	20.2	30.3	3.9	31.3
Georgia	576,113	100.0	67.8	8.0	2.5	1.2	20.4
Hawaii	96,778	100.0	28.4	35.0	1.9	0.1	34.6
Idaho	121,398	100.0	86.5	0.9	0.2	0.0	12.4
Illinois	1,739,870	100.0	78.3	8.4	1.2	0.5	11.7
Indiana	264,936	100.0	81.0	6.4	0.9	0.3	11.5
Iowa	104,688	100.0	80.3	1.9	0.9	0.0	16.9
Kansas	160,808	100.0	80.0	4.6	2.3	0.1	13.0
Kentucky	74,613	100.0	63.7	7.6	7.1	0.3	21.3
Louisiana	118,273	100.0	26.6	4.7	7.4	1.4	60.0
Maine	11,419	100.0	26.9	27.3	5.5	0.0	40.4
Maryland	294,052	100.0	21.0	9.3	3.8	2.7	63.2
Massachusetts	478,929	100.0	3.9	45.7	1.3	15.6	33.6
Michigan	359,111	100.0	72.4	9.8	2.0	0.1	15.7
Minnesota	173,124	100.0	68.9	4.2	2.2	0.6	24.1
Mississippi	41,706	100.0	66.1	3.8	1.9	0.0	28.1
Missouri	143,729	100.0	69.5	8.3	2.3	0.6	19.3
Montana	20,227	100.0	79.0	4.2	1.2	0.9	14.7
Nebraska	118,227	100.0	81.4	3.4	1.1	0.3	13.8
Nevada	527,570	100.0	77.7	2.6	2.3	0.1	17.2
New Hampshire	26,108	100.0	25.0	27.8	4.9	13.7	28.6
New Jersey	1,274,500	100.0	9.1	34.6	6.3	11.5	38.4
New Mexico	808,693	100.0	54.4	0.7	0.4	0.0	44.5
New York	3,003,572	100.0	10.5	36.9	2.5	19.0	31.0
North Carolina	506,206	100.0	70.9	6.6	1.0	0.4	21.1
North Dakota	6,936	100.0	74.4	3.1	2.9	0.0	19.6
Ohio	242,100	100.0	44.1	33.8	1.2	1.5	19.3
Oklahoma	218,775	100.0	79.9	3.2	0.1	0.0	16.7
Oregon	336,925	100.0	80.7	2.3	1.0	0.2	15.8

(continued)

| | total | | | Puerto | | | other |
	number	percent	Mexican	Rican	Cuban	Dominican	Hispanic
Pennsylvania	447,846	100.0%	15.7%	57.3%	2.2%	5.8%	19.0%
Rhode Island	109,192	100.0	6.3	35.8	0.9	21.6	35.4
South Carolina	120,681	100.0	60.9	7.9	2.1	1.6	27.6
South Dakota	12,773	100.0	70.0	3.5	0.0	0.0	26.5
Tennessee	165,155	100.0	69.8	5.1	4.4	0.2	20.5
Texas	7,656,151	100.0	85.5	1.0	0.4	0.1	12.9
Utah	249,091	100.0	75.6	0.8	1.3	0.1	22.2
Vermont	5,124	100.0	26.9	41.8	4.1	0.0	27.2
Virginia	418,130	100.0	26.4	11.9	3.9	1.3	56.5
Washington	517,055	100.0	80.8	2.9	0.9	0.1	15.4
West Virginia	10,935	100.0	50.7	24.2	4.4	0.0	20.7
Wisconsin	234,453	100.0	71.5	13.9	1.0	1.1	12.4
Wyoming	33,011	100.0	66.3	3.4	0.2	0.0	30.1

Source: Bureau of the Census, 2004 American Community Survey, Internet site http://factfinder.census.gov/servlet/ DatasetMainPageServlet?_lang=en&_ts=143469461584&_ds_name=ACS_2004_EST_G00_&_program=ACS; calculations by New Strategist

Table 4.109 Hispanics by Metropolitan Area, 2004

(total number of people, number of Hispanics, and Hispanic share of total, for selected metropolitan areas, 2004)

	total population	Hispanic number	Hispanic share of total
Albany–Schenectady–Troy, NY MSA	860,976	26,108	3.0%
Allentown–Bethlehem–Easton, PA MSA	650,230	63,513	9.8
Anchorage, AK MSA	265,176	18,252	6.9
Appleton–Oshkosh–Neenah, WI MSA	359,711	8,278	2.3
Atlanta, GA MSA	4,477,579	381,192	8.5
Augusta–Aiken, GA–SC MSA	476,167	12,183	2.6
Austin–San Marcos, TX MSA	1,373,125	397,684	29.0
Bakersfield, CA MSA	702,855	300,758	42.8
Baton Rouge, LA MSA	610,743	13,269	2.2
Beaumont–Port Arthur, TX MSA	366,244	31,704	8.7
Biloxi–Gulfport–Pascagoula, MS MSA	363,966	9,161	2.5
Binghamton, NY MSA	239,012	4,637	1.9
Birmingham, AL MSA	929,694	22,906	2.5
Boise City, ID MSA	479,284	48,370	10.1
Boston–Worcester–Lawrence, MA–NH–ME–CT CMSA	5,749,197	405,342	7.1
Brownsville–Harlingen–San Benito, TX MSA	367,603	315,832	85.9
Buffalo–Niagara Falls, NY MSA	1,119,037	33,954	3.0
Canton–Massillon, OH MSA	400,919	3,612	0.9
Charleston–North Charleston, SC MSA	563,828	15,991	2.8
Chicago, IL PMSA	8,388,723	1,623,313	19.4
Cleveland–Akron, OH CMSA	2,878,475	86,702	3.0
Colorado Springs, CO MSA	539,225	67,740	12.6
Columbia, SC MSA	543,126	10,848	2.0
Corpus Christi, TX MSA	381,422	215,139	56.4
Dallas–Fort Worth, TX CMSA	5,676,651	1,416,176	24.9
Davenport–Moline–Rock Island, IA–IL MSA	350,022	23,139	6.6
Dayton–Springfield, OH MSA	916,635	13,227	1.4
Daytona Beach, FL MSA	530,553	42,218	8.0
Denver–Boulder–Greeley, CO CMSA*	2,514,628	516,842	20.6
Des Moines, IA MSA	476,699	23,986	5.0
Detroit–Ann Arbor–Flint, MI CMSA	5,437,277	177,864	3.3
El Paso, TX MSA	700,225	568,527	81.2
Erie, PA MSA	267,426	6,379	2.4
Eugene–Springfield, OR MSA	324,176	17,628	5.4
Fayetteville, NC MSA	287,220	17,243	6.0
Fayetteville–Springdale–Rogers, AR MSA	345,308	41,334	12.0
Fort Myers–Cape Coral, FL MSA	508,634	66,099	13.0
Fort Pierce–Port St. Lucie, FL MSA	358,578	36,906	10.3
Fort Wayne, IN MSA	506,545	20,281	4.0

(continued)

	total population	Hispanic number	share of total
Fresno, CA MSA	978,274	453,903	46.4%
Grand Rapids–Muskegon–Holland, MI MSA	1,102,729	81,488	7.4
Greensboro–Winston-Salem–High Point, NC MSA	1,283,261	86,482	6.7
Greenville–Spartanburg–Anderson, SC MSA	976,678	37,919	3.9
Harrisburg–Lebanon–Carlisle, PA MSA	617,676	22,004	3.6
Hartford, CT MSA	1,163,367	124,845	10.7
Hickory–Morganton–Lenoir, NC MSA	345,590	19,350	5.6
Honolulu, HI MSA	868,751	61,436	7.1
Houston–Galveston–Brazoria, TX CMSA*	4,794,384	1,554,510	32.4
Huntsville, AL MSA	354,936	6,171	1.7
Indianapolis, IN MSA	1,664,412	61,896	3.7
Jackson, MS MSA	443,275	5,212	1.2
Jacksonville, FL MSA	1,182,453	56,952	4.8
Johnson City–Kingsport–Bristol, TN–VA MSA	482,047	6,589	1.4
Kalamazoo–Battle Creek, MI MSA	441,059	17,354	3.9
Kansas City, MO–KS MSA	1,823,092	116,805	6.4
Killeen–Temple, TX MSA	298,933	52,364	17.5
Knoxville, TN MSA	707,617	11,368	1.6
Lafayette, LA MSA	386,812	5,852	1.5
Lakeland–Winter Haven, FL MSA	511,565	63,343	12.4
Lancaster, PA MSA	473,104	31,038	6.6
Lansing–East Lansing, MI MSA	436,485	22,080	5.1
Lexington, KY MSA	478,625	15,661	3.3
Lincoln, NE MSA	249,670	10,202	4.1
Little Rock–North Little Rock, AR MSA	593,032	15,873	2.7
Los Angeles–Riverside–Orange County, CA CMSA	17,199,115	7,375,686	42.9
Lubbock, TX MSA	240,721	72,494	30.1
Macon, GA MSA	329,432	8,289	2.5
Madison, WI MSA	437,843	18,816	4.3
McAllen–Edinburg–Mission, TX MSA	651,974	582,072	89.3
Melbourne–Titusville–Palm Bay, FL MSA	509,248	29,333	5.8
Miami–Fort Lauderdale, FL CMSA	4,051,442	1,772,206	43.7
Milwaukee–Waukesha, WI PMSA	1,483,023	111,544	7.5
Mobile, AL MSA	547,153	2,853	0.5
Modesto, CA MSA	490,860	179,888	36.6
Montgomery, AL MSA	323,220	4,529	1.4
Nashville, TN MSA	1,275,212	58,131	4.6
New Orleans, LA MSA	1,313,694	63,911	4.9
New York–Northern New Jersey–Long Island, NY–NJ–CT–PA CMSA*	20,345,959	4,069,863	20.0
Oklahoma City, OK MSA	1,095,252	91,524	8.4
Orlando, FL MSA	1,831,212	370,628	20.2
Pensacola, FL MSA	410,542	8,886	2.2
Peoria–Pekin, IL MSA	337,020	6,069	1.8
Philadelphia–Wilmington–Atlantic City, PA–NJ–DE–MD CMSA*	5,383,262	328,101	6.1

(continued)

	total population	Hispanic number	share of total
Pittsburgh, PA MSA	2,260,551	17,116	0.8%
Portland, ME MSA	248,827	2,455	1.0
Providence–Fall River–Warwick, RI–MA MSA	1,165,549	113,593	9.7
Provo–Orem, UT MSA	395,173	32,803	8.3
Raleigh–Durham–Chapel Hill, NC MSA	1,278,372	106,920	8.4
Reading, PA MSA	378,456	44,975	11.9
Reno, NV MSA	375,344	73,188	19.5
Richmond–Petersburg, VA MSA	1,013,399	31,189	3.1
Rochester, NY MSA	1,057,917	47,945	4.5
Rockford, IL MSA	382,901	37,019	9.7
Sacramento, CA PMSA	1,803,160	290,331	16.1
Saginaw–Bay City–Midland, MI MSA	393,837	19,892	5.1
St. Louis, MO–IL MSA	2,620,334	47,411	1.8
Salinas, CA MSA	392,192	199,828	51.0
Salt Lake City–Ogden, UT MSA	1,384,041	177,839	12.8
San Antonio, TX MSA	1,683,872	899,192	53.4
San Diego, CA MSA	2,833,275	831,580	29.4
San Francisco–Oakland–San Jose, CA CMSA	6,951,260	1,471,359	21.2
San Luis Obispo–Atascadero–Paso Robles, CA MSA	238,502	40,433	17.0
Santa Barbara–Santa Maria–Lompoc, CA MSA	385,238	144,459	37.5
Sarasota–Bradenton, FL MSA	639,438	52,218	8.2
Savannah, GA MSA	299,920	7,638	2.5
Scranton–Wilkes-Barre–Hazleton, PA MSA	587,557	11,243	1.9
Seattle–Tacoma–Bremerton, WA CMSA*	3,184,924	218,504	6.9
Shreveport–Bossier City, LA MSA	387,312	8,770	2.3
South Bend, IN MSA	252,944	14,068	5.6
Spokane, WA MSA	420,592	13,165	3.1
Springfield, MA MSA	560,472	78,801	14.1
Springfield, MO MSA	332,918	6,356	1.9
Stockton–Lodi, CA MSA	632,143	214,351	33.9
Syracuse, NY MSA	707,901	14,752	2.1
Tallahassee, FL MSA	274,945	12,053	4.4
Tampa–St. Petersburg–Clearwater, FL MSA	2,537,586	320,798	12.6
Toledo, OH MSA	598,283	29,241	4.9
Tucson, AZ MSA	885,025	283,871	32.1
Tulsa, OK MSA	810,062	50,536	6.2
Utica–Rome, NY MSA	282,844	6,992	2.5
Visalia–Tulare–Porterville, CA MSA	395,493	215,888	54.6
West Palm Beach–Boca Raton, FL MSA	1,223,206	190,348	15.6
Wichita, KS MSA	546,308	49,024	9.0
York, PA MSA	393,426	14,082	3.6
Youngstown–Warren, OH MSA	566,597	10,306	1.8

* Population figures are for only part of the metropolitan area.

Note: Some metropolitan areas are not shown because data are not available. For the definition of CMSA, MSA, and PMSA, see the glossary.

Source: Bureau of the Census, 2004 American Community Survey, Internet site http://factfinder.census.gov/servlet/ DatasetMainPageServlet?_program=ACS&_lang=en&_ts=; calculations by New Strategist

Table 4.110 Immigrants from Latin America and Spain, 2004

(total number of immigrants admitted for legal permanent residence, and number and percent distribution of immigrants from Latin America and Spain, by country of birth, 2004)

	number	percent distribution
Total immigrants	**946,142**	**100.0%**
Immigrants from Latin America and Spain	398,742	42.1
Immigrants from Latin America and Spain	**398,742**	**100.0%**
Mexico	175,364	44.0
Caribbean	88,921	22.3
Dominican Republic	30,492	7.6
Cuba	20,488	5.1
Jamaica	14,414	3.6
Haiti	13,998	3.5
Trinidad and Tobago	5,384	1.4
Barbados	630	0.2
St. Lucia	616	0.2
Grenada	609	0.2
Bahamas	586	0.1
Antigua-Barbuda	414	0.1
St. Vincent and the Grenadines	400	0.1
St. Kitts-Nevis	299	0.1
Dominica	132	0.0
Bermuda	100	0.0
Netherlands Antilles	72	0.0
Guadeloupe	59	0.0
Cayman Islands	38	0.0
British Virgin Islands	35	0.0
Montserrat	33	0.0
Aruba	31	0.0
Turks and Caicos Islands	28	0.0
Martinique	26	0.0
Anguilla	22	0.0
South America	71,785	18.0
Colombia	18,678	4.7
Peru	11,781	3.0
Brazil	10,504	2.6
Ecuador	8,611	2.2
Guyana	6,329	1.6
Venezuela	6,220	1.6
Argentina	4,805	1.2
Chile	1,808	0.5
Bolivia	1,765	0.4
Uruguay	787	0.2
Paraguay	328	0.1
Suriname	166	0.0
French Guiana	3	0.0

(continued)

	number	percent distribution
Central America	61,333	15.4%
El Salvador	29,795	7.5
Guatemala	17,999	4.5
Honduras	5,505	1.4
Nicaragua	4,000	1.0
Costa Rica	1,754	0.4
Panama	1,415	0.4
Belize	865	0.2
Spain	1,339	0.3

Source: Office of Immigration Statistics, 2004 Yearbook of Immigration Statistics, Internet site http://uscis.gov/graphics/shared/statistics/yearbook/YrBk04Im.htm; calculations by New Strategist

Table 4.111 Total and Latin American Foreign-Born by Age, 2004

(number of total foreign-born, number and percent distribution of Latin American foreign-born, and Latin American share of total by age, 2004; numbers in thousands)

| | | Latin American foreign-born | | |
	total	number	percent distribution	share of total
Total foreign-born	**34,244**	**18,314**	**100.0%**	**53.5%**
Under age 5	334	181	1.0	54.2
Aged 5 to 9	709	461	2.5	65.0
Aged 10 to 14	1,113	674	3.7	60.6
Aged 15 to 19	1,677	1,019	5.6	60.8
Aged 20 to 24	2,884	1,890	10.3	65.5
Aged 25 to 29	3,751	2,390	13.1	63.7
Aged 30 to 34	4,033	2,405	13.1	59.6
Aged 35 to 39	3,873	2,137	11.7	55.2
Aged 40 to 44	3,686	2,052	11.2	55.7
Aged 45 to 49	3,049	1,524	8.3	50.0
Aged 50 to 54	2,267	1,044	5.7	46.1
Aged 55 to 59	1,811	739	4.0	40.8
Aged 60 to 64	1,360	570	3.1	41.9
Aged 65 or older	3,697	1,228	6.7	33.2

Source: Bureau of the Census, Foreign-Born Population of the United States, Current Population Survey, March 2004, detailed tables (PPL-176), Internet site http://www.census.gov/population/www/socdemo/foreign/ppl-176.html; calculations by New Strategist

Table 4.112 Latin American Foreign-Born by Selected Characteristics and Region of Birth, 2004

(number and percent distribution of the Latin American foreign-born by selected characteristics and region of birth, 2004; numbers in thousands)

	total	Caribbean	Central America	South America
Total Latin American foreign-born	**18,314**	**3,323**	**12,924**	**2,066**
Under age 18	2,388	262	1,900	228
Aged 18 to 24	1,836	252	1,364	221
Aged 25 to 34	4,795	521	3,842	431
Aged 35 to 44	4,189	749	2,962	479
Aged 45 to 54	2,568	643	1,566	359
Aged 55 to 64	1,309	394	714	200
Aged 65 or older	1,228	502	576	149
Sex				
Male	9,650	1,536	7,078	1,037
Female	8,663	1,787	5,846	1,030
Year of arrival				
Arrived 2000 or later	3,547	353	2,687	507
Arrived 1990 to 1999	6,611	1,044	4,883	684
Arrived before 1990	8,156	1,925	5,355	875

PERCENT DISTRIBUTION BY REGION OF BIRTH

	total	Caribbean	Central America	South America
Total Latin American foreign-born	**100.0%**	**18.1%**	**70.6%**	**11.3%**
Under age 18	100.0	11.0	79.6	9.5
Aged 18 to 24	100.0	13.7	74.3	12.0
Aged 25 to 34	100.0	10.9	80.1	9.0
Aged 35 to 44	100.0	17.9	70.7	11.4
Aged 45 to 54	100.0	25.0	61.0	14.0
Aged 55 to 64	100.0	30.1	54.5	15.3
Aged 65 or older	100.0	40.9	46.9	12.1
Sex				
Male	100.0	15.9	73.3	10.7
Female	100.0	20.6	67.5	11.9
Year of arrival				
Arrived 2000 or later	100.0	10.0	75.8	14.3
Arrived 1990 to 1999	100.0	15.8	73.9	10.3
Arrived before 1990	100.0	23.6	65.7	10.7

(continued)

PERCENT DISTRIBUTION BY CHARACTERISTIC	total	Caribbean	Central America	South America
Total Latin American foreign-born	**100.0%**	**100.0%**	**100.0%**	**100.0%**
Under age 18	13.0	7.9	14.7	11.0
Aged 18 to 24	10.0	7.6	10.6	10.7
Aged 25 to 34	26.2	15.7	29.7	20.9
Aged 35 to 44	22.9	22.5	22.9	23.2
Aged 45 to 54	14.0	19.3	12.1	17.4
Aged 55 to 64	7.1	11.9	5.5	9.7
Aged 65 or older	6.7	15.1	4.5	7.2
Sex				
Male	52.7	46.2	54.8	50.2
Female	47.3	53.8	45.2	49.9
Year of arrival				
Arrived 2000 or later	19.4	10.6	20.8	24.5
Arrived 1990 to 1999	36.1	31.4	37.8	33.1
Arrived before 1990	44.5	57.9	41.4	42.4

Note: Most of the foreign-born from Central America are from Mexico.

Source: Bureau of the Census, Foreign-born Population of the United States, Current Population Survey, March 2004, detailed tables (PPL-176), Internet site http://www.census.gov/population/www/socdemo/foreign/ppl-176.html; calculations by New Strategist

Table 4.113 Latin American Foreign-Born by U.S. Region of Residence, 2004

(number and percent distribution of total people and Latin American foreign-born by U.S. region of residence and world region of birth, 2004; numbers in thousands)

| | total | Latin American foreign-born | | | |
		total	Caribbean	Central America	South America
Total people	**288,280**	**18,314**	**3,323**	**12,924**	**2,066**
Northeast	53,703	3,237	1,548	854	836
Midwest	64,784	1,365	54	1,216	95
South	103,545	6,661	1,581	4,240	840
West	66,247	7,051	141	6,614	296
PERCENT DISTRIBUTION BY FOREIGN-BORN STATUS					
Total people	**100.0%**	**6.4%**	**1.2%**	**4.5%**	**0.7%**
Northeast	100.0	6.0	2.9	1.6	1.6
Midwest	100.0	2.1	0.1	1.9	0.1
South	100.0	6.4	1.5	4.1	0.8
West	100.0	10.6	0.2	10.0	0.4
PERCENT DISTRIBUTION BY U.S. REGION OF RESIDENCE					
Total people	**100.0%**	**100.0%**	**100.0%**	**100.0%**	**100.0%**
Northeast	18.6	17.7	46.6	6.6	40.5
Midwest	22.5	7.5	1.6	9.4	4.6
South	35.9	36.4	47.6	32.8	40.7
West	23.0	38.5	4.2	51.2	14.3

Note: Most of the foreign-born from Central America are from Mexico.
Source: Bureau of the Census, Foreign-Born Population of the United States, Current Population Survey, March 2004, detailed tables (PPL-176), Internet site http://www.census.gov/population/www/socdemo/foreign/ppl-176.html; calculations by New Strategist

Table 4.114 People Who Speak Spanish at Home, by State, 2003

(total number of people aged 5 or older and number and percent who speak Spanish at home, by state, 2003)

	total aged 5 or older	speak Spanish at home	
		number	percent
United States	**263,230,104**	**26,922,425**	**10.2%**
Alabama	4,087,909	50,984	1.2
Alaska	581,706	11,090	1.9
Arizona	5,031,761	968,681	19.3
Arkansas	2,460,507	64,941	2.6
California	32,115,612	8,275,568	25.8
Colorado	4,123,589	397,573	9.6
Connecticut	3,157,963	231,514	7.3
Delaware	738,327	29,650	4.0
District of Columbia	495,397	40,318	8.1
Florida	15,572,360	2,497,360	16.0
Georgia	7,779,928	389,234	5.0
Hawaii	1,136,645	11,134	1.0
Idaho	1,229,675	72,026	5.9
Illinois	11,442,014	1,253,997	11.0
Indiana	5,595,593	152,499	2.7
Iowa	2,660,537	50,755	1.9
Kansas	2,450,103	79,787	3.3
Kentucky	3,732,957	38,312	1.0
Louisiana	4,038,853	58,570	1.5
Maine	1,203,618	3,675	0.3
Maryland	5,006,754	177,287	3.5
Massachusetts	5,822,123	332,505	5.7
Michigan	9,178,031	178,989	2.0
Minnesota	4,591,314	85,118	1.9
Mississippi	2,577,551	19,240	0.7
Missouri	5,159,771	60,134	1.2
Montana	840,297	3,669	0.4
Nebraska	1,568,543	61,329	3.9
Nevada	2,045,157	335,124	16.4
New Hampshire	1,179,322	12,124	1.0
New Jersey	7,887,106	955,373	12.1
New Mexico	1,708,107	454,113	26.6
New York	17,394,711	2,267,384	13.0
North Carolina	7,557,056	316,920	4.2
North Dakota	572,574	3,423	0.6
Ohio	10,396,176	103,638	1.0
Oklahoma	3,162,666	105,051	3.3
Oregon	3,256,681	192,538	5.9

(continued)

	total aged 5 or older	speak Spanish at home	
		number	percent
Pennsylvania	11,218,258	264,653	2.4%
Rhode Island	976,471	75,201	7.7
South Carolina	3,736,487	60,735	1.6
South Dakota	683,219	3,447	0.5
Tennessee	5,309,621	94,225	1.8
Texas	19,751,381	5,298,818	26.8
Utah	2,082,635	130,351	6.3
Vermont	567,271	1,155	0.2
Virginia	6,667,441	254,626	3.8
Washington	5,600,233	246,260	4.4
West Virginia	1,663,592	4,653	0.3
Wisconsin	4,978,150	135,231	2.7
Wyoming	456,351	11,443	2.5

Source: Bureau of the Census, 2003 American Community Survey, Internet site http://factfinder.census.gov/servlet/ DatasetMainPageServlet?_lang=en&_ts=143386397087&_ds_name=ACS_2003_EST_G00_&_program=; calculations by New Strategist

Hispanic Households Spend 85 Percent as Much as the Average Household

The nation's 12 million Hispanic households spent an average of $34,575 in 2003, according to the Consumer Expenditure Survey. While the annual spending of Hispanic households (called consumer units by the Bureau of Labor Statistics) is less than the $40,817 spent by the average household, on many items Hispanics spend more.

Hispanic households spend less than average because their incomes are relatively low. Hispanic incomes are low because many Hispanics have little education or earning power. Nevertheless, Hispanics spend 15 percent more than the average household on food at home because of their large household size—3.3 people versus 2.5 people in the average household. Hispanics spend 59 percent more than average on eggs and 40 percent more than average on fresh vegetables. They are also big consumers of infants' clothes, spending 49 percent more than the average household on this item and accounting for 15 percent of the market. Hispanic households spend 25 percent more than average on laundry and cleaning supplies.

■ Hispanic spending will remain below average as long as poorly educated immigrants account for a large share of the Hispanic population.

Hispanic households spend 15 percent less than the average household

(average annual spending of total and Hispanic consumer units, 2003)

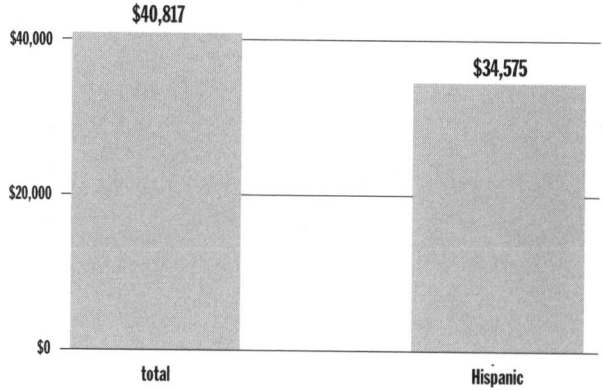

Table 4.115 Spending of Households Headed by Hispanics, 2003

(average annual spending of total consumer units (CU), and average annual, indexed, and market share of spending of consumer units headed by Hispanics, by product and service category, 2003)

	total consumer units	Hispanic consumer units		
		average spending	indexed spending	market share
Number of consumer units (000s)	115,356	11,727	–	10.2%
Persons per consumer unit	2.5	3.3	–	–
Average income before taxes	$51,128	$37,150	73	7.4
Average annual spending	40,817	34,575	85	8.6
FOOD	5,340	5,717	107	10.9
Food at home	3,129	3,597	115	11.7
Cereals and bakery products	442	486	110	11.2
Cereals and cereal products	150	183	122	12.4
Bakery products	292	303	104	10.5
Meats, poultry, fish, and eggs	825	1,059	128	13.0
Beef	246	327	133	13.5
Pork	171	212	124	12.6
Other meats	102	113	111	11.3
Poultry	145	190	131	13.3
Fish and seafood	124	158	127	13.0
Eggs	37	59	159	16.2
Dairy products	328	374	114	11.6
Fresh milk and cream	127	160	126	12.8
Other dairy products	201	214	106	10.8
Fruits and vegetables	535	686	128	13.0
Fresh fruits	171	231	135	13.7
Fresh vegetables	172	240	140	14.2
Processed fruits	108	131	121	12.3
Processed vegetables	84	83	99	10.0
Other food at home	999	992	99	10.1
Sugar and other sweets	119	128	108	10.9
Fats and oils	86	97	113	11.5
Miscellaneous foods	490	452	92	9.4
Nonalcoholic beverages	268	289	108	11.0
Food prepared by CU on trips	36	25	69	7.1
Food away from home	2,211	2,120	96	9.7
ALCOHOLIC BEVERAGES	391	315	81	8.2
HOUSING	13,432	12,300	92	9.3
Shelter	7,887	7,672	97	9.9
Owned dwellings	5,263	3,889	74	7.5
Mortgage interest and charges	2,954	2,471	84	8.5
Property taxes	1,344	779	58	5.9
Maintenance, repair, insurance, other expenses	965	638	66	6.7
Rented dwellings	2,179	3,560	163	16.6
Other lodging	445	224	50	5.1
Utilities, fuels, and public services	2,811	2,490	89	9.0
Natural gas	392	301	77	7.8
Electricity	1,028	860	84	8.5

(continued)

	total consumer units	Hispanic consumer units average spending	Hispanic consumer units indexed spending	Hispanic consumer units market share
Fuel oil and other fuels	$110	$57	52	5.3%
Telephone	956	968	101	10.3
Water and other public services	326	305	94	9.5
Household services	**707**	**454**	**64**	**6.5**
Personal services	294	238	81	8.2
Other household services	414	216	52	5.3
Housekeeping supplies	**529**	**476**	**90**	**9.1**
Laundry and cleaning supplies	132	165	125	12.7
Other household products	263	199	76	7.7
Postage and stationery	133	111	83	8.5
Household furnishings and equipment	**1,497**	**1,208**	**81**	**8.2**
Household textiles	113	89	79	8.0
Furniture	401	403	100	10.2
Floor coverings	52	19	37	3.7
Major appliances	196	201	103	10.4
Small appliances, misc. housewares	88	82	93	9.5
Miscellaneous household equipment	648	415	64	6.5
APPAREL AND RELATED SERVICES	**1,640**	**1,756**	**107**	**10.9**
Men and boys	**372**	**435**	**117**	**11.9**
Men, aged 16 or older	282	307	109	11.1
Boys, aged 2 to 15	89	128	144	14.6
Women and girls	**634**	**564**	**89**	**9.0**
Women, aged 16 or older	529	438	83	8.4
Girls, aged 2 to 15	106	126	119	12.1
Children under age 2	**81**	**121**	**149**	**15.2**
Footwear	**294**	**368**	**125**	**12.7**
Other apparel products and services	**258**	**268**	**104**	**10.6**
TRANSPORTATION	**7,781**	**6,780**	**87**	**8.9**
Vehicle purchases	**3,732**	**3,063**	**82**	**8.3**
Cars and trucks, new	2,052	1,441	70	7.1
Cars and trucks, used	1,611	1,562	97	9.9
Other vehicles	68	60	88	9.0
Gasoline and motor oil	**1,333**	**1,328**	**100**	**10.1**
Other vehicle expenses	**2,331**	**2,057**	**88**	**9.0**
Vehicle finance charges	371	331	89	9.1
Maintenance and repairs	619	520	84	8.5
Vehicle insurance	905	812	90	9.1
Vehicle rentals, leases, licenses, other charges	436	393	90	9.2
Public transportation	**385**	**331**	**86**	**8.7**
HEALTH CARE	**2,416**	**1,439**	**60**	**6.1**
Health insurance	1,252	747	60	6.1
Medical services	591	365	62	6.3
Drugs	467	263	56	5.7
Medical supplies	107	65	61	6.2
ENTERTAINMENT	**2,060**	**1,245**	**60**	**6.1**
Fees and admissions	494	250	51	5.1
Television, radio, sound equipment	730	621	85	8.6
Pets, toys, and playground equipment	378	194	51	5.2
Other entertainment products and services	457	179	39	4.0

(continued)

	total consumer units	Hispanic consumer units		
		average spending	indexed spending	market share
PERSONAL CARE PRODUCTS, SERVICES	$527	$490	93	9.5%
READING	127	48	38	3.8
EDUCATION	783	477	61	6.2
TOBACCO PRODUCTS, SMOKING SUPPLIES	290	171	59	6.0
MISCELLANEOUS	606	419	69	7.0
CASH CONTRIBUTIONS	1,370	594	43	4.4
PERSONAL INSURANCE AND PENSIONS	4,055	2,824	70	7.1
Life and other personal insurance	397	160	40	4.1
Pensions and Social Security	3,658	2,664	73	7.4
PERSONAL TAXES	2,532	680	27	2.7
Federal income taxes	1,843	413	22	2.3
State and local income taxes	502	197	39	4.0
Other taxes	187	70	37	3.8
GIFTS FOR NONHOUSEHOLD MEMBERS	1,007	745	74	7.5
Food	78	74	95	9.6
Alcoholic beverages	16	13	81	8.3
Housing	220	138	63	6.4
Housekeeping supplies	42	37	88	9.0
Household textiles	13	5	38	3.9
Appliances and misc. housewares	25	12	48	4.9
Major appliances	7	1	14	1.5
Small appliances and misc. housewares	18	11	61	6.2
Miscellaneous household equipment	57	31	54	5.5
Other housing	85	52	61	6.2
Apparel and services	225	187	83	8.4
Males, aged 2 or older	56	52	93	9.4
Females, aged 2 or older	80	51	64	6.5
Children under age 2	39	49	126	12.8
Other apparel products and services	50	35	70	7.1
Jewelry and watches	26	13	50	5.1
All other apparel products and services	25	21	84	8.5
Transportation	60	142	237	24.1
Health care	48	7	15	1.5
Entertainment	69	42	61	6.2
Toys, games, hobbies, and tricycles	26	13	50	5.1
Other entertainment	43	28	65	6.6
Personal care products and services	16	13	81	8.3
Reading	1	–	–	–
Education	200	98	49	5.0
All other gifts	74	33	45	4.5

Definitions: The index compares the spending of the average Hispanic consumer unit with the spending of the average consumer unit by dividing Hispanic spending by average spending in each category and multiplying by 100. An index of 100 means Hispanic spending in the category equals average spending. An index of 125 means Hispanic spending is 25 percent above average, while an index of 75 means Hispanic spending is 25 percent below average. The market share is the percentage of total spending on a product or service category that is accounted for by consumer units headed by Hispanics.

Note: The Bureau of Labor Statistics uses consumer unit rather than household as the sampling unit in the Consumer Expenditure Survey. For the definition of consumer unit, see the glossary. Spending by category will not add to total spending because gift spending is also included in the preceding product and service categories and personal taxes are not included in the total. (–) means sample is too small to make a reliable estimate or not applicable.

Source: Bureau of Labor Statistics, 2003 Consumer Expenditure Survey, Internet site http://www.bls.gov/cex/; calculations by New Strategist

Hispanic Households Have Little Wealth

The median net worth (assets minus debts) of Hispanic and nonwhite households amounted to just $17,100 in 2001 (the latest data available), far below the $86,100 net worth of the average American household. On every measure of wealth, Hispanics and nonwhites have less than the average household. Their financial assets are just 26 percent as high as the average, and their nonfinancial assets are only 51 percent of the average. (Note: The Federal Reserve collects wealth data for only two racial and ethnic categories: non-Hispanic whites, and Hispanics and nonwhites. The Hispanic-and-nonwhite category includes primarily Hispanics and blacks, but also Asians and American Indians.)

The net worth of Hispanic and nonwhite households is below average in large part because Hispanics and blacks are less likely to own a home than the average householder. Home equity accounts for the largest share of Americans' net worth. In 2001, just 47 percent of Hispanic and nonwhite householders owned their home.

Hispanic and nonwhite householders have a median of only $7,200 in financial assets. The median debt of Hispanic and nonwhite householders stood at $20,000 in 2001, much lower than average in part because fewer have mortgage debt.

Hispanics not only have little wealth, but they are short on retirement savings as well. Only 18 percent of Hispanic workers have an IRA or participate in a 401(k)-type retirement plan. Among the 15 percent who participate in a retirement plan, the median balance is just $10,000. This may explain why only 13 percent of Hispanic workers are "very confident" they will have enough money to live comfortably throughout their retirement years.

■ Among Hispanics aged 65 or older, 83 percent receive Social Security benefits. Only 19 percent receive retirement income from pensions or IRAs.

The net worth of Hispanic and nonwhite households is well below average

(median net worth of total and Hispanic/nonwhite households, 2001)

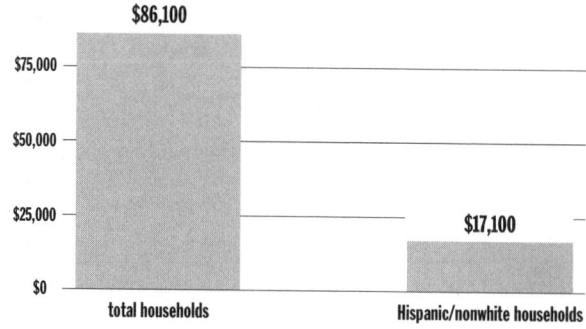

Table 4.116 Net Worth, Assets, and Debt of Hispanic and Nonwhite Households, 2001

(median net worth, median value of assets for owners, and median amount of debt for debtors, for total and Hispanic/nonwhite households, and index of Hispanic/nonwhite to total, 2001)

		Hispanic/nonwhite households	
	total households	median	index
Median net worth	**$86,100**	**$17,100**	**20**
Median value of financial assets	28,000	7,200	26
Median value of nonfinancial assets	113,500	58,200	51
Median amount of debt	38,775	20,000	52

Note: The index is calculated by dividing the Hispanic/nonwhite figure by the total figure and multiplying by 100.
Source: Federal Reserve Board, "Recent Changes in U.S. Family Finances: Evidence from the 1998 and 2001 Survey of Consumer Finances," Federal Reserve Bulletin, January 2003; calculations by New Strategist

Table 4.117 Financial Assets of Hispanic and Nonwhite Households, 2001

(percent of Hispanic/nonwhite households owning financial assets, and median value of assets for owners, 2001)

	percent owning asset	median value
Any financial asset	**82.4%**	**$7,200**
Transaction accounts	78.2	1,700
Certificates of deposit	6.7	9,000
Savings bonds	7.8	700
Bonds	0.4	7,600
Stocks	11.0	8,000
Mutual funds	7.2	17,500
Retirement accounts	37.3	10,000
Life insurance	22.3	8,100
Other managed assets	1.8	45,000
Other financial assets	9.7	1,700

Source: Federal Reserve Board, "Recent Changes in U.S. Family Finances: Evidence from the 1998 and 2001 Survey of Consumer Finances," Federal Reserve Bulletin, January 2003; calculations by New Strategist

Table 4.118 Nonfinancial Assets of Hispanic and Nonwhite Households, 2001

(percent of Hispanic/nonwhite households owning nonfinancial assets, and median value of assets for owners, 2001)

	percent owning asset	median value
Any nonfinancial asset	**77.9%**	**$58,200**
Vehicles	70.9	10,000
Primary residence	47.0	92,000
Other residential property	6.4	60,000
Nonresidential property	4.1	22,500
Business	5.1	50,000
Other nonfinancial asset	2.9	5,000

Source: Federal Reserve Board, "Recent Changes in U.S. Family Finances: Evidence from the 1998 and 2001 Survey of Consumer Finances," Federal Reserve Bulletin, *January 2003*

Table 4.119 Debt of Hispanic and Nonwhite Households, 2001

(percent of Hispanic/nonwhite households with debt, and median amount of debt for those with debt, 2001)

	percent with debt	median amount
Any debt	**72.9%**	**$20,000**
Home-secured	35.1	60,958
Other residential property	2.5	40,000
Installment loans	44.6	8,133
Other lines of credit	47.7	1,527
Credit card	1.1	1,000
Other debt	6.5	2,000

Source: Federal Reserve Board, "Recent Changes in U.S. Family Finances: Evidence from the 1998 and 2001 Survey of Consumer Finances," Federal Reserve Bulletin, *January 2003*

Table 4.120 Hispanic Ownership of IRAs and 401(k)-Type Plans, 2002

(percent of total and Hispanic workers aged 21 to 64 owning IRAs and 401(k)-type plans, 2002)

	total workers	Hispanic workers
IRA or 401(k)-type plan	**40.4%**	**18.0%**
IRA only	9.6	2.8
401(k)-type plan only	21.7	13.1
Both IRA and 401(k)-type plan	9.2	2.1
Neither IRA nor 401(k)-type plan	**59.6**	**82.0**

Source: Employee Benefit Research Institute, "401(k)-Type Plan and IRA Ownership," by Craig Copeland, EBRI Notes, Vol. 26, No. 1, January 2005; Internet site http://www.ebri.org/

Table 4.121 Hispanic Participation and Savings in IRAs and 401(k)s, 2002

(percent of total and Hispanic workers aged 21 to 64 owning an IRA or participating in 401(k)-type plan, and average and median balance of IRA and 401(k), 2002)

	percent owning IRA	IRA balance		percent participating in 401(k)	401(k) balance	
		average	median		average	median
Total workers	**18.7%**	**$26,951**	**$10,000**	**30.9%**	**$33,647**	**$14,000**
Hispanic workers	4.9	15,711	6,500	15.2	21,481	10,000

Source: Employee Benefit Research Institute, "401(k)-Type Plan and IRA Ownership," by Craig Copeland, EBRI Notes, Vol. 26, No. 1, January 2005; Internet site http://www.ebri.org/

Table 4.122 Retirement Confidence among Hispanic Workers, 2003

(percent distribution of Hispanic workers aged 25 or older by degree of confidence in retirement savings and planning, 2003)

	very confident	somewhat confident	not too confident	not at all confident
Having enough money to live comfortably throughout retirement years	13%	38%	23%	22%
Having enough money to take care of basic expenses	15	40	16	27
Doing a good job of preparing financially for retirement	20	35	24	21
Not outliving retirement savings	14	30	16	36
Having enough money to take care of medical expenses	11	30	26	31
Having enough money to pay for long-term care	10	16	32	40

Source: The 2003 Minority Retirement Confidence Survey Summary of Findings, *Employee Benefit Research Institute, American Savings Education Council, and Mathew Greenwald & Associates; Internet site http://www.ebri.org/surveys/rcs/2003/*

Table 4.123 Sources of Income for Hispanics Aged 65 or Older, 2003

(number and percent of Hispanics aged 65 or older with income from selected sources and average income for those with income, ranked by number receiving income, 2003; people in thousands as of 2004)

	number with income	percent with income	average amount received by those with income
Hispanics aged 65 or older with income	**1,916**	**100.0%**	**$9,677**
Social Security	1,590	83.0	8,091
Interest	490	25.6	1,512
Retirement income, including pensions	357	18.6	6,833
Earnings	346	18.1	16,783
SSI (Supplemental Security Income)	233	12.2	3,613
Dividends	100	5.2	1,736
Rents, royalties, estates, or trusts	72	3.8	–
Survivor's benefits	41	2.1	–
Veteran's benefits	32	1.7	–

Note: (–) means sample is too small to make a reliable estimate.
Source: Bureau of the Census, 2004 Current Population Survey, Internet site http://pubdb3.census.gov/macro/032004/perinc/new09_001.htm; calculations by New Strategist

Non-Hispanic Whites

■ The non-Hispanic white population accounted for 67 percent of the total U.S. population in 2004, down from 69 percent in 2000.

■ Thirty-one percent of non-Hispanic whites have a college degree, second only to the 49 percent of Asians who are college graduates.

■ Fifty-seven percent of the nation's births are to non-Hispanic white women.

■ Seventy-six percent of the nation's non-Hispanic white households own their home.

■ The $47,777 median income of non-Hispanic white households in 2003 was 10 percent greater than the all-household average.

■ Between 2002 and 2012, the number of non-Hispanic white workers will expand by only 3 percent, much more slowly than the number of Asian, black, or Hispanic workers.

■ Only 29 percent of non-Hispanic white households include children under age 18.

■ The non-Hispanic white share of the population ranges from a low of 56 percent in the West to a high of 80 percent in the Midwest.

■ The nation's non-Hispanic white and other households spent an average of $43,459 in 2003, or 6 percent more than the average household.

■ The median net worth of non-Hispanic white households stood at $120,900 in 2001, far above the $86,100 net worth of the average American household.

Non-Hispanic whites account for 67.4 percent of the U.S. population

(percent distribution of people by race and Hispanic origin, 2004)

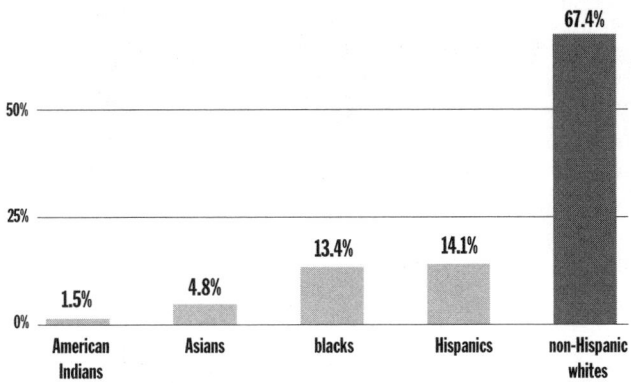

Non-Hispanic Whites Are Better Educated than Blacks and Hispanics

The educational attainment of non-Hispanic whites is above average. Thirty-one percent of non-Hispanic whites have a college degree versus 28 percent of the total population. Only Asians are more likely to have a college degree (49 percent). Ninety percent of non-Hispanic whites are high school graduates—the largest proportion among all racial and ethnic groups.

Because non-Hispanic whites account for the majority of Americans, they also earn most college degrees. Non-Hispanic whites earned 70 percent of associate's degree in 2001–02. They were awarded 74 percent of bachelor's degrees, 68 percent of master's degrees, and 61 percent of doctorates. Among first-professional degrees, non-Hispanic whites earned 90 percent of those awarded in veterinary medicine but only 62 percent of degrees in dentistry.

■ The share of college degrees earned by non-Hispanic whites is shrinking as minorities make up a growing proportion of college students.

More than 30 percent of non-Hispanic whites are college graduates

(percent of non-Hispanic whites aged 25 or older who are high school graduates or more, have some college or more, or are college graduates, 2003)

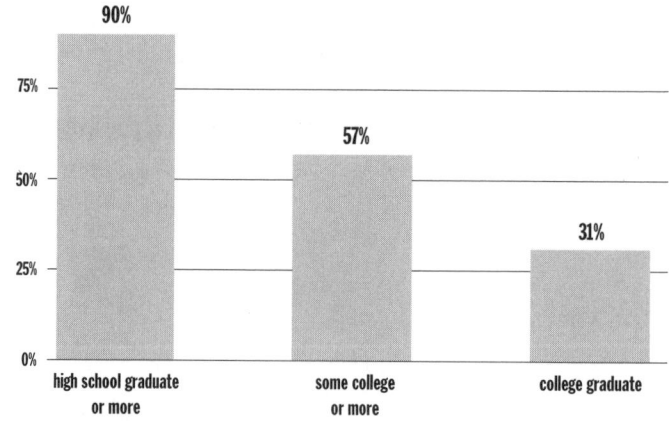

Table 5.1 Educational Attainment of Non-Hispanic Whites by Age, 2004

(number and percent distribution of non-Hispanic whites aged 25 or older by educational attainment and age, 2004; numbers in thousands)

	total	25 to 34	35 to 44	45 to 54	55 to 64	65 or older
Total non-Hispanic whites	**134,063**	**23,900**	**29,560**	**30,219**	**22,047**	**28,335**
Not a high school graduate	13,415	1,467	1,926	1,736	2,066	6,223
High school graduate only	44,022	6,704	9,362	9,502	7,493	10,960
Some college, no degree	23,539	4,739	5,225	5,505	3,898	4,170
Associate's degree	12,092	2,417	3,188	3,291	1,831	1,366
Bachelor's degree	26,569	6,423	6,760	6,311	3,778	3,297
Master's degree	10,192	1,577	2,221	2,806	2,113	1,476
Professional degree	2,320	358	543	581	387	450
Doctoral degree	1,914	217	335	487	483	393
High school graduate or more	120,648	22,435	27,634	28,483	19,983	22,112
Some college or more	76,626	15,731	18,272	18,981	12,490	11,152
Bachelor's degree or more	40,995	8,575	9,859	10,185	6,761	5,616
PERCENT DISTRIBUTION						
Total non-Hispanic whites	**100.0%**	**100.0%**	**100.0%**	**100.0%**	**100.0%**	**100.0%**
Not a high school graduate	10.0	6.1	6.5	5.7	9.4	22.0
High school graduate only	32.8	28.1	31.7	31.4	34.0	38.7
Some college, no degree	17.6	19.8	17.7	18.2	17.7	14.7
Associate's degree	9.0	10.1	10.8	10.9	8.3	4.8
Bachelor's degree	19.8	26.9	22.9	20.9	17.1	11.6
Master's degree	7.6	6.6	7.5	9.3	9.6	5.2
Professional degree	1.7	1.5	1.8	1.9	1.8	1.6
Doctoral degree	1.4	0.9	1.1	1.6	2.2	1.4
High school graduate or more	90.0	93.9	93.5	94.3	90.6	78.0
Some college or more	57.2	65.8	61.8	62.8	56.7	39.4
Bachelor's degree or more	30.6	35.9	33.4	33.7	30.7	19.8

Note: Non-Hispanic whites include only those identifying themselves as being white alone and not Hispanic.
Source: Bureau of the Census, 2004 Current Population Survey Annual Social and Economic Supplement, Educational Attainment in the United States: 2004, Detailed Tables, Internet site http://www.census.gov/population/www/socdemo/education/cps2004.html; calculations by New Strategist

Table 5.2 Educational Attainment of Non-Hispanic White Men by Age, 2004

(number and percent distribution of non-Hispanic white men aged 25 or older by educational attainment and age, 2004; numbers in thousands)

	total	25 to 34	35 to 44	45 to 54	55 to 64	65 or older
Total non-Hispanic white men	**64,397**	**11,912**	**14,683**	**14,963**	**10,647**	**12,194**
Not a high school graduate	6,523	846	1,108	917	1,049	2,603
High school graduate only	20,343	3,643	4,855	4,632	3,199	4,013
Some college, no degree	11,104	2,300	2,459	2,751	1,834	1,761
Associate's degree	5,209	1,148	1,368	1,417	782	493
Bachelor's degree	13,371	3,005	3,306	3,229	2,033	1,798
Master's degree	4,963	640	1,071	1,325	1,082	845
Professional degree	1,588	215	328	383	307	356
Doctoral degree	1,297	118	186	310	359	324
High school graduate or more	57,875	11,069	13,573	14,047	9,596	9,590
Some college or more	37,532	7,426	8,718	9,415	6,397	5,577
Bachelor's degree or more	21,219	3,978	4,891	5,247	3,781	3,323
PERCENT DISTRIBUTION						
Total non-Hispanic white men	**100.0%**	**100.0%**	**100.0%**	**100.0%**	**100.0%**	**100.0%**
Not a high school graduate	10.1	7.1	7.5	6.1	9.9	21.3
High school graduate only	31.6	30.6	33.1	31.0	30.0	32.9
Some college, no degree	17.2	19.3	16.7	18.4	17.2	14.4
Associate's degree	8.1	9.6	9.3	9.5	7.3	4.0
Bachelor's degree	20.8	25.2	22.5	21.6	19.1	14.7
Master's degree	7.7	5.4	7.3	8.9	10.2	6.9
Professional degree	2.5	1.8	2.2	2.6	2.9	2.9
Doctoral degree	2.0	1.0	1.3	2.1	3.4	2.7
High school graduate or more	89.9	92.9	92.4	93.9	90.1	78.6
Some college or more	58.3	62.3	59.4	62.9	60.1	45.7
Bachelor's degree or more	33.0	33.4	33.3	35.1	35.5	27.3

Note: Non-Hispanic whites include only those identifying themselves as being white alone and not Hispanic.
Source: Bureau of the Census, 2004 Current Population Survey Annual Social and Economic Supplement, Educational Attainment in the United States: 2004, Detailed Tables, Internet site http://www.census.gov/population/www/socdemo/education/cps2004.html; calculations by New Strategist

Table 5.3 Educational Attainment of Non-Hispanic White Women by Age, 2004

(number and percent distribution of non-Hispanic white women aged 25 or older by educational attainment and age, 2004; numbers in thousands)

	total	25 to 34	35 to 44	45 to 54	55 to 64	65 or older
Total non-Hispanic white women	**69,666**	**11,988**	**14,878**	**15,257**	**11,401**	**16,142**
Not a high school graduate	6,892	621	816	821	1,017	3,621
High school graduate only	23,679	3,061	4,507	4,869	4,293	6,947
Some college, no degree	12,435	2,440	2,767	2,754	2,063	2,410
Associate's degree	6,883	1,268	1,819	1,874	1,048	873
Bachelor's degree	13,198	3,418	3,453	3,082	1,745	1,499
Master's degree	5,229	937	1,150	1,481	1,031	631
Professional degree	732	143	216	198	80	94
Doctoral degree	617	100	148	177	124	68
High school graduate or more	62,773	11,367	14,060	14,435	10,384	12,522
Some college or more	39,094	8,306	9,553	9,566	6,091	5,575
Bachelor's degree or more	19,776	4,598	4,967	4,938	2,980	2,292

PERCENT DISTRIBUTION

	total	25 to 34	35 to 44	45 to 54	55 to 64	65 or older
Total non-Hispanic white women	**100.0%**	**100.0%**	**100.0%**	**100.0%**	**100.0%**	**100.0%**
Not a high school graduate	9.9	5.2	5.5	5.4	8.9	22.4
High school graduate only	34.0	25.5	30.3	31.9	37.7	43.0
Some college, no degree	17.8	20.4	18.6	18.1	18.1	14.9
Associate's degree	9.9	10.6	12.2	12.3	9.2	5.4
Bachelor's degree	18.9	28.5	23.2	20.2	15.3	9.3
Master's degree	7.5	7.8	7.7	9.7	9.0	3.9
Professional degree	1.1	1.2	1.5	1.3	0.7	0.6
Doctoral degree	0.9	0.8	1.0	1.2	1.1	0.4
High school graduate or more	90.1	94.8	94.5	94.6	91.1	77.6
Some college or more	56.1	69.3	64.2	62.7	53.4	34.5
Bachelor's degree or more	28.4	38.4	33.4	32.4	26.1	14.2

Note: Non-Hispanic whites include only those identifying themselves as being white alone and not Hispanic.
Source: Bureau of the Census, 2004 Current Population Survey Annual Social and Economic Supplement, Educational Attainment in the United States: 2004, Detailed Tables, Internet site http://www.census.gov/population/www/socdemo/education/cps2004.html; calculations by New Strategist

Table 5.4 Educational Attainment of Non-Hispanic Whites by Age and Region, 2004

(percent of non-Hispanic whites aged 25 or older by selected educational attainment, age, and region, 2004)

	Northeast	Midwest	South	West
HIGH SCHOOL GRADUATE OR MORE				
Total non-Hispanic whites	**89.9%**	**90.4%**	**87.8%**	**93.3%**
Aged 25 to 34	94.3	94.2	92.5	95.2
Aged 35 to 44	94.8	94.2	91.3	94.9
Aged 45 to 54	95.2	94.6	92.1	96.3
Aged 55 to 64	90.9	91.2	87.8	94.3
Aged 65 or older	75.6	76.9	76.6	85.3
SOME COLLEGE OR MORE				
Total non-Hispanic whites	**54.3**	**54.4**	**55.2**	**67.4**
Aged 25 to 34	65.2	64.0	63.6	72.5
Aged 35 to 44	61.6	60.1	58.7	69.8
Aged 45 to 54	61.5	59.0	60.8	72.5
Aged 55 to 64	52.4	52.2	54.7	69.6
Aged 65 or older	32.7	35.0	39.8	52.2
BACHELOR'S DEGREE OR MORE				
Total non-Hispanic whites	**33.3**	**27.0**	**28.8**	**35.6**
Aged 25 to 34	42.3	32.3	34.1	37.5
Aged 35 to 44	38.7	30.6	30.8	35.8
Aged 45 to 54	36.9	28.4	32.5	39.4
Aged 55 to 64	31.6	26.3	29.3	37.5
Aged 65 or older	18.4	17.0	18.8	27.4

Note: Non-Hispanic whites include only those identifying themselves as being white alone and not Hispanic.
Source: Bureau of the Census, 2004 Current Population Survey Annual Social and Economic Supplement, Educational Attainment in the United States: 2004, Detailed Tables, Internet site http://www.census.gov/population/www/socdemo/education/cps2004.html; calculations by New Strategist

Table 5.5 Educational Attainment of Non-Hispanic Whites by State, 2004

(percent of non-Hispanic whites aged 25 or older who are high school or college graduates, for the 25 largest states, 2004)

	high school graduate or more	college graduate
Total non-Hispanic whites	**90.0%**	**30.6%**
Alabama	84.3	25.1
Arizona	93.4	33.7
California	93.6	39.5
Colorado	94.2	41.3
Florida	91.8	28.7
Georgia	87.3	30.3
Illinois	91.3	30.2
Indiana	88.0	21.2
Kentucky	81.5	21.4
Louisiana	82.6	27.0
Maryland	90.3	39.2
Massachusetts	89.9	38.9
Michigan	89.5	25.0
Minnesota	93.3	32.6
Missouri	89.2	28.7
New Jersey	91.5	37.0
New York	91.3	35.1
North Carolina	84.7	25.6
Ohio	89.2	25.2
Pennsylvania	87.7	26.0
Tennessee	83.8	25.2
Texas	91.7	32.7
Virginia	91.2	36.0
Washington	92.4	31.0
Wisconsin	91.4	27.2

Note: Non-Hispanic whites include only those identifying themselves as being white alone and not Hispanic.
Source: Bureau of the Census, 2004 Current Population Survey Annual Social and Economic Supplement, Educational Attainment in the United States: 2004, Detailed Tables, Internet site http://www.census.gov/population/www/socdemo/education/cps2004 .html; calculations by New Strategist

Table 5.6 School Enrollment of Non-Hispanic Whites, 2003

(total number of people aged 3 or older enrolled in school, number of non-Hispanic whites enrolled, and non-Hispanic white share of total, by age, October 2003; numbers in thousands)

		non-Hispanic white	
	total	number	share of total
Total aged 3 or older	**74,911**	**46,440**	**62.0%**
Aged 3 to 4	4,590	2,874	62.6
Aged 5 to 6	7,309	4,409	60.3
Aged 7 to 9	11,706	6,789	58.0
Aged 10 to 13	16,478	9,957	60.4
Aged 14 to 15	8,329	5,110	61.4
Aged 16 to 17	8,177	5,169	63.2
Aged 18 to 19	4,856	3,243	66.8
Aged 20 to 21	3,684	2,467	67.0
Aged 22 to 24	3,397	2,239	65.9
Aged 25 to 29	2,212	1,390	62.8
Aged 30 to 34	1,378	855	62.0
Aged 35 to 44	1,635	1,082	66.2
Aged 45 to 54	879	649	73.8
Aged 55 or older	283	205	72.4

Note: Non-Hispanic whites include only those identifying themselves as being white alone and not Hispanic.
Source: Bureau of the Census, School Enrollment—Social and Economic Characteristics of Students: October 2003, Detailed Tables, Internet site http://www.census.gov/population/www/socdemo/school/cps2003.html; calculations by New Strategist

Table 5.7 School Enrollment of Non-Hispanic Whites by Age and Sex, 2003

(number and percent of non-Hispanic whites aged 3 or older enrolled in school, by age and sex, October 2003; numbers in thousands)

	total		female		male	
	number	percent	number	percent	number	percent
Total non-Hispanic whites enrolled	**46,440**	**24.7%**	**23,189**	**24.1%**	**23,250**	**25.4%**
Aged 3 to 4	2,874	58.8	1,340	56.9	1,533	60.6
Aged 5 to 6	4,409	95.8	2,163	95.3	2,246	96.2
Aged 7 to 9	6,789	98.2	3,298	98.6	3,491	97.7
Aged 10 to 13	9,957	98.5	4,747	98.8	5,210	98.2
Aged 14 to 15	5,110	97.5	2,596	97.6	2,514	97.4
Aged 16 to 17	5,169	95.6	2,488	95.1	2,681	96.1
Aged 18 to 19	3,243	67.9	1,669	70.3	1,574	65.4
Aged 20 to 21	2,467	51.8	1,364	55.6	1,104	47.9
Aged 22 to 24	2,239	29.4	1,134	29.9	1,106	28.9
Aged 25 to 29	1,390	12.5	742	13.2	648	11.7
Aged 30 to 34	855	6.8	462	7.3	393	6.3
Aged 35 to 44	1,082	3.7	666	4.5	416	2.8
Aged 45 to 54	649	2.2	402	2.7	246	1.7
Aged 55 or older	205	0	118	0.4	87	0.4

Note: Non-Hispanic whites include only those identifying themselves as being white alone and not Hispanic.
Source: Bureau of the Census, School Enrollment—Social and Economic Characteristics of Students: October 2003, Detailed Tables, Internet site http://www.census.gov/population/www/socdemo/school/cps2003.html

Table 5.8 Non-Hispanic White Families with Children in College, 2003

(total number of non-Hispanic white families, number with dependent children aged 5 to 24, and number and percent with children enrolled in college by household income, 2003; numbers in thousands)

| | | | with one or more children enrolled in college | | |
	total	with children aged 5–24	number	percent of total non-Hispanic white families	percent of non-Hispanic white families with children 5–24
Total non-Hispanic white families	**53,953**	**23,947**	**3,903**	**7.2%**	**16.3%**
Less than $10,000	1,476	773	45	3.0	5.8
$10,000 to $14,999	1,718	659	46	2.7	7.0
$15,000 to $19,999	1,496	518	52	3.5	10.0
$20,000 to $24,999	4,813	1,849	160	3.3	8.7
$25,000 to $29,999	5,364	2,216	271	5.1	12.2
$30,000 to $34,999	4,437	2,013	240	5.4	11.9
$35,000 to $39,999	10,163	4,719	794	7.8	16.8
$40,000 to $49,999	6,527	3,268	685	10.5	21.0
$50,000 to $74,999	4,804	2,579	610	12.7	23.7
$75,000 and over	3,142	1,598	351	11.2	22.0

Note: Non-Hispanic whites include only those identifying themselves as being white alone and not Hispanic. Numbers will not add to total because not reported is not shown.
Source: Bureau of the Census, School Enrollment—Social and Economic Characteristics of Students: October 2003, Detailed Tables, Internet site http://www.census.gov/population/www/socdemo/school/cps2003.html; calculations by New Strategist

Table 5.9 Non-Hispanic White College Enrollment Rate, 1990 to 2001

(percent of total people and non-Hispanic whites aged 16 to 24 graduating from high school in the previous 12 months who were enrolled in college as of October of each year, percentage point change in enrollment rate, 1990–2001)

	total	non-Hispanic white
2001	61.7%	64.2%
2000	63.3	65.7
1999	62.9	66.3
1998	65.6	68.5
1997	67.0	68.2
1996	65.0	67.4
1995	61.9	64.3
1994	61.9	64.5
1993	62.6	62.9
1992	61.9	64.3
1991	62.5	65.4
1990	60.1	63.0

Percentage point change

1990–2001	1.5	1.2

Source: National Center for Education Statistics, Digest of Education Statistics 2003; *Internet site http://nces.ed.gov/programs/digest/d03/list_tables3.asp#c3; calculations by New Strategist*

Table 5.10 College Enrollment of Non-Hispanic Whites, 2003

(total number of people aged 15 or older enrolled in college, number of non-Hispanic whites enrolled, and non-Hispanic white share of total, by age, October 2003; numbers in thousands)

	total	non-Hispanic white number	share of total
Total enrolled in college	**16,638**	**11,295**	**67.9%**
Under age 20	3,661	2,576	70.4
Aged 20 to 21	3,534	2,419	68.4
Aged 22 to 24	3,320	2,224	67.0
Aged 25 to 29	2,164	1,372	63.4
Aged 30 to 34	1,330	833	62.6
Aged 35 to 39	769	509	66.2
Aged 40 to 44	757	534	70.5
Aged 45 to 49	479	359	74.9
Aged 50 to 54	357	268	75.1
Aged 55 or older	268	203	75.7

Note: Non-Hispanic whites include only those identifying themselves as being white alone and not Hispanic.
Source: Bureau of the Census, School Enrollment—Social and Economic Characteristics of Students: October 2003, Detailed Tables, *Internet site http://www.census.gov/population/www/socdemo/school/cps2003.html; calculations by New Strategist*

Table 5.11 College Enrollment of Non-Hispanic Whites by Age and Type of School, 2003

(number and percent distribution of non-Hispanic whites aged 15 or older enrolled in college by age and type of school, October 2003; numbers in thousands)

	total	two-year college	four-year college	graduate school
Total non-Hispanic whites enrolled	**11,295**	**2,739**	**6,223**	**2,331**
Under age 20	2,576	763	1,795	18
Aged 20 to 21	2,419	449	1,910	60
Aged 22 to 24	2,224	510	1,248	468
Aged 25 to 29	1,372	259	478	632
Aged 30 to 34	833	224	284	323
Aged 35 to 39	509	161	122	224
Aged 40 to 44	534	156	155	223
Aged 45 to 49	359	79	117	162
Aged 50 to 54	268	82	66	120
Aged 55 or older	203	56	46	101

PERCENT DISTRIBUTION BY TYPE OF SCHOOL

	total	two-year college	four-year college	graduate school
Total non-Hispanic whites enrolled	**100.0%**	**24.2%**	**55.1%**	**20.6%**
Under age 20	100.0	29.6	69.7	0.7
Aged 20 to 21	100.0	18.6	79.0	2.5
Aged 22 to 24	100.0	22.9	56.1	21.0
Aged 25 to 29	100.0	18.9	34.8	46.1
Aged 30 to 34	100.0	26.9	34.1	38.8
Aged 35 to 39	100.0	31.6	24.0	44.0
Aged 40 to 44	100.0	29.2	29.0	41.8
Aged 45 to 49	100.0	22.0	32.6	45.1
Aged 50 to 54	100.0	30.6	24.6	44.8
Aged 55 or older	100.0	27.6	22.7	49.8

PERCENT DISTRIBUTION BY AGE

	total	two-year college	four-year college	graduate school
Total non-Hispanic whites enrolled	**100.0%**	**100.0%**	**100.0%**	**100.0%**
Under age 20	22.8	27.9	28.8	0.8
Aged 20 to 21	21.4	16.4	30.7	2.6
Aged 22 to 24	19.7	18.6	20.1	20.1
Aged 25 to 29	12.1	9.5	7.7	27.1
Aged 30 to 34	7.4	8.2	4.6	13.9
Aged 35 to 39	4.5	5.9	2.0	9.6
Aged 40 to 44	4.7	5.7	2.5	9.6
Aged 45 to 49	3.2	2.9	1.9	6.9
Aged 50 to 54	2.4	3.0	1.1	5.1
Aged 55 or older	1.8	2.0	0.7	4.3

Note: Non-Hispanic whites include only those identifying themselves as being white alone and not Hispanic.
Source: Bureau of the Census, School Enrollment—Social and Economic Characteristics of Students: October 2003, Detailed Tables, Internet site http://www.census.gov/population/www/socdemo/school/cps2003.html; calculations by New Strategist

Table 5.12 Associate's Degrees Earned by Non-Hispanic Whites by Field of Study, 2001–02

(total number of associate's degrees conferred and number and percent earned by non-Hispanic whites, by field of study, 2001–02)

	total	earned by non-Hispanic whites	
		number	percent
Total associate's degrees	**595,133**	**417,739**	**70.2%**
Agriculture and natural resources	6,494	6,118	94.2
Architecture and related programs	443	331	74.7
Area, ethnic, and cultural studies	319	240	75.2
Biological and life sciences	1,517	1,074	70.8
Business	108,911	73,361	67.4
Communications	2,819	2,252	79.9
Communications technologies	2,021	1,518	75.1
Computer and information sciences	30,965	19,943	64.4
Construction trades	2,639	2,216	84.0
Education	9,267	6,318	68.2
Engineering	1,724	1,284	74.5
Engineering-related technologies	32,895	22,920	69.7
English language and literature, letters	864	625	72.3
Foreign languages and literatures	517	298	57.6
Health professions and related sciences	79,888	60,300	75.5
Home economics	9,480	5,652	59.6
Law and legal studies	6,825	4,785	70.1
Liberal arts and sciences, general studies, humanities	207,163	144,594	69.8
Library science	96	85	88.5
Mathematics	685	407	59.4
Mechanics and repairers	12,086	9,012	74.6
Multi- and interdisciplinary studies	13,204	8,826	66.8
Parks, recreation, leisure, and fitness	830	629	75.8
Philosophy and religion	134	67	50.0
Physical sciences	2,308	1,707	74.0
Precision production trades	10,818	8,470	78.3
Protective services	16,689	12,276	73.6
Psychology	1,705	1,166	68.4
Public administration and services	3,323	1,862	56.0
R.O.T.C. and military technologies	62	32	51.6
Social sciences and history	5,593	3,326	59.5
Theological studies, religious vocations	414	314	75.8
Transportation and material moving	1,159	901	77.7
Visual and performing arts	20,911	14,546	69.6
Not classified	365	284	77.8

Source: National Center for Education Statistics, Digest of Education Statistics 2003, *Internet site http://nces.ed.gov//programs/ digest/d03/list_tables.asp; calculations by New Strategist*

Table 5.13 Bachelor's Degrees Earned by Non-Hispanic Whites by Field of Study, 2001–02

(total number of bachelor's degrees conferred and number and percent earned by non-Hispanic whites, by field of study, 2001–02)

	total	earned by non-Hispanic whites	
		number	percent
Total bachelor's degrees	**1,291,900**	**958,585**	**74.2%**
Agriculture and natural resources	23,353	20,659	88.5
Architecture and related programs	8,808	6,518	74.0
Area, ethnic, and cultural studies	6,557	3,841	58.6
Biological and life sciences	60,256	42,831	71.1
Business	281,330	199,906	71.1
Communications	62,791	49,483	78.8
Communications technologies	1,110	781	70.4
Computer and information sciences	47,299	28,311	59.9
Construction trades	202	182	90.1
Education	106,383	90,475	85.0
Engineering	59,481	41,192	69.3
Engineering-related technologies	14,117	10,567	74.9
English language and literature, letters	53,162	43,129	81.1
Foreign languages and literatures	15,318	10,885	71.1
Health professions and related sciences	70,517	53,533	75.9
Home economics	18,153	14,722	81.1
Law and legal studies	1,971	1,359	68.9
Liberal arts and sciences, general studies, humanities	39,333	27,786	70.6
Library science	74	67	90.5
Mathematics	12,395	9,190	74.1
Mechanics and repairers	164	104	63.4
Multi- and interdisciplinary studies	27,629	19,866	71.9
Parks, recreation, leisure, and fitness	20,554	16,795	81.7
Philosophy and religion	9,306	7,661	82.3
Physical sciences	17,851	13,900	77.9
Precision production trades	468	391	83.5
Protective services	25,536	17,262	67.6
Psychology	76,671	55,824	72.8
Public administration and services	19,392	12,529	64.6
R.O.T.C. and military technologies	3	3	100.0
Social sciences and history	132,874	96,346	72.5
Theological studies, religious vocations	7,785	6,699	86.1
Transportation and material moving	4,020	3,339	83.1
Visual and performing arts	66,773	52,224	78.2
Not classified	264	225	85.2

Source: National Center for Education Statistics, Digest of Education Statistics 2003, *Internet site http://nces.ed.gov//programs/ digest/d03/list_tables.asp; calculations by New Strategist*

Table 5.14 Master's Degrees Earned by Non-Hispanic Whites by Field of Study, 2001–02

(total number of master's degrees conferred and number and percent earned by non-Hispanic whites, by field of study, 2001–02)

		earned by non-Hispanic whites	
	total	number	percent
Total master's degrees	**482,118**	**327,635**	**68.0%**
Agriculture and natural resources	4,519	3,454	76.4
Architecture and related programs	4,566	2,797	61.3
Area, ethnic, and cultural studies	1,578	959	60.8
Biological and life sciences	6,205	4,265	68.7
Business	120,785	76,435	63.3
Communications	5,510	3,512	63.7
Communications technologies	549	312	56.8
Computer and information sciences	16,113	5,144	31.9
Construction trades	9	2	22.2
Education	136,579	107,793	78.9
Engineering	26,015	11,215	43.1
Engineering-related technologies	896	583	65.1
English language and literature, letters	7,268	5,897	81.1
Foreign languages and literatures	2,861	1,598	55.9
Health professions and related sciences	43,644	33,012	75.6
Home economics	2,616	1,911	73.1
Law and legal studies	4,053	1,304	32.2
Liberal arts and sciences, general studies, humanities	2,754	2,156	78.3
Library science	5,113	4,280	83.7
Mathematics	3,487	1,727	49.5
Multi- and interdisciplinary studies	3,211	2,236	69.6
Parks, recreation, leisure, and fitness	2,754	2,231	81.0
Philosophy and religion	1,334	1,063	79.7
Physical sciences	5,034	3,056	60.7
Precision production trades	2	0	0.0
Protective services	2,935	2,119	72.2
Psychology	14,888	10,931	73.4
Public administration and services	25,448	16,889	66.4
Social sciences and history	14,112	8,660	61.4
Theological studies, religious vocations	4,952	3,570	72.1
Transportation and material moving	709	604	85.2
Visual and performing arts	11,595	7,906	68.2
Not classified	24	14	58.3

Source: National Center for Education Statistics, Digest of Education Statistics 2003, *Internet site http://nces.ed.gov//programs/ digest/d03/list_tables.asp; calculations by New Strategist*

Table 5.15 Doctoral Degrees Earned by Non-Hispanic Whites by Field of Study, 2001–02

(total number of doctoral degrees conferred and number and percent earned by non-Hispanic whites, by field of study, 2001–02)

	total	earned by non-Hispanic whites	
		number	percent
Total doctoral degrees	**44,160**	**26,905**	**60.9%**
Agriculture and natural resources	1,166	562	48.2
Architecture and related programs	183	71	38.8
Area, ethnic, and cultural studies	216	125	57.9
Biological and life sciences	4,489	2,691	59.9
Business	1,158	612	52.8
Communications	374	243	65.0
Communications technologies	9	6	66.7
Computer and information sciences	750	288	38.4
Education	6,967	4,938	70.9
Engineering	5,195	1,696	32.6
Engineering-related technologies	15	5	33.3
English language and literature, letters	1,446	1,101	76.1
Foreign languages and literatures	843	463	54.9
Health professions and related sciences	3,523	2,461	69.9
Home economics	355	227	63.9
Law and legal studies	79	18	22.8
Liberal arts and sciences, general studies, humanities	113	94	83.2
Library science	45	25	55.6
Mathematics	958	396	41.3
Multi- and interdisciplinary studies	384	259	67.4
Parks, recreation, leisure, and fitness	151	107	70.9
Philosophy and religion	606	466	76.9
Physical sciences	3,803	2,054	54.0
Protective services	49	43	87.8
Psychology	4,341	3,454	79.6
Public administration and services	571	386	67.6
Social sciences and history	3,902	2,485	63.7
Theological studies, religious vocations	1,355	862	63.6
Visual and performing arts	1,114	767	68.9

Source: National Center for Education Statistics, Digest of Education Statistics 2003, *Internet site http://nces.ed.gov//programs/ digest/d03/list_tables.asp; calculations by New Strategist*

Table 5.16 First-Professional Degrees Earned by Non-Hispanic Whites by Field of Study, 2001–02

(total number of first-professional degrees conferred and number and percent earned by non-Hispanic whites, by field of study, 2001–02)

		earned by non-Hispanic whites	
	total	number	percent
Total first-professional degrees	**80,698**	**58,874**	**73.0%**
Dentistry (D.D.S. or D.M.D.)	4,239	2,630	62.0
Medicine (M.D.)	15,237	10,148	66.6
Optometry (O.D.)	1,280	800	62.5
Osteopathic medicine (D.O.)	2,416	1,825	75.5
Pharmacy (Pharm.D.)	7,076	4,551	64.3
Podiatry (Pod.D., D.P., or D.P.M.)	474	332	70.0
Veterinary medicine (D.V.M.)	2,289	2,055	89.8
Chiropractic (D.C. or D.C.M.)	3,284	2,426	73.9
Naturopathic medicine	227	200	88.1
Law (LL.B. or J.D.)	38,981	30,125	77.3
Theology (M.Div., M.H.L., B.D., or Ord.)	5,195	3,782	72.8

Source: National Center for Education Statistics, Digest of Education Statistics 2003, *Internet site http://nces.ed.gov//programs/ digest/d03/list_tables.asp; calculations by New Strategist*

Table 5.17 Non-Hispanic White Participation in Adult Education, 2001

(percent of total people and non-Hispanic whites aged 16 or older participating in adult education activities, by type of adult education activity, 2001)

	percent participating	
	total	non-Hispanic whites
Any adult education course	**47.4%**	**48.3%**
College or university credential programs	7.3	7.0
Work-related courses	29.7	31.7
Personal interest courses	21.3	21.6
Other educational activities	3.6	2.4

Note: Adult education activities include apprenticeships, courses for basic skills, English as a second language, work-related courses, and personal development. For those aged 25 or older, credential programs in postsecondary institutions are counted as adult education activities. For those aged 16 to 24, full-time participation (full-year or part-year) in college or university credential programs or vocational or technical diploma programs are excluded.
Source: National Center for Education Statistics, Adult Education and Lifelong Learning Survey of the National Household Education Surveys Program; Internet site http://nces.ed.gov/programs/coe/2003/section1/tables/t08_2.asp

Most Non-Hispanic Whites Say Their Health Is Very Good or Excellent

Sixty-six percent of non-Hispanic whites report being in very good or excellent health. Only 11 percent say their health is fair or poor. Non-Hispanic whites rate their health highly even though 57 percent are overweight. Twenty-three percent of non-Hispanic whites smoke cigarettes, and the majority are regular drinkers—60 percent of men and 45 percent of women.

Fifty-seven percent of the nation's births in 2003 were to non-Hispanic white women. In eight states (Alaska, Arizona, California, Florida, Hawaii, Nevada, New Mexico, and Texas), non-Hispanic whites account for a minority of births. In California, the most populous state, only 31 percent of births are to non-Hispanic whites.

Among all racial and ethnic groups, non-Hispanic whites are least likely to be without health insurance. Only 11 percent are uninsured. Two-thirds of non-Hispanic whites are covered by employment-based private health insurance. Among Hispanics, in contrast, only 42 percent are covered by health insurance through an employer.

Because the non-Hispanic white population is older than the Asian, black, and Hispanic populations, non-Hispanic whites account for a disproportionate 76 percent of adults with difficulties in physical functioning. Fifteen percent of non-Hispanic whites aged 18 or older have physical difficulties.

Among non-Hispanic whites, heart disease and cancer are the leading causes of death, accounting for 52 percent of the total. Alzheimer's disease is the seventh leading cause of death among non-Hispanic whites.

■ As the non-Hispanic white population ages, the percentage of Americans with disabilities will rise.

Non-Hispanic whites are most likely to be covered by employment-based health insurance

(percent of people covered by employment-based private health insurance, by race and Hispanic origin, 2003)

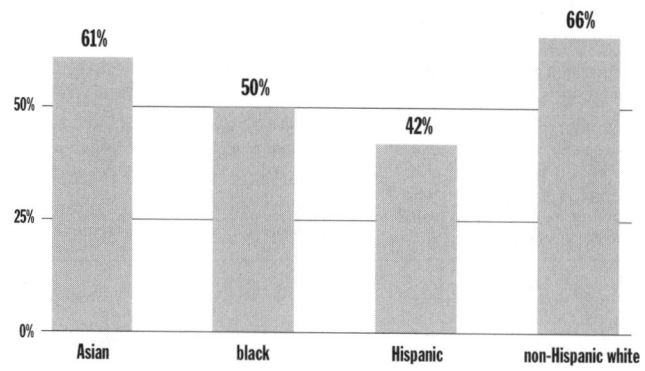

Table 5.18 Non-Hispanic White Health Status, 2003

(percent distribution of total people and non-Hispanic whites aged 18 or older by self-reported health status, and index of non-Hispanic white to total, 2003)

	total	non-Hispanic white	index of non-Hispanic white to total
Total people	**100.0%**	**100.0%**	–
Excellent/very good	62.3	65.9	106
Good	25.5	23.5	92
Fair/poor	12.2	10.5	86

Note: Non-Hispanic whites are those identifying themselves as being white alone and not Hispanic. The index is calculated by dividing the non-Hispanic white figure by the total figure and multiplying by 100. (–) means not applicable.
Source: National Center for Health Statistics, Summary Health Statistics for U.S. Adults: National Health Interview Survey, 2003, *Series 10, No. 225, 2005; Internet site http://www.cdc.gov/nchs/nhis.htm; calculations by New Strategist*

Table 5.19 Smoking and Drinking Status of Non-Hispanic Whites by Sex, 2003

(percent distribution of non-Hispanic whites aged 18 or older by smoking and drinking status and sex, 2003)

	total	men	women
SMOKING STATUS			
Total non-Hispanic whites	**100.0%**	**100.0%**	**100.0%**
Never smoked	52.9	48.3	56.7
Former smoker	23.9	27.2	21.2
Current smoker	23.3	24.5	22.1
DRINKING STATUS			
Total non-Hispanic whites	**100.0**	**100.0**	**100.0**
Lifetime abstainer	19.9	14.6	24.5
Former drinker	14.0	14.5	13.4
Current infrequent drinker	13.0	9.5	16.3
Current regular drinker	52.3	60.1	45.0

Note: Never smoked means haaving had fewer than 100 cigarettes in lifetime. Former smokers have had 100 or more cigarettes in lifetime but did not smoke at time of interview. Current smokers have had at least 100 cigarettes in lifetime and currently smoke. Lifetime abstainers have had fewer than 12 drinks in lifetime. Former drinkers have had 12 or more drinks in lifetime, none in past year. Current infrequent drinkers have had 12 or more drinks in lifetime and fewer than 12 drinks in past year. Current regular drinkers have had at least 12 drinks in past year. Non-Hispanic whites are those identifying themselves as being white alone and not Hispanic.
Source: National Center for Health Statistics, Summary Health Statistics for U.S. Adults: National Health Interview Survey, 2003, *Series 10, No. 225, 2005; Internet site http://www.cdc.gov/nchs/nhis.htm*

Table 5.20 Weight in Pounds of Non-Hispanic Whites by Age and Sex, 1999–2002

(average weight in pounds of non-Hispanic whites aged 20 or older by age and sex, 1999–2002)

	men	women
WEIGHT IN POUNDS		
Total non-Hispanic whites	**193.1**	**161.7**
Aged 20 to 39	189.7	158.4
Aged 40 to 59	199.5	167.6
Aged 60 or older	188.8	158.0

Note: Data are based on measured weight of a sample of the civilian noninstitutionalized population.
Source: National Center for Health Statistics, Mean Body Weight, Height, and Body Mass Index, United States 1960–2002; Advance Data, No. 347, 2004; Internet site http://www.cdc.gov/nchs/products/pubs/pubd/ad/341-350/341-350.htm

Table 5.21 Weight Status of Non-Hispanic Whites by Sex, 2003

(percent distribution of non-Hispanic whites aged 18 or older by weight status and sex, 2003)

	total	men	women
Total non-Hispanic whites	**100.0%**	**100.0%**	**100.0%**
Underweight	2.1	0.9	3.4
Healthy weight	40.5	31.7	49.2
Overweight, total	57.4	67.5	47.5
Overweight, but not obese	35.7	45.0	26.6
Obese	21.7	22.5	20.9

Note: Being overweight is defined as having a body mass index of 25 or higher. Being obese is defined as having a body mass index of 30 or higher. Body mass index is calculated by dividing weight in kilograms by height in meters squared. Data are based on measured height and weight of a sample of the civilian noninstitutionalized population. Non-Hispanic whites are those identifying themselves as being white alone and not Hispanic.
Source: National Center for Health Statistics, Summary Health Statistics for U.S. Adults: National Health Interview Survey, 2003, Series 10, No. 225, 2005; Internet site http://www.cdc.gov/nchs/nhis.htm

Table 5.22   Births to Non-Hispanic White Women by Age, 2003

(total number of births, number and percent distribution of births to non-Hispanic whites, and non-Hispanic white share of total, by age, 2003)

| | | non-Hispanic white | | |
	total	number	percent distribution	share of total
Total births	**4,089,950**	**2,321,904**	**100.0%**	**56.8%**
Under age 15	6,661	1,399	0.1	21.0
Aged 15 to 19	414,580	172,620	7.4	41.6
Aged 20 to 24	1,032,305	522,275	22.5	50.6
Aged 25 to 29	1,086,366	627,437	27.0	57.8
Aged 30 to 34	975,546	626,315	27.0	64.2
Aged 35 to 39	467,642	303,354	13.1	64.9
Aged 40 to 44	101,005	64,600	2.8	64.0
Aged 45 to 54	5,845	3,904	0.2	66.8

Source: National Center for Health Statistics, Births: Final Data for 2003, *National Vital Statistics Reports, Vol. 54, No. 2, 2005; Internet site http://www.cdc.gov/nchs/products/pubs/pubd/nvsr/54/54-pre.htm; calculations by New Strategist*

Table 5.23   Births to Non-Hispanic White Women by Age and Marital Status, 2003

(total number of births to non-Hispanic whites, number of births to unmarried non-Hispanic whites, and unmarried share of total, by age, 2003)

| | | unmarried non-Hispanic whites | |
	total	number	share of total
Births to non-Hispanic whites	**2,321,904**	**546,991**	**23.6%**
Under age 15	1,399	1,353	96.7
Aged 15 to 19	172,620	132,482	76.7
Aged 20 to 24	522,275	224,941	43.1
Aged 25 to 29	627,437	101,454	16.2
Aged 30 to 34	626,315	52,167	8.3
Aged 35 to 39	303,354	26,352	8.7
Aged 40 or older	68,504	8,242	12.0

Source: National Center for Health Statistics, Births: Final Data for 2003, *National Vital Statistics Reports, Vol. 54, No. 2, 2005; Internet site http://www.cdc.gov/nchs/products/pubs/pubd/nvsr/54/54-pre.htm; calculations by New Strategist*

Table 5.24 Births to Non-Hispanic White Women by Birth Order, 2003

(total number of births, number and percent distribution of births to non-Hispanic whites, and non-Hispanic white share of total, by birth order, 2003)

	total	non-Hispanic white		
		number	percent distribution	share of total
Total births	**4,089,950**	**2,321,904**	**100.0%**	**56.8%**
First child	1,633,987	961,897	41.4	58.9
Second child	1,320,477	780,026	33.6	59.1
Third child	684,296	370,971	16.0	54.2
Fourth or later child	439,235	203,511	8.8	46.3

Note: Numbers will not add to total because "not stated" is not shown.
Source: National Center for Health Statistics, Births: Final Data for 2003, National Vital Statistics Reports, Vol. 54, No. 2, 2005; Internet site http://www.cdc.gov/nchs/products/pubs/pubd/nvsr/54/54-pre.htm; calculations by New Strategist

Table 5.25 Births to Non-Hispanic White Women by State, 2003

(total number of births, number and percent distribution of births to non-Hispanic whites, and non-Hispanic white share of total, by state, 2003)

	total	non-Hispanic white births number	non-Hispanic white births percent distribution	share of total
Total births	**4,089,950**	**2,321,904**	**100.0%**	**56.8%**
Alabama	59,552	37,996	1.6	63.8
Alaska	10,086	4,917	0.2	48.8
Arizona	90,967	39,222	1.7	43.1
Arkansas	37,784	26,480	1.1	70.1
California	540,997	166,764	7.2	30.8
Colorado	69,339	42,348	1.8	61.1
Connecticut	42,873	28,047	1.2	65.4
Delaware	11,329	6,584	0.3	58.1
District of Columbia	7,619	1,844	0.1	24.2
Florida	212,250	104,289	4.5	49.1
Georgia	135,979	68,900	3.0	50.7
Hawaii	18,100	4,275	0.2	23.6
Idaho	21,800	17,923	0.8	82.2
Illinois	182,495	99,565	4.3	54.6
Indiana	86,434	68,511	3.0	79.3
Iowa	38,174	33,185	1.4	86.9
Kansas	39,476	29,230	1.3	74.0
Kentucky	55,236	47,568	2.0	86.1
Louisiana	65,040	35,726	1.5	54.9
Maine	13,855	13,153	0.6	94.9
Maryland	74,930	39,234	1.7	52.4
Massachusetts	80,184	57,884	2.5	72.2
Michigan	131,094	93,630	4.0	71.4
Minnesota	70,050	54,074	2.3	77.2
Mississippi	42,380	22,664	1.0	53.5
Missouri	77,045	60,488	2.6	78.5
Montana	11,422	9,299	0.4	81.4
Nebraska	25,917	19,404	0.8	74.9
Nevada	33,647	15,612	0.7	46.4
New Hampshire	14,393	12,590	0.5	87.5
New Jersey	116,983	61,911	2.7	52.9
New Mexico	27,821	8,606	0.4	30.9
New York	253,714	132,088	5.7	52.1
North Carolina	118,323	70,473	3.0	59.6
North Dakota	7,972	6,571	0.3	82.4
Ohio	149,679	118,304	5.1	79.0
Oklahoma	50,981	34,349	1.5	67.4
Oregon	45,953	33,074	1.4	72.0

(continued)

	total	non-Hispanic white births		
		number	percent distribution	share of total
Pennsylvania	145,959	109,259	4.7%	74.9%
Rhode Island	13,209	7,251	0.3	54.9
South Carolina	55,649	32,677	1.4	58.7
South Dakota	11,027	8,616	0.4	78.1
Tennessee	78,890	56,119	2.4	71.1
Texas	377,476	138,194	6.0	36.6
Utah	49,860	40,154	1.7	80.5
Vermont	6,589	6,311	0.3	95.8
Virginia	101,254	62,347	2.7	61.6
Washington	80,489	53,848	2.3	66.9
West Virginia	20,935	19,874	0.9	94.9
Wisconsin	70,040	54,845	2.4	78.3
Wyoming	6,700	5,627	0.2	84.0

Source: National Center for Health Statistics, Births: Final Data for 2003, *National Vital Statistics Reports, Vol. 54, No. 2, 2005; Internet site http://www.cdc.gov/nchs/products/pubs/pubd/nvsr/54/54-pre.htm; calculations by New Strategist*

Table 5.26 Health Insurance Coverage of Non-Hispanic Whites by Age, 2003

(number and percent distribution of non-Hispanic whites by age and health insurance coverage status, 2003; numbers in thousands)

	total	with health insurance coverage during year			not covered at any time during the year
		total	private	government	
Total non-Hispanic whites	**194,877**	**173,295**	**149,084**	**49,743**	**21,582**
Under age 18	43,432	40,222	33,989	8,917	3,210
Aged 18 to 24	17,382	13,374	12,007	2,071	4,008
Aged 25 to 34	23,900	19,311	17,697	2,262	4,590
Aged 35 to 44	29,560	25,671	23,882	2,669	3,889
Aged 45 to 54	30,219	26,817	25,055	2,880	3,402
Aged 55 to 64	22,048	19,663	17,682	3,427	2,385
Aged 65 or older	28,335	28,237	18,771	27,517	98

PERCENT DISTRIBUTION BY COVERAGE STATUS

	total	with health insurance coverage during year			not covered at any time during the year
Total non-Hispanic whites	**100.0%**	**88.9%**	**76.5%**	**25.5%**	**11.1%**
Under age 18	100.0	92.6	78.3	20.5	7.4
Aged 18 to 24	100.0	76.9	69.1	11.9	23.1
Aged 25 to 34	100.0	80.8	74.0	9.5	19.2
Aged 35 to 44	100.0	86.8	80.8	9.0	13.2
Aged 45 to 54	100.0	88.7	82.9	9.5	11.3
Aged 55 to 64	100.0	89.2	80.2	15.5	10.8
Aged 65 or older	100.0	99.7	66.2	97.1	0.3

Note: Non-Hispanic whites are those identifying themselves as being white alone and not Hispanic. Numbers may not add to total because some people have more than one type of health insurance.
Source: Bureau of the Census, 2004 Current Population Survey, Annual Social and Economic Supplement, detailed tables, Internet site http://pubdb3.census.gov/macro/032004/health/h01_000.htm; calculations by New Strategist

Table 5.27 Non-Hispanic Whites with Private Health Insurance Coverage by Age, 2003

(number and percent distribution of non-Hispanic whites by age and private health insurance coverage status, 2003; numbers in thousands)

| | | with private health insurance | | | |
| | total | total | employment-based | | direct purchase |
			total	own	
Total non-Hispanic whites	**194,877**	**149,084**	**129,261**	**68,451**	**21,865**
Under age 18	43,432	33,989	31,422	122	2,861
Aged 18 to 24	17,382	12,007	9,624	3,543	1,172
Aged 25 to 34	23,900	17,697	16,519	12,449	1,461
Aged 35 to 44	29,560	23,882	22,216	15,498	2,141
Aged 45 to 54	30,219	25,055	23,173	16,918	2,594
Aged 55 to 64	22,048	17,682	15,779	11,764	2,530
Aged 65 or older	28,335	18,771	10,529	8,155	9,107
PERCENT DISTRIBUTION BY COVERAGE STATUS					
Total non-Hispanic whites	**100.0%**	**76.5%**	**66.3%**	**35.1%**	**11.2%**
Under age 18	100.0	78.3	72.3	0.3	6.6
Aged 18 to 24	100.0	69.1	55.4	20.4	6.7
Aged 25 to 34	100.0	74.0	69.1	52.1	6.1
Aged 35 to 44	100.0	80.8	75.2	52.4	7.2
Aged 45 to 54	100.0	82.9	76.7	56.0	8.6
Aged 55 to 64	100.0	80.2	71.6	53.4	11.5
Aged 65 or older	100.0	66.2	37.2	28.8	32.1

Note: Non-Hispanic whites are those identifying themselves as being white alone and not Hispanic. Numbers will not add to total because some people have more than one type of health insurance.
Source: Bureau of the Census, 2004 Current Population Survey, Annual Social and Economic Supplement, detailed tables, Internet site http://pubdb3.census.gov/macro/032004/health/h01_000.htm; calculations by New Strategist

Table 5.28 Non-Hispanic Whites with Government Health Insurance Coverage by Age, 2003

(number and percent distribution of non-Hispanic whites by age and government health insurance coverage status, 2003; numbers in thousands)

	total	with government health insurance			
		total	Medicaid	Medicare	military
Total non-Hispanic whites	**194,877**	**49,743**	**16,247**	**31,458**	**7,563**
Under age 18	43,432	8,917	7,637	165	1,351
Aged 18 to 24	17,382	2,071	1,432	104	624
Aged 25 to 34	23,900	2,262	1,449	331	635
Aged 35 to 44	29,560	2,669	1,570	628	781
Aged 45 to 54	30,219	2,880	1,274	1,035	1,034
Aged 55 to 64	22,048	3,427	1,009	1,735	1,215
Aged 65 or older	28,335	27,517	1,876	27,460	1,922
PERCENT DISTRIBUTION BY COVERAGE STATUS					
Total non-Hispanic whites	**100.0%**	**25.5%**	**8.3%**	**16.1%**	**3.9%**
Under age 18	100.0	20.5	17.6	0.4	3.1
Aged 18 to 24	100.0	11.9	8.2	0.6	3.6
Aged 25 to 34	100.0	9.5	6.1	1.4	2.7
Aged 35 to 44	100.0	9.0	5.3	2.1	2.6
Aged 45 to 54	100.0	9.5	4.2	3.4	3.4
Aged 55 to 64	100.0	15.5	4.6	7.9	5.5
Aged 65 or older	100.0	97.1	6.6	96.9	6.8

Note: Non-Hispanic whites are those identifying themselves as being white alone and not Hispanic. Numbers will not add to total because some people have more than one type of health insurance.
Source: Bureau of the Census, 2004 Current Population Survey, Annual Social and Economic Supplement, detailed tables, Internet site http://pubdb3.census.gov/macro/032004/health/h01_000.htm; calculations by New Strategist

Table 5.29 Health Conditions among Non-Hispanic Whites Aged 18 or Older, 2003

(number of total people and non-Hispanic whites aged 18 or older with selected health conditions, percent of non-Hispanic whites with condition, and non-Hispanic white share of total with condition, 2003; numbers in thousands)

| | | non-Hispanic white | | |
	total	number	percent with condition	share of total
Total people	213,042	153,032	–	71.8%
Selected circulatory diseases				
Heart disease, all types	23,536	19,289	11.8%	82.0
Coronary	12,254	10,043	6.0	82.0
Hypertension	45,927	34,101	20.8	74.3
Stroke	5,070	3,862	2.3	76.2
Selected respiratory conditions				
Emphysema	3,115	2,778	1.6	89.2
Asthma				
Ever	20,697	15,404	10.2	74.4
Still	13,623	10,265	6.7	75.4
Hay fever	18,356	14,436	9.5	78.6
Sinusitis	29,673	23,476	15.2	79.1
Chronic bronchitis	8,560	6,791	4.3	79.3
Cancer				
Any cancer	13,973	12,377	7.5	88.6
Breast cancer (all adults)	2,426	2,139	1.3	88.2
Cervical cancer (women only)	1,082	951	1.2	87.9
Prostate cancer (men only)	1,332	1,080	1.5	81.1
Other selected diseases and conditions				
Diabetes	14,012	9,729	6.0	69.4
Ulcers	14,456	11,323	7.1	78.3
Kidney disease	3,017	2,065	1.2	68.4
Liver disease	2,511	1,751	1.1	69.7
Arthritis	45,793	36,931	22.7	80.6
Chronic joint symptoms	57,242	45,685	28.8	79.8
Migraines or severe headaches	32,268	22,813	15.3	70.7
Pain in neck	31,368	24,154	15.6	77.0
Pain in lower back	58,430	43,911	28.4	75.2
Pain in face or jaw	9,464	7,372	4.9	77.9
Selected sensory problems				
Hearing	32,533	27,897	17.2	85.7
Vision	18,628	13,691	8.6	73.5
Absence of all natural teeth	15,927	12,494	7.6	78.4

Note: The conditions shown are those that have ever been diagnosed by a doctor, except as noted. Hay fever, sinusitis, and chronic bronchitis have been diagnosed in the past twelve months. Kidney and liver disease have been diagnosed in the past twelve months and exclude kidney stones, bladder infections, and incontinence. Chronic joint symptoms are shown if respondent had pain, aching, or stiffness in or around a joint (excluding back and neck) and the condition began more than three months ago. Migraines, pain in neck, lower back, face, or jaw are shown only if pain lasted a whole day or more. Non-Hispanic whites are those identifying themselves as being white alone and not Hispanic. (–) means not applicable.
Source: National Center for Health Statistics, Summary Health Statistics for U.S. Adults: National Health Interview Survey, 2003, Series 10, No. 225, 2005; Internet site http://www.cdc.gov/nchs/nhis.htm; calculations by New Strategist

Table 5.30 Health Conditions among Non-Hispanic White Children, 2003

(number of total people and non-Hispanic whites under age 18 with selected health conditions, percent of non-Hispanic whites with condition, and non-Hispanic white share of total, 2003; numbers in thousands)

		non-Hispanic white		
	total	number	percent with condition	share of total
Total children	72,973	44,038	–	60.3%
Diagnosed with asthma	9,071	4,978	11.3%	54.9
Experienced in last 12 months				
Asthma attack	3,975	2,132	4.8	53.6
Hay fever	7,059	4,708	10.6	66.7
Respiratory allergies	8,347	5,668	12.9	67.9
Other allergies	8,407	5,146	11.7	61.2
Ever told had*				
Learning disability	4,561	2,996	8.0	65.7
Attention deficit hyperactivity disorder	3,881	2,767	7.4	71.3
Prescription medication taken regularly for at least 3 months	9,287	6,452	14.5	69.5

* *"Ever told" by a school representative or health professional. Data exclude children under age 3.*
Note: Other allergies include food or digestive allergies, eczema, and other skin allergies. Non-Hispanic whites are those identifying themselves as being white alone and not Hispanic. (–) means not applicable.
Source: National Center for Health Statistics, Summary Health Statistics for U.S. Children: National Health Interview Survey, *2003, Series 10, No. 223, 2005; Internet site http://www.cdc.gov/nchs/nhis.htm; calculations by New Strategist*

Table 5.31 Physician Office Visits by Whites by Age, 2002

(number of total physician office visits, number and percent distribution of visits by whites, white share of total, and average number of visits by whites per person per year, by age, 2002)

		visits by whites			
	total (000s)	number (000s)	percent distribution	share of total	per person per year
Total visits	889,980	766,096	100.0%	86.1%	3.3
Under age 15	159,235	131,023	17.1	82.3	2.8
Aged 15 to 24	71,865	61,012	8.0	84.9	2.0
Aged 25 to 44	192,359	164,890	21.5	85.7	2.5
Aged 45 to 64	242,142	211,162	27.6	87.2	3.8
Aged 65 to 74	109,331	95,465	12.5	87.3	6.1
Aged 75 or older	115,049	102,544	13.4	89.1	7.2

Source: National Center for Health Statistics, National Ambulatory Medical Care Survey: 2002 Summary, *Advance Data No. 346, 2004; Internet site http://www.cdc.gov/nchs/about/major/ahcd/adata.htm; calculations by New Strategist*

Table 5.32 Difficulties in Physical Functioning among Non-Hispanic Whites, 2003

(number of total people and non-Hispanic whites aged 18 or older, number with difficulties in physical functioning, percent of non-Hispanic whites with difficulty, and non-Hispanic white share of total, by type of difficulty, 2003; numbers in thousands)

| | | non-Hispanic white | | |
	total	number	percent with difficulty	share of total
TOTAL PEOPLE	**213,042**	**153,032**	–	**71.8%**
Total with any physical difficulty	**31,322**	**23,858**	**14.6%**	**76.2**
Walk quarter of a mile	14,910	11,156	6.8	74.8
Climb up ten steps without resting	11,107	7,838	4.7	70.6
Stand for two hours	18,663	13,974	8.5	74.9
Sit for two hours	7,211	5,102	3.2	70.8
Stoop, bend, or kneel	18,250	13,735	8.4	75.3
Reach over head	6,264	4,576	2.8	73.1
Grasp or handle small objects	3,943	2,944	1.8	74.7
Lift or carry ten pounds	9,194	6,533	4.0	71.1
Push or pull large objects	13,463	10,097	6.2	75.0

Note: Respondents were classified as having difficulties if they responded "very difficult" or "can't do at all." Non-Hispanic whites are those identifying themselves as being white alone and not Hispanic. (–) means not applicable.
Source: National Center for Health Statistics, Summary Health Statistics for U.S. Adults: National Health Interview Survey, 2003, Series 10, No. 225, 2005; Internet site http://www.cdc.gov/nchs/nhis.htm; calculations by New Strategist

Table 5.33 AIDS Cases among Non-Hispanic Whites, through December 2003

(total number of AIDS cases diagnosed, number and percent distribution of AIDS cases diagnosed among non-Hispanic whites, and non-Hispanic white share of total, by sex and age at diagnosis, through December 2003)

| | | non-Hispanic white | | |
	total	number	percent distribution	share of total
Total AIDS cases	**874,230**	**369,252**	**100.0%**	**42.2%**
Males aged 13 or older	708,452	333,873	90.4	47.1
Females aged 13 or older	156,837	33,766	9.1	21.5
Children under age 13	8,939	1,613	0.4	18.0

Source: National Center for Health Statistics, Health, United States, 2004; Internet site http://www.cdc.gov/nchs/hus.htm; calculations by New Strategist

Table 5.34 Leading Causes of Death Among Non-Hispanic Whites, 2002

(number and percent distribution of deaths to non-Hispanic whites accounted for by the ten leading causes of death among non-Hispanic whites, 2002)

	number	percent distribution
Total non-Hispanic white deaths	**1,981,973**	**100.0%**
1. Diseases of the heart (1)	577,761	29.2
2. Malignant neoplasms (cancer) (2)	458,754	23.1
3. Cerebrovascular diseases (3)	133,118	6.7
4. Chronic lower respiratory disease (4)	112,128	5.7
5. Accidents (unintentional injuries) (5)	80,605	4.1
6. Influenza and pneumonia (7)	55,419	2.8
7. Alzheimer's disease (8)	53,486	2.7
8. Diabetes mellitus (6)	52,463	2.6
9. Nephritis, nephrotic syndrome, nephrosis (9)	30,669	1.5
10. Suicide (11)	26,691	1.3
All other causes	400,879	20.2

Note: Number in parentheses shows rank for all Americans.
Source: National Center for Health Statistics, Health, United States, 2004*; Internet site http://www.cdc.gov/nchs/hus.htm; calculations by New Strategist*

Table 5.35 Life Expectancy of Whites at Birth and Age 65 by Sex, 1990 to 2002

(number of years of life remaining for whites at birth and age 65, by sex, 1990 to 2002; change in years, 1990 to 2002)

	total whites	white females	white males
Birth			
2002	77.7	80.3	75.1
2000	77.6	80.1	74.9
1990	76.1	79.4	72.7
Change, 1990 to 2002	1.6	0.9	2.4
Age 65			
2002	18.2	19.5	16.6
2000	18.0	19.4	16.3
1990	17.3	19.1	15.2
Change, 1990 to 2002	0.9	0.4	1.4

Source: National Center for Health Statistics, Health, United States, 2004*; Internet site http://www.cdc.gov/nchs/hus.htm; calculations by New Strategist*

More than Three out of Four Non-Hispanic White Households Own Their Home

Seventy-six percent of the nation's non-Hispanic white households owned their home in 2004, a greater proportion than the 69 percent of all households that are homeowners. Homeownership among non-Hispanic whites does not vary much by region, ranging from a low of 71 percent in the West to a high of 78 percent in the Midwest.

Among non-Hispanic white married couples, 88 percent are homeowners. Homeownership claims a majority of non-Hispanic white householders regardless of household type. Even among female-headed families, 61 percent are homeowners.

Only 12 percent of non-Hispanic whites moved between 2003 and 2004, a lower mobility rate than that for Asians, blacks, or Hispanics. One reason for the lower mobility of non-Hispanic whites is their higher homeownership rate. Homeowners are much less likely to move than renters. Non-Hispanic whites aged 20 to 24 are most likely to move, with 30 percent moving between 2003 and 2004.

■ The homeownership rate of non-Hispanic whites will continue to climb as the baby-boom generation enters the ages of peak homeownership.

Non-Hispanic white homeownership is lowest in the West

(percent of non-Hispanic white households that own their home, by region, 2004)

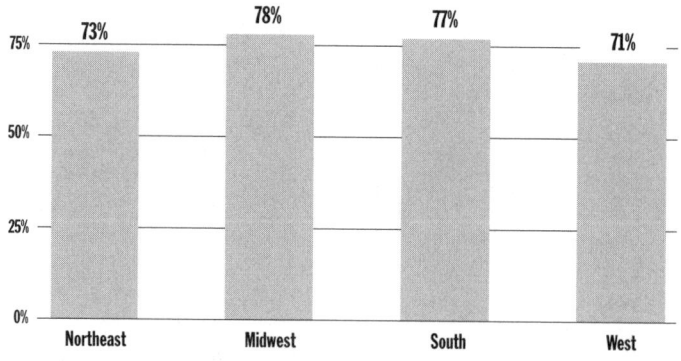

Table 5.36 Non-Hispanic White Homeownership Rate, 1994 to 2004

(homeownership rate of total and non-Hispanic white households and index of non-Hispanic white to total, 1994 to 2004; percentage point change in homeownership rate, 1994–2004)

	total households	non-Hispanic white households	index
2004	69.0%	76.0%	110
2003	68.3	75.4	110
2002	67.9	74.5	110
2001	67.8	74.3	110
2000	67.4	73.8	109
1999	66.8	73.2	110
1998	66.3	72.6	110
1997	65.7	72.0	110
1996	65.4	71.7	110
1995	64.7	70.9	110
1994	64.0	70.0	109
Percentage point change			
1994 to 2004	5.0	6.0	–

Note: Non-Hispanic whites are those identifying themselves as being white alone and not Hispanic. The index is calculated by dividing the non-Hispanic white homeownership rate by the total rate and multiplying by 100. (–) means not applicable.
Source: Bureau of the Census, American Housing Survey for the United States: 2003, *Current Housing Reports, Internet site http://www.census.gov/hhes/www/ahs.html; calculations by New Strategist*

Table 5.37 Non-Hispanic White Homeownership Status by Household Type, 2003

(number and percent of non-Hispanic white households by household type and homeownership status, 2003; numbers in thousands)

	total	owner		renter	
		number	percent	number	percent
TOTAL NON-HISPANIC WHITE HOUSEHOLDS	**81,166**	**60,980**	**75.1%**	**20,185**	**24.9%**
Family households	**53,845**	**45,162**	**83.9**	**8,683**	**16.1**
Married couples	44,101	38,981	88.4	5,120	11.6
Female householder, no spouse present	7,070	4,339	61.4	2,731	38.6
Male householder, no spouse present	2,674	1,841	68.8	833	31.2
Nonfamily households	**27,321**	**15,818**	**57.9**	**11,503**	**42.1**
Female householder	15,353	9,283	60.5	6,070	39.5
Male householder	11,968	6,535	54.6	5,433	45.4

Note: Non-Hispanic whites include only those identifying themselves as being white alone and not Hispanic.
Source: Bureau of the Census, America's Families and Living Arrangements, 2003 Current Population Survey Annual Social and Economic Supplement; Internet site http://www.census.gov/population/www/socdemo/hh-fam/cps2003.html; calculations by New Strategist

Table 5.38 Non-Hispanic White Homeowners by Type of Household, 2003

(number of total homeowners, number and percent distribution of non-Hispanic white homeowners, and non-Hispanic white share of total, by type of household, 2003; numbers in thousands)

	total	non-Hispanic white		
		number	percent distribution	share of total
TOTAL HOMEOWNERS	**75,909**	**60,980**	**100.0%**	**80.3%**
Family households	**57,092**	**45,162**	**74.1**	**79.1**
Married couples	47,676	38,981	63.9	81.8
Female householder, no spouse present	6,695	4,339	7.1	64.8
Male householder, no spouse present	2,721	1,841	3.0	67.7
Nonfamily households	**18,817**	**15,818**	**25.9**	**84.1**
Female householder	11,075	9,283	15.2	83.8
Male householder	7,742	6,535	10.7	84.4

Note: Non-Hispanic whites include only those identifying themselves as being white alone and not Hispanic.
Source: Bureau of the Census, America's Families and Living Arrangements, 2003 Current Population Survey Annual Social and Economic Supplement; Internet site http://www.census.gov/population/www/socdemo/hh-fam/cps2003.html; calculations by New Strategist

Table 5.39 Non-Hispanic White Homeownership Status by Region, 2003

(number and percent of non-Hispanic white households by homeownership status and region, 2003; numbers in thousands)

| | | owners | | renters | |
	total	number	share of total	number	share of total
Total non-Hispanic white households	**77,358**	**58,366**	**75.4%**	**18,992**	**24.6%**
Northeast	15,482	11,337	73.2	4,145	26.8
Midwest	20,485	15,990	78.1	4,496	21.9
South	26,254	20,274	77.2	5,980	22.8
West	15,137	10,765	71.1	4,372	28.9

Note: Non-Hispanic whites include only those identifying themselves as being white alone and not Hispanic.
Source: Bureau of the Census, American Housing Survey for the United States: 2003, *Current Housing Reports, Internet site http://www.census.gov/hhes/www/ahs.html; calculations by New Strategist*

Table 5.40 Non-Hispanic White Homeowners by Region, 2003

(number of total homeowners, number and percent distribution of non-Hispanic white homeowners, and non-Hispanic white share of total, by region, 2003; numbers in thousands)

| | | non-Hispanic white | | |
	total	number	percent distribution	share of total
Total homeowners	**72,238**	**58,366**	**100.0%**	**80.8%**
Northeast	12,964	11,337	19.4	87.4
Midwest	17,889	15,990	27.4	89.4
South	26,699	20,274	34.7	75.9
West	14,686	10,765	18.4	73.3

Note: Non-Hispanic whites include only those identifying themselves as being white alone and not Hispanic.
Source: Bureau of the Census, American Housing Survey for the United States: 2003, *Current Housing Reports, Internet site http://www.census.gov/hhes/www/ahs.html; calculations by New Strategist*

Table 5.41 Housing Units Occupied by Non-Hispanic Whites by Type, 2003

(number of total occupied housing units, number and percent distribution of housing units occupied by non-Hispanic whites, and non-Hispanic white share of total, by number of units in structure, 2003)

| | | non-Hispanic whites | | |
	total	number	percent distribution	share of total
Total occupied housing units	**108,419,506**	**79,438,806**	**100.0%**	**73.3%**
One, detached or attached	73,740,642	57,656,905	72.6	78.2
Two to four	9,374,261	5,609,209	7.1	59.8
Five or more	18,089,052	10,377,254	13.1	57.4
Mobile home	7,128,265	5,725,576	7.2	80.3
Boat, RV, van, etc.	87,286	69,862	0.1	80.0

Note: Non-Hispanic whites include only those identifying themselves as being white alone and not Hispanic.
Source: Bureau of the Census, 2003 American Community Survey, Internet site http://factfinder.census.gov/servlet/ DatasetMainPageServlet?_program=ACS&_lang=en&_ts=; calculations by New Strategist

Table 5.42   Geographical Mobility of Non-Hispanic Whites by Age, 2003–04

(total number of non-Hispanic whites aged 1 or older, and number and percent who moved between March 2003 and March 2004, by age and type of move; numbers in thousands)

| | | movers | | | | |
	total	total	same county	different county, same state	different state	abroad
Total non-Hispanic whites	**192,629**	**23,474**	**12,958**	**5,178**	**4,926**	**412**
Aged 1 to 4	9,043	1,605	935	302	334	34
Aged 5 to 9	11,508	1,562	900	356	281	25
Aged 10 to 14	12,652	1,309	767	267	257	18
Aged 15 to 17	7,981	669	376	135	144	14
Aged 18 to 19	4,833	744	375	194	167	8
Aged 20 to 24	12,549	3,822	2,074	931	753	64
Aged 25 to 29	11,372	3,263	1,827	696	676	64
Aged 30 to 34	12,528	2,309	1,278	530	455	46
Aged 35 to 39	13,646	1,812	983	408	365	56
Aged 40 to 44	15,914	1,683	984	320	355	24
Aged 45 to 49	15,842	1,233	675	239	306	13
Aged 50 to 54	14,377	962	529	197	210	26
Aged 55 to 59	12,510	769	367	199	194	9
Aged 60 to 61	4,305	257	126	60	71	0
Aged 62 to 64	5,233	270	120	71	76	3
Aged 65 or older	28,335	1,202	642	274	279	7

PERCENT DISTRIBUTION BY MOBILITY STATUS

Total non-Hispanic whites	**100.0%**	**12.2%**	**6.7%**	**2.7%**	**2.6%**	**0.2%**
Aged 1 to 4	100.0	17.7	10.3	3.3	3.7	0.4
Aged 5 to 9	100.0	13.6	7.8	3.1	2.4	0.2
Aged 10 to 14	100.0	10.3	6.1	2.1	2.0	0.1
Aged 15 to 17	100.0	8.4	4.7	1.7	1.8	0.2
Aged 18 to 19	100.0	15.4	7.8	4.0	3.5	0.2
Aged 20 to 24	100.0	30.5	16.5	7.4	6.0	0.5
Aged 25 to 29	100.0	28.7	16.1	6.1	5.9	0.6
Aged 30 to 34	100.0	18.4	10.2	4.2	3.6	0.4
Aged 35 to 39	100.0	13.3	7.2	3.0	2.7	0.4
Aged 40 to 44	100.0	10.6	6.2	2.0	2.2	0.2
Aged 45 to 49	100.0	7.8	4.3	1.5	1.9	0.1
Aged 50 to 54	100.0	6.7	3.7	1.4	1.5	0.2
Aged 55 to 59	100.0	6.1	2.9	1.6	1.6	0.1
Aged 60 to 61	100.0	6.0	2.9	1.4	1.6	0.0
Aged 62 to 64	100.0	5.2	2.3	1.4	1.5	0.1
Aged 65 or older	100.0	4.2	2.3	1.0	1.0	0.0

Note: Non-Hispanic whites include only those identifying themselves as being white alone and not Hispanic.
Source: Bureau of the Census, Geographic Mobility: 2004, Detailed Tables, Internet site http://www.census.gov/population/www/socdemo/migrate/cps2004.html; calculations by New Strategist

Non-Hispanic Whites Have Above-Average Incomes

The $47,777 median income of non-Hispanic white households in 2003 was 10 percent greater than the all-household median. Between 1990 and 2003, the median income of non-Hispanic white households grew 10 percent, faster than the 6 percent gain for all households during those years.

Among non-Hispanic white households, median income peaks at $66,811 for householders aged 45 to 54. By household type, non-Hispanic white married couples have the highest median income—$66,677 in 2003. Seventeen percent of non-Hispanic white households have incomes of $100,000 or more.

Among full-time workers, the median income of non-Hispanic white men rose 10 percent between 1990 and 2003, while their female counterparts saw an 18 percent increase. Even during the 2000 to 2003 time period, when many workers lost ground, non-Hispanic whites with full-time jobs saw their incomes grow.

Non-Hispanic whites are less likely to be poor than Asians, blacks, or Hispanics. The poverty rate of non-Hispanic white couples stood at less than 4 percent in 2003. Among non-Hispanic white female-headed families, the poverty rate fell from 23 to 20 percent between 1990 and 2003. Among male-headed families, the poverty rate rose slightly during those years to just below 9 percent.

■ Non-Hispanic white households have much higher incomes than black or Hispanic households. Behind the income gap is the higher educational level of non-Hispanic whites and the larger proportion of households headed by dual-earner married couples.

Non-Hispanic white household income grew slightly faster than average

(percent change in total and non-Hispanic white median household income, 1990 to 2003; in 2003 dollars)

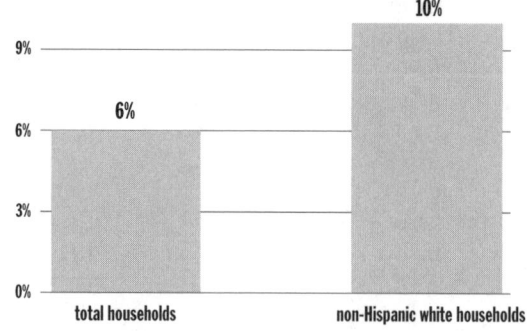

Table 5.43 Median Income of Non-Hispanic White Households, 1990 to 2003

(median income of total and non-Hispanic white households, and index of non-Hispanic white to total, 1990 to 2003; percent change in incomes, 2000–03 and 1990–2003; in 2003 dollars)

	total households	non-Hispanic white households	index
2003	$43,318	$47,777	110
2002	43,381	47,974	111
2001	43,882	48,119	110
2000	44,853	48,734	109
1999	44,922	48,742	109
1998	43,825	47,831	109
1997	42,294	46,376	110
1996	41,431	45,277	109
1995	40,845	44,564	109
1994	39,613	43,127	109
1993	39,165	42,840	109
1992	39,364	42,774	109
1991	39,679	42,573	107
1990	40,865	43,597	107
Percent change			
2000 to 2003	–3.4%	–2.0%	–
1990 to 2003	6.0	9.6	–

Note: Non-Hispanic whites in 2002 and 2003 are those identifying their race as white alone and not Hispanic. (–) means not applicable.
Source: Bureau of the Census, Current Population Surveys, Internet site http://www.census.gov/hhes/income/histinc/h05.html; calculations by New Strategist

Table 5.44 High-Income Non-Hispanic White Households, 2003

(number and percent distribution of non-Hispanic white households with incomes of $100,000 or more, 2003; households in thousands as of 2004)

	total	percent
TOTAL NON-HISPANIC WHITE HOUSEHOLDS	**81,148**	**100.0%**
$100,000 or more	**14,031**	**17.3**
$100,000 to $149,999	8,797	10.8
$150,000 to $199,999	2,774	3.4
$200,000 to $249,999	1,105	1.4
$250,000 or more	1,355	1.7

Note: Non-Hispanic whites are those identifying themselves as being white alone and not Hispanic.
Source: Bureau of the Census, 2004 Current Population Survey, Internet site http://pubdb3.census.gov/macro/032004/hhinc/new06_000.htm; calculations by New Strategist

Table 5.45 Non-Hispanic White Household Income by Age of Householder, 2003

(number and percent distribution of non-Hispanic white households by household income and age of householder, 2003; households in thousands as of 2004)

	total	15 to 24	25 to 34	35 to 44	45 to 54	55 to 64	aged 65 or older total	65 to 74	75 or older
Non-Hispanic white households	**81,148**	**3,979**	**11,988**	**15,902**	**17,099**	**13,037**	**19,144**	**9,262**	**9,882**
Under $10,000	5,840	567	583	700	807	976	2,207	831	1,377
$10,000 to $19,999	10,103	650	919	932	964	1,261	5,378	1,885	3,493
$20,000 to $29,999	9,514	749	1,299	1,265	1,261	1,296	3,645	1,680	1,964
$30,000 to $39,999	8,830	629	1,582	1,483	1,504	1,406	2,227	1,203	1,023
$40,000 to $49,999	7,752	423	1,427	1,594	1,557	1,232	1,519	894	625
$50,000 to $59,999	6,855	295	1,340	1,617	1,455	1,112	1,036	638	398
$60,000 to $69,999	5,849	225	1,064	1,445	1,436	924	752	463	289
$70,000 to $79,999	5,002	124	922	1,252	1,362	836	505	339	167
$80,000 to $89,999	4,023	98	720	1,081	1,118	654	351	228	123
$90,000 to $99,999	3,349	68	540	898	943	583	319	215	106
$100,000 or more	14,032	154	1,591	3,635	4,690	2,758	1,202	888	315
Median income	$47,777	$30,266	$50,971	$61,884	$66,811	$52,825	$24,910	$31,791	$20,298

PERCENT DISTRIBUTION BY INCOME

	total	15 to 24	25 to 34	35 to 44	45 to 54	55 to 64	aged 65 or older total	65 to 74	75 or older
Non-Hispanic white households	**100.0%**	**100.0%**	**100.0%**	**100.0%**	**100.0%**	**100.0%**	**100.0%**	**100.0%**	**100.0%**
Under $10,000	7.2	14.2	4.9	4.4	4.7	7.5	11.5	9.0	13.9
$10,000 to $19,999	12.5	16.3	7.7	5.9	5.6	9.7	28.1	20.4	35.3
$20,000 to $29,999	11.7	18.8	10.8	8.0	7.4	9.9	19.0	18.1	19.9
$30,000 to $39,999	10.9	15.8	13.2	9.3	8.8	10.8	11.6	13.0	10.4
$40,000 to $49,999	9.6	10.6	11.9	10.0	9.1	9.5	7.9	9.7	6.3
$50,000 to $59,999	8.4	7.4	11.2	10.2	8.5	8.5	5.4	6.9	4.0
$60,000 to $69,999	7.2	5.7	8.9	9.1	8.4	7.1	3.9	5.0	2.9
$70,000 to $79,999	6.2	3.1	7.7	7.9	8.0	6.4	2.6	3.7	1.7
$80,000 to $89,999	5.0	2.5	6.0	6.8	6.5	5.0	1.8	2.5	1.2
$90,000 to $99,999	4.1	1.7	.4.5	5.6	5.5	4.5	1.7	2.3	1.1
$100,000 or more	17.3	3.9	13.3	22.9	27.4	21.2	6.3	9.6	3.2

Note: Non-Hispanic whites are those identifying themselves as being white alone and not Hispanic.
Source: Bureau of the Census, 2004 Current Population Survey, Internet site http://pubdb3.census.gov/macro/032004/hhinc/new02_001.htm; calculations by New Strategist

Table 5.46 Non-Hispanic White Household Income by Household Type, 2003

(number and percent distribution of households headed by non-Hispanic whites by household income and household type, 2003; households in thousands as of 2004)

| | | family households | | | nonfamily households | | | |
| | | | female hh, no spouse present | male hh, no spouse present | female householder | | male householder | |
	total	married couples			total	living alone	total	living alone
Non-Hispanic white households	**81,148**	**44,197**	**7,115**	**2,710**	**15,089**	**13,072**	**12,037**	**9,402**
Under $10,000	5,840	866	724	116	2,757	2,658	1,378	1,276
$10,000 to $19,999	10,103	2,415	1,112	267	4,138	3,965	2,170	1,988
$20,000 to $29,999	9,514	3,891	1,159	377	2,425	2,205	1,660	1,406
$30,000 to $39,999	8,830	3,941	1,113	403	1,732	1,472	1,639	1,349
$40,000 to $49,999	7,752	4,147	774	302	1,212	979	1,318	988
$50,000 to $59,999	6,855	4,117	587	300	824	608	1,028	741
$60,000 to $69,999	5,849	3,917	502	185	523	353	721	475
$70,000 to $79,999	5,002	3,586	343	148	402	280	522	306
$80,000 to $89,999	4,023	3,001	215	155	270	142	381	252
$90,000 to $99,999	3,349	2,631	148	101	204	83	267	135
$100,000 or more	14,032	11,686	439	356	600	330	952	486
Median income	$47,777	$66,677	$34,686	$45,416	$22,307	$19,674	$34,280	$30,156

PERCENT DISTRIBUTION BY INCOME

Non-Hispanic white households	**100.0%**	**100.0%**	**100.0%**	**100.0%**	**100.0%**	**100.0%**	**100.0%**	**100.0%**
Under $10,000	7.2	2.0	10.2	4.3	18.3	20.3	11.4	13.6
$10,000 to $19,999	12.5	5.5	15.6	9.9	27.4	30.3	18.0	21.1
$20,000 to $29,999	11.7	8.8	16.3	13.9	16.1	16.9	13.8	15.0
$30,000 to $39,999	10.9	8.9	15.6	14.9	11.5	11.3	13.6	14.3
$40,000 to $49,999	9.6	9.4	10.9	11.1	8.0	7.5	10.9	10.5
$50,000 to $59,999	8.4	9.3	8.3	11.1	5.5	4.7	8.5	7.9
$60,000 to $69,999	7.2	8.9	7.1	6.8	3.5	2.7	6.0	5.1
$70,000 to $79,999	6.2	8.1	4.8	5.5	2.7	2.1	4.3	3.3
$80,000 to $89,999	5.0	6.8	3.0	5.7	1.8	1.1	3.2	2.7
$90,000 to $99,999	4.1	6.0	2.1	3.7	1.4	0.6	2.2	1.4
$100,000 or more	17.3	26.4	6.2	13.1	4.0	2.5	7.9	5.2

Note: Non-Hispanic whites are those identifying themselves as being white alone and not Hispanic.
Source: Bureau of the Census, 2004 Current Population Survey, Internet site http://pubdb3.census.gov/macro/032004/hhinc/new02_000.htm; calculations by New Strategist

Table 5.47 Income of Non-Hispanic White Men by Age, 2003

(number and percent distribution of non-Hispanic white men aged 15 or older by income and age, median income of men with income and of men working full-time, year-round, and percent working full-time, year-round, 2003; men in thousands as of 2004)

	total	under 25	25 to 34	35 to 44	45 to 54	55 to 64	65 or older
TOTAL NON-HISPANIC WHITE MEN	**77,336**	**12,939**	**11,912**	**14,682**	**14,963**	**10,647**	**12,194**
Without income	**4,801**	**3,367**	**323**	**363**	**356**	**266**	**126**
With income	**72,535**	**9,572**	**11,589**	**14,319**	**14,607**	**10,381**	**12,068**
Under $10,000	10,208	4,935	996	1,057	1,007	852	1,362
$10,000 to $19,999	12,070	2,199	1,641	1,333	1,387	1,396	4,116
$20,000 to $29,999	10,602	1,336	2,118	1,792	1,527	1,359	2,469
$30,000 to $39,999	9,520	643	2,193	2,098	1,948	1,324	1,313
$40,000 to $49,999	7,557	221	1,565	1,945	1,928	1,157	738
$50,000 to $59,999	5,809	100	993	1,548	1,641	958	571
$60,000 to $69,999	4,212	51	683	1,126	1,209	740	401
$70,000 to $79,999	3,023	31	479	758	976	556	225
$80,000 to $89,999	2,081	7	285	566	652	415	156
$90,000 to $99,999	1,386	19	143	389	425	264	148
$100,000 or more	6,064	30	492	1,709	1,906	1,361	566
Median income of men with income	$32,331	$9,424	$33,775	$43,105	$46,850	$41,291	$21,861
Median income of men working full-time	46,294	22,905	38,299	49,991	52,076	55,514	60,338
Percent of men working full-time	54.0%	22.2%	73.7%	77.2%	76.8%	57.4%	9.8%
TOTAL NON-HISPANIC WHITE MEN	**100.0%**	**100.0%**	**100.0%**	**100.0%**	**100.0%**	**100.0%**	**100.0%**
Without income	**6.2**	**26.0**	**2.7**	**2.5**	**2.4**	**2.5**	**1.0**
With income	**93.8**	**74.0**	**97.3**	**97.5**	**97.6**	**97.5**	**99.0**
Under $10,000	13.2	38.1	8.4	7.2	6.7	8.0	11.2
$10,000 to $19,999	15.6	17.0	13.8	9.1	9.3	13.1	33.8
$20,000 to $29,999	13.7	10.3	17.8	12.2	10.2	12.8	20.2
$30,000 to $39,999	12.3	5.0	18.4	14.3	13.0	12.4	10.8
$40,000 to $49,999	9.8	1.7	13.1	13.2	12.9	10.9	6.1
$50,000 to $59,999	7.5	0.8	8.3	10.5	11.0	9.0	4.7
$60,000 to $69,999	5.4	0.4	5.7	7.7	8.1	7.0	3.3
$70,000 to $79,999	3.9	0.2	4.0	5.2	6.5	5.2	1.8
$80,000 to $89,999	2.7	0.1	2.4	3.9	4.4	3.9	1.3
$90,000 to $99,999	1.8	0.1	1.2	2.6	2.8	2.5	1.2
$100,000 or more	7.8	0.2	4.1	11.6	12.7	12.8	4.6

Note: Non-Hispanic whites are those identifying themselves as being white alone and not Hispanic.
Source: Bureau of the Census, 2004 Current Population Survey, Internet site http://pubdb3.census.gov/macro/032004/perinc/new01_000.htm; calculations by New Strategist

Table 5.48 Income of Non-Hispanic White Women by Age, 2003

(number and percent distribution of non-Hispanic white women aged 15 or older by income and age, median income of women with income and of women working full-time, year-round, and percent working full-time, year-round, 2003; women in thousands as of 2004)

	total	under 25	25 to 34	35 to 44	45 to 54	55 to 64	65 or older
TOTAL NON-HISPANIC WHITE WOMEN	**82,120**	**12,455**	**11,988**	**14,878**	**15,257**	**11,401**	**16,142**
Without income	**7,634**	**3,270**	**1,048**	**1,060**	**968**	**917**	**372**
With income	**74,486**	**9,185**	**10,940**	**13,818**	**14,289**	**10,484**	**15,770**
Under $10,000	22,703	5,348	2,453	3,350	2,732	3,049	5,771
$10,000 to $19,999	16,573	2,105	2,017	2,321	2,351	1,902	5,875
$20,000 to $29,999	11,965	1,120	2,209	2,327	2,589	1,749	1,973
$30,000 to $39,999	8,676	438	1,891	1,958	2,130	1,257	1,000
$40,000 to $49,999	5,369	124	1,084	1,358	1,546	821	435
$50,000 to $59,999	3,121	28	492	817	957	573	255
$60,000 to $69,999	1,982	16	261	546	673	344	145
$70,000 to $79,999	1,277	3	186	345	391	260	93
$80,000 to $89,999	771	–	102	239	245	130	56
$90,000 to $99,999	438	2	45	126	151	73	40
$100,000 or more	1,610	3	202	431	523	327	125
Median income of women with income	$18,301	$7,388	$24,221	$25,127	$27,314	$21,461	$12,471
Median income of women working full-time	34,037	21,129	32,078	36,415	36,689	35,872	37,062
Percent of women working full-time	35.3%	16.5%	50.5%	49.5%	54.7%	38.6%	4.7%
TOTAL NON-HISPANIC WHITE WOMEN	**100.0%**	**100.0%**	**100.0%**	**100.0%**	**100.0%**	**100.0%**	**100.0%**
Without income	**9.3**	**26.3**	**8.7**	**7.1**	**6.3**	**8.0**	**2.3**
With income	**90.7**	**73.7**	**91.3**	**92.9**	**93.7**	**92.0**	**97.7**
Under $10,000	27.6	42.9	20.5	22.5	17.9	26.7	35.8
$10,000 to $19,999	20.2	16.9	16.8	15.6	15.4	16.7	36.4
$20,000 to $29,999	14.6	9.0	18.4	15.6	17.0	15.3	12.2
$30,000 to $39,999	10.6	3.5	15.8	13.2	14.0	11.0	6.2
$40,000 to $49,999	6.5	1.0	9.0	9.1	10.1	7.2	2.7
$50,000 to $59,999	3.8	0.2	4.1	5.5	6.3	5.0	1.6
$60,000 to $69,999	2.4	0.1	2.2	3.7	4.4	3.0	0.9
$70,000 to $79,999	1.6	0.0	1.6	2.3	2.6	2.3	0.6
$80,000 to $89,999	0.9	–	0.9	1.6	1.6	1.1	0.3
$90,000 to $99,999	0.5	0.0	0.4	0.8	1.0	0.6	0.2
$100,000 or more	2.0	0.0	1.7	2.9	3.4	2.9	0.8

Note: Non-Hispanic whites are those identifying themselves as being white alone and not Hispanic. (–) means sample is too small to make a reliable estimate.
Source: Bureau of the Census, 2004 Current Population Survey, Internet site http://pubdb3.census.gov/macro/032004/perinc/new01_000.htm; calculations by New Strategist

Table 5.49 Median Income of Non-Hispanic Whites Working Full-Time by Sex, 1990 to 2003

(median income of non-Hispanic whites working full-time, year-round by sex; index of non-Hispanic white to total population median income, and non-Hispanic white women's income as a percent of non-Hispanic white men's income, 1990 to 2003; percent change in income, 2000–03 and 1990–2003; in 2003 dollars)

	non-Hispanic white men		non-Hispanic white women		non-Hispanic white women's income as a percent of non-Hispanic white men's income
	median income	index white/total	median income	index white/total	
2003	$46,294	112	$34,037	108	73.5%
2002	46,187	111	33,088	104	71.6
2001	44,886	108	33,040	105	73.6
2000	45,213	109	33,100	106	73.2
1999	45,864	111	32,457	107	70.8
1998	44,973	110	31,882	105	70.9
1997	43,352	108	31,029	104	71.6
1996	42,489	109	30,347	104	71.4
1995	42,678	111	29,972	105	70.2
1994	42,219	109	30,064	105	71.2
1993	41,459	106	29,559	105	71.3
1992	41,840	106	29,222	103	69.8
1991	41,904	105	28,838	103	68.8
1990	42,104	106	28,919	103	68.7
Percent change					
2000 to 2003	2.4%	–	2.8%	1.1%	–
1990 to 2003	10.0	–	17.7	4.5	–

Note: Data for non-Hispanic whites in 2002 and 2003 are for those identifying themselves as being white alone and not Hispanic. The non-Hispanic white/total indexes are calculated by dividing the median income of non-Hispanic white men and women by the median income of total men and women and multiplying by 100. (–) means not applicable.
Source: Bureau of the Census, Current Population Surveys, Internet site http://www.census.gov/hhes/income/histinc/p36b.html; calculations by New Strategist

Table 5.50 Median Earnings of Non-Hispanic Whites Working Full-Time by Education and Sex, 2003

(median earnings of non-Hispanic whites aged 25 or older working full-time, year-round, by educational attainment and sex, and non-Hispanic white women's earnings as a percent of non-Hispanic white men's earnings, 2003)

	men	women	non-Hispanic white women's earnings as a percent of non-Hispanic white men's earnings
Total non-Hispanic whites	**$46,579**	**$33,536**	**72.0%**
Less than 9th grade	29,150	21,419	73.5
9th to 12th grade, no diploma	30,479	20,486	67.2
High school graduate	37,434	26,946	72.0
Some college, no degree	42,688	30,826	72.2
Associate's degree	45,140	34,266	75.9
Bachelor's degree or more	65,471	45,460	69.4

Note: Non-Hispanic whites are those identifying themselves as being white alone and not Hispanic.
Source: Bureau of the Census, 2004 Current Population Survey, Internet site http://pubdb3.census.gov/macro/032004/perinc/new03_000.htm; calculations by New Strategist

Table 5.51 Poverty Status of Non-Hispanic White Married Couples, 1990 to 2003

(total number of non-Hispanic white married couples, and number and percent below poverty level by presence of children under age 18 at home, 1990 to 2003; percent change in numbers and percentage point change in rates, 2000–03 and 1990–2003; married couples in thousands as of March the following year)

		in poverty	
	total	number	percent
Total non-Hispanic white married couples			
2003	44,200	1,575	3.6%
2002	44,109	1,628	3.7
2001	44,124	1,477	3.3
2000	44,278	1,435	3.2
1999	44,443	1,474	3.3
1998	43,669	1,639	3.8
1997	43,427	1,501	3.5
1996	43,276	1,628	3.8
1995	43,771	1,664	3.8
1994	44,178	1,915	4.3
1993	43,745	2,042	4.7
1992	43,661	1,978	4.5
1991	43,724	1,918	4.4
1990	43,682	1,799	4.1

	percent change		percentage point change
2000 to 2003	−0.2%	9.8%	0.4
1990 to 2003	1.2	−12.5	−0.5

Non-Hispanic white married couples with children			
2003	18,628	746	4.0%
2002	18,879	781	4.1
2001	19,076	696	3.6
2000	19,356	709	3.7
1999	19,209	743	3.9
1998	19,327	859	4.5
1997	19,588	842	4.3
1996	19,729	884	4.5
1995	19,866	948	4.8
1994	20,276	1,101	5.4
1993	20,166	1,263	6.3
1992	19,905	1,177	5.9
1991	19,845	1,152	5.8
1990	19,957	1,085	5.4

	percent change		percentage point change
2000 to 2003	−3.8%	5.2%	0.3
1990 to 2003	−6.7	−31.2	−1.4

Note: Data for non-Hispanic whites in 2002 and 2003 are for those identifying themselves as being white alone and not Hispanic.
Source: Bureau of the Census, Current Population Surveys, Internet site http://www.census.gov/hhes/www/poverty/histpov/hstpov4.html; calculations by New Strategist

Table 5.52   Poverty Status of Non-Hispanic White Female-Headed Families, 1990 to 2003

(total number of non-Hispanic white female-headed families, and number and percent below poverty level by presence of children under age 18 at home, 1990 to 2003; percent change in numbers and percentage point change in rates, 2000–03 and 1990–2003; families in thousands as of March the following year)

		in poverty	
	total	number	percent
Total non-Hispanic white female-headed families			
2003	7,121	1,455	20.4%
2002	7,072	1,374	19.4
2001	6,886	1,305	19.0
2000	6,891	1,226	17.8
1999	6,770	1,248	18.4
1998	6,909	1,428	20.7
1997	6,826	1,598	23.4
1996	6,875	1,538	22.4
1995	6,792	1,463	21.5
1994	6,764	1,678	24.8
1993	6,798	1,699	25.0
1992	6,629	1,637	24.7
1991	6,553	1,610	24.6
1990	6,408	1,480	23.1

	percent change		percentage point change
2000 to 2003	3.3%	18.7%	2.6
1990 to 2003	11.1	−1.7	−2.7

Non-Hispanic white female-headed families with children			
2003	4,518	1,269	28.1%
2002	4,470	1,170	26.2
2001	4,414	1,135	25.7
2000	4,305	1,058	24.6
1999	4,233	1,069	25.3
1998	4,427	1,275	28.8
1997	4,320	1,420	32.9
1996	4,357	1,351	31.0
1995	4,361	1,294	29.7
1994	4,386	1,471	33.5
1993	4,330	1,506	34.8
1992	4,150	1,474	35.5
1991	4,067	1,429	35.1
1990	3,929	1,317	33.5

	percent change		percentage point change
2000 to 2003	4.9%	19.9%	3.5
1990 to 2003	15.0	−3.6	−5.4

Note: Data for non-Hispanic whites in 2002 and 2003 are for those identifying themselves as being white alone and not Hispanic.
Source: Bureau of the Census, Current Population Surveys, Internet site http://www.census.gov/hhes/www/poverty/histpov/hstpov4.html; calculations by New Strategist

Table 5.53 Poverty Status of Non-Hispanic White Male-Headed Families, 1990 to 2003

(total number of non-Hispanic white male-headed families, and number and percent below poverty level by presence of children under age 18 at home, 1990 to 2003; percent change in numbers and percentage point change in rates, 2000–03 and 1990–2003; families in thousands as of March the following year)

	total	in poverty number	in poverty percent
Total non-Hispanic white male-headed families			
2003	2,710	241	8.9%
2002	2,679	207	7.7
2001	2,618	270	10.3
2000	2,559	236	9.2
1999	2,481	231	9.3
1998	2,530	197	7.8
1997	2,622	258	9.8
1996	2,475	267	10.8
1995	2,298	257	11.2
1994	2,087	241	11.5
1993	1,927	248	12.9
1992	2,011	225	11.2
1991	2,011	190	9.4
1990	1,948	163	8.4

	percent change		percentage point change
2000 to 2003	5.9%	2.1%	−0.3
1990 to 2003	39.1	47.9	0.5

	total	in poverty number	in poverty percent
Non-Hispanic white male-headed families with children			
2003	1,358	170	12.5%
2002	1,315	137	10.4
2001	1,371	184	13.4
2000	1,404	173	12.3
1999	1,347	161	12.0
1998	1,355	148	10.9
1997	1,466	215	14.7
1996	1,295	190	14.7
1995	1,270	202	15.9
1994	1,072	161	15.0
1993	981	177	18.0
1992	1,034	166	16.1
1991	997	141	14.1
1990	878	119	13.6

	percent change		percentage point change
2000 to 2003	−3.3%	−1.7%	0.2
1990 to 2003	54.7	42.9	−1.1

Note: Data for non-Hispanic whites in 2002 and 2003 are for those identifying themselves as being white alone and not Hispanic.
Source: Bureau of the Census, Current Population Surveys, Internet site http://www.census.gov/hhes/www/poverty/histpov/hstpov4.html; calculations by New Strategist

Table 5.54 Poverty Status of Non-Hispanic Whites by Sex and Age, 2003

(total number of non-Hispanic whites, and number and percent below poverty level by sex and age, 2003; people in thousands as of 2004)

	total	in poverty	
		number	percent
Total non-Hispanic whites	**194,595**	**15,902**	**8.2%**
Under age 18	43,150	4,233	9.8
Aged 18 to 24	17,382	2,242	12.9
Aged 25 to 34	23,900	1,949	8.2
Aged 35 to 44	29,560	1,980	6.7
Aged 45 to 54	30,219	1,675	5.5
Aged 55 to 59	12,510	826	6.6
Aged 60 to 64	9,537	719	7.5
Aged 65 or older	28,335	2,277	8.0
Non-Hispanic white females	**99,287**	**9,024**	**9.1**
Under age 18	21,055	2,028	9.6
Aged 18 to 24	8,567	1,323	15.4
Aged 25 to 34	11,988	1,176	9.8
Aged 35 to 44	14,878	1,098	7.4
Aged 45 to 54	15,257	881	5.8
Aged 55 to 59	6,348	475	7.5
Aged 60 to 64	5,053	428	8.5
Aged 65 or older	16,142	1,617	10.0
Non-Hispanic white males	**95,307**	**6,878**	**7.2**
Under age 18	22,094	2,206	10.0
Aged 18 to 24	8,816	919	10.4
Aged 25 to 34	11,912	773	6.5
Aged 35 to 44	14,682	883	6.0
Aged 45 to 54	14,963	794	5.3
Aged 55 to 59	6,162	351	5.7
Aged 60 to 64	4,485	292	6.5
Aged 65 or older	12,194	661	5.4

Note: Non-Hispanic whites are those identifying themselves as being white alone and not Hispanic.
Source: Bureau of the Census, 2004 Current Population Survey, Internet site http://pubdb3.census.gov/macro/032004/pov/new01_100.htm

Thirty-Six Percent of White Workers Are Employed in Managerial or Professional Occupations

Seventy-four percent of white men and 59 percent of white women were in the labor force in 2004. Because whites comprise the great majority of the population, their labor force participation rate closely matches that of the total population. (The Bureau of Labor Statistics' employment figures for whites include most Hispanics, since Hispanics may be of any race and most are white.)

The largest share of whites (36 percent) is employed in managerial or professional occupations. Another 26 percent work in sales and office occupations. Only 15 percent of whites work in service occupations.

Forty-three percent of non-Hispanic white households have two or more earners. Among non-Hispanic white couples, the 56 percent majority are dual earners. Only 20 percent have only the husband in the labor force.

Between 2002 and 2012, the number of non-Hispanic white workers will expand only 3 percent, much more slowly than the number of Asian, black, or Hispanic workers. In the year 2012, non-Hispanic white workers will account for just 66 percent of the labor force.

■ Non-Hispanic white households have higher incomes than black or Hispanic households because a larger share are headed by dual-earner married couples.

Three out of four white men are in the labor force

(percent of whites aged 16 or older in the labor force, by sex, 2004)

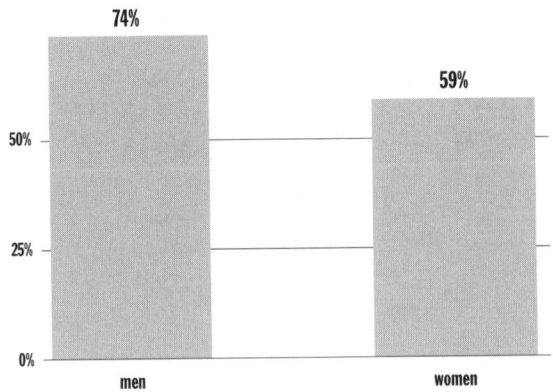

Table 5.55 Labor Force Participation Rate of Whites by Age and Sex, 2004

(percent of whites aged 16 or older in the civilian labor force, by age and sex, 2004)

	total	men	women
Total whites	**66.3%**	**74.1%**	**58.9%**
Aged 16 to 19	47.1	47.4	46.7
Aged 20 to 24	77.1	82.1	71.9
Aged 25 to 29	83.3	92.6	73.7
Aged 30 to 34	83.7	93.7	73.6
Aged 35 to 39	83.8	93.7	73.9
Aged 40 to 44	84.4	92.5	76.3
Aged 45 to 49	84.6	90.6	78.7
Aged 50 to 54	81.0	86.6	75.4
Aged 55 to 59	71.9	78.6	65.6
Aged 60 to 64	51.9	58.3	46.0
Aged 65 or older	14.6	19.1	11.2
Aged 65 to 69	28.3	33.3	23.9
Aged 70 to 74	15.7	19.7	12.3
Aged 75 or older	6.2	9.1	4.3

Note: Whites include white Hispanics. The civilian labor force equals the number of employed plus the number of unemployed.
Source: Bureau of Labor Statistics, 2004 Current Population Survey, http://www.bls.gov/cps/home.htm

Table 5.56 Employment Status of Whites by Sex and Age, 2004

(number and percent of whites aged 16 or older in the civilian labor force by sex, age, and employment status, 2004; numbers in thousands)

		civilian labor force			unemployed	
	civilian non-institutional population	total	percent of population	employed	number	percent of labor force
Total whites	**182,643**	**121,086**	**66.3%**	**115,239**	**5,847**	**4.8%**
Aged 16 to 19	12,599	5,929	47.1	5,039	890	15.0
Aged 20 to 24	15,817	12,192	77.1	11,233	959	7.9
Aged 25 to 34	30,585	25,548	83.5	24,337	1,211	4.7
Aged 35 to 44	34,845	29,305	84.1	28,176	1,130	3.9
Aged 45 to 54	34,005	28,181	82.9	27,228	953	3.4
Aged 55 to 64	24,549	15,522	63.2	14,965	557	3.6
Aged 65 or older	30,245	4,408	14.6	4,260	148	3.3
Total white men	**89,044**	**65,994**	**74.1**	**62,712**	**3,282**	**5.0**
Aged 16 to 19	6,429	3,050	47.4	2,553	497	16.3
Aged 20 to 24	8,024	6,586	82.1	6,026	560	8.5
Aged 25 to 34	15,486	14,429	93.2	13,735	694	4.8
Aged 35 to 44	17,404	16,192	93.0	15,572	620	3.8
Aged 45 to 54	16,834	14,934	88.7	14,418	516	3.5
Aged 55 to 64	11,922	8,326	69.8	8,018	307	3.7
Aged 65 or older	12,946	2,478	19.1	2,390	88	3.5
Total white women	**93,599**	**55,092**	**58.9**	**52,527**	**2,565**	**4.7**
Aged 16 to 19	6,169	2,879	46.7	2,486	393	13.6
Aged 20 to 24	7,794	5,606	71.9	5,207	399	7.1
Aged 25 to 34	15,099	11,119	73.6	10,602	516	4.6
Aged 35 to 44	17,441	13,114	75.2	12,604	510	3.9
Aged 45 to 54	17,170	13,247	77.1	12,810	437	3.3
Aged 55 to 64	12,627	7,197	57.0	6,947	250	3.5
Aged 65 or older	17,299	1,930	11.2	1,870	60	3.1

Note: Whites include white Hispanics. The civilian labor force equals the number of employed plus the number of unemployed. The civilian population equals the number in the labor force plus the number not in the labor force.
Source: Bureau of Labor Statistics, 2004 Current Population Survey, http://www.bls.gov/cps/home.htm

Table 5.57 White Workers by Occupation, 2004

(total number of employed persons aged 16 or older in the civilian labor force, number and percent distribution of employed whites, and white share of total, by occupation, 2004; numbers in thousands)

	total	white number	white percent distribution	white share of total
TOTAL EMPLOYED	**139,252**	**115,239**	**100.0%**	**82.8%**
Management, professional and related occupations	**48,532**	**41,027**	**35.6**	**84.5**
Management, business, and financial operations	20,235	17,590	15.3	86.9
Management occupations	14,555	12,873	11.2	88.4
Business and financial operations occupations	5,860	4,717	4.1	80.5
Professional and related occupations	28,297	23,438	20.3	82.8
Computer and mathematical occupations	3,140	2,410	2.1	76.8
Architecture and engineering occupations	2,760	2,343	2.0	84.9
Life, physical, and social science occupations	1,365	1,143	1.0	83.7
Community and social services occupations	2,170	1,650	1.4	76.0
Legal occupations	1,554	1,380	1.2	88.8
Education, training, and library occupations	7,900	6,741	5.8	85.3
Arts, design, entertainment, sports, and media occupations	2,687	2,336	2.0	86.9
Health care practitioner and technical occupations	6,721	5,435	4.7	80.9
Service occupations	**22,720**	**17,544**	**15.2**	**77.2**
Health care support occupations	2,921	1,991	1.7	68.2
Protective service occupations	2,847	2,197	1.9	77.2
Food preparation and serving-related occupations	7,279	5,854	5.1	80.4
Building and grounds cleaning and maintenance occupations	5,185	4,094	3.6	79.0
Personal care and service occupations	4,488	3,407	3.0	75.9
Sales and office occupations	**35,464**	**29,399**	**25.5**	**82.9**
Sales and related occupations	15,983	13,557	11.8	84.8
Office and administrative support occupations	19,481	15,842	13.7	81.3
Natural resources, construction, maintenance occupations	**14,582**	**12,928**	**11.2**	**88.7**
Farming, fishing, and forestry occupations	991	885	0.8	89.3
Construction and extraction occupations	8,522	7,642	6.6	89.7
Installation, maintenance, and repair occupations	5,069	4,401	3.8	86.8
Production, transportation, and material moving occupations	**17,954**	**14,340**	**12.4**	**79.9**
Production occupations	9,462	7,594	6.6	80.3
Transportation and material moving occupations	8,491	6,746	5.9	79.4

Note: Whites include white Hispanics.
Source: Bureau of Labor Statistics, 2004 Current Population Survey, Internet site http://www.bls.gov/cps/home.htm; calculations by New Strategist

Table 5.58 White Workers by Industry, 2004

(total number of employed people aged 16 or older in the civilian labor force; number and percent distribution of employed whites, and white share of total, by industry, 2004; numbers in thousands)

	total	white number	white percent distribution	white share of total
Total employed	**139,252**	**115,238**	**100.0%**	**82.8%**
Agriculture, forestry, fishing, and hunting	2,232	2,100	1.8	94.1
Mining	539	498	0.4	92.4
Construction	10,768	9,741	8.5	90.5
Manufacturing	16,484	13,766	11.9	83.5
Durable goods	10,329	8,717	7.6	84.4
Nondurable goods	6,155	5,050	4.4	82.0
Wholesale and retail trade	20,869	17,574	15.3	84.2
Wholesale trade	4,600	3,976	3.5	86.4
Retail trade	16,269	13,598	11.8	83.6
Transportation and utilities	7,013	5,535	4.8	78.9
Information	3,463	2,857	2.5	82.5
Financial activities	9,969	8,378	7.3	84.0
Professional and business services	14,108	11,837	10.3	83.9
Educational and health services	28,719	22,886	19.9	79.7
Leisure and hospitality	11,820	9,496	8.2	80.3
Other services	6,903	5,626	4.9	81.5
Other services, except private households	6,124	4,998	4.3	81.6
Private households	779	628	0.5	80.6
Public administration	6,365	4,944	4.3	77.7

Note: Whites includes white Hispanics.
Source: Bureau of Labor Statistics, 2004 Current Population Survey, Internet site http://www.bls.gov/cps/home.htm; calculations by New Strategist

Table 5.59 White Workers by Full-Time and Part-Time Status, Age, and Sex, 2004

(number and percent distribution of employed whites aged 16 or older by age, employment status, and sex, 2004; numbers in thousands)

	men			women		
	total	full-time	part-time	total	full-time	part-time
Total employed whites	**62,712**	**55,926**	**6,786**	**52,527**	**38,240**	**14,287**
Aged 16 to 19	2,553	921	1,632	2,486	576	1,910
Aged 20 to 24	6,026	4,677	1,349	5,206	3,312	1,894
Aged 25 to 54	43,725	41,744	1,981	36,016	28,368	7,648
Aged 55 or older	10,409	8,584	1,825	8,817	5,983	2,834
PERCENT DISTRIBUTION BY EMPLOYMENT STATUS						
Total employed whites	**100.0%**	**89.2%**	**10.8%**	**100.0%**	**72.8%**	**27.2%**
Aged 16 to 19	100.0	36.1	63.9	100.0	23.2	76.8
Aged 20 to 24	100.0	77.6	22.4	100.0	63.6	36.4
Aged 25 to 54	100.0	95.5	4.5	100.0	78.8	21.2
Aged 55 or older	100.0	82.5	17.5	100.0	67.9	32.1
PERCENT DISTRIBUTION BY AGE						
Total employed whites	**100.0%**	**100.0%**	**100.0%**	**100.0%**	**100.0%**	**100.0%**
Aged 16 to 19	4.1	1.6	24.0	4.7	1.5	13.4
Aged 20 to 24	9.6	8.4	19.9	9.9	8.7	13.3
Aged 25 to 54	69.7	74.6	29.2	68.6	74.2	53.5
Aged 55 or older	16.6	15.3	26.9	16.8	15.6	19.8

Note: Whites include white Hispanics.
Source: Bureau of Labor Statistics, 2004 Current Population Survey, Internet site http://www.bls.gov/cps/home.htm; calculations by New Strategist

Table 5.60 White Workers by Educational Attainment, 2004

(number of total people and whites aged 25 or older in the civilian labor force, white labor force participation rate, distribution of whites in the labor force, and white share of total labor force, by educational attainment, 2004; numbers in thousands)

	total labor force	white labor force			
		number	participation rate	percent distribution	share of total
Total aged 25 or older	**125,133**	**102,965**	**66.8%**	**100.0%**	**82.3%**
Not a high school graduate	12,470	10,086	46.0	9.8	80.9
High school graduate only	37,834	30,925	62.4	30.0	81.7
Some college	22,298	18,144	69.7	17.6	81.4
Associate's degree	12,141	10,157	76.6	9.9	83.7
Bachelor's degree or more	40,390	33,653	77.5	32.7	83.3

Note: Whites include white Hispanics.
Source: Bureau of Labor Statistics, 2004 Current Population Survey, Internet site http://www.bls.gov/cps/home.htm; calculations by New Strategist

Table 5.61 White Workers by Job Tenure and Sex, 2004

(total number of employed white wage and salary workers aged 16 or older and percent distribution by tenure with current employer, by sex, 2004; numbers in thousands)

	total	men	women
Total white workers, number	**100,243**	**52,758**	**47,485**
Total white workers, percent	**100.0%**	**100.0%**	**100.0%**
12 months or less	22.7	22.3	23.2
13 to 23 months	7.1	6.7	7.6
2 years	5.4	5.3	5.5
3 to 4 years	18.2	17.9	18.5
5 to 9 years	19.6	19.3	20.0
10 to 14 years	10.2	10.3	10.1
15 to 19 years	6.6	6.7	6.4
20 or more years	10.2	11.5	8.7

Note: Whites include white Hispanics. Whites include only those identifying themselves as being white alone.
Source: Bureau of Labor Statistics, 2004 Current Population Survey, Internet site http://www.bls.gov/cps/home.htm; calculations by New Strategist

Table 5.62 Non-Hispanic White Households by Number of Earners, 2004

(number of total households, number and percent distribution of non-Hispanic white households and non-Hispanic white share of total, by number of earners per household, 2004; numbers in thousands)

		non-Hispanic white		
	total	number	percent distribution	share of total
Total households	**112,000**	**81,148**	**100.0%**	**72.5%**
No earners	23,932	18,451	22.7	77.1
One earner	40,769	27,933	34.4	68.5
Two or more earners	47,299	34,764	42.8	73.5
Two earners	37,917	28,138	34.7	74.2
Three earners	6,998	4,980	6.1	71.2
Four or more earners	2,384	1,646	2.0	69.0
Average number of earners per household	1.36	1.33	–	–

Note: Non-Hispanic whites include those identifying themselves as being white alone and not Hispanic. (–) means not applicable.
Source: Bureau of the Census, 2004 Current Population Survey, Annual Social and Economic Supplement, Internet site http://pubdb3.census.gov/macro/032004/hhinc/new01_000.htm; calculations by New Strategist

Table 5.63 Non-Hispanic White Married Couples by Labor Force Status of Husband and Wife, 2003

(number and percent distribution of non-Hispanic white married couples aged 20 or older by age of householder and labor force status of husband and wife, 2003; numbers in thousands)

	total	husband and/or wife in labor force			neither husband nor wife in labor force
		husband and wife	husband only	wife only	
Total non-Hispanic white couples	**44,052**	**24,793**	**8,852**	**2,655**	**7,753**
Aged 20 to 24	821	518	237	46	20
Aged 25 to 29	2,589	1,838	646	76	28
Aged 30 to 34	3,998	2,812	1,035	79	71
Aged 35 to 39	4,718	3,321	1,189	135	73
Aged 40 to 44	5,479	3,968	1,254	178	78
Aged 45 to 54	10,479	7,729	1,986	492	271
Aged 55 to 64	7,825	3,895	1,628	929	1,374
Aged 65 or older	8,144	710	877	720	5,838
Total non-Hispanic white couples	**100.0%**	**56.3%**	**20.1%**	**6.0%**	**17.6%**
Aged 20 to 24	100.0	63.1	28.9	5.6	2.4
Aged 25 to 29	100.0	71.0	25.0	2.9	1.1
Aged 30 to 34	100.0	70.3	25.9	2.0	1.8
Aged 35 to 39	100.0	70.4	25.2	2.9	1.5
Aged 40 to 44	100.0	72.4	22.9	3.2	1.4
Aged 45 to 54	100.0	73.8	19.0	4.7	2.6
Aged 55 to 64	100.0	49.8	20.8	11.9	17.6
Aged 65 or older	100.0	8.7	10.8	8.8	71.7

Note: Non-Hispanic whites include those identifying themselves as being white alone and not Hispanic.
Source: Bureau of the Census, America's Families and Living Arrangements: 2003, detailed tables, Internet site http://www
.census.gov/population/www/socdemo/hh-fam/cps2003.html; calculations by New Strategist

Table 5.64 White Minimum Wage Workers by Sex, 2004

(number and percent distribution of total and white wage-and-salary workers aged 16 or older paid hourly rates and those paid at or below minimum wage, by sex, 2004; numbers in thousands)

	total paid hourly rates	at or below minimum wage		
		total	at $5.15/hour	below $5.15/hour
Total workers aged 16 or older	**73,939**	**2,003**	**520**	**1,483**
White workers aged 16 or older	59,877	1,681	395	1,286
White men	30,255	555	161	393
White women	29,621	1,126	234	892
PERCENT DISTRIBUTION BY RACE/SEX				
Total workers aged 16 or older	**100.0%**	**100.0%**	**100.0%**	**100.0%**
White workers aged 16 or older	81.0	83.9	76.0	86.7
White men	40.9	27.7	31.0	26.5
White women	40.1	56.2	45.0	60.1
PERCENT DISTRIBUTION BY WAGE STATUS				
Total workers aged 16 or older	**100.0%**	**2.7%**	**0.7%**	**2.0%**
White workers aged 16 or older	100.0	2.8	0.7	2.1
White men	100.0	1.8	0.5	1.3
White women	100.0	3.8	0.8	3.0

Note: Whites include white Hispanics.
Source: Bureau of Labor Statistics, 2004 Current Population Survey, Internet site http://www.bls.gov/cps/home.htm

Table 5.65 White Multiple Job Holders by Sex, 2004

(total number of employed people aged 16 or older who hold more than one job, number and percent of whites holding more than one job, and white share of total, by sex, 2004; numbers in thousands)

		white multiple job holders		
	total	number	percent	share of total
Total multiple job holders	**7,473**	**6,357**	**5.5%**	**85.1%**
Men	3,835	3,266	5.2	85.2
Women	3,638	3,091	5.9	85.0

Note: Whites include white Hispanics.
Source: Bureau of Labor Statistics, 2004 Current Population Survey, Internet site http://www.bls.gov/cps/home.htm

Table 5.66 Union Representation of White Workers by Sex, 2004

(number of employed white wage and salary workers aged 16 or older, number and percent represented by unions, and median weekly earnings of those working full-time by union representation status, by sex, 2004; number in thousands)

	total	men	women
Total employed whites	**101,340**	**53,432**	**47,908**
Number represented by unions	13,657	7,854	5,803
Percent represented by unions	13.5%	14.7%	12.1%
Median weekly earnings of white full-time workers	**$657**	**$732**	**$584**
White workers represented by unions	802	854	734
White workers not represented by unions	626	704	557

Note: Workers represented by unions are either members of a labor union or similar employee association or workers who report no union affiliation but whose jobs are covered by a union or an employee association contract. Whites include white Hispanics.
Source: Bureau of Labor Statistics, 2004 Current Population Survey, Internet site http://www.bls.gov/cps/home.htm

Table 5.67 Non-Hispanic White Labor Force Projections, 2002 and 2012

(number and percent of total people and non-Hispanic whites aged 16 or older in the civilian labor force by sex, 2002 and 2012; percent change in number and percentage point change in rate, 2002–12; numbers in thousands)

	2002	2012	percent change
NUMBER			
Total labor force	**144,863**	**162,269**	**12.0%**
Non-Hispanic white labor force	103,348	106,237	2.8
Total men in labor force	**77,500**	**85,252**	**10.0**
Non-Hispanic white men in labor force	55,340	56,849	2.7
Total women in labor force	**67,363**	**77,017**	**14.3**
Non-Hispanic white women in labor force	48,008	49,388	2.9

	2002	2012	percentage point change
PARTICIPATION RATE			
Total people	**66.6%**	**67.2%**	**0.6**
Total non-Hispanic whites	66.5	65.7	−0.8
Total men	**74.1**	**73.1**	**−1.0**
Non-Hispanic white men	73.8	72.4	−1.4
Total women	**59.6**	**61.6**	**2.0**
Non-Hispanic white women	59.6	59.4	−0.2

Note: Non-Hispanic whites include only those who identified themselves as being white alone and not Hispanic.
Source: Bureau of Labor Statistics, "Labor Force Projections to 2012: The graying of the U.S. workforce," Monthly Labor Review, February 2004, Internet site http://www.bls.gov/opub/mlr/2004/02/art3exc.htm; calculations by New Strategist

Married Couples Head Most Non-Hispanic White Households

Non-Hispanic whites account for 72 percent of the nation's 112 million households. The proportion ranges from a low of 60 percent among householders under age 25 to a high of 83 percent among householders aged 65 or older.

Married couples account for the 54 percent majority of non-Hispanic white households. Only 9 percent are female-headed families. People who live alone head a substantial 28 percent of non-Hispanic white households. Among non-Hispanic white women aged 75 or older, 51 percent live by themselves.

Only 29 percent of non-Hispanic white households include children under age 18. Even among non-Hispanic white married couples, just 41 percent have children under age 18 living with them. Seventy-seven percent of non-Hispanic white children live with both parents, while 16 percent live with only their mother.

Sixty-one percent of non-Hispanic white men aged 18 or older are currently married. The proportion is a slightly smaller 57 percent among non-Hispanic white women. Twenty-three percent of non-Hispanic white men have ever divorced, with the proportion peaking at 43 percent among men aged 50 to 59. The figures are even higher for non-Hispanic white women: 25 percent have been divorced, and the proportion reaches 40 percent among women in their fifties.

■ Non-Hispanic white households are more likely than average to be headed by people living alone because of the older age of the non-Hispanic white population.

Many non-Hispanic white households are headed by people living alone

(percent distribution of non-Hispanic white households, by household type, 2004)

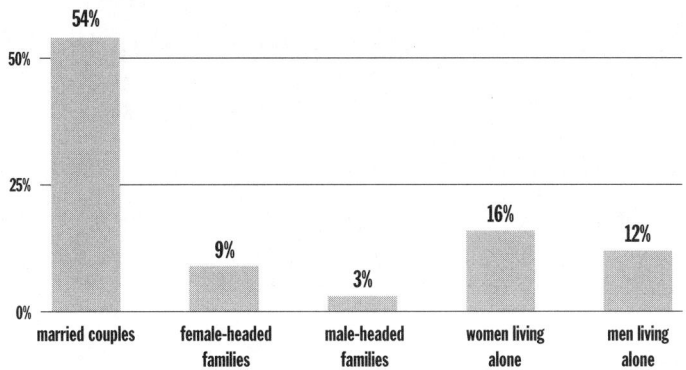

Table 5.68 Non-Hispanic White Households by Age of Householder, 2004

(number of total households, number and percent distribution of non-Hispanic white households, and non-Hispanic white share of total, by age of householder, 2004, numbers in thousands)

	total	non-Hispanic white number	percent distribution	share of total
Total households	**112,000**	**81,148**	**100.0%**	**72.5%**
Under age 25	6,610	3,979	4.9	60.2
Aged 25 to 29	8,737	5,480	6.8	62.7
Aged 30 to 34	10,421	6,508	8.0	62.5
Aged 35 to 39	10,997	7,335	9.0	66.7
Aged 40 to 44	12,225	8,567	10.6	70.1
Aged 45 to 49	12,360	8,960	11.0	72.5
Aged 50 to 54	10,777	8,138	10.0	75.5
Aged 55 to 59	9,504	7,356	9.1	77.4
Aged 60 to 64	7,320	5,681	7.0	77.6
Aged 65 or older	23,048	19,144	23.6	83.1

Note: Non-Hispanic whites include only those who identify themselves as being white alone and not Hispanic.
Source: Bureau of the Census, 2004 Current Population Survey Annual Social and Economic Supplement, Internet site http://pubdb3.census.gov/macro/032004/hhinc/toc.htm; calculations by New Strategist

Table 5.69 Non-Hispanic White Households by Household Type, 2004

(number of total households, number and percent distribution of non-Hispanic white households, and non-Hispanic white share of total, by type, 2004; numbers in thousands)

	total	non-Hispanic white number	percent distribution	share of total
TOTAL HOUSEHOLDS	**112,000**	**81,148**	**100.0%**	**72.5%**
Family households	**76,217**	**54,022**	**66.6**	**70.9**
Married couples	57,719	44,197	54.5	76.6
Female householder, no spouse present	13,781	7,115	8.8	51.6
Male householder, no spouse present	4,717	2,710	3.3	57.5
Nonfamily households	**35,783**	**27,126**	**33.4**	**75.8**
Female householder	19,647	15,089	18.6	76.8
Living alone	17,024	13,072	16.1	76.8
Male householder	16,136	12,037	14.8	74.6
Living alone	12,562	9,402	11.6	74.8

Note: Non-Hispanic whites include only those identifying themselves as being white alone and not Hispanic.
Source: Bureau of the Census, 2004 Current Population Survey Annual Social and Economic Supplement, Internet site http://pubdb3.census.gov/macro/032004/hhinc/toc.htm; calculations by New Strategist

Table 5.70 Non-Hispanic White Households by Age of Householder and Household Type, 2004

(number and percent distribution of non-Hispanic white households by age of householder and household type, 2004; numbers in thousands)

| | | family households | | | nonfamily households | | | |
| | | | female hh, | male hh, | female householder | | male householder | |
	total	married couples	no spouse present	no spouse present	total	living alone	total	living alone
Total non-Hispanic white households	**81,148**	**44,197**	**7,115**	**2,710**	**15,089**	**13,072**	**12,037**	**9,402**
Under age 25	3,979	905	569	339	1,073	498	1,092	533
Aged 25 to 34	11,988	6,432	1,239	460	1,545	1,068	2,312	1,529
Aged 35 to 44	15,902	9,905	1,864	673	1,277	1,020	2,184	1,706
Aged 45 to 54	17,098	10,533	1,463	636	2,072	1,766	2,394	1,973
Aged 55 to 64	13,037	7,986	809	283	2,328	2,098	1,631	1,383
Aged 65 or older	19,144	8,436	1,170	319	6,794	6,621	2,424	2,277

PERCENT DISTRIBUTION BY HOUSEHOLD TYPE

Total non-Hispanic white households	**100.0%**	**54.5%**	**8.8%**	**3.3%**	**18.6%**	**16.1%**	**14.8%**	**11.6%**
Under age 25	100.0	22.7	14.3	8.5	27.0	12.5	27.4	13.4
Aged 25 to 34	100.0	53.7	10.3	3.8	12.9	8.9	19.3	12.8
Aged 35 to 44	100.0	62.3	11.7	4.2	8.0	6.4	13.7	10.7
Aged 45 to 54	100.0	61.6	8.6	3.7	12.1	10.3	14.0	11.5
Aged 55 to 64	100.0	61.3	6.2	2.2	17.9	16.1	12.5	10.6
Aged 65 or older	100.0	44.1	6.1	1.7	35.5	34.6	12.7	11.9

PERCENT DISTRIBUTION BY AGE

Total non-Hispanic white households	**100.0%**	**100.0%**	**100.0%**	**100.0%**	**100.0%**	**100.0%**	**100.0%**	**100.0%**
Under age 25	4.9	2.0	8.0	12.5	7.1	3.8	9.1	5.7
Aged 25 to 34	14.8	14.6	17.4	17.0	10.2	8.2	19.2	16.3
Aged 35 to 44	19.6	22.4	26.2	24.8	8.5	7.8	18.1	18.1
Aged 45 to 54	21.1	23.8	20.6	23.5	13.7	13.5	19.9	21.0
Aged 55 to 64	16.1	18.1	11.4	10.4	15.4	16.0	13.5	14.7
Aged 65 or older	23.6	19.1	16.4	11.8	45.0	50.7	20.1	24.2

Note: Non-Hispanic whites include only those identifying themselves as being white alone and not Hispanic.
Source: Bureau of the Census, 2004 Current Population Survey Annual Social and Economic Supplement, Internet site http:// pubdb3.census.gov/macro/032004/hhinc/toc.htm; calculations by New Strategist

Table 5.71 Non-Hispanic White Households by Size, 2004

(number of total households, number and percent distribution of non-Hispanic white households, and non-Hispanic white share of total, by size, 2004; numbers in thousands)

	total	non-Hispanic white number	percent distribution	share of total
Total households	**112,000**	**81,148**	**100.0%**	**72.5%**
One person	29,586	22,474	27.7	76.0
Two people	37,366	29,547	36.4	79.1
Three people	17,968	12,169	15.0	67.7
Four people	16,065	10,809	13.3	67.3
Five people	7,150	4,280	5.3	59.9
Six people	2,476	1,289	1.6	52.1
Seven or more people	1,388	580	0.7	41.8
Average number of persons per household	2.57	2.43	–	–

Note: Non-Hispanic whites include only those identifying themselves as being white alone and not Hispanic. (–) means not applicable.
Source: Bureau of the Census, 2004 Current Population Survey Annual Social and Economic Supplement, Internet site http:// pubdb3.census.gov/macro/032004/hhinc/toc.htm; calculations by New Strategist

Table 5.72 Non-Hispanic Whites Living Alone by Sex and Age, 2004

(total number of non-Hispanic white households, number and percent distribution of non-Hispanic white single-person households, and single-person household share of total, by age of householder, 2004; numbers in thousands)

		living alone		
	total	number	percent distribution	share of total
Total non-Hispanic whites	**159,456**	**22,474**	**100.0%**	**14.1%**
Under age 25	25,394	1,031	4.6	4.1
Aged 25 to 34	23,900	2,597	11.6	10.9
Aged 35 to 44	29,560	2,726	12.1	9.2
Aged 45 to 54	30,219	3,739	16.6	12.4
Aged 55 to 64	22,048	3,481	15.5	15.8
Aged 65 to 74	14,519	3,336	14.8	23.0
Aged 75 or older	13,816	5,562	24.7	40.3
Non-Hispanic white men	**77,336**	**9,402**	**100.0**	**12.2**
Under age 25	12,939	533	5.7	4.1
Aged 25 to 34	11,912	1,529	16.3	12.8
Aged 35 to 44	14,682	1,706	18.1	11.6
Aged 45 to 54	14,963	1,973	21.0	13.2
Aged 55 to 64	10,647	1,383	14.7	13.0
Aged 65 to 74	6,756	1,007	10.7	14.9
Aged 75 or older	5,438	1,270	13.5	23.4
Non-Hispanic white women	**82,120**	**13,072**	**100.0**	**15.9**
Under age 25	12,455	498	3.8	4.0
Aged 25 to 34	11,988	1,068	8.2	8.9
Aged 35 to 44	14,878	1,020	7.8	6.9
Aged 45 to 54	15,257	1,766	13.5	11.6
Aged 55 to 64	11,401	2,098	16.0	18.4
Aged 65 to 74	7,763	2,329	17.8	30.0
Aged 75 or older	8,378	4,292	32.8	51.2

Note: Non-Hispanic whites include only those identifying themselves as being white alone and not Hispanic.
Source: Bureau of the Census, 2004 Current Population Survey Annual Social and Economic Supplement, Internet site http:// pubdb3.census.gov/macro/032004/hhinc/toc.htm; calculations by New Strategist

Table 5.73 Non-Hispanic White Households by Age of Householder, Type of Household, and Presence of Children, 2003

(number and percent distribution of non-Hispanic white households by age of householder, type of household, and presence of own children under age 18, and average age of householder, 2003; numbers in thousands)

	all households		married couples		female-headed families		male-headed families	
	total	with children	total	with children	total	with children	total	with children
Total non-Hispanic white households	**81,166**	**23,378**	**44,101**	**18,242**	**7,070**	**3,960**	**2,674**	**1,176**
Under age 25	3,979	951	870	491	570	389	333	71
Aged 25 to 29	5,465	2,193	2,589	1,540	584	511	253	142
Aged 30 to 34	6,782	3,843	3,998	3,045	663	630	252	167
Aged 35 to 39	7,702	4,896	4,718	3,842	908	846	266	208
Aged 40 to 44	8,851	5,249	5,479	4,207	952	779	353	262
Aged 45 to 49	8,795	3,756	5,512	3,079	826	509	353	168
Aged 50 to 54	8,080	1,708	4,966	1,381	660	224	273	102
Aged 55 to 64	12,668	686	7,825	585	759	54	265	47
Aged 65 or older	18,844	96	8,144	72	1,148	17	326	8
Average age of householder	50.7	39.2	49.9	39.7	46.4	36.9	44.0	39.0

PERCENT OF HOUSEHOLDS WITH CHILDREN BY TYPE

	all households		married couples		female-headed families		male-headed families	
	total	with children	total	with children	total	with children	total	with children
Total non-Hispanic white households	**100.0%**	**28.8%**	**100.0%**	**41.4%**	**100.0%**	**56.0%**	**100.0%**	**44.0%**
Under age 25	100.0	23.9	100.0	56.4	100.0	68.2	100.0	21.3
Aged 25 to 29	100.0	40.1	100.0	59.5	100.0	87.5	100.0	56.1
Aged 30 to 34	100.0	56.7	100.0	76.2	100.0	95.0	100.0	66.3
Aged 35 to 39	100.0	63.6	100.0	81.4	100.0	93.2	100.0	78.2
Aged 40 to 44	100.0	59.3	100.0	76.8	100.0	81.8	100.0	74.2
Aged 45 to 49	100.0	42.7	100.0	55.9	100.0	61.6	100.0	47.6
Aged 50 to 54	100.0	21.1	100.0	27.8	100.0	33.9	100.0	37.4
Aged 55 to 64	100.0	5.4	100.0	7.5	100.0	7.1	100.0	17.7
Aged 65 or older	100.0	0.5	100.0	0.9	100.0	1.5	100.0	2.5

Note: Non-Hispanic whites include only those identifying themselves as being white alone and not Hispanic.
Source: Bureau of the Census, America's Families and Living Arrangements, 2003 Current Population Survey Annual Social and Economic Supplement; Internet site http://www.census.gov/population/www/socdemo/hh-fam/cps2003.html; calculations by New Strategist

Table 5.74 Living Arrangements of Non-Hispanic White Children, 2003

(number of total children under age 18, number and percent distribution of non-Hispanic white children, and non-Hispanic white share of total, by living arrangement, 2003; numbers in thousands)

| | | non-Hispanic white | | |
	total	number	percent distribution	share of total
Total children	**73,001**	**43,759**	**100.0%**	**59.9%**
Living with both parents	49,903	33,824	77.3	67.8
Living with mother only	16,771	6,925	15.8	41.3
Never married	7,006	1,734	4.0	24.8
Divorced or separated	9,102	4,868	11.1	53.5
Widowed	663	323	0.7	48.7
Living with father only	3,324	1,860	4.3	56.0
Never married	1,172	425	1.0	36.3
Divorced or separated	1,979	1,329	3.0	67.2
Widowed	173	106	0.2	61.3
Living with neither parent	3,004	1,150	2.6	38.3

Note: Non-Hispanic whites are only those identifying themselves as being white alone and not Hispanic.
Source: Bureau of the Census, America's Families and Living Arrangements, 2003 Current Population Survey Annual Social and Economic Supplement; Internet site http://www.census.gov/population/www/socdemo/hh-fam/cps2003.html; calculations by New Strategist

Table 5.75 Non-Hispanic White Men by Living Arrangement and Age, 2003

(number and percent distribution of non-Hispanic white men aged 15 or older by living arrangement and age, 2003; numbers in thousands)

	total	under 25	25 to 29	30 to 34	35 to 44	45 to 54	55 to 64	65 or older
Total non-Hispanic white men	**76,656**	**12,619**	**5,563**	**6,419**	**14,962**	**14,785**	**10,400**	**11,909**
Married-couple householder or spouse	44,071	679	2,326	3,830	10,037	10,610	7,988	8,601
Other householder	14,641	1,412	1,415	1,413	2,996	2,884	1,844	2,677
Male family householder	2,674	333	253	252	619	626	265	326
Living alone	9,421	490	709	823	1,872	1,927	1,374	2,226
Living with nonrelatives	2,546	589	453	338	505	331	205	125
Nonhouseholder	17,944	10,527	1,820	1,176	1,928	1,293	569	632
Child of householder	11,681	8,775	898	533	861	487	116	11
Other relative of householder	2,144	618	200	137	264	313	190	423
Living with nonrelatives	4,119	1,134	722	506	803	493	263	198
Total non-Hispanic white men	**100.0%**	**100.0%**	**100.0%**	**100.0%**	**100.0%**	**100.0%**	**100.0%**	**100.0%**
Married-couple householder or spouse	57.5	5.4	41.8	59.7	67.1	71.8	76.8	72.2
Other householder	19.1	11.2	25.4	22.0	20.0	19.5	17.7	22.5
Male family householder	3.5	2.6	4.5	3.9	4.1	4.2	2.5	2.7
Living alone	12.3	3.9	12.7	12.8	12.5	13.0	13.2	18.7
Living with nonrelatives	3.3	4.7	8.1	5.3	3.4	2.2	2.0	1.0
Nonhouseholder	23.4	83.4	32.7	18.3	12.9	8.7	5.5	5.3
Child of householder	15.2	69.5	16.1	8.3	5.8	3.3	1.1	0.1
Other relative of householder	2.8	4.9	3.6	2.1	1.8	2.1	1.8	3.6
Living with nonrelatives	5.4	9.0	13.0	7.9	5.4	3.3	2.5	1.7

Note: Non-Hispanic whites include only those identifying themselves as being white alone and not Hispanic.
Source: Bureau of the Census, America's Families and Living Arrangements, 2003 Current Population Survey Annual Social and Economic Supplement; Internet site http://www.census.gov/population/www/socdemo/hh-fam/cps2003.html; calculations by New Strategist

Table 5.76 Non-Hispanic White Women by Living Arrangement and Age, 2003

(number and percent distribution of non-Hispanic white women aged 15 or older by living arrangement and age, 2003; numbers in thousands)

	total	under 25	25 to 29	30 to 34	35 to 44	45 to 54	55 to 64	65 or older
Total non-Hispanic white women	**81,802**	**12,443**	**5,603**	**6,469**	**15,161**	**15,067**	**10,966**	**16,093**
Married-couple householder or spouse	43,733	1,288	2,912	4,375	10,528	10,486	7,308	6,837
Other householder	22,423	1,697	1,460	1,371	3,359	3,513	2,999	8,025
Female family householder	7,070	570	584	663	1,860	1,486	759	1,148
Living alone	13,233	556	541	532	1,174	1,652	2,057	6,722
Living with nonrelatives	2,120	571	335	176	325	375	183	155
Nonhouseholder	15,646	9,457	1,232	724	1,274	1,069	660	1,231
Child of householder	9,494	7,827	529	276	431	294	120	19
Other relative of householder	2,624	435	115	90	253	325	313	1,092
Living with nonrelatives	3,528	1,195	588	358	590	450	227	120
Total non-Hispanic white women	**100.0%**	**100.0%**	**100.0%**	**100.0%**	**100.0%**	**100.0%**	**100.0%**	**100.0%**
Married-couple householder or spouse	53.5	10.4	52.0	67.6	69.4	69.6	66.6	42.5
Other householder	27.4	13.6	26.1	21.2	22.2	23.3	27.3	49.9
Female family householder	8.6	4.6	10.4	10.2	12.3	9.9	6.9	7.1
Living alone	16.2	4.5	9.7	8.2	7.7	11.0	18.8	41.8
Living with nonrelatives	2.6	4.6	6.0	2.7	2.1	2.5	1.7	1.0
Nonhouseholder	19.1	76.0	22.0	11.2	8.4	7.1	6.0	7.6
Child of householder	11.6	62.9	9.4	4.3	2.8	2.0	1.1	0.1
Other relative of householder	3.2	3.5	2.1	1.4	1.7	2.2	2.9	6.8
Living with nonrelatives	4.3	9.6	10.5	5.5	3.9	3.0	2.1	0.7

Note: Non-Hispanic whites include only those identifying themselves as being white alone and not Hispanic.
Source: Bureau of the Census, America's Families and Living Arrangements, 2003 Current Population Survey Annual Social and Economic Supplement; Internet site http://www.census.gov/population/www/socdemo/hh-fam/cps2003.html; calculations by New Strategist

Table 5.77 Marital Status of Non-Hispanic White Men by Age, 2003

(number and percent distribution of non-Hispanic white men aged 18 or older by age and current marital status, 2003; numbers in thousands)

	total	never married	married, spouse present	married, spouse absent	separated	divorced	widowed
Total non-Hispanic white men	**72,586**	**17,463**	**44,621**	**619**	**978**	**6,827**	**2,078**
Aged 18 to 19	2,439	2,399	38	0	1	1	0
Aged 20 to 24	6,110	5,287	704	13	36	71	0
Aged 25 to 29	5,563	2,860	2,383	36	80	199	4
Aged 30 to 34	6,419	1,890	3,888	50	87	494	10
Aged 35 to 39	7,014	1,374	4,654	41	171	763	10
Aged 40 to 44	7,948	1,252	5,460	75	151	963	47
Aged 45 to 49	7,803	868	5,548	85	106	1,137	60
Aged 50 to 54	6,982	513	5,189	53	106	1,053	68
Aged 55 to 64	10,400	548	8,070	92	140	1,341	209
Aged 65 to 74	6,615	295	5,052	76	67	576	548
Aged 75 to 84	4,252	152	3,032	70	29	198	771
Aged 85 or older	1,042	26	603	28	5	30	351
Total non-Hispanic white men	**100.0%**	**24.1%**	**61.5%**	**0.9%**	**1.3%**	**9.4%**	**2.9%**
Aged 18 to 19	100.0	98.4	1.6	0.0	0.0	0.0	0.0
Aged 20 to 24	100.0	86.5	11.5	0.2	0.6	1.2	0.0
Aged 25 to 29	100.0	51.4	42.8	0.6	1.4	3.6	0.1
Aged 30 to 34	100.0	29.4	60.6	0.8	1.4	7.7	0.2
Aged 35 to 39	100.0	19.6	66.4	0.6	2.4	10.9	0.1
Aged 40 to 44	100.0	15.8	68.7	0.9	1.9	12.1	0.6
Aged 45 to 49	100.0	11.1	71.1	1.1	1.4	14.6	0.8
Aged 50 to 54	100.0	7.3	74.3	0.8	1.5	15.1	1.0
Aged 55 to 64	100.0	5.3	77.6	0.9	1.3	12.9	2.0
Aged 65 to 74	100.0	4.5	76.4	1.1	1.0	8.7	8.3
Aged 75 to 84	100.0	3.6	71.3	1.6	0.7	4.7	18.1
Aged 85 or older	100.0	2.5	57.9	2.7	0.5	2.9	33.7

Note: Non-Hispanic whites are those who identified themselves as being white alone and not Hispanic.
Source: Bureau of the Census, America's Families and Living Arrangements, 2003 Current Population Survey Annual Social and Economic Supplement; Internet site http://www.census.gov/population/www/socdemo/hh-fam/cps2003.html

Table 5.78 Marital Status of Non-Hispanic White Women by Age, 2003

(number and percent distribution of non-Hispanic white women aged 18 or older by age and current marital status, 2003; numbers in thousands)

	total	never married	married, spouse present	married, spouse absent	separated	divorced	widowed
Total non-Hispanic white women	**77,828**	**13,618**	**44,298**	**744**	**1,225**	**9,240**	**8,703**
Aged 18 to 19	2,301	2,210	80	5	2	4	0
Aged 20 to 24	6,168	4,618	1,293	45	86	117	9
Aged 25 to 29	5,603	2,057	2,975	58	125	375	13
Aged 30 to 34	6,469	1,183	4,438	37	144	634	33
Aged 35 to 39	7,102	740	4,972	81	193	1,031	86
Aged 40 to 44	8,059	800	5,653	71	205	1,223	107
Aged 45 to 49	7,912	578	5,620	63	156	1,351	143
Aged 50 to 54	7,155	459	5,003	68	114	1,284	227
Aged 55 to 64	10,966	476	7,363	116	135	1,875	1,000
Aged 65 to 74	7,778	187	4,398	74	40	840	2,239
Aged 75 to 84	6,355	224	2,246	103	24	436	3,322
Aged 85 or older	1,960	85	257	22	0	72	1,524
Total non-Hispanic white women	**100.0%**	**17.5%**	**56.9%**	**1.0%**	**1.6%**	**11.9%**	**11.2%**
Aged 18 to 19	100.0	96.0	3.5	0.2	0.1	0.2	0.0
Aged 20 to 24	100.0	74.9	21.0	0.7	1.4	1.9	0.1
Aged 25 to 29	100.0	36.7	53.1	1.0	2.2	6.7	0.2
Aged 30 to 34	100.0	18.3	68.6	0.6	2.2	9.8	0.5
Aged 35 to 39	100.0	10.4	70.0	1.1	2.7	14.5	1.2
Aged 40 to 44	100.0	9.9	70.1	0.9	2.5	15.2	1.3
Aged 45 to 49	100.0	7.3	71.0	0.8	2.0	17.1	1.8
Aged 50 to 54	100.0	6.4	69.9	1.0	1.6	17.9	3.2
Aged 55 to 64	100.0	4.3	67.1	1.1	1.2	17.1	9.1
Aged 65 to 74	100.0	2.4	56.5	1.0	0.5	10.8	28.8
Aged 75 to 84	100.0	3.5	35.3	1.6	0.4	6.9	52.3
Aged 85 or older	100.0	4.3	13.1	1.1	0.0	3.7	77.8

Note: Non-Hispanic whites are those who identified themselves as being white alone and not Hispanic.
Source: Bureau of the Census, America's Families and Living Arrangements, 2003 Current Population Survey Annual Social and Economic Supplement; Internet site http://www.census.gov/population/www/socdemo/hh-fam/cps2003.html

Table 5.79 Marital History of Non-Hispanic White Men by Age, 2001

(number of non-Hispanic white men aged 15 or older and percent distribution by marital history and age, 2001; numbers in thousands)

	total	15 to 19	20 to 24	25 to 29	30 to 34	35 to 39	40 to 49	50 to 59	60 to 69	70 or older
Total non-Hispanic white men, number	77,085	6,679	5,981	5,811	6,680	7,691	15,781	12,378	7,807	8,277
Total non-Hispanic white men, percent	100.0%	100.0%	100.0%	100.0%	100.0%	100.0%	100.0%	100.0%	100.0%	100.0%
Never married	27.4	99.4	83.7	48.3	28.1	19.0	12.8	5.7	4.0	3.5
Ever married	72.6	0.6	16.3	51.7	71.9	81.0	87.2	94.3	96.0	96.5
Married once	54.8	0.5	16.2	48.0	61.3	67.1	64.5	60.8	67.3	75.1
Still married	45.1	0.3	14.4	41.0	52.7	53.2	52.8	48.9	58.7	59.2
Married twice	14.0	0.1	0.1	3.6	9.3	12.2	18.9	24.4	21.5	16.5
Still married	11.3	0.1	0.1	3.3	7.9	10.2	15.2	19.2	17.3	12.5
Married three or more times	3.8	0.0	0.0	0.1	1.3	1.6	3.8	9.1	7.3	4.9
Still married	2.9	0.0	0.0	0.1	1.0	1.5	3.1	6.7	5.6	3.7
Ever divorced	23.3	0.1	1.1	8.7	16.8	25.7	32.1	42.8	31.3	18.1
Currently divorced	9.4	0.0	1.0	5.1	7.8	13.8	13.4	16.6	9.5	5.0
Ever widowed	3.8	0.0	0.0	0.1	0.3	0.4	1.2	2.5	7.2	22.3
Currently widowed	2.5	0.0	0.0	0.1	0.1	0.1	0.7	1.4	4.0	15.7

Note: Non-Hispanic whites are those who identified themselves as being white alone and not Hispanic.
Source: Bureau of the Census, Number, Timing, and Duration of Marriages and Divorces: 2001, *Current Population Report P70-97, 2005; Internet site http://www.census.gov/population/www/socdemo/marr-div.html*

Table 5.80 Marital History of Non-Hispanic White Women by Age, 2001

(number of non-Hispanic white women aged 15 or older and percent distribution by marital history and age, 2001; numbers in thousands)

	total	15 to 19	20 to 24	25 to 29	30 to 34	35 to 39	40 to 49	50 to 59	60 to 69	70 or older
Total non-Hispanic white women, number	82,128	6,310	6,015	5,904	6,696	7,584	15,977	12,880	8,525	12,237
Total non-Hispanic white women, percent	100.0%	100.0%	100.0%	100.0%	100.0%	100.0%	100.0%	100.0%	100.0%	100.0%
Never married	20.7	97.3	70.9	34.1	17.1	12.3	8.1	5.0	2.9	2.9
Ever married	79.3	2.7	29.1	65.9	82.9	87.7	91.9	95.0	97.1	97.1
Married once	60.0	2.7	27.6	59.2	69.6	67.1	64.1	63.8	72.8	78.1
Still married	42.1	2.3	23.4	48.2	58.7	55.0	49.5	48.0	50.2	30.5
Married twice	15.5	0.0	1.4	6.3	12.0	18.3	22.2	24.1	18.3	15.5
Still married	10.6	0.0	1.1	5.0	9.5	14.3	16.4	17.0	11.7	6.6
Married three or more times	3.7	0.0	0.0	0.4	1.4	2.3	5.6	7.1	6.1	3.6
Still married	2.3	0.0	0.0	0.3	1.0	2.0	3.9	4.7	3.4	1.2
Ever divorced	25.4	0.1	3.3	14.5	21.9	30.4	38.8	40.4	29.1	17.4
Currently divorced	11.1	0.1	1.9	8.9	10.8	13.5	17.6	17.0	12.1	6.0
Ever widowed	12.9	0.0	0.2	0.4	0.5	1.2	3.2	8.9	22.2	56.5
Currently widowed	11.3	0.0	0.2	0.4	0.3	0.7	2.0	6.4	18.4	52.6

Note: Non-Hispanic whites are those who identified themselves as being white alone and not Hispanic.
Source: Bureau of the Census, Number, Timing, and Duration of Marriages and Divorces: 2001, *Current Population Report P70-97, 2005; Internet site http://www.census.gov/population/www/socdemo/marr-div.html*

The Non-Hispanic White Population Barely Grew between 2000 and 2004

Non-Hispanic whites accounted for 67 percent of the total population in 2004, down from 69 percent in 2000. The non-Hispanic white population grew only 1 percent during those years, well below the 4 percent gain for the population as a whole.

Non-Hispanic whites account for a much smaller share of children and young adults than of older Americans because Hispanics (who may be of any race, with most being white) are a growing proportion of the younger age groups. Just 56 percent of children under age 5 are non-Hispanic white, versus 86 percent of people aged 85 or older.

The non-Hispanic white share of regional populations varies substantially. In the Midwest, 80 percent of the population is non-Hispanic white. In the West, only 56 percent of residents are non-Hispanic white. Variations by state are even greater. In Maine and Vermont, 96 percent of the population is non-Hispanic white. In California, Hawaii, New Mexico, and Texas, fewer than 50 percent of residents are non-Hispanic white. Fully 95 percent of the population of Scranton–Wilkes-Barre–Hazelton, Pennsylvania, is non-Hispanic white. In contrast, non-Hispanic whites account for only 9 percent of the residents of McAllen–Edinburg–Mission, Texas.

■ In a growing number of states and metropolitan areas, non-Hispanic whites are no longer in the majority, changing America's social fabric.

The non-Hispanic white share of regional populations varies substantially

(non-Hispanic white share of population by region, 2004)

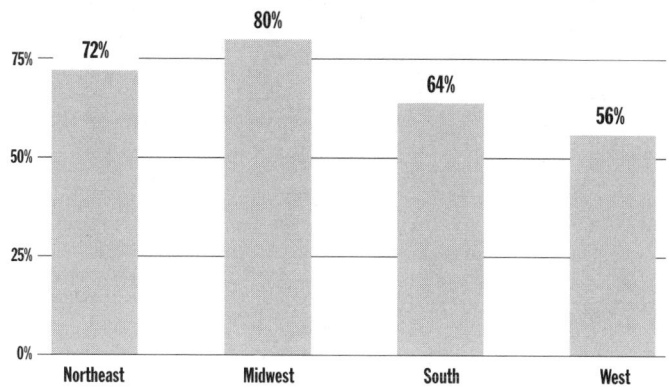

Table 5.81 Whites by Racial Identification, 2000 and 2004

(total number of people, and number and percent distribution of whites by racial identification, 2000 and 2004; percent change, 2000–04)

	2004 number	2004 percent distribution	2000 number	2000 percent distribution	percent change 2000–04
TOTAL PEOPLE	**293,655,404**	**100.0%**	**282,192,162**	**100.0%**	**4.1%**
White alone or in combination with one or more other races	**239,880,132**	**81.7**	**231,978,329**	**82.2**	**3.4**
White alone	236,057,761	80.4	228,620,482	81.0	3.3
White alone, not Hispanic	197,840,821	67.4	195,769,452	69.4	1.1
White in combination	3,822,371	1.3	3,357,847	1.2	13.8

Source: Bureau of the Census, National Population Estimates, Internet site http://www.census.gov/popest/national/asrh/ NC-EST2004-srh.html; calculations by New Strategist

Table 5.82 Whites by Hispanic Origin, 2004

(number and percent distribution of whites by Hispanic origin and racial identification, 2004)

	white alone or in combination number	white alone or in combination percent distribution	white alone number	white alone percent distribution
Total whites	**239,880,132**	**100.0%**	**236,057,761**	**100.0%**
Not Hispanic	201,148,336	83.9	197,840,821	83.8
Hispanic	38,731,796	16.1	38,216,940	16.2

Source: Bureau of the Census, National Population Estimates, Internet site http://www.census.gov/popest/national/asrh/ NC-EST2004-asrh.html; calculations by New Strategist

Table 5.83 Non-Hispanic Whites in the Armed Forces, 2003

(number and percent distribution of non-Hispanic whites aged 18 or older who are in the armed forces or who are veterans, by sex and age, 2003)

	total	in armed forces	veteran
Total non-Hispanic whites aged 18 or older	**148,604,400**	**458,950**	**19,881,122**
Men	71,801,242	401,961	18,757,563
Aged 18 to 64	59,888,189	401,961	10,948,673
Aged 65 or older	11,913,053	0	7,808,890
Women	76,803,158	56,989	1,123,559
Aged 18 to 64	60,917,343	56,989	834,574
Aged 65 or older	15,885,815	0	288,985
Total non-Hispanic whites aged 18 or older	**100.0%**	**0.3%**	**13.4%**
Men	100.0	0.6	26.1
Aged 18 to 64	100.0	0.7	18.3
Aged 65 or older	100.0	0.0	65.5
Women	100.0	0.1	1.5
Aged 18 to 64	100.0	0.1	1.4
Aged 65 or older	100.0	0.0	1.8

Note: Non-Hispanic whites are those identifying themselves as being white alone and not Hispanic.
Source: Bureau of the Census, 2003 American Community Survey, Internet site http://factfinder.census.gov/servlet/ DatasetMainPageServlet?_program=ACS&_lang=en&_ts=; calculations by New Strategist

Table 5.84 Non-Hispanic Whites by Age, 2000 and 2004

(number of non-Hispanic whites by age, 2000 and 2004; percent change, 2000–04)

	2004	2000	percent change 2000–04
Total non-Hispanic whites	**197,840,821**	**195,769,452**	**1.1%**
Under age 5	11,246,247	11,267,932	–0.2
Aged 5 to 9	11,447,644	12,321,560	–7.1
Aged 10 to 14	12,675,858	12,985,055	–2.4
Aged 15 to 19	12,967,292	12,860,388	0.8
Aged 20 to 24	12,839,493	11,773,414	9.1
Aged 25 to 29	11,604,739	11,970,409	–3.1
Aged 30 to 34	12,559,304	13,434,011	–6.5
Aged 35 to 39	13,698,389	15,671,501	–12.6
Aged 40 to 44	15,966,017	16,234,442	–1.7
Aged 45 to 49	15,982,993	15,052,430	6.2
Aged 50 to 54	14,522,772	13,652,179	6.4
Aged 55 to 59	12,719,105	10,641,426	19.5
Aged 60 to 64	9,878,716	8,543,551	15.6
Aged 65 to 69	7,837,395	7,647,381	2.5
Aged 70 to 74	6,851,665	7,332,777	–6.6
Aged 75 to 79	6,150,091	6,331,265	–2.9
Aged 80 to 84	4,725,199	4,327,413	9.2
Aged 85 or older	4,167,902	3,722,318	12.0
Aged 18 or older	154,713,671	151,484,905	2.1
Aged 18 to 24	18,049,384	16,923,802	6.7
Aged 65 or older	29,732,252	29,361,154	1.3

Note: Non-Hispanic whites are those identifying themselves as being white alone and not Hispanic.
Source: Bureau of the Census, National Population Estimates, Internet site http://www.census.gov/popest/national/asrh/ NC-EST2004-asrh.html; calculations by New Strategist

Table 5.85 Non-Hispanic White Share of Total Population by Age, 2004

(total number of people, number and percent distribution of non-Hispanic whites, and non-Hispanic white share of total, by age, 2004)

		non-Hispanic white		
	total	number	percent distribution	share of total
Total people	**293,655,404**	**197,840,821**	**100.0%**	**67.4%**
Under age 5	20,071,268	11,246,247	5.7	56.0
Aged 5 to 9	19,605,572	11,447,644	5.8	58.4
Aged 10 to 14	21,145,156	12,675,858	6.4	59.9
Aged 15 to 19	20,729,802	12,967,292	6.6	62.6
Aged 20 to 24	20,971,302	12,839,493	6.5	61.2
Aged 25 to 29	19,560,906	11,604,739	5.9	59.3
Aged 30 to 34	20,471,032	12,559,304	6.3	61.4
Aged 35 to 39	21,052,318	13,698,389	6.9	65.1
Aged 40 to 44	23,056,334	15,966,017	8.1	69.2
Aged 45 to 49	22,122,629	15,982,993	8.1	72.2
Aged 50 to 54	19,496,176	14,522,772	7.3	74.5
Aged 55 to 59	16,489,501	12,719,105	6.4	77.1
Aged 60 to 64	12,589,423	9,878,716	5.0	78.5
Aged 65 to 69	9,956,467	7,837,395	4.0	78.7
Aged 70 to 74	8,507,005	6,851,665	3.5	80.5
Aged 75 to 79	7,410,757	6,150,091	3.1	83.0
Aged 80 to 84	5,560,125	4,725,199	2.4	85.0
Aged 85 or older	4,859,631	4,167,902	2.1	85.8
Aged 18 or older	220,377,406	154,713,671	78.2	70.2
Aged 18 to 24	29,245,102	18,049,384	9.1	61.7
Aged 65 or older	36,293,985	29,732,252	15.0	81.9

Note: Non-Hispanic whites are those identifying themselves as being white alone and not Hispanic.
Source: Bureau of the Census, National Population Estimates, Internet site http://www.census.gov/popest/national/asrh/NC-EST2004-sa.html; calculations by New Strategist

Table 5.86 Non-Hispanic Whites by Age and Sex, 2004

(number of non-Hispanic whites by age and sex, and sex ratio by age, 2004)

	total	females	males	sex ratio
Total non-Hispanic whites	**197,840,821**	**100,801,786**	**97,039,035**	**96**
Under age 5	11,246,247	5,481,101	5,765,146	105
Aged 5 to 9	11,447,644	5,570,123	5,877,521	106
Aged 10 to 14	12,675,858	6,163,133	6,512,725	106
Aged 15 to 19	12,967,292	6,304,886	6,662,406	106
Aged 20 to 24	12,839,493	6,301,174	6,538,319	104
Aged 25 to 29	11,604,739	5,742,354	5,862,385	102
Aged 30 to 34	12,559,304	6,233,901	6,325,403	101
Aged 35 to 39	13,698,389	6,817,293	6,881,096	101
Aged 40 to 44	15,966,017	7,991,281	7,974,736	100
Aged 45 to 49	15,982,993	8,029,702	7,953,291	99
Aged 50 to 54	14,522,772	7,337,985	7,184,787	98
Aged 55 to 59	12,719,105	6,472,969	6,246,136	96
Aged 60 to 64	9,878,716	5,112,870	4,765,846	93
Aged 65 to 69	7,837,395	4,142,577	3,694,818	89
Aged 70 to 74	6,851,665	3,753,337	3,098,328	83
Aged 75 to 79	6,150,091	3,549,864	2,600,227	73
Aged 80 to 84	4,725,199	2,918,595	1,806,604	62
Aged 85 or older	4,167,902	2,878,641	1,289,261	45
Aged 18 or older	154,713,671	79,814,916	74,898,755	94
Aged 18 to 24	18,049,384	8,833,547	9,215,837	104
Aged 65 or older	29,732,252	17,243,014	12,489,238	72

Note: Non-Hispanic whites are those identifying themselves as being white alone and not Hispanic. The sex ratio is the number of males divided by the number of females multiplied by 100.
Source: Bureau of the Census, National Population Estimates, Internet site http://www.census.gov/popest/national/asrh/ NC-EST2004-sa.html; calculations by New Strategist

Table 5.87 Non-Hispanic Whites by Age, 2000 to 2020

(number and percent distribution of non-Hispanic whites by age, 2000 to 2020, percent change, 2000–10 and 2010–20; numbers in thousands)

	2000	2010	2020	percent change 2000–10	percent change 2010–20
Total non-Hispanic whites	**195,729**	**201,112**	**205,936**	**2.8%**	**2.4%**
Under age 5	11,293	11,647	11,909	3.1	2.3
Aged 5 to 9	12,327	11,553	11,908	–6.3	3.1
Aged 10 to 14	12,970	11,361	11,696	–12.4	2.9
Aged 15 to 19	12,843	12,401	11,606	–3.4	–6.4
Aged 20 to 24	11,780	12,992	11,380	10.3	–12.4
Aged 25 to 29	11,952	12,919	12,467	8.1	–3.5
Aged 30 to 34	13,442	11,977	13,159	–10.9	9.9
Aged 35 to 39	15,633	12,096	13,036	–22.6	7.8
Aged 40 to 44	16,239	13,466	12,010	–17.1	–10.8
Aged 45 to 49	15,050	15,489	12,018	2.9	–22.4
Aged 50 to 54	13,665	15,870	13,196	16.1	–16.9
Aged 55 to 59	10,636	14,431	14,905	35.7	3.3
Aged 60 to 64	8,550	12,736	14,897	49.0	17.0
Aged 65 or older	29,349	32,171	41,748	9.6	29.8

Note: Non-Hispanic whites are those identifying themselves as being white alone and not Hispanic.
Source: Bureau of the Census, Internet site http://www.census.gov/ipc/www/usinterimproj/; calculations by New Strategist

Table 5.88 Non-Hispanic Whites by Region, 2000 and 2004

(number of non-Hispanic whites by region, 2000 and 2004; percent change, 2000–04)

	2004	2000	percent change 2000–04
Total non-Hispanic whites	**197,840,821**	**194,552,774**	**1.7%**
Northeast	39,380,123	39,327,262	0.1
Midwest	52,781,798	52,386,131	0.8
South	67,615,334	65,927,794	2.6
West	38,063,566	36,911,587	3.1

Note: Non-Hispanic whites are those identifying themselves as being white alone and not Hispanic. Total number of non-Hispanic whites in 2000 differs from the total in previous tables of this chapter because these are census counts from April 1, 2000, whereas the others are population estimates.
Source: Bureau of the Census, 2000 Census, Internet site http://factfinder.census.gov/servlet/DatasetMainPageServlet?_program=DEC&_lang=en&_ts=; and State Population Estimates, Internet site http://www.census.gov/popest/states/asrh/SC-EST2004-04.html; calculations by New Strategist

Table 5.89 Non-Hispanic White Share of the Total Population by Region, 2004

(total number of people, number and percent distribution of non-Hispanic whites, and non-Hispanic white share of total, by region, 2004)

	total	non-Hispanic white		
		number	percent distribution	share of total
Total people	**293,655,404**	**197,840,821**	**100.0%**	**67.4%**
Northeast	54,571,147	39,380,123	19.9	72.2
Midwest	65,729,852	52,781,798	26.7	80.3
South	105,944,965	67,615,334	34.2	63.8
West	67,409,440	38,063,566	19.2	56.5

Note: Non-Hispanic whites are those identifying themselves as being white alone and not Hispanic.
Source: Bureau of the Census, State Population Estimates, Internet site http://www.census.gov/popest/states/asrh/SC-EST2004-04.html; calculations by New Strategist

Table 5.90 Non-Hispanic Whites by State, 2000 and 2004

(number of non-Hispanic whites by state, 2000 and 2004; percent change, 2000–04)

	2004	2000	percent change 2000–04
Total non-Hispanic whites	**197,840,821**	**194,552,774**	**1.7%**
Alabama	3,147,620	3,125,819	0.7
Alaska	438,177	423,788	3.4
Arizona	3,509,599	3,274,258	7.2
Arkansas	2,126,382	2,100,135	1.2
California	15,982,109	15,816,790	1.0
Colorado	3,334,447	3,202,880	4.1
Connecticut	2,657,671	2,638,845	0.7
Delaware	583,119	567,973	2.7
District of Columbia	167,563	159,178	5.3
Florida	10,919,745	10,458,509	4.4
Georgia	5,318,847	5,128,661	3.7
Hawaii	294,558	277,091	6.3
Idaho	1,214,571	1,139,291	6.6
Illinois	8,414,026	8,424,140	–0.1
Indiana	5,279,777	5,219,373	1.2
Iowa	2,709,712	2,710,344	0.0
Kansas	2,239,170	2,233,997	0.2
Kentucky	3,677,961	3,608,013	1.9
Louisiana	2,788,717	2,794,391	–0.2
Maine	1,266,068	1,230,297	2.9
Maryland	3,324,989	3,286,547	1.2
Massachusetts	5,181,427	5,198,359	–0.3
Michigan	7,895,516	7,806,691	1.1
Minnesota	4,420,829	4,337,143	1.9
Mississippi	1,739,026	1,727,908	0.6
Missouri	4,781,115	4,686,474	2.0
Montana	825,827	807,823	2.2
Nebraska	1,496,640	1,494,494	0.1
Nevada	1,429,272	1,303,001	9.7
New Hampshire	1,225,145	1,175,252	4.2
New Jersey	5,549,273	5,557,209	–0.1
New Mexico	827,230	813,495	1.7
New York	11,745,589	11,760,981	–0.1
North Carolina	5,860,777	5,647,155	3.8
North Dakota	577,639	589,149	–2.0
Ohio	9,547,385	9,538,111	0.1
Oklahoma	2,569,827	2,556,368	0.5
Oregon	2,948,024	2,857,616	3.2

(continued)

	2004	2000	percent change 2000–04
Pennsylvania	10,288,227	10,322,455	–0.3%
Rhode Island	870,209	858,433	1.4
South Carolina	2,753,295	2,652,291	3.8
South Dakota	671,072	664,585	1.0
Tennessee	4,610,827	4,505,930	2.3
Texas	11,190,222	10,933,313	2.3
Utah	2,002,538	1,904,265	5.2
Vermont	596,514	585,431	1.9
Virginia	5,121,944	4,965,637	3.1
Washington	4,808,520	4,652,490	3.4
West Virginia	1,714,473	1,709,966	0.3
Wisconsin	4,748,917	4,681,630	1.4
Wyoming	448,694	438,799	2.3

Note: Non-Hispanic whites are those identifying themselves as being white alone and not Hispanic. Total number of non-Hispanic whites in 2000 differs from the total in previous tables of this chapter because these are census counts from April 1, 2000, whereas the others are population estimates.

Source: Bureau of the Census, 2000 Census, Internet site http://factfinder.census.gov/servlet/DatasetMainPageServlet?_program=DEC&_lang=en&_ts=; and State Population Estimates, Internet site http://www.census.gov/popest/states/asrh/SC-EST2004-04.html; calculations by New Strategist

Table 5.91 Non-Hispanic White Share of Total Population by State, 2004

(total number of people, number and percent distribution of non-Hispanic whites, and non-Hispanic white share of total, by state, 2004)

| | | non-Hispanic white | | |
	total	number	percent distribution	share of total
Total people	**293,655,404**	**197,840,821**	**100.0%**	**67.4%**
Alabama	4,530,182	3,147,620	1.6	69.5
Alaska	655,435	438,177	0.2	66.9
Arizona	5,743,834	3,509,599	1.8	61.1
Arkansas	2,752,629	2,126,382	1.1	77.2
California	35,893,799	15,982,109	8.1	44.5
Colorado	4,601,403	3,334,447	1.7	72.5
Connecticut	3,503,604	2,657,671	1.3	75.9
Delaware	830,364	583,119	0.3	70.2
District of Columbia	553,523	167,563	0.1	30.3
Florida	17,397,161	10,919,745	5.5	62.8
Georgia	8,829,383	5,318,847	2.7	60.2
Hawaii	1,262,840	294,558	0.1	23.3
Idaho	1,393,262	1,214,571	0.6	87.2
Illinois	12,713,634	8,414,026	4.3	66.2
Indiana	6,237,569	5,279,777	2.7	84.6
Iowa	2,954,451	2,709,712	1.4	91.7
Kansas	2,735,502	2,239,170	1.1	81.9
Kentucky	4,145,922	3,677,961	1.9	88.7
Louisiana	4,515,770	2,788,717	1.4	61.8
Maine	1,317,253	1,266,068	0.6	96.1
Maryland	5,558,058	3,324,989	1.7	59.8
Massachusetts	6,416,505	5,181,427	2.6	80.8
Michigan	10,112,620	7,895,516	4.0	78.1
Minnesota	5,100,958	4,420,829	2.2	86.7
Mississippi	2,902,966	1,739,026	0.9	59.9
Missouri	5,754,618	4,781,115	2.4	83.1
Montana	926,865	825,827	0.4	89.1
Nebraska	1,747,214	1,496,640	0.8	85.7
Nevada	2,334,771	1,429,272	0.7	61.2
New Hampshire	1,299,500	1,225,145	0.6	94.3
New Jersey	8,698,879	5,549,273	2.8	63.8
New Mexico	1,903,289	827,230	0.4	43.5
New York	19,227,088	11,745,589	5.9	61.1
North Carolina	8,541,221	5,860,777	3.0	68.6
North Dakota	634,366	577,639	0.3	91.1
Ohio	11,459,011	9,547,385	4.8	83.3
Oklahoma	3,523,553	2,569,827	1.3	72.9
Oregon	3,594,586	2,948,024	1.5	82.0

(continued)

	total	non-Hispanic white		
		number	percent distribution	share of total
Pennsylvania	12,406,292	10,288,227	5.2%	82.9%
Rhode Island	1,080,632	870,209	0.4	80.5
South Carolina	4,198,068	2,753,295	1.4	65.6
South Dakota	770,883	671,072	0.3	87.1
Tennessee	5,900,962	4,610,827	2.3	78.1
Texas	22,490,022	11,190,222	5.7	49.8
Utah	2,389,039	2,002,538	1.0	83.8
Vermont	621,394	596,514	0.3	96.0
Virginia	7,459,827	5,121,944	2.6	68.7
Washington	6,203,788	4,808,520	2.4	77.5
West Virginia	1,815,354	1,714,473	0.9	94.4
Wisconsin	5,509,026	4,748,917	2.4	86.2
Wyoming	506,529	448,694	0.2	88.6

Note: Non-Hispanic whites are those identifying themselves as being white alone and not Hispanic.
Source: Bureau of the Census, State Population Estimates, Internet site http://www.census.gov/popest/states/asrh/ SC-EST2004-04.html; calculations by New Strategist

Table 5.92 Non-Hispanic Whites by Metropolitan Area, 2004

(total number of people, number of non-Hispanic whites, and non-Hispanic white share of total, for selected metropolitan areas, 2004)

	total population	non-Hispanic white number	non-Hispanic white share of total
Albany–Schenectady–Troy, NY MSA	860,976	748,680	87.0%
Allentown–Bethlehem–Easton, PA MSA	650,230	545,385	83.9
Anchorage, AK MSA	265,176	179,231	67.6
Appleton–Oshkosh–Neenah, WI MSA	359,711	335,280	93.2
Atlanta, GA MSA	4,477,579	2,507,385	56.0
Augusta–Aiken, GA–SC MSA	476,167	284,501	59.7
Austin–San Marcos, TX MSA	1,373,125	794,475	57.9
Bakersfield, CA MSA	702,855	324,519	46.2
Baton Rouge, LA MSA	610,743	384,871	63.0
Beaumont–Port Arthur, TX MSA	366,244	232,445	63.5
Biloxi–Gulfport–Pascagoula, MS MSA	363,966	267,448	73.5
Binghamton, NY MSA	239,012	216,022	90.4
Birmingham, AL MSA	929,694	608,284	65.4
Boise City, ID MSA	479,284	408,762	85.3
Boston–Worcester–Lawrence, MA–NH–ME–CT CMSA	5,749,197	4,652,027	80.9
Brownsville–Harlingen–San Benito, TX MSA	367,603	47,798	13.0
Buffalo–Niagara Falls, NY MSA	1,119,037	919,616	82.2
Canton–Massillon, OH MSA	400,919	361,137	90.1
Charleston–North Charleston, SC MSA	563,828	361,409	64.1
Chicago, IL PMSA	8,388,723	4,706,417	56.1
Cleveland–Akron, OH CMSA	2,878,475	2,221,674	77.2
Colorado Springs, CO MSA	539,225	404,363	75.0
Columbia, SC MSA	543,126	336,453	61.9
Corpus Christi, TX MSA	381,422	141,936	37.2
Dallas–Fort Worth, TX CMSA	5,676,651	3,135,974	55.2
Davenport–Moline–Rock Island, IA–IL MSA	350,022	296,177	84.6
Dayton–Springfield, OH MSA	916,635	742,768	81.0
Daytona Beach, FL MSA	530,553	425,807	80.3
Denver–Boulder–Greeley, CO CMSA*	2,514,628	1,732,541	68.9
Des Moines, IA MSA	476,699	415,764	87.2
Detroit–Ann Arbor–Flint, MI CMSA	5,437,277	3,869,258	71.2
El Paso, TX MSA	700,225	101,965	14.6
Erie, PA MSA	267,426	238,217	89.1
Eugene–Springfield, OR MSA	324,176	283,861	87.6
Fayetteville, NC MSA	287,220	147,454	51.3
Fayetteville–Springdale–Rogers, AR MSA	345,308	281,780	81.6
Fort Myers–Cape Coral, FL MSA	508,634	392,124	77.1
Fort Pierce–Port St. Lucie, FL MSA	358,578	272,081	75.9
Fort Wayne, IN MSA	506,545	434,174	85.7

(continued)

	total population	non-Hispanic white	
		number	share of total
Fresno, CA MSA	978,274	382,355	39.1%
Grand Rapids–Muskegon–Holland, MI MSA	1,102,729	903,229	81.9
Greensboro–Winston-Salem–High Point, NC MSA	1,283,261	900,548	70.2
Greenville–Spartanburg–Anderson, SC MSA	976,678	744,993	76.3
Harrisburg–Lebanon–Carlisle, PA MSA	617,676	528,293	85.5
Hartford, CT MSA	1,163,367	872,040	75.0
Hickory–Morganton–Lenoir, NC MSA	345,590	292,194	84.5
Honolulu, HI MSA	868,751	166,041	19.1
Houston–Galveston–Brazoria, TX CMSA*	4,794,384	2,118,076	44.2
Huntsville, AL MSA	354,936	259,983	73.2
Indianapolis, IN MSA	1,664,412	1,318,647	79.2
Jackson, MS MSA	443,275	223,779	50.5
Jacksonville, FL MSA	1,182,453	812,284	68.7
Johnson City–Kingsport–Bristol, TN–VA MSA	482,047	459,257	95.3
Kalamazoo–Battle Creek, MI MSA	441,059	365,078	82.8
Kansas City, MO–KS MSA	1,823,092	1,412,083	77.5
Killeen–Temple, TX MSA	298,933	167,567	56.1
Knoxville, TN MSA	707,617	638,498	90.2
Lafayette, LA MSA	386,812	263,972	68.2
Lakeland–Winter Haven, FL MSA	511,565	366,480	71.6
Lancaster, PA MSA	473,104	416,291	88.0
Lansing–East Lansing, MI MSA	436,485	351,507	80.5
Lexington, KY MSA	478,625	403,613	84.3
Lincoln, NE MSA	249,670	219,590	88.0
Little Rock–North Little Rock, AR MSA	593,032	427,726	72.1
Los Angeles–Riverside–Orange County, CA CMSA	17,199,115	6,323,085	36.8
Lubbock, TX MSA	240,721	144,727	60.1
Macon, GA MSA	329,432	185,203	56.2
Madison, WI MSA	437,843	374,722	85.6
McAllen–Edinburg–Mission, TX MSA	651,974	61,813	9.5
Melbourne–Titusville–Palm Bay, FL MSA	509,248	417,750	82.0
Miami–Fort Lauderdale, FL CMSA	4,051,442	1,311,805	32.4
Milwaukee–Waukesha, WI PMSA	1,483,023	1,072,922	72.3
Mobile, AL MSA	547,153	373,606	68.3
Modesto, CA MSA	490,860	256,867	52.3
Montgomery, AL MSA	323,220	184,535	57.1
Nashville, TN MSA	1,275,212	977,618	76.7
New Orleans, LA MSA	1,313,694	701,973	53.4
New York–Northern New Jersey–Long Island, NY–NJ–CT–PA CMSA*	20,345,959	10,941,478	53.8
Oklahoma City, OK MSA	1,095,252	778,349	71.1
Orlando, FL MSA	1,831,212	1,104,434	60.3
Pensacola, FL MSA	410,542	311,023	75.8
Peoria–Pekin, IL MSA	337,020	290,838	86.3
Philadelphia–Wilmington–Atlantic City, PA–NJ–DE–MD CMSA*	5,383,262	3,712,235	69.0

(continued)

	total population	non-Hispanic white	
		number	share of total
Pittsburgh, PA MSA	2,260,551	2,005,122	88.7%
Portland, ME MSA	248,827	235,307	94.6
Providence–Fall River–Warwick, RI–MA MSA	1,165,549	948,656	81.4
Provo–Orem, UT MSA	395,173	346,845	87.8
Raleigh–Durham–Chapel Hill, NC MSA	1,278,372	825,527	64.6
Reading, PA MSA	378,456	312,130	82.5
Reno, NV MSA	375,344	261,681	69.7
Richmond–Petersburg, VA MSA	1,013,399	639,642	63.1
Rochester, NY MSA	1,057,917	865,303	81.8
Rockford, IL MSA	382,901	305,655	79.8
Sacramento, CA PMSA	1,803,160	1,108,510	61.5
Saginaw–Bay City–Midland, MI MSA	393,837	324,355	82.4
St. Louis, MO–IL MSA	2,620,334	2,010,888	76.7
Salinas, CA MSA	392,192	148,407	37.8
Salt Lake City–Ogden, UT MSA	1,384,041	1,119,560	80.9
San Antonio, TX MSA	1,683,872	631,107	37.5
San Diego, CA MSA	2,833,275	1,483,817	52.4
San Francisco–Oakland–San Jose, CA CMSA	6,951,260	3,324,362	47.8
San Luis Obispo–Atascadero–Paso Robles, CA MSA	238,502	182,812	76.7
Santa Barbara–Santa Maria–Lompoc, CA MSA	385,238	207,886	54.0
Sarasota–Bradenton, FL MSA	639,438	533,490	83.4
Savannah, GA MSA	299,920	180,377	60.1
Scranton–Wilkes-Barre–Hazleton, PA MSA	587,557	561,085	95.5
Seattle–Tacoma–Bremerton, WA CMSA*	3,184,924	2,343,335	73.6
Shreveport–Bossier City, LA MSA	387,312	222,355	57.4
South Bend, IN MSA	252,944	199,130	78.7
Spokane, WA MSA	420,592	376,780	89.6
Springfield, MA MSA	560,472	424,472	75.7
Springfield, MO MSA	332,918	311,018	93.4
Stockton–Lodi, CA MSA	632,143	267,733	42.4
Syracuse, NY MSA	707,901	618,552	87.4
Tallahassee, FL MSA	274,945	161,150	58.6
Tampa–St. Petersburg–Clearwater, FL MSA	2,537,586	1,848,645	72.9
Toledo, OH MSA	598,283	473,234	79.1
Tucson, AZ MSA	885,025	515,785	58.3
Tulsa, OK MSA	810,062	587,677	72.5
Utica–Rome, NY MSA	282,844	259,361	91.7
Visalia–Tulare–Porterville, CA MSA	395,493	152,386	38.5
West Palm Beach–Boca Raton, FL MSA	1,223,206	805,740	65.9
Wichita, KS MSA	546,308	421,776	77.2
York, PA MSA	393,426	356,218	90.5
Youngstown–Warren, OH MSA	566,597	492,563	86.9

Population figures are for only part of the metropolitan area.
Note: Some metropolitan areas are not shown because data are not available. Non-Hispanic whites are those identifying themselves as being white alone and not Hispanic. For the definition of CMSA, MSA, and PMSA, see the glossary.
Source: Bureau of the Census, 2004 American Community Survey, Internet site http://factfinder.census.gov/servlet/ DatasetMainPageServlet?_program=ACS&_lang=en&_ts=; calculations by New Strategist

The Spending of Non-Hispanic Whites and "Others" Is Above Average

The nation's 90 million non-Hispanic white and "other" households spent an average of $43,459 in 2003, according to the Bureau of Labor Statistics' Consumer Expenditure Survey. The "others" include Asians, American Indians, Alaska Natives, Pacific Islanders, and those identifying themselves as being of two or more races.

Non-Hispanic white and other households spend 12 percent more than the average household on health care, 12 percent more on alcoholic beverages, and 17 percent more on other lodging (a category that includes hotel and motel expenses). The segment spends 8 percent less than average on eggs, 6 percent less on fish and seafood, 13 percent less on rent, and 10 percent less on infants' clothes.

■ Because the non-Hispanic white population is older than the black or Hispanic population, its spending on health care is above average.

Non-Hispanic white and other households spend 6 percent more than the average household

(average annual spending of total and non-Hispanic white and other consumer units, 2003)

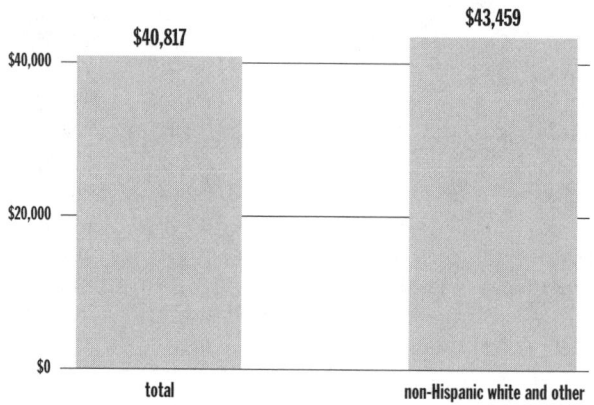

Table 5.93 Spending of Households Headed by Non-Hispanic Whites and Others, 2003

(average annual spending of total consumer units (CU), and average annual, indexed, and market share of spending of consumer units headed by non-Hispanic whites and others, by product and service category, 2003)

	total consumer units	non-Hispanic white and other consumer units		
		average spending	indexed spending	market share
Number of consumer units (000s)	115,356	90,019	–	78.0%
Persons per CU	2.5	2.4	–	–
Average income before taxes	$51,128	$55,463	108	84.7
Average annual spending	40,817	43,459	106	83.1
FOOD	$5,340	5,486	103	80.2
Food at home	3,129	3,134	100	78.2
Cereals and bakery products	442	447	101	78.9
Cereals and cereal products	150	147	98	76.5
Bakery products	292	300	103	80.2
Meats, poultry, fish, and eggs	825	783	95	74.1
Beef	246	236	96	74.9
Pork	171	159	93	72.6
Other meats	102	102	100	78.0
Poultry	145	133	92	71.6
Fish and seafood	124	117	94	73.6
Eggs	37	34	92	71.7
Dairy products	328	337	103	80.2
Fresh milk and cream	127	127	100	78.0
Other dairy products	201	210	104	81.5
Fruits and vegetables	535	529	99	77.2
Fresh fruits	171	169	99	77.1
Fresh vegetables	172	168	98	76.2
Processed fruits	108	106	98	76.6
Processed vegetables	84	85	101	79.0
Other food at home	999	1,038	104	81.1
Sugar and other sweets	119	122	103	80.0
Fats and oils	86	85	99	77.1
Miscellaneous foods	490	514	105	81.9
Nonalcoholic beverages	268	275	103	80.1
Food prepared by CU on trips	36	41	114	88.9
Food away from home	2,211	2,353	106	83.0
ALCOHOLIC BEVERAGES	391	437	112	87.2
HOUSING	13,432	14,005	104	81.4
Shelter	7,887	8,185	104	81.0
Owned dwellings	5,263	5,775	110	85.6
Mortgage interest and charges	2,954	3,182	108	84.1
Property taxes	1,344	1,507	112	87.5
Maintenance, repair, insurance, other expenses	965	1,086	113	87.8
Rented dwellings	2,179	1,889	87	67.7
Other lodging	445	521	117	91.4
Utilities, fuels, and public services	2,811	2,837	101	78.8
Natural gas	392	392	100	78.0
Electricity	1,028	1,039	101	78.9

(continued)

	total consumer units	non-Hispanic white and other consumer units		
		average spending	indexed spending	market share
Fuel oil and other fuels	$110	$126	115	89.4%
Telephone	956	944	99	77.1
Water and other public services	326	336	103	80.4
Household services	**707**	**779**	**110**	**86.0**
Personal services	294	308	105	81.8
Other household services	414	471	114	88.8
Housekeeping supplies	**529**	**563**	**106**	**83.1**
Laundry and cleaning supplies	132	127	96	75.1
Other household products	263	287	109	85.2
Postage and stationery	133	148	111	86.8
Household furnishings and equipment	**1,497**	**1,642**	**110**	**85.6**
Household textiles	113	125	111	86.3
Furniture	401	426	106	82.9
Floor coverings	52	62	119	93.0
Major appliances	196	206	105	82.0
Small appliances, misc. housewares	88	95	108	84.2
Miscellaneous household equipment	648	729	113	87.8
APPAREL AND RELATED SERVICES	**1,640**	**1,631**	**99**	**77.6**
Men and boys	**372**	**374**	**101**	**78.5**
Men, aged 16 or older	282	294	104	81.4
Boys, aged 2 to 15	89	81	91	71.0
Women and girls	**634**	**655**	**103**	**80.6**
Women, aged 16 or older	529	554	105	81.7
Girls, aged 2 to 15	106	101	95	74.4
Children under age 2	**81**	**73**	**90**	**70.3**
Footwear	**294**	**262**	**89**	**69.5**
Other apparel products and services	**258**	**266**	**103**	**80.5**
TRANSPORTATION	**7,781**	**8,317**	**107**	**83.4**
Vehicle purchases	**3,732**	**4,063**	**109**	**85.0**
Cars and trucks, new	2,052	2,301	112	87.5
Cars and trucks, used	1,611	1,684	105	81.6
Other vehicles	68	79	116	90.7
Gasoline and motor oil	**1,333**	**1,381**	**104**	**80.8**
Other vehicle expenses	**2,331**	**2,458**	**105**	**82.3**
Vehicle finance charges	371	385	104	81.0
Maintenance and repairs	619	663	107	83.6
Vehicle insurance	905	944	104	81.4
Vehicle rentals, leases, licenses, other charges	436	466	107	83.4
Public transportation	**385**	**416**	**108**	**84.3**
HEALTH CARE	**2,416**	**2,711**	**112**	**87.6**
Health insurance	1,252	1,389	111	86.6
Medical services	591	675	114	89.1
Drugs	467	524	112	87.6
Medical supplies	107	122	114	89.0
ENTERTAINMENT	**2,060**	**2,326**	**113**	**88.1**
Fees and admissions	494	576	117	91.0
Television, radio, sound equipment	730	761	104	81.3
Pets, toys, and playground equipment	378	441	117	91.0
Other entertainment products and services	457	546	119	93.2

(continued)

	total consumer units	non-Hispanic white and other consumer units		
		average spending	indexed spending	market share
PERSONAL CARE PRODUCTS, SERVICES	$527	$541	103	80.1%
READING	127	149	117	91.6
EDUCATION	783	877	112	87.4
TOBACCO PRODUCTS, SMOKING SUPPLIES	290	322	111	86.6
MISCELLANEOUS	606	655	108	84.3
CASH CONTRIBUTIONS	1,370	1,552	113	88.4
PERSONAL INSURANCE AND PENSIONS	4,055	4,450	110	85.6
Life and other personal insurance	397	444	112	87.3
Pensions and Social Security	3,658	4,006	110	85.5
PERSONAL TAXES	2,532	3,013	119	92.9
Federal income taxes	1,843	2,221	121	94.0
State and local income taxes	502	570	114	88.6
Other taxes	187	222	119	92.6
GIFTS FOR NONHOUSEHOLD MEMBERS	1,007	1,115	111	86.4
Food	78	85	109	85.0
Alcoholic beverages	16	18	113	87.8
Housing	220	250	114	88.7
Housekeeping supplies	42	47	112	87.3
Household textiles	13	15	115	90.0
Appliances and misc. housewares	25	28	112	87.4
Major appliances	7	7	100	78.0
Small appliances and misc. housewares	18	21	117	91.0
Miscellaneous household equipment	57	66	116	90.4
Other housing	85	94	111	86.3
Apparel and services	225	231	103	80.1
Males, aged 2 or older	56	60	107	83.6
Females, aged 2 or older	80	82	103	80.0
Children under age 2	39	37	95	74.0
Other apparel products and services	50	52	104	81.2
Jewelry and watches	26	28	108	84.0
All other apparel products and services	25	24	96	74.9
Transportation	60	52	87	67.6
Health care	48	57	119	92.7
Entertainment	69	79	114	89.3
Toys, games, hobbies, and tricycles	26	30	115	90.0
Other entertainment	43	49	114	88.9
Personal care products and services	16	17	106	82.9
Reading	1	2	200	–
Education	200	237	119	92.5
All other gifts	74	86	116	90.7

Definitions: The index compares the spending of the average non-Hispanic white and other consumer unit with the spending of the average consumer unit by dividing non-Hispanic white and other spending by average spending in each category and multiplying by 100. An index of 100 means non-Hispanic white and other spending in the category equals average spending. An index of 125 means non-Hispanic white and other spending is 25 percent above average, while an index of 75 means non-Hispanic white and other spending is 25 percent below average. The market share is the percentage of total spending on a product or service category that is accounted for by consumer units headed by non-Hispanic whites and others.

Note: Non-Hispanic whites and others include Asians, Alaska Natives, American Indians, Native Hawaiians, and other Pacific Islanders as well as those reporting more than one race. The Bureau of labor Statistics uses consumer unit rather than household as the sampling unit in the Consumer Expenditure Survey. For the definition of consumer unit, see the glossary. Spending by category will not add to total spending because gift spending is also included in the preceding product and service categories and personal taxes are not included in the total. (–) means sample is too small to make a reliable estimate or not applicable.

Source: Bureau of Labor Statistics, 2003 Consumer Expenditure Survey, Internet site http://www.bls.gov/cex/; calculations by New Strategist

Non-Hispanic Whites Are the Only Population Segment With Significant Wealth

The median net worth (assets minus debts) of non-Hispanic white households stood at $120,900 in 2001 (the latest data available), far above the $86,100 net worth of the average American household. The net worth of non-Hispanic white householders is above average because the group is much more likely to own a home than other segments of the population. Home equity accounts for the largest share of Americans' net worth. Fully 74 percent of non-Hispanic white householders owned their home in 2001. Their homes were worth a median of $130,000.

Non-Hispanic white householders had $38,500 in financial assets in 2001. Twenty-five percent owned stock, worth a median of $22,000. The 57 percent majority owned retirement accounts, worth a median of $35,000. Seventy-six percent of non-Hispanic white households were in debt in 2001, with mortgages accounting for the largest share of debt.

Fewer than half of white workers have an IRA or participate in a 401(k)-type retirement plan, according to the Employee Benefit Research Institute. Among the 35 percent who participate in a 401(k)-type plan, the median balance is just $15,000. These dismal savings figures among the nation's majority population may explain why few Americans say they are "very confident" they will have enough money to live comfortably throughout their retirement years.

■ Among non-Hispanic whites aged 65 or older, 93 percent receive Social Security benefits. Thirty-nine percent receive retirement income from a pension or IRA.

The net worth of non-Hispanic whites is well above average

(median net worth of total and non-Hispanic white households, 2001)

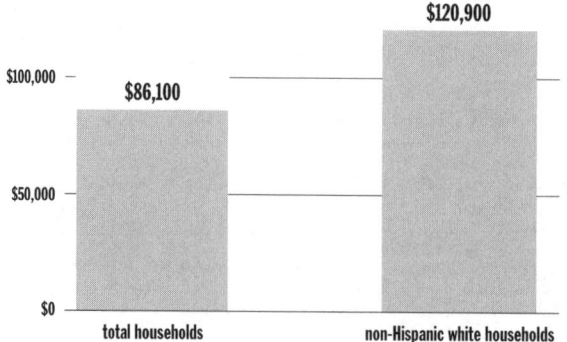

Table 5.94 Net Worth, Assets, and Debt of Non-Hispanic White Households, 2001

(median net worth, median value of assets for owners, and median amount of debt for debtors, for total and non-Hispanic white households, and index of non-Hispanic whites to total, 2001)

		non-Hispanic white households	
	total households	median	index
Median net worth	**$86,100**	**$120,900**	**140**
Median value of financial assets	28,000	38,500	138
Median value of nonfinancial assets	113,500	131,500	116
Median amount of debt	38,775	44,478	115

Note: The index is calculated by dividing the non-Hispanic white figure by the total figure and multiplying by 100.
Source: Federal Reserve Board, "Recent Changes in U.S. Family Finances: Evidence from the 1998 and 2001 Survey of Consumer Finances," Federal Reserve Bulletin, January 2003; calculations by New Strategist

Table 5.95 Financial Assets of Non-Hispanic White Households, 2001

(percent of non-Hispanic white households owning financial assets, and median value of assets for owners, 2001)

	percent owning asset	median value
Any financial asset	**96.5%**	**$38,500**
Transaction accounts	94.9	4,800
Certificates of deposit	18.5	15,000
Savings bonds	19.4	1,000
Bonds	3.8	50,000
Stocks	24.5	22,000
Mutual funds	20.9	40,000
Retirement accounts	56.9	35,000
Life insurance	29.8	10,000
Other managed assets	8.2	70,000
Other financial assets	9.2	5,000

Source: Federal Reserve Board, "Recent Changes in U.S. Family Finances: Evidence from the 1998 and 2001 Survey of Consumer Finances," Federal Reserve Bulletin, January 2003; calculations by New Strategist

Table 5.96 Nonfinancial Assets of Non-Hispanic White Households, 2001

(percent of non-Hispanic white households owning nonfinancial assets, and median value of assets for owners, 2001)

	percent owning asset	median value
Any nonfinancial asset	**94.7%**	**$131,500**
Vehicles	89.1	14,600
Primary residence	74.1	130,000
Other residential property	12.9	80,000
Nonresidential property	9.6	50,000
Business	13.9	100,000
Other nonfinancial asset	9.0	15,000

Source: Federal Reserve Board, "Recent Changes in U.S. Family Finances: Evidence from the 1998 and 2001 Survey of Consumer Finances," Federal Reserve Bulletin, January 2003

Table 5.97 Debt of Non-Hispanic White Households, 2001

(percent of non-Hispanic white households with debt, and median amount of debt for those with debt, 2001)

	percent with debt	median amount
Any debt	**75.8%**	**$44,478**
Home-secured	47.6	74,000
Other residential property	5.4	40,000
Installment loans	45.3	10,000
Other lines of credit	43.3	2,000
Credit card	1.7	4,000
Other debt	7.4	3,600

Source: Federal Reserve Board, "Recent Changes in U.S. Family Finances: Evidence from the 1998 and 2001 Survey of Consumer Finances," Federal Reserve Bulletin, January 2003

Table 5.98 White Ownership of IRAs and 401(k)-Type Plans, 2002

(percent of total and white workers aged 21 to 64 owning IRAs and 401(k)-type plans, 2002)

	total workers	white workers
IRA or 401(k)-type plan	**40.4%**	**46.5%**
IRA only	9.6	11.9
401(k)-type plan only	21.7	23.4
Both IRA and 401(k)-type plan	9.2	11.3
Neither IRA nor 401(k)-type plan	**59.6**	**53.5**

Source: Employee Benefit Research Institute, "401(k)-Type Plan and IRA Ownership," by Craig Copeland, EBRI Notes, *Vol. 26, No. 1, January 2005; Internet site http://www.ebri.org/*

Table 5.99 White Participation and Savings in IRAs and 401(k)s, 2002

(percent of total and white workers aged 21 to 64 owning an IRA or participating in 401(k) type plan, and average and median balance of IRA and 401(k), 2002)

	percent owning IRA	IRA balance		percent participating in 401(k)	401(k) balance	
		average	median		average	median
Total workers	**18.7%**	**$26,951**	**$10,000**	**30.9%**	**$33,647**	**$14,000**
White workers	23.2	27,873	10,000	34.6	35,808	15,000

Source: Employee Benefit Research Institute, "401(k)-Type Plan and IRA Ownership," by Craig Copeland, EBRI Notes, *Vol. 26, No. 1, January 2005; Internet site http://www.ebri.org/*

Table 5.100 Sources of Income for Non-Hispanic Whites Aged 65 or Older, 2003

(number and percent of non-Hispanic whites aged 65 or older with income by selected source and average income for those with income, ranked by number receiving income, 2003; people in thousands as of 2004)

	number with income	percent with income	average amount received by those with income
Non-Hispanic whites aged 65 or older with income	**27,838**	**100.0%**	**$15,650**
Social Security	25,857	92.9	10,620
Interest	16,593	59.6	1,656
Retirement income, including pensions	10,776	38.7	9,217
Dividends	6,447	23.2	1,833
Earnings	5,074	18.2	16,229
Rents, royalties, estates, or trusts	2,494	9.0	2,194
Survivor's benefits	1,535	5.5	6,273
Veteran's benefits	795	2.9	4,944
SSI (Supplemental Security Income)	541	1.9	3,654

Note: Non-Hispanic whites include only those identifying themselves as being white alone and not Hispanic.
Source: Bureau of the Census, 2004 Current Population Survey, Internet site http://pubdb3.census.gov/macro/032004/perinc/new09_001.htm; calculations by New Strategist

Total Population

■ The U.S. population grew from 282 million in 2000 to 294 million in 2004. The non-Hispanic white share of the population fell from 69 to 67 percent during those years.

■ Twenty-eight percent of Americans had a college degree in 2004. The proportion ranges from a low of 12 percent among Hispanics to a high of 49 percent among Asians.

■ More than 4 million babies were born to American women in 2003, and only a slim majority—57 percent—was non-Hispanic white.

■ More than 80 percent of the nation's homeowners are non-Hispanic white.

■ The median income of U.S. households climbed 6 percent between 1990 and 2003, to $43,318 after adjusting for inflation.

■ The non-Hispanic white share of workers will fall from 71 to 65 percent between 2002 and 2012.

■ Among householders under age 40, more than one in three are Asian, black, Hispanic, or another minority.

■ Fully 34 million Americans are foreign-born, accounting for 12 percent of the total population. Among people aged 30 to 34, one in five is foreign-born.

■ Asian households spend the most—10 percent more than the average household. Black households spend the least—30 percent less than average.

■ The median net worth of non-Hispanic white households stood at $120,900 in 2001, much greater than the $17,100 net worth of nonwhite and Hispanic household.

One-third of Americans are minorities

(percent distribution of people by race and Hispanic origin, 2004)

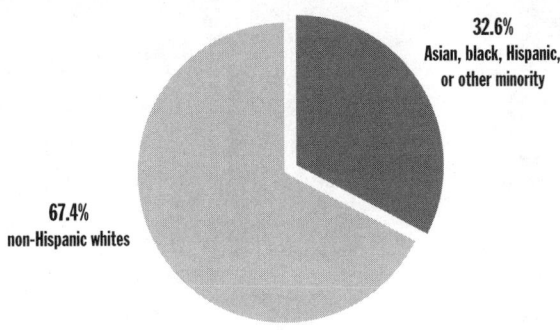

32.6%
Asian, black, Hispanic,
or other minority

67.4%
non-Hispanic whites

The Educational Attainment of Americans Varies Greatly by Race and Hispanic Origin

Overall, 85 percent of Americans had a high school diploma in 2004. But the figure ranges from a low of 58 percent among Hispanics to a high of 90 percent among non-Hispanic whites. The proportion of all Americans with a high school diploma did not top 50 percent until the late 1960s, then rose rapidly as the well-educated baby-boom generation entered adulthood.

Twenty-eight percent of Americans had a college degree in 2004. Again, the proportion varies greatly by race and Hispanic origin—ranging from a low of 12 percent among Hispanics to a high of 49 percent among Asians.

Seventy-five million Americans aged 3 or older are enrolled in school, or 27 percent of the population. Blacks, Hispanics, Asians, and other minorities are an ever-growing proportion of the student population. The minority share of public school students ranges from a low of 26 percent in the Midwest to a high of 54 percent in the West. At the college level, the minority share is 32 percent.

■ The educational attainment of Americans will continue to rise as well-educated younger adults replace less educated older people.

Most Americans have at least some college experience

(percent of total people aged 25 or older who are high school graduates or more, have some college or more, or are college graduates, 2004)

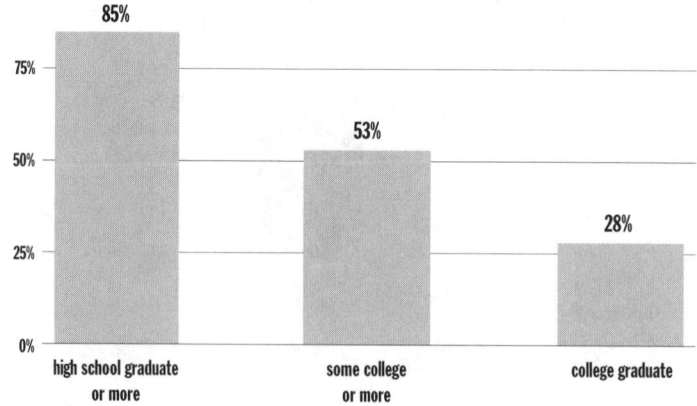

Table 6.1 Educational Attainment of Total People by Age, 2004

(number and percent distribution of people aged 25 or older by educational attainment and age, 2004; numbers in thousands)

	total	25 to 34	35 to 44	45 to 54	55 to 64	65 or older
Total people	**186,877**	**39,201**	**43,573**	**41,069**	**28,375**	**34,659**
Not a high school graduate	27,744	5,072	5,232	4,251	3,856	9,339
High school graduate only	59,810	11,244	13,739	12,910	9,436	12,482
Some college, no degree	31,808	7,583	7,420	7,210	4,824	4,771
Associate's degree	15,764	3,462	4,312	4,152	2,238	1,600
Bachelor's degree	33,766	8,758	8,821	7,838	4,555	3,794
Master's degree	12,609	2,234	2,879	3,369	2,432	1,694
Professional degree	2,952	556	695	715	468	517
Doctoral degree	2,422	294	476	625	565	462
High school graduate or more	159,131	34,131	38,342	36,819	24,518	25,320
Some college or more	99,321	22,887	24,603	23,909	15,082	12,838
Bachelor's degree or more	51,749	11,842	12,871	12,547	8,020	6,467

PERCENT DISTRIBUTION

Total people	**100.0%**	**100.0%**	**100.0%**	**100.0%**	**100.0%**	**100.0%**
Not a high school graduate	14.8	12.9	12.0	10.4	13.6	26.9
High school graduate only	32.0	28.7	31.5	31.4	33.3	36.0
Some college, no degree	17.0	19.3	17.0	17.6	17.0	13.8
Associate's degree	8.4	8.8	9.9	10.1	7.9	4.6
Bachelor's degree	18.1	22.3	20.2	19.1	16.1	10.9
Master's degree	6.7	5.7	6.6	8.2	8.6	4.9
Professional degree	1.6	1.4	1.6	1.7	1.6	1.5
Doctoral degree	1.3	0.7	1.1	1.5	2.0	1.3
High school graduate or more	85.2	87.1	88.0	89.7	86.4	73.1
Some college or more	53.1	58.4	56.5	58.2	53.2	37.0
Bachelor's degree or more	27.7	30.2	29.5	30.6	28.3	18.7

Source: Bureau of the Census, 2004 Current Population Survey Annual Social and Economic Supplement, Educational Attainment in the United States: 2004, Detailed Tables, Internet site http://www.census.gov/population/www/socdemo/education/cps2004.html; calculations by New Strategist

Table 6.2 Educational Attainment of Total Men by Age, 2004

(number and percent distribution of men aged 25 or older by educational attainment and age, 2004; numbers in thousands)

	total	25 to 34	35 to 44	45 to 54	55 to 64	65 or older
Total men	**89,558**	**19,599**	**21,531**	**20,082**	**13,551**	**14,797**
Not a high school graduate	13,569	2,798	2,872	2,185	1,879	3,837
High school graduate only	27,889	6,020	7,020	6,218	4,056	4,575
Some college, no degree	15,012	3,681	3,504	3,537	2,254	2,035
Associate's degree	6,751	1,605	1,823	1,772	958	594
Bachelor's degree	16,632	4,072	4,233	3,911	2,390	2,026
Master's degree	6,158	970	1,398	1,599	1,239	952
Professional degree	1,925	291	410	468	352	404
Doctoral degree	1,621	162	269	392	423	373
High school graduate or more	75,988	16,801	18,657	17,897	11,672	10,959
Some college or more	48,099	10,781	11,637	11,679	7,616	6,384
Bachelor's degree or more	26,336	5,495	6,310	6,370	4,404	3,755
PERCENT DISTRIBUTION						
Total men	**100.0%**	**100.0%**	**100.0%**	**100.0%**	**100.0%**	**100.0%**
Not a high school graduate	15.2	14.3	13.3	10.9	13.9	25.9
High school graduate only	31.1	30.7	32.6	31.0	29.9	30.9
Some college, no degree	16.8	18.8	16.3	17.6	16.6	13.8
Associate's degree	7.5	8.2	8.5	8.8	7.1	4.0
Bachelor's degree	18.6	20.8	19.7	19.5	17.6	13.7
Master's degree	6.9	4.9	6.5	8.0	9.1	6.4
Professional degree	2.1	1.5	1.9	2.3	2.6	2.7
Doctoral degree	1.8	0.8	1.2	2.0	3.1	2.5
High school graduate or more	84.8	85.7	86.7	89.1	86.1	74.1
Some college or more	53.7	55.0	54.0	58.2	56.2	43.1
Bachelor's degree or more	29.4	28.0	29.3	31.7	32.5	25.4

Source: Bureau of the Census, 2004 Current Population Survey Annual Social and Economic Supplement, Educational Attainment in the United States: 2004, Detailed Tables, Internet site http://www.census.gov/population/www/socdemo/education/cps2004.html; calculations by New Strategist

Table 6.3 Educational Attainment of Total Women by Age, 2004

(number and percent distribution of women aged 25 or older by educational attainment and age, 2004; numbers in thousands)

	total	25 to 34	35 to 44	45 to 54	55 to 64	65 or older
Total women	**97,319**	**19,603**	**22,043**	**20,986**	**14,824**	**19,862**
Not a high school graduate	14,175	2,273	2,361	2,066	1,975	5,502
High school graduate only	31,921	5,224	6,719	6,692	5,380	7,907
Some college, no degree	16,796	3,901	3,916	3,673	2,569	2,736
Associate's degree	9,013	1,855	2,490	2,381	1,283	1,006
Bachelor's degree	17,134	4,686	4,588	3,929	2,164	1,767
Master's degree	6,451	1,265	1,481	1,769	1,194	742
Professional degree	1,027	266	284	247	117	114
Doctoral degree	801	132	206	232	142	89
High school graduate or more	83,143	17,329	19,684	18,923	12,849	14,361
Some college or more	51,222	12,105	12,965	12,231	7,469	6,454
Bachelor's degree or more	25,413	6,349	6,559	6,177	3,617	2,712

PERCENT DISTRIBUTION

	total	25 to 34	35 to 44	45 to 54	55 to 64	65 or older
Total women	**100.0%**	**100.0%**	**100.0%**	**100.0%**	**100.0%**	**100.0%**
Not a high school graduate	14.6	11.6	10.7	9.8	13.3	27.7
High school graduate only	32.8	26.6	30.5	31.9	36.3	39.8
Some college, no degree	17.3	19.9	17.8	17.5	17.3	13.8
Associate's degree	9.3	9.5	11.3	11.3	8.7	5.1
Bachelor's degree	17.6	23.9	20.8	18.7	14.6	8.9
Master's degree	6.6	6.5	6.7	8.4	8.1	3.7
Professional degree	1.1	1.4	1.3	1.2	0.8	0.6
Doctoral degree	0.8	0.7	0.9	1.1	1.0	0.4
High school graduate or more	85.4	88.4	89.3	90.2	86.7	72.3
Some college or more	52.6	61.8	58.8	58.3	50.4	32.5
Bachelor's degree or more	26.1	32.4	29.8	29.4	24.4	13.7

Source: Bureau of the Census, 2004 Current Population Survey Annual Social and Economic Supplement, Educational Attainment in the United States: 2004, Detailed Tables, Internet site http://www.census.gov/population/www/socdemo/education/cps2004.html; calculations by New Strategist

Table 6.4 Educational Attainment by Race and Hispanic Origin, 2004

(number and percent distribution of people aged 25 or older by educational attainment, race, and Hispanic origin, 2004; numbers in thousands)

	total	Asian	black	Hispanic	non-Hispanic white
Total people	**186,877**	**8,312**	**21,290**	**21,596**	**134,063**
Not a high school graduate	27,744	1,089	4,122	8,986	13,415
High school graduate or more	159,131	7,224	17,169	12,610	120,648
Some college or more	99,321	5,567	9,545	6,633	76,626
Bachelor's degree or more	51,749	4,063	3,761	2,606	40,995

PERCENT DISTRIBUTION BY EDUCATIONAL ATTAINMENT

Total people	**100.0%**	**100.0%**	**100.0%**	**100.0%**	**100.0%**
Not a high school graduate	14.8	13.1	19.4	41.6	10.0
High school graduate or more	85.2	86.9	80.6	58.4	90.0
Some college or more	53.1	67.0	44.8	30.7	57.2
Bachelor's degree or more	27.7	48.9	17.7	12.1	30.6

PERCENT DISTRIBUTION BY RACE AND HISPANIC ORIGIN

Total people	**100.0%**	**4.4%**	**11.4%**	**11.6%**	**71.7%**
Not a high school graduate	100.0	3.9	14.9	32.4	48.4
High school graduate or more	100.0	4.5	10.8	7.9	75.8
Some college or more	100.0	5.6	9.6	6.7	77.1
Bachelor's degree or more	100.0	7.9	7.3	5.0	79.2

Note: Numbers by race and Hispanic origin will not sum to total because Asians and blacks include those identifying themselves as being of the race alone and those identifying themselves as being of the race in combination with one or more other races, Hispanics may be of any race, and not all races are shown. Non-Hispanic whites are those identifying themselves as being white alone and not Hispanic.

Source: Bureau of the Census, 2004 Current Population Survey Annual Social and Economic Supplement, Educational Attainment in the United States: 2004, Detailed Tables, Internet site http://www.census.gov/population/www/socdemo/education/cps2004 .html; calculations by New Strategist

Table 6.5 Educational Attainment of Total People by Age and Region, 2004

(percent of people aged 25 or older by selected educational attainment, age, and region, 2004)

	Northeast	Midwest	South	West
HIGH SCHOOL GRADUATE OR MORE				
Total people	**86.5%**	**88.3%**	**83.0%**	**84.3%**
Aged 25 to 34	90.1	90.6	85.7	83.6
Aged 35 to 44	91.0	92.2	86.5	83.6
Aged 45 to 54	90.6	93.0	88.0	87.9
Aged 55 to 64	87.6	89.3	83.0	88.2
Aged 65 or older	72.6	74.4	69.8	77.9
SOME COLLEGE OR MORE				
Total people	**51.4**	**53.1**	**50.4**	**59.1**
Aged 25 to 34	59.5	60.4	56.0	59.4
Aged 35 to 44	57.6	58.3	53.1	59.0
Aged 45 to 54	57.1	57.5	55.5	64.1
Aged 55 to 64	49.1	51.2	49.9	63.9
Aged 65 or older	31.6	34.4	35.7	48.1
BACHELOR'S DEGREE OR MORE				
Total people	**30.9**	**26.0**	**25.5**	**30.2**
Aged 25 to 34	36.8	29.8	28.1	28.9
Aged 35 to 44	35.0	29.1	26.9	29.4
Aged 45 to 54	34.1	27.4	28.5	33.8
Aged 55 to 64	29.4	25.6	25.7	34.2
Aged 65 or older	18.0	16.5	17.1	24.6

Source: Bureau of the Census, 2004 Current Population Survey Annual Social and Economic Supplement, Educational Attainment in the United States: 2004, Detailed Tables, Internet site http://www.census.gov/population/www/socdemo/education/cps2004.html; calculations by New Strategist

Table 6.6 Educational Attainment of Total People by State, 2004

(percent of people aged 25 or older who are high school or college graduates, for the 25 largest states, 2004)

	high school graduate or more	college graduate
Total people	**85.2%**	**27.7%**
Alabama	82.4	22.3
Arizona	84.4	28.0
California	81.3	31.7
Colorado	88.3	35.5
Florida	85.9	26.0
Georgia	85.2	27.6
Illinois	86.8	27.4
Indiana	87.2	21.1
Kentucky	81.8	21.0
Louisiana	78.7	22.4
Maryland	87.4	35.2
Massachusetts	86.9	36.7
Michigan	87.9	24.4
Minnesota	92.3	32.5
Missouri	87.9	28.1
New Jersey	87.6	34.6
New York	85.4	30.6
North Carolina	80.9	23.4
Ohio	88.1	24.6
Pennsylvania	86.5	25.3
Tennessee	82.9	24.3
Texas	78.3	24.5
Virginia	88.4	33.1
Washington	89.7	29.9
Wisconsin	88.8	25.6

Source: Bureau of the Census, 2004 Current Population Survey Annual Social and Economic Supplement, Educational Attainment in the United States: 2004, Detailed Tables, Internet site http://www.census.gov/population/www/socdemo/education/cps2004. html; calculations by New Strategist

Table 6.7 School Enrollment of Total People by Age and Sex, 2003

(number and percent of people aged 3 or older enrolled in school, by age and sex, October 2003; numbers in thousands)

	total		female		male	
	number	percent	number	percent	number	percent
Total people enrolled	**74,911**	**27.2%**	**37,588**	**26.6%**	**37,323**	**27.8%**
Aged 3 to 4	4,590	55.1	2,154	54.1	2,437	55.9
Aged 5 to 6	7,309	94.5	3,620	94.4	3,689	94.7
Aged 7 to 9	11,706	98.1	5,692	98.3	6,014	97.9
Aged 10 to 13	16,478	98.4	7,925	98.6	8,553	98.3
Aged 14 to 15	8,329	97.5	4,173	97.5	4,155	97.5
Aged 16 to 17	8,177	94.9	3,978	94.8	4,199	95.0
Aged 18 to 19	4,856	64.5	2,508	66.6	2,348	62.4
Aged 20 to 21	3,684	48.3	2,059	52.9	1,625	43.4
Aged 22 to 24	3,397	27.8	1,786	29.5	1,611	26.1
Aged 25 to 29	2,212	11.8	1,203	12.8	1,009	10.8
Aged 30 to 34	1,378	6.8	749	7.3	629	6.3
Aged 35 to 44	1,635	3.7	1,024	4.6	611	2.9
Aged 45 to 54	879	2.2	547	2.6	333	1.7
Aged 55 or older	283	0.5	171	0.5	111	0.4

Source: Bureau of the Census, School Enrollment—Social and Economic Characteristics of Students: October 2003, Detailed Tables, Internet site http://www.census.gov/population/www/socdemo/school/cps2003.html

Table 6.8 School Enrollment by Age, Race, and Hispanic Origin, 2003

(number and percent distribution of people aged 3 or older enrolled in school, by age, race, and Hispanic origin, October 2003; numbers in thousands)

	total	Asian	black	Hispanic	non-Hispanic white
Total people enrolled	**74,911**	**3,817**	**12,144**	**11,929**	**46,440**
Aged 3 to 4	4,590	179	798	728	2,874
Aged 5 to 6	7,309	295	1,204	1,386	4,409
Aged 7 to 9	11,706	577	2,015	2,230	6,789
Aged 10 to 13	16,478	767	2,804	2,843	9,957
Aged 14 to 15	8,329	328	1,379	1,415	5,110
Aged 16 to 17	8,177	356	1,321	1,242	5,169
Aged 18 to 19	4,856	279	688	614	3,243
Aged 20 to 21	3,684	252	490	454	2,467
Aged 22 to 24	3,397	304	469	353	2,239
Aged 25 to 29	2,212	232	311	240	1,390
Aged 30 to 34	1,378	117	220	174	855
Aged 35 to 44	1,635	87	255	185	1,082
Aged 45 to 54	879	30	150	42	649
Aged 55 or older	283	15	40	23	205

PERCENT DISTRIBUTION BY RACE AND HISPANIC ORIGIN

	total	Asian	black	Hispanic	non-Hispanic white
Total people enrolled	**100.0%**	**5.1%**	**16.2%**	**15.9%**	**62.0%**
Aged 3 to 4	100.0	3.9	17.4	15.9	62.6
Aged 5 to 6	100.0	4.0	16.5	19.0	60.3
Aged 7 to 9	100.0	4.9	17.2	19.1	58.0
Aged 10 to 13	100.0	4.7	17.0	17.3	60.4
Aged 14 to 15	100.0	3.9	16.6	17.0	61.4
Aged 16 to 17	100.0	4.4	16.2	15.2	63.2
Aged 18 to 19	100.0	5.7	14.2	12.6	66.8
Aged 20 to 21	100.0	6.8	13.3	12.3	67.0
Aged 22 to 24	100.0	8.9	13.8	10.4	65.9
Aged 25 to 29	100.0	10.5	14.1	10.8	62.8
Aged 30 to 34	100.0	8.5	16.0	12.6	62.0
Aged 35 to 44	100.0	5.3	15.6	11.3	66.2
Aged 45 to 54	100.0	3.4	17.1	4.8	73.8
Aged 55 or older	100.0	5.3	14.1	8.1	72.4

Note: Numbers by race and Hispanic origin will not sum to total because Asians and blacks include those identifying themselves as being of the race alone and those identifying themselves as being of the race in combination with one or more other races, Hispanics may be of any race, and not all races are shown. Non-Hispanic whites are those identifying themselves as being white alone and not Hispanic.
Source: Bureau of the Census, School Enrollment—Social and Economic Characteristics of Students: October 2003, Detailed Tables, Internet site http://www.census.gov/population/www/socdemo/school/cps2003.html; calculations by New Strategist

Table 6.9 Minority Enrollment in Public Schools by Region, 2003

(percent distribution of public school students in kindergarten through 12th grade, by race and Hispanic origin, fall 2003)

	Northeast	Midwest	South	West
Total enrolled	**100.0%**	**100.0%**	**100.0%**	**100.0%**
Non-Hispanic white	64.8	74.4	53.6	45.9
Total minority	35.2	25.6	46.4	54.1
Black	16.0	14.2	24.8	5.2
Hispanic	13.7	6.4	16.9	35.5
Other	5.4	5.0	4.6	13.4

Note: Other includes American Indians, Asians, and those identifying themselves as being of two or more races.
Source: National Center for Education Statistics, The Condition of Education, *Internet site http://nces.ed.gov/programs/coe/2005/section1/indicator04.asp*

Table 6.10 Total Families with Children in College, 2003

(total number of families, number with dependent children aged 5 to 24, and number and percent with children enrolled in college by household income, 2003; numbers in thousands)

	total	with children aged 5–24	with one or more children enrolled in college		
			number	percent of total families	percent of families with children 5–24
Total families	**76,727**	**38,005**	**5,719**	**7.5%**	**15.0%**
Less than $10,000	3,701	2,227	123	3.3	5.5
$10,000 to $14,999	3,571	1,776	152	4.3	8.6
$15,000 to $19,999	2,803	1,328	101	3.6	7.6
$20,000 to $24,999	8,009	3,911	359	4.5	9.2
$25,000 to $29,999	8,076	3,984	474	5.9	11.9
$30,000 to $34,999	5,963	2,970	388	6.5	13.1
$35,000 to $39,999	13,039	6,480	1,091	8.4	16.8
$40,000 to $49,999	7,970	4,102	832	10.4	20.3
$50,000 to $74,999	5,733	3,129	716	12.5	22.9
$75,000 and over	3,629	1,896	436	12.0	23.0

Note: Numbers will not add to total because not reported is not shown.
Source: Bureau of the Census, School Enrollment—Social and Economic Characteristics of Students: October 2003, Detailed Tables, *Internet site http://www.census.gov/population/www/socdemo/school/cps2003.html; calculations by New Strategist*

Table 6.11 Scholastic Assessment Test Scores by Race and Hispanic Origin, 1990–91 and 2002–03

(average SAT scores and change in scores by race and Hispanic origin of student, 1990–91 and 2002–03)

	2002–03	1990–91	change
VERBAL SAT			
Total students	**507**	**499**	**8**
American Indian	480	470	10
Asian	508	485	23
Black	431	427	4
Hispanic or Latino	457	458	–1
Mexican American	448	454	–6
Puerto Rican	456	436	20
White	529	518	11
Other	501	486	15
MATH SAT			
Total students	**519**	**500**	**19**
American Indian	482	468	14
Asian	575	548	27
Black	426	419	7
Hispanic or Latino	464	462	2
Mexican American	457	459	–2
Puerto Rican	453	439	14
White	534	513	21
Other	513	492	21

Source: National Center for Education Statistics, Digest of Education Statistics 2003; *Internet site http://nces.ed.gov/programs/ digest/d03/list_tables3.asp#c3; calculations by New Strategist*

Table 6.12   College Enrollment of Total People by Age and Type of School, 2003

(number and percent distribution of people aged 15 or older enrolled in college by age and type of school, October 2003; numbers in thousands)

	total	two-year college	four-year college	graduate school
Total people enrolled	**16,638**	**4,384**	**8,985**	**3,268**
Under age 20	3,661	1,178	2,455	30
Aged 20 to 21	3,534	747	2,703	84
Aged 22 to 24	3,320	843	1,844	632
Aged 25 to 29	2,164	476	786	903
Aged 30 to 34	1,330	358	475	496
Aged 35 to 39	769	248	196	325
Aged 40 to 44	757	239	224	294
Aged 45 to 49	479	120	149	209
Aged 50 to 54	357	111	83	162
Aged 55 or older	268	66	68	133
PERCENT DISTRIBUTION BY TYPE OF SCHOOL				
Total people enrolled	**100.0%**	**26.3%**	**54.0%**	**19.6%**
Under age 20	100.0	32.2	67.1	0.8
Aged 20 to 21	100.0	21.1	76.5	2.4
Aged 22 to 24	100.0	25.4	55.5	19.0
Aged 25 to 29	100.0	22.0	36.3	41.7
Aged 30 to 34	100.0	26.9	35.7	37.3
Aged 35 to 39	100.0	32.2	25.5	42.3
Aged 40 to 44	100.0	31.6	29.6	38.8
Aged 45 to 49	100.0	25.1	31.1	43.6
Aged 50 to 54	100.0	31.1	23.2	45.4
Aged 55 or older	100.0	24.6	25.4	49.6
PERCENT DISTRIBUTION BY AGE				
Total people enrolled	**100.0%**	**100.0%**	**100.0%**	**100.0%**
Under age 20	22.0	26.9	27.3	0.9
Aged 20 to 21	21.2	17.0	30.1	2.6
Aged 22 to 24	20.0	19.2	20.5	19.3
Aged 25 to 29	13.0	10.9	8.7	27.6
Aged 30 to 34	8.0	8.2	5.3	15.2
Aged 35 to 39	4.6	5.7	2.2	9.9
Aged 40 to 44	4.5	5.5	2.5	9.0
Aged 45 to 49	2.9	2.7	1.7	6.4
Aged 50 to 54	2.1	2.5	0.9	5.0
Aged 55 or older	1.6	1.5	0.8	4.1

Source: Bureau of the Census, School Enrollment—Social and Economic Characteristics of Students: October 2003, Detailed Tables, Internet site http://www.census.gov/population/www/socdemo/school/cps2003.html; calculations by New Strategist

Table 6.13 College Enrollment by Age, Race, and Hispanic Origin, 2003

(number and percent distribution of people aged 15 or older enrolled in college by age, race, and Hispanic origin, October 2003; numbers in thousands)

	total	Asian	black	Hispanic	non-Hispanic white
Total people enrolled	**16,638**	**1,263**	**2,227**	**1,715**	**11,295**
Under age 20	3,661	254	430	390	2,576
Aged 20 to 21	3,534	248	441	408	2,419
Aged 22 to 24	3,320	290	445	330	2,224
Aged 25 to 29	2,164	231	303	224	1,372
Aged 30 to 34	1,330	117	214	155	833
Aged 35 to 39	769	42	129	84	509
Aged 40 to 44	757	42	95	68	534
Aged 45 to 49	479	15	81	19	359
Aged 50 to 54	357	12	58	17	268
Aged 55 or older	268	11	34	19	203

PERCENT DISTRIBUTION BY RACE AND HISPANIC ORIGIN

	total	Asian	black	Hispanic	non-Hispanic white
Total people enrolled	**100.0%**	**7.6%**	**13.4%**	**10.3%**	**67.9%**
Under age 20	100.0	6.9	11.7	10.7	70.4
Aged 20 to 21	100.0	7.0	12.5	11.5	68.4
Aged 22 to 24	100.0	8.7	13.4	9.9	67.0
Aged 25 to 29	100.0	10.7	14.0	10.4	63.4
Aged 30 to 34	100.0	8.8	16.1	11.7	62.6
Aged 35 to 39	100.0	5.5	16.8	10.9	66.2
Aged 40 to 44	100.0	5.5	12.5	9.0	70.5
Aged 45 to 49	100.0	3.1	16.9	4.0	74.9
Aged 50 to 54	100.0	3.4	16.2	4.8	75.1
Aged 55 or older	100.0	4.1	12.7	7.1	75.7

Note: Numbers by race and Hispanic origin will not sum to total because Asians and blacks include those identifying themselves as being of the race alone and those identifying themselves as being of the race in combination with one or more other races, Hispanics may be of any race, and not all races are shown. Non-Hispanic whites are those identifying themselves as being white alone and not Hispanic.
Source: Bureau of the Census, School Enrollment—Social and Economic Characteristics of Students: October 2003, Detailed Tables, Internet site http://www.census.gov/population/www/socdemo/school/cps2003.html; calculations by New Strategist

Table 6.14 Degrees Earned by Race and Hispanic Origin, 2001–02

(total number of degrees conferred and percent distribution by race and Hispanic origin, 2001–02)

	total	American Indian	Asian	black	Hispanic	non-Hispanic white	non-resident alien
Number of degrees							
Associate's degrees	595,133	6,830	30,947	67,337	60,003	417,739	12,277
Bachelor's degrees	1,291,900	9,165	83,101	116,624	82,969	958,585	41,456
Master's degrees	482,118	2,626	25,414	40,373	22,387	327,635	63,683
Doctoral degrees	44,160	180	2,317	2,397	1,432	26,905	10,929
First-professional degrees	80,698	581	9,584	5,811	3,965	58,874	1,883
Percent distribution by race and Hispanic origin							
Associate's degrees	100.0%	1.1%	5.2%	11.3%	10.1%	70.2%	2.1%
Bachelor's degrees	100.0	0.7	6.4	9.0	6.4	74.2	3.2
Master's degrees	100.0	0.5	5.3	8.4	4.6	68.0	13.2
Doctoral degrees	100.0	0.4	5.2	5.4	3.2	60.9	24.7
First-professional degrees	100.0	0.7	11.9	7.2	4.9	73.0	2.3

Source: National Center for Education Statistics, Digest of Education Statistics 2003, *Internet site http://nces.ed.gov//programs/digest/d03/list_tables.asp; calculations by New Strategist*

As the Asian, Black, and Hispanic Populations Grow, a Smaller Share of Newborns Are Non-Hispanic White

More than 4 million babies were born to American women in 2003, and only a slim major-ity—57 percent—was non-Hispanic white. Twenty-two percent of babies born in 2003 were Hispanic, 15 percent were black, and 5 percent were Asian. As these children grow up, the United States will become an increasingly multicultural society.

Eighty-four percent of Americans have health insurance, leaving a substantial 16 per-cent without coverage. The majority of those without health insurance are Asian, black, or Hispanic. Non-Hispanic whites account for only 48 percent of the uninsured.

Twenty-two percent of adults have hypertension, according to the National Center for Health Statistics. Fifteen percent have difficulties in physical functioning, with 7 percent say-ing they would find it very difficult or impossible to walk a quarter of a mile. Heart disease and cancer are the leading causes of death, accounting for 51 percent of all deaths in 2002. At birth, the average American male can expect to live 74.5 years, while the average female can expect to live 79.9 years. At age 65, people have an average of 18.2 more years of life.

■ Because of the aging of the population, the proportion of Americans with disabilities is certain to rise.

Minorities are the majority of those without health insurance

(percent distribution of people without health insurance by race and Hispanic origin, 2003)

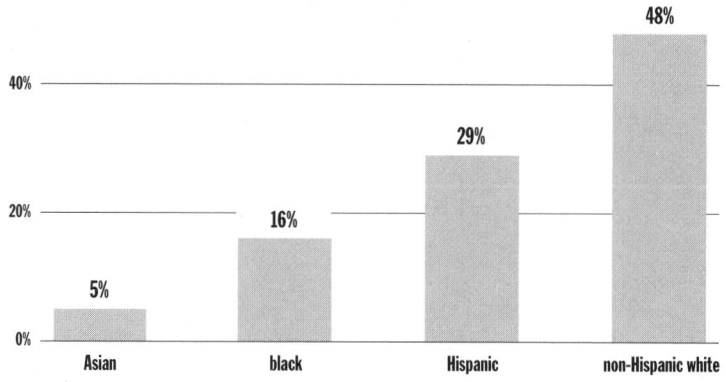

Table 6.15 Smoking and Drinking Status of Total People by Sex, 2003

(percent distribution of people aged 18 or older by smoking and drinking status and sex, 2003)

	total	men	women
SMOKING STATUS			
Total people	100.0%	100.0%	100.0%
Never smoked	56.6	50.5	62.2
Former smoker	21.8	25.9	18.4
Current smoker	21.6	23.6	19.4
DRINKING STATUS			
Total people	100.0	100.0	100.0
Lifetime abstainer	24.7	17.8	31.2
Former drinker	14.1	15.0	13.4
Current infrequent drinker	12.9	9.7	15.9
Current regular drinker	47.3	56.4	38.8

Note: Never smoked means having had fewer than 100 cigarettes in lifetime. Former smokers have had 100 or more cigarettes in lifetime but did not smoke at time of interview. Current smokers have had at least 100 cigarettes in lifetime and currently smoke. Lifetime abstainers have had fewer than 12 drinks in lifetime. Former drinkers have had 12 or more drinks in lifetime, none in past year. Current infrequent drinkers have had 12 or more drinks in lifetime and fewer than 12 drinks in past year. Current regular drinkers have had at least 12 drinks in past year.
Source: National Center for Health Statistics, Summary Health Statistics for U.S. Adults: National Health Interview Survey, 2003, *Series 10, No. 225, 2005; Internet site http://www.cdc.gov/nchs/nhis.htm*

Table 6.16 Weight in Pounds of Total People by Age and Sex, 1999–2002

(average weight in pounds of people aged 20 to 74 by sex and age, 1999–2002)

	men	women
WEIGHT IN POUNDS		
Total people	**191.0**	**164.3**
Aged 20 to 29	183.4	156.5
Aged 30 to 39	189.1	163.0
Aged 40 to 49	196.0	168.2
Aged 50 to 59	195.4	169.2
Aged 60 to 74	191.5	164.7

Note: Data are based on measured weight of a sample of the civilian noninstitutionalized population.
Source: National Center for Health Statistics, Mean Body Weight, Height, and Body Mass Index, United States 1960–2002; *Advance Data, No. 347, 2004; Internet site http://www.cdc.gov/nchs/products/pubs/pubd/ad/341-350/341-350.htm*

Table 6.17 Weight Status of Total People by Sex, 2003

(percent distribution of people aged 18 or older by weight status and sex, 2003)

	total	men	women
Total people	**100.0%**	**100.0%**	**100.0%**
Underweight	2.0	0.9	3.0
Healthy weight	39.2	32.2	46.1
Overweight, total	58.7	66.8	50.9
Overweight, but not obese	35.7	44.1	27.6
Obese	23.0	22.7	23.3

Note: Being overweight is defined as having a body mass index of 25 or higher. Being obese is defined as having a body mass index of 30 or higher. Body mass index is calculated by dividing weight in kilograms by height in meters squared. Data are based on measured height and weight of a sample of the civilian noninstitutionalized population.
Source: National Center for Health Statistics, Summary Health Statistics for U.S. Adults: National Health Interview Survey, 2003, *Series 10, No. 225, 2005; Internet site http://www.cdc.gov/nchs/nhis.htm*

Table 6.18 Births to Total Women by Age, 2003

(number and percent distribution of births to women by age, 2003)

	number	percent distribution
Total births	**4,089,950**	**100.0%**
Under age 15	6,661	0.2
Aged 15 to 19	414,580	10.1
Aged 20 to 24	1,032,305	25.2
Aged 25 to 29	1,086,366	26.6
Aged 30 to 34	975,546	23.9
Aged 35 to 39	467,642	11.4
Aged 40 to 44	101,005	2.5
Aged 45 to 54	5,845	0.1

Source: National Center for Health Statistics, Births: Final Data for 2003, *National Vital Statistics Reports, Vol. 54, No. 2, 2005; Internet site http://www.cdc.gov/nchs/products/pubs/pubd/nvsr/54/54-pre.htm; calculations by New Strategist*

Table 6.19 Births by Age, Race, and Hispanic Origin, 2003

(number and percent distribution of births by age, race, and Hispanic origin of mother, 2003)

	total	American Indian	Asian	black	Hispanic	non-Hispanic white
Total births	4,089,950	43,052	221,203	599,847	912,329	2,321,904
Under age 15	6,661	154	104	2,726	2,356	1,399
Aged 15 to 19	414,580	7,690	7,592	100,951	128,524	172,620
Aged 20 to 24	1,032,305	14,645	30,482	196,268	273,311	522,275
Aged 25 to 29	1,086,366	10,524	64,399	139,947	246,361	627,437
Aged 30 to 34	975,546	6,423	75,692	97,529	169,054	626,315
Aged 35 to 39	467,642	2,906	35,074	49,889	75,801	303,354
Aged 40 to 44	101,005	666	7,413	11,895	16,172	64,600
Aged 45 to 54	5,845	44	447	642	750	3,904

PERCENT DISTRIBUTION BY RACE AND HISPANIC ORIGIN

	total	American Indian	Asian	black	Hispanic	non-Hispanic white
Total births	100.0%	1.1%	5.4%	14.7%	22.3%	56.8%
Under age 15	100.0	2.3	1.6	40.9	35.4	21.0
Aged 15 to 19	100.0	1.9	1.8	24.4	31.0	41.6
Aged 20 to 24	100.0	1.4	3.0	19.0	26.5	50.6
Aged 25 to 29	100.0	1.0	5.9	12.9	22.7	57.8
Aged 30 to 34	100.0	0.7	7.8	10.0	17.3	64.2
Aged 35 to 39	100.0	0.6	7.5	10.7	16.2	64.9
Aged 40 to 44	100.0	0.7	7.3	11.8	16.0	64.0
Aged 45 to 54	100.0	0.8	7.6	11.0	12.8	66.8

Source: National Center for Health Statistics, Births: Final Data for 2003, *National Vital Statistics Reports, Vol. 54, No. 2, 2005; Internet site http://www.cdc.gov/nchs/products/pubs/pubd/nvsr/54/54-pre.htm; calculations by New Strategist*

Table 6.20 Births to Total Women by Age and Marital Status, 2003

(total number of births and number and percent to unmarried women, by age, 2003)

		unmarried women	
	total	number	share of total
Total births	4,089,950	1,415,995	34.6%
Under age 15	6,661	6,469	97.1
Aged 15 to 19	414,580	337,201	81.3
Aged 20 to 24	1,032,305	549,353	53.2
Aged 25 to 29	1,086,366	287,205	26.4
Aged 30 to 34	975,546	147,555	15.1
Aged 35 to 39	467,642	69,071	14.8
Aged 40 or older	106,850	19,141	17.9

Source: National Center for Health Statistics, Births: Final Data for 2003, *National Vital Statistics Reports, Vol. 54, No. 2, 2005; Internet site http://www.cdc.gov/nchs/products/pubs/pubd/nvsr/54/54-pre.htm; calculations by New Strategist*

Table 6.21 Births to Unmarried Women by Age, Race, and Hispanic Origin, 2003

(number and percent distribution of births to unmarried women by age, race, and Hispanic origin of mother, 2002)

	total		American Indian	Asian	black	Hispanic	non-Hispanic white
	number	percent					
Total births to unmarried women	**1,415,995**	**100.0%**	**1.9%**	**2.3%**	**28.9%**	**29.0%**	**38.6%**
Under age 15	6,469	100.0	2.3	1.6	42.0	34.4	20.9
Aged 15 to 19	337,201	100.0	2.0	1.6	28.8	29.0	39.3
Aged 20 to 24	549,353	100.0	1.8	2.0	29.2	26.7	40.9
Aged 25 to 29	287,205	100.0	1.8	2.7	29.0	31.9	35.3
Aged 30 to 34	147,555	100.0	1.8	3.5	28.3	31.8	35.4
Aged 35 to 39	69,071	100.0	1.7	3.7	27.9	29.2	38.2
Aged 40 or older	19,141	100.0	1.6	4.1	25.8	25.8	43.1

Note: Births by race and Hispanic origin will not add to total because Hispanics may be of any race and "not stated" is not shown. American Indians include Alaska Natives. Asians include Pacific Islanders.
Source: National Center for Health Statistics, Births: Final Data for 2003, *National Vital Statistics Reports, Vol. 54, No. 2, 2005; Internet site http://www.cdc.gov/nchs/products/pubs/pubd/nvsr/54/54-pre.htm; calculations by New Strategist*

Table 6.22 Births to Total Women by Birth Order, 2003

(number and percent distribution of births by birth order, 2003)

	number	percent distribution
Total births	**4,089,950**	**100.0%**
First child	1,633,987	40.0
Second child	1,320,477	32.3
Third child	684,296	16.7
Fourth or later child	439,235	10.7

Note: Numbers will not add to total because "not stated" is not shown.
Source: National Center for Health Statistics, Births: Final Data for 2003, *National Vital Statistics Reports, Vol. 54, No. 2, 2005; Internet site http://www.cdc.gov/nchs/products/pubs/pubd/nvsr/54/54-pre.htm; calculations by New Strategist*

Table 6.23 Births by State, Race, and Hispanic Origin, 2003

(total number of births and percent distribution by race and Hispanic origin of mother, by state, 2003

	total		American Indian	Asian	black	Hispanic	non-Hispanic white
	number	percent					
Total births	**4,089,950**	**100.0%**	**1.1%**	**5.4%**	**14.7%**	**22.3%**	**56.8%**
Alabama	59,552	100.0	0.2	1.0	30.1	4.9	63.8
Alaska	10,086	100.0	24.6	7.1	4.0	7.6	48.8
Arizona	90,967	100.0	6.7	3.0	3.6	43.7	43.1
Arkansas	37,784	100.0	0.7	1.4	19.2	8.7	70.1
California	540,997	100.0	0.5	12.5	6.0	49.9	30.8
Colorado	69,339	100.0	0.8	3.9	4.2	30.8	61.1
Connecticut	42,873	100.0	0.6	4.7	12.1	17.6	65.4
Delaware	11,329	100.0	0.3	4.0	25.7	12.2	58.1
District of Columbia	7,619	100.0	0.1	3.4	68.9	12.6	24.2
Florida	212,250	100.0	0.5	2.7	22.3	25.8	49.1
Georgia	135,979	100.0	0.2	3.3	31.7	13.4	50.7
Hawaii	18,100	100.0	0.4	68.3	3.2	14.5	23.6
Idaho	21,800	100.0	1.7	1.6	0.5	13.5	82.2
Illinois	182,495	100.0	0.1	4.8	17.3	23.3	54.6
Indiana	86,434	100.0	0.2	1.6	10.8	7.8	79.3
Iowa	38,174	100.0	0.7	2.5	3.4	6.6	86.9
Kansas	39,476	100.0	1.2	3.1	7.0	13.8	74.0
Kentucky	55,236	100.0	0.2	1.6	8.8	3.5	86.1
Louisiana	65,040	100.0	0.6	1.7	40.3	2.6	54.9
Maine	13,855	100.0	0.7	1.5	1.3	1.2	94.9
Maryland	74,930	100.0	0.3	6.0	34.1	9.3	52.4
Massachusetts	80,184	100.0	0.2	6.7	10.7	12.2	72.2
Michigan	131,094	100.0	0.5	3.6	17.2	5.9	71.4
Minnesota	70,050	100.0	2.0	5.5	7.7	7.0	77.2
Mississippi	42,380	100.0	0.7	0.7	43.8	1.3	53.5
Missouri	77,045	100.0	0.5	2.2	14.5	4.5	78.5
Montana	11,422	100.0	12.3	1.1	0.4	3.3	81.4
Nebraska	25,917	100.0	1.8	2.3	5.7	13.3	74.9
Nevada	33,647	100.0	1.5	7.5	8.6	36.3	46.4
New Hampshire	14,393	100.0	0.2	3.3	1.7	3.7	87.5
New Jersey	116,983	100.0	0.2	9.2	17.3	22.7	52.9
New Mexico	27,821	100.0	13.0	1.4	1.9	53.4	30.9
New York	253,714	100.0	0.3	8.4	18.9	21.8	52.1
North Carolina	118,323	100.0	1.4	2.6	23.0	13.6	59.6
North Dakota	7,972	100.0	10.8	1.4	1.4	2.1	82.4
Ohio	149,679	100.0	0.2	2.1	15.2	3.6	79.0
Oklahoma	50,981	100.0	10.4	2.1	9.1	11.2	67.4
Oregon	45,953	100.0	1.9	5.4	2.2	18.4	72.0

(continued)

| | total | | American | | | | non-Hispanic |
	number	percent	Indian	Asian	black	Hispanic	white
Pennsylvania	145,959	100.0%	0.2%	3.5%	15.1%	7.4%	74.9%
Rhode Island	13,209	100.0	1.2	4.3	9.5	18.8	54.9
South Carolina	55,649	100.0	0.3	1.6	32.9	6.6	58.7
South Dakota	11,027	100.0	17.0	1.2	1.1	3.1	78.1
Tennessee	78,890	100.0	0.2	1.9	20.6	6.3	71.1
Texas	377,476	100.0	0.2	3.5	11.1	48.5	36.6
Utah	49,860	100.0	1.2	3.1	0.8	14.2	80.5
Vermont	6,589	100.0	0.1	1.8	0.8	0.9	95.8
Virginia	101,254	100.0	0.2	6.5	22.3	10.3	61.6
Washington	80,489	100.0	2.5	9.7	5.0	16.5	66.9
West Virginia	20,935	100.0	0.1	0.7	3.4	0.5	94.9
Wisconsin	70,040	100.0	1.5	3.2	9.3	7.9	78.3
Wyoming	6,700	100.0	4.3	1.0	0.8	10.0	84.0

Note: Numbers will not add to total because not all races are shown and Hispanics may be of any race. American Indians include Alaskan Natives. Asians include Pacific Islanders.
Source: National Center for Health Statistics, Births: Final Data for 2003, National Vital Statistics Reports, Vol. 54, No. 2, 2005; Internet site http://www.cdc.gov/nchs/products/pubs/pubd/nvsr/54/54-pre.htm; calculations by New Strategist

Table 6.24 Health Insurance Coverage of Total People by Age, 2003

(number and percent distribution of people by age and health insurance coverage status, 2003; numbers in thousands)

	total	with health insurance coverage during year			not covered at any time during the year
		total	private	government	
Total people	**288,280**	**243,320**	**197,869**	**76,755**	**44,961**
Under age 18	73,580	65,207	48,475	21,389	8,373
Aged 18 to 24	27,824	19,410	16,526	3,929	8,414
Aged 25 to 34	39,201	28,856	25,606	4,210	10,345
Aged 35 to 44	43,573	35,688	32,533	4,420	7,885
Aged 45 to 54	41,068	35,108	32,000	4,569	5,961
Aged 55 to 64	28,375	24,679	21,569	4,893	3,696
Aged 65 or older	34,659	34,373	21,159	33,345	286
PERCENT DISTRIBUTION BY COVERAGE STATUS					
Total people	**100.0%**	**84.4%**	**68.6%**	**26.6%**	**15.6%**
Under age 18	100.0	88.6	65.9	29.1	11.4
Aged 18 to 24	100.0	69.8	59.4	14.1	30.2
Aged 25 to 34	100.0	73.6	65.3	10.7	26.4
Aged 35 to 44	100.0	81.9	74.7	10.1	18.1
Aged 45 to 54	100.0	85.5	77.9	11.1	14.5
Aged 55 to 64	100.0	87.0	76.0	17.2	13.0
Aged 65 or older	100.0	99.2	61.0	96.2	0.8

Note: Numbers may not add to total because some people have more than one type of health insurance.
Source: Bureau of the Census, 2004 Current Population Survey, Annual Social and Economic Supplement, detailed tables, Internet site http://pubdb3.census.gov/macro/032004/health/h01_000.htm; calculations by New Strategist

Table 6.25 Total People with Private Health Insurance Coverage by Age, 2003

(number and percent distribution of people by age and private health insurance coverage status, 2003; numbers in thousands)

	total	with private health insurance			
		total	employment-based		direct purchase
			total	own	
Total people	**288,280**	**197,869**	**174,020**	**91,353**	**26,486**
Under age 18	73,580	48,475	45,004	185	3,893
Aged 18 to 24	27,824	16,526	13,434	5,103	1,596
Aged 25 to 34	39,201	25,606	23,946	18,262	2,058
Aged 35 to 44	43,573	32,533	30,386	21,705	2,793
Aged 45 to 54	41,068	32,000	29,722	22,044	3,198
Aged 55 to 64	28,375	21,569	19,324	14,543	2,987
Aged 65 or older	34,659	21,159	12,204	9,511	9,962

PERCENT DISTRIBUTION BY COVERAGE STATUS

Total people	**100.0%**	**68.6%**	**60.4%**	**31.7%**	**9.2%**
Under age 18	100.0	65.9	61.2	0.3	5.3
Aged 18 to 24	100.0	59.4	48.3	18.3	5.7
Aged 25 to 34	100.0	65.3	61.1	46.6	5.2
Aged 35 to 44	100.0	74.7	69.7	49.8	6.4
Aged 45 to 54	100.0	77.9	72.4	53.7	7.8
Aged 55 to 64	100.0	76.0	68.1	51.3	10.5
Aged 65 or older	100.0	61.0	35.2	27.4	28.7

Note: Numbers will not add to total because some people have more than one type of health insurance.
Source: Bureau of the Census, 2004 Current Population Survey, Annual Social and Economic Supplement, detailed tables, Internet site http://pubdb3.census.gov/macro/032004/health/h01_000.htm; calculations by New Strategist

Table 6.26 Total People with Government Health Insurance Coverage by Age, 2003

(number and percent distribution of people by age and government health insurance coverage status, 2003; numbers in thousands)

	total	with government health insurance			
		total	Medicaid	Medicare	military
Total people	**288,280**	**76,755**	**35,647**	**39,456**	**9,979**
Under age 18	73,580	21,389	19,392	483	2,021
Aged 18 to 24	27,824	3,929	3,016	176	902
Aged 25 to 34	39,201	4,210	3,073	538	898
Aged 35 to 44	43,573	4,420	2,860	940	1,111
Aged 45 to 54	41,068	4,569	2,359	1,569	1,369
Aged 55 to 64	28,375	4,893	1,757	2,494	1,471
Aged 65 or older	34,659	33,345	3,190	33,257	2,206
PERCENT DISTRIBUTION BY COVERAGE STATUS					
Total people	**100.0%**	**26.6%**	**12.4%**	**13.7%**	**3.5%**
Under age 18	100.0	29.1	26.4	0.7	2.7
Aged 18 to 24	100.0	14.1	10.8	0.6	3.2
Aged 25 to 34	100.0	10.7	7.8	1.4	2.3
Aged 35 to 44	100.0	10.1	6.6	2.2	2.5
Aged 45 to 54	100.0	11.1	5.7	3.8	3.3
Aged 55 to 64	100.0	17.2	6.2	8.8	5.2
Aged 65 or older	100.0	96.2	9.2	96.0	6.4

Note: Numbers will not add to total because some people have more than one type of health insurance.
Source: Bureau of the Census, 2004 Current Population Survey, Annual Social and Economic Supplement, detailed tables, Internet site http://pubdb3.census.gov/macro/032004/health/h01_000.htm; calculations by New Strategist

Table 6.27 People without Health Insurance Coverage by Age, Race, and Hispanic Origin, 2003

(total number of people with no health insurance coverage during the year and percent distribution by age, race, and Hispanic origin, 2003; numbers in thousands)

	total		Asian	black	Hispanic	non-Hispanic white
	number	percent				
Total people without health insurance coverage	**44,961**	**100.0%**	**5.3%**	**16.3%**	**29.4%**	**48.0%**
Under age 18	8,373	100.0	4.7	20.6	34.8	38.3
Aged 18 to 24	8,414	100.0	4.9	16.6	30.2	47.6
Aged 25 to 34	10,345	100.0	5.6	14.6	34.7	44.4
Aged 35 to 44	7,885	100.0	5.2	16.0	28.6	49.3
Aged 45 to 54	5,961	100.0	6.1	15.7	19.9	57.1
Aged 55 to 64	3,696	100.0	5.6	11.7	17.2	64.5
Aged 65 or older	286	100.0	12.6	12.6	41.3	34.3

Note: Percentages will not sum to total because Asians and blacks include those identifying themselves as being of the race alone and those identifying themselves as being of the race in combination with one or more other races, not all races are shown, and Hispanics may be of any race. Non-Hispanic whites include only those identifying themselves as being white alone and not Hispanic.
Source: Bureau of the Census, 2004 Current Population Survey, Annual Social and Economic Supplement, detailed tables, Internet site http://pubdb3.census.gov/macro/032004/health/h01_000.htm; calculations by New Strategist

Table 6.28 Health Conditions among Total People Aged 18 or Older, 2003

(number and percent of total people aged 18 or older with selected health conditions, 2003; numbers in thousands)

	number	percent with condition
Total people	**213,042**	–
Selected circulatory diseases		
Heart disease, all types	23,536	11.1%
Coronary	12,254	5.8
Hypertension	45,927	21.6
Stroke	5,070	2.4
Selected respiratory conditions		
Emphysema	3,115	1.5
Asthma		
Ever	20,697	9.7
Still	13,623	6.4
Hay fever	18,356	8.6
Sinusitis	29,673	14.0
Chronic bronchitis	8,560	4.0
Cancer		
Any cancer	13,973	6.6
Breast cancer (all adults)	2,426	1.1
Cervical cancer (women only)	1,082	1.0
Prostate cancer (men only)	1,332	1.3
Other selected diseases and conditions		
Diabetes	14,012	6.6
Ulcers	14,456	6.8
Kidney disease	3,017	1.4
Liver disease	2,511	1.2
Arthritis	45,793	21.6
Chronic joint symptoms	57,242	26.9
Migraines or severe headaches	32,268	15.2
Pain in neck	31,368	14.8
Pain in lower back	58,430	27.5
Pain in face or jaw	9,464	4.4
Selected sensory problems		
Hearing	32,533	15.3
Vision	18,628	8.7
Absence of all natural teeth	15,927	7.5

Note: The conditions shown are those that have ever been diagnosed by a doctor, except as noted. Hay fever, sinusitis, and chronic bronchitis have been diagnosed in the past twelve months. Kidney and liver disease have been diagnosed in the past twelve months and exclude kidney stones, bladder infections, and incontinence. Chronic joint symptoms are shown if respondent had pain, aching, or stiffness in or around a joint (excluding back and neck) and the condition began more than three months ago. Migraines, pain in neck, lower back, face, or jaw are shown only if pain lasted a whole day or more. (–) means not applicable.
Source: National Center for Health Statistics, Summary Health Statistics for U.S. Adults: National Health Interview Survey, 2003, *Series 10, No. 225, 2005; Internet site http://www.cdc.gov/nchs/nhis.htm*

Table 6.29 Health Conditions among Total Children, 2003

(number and percent of people under age 18 with selected health conditions, 2003; numbers in thousands)

	number	percent with condition
Total children	**72,973**	–
Diagnosed with asthma	9,071	12.5%
Experienced in last 12 months		
Asthma attack	3,975	5.4
Hay fever	7,059	9.7
Respiratory allergies	8,347	11.5
Other allergies	8,407	11.5
Ever told had*		
Learning disability	4,561	7.5
Attention deficit hyperactivity disorder	3,881	6.4
Prescription medication taken regularly for at least 3 months	9,287	12.7

* *"Ever told" by a school representative or health professional. Data exclude children under age 3.*
Note: Other allergies include food or digestive allergies, eczema, and other skin allergies. (–) means not applicable.
Source: National Center for Health Statistics, Summary Health Statistics for U.S. Children: National Health Interview Survey, *2003, Series 10, No. 223, 2005; Internet site http://www.cdc.gov/nchs/nhis.htm*

Table 6.30 Physician Office Visits by Total People by Age, 2002

(number and percent distribution of physician office visits, and average number of visits per person per year, by age, 2002)

	number (000s)	percent distribution	per person per year
Total visits	**889,980**	**100.0%**	**3.1**
Under age 15	159,235	17.9	2.6
Aged 15 to 24	71,865	8.1	1.8
Aged 25 to 44	192,359	21.6	2.3
Aged 45 to 64	242,142	27.2	3.7
Aged 65 to 74	109,331	12.3	6.1
Aged 75 or older	115,049	12.9	7.2

Source: National Center for Health Statistics, National Ambulatory Medical Care Survey: 2002 Summary, *Advance Data No. 346, 2004; Internet site http://www.cdc.gov/nchs/about/major/ahcd/adata.htm; calculations by New Strategist*

Table 6.31 Difficulties in Physical Functioning among Total People, 2003

(number and percent of people aged 18 or older with difficulties in physical functioning, by type of difficulty, 2003; numbers in thousands)

	number	percent with difficulty
TOTAL PEOPLE	**213,042**	–
Total with any physical difficulty	**31,322**	**14.7%**
Walk quarter of a mile	14,910	7.0
Climb up ten steps without resting	11,107	5.2
Stand for two hours	18,663	8.8
Sit for two hours	7,211	3.4
Stoop, bend, or kneel	18,250	8.6
Reach over head	6,264	2.9
Grasp or handle small objects	3,943	1.9
Lift or carry ten pounds	9,194	4.3
Push or pull large objects	13,463	6.3

Note: Respondents were classified as having difficulties if they responded "very difficult" or "can't do at all." (–) means not applicable.
Source: National Center for Health Statistics, Summary Health Statistics for U.S. Adults: National Health Interview Survey, 2003, *Series 10, No. 225, 2005; Internet site http://www.cdc.gov/nchs/nhis.htm*

Table 6.32 Leading Causes of Death among Total People, 2002

(number and percent distribution of deaths accounted for by the ten leading causes of death, 2002)

	number	percent distribution
Total deaths	**2,443,387**	**100.0%**
1. Diseases of the heart	696,947	28.5
2. Malignant neoplasms (cancer)	557,271	22.8
3. Cerebrovascular diseases	162,672	6.7
4. Chronic lower respiratory disease	124,816	5.1
5. Accidents (unintentional injuries)	106,742	4.4
6. Diabetes mellitus	73,249	3.0
7. Influenza and pneumonia	65,681	2.7
8. Alzheimer's disease	58,866	2.4
9. Nephritis, nephrotic syndrome, nephrosis	40,974	1.7
10. Septicemia	33,865	1.4
All other causes	522,304	21.4

Source: National Center for Health Statistics, Deaths: Final Data for 2002, National Vital Statistics Reports, Vol. 53, No. 5, 2004; calculations by New Strategist

Table 6.33 Life Expectancy of Total People at Birth and Age 65 by Sex, 1990 to 2002

(number of years of life remaining at birth and age 65, by sex, 1990 to 2002; change in years, 1990 to 2002)

	total	females	males
Birth			
2002	77.3	79.9	74.5
2000	77.0	79.7	74.3
1990	75.4	78.8	71.8
Change, 1990 to 2002	1.9	1.1	2.7
Age 65			
2002	18.2	19.5	16.6
2000	18.0	19.3	16.2
1990	17.2	18.9	15.1
Change, 1990 to 2002	1.0	0.6	1.5

Source: National Center for Health Statistics, Health, United States, 2004; Internet site http://www.cdc.gov/nchs/hus.htm; calculations by New Strategist

Homeownership Is at a Record High in the United States

Homeownership stood at a record high in 2004, when 69 percent of American households owned their home. Because non-Hispanic whites are the largest population segment and have the highest homeownership rate, they are the great majority of homeowners. In 2003, more than 80 percent of the nation's homeowners were non-Hispanic white. Only 9 percent of homeowners are black, 7 percent are Hispanic, and fewer than 3 percent are Asian.

Married couples are most likely to be homeowners, with a homeownership rate of 83 percent. Among the nation's married-couple homeowners, 82 percent are non-Hispanic white. Among female-headed families, in contrast, only 65 percent of homeowners are non-Hispanic white, while a substantial 21 percent are black and 10 percent Hispanic.

Among all homeowners, median housing value stood at $140,201 in 2003. When asked to rate their home on a scale of one to ten, 75 percent of the nation's homeowners give their home a rating of eight or higher. Among renters, only 55 percent rate their home an eight or higher. Seven percent of homeowners and 13 percent of renters say crime is a bothersome problem in their neighborhood.

Fourteen percent of Americans moved between March 2003 and March 2004. Non-Hispanic whites account for only 60 percent of movers. Hispanics are 18 percent of movers, blacks 16 percent, and Asians 5 percent.

■ Asians, blacks, and Hispanics will account for a growing share of the nation's homeowners in the years ahead as minority populations expand.

Non-Hispanic whites are the great majority of homeowners

(percent distribution of households owning their home, by race and Hispanic origin of householder, 2003)

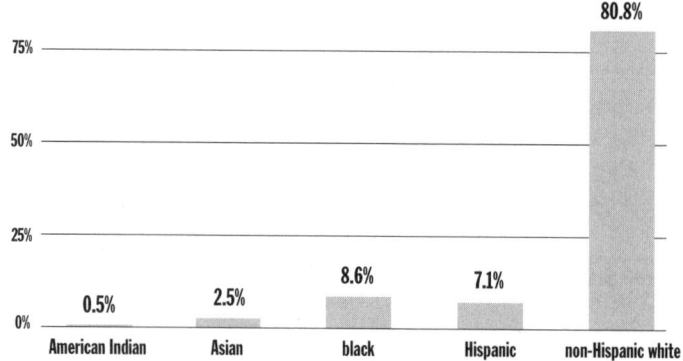

Table 6.34 Homeowners by Race and Hispanic Origin, 2003

(number of total households, and number, percent, and percent distribution of households that own their home, by race and Hispanic origin of householder, 2003; numbers in thousands)

| | | homeowners | | |
	total	number	percent of total	percent distribution
Total households	**105,842**	**72,238**	**68.3%**	**100.0%**
Race				
American Indian alone	664	341	51.4	0.5
Asian alone	3,183	1,811	56.9	2.5
Black alone	13,004	6,193	47.6	8.6
Pacific Islander alone	295	148	50.2	0.2
White alone	87,483	63,126	72.2	87.4
Two or more races	1,215	620	51.0	0.9
Hispanic origin				
Hispanic	11,038	5,106	46.3	7.1
Non-Hispanic white	77,358	58,366	75.4	80.8

Note: Hispanics may be of any race. Non-Hispanic whites are those identifying themselves as being white alone and not Hispanic.
Source: Bureau of the Census, American Housing Survey for the United States: 2003, *Current Housing Reports, Internet site http://www.census.gov/hhes/www/ahs.html; calculations by New Strategist*

Table 6.35 Homeownership Status by Age of Householder, 2003

(number and percent of total households by age of householder and homeownership status, 2003; numbers in thousands)

	total	owner number	owner percent	renter number	renter percent
Total households	**105,842**	**72,238**	**68.3%**	**33,604**	**31.7%**
Under age 25	6,087	1,272	20.9	4,815	79.1
Aged 25 to 29	7,805	3,207	41.1	4,598	58.9
Aged 30 to 34	10,575	5,845	55.3	4,730	44.7
Aged 35 to 44	22,516	15,406	68.4	7,110	31.6
Aged 45 to 54	21,828	16,661	76.3	5,167	23.7
Aged 55 to 64	15,404	12,497	81.1	2,906	18.9
Aged 65 to 74	10,782	8,876	82.3	1,907	17.7
Aged 75 or older	10,845	8,474	78.1	2,370	21.9
Median age	48	51	–	38	–

Note: (–) means not applicable.
Source: Bureau of the Census, American Housing Survey for the United States: 2003, Current Housing Reports, Internet site http://www.census.gov/hhes/www/ahs.html; calculations by New Strategist

Table 6.36 Homeowners by Age of Householder, 2003

(number and percent distribution of total homeowners, by age, 2003; numbers in thousands)

	number	percent distribution
Total homeowners	**72,238**	**100.0%**
Under age 25	1,272	1.8
Aged 25 to 29	3,207	4.4
Aged 30 to 34	5,845	8.1
Aged 35 to 44	15,406	21.3
Aged 45 to 54	16,661	23.1
Aged 55 to 64	12,497	17.3
Aged 65 to 74	8,876	12.3
Aged 75 or older	8,474	11.7

Source: Bureau of the Census, American Housing Survey for the United States: 2003, Current Housing Reports, Internet site http://www.census.gov/hhes/www/ahs.html; calculations by New Strategist

Table 6.37 Homeownership Status by Household Type, 2003

(number and percent of total households by household type and homeownership status, 2003; numbers in thousands)

	total	owner		renter	
		number	percent	number	percent
TOTAL HOUSEHOLDS	**111,278**	**75,909**	**68.2%**	**35,369**	**31.8%**
Family households	**75,596**	**57,092**	**75.5**	**18,504**	**24.5**
Married couples	57,320	47,676	83.2	9,644	16.8
Female householder, no spouse present	13,620	6,695	49.2	6,925	50.8
Male householder, no spouse present	4,656	2,721	58.4	1,935	41.6
Nonfamily households	**35,682**	**18,817**	**52.7**	**16,865**	**47.3**
Female householder	19,662	11,075	56.3	8,587	43.7
Male householder	16,020	7,742	48.3	8,278	51.7

Source: Bureau of the Census, America's Families and Living Arrangements, 2003 Current Population Survey Annual Social and Economic Supplement; Internet site http://www.census.gov/population/www/socdemo/hh-fam/cps2003.html; calculations by New Strategist

Table 6.38 Homeowners by Type of Household, 2003

(number and percent distribution of total homeowners by household type, 2003; numbers in thousands)

	number	percent distribution
TOTAL HOMEOWNERS	**75,909**	**100.0%**
Family households	**57,092**	**75.2**
Married couples	47,676	62.8
Female householder, no spouse present	6,695	8.8
Male householder, no spouse present	2,721	3.6
Nonfamily households	**18,817**	**24.8**
Female householder	11,075	14.6
Male householder	7,742	10.2

Source: Bureau of the Census, America's Families and Living Arrangements, 2003 Current Population Survey Annual Social and Economic Supplement; Internet site http://www.census.gov/population/www/socdemo/hh-fam/cps2003.html; calculations by New Strategist

Table 6.39 Homeowners by Type of Household, Race, and Hispanic Origin of Householder, 2003

(total number of homeowners and percent distribution by race and Hispanic origin of householder, by household type, 2003; numbers in thousands)

	total number	total percent	Asian	black	Hispanic	non-Hispanic white
TOTAL HOMEOWNERS	**75,909**	**100.0%**	**3.0%**	**8.6%**	**7.1%**	**80.3%**
Family households	**57,092**	**100.0**	**3.4**	**8.4**	**8.2**	**79.1**
Married couples	47,676	100.0	3.4	6.3	7.7	81.8
Female householder, no spouse present	6,695	100.0	2.9	21.0	10.1	64.8
Male householder, no spouse present	2,721	100.0	4.5	14.0	11.9	67.7
Nonfamily households	**18,817**	**100.0**	**1.9**	**9.3**	**3.7**	**84.1**
Female householder	11,075	100.0	1.9	9.9	3.4	83.8
Male householder	7,742	100.0	1.8	8.5	4.1	84.4

Note: Percentages will not sum to 100 because Asians and blacks include those identifying themselves as being of the race alone and those identifying themselves as being of the race in combination with one or more other races, Hispanics may be of any race, and non-Hispanic whites are those identifying themselves as being white alone and not Hispanic.
Source: Bureau of the Census, America's Families and Living Arrangements, 2003 Current Population Survey Annual Social and Economic Supplement; Internet site http://www.census.gov/population/www/socdemo/hh-fam/cps2003.html; calculations by New Strategist

Table 6.40 Homeownership Status by Region, 2003

(number and percent of total households by region and homeownership status, 2003; numbers in thousands)

	total	owners number	owners percent	renters number	renters percent
Total households	**105,842**	**72,238**	**68.3%**	**33,604**	**31.7%**
Northeast	20,133	12,964	64.4	7,169	35.6
Midwest	24,488	17,889	73.1	6,599	26.9
South	38,145	26,699	70.0	11,446	30.0
West	23,077	14,686	63.6	8,390	36.4

Source: Bureau of the Census, American Housing Survey for the United States: 2003, Current Housing Reports, Internet site http://www.census.gov/hhes/www/ahs.html; calculations by New Strategist

Table 6.41 Homeowners by Region, 2003

(number and percent distribution of total homeowners by region, 2003; numbers in thousands)

	number	percent distribution
Total homeowners	**72,238**	**100.0%**
Northeast	12,964	17.9
Midwest	17,889	24.8
South	26,699	37.0
West	14,686	20.3

Source: Bureau of the Census, American Housing Survey for the United States: 2003, *Current Housing Reports, Internet site http://www.census.gov/hhes/www/ahs.html; calculations by New Strategist*

Table 6.42 Homeowners by Region, Race, and Hispanic Origin, 2003

(number of total homeowners and percent distribution of homeowners by race and Hispanic origin, by region, 2003; numbers in thousands)

	total		American Indian	Asian	black	Hispanic	non-Hispanic white
	number	percent					
Total homeowners	**72,238**	**100.0%**	**0.5%**	**2.5%**	**8.6%**	**7.1%**	**80.8%**
Northeast	12,964	100.0	0.2	2.4	6.4	3.4	87.4
Midwest	17,889	100.0	0.2	1.0	6.1	2.8	89.4
South	26,699	100.0	0.3	1.5	14.0	7.6	75.9
West	14,686	100.0	1.3	6.3	3.5	14.6	73.3

Note: American Indians, Asians, and blacks are those identifying themselves as being of the race alone. Hispanics may be of any race. Non-Hispanic whites are those identifying themselves as being white alone and not Hispanic. Percentages will not sum to 100 because not all races are shown.
Source: Bureau of the Census, American Housing Survey for the United States: 2003, *Current Housing Reports, Internet site http://www.census.gov/hhes/www/ahs.html; calculations by New Strategist*

Table 6.43 Characteristics of Total Occupied Housing Units, 2003

(number and percent distribution of total occupied housing units by selected housing characteristics and homeownership status, 2003; numbers in thousands)

	total	owner-occupied		renter-occupied	
		number	percent distribution	number	percent distribution
UNITS IN STRUCTURE					
Total households	**105,842**	**72,238**	**100.0%**	**33,604**	**100.0%**
One, detached	67,753	59,642	82.6	8,111	24.1
One, attached	6,272	3,679	5.1	2,593	7.7
Two to four	8,474	1,426	2.0	7,048	21.0
Five to nine	5,135	501	0.7	4,634	13.8
10 to 19	4,468	485	0.7	3,983	11.9
20 to 49	3,294	389	0.5	2,905	8.6
50 or more	3,592	601	0.8	2,991	8.9
Mobile home or trailer	6,854	5,514	7.6	1,340	4.0
Median square footage of unit*	1,756	1,822	–	1,299	–
NUMBER OF BEDROOMS					
Total households	**105,842**	**72,238**	**100.0**	**33,604**	**100.0**
None	811	35	0.0	776	2.3
One	11,557	1,729	2.4	9,828	29.2
Two	28,595	14,183	19.6	14,412	42.9
Three	44,592	37,602	52.1	6,990	20.8
Four or more	20,286	18,689	25.9	1,597	4.8
NUMBER OF BATHROOMS					
Total households	**105,842**	**72,238**	**100.0**	**33,604**	**100.0**
None	642	270	0.4	372	1.1
One	40,814	17,620	24.4	23,194	69.0
One-and-one-half	16,240	12,716	17.6	3,524	10.5
Two or more	48,147	41,631	57.6	6,516	19.4
ROOM USED FOR BUSINESS					
Total households	**105,842**	**72,238**	**100.0**	**33,604**	**100.0**
With room(s) used for business	22,373	17,668	24.5	4,704	14.0
SELECTED AMENITIES					
Porch, deck, balcony, or patio	89,562	66,021	91.4	23,541	70.1
Telephone available	102,873	70,601	97.7	32,272	96.0
Usable fireplace	35,458	31,593	43.7	3,865	11.5
Separate dining room	50,690	41,317	57.2	9,373	27.9
Two or more living or recreation rooms	30,254	28,149	39.0	2,105	6.3
Garage or carport	65,251	54,664	75.7	10,587	31.5
No cars, trucks, or vans available	9,089	2,416	3.3	6,673	19.9

* Single-family detached and mobile/manufactured homes only.
Source: Bureau of the Census, American Housing Survey for the United States: 2003, *Current Housing Reports, Internet site http://www.census.gov/hhes/www/ahs.html; calculations by New Strategist*

Table 6.44 Housing Value for Total Homeowners, 2003

(number and percent distribution of total homeowners by value of home, 2003; numbers in thousands)

	number	percent distribution
Total homeowners	**72,238**	**100.0%**
Under $10,000	1,880	2.6
$10,000 to $19,999	1,359	1.9
$20,000 to $29,999	1,475	2.0
$30,000 to $39,999	1,627	2.3
$40,000 to $49,999	1,936	2.7
$50,000 to $59,999	2,486	3.4
$60,000 to $69,999	2,821	3.9
$70,000 to $79,999	3,606	5.0
$80,000 to $99,999	7,440	10.3
$100,000 to $119,999	5,766	8.0
$120,000 to $149,999	8,500	11.8
$150,000 to $199,999	9,989	13.8
$200,000 to $249,999	6,358	8.8
$250,000 to $299,999	4,561	6.3
$300,000 or more	12,434	17.2
Median home value	$140,201	–

Note: (–) means not applicable.
Source: Bureau of the Census, American Housing Survey for the United States: 2003, Current Housing Reports, Internet site http://www.census.gov/hhes/www/ahs.html; calculations by New Strategist

Table 6.45 Neighborhood Characteristics of Total Occupied Housing Units, 2003

(number and percent distribution of total occupied housing units by selected neighborhood characteristics and homeownership status, 2003; numbers in thousands)

	total	owner-occupied		renter-occupied	
		number	percent distribution	number	percent distribution
DESCRIPTION OF AREA WITHIN 300 FEET OF HOME					
Total households	**105,842**	**72,238**	**100.0%**	**33,604**	**100.0%**
Single-family detached homes	83,540	61,049	84.5	22,491	66.9
Single-family attached homes	13,754	7,199	10.0	6,555	19.5
One-to-three-story multiunit	23,684	7,157	9.9	16,527	49.2
Four-to-six-story multiunit	5,641	1,421	2.0	4,220	12.6
Seven-or-more story multiunit	2,823	746	1.0	2,077	6.2
Manufactured/mobile homes	11,247	8,733	12.1	2,514	7.5
Commercial or institutional	25,995	11,505	15.9	14,490	43.1
Industrial or factories	3,594	1,660	2.3	1,934	5.8
Open space, park, woods, farm, or ranch	38,287	27,888	38.6	10,399	30.9
Four-or-more-lane highway, railroad, or airport	13,355	6,788	9.4	6,567	19.5
Waterfront property	2,749	2,194	3.0	555	1.7
NEIGHBORHOOD PROBLEMS					
Total households	**105,842**	**72,238**	**100.0**	**33,604**	**100.0**
Bothersome street noise problem	11,235	6,712	9.3	4,523	13.5
Bothersome neighborhood crime problem	9,021	4,765	6.6	4,256	12.7
Bothersome odor problem	3,554	1,960	2.7	1,594	4.7
Noise problem	2,487	1,391	1.9	1,096	3.3
Litter or housing deterioration	1,902	1,182	1.6	720	2.1
Poor city or county services	779	494	0.7	285	0.8
Undesirable commercial, institutional, industrial	750	518	0.7	232	0.7
People problem	4,005	2,358	3.3	1,647	4.9
Other problems	7,956	5,486	7.6	2,470	7.4
PUBLIC SCHOOLS					
Total households with children under age 14	**31,081**	**20,686**	**100.0**	**10,395**	**100.0**
Satisfactory public elementary school	24,010	16,530	79.9	7,480	72.0
PUBLIC SERVICES					
Total households	**105,842**	**72,238**	**100.0**	**33,604**	**100.0**
With public transportation	57,910	34,211	47.4	23,699	70.5
Satisfactory neighborhood shopping	86,800	57,847	80.1	28,953	86.2
Satisfactory police protection	93,968	64,487	89.3	29,481	87.7

Source: Bureau of the Census, American Housing Survey for the United States: 2003, *Current Housing Reports, Internet site http://www.census.gov/hhes/www/ahs.html; calculations by New Strategist*

Table 6.46 Opinion of Housing Unit and Neighborhood, 2003

(number and percent distribution of total households by opinion of housing unit and neighborhood, by homeownership status, 2003; numbers in thousands)

	total	owner-occupied number	owner-occupied percent distribution	renter-occupied number	renter-occupied percent distribution
OPINION OF HOUSING UNIT					
Total households	**105,842**	**72,238**	**100.0%**	**33,604**	**100.0%**
1 (worst)	472	162	0.2	310	0.9
2	393	102	0.1	291	0.9
3	819	287	0.4	532	1.6
4	1,092	384	0.5	708	2.1
5	5,660	2,443	3.4	3,217	9.6
6	5,642	2,815	3.9	2,827	8.4
7	14,349	8,419	11.7	5,930	17.6
8	28,684	20,014	27.7	8,670	25.8
9	15,947	12,265	17.0	3,682	11.0
10 (best)	28,132	22,114	30.6	6,018	17.9
Not reported	4,654	3,234	4.5	1,420	4.2
OPINION OF NEIGHBORHOOD					
Total households	**105,842**	**72,238**	**100.0**	**33,604**	**100.0**
1 (worst)	771	278	0.4	493	1.5
2	604	267	0.4	337	1.0
3	1,089	450	0.6	639	1.9
4	1,516	702	1.0	814	2.4
5	6,896	3,548	4.9	3,348	10.0
6	5,942	3,371	4.7	2,571	7.7
7	13,914	8,715	12.1	5,199	15.5
8	27,639	19,651	27.2	7,988	23.8
9	16,226	12,129	16.8	4,097	12.2
10 (best)	26,019	19,481	27.0	6,538	19.5
No neighborhood	454	362	0.5	92	0.3
Not reported	4,772	3,282	4.5	1,490	4.4

Source: Bureau of the Census, American Housing Survey for the United States: 2003, *Current Housing Reports, Internet site http://www.census.gov/hhes/www/ahs.html; calculations by New Strategist*

Table 6.47 Geographical Mobility of Total People by Age, 2003–04

(total number of people aged 1 or older, and number and percent who moved between March 2003 and March 2004, by age and type of move; numbers in thousands)

	total	movers total	same county	different county, same state	different state	abroad
Total people	284,367	38,995	22,551	7,842	7,330	1,272
Aged 1 to 4	16,026	3,324	2,109	600	542	73
Aged 5 to 9	19,636	3,105	1,914	625	490	76
Aged 10 to 14	21,176	2,663	1,613	509	481	60
Aged 15 to 17	12,829	1,418	849	263	257	49
Aged 18 to 19	7,485	1,218	666	282	232	38
Aged 20 to 24	20,339	5,882	3,343	1,281	1,038	220
Aged 25 to 29	19,008	5,249	3,020	1,030	966	233
Aged 30 to 34	20,193	3,878	2,253	781	700	144
Aged 35 to 39	20,791	3,034	1,686	643	576	129
Aged 40 to 44	22,782	2,677	1,627	459	495	96
Aged 45 to 49	21,823	1,841	1,005	370	428	38
Aged 50 to 54	19,246	1,425	792	263	315	55
Aged 55 to 59	16,158	1,047	533	241	252	21
Aged 60 to 61	5,454	334	159	69	100	6
Aged 62 to 64	6,762	385	169	88	112	16
Aged 65 or older	34,660	1,513	812	338	344	19
PERCENT DISTRIBUTION BY MOBILITY STATUS						
Total people	100.0%	13.7%	7.9%	2.8%	2.6%	0.4%
Aged 1 to 4	100.0	20.7	13.2	3.7	3.4	0.5
Aged 5 to 9	100.0	15.8	9.7	3.2	2.5	0.4
Aged 10 to 14	100.0	12.6	7.6	2.4	2.3	0.3
Aged 15 to 17	100.0	11.1	6.6	2.1	2.0	0.4
Aged 18 to 19	100.0	16.3	8.9	3.8	3.1	0.5
Aged 20 to 24	100.0	28.9	16.4	6.3	5.1	1.1
Aged 25 to 29	100.0	27.6	15.9	5.4	5.1	1.2
Aged 30 to 34	100.0	19.2	11.2	3.9	3.5	0.7
Aged 35 to 39	100.0	14.6	8.1	3.1	2.8	0.6
Aged 40 to 44	100.0	11.8	7.1	2.0	2.2	0.4
Aged 45 to 49	100.0	8.4	4.6	1.7	2.0	0.2
Aged 50 to 54	100.0	7.4	4.1	1.4	1.6	0.3
Aged 55 to 59	100.0	6.5	3.3	1.5	1.6	0.1
Aged 60 to 61	100.0	6.1	2.9	1.3	1.8	0.1
Aged 62 to 64	100.0	5.7	2.5	1.3	1.7	0.2
Aged 65 or older	100.0	4.4	2.3	1.0	1.0	0.1

Source: Bureau of the Census, Geographic Mobility: 2004, Detailed Tables, Internet site http://www.census.gov/population/www/socdemo/migrate/cps2004.html; calculations by New Strategist

Table 6.48 Geographical Mobility by Age, Race, and Hispanic Origin, 2003–04

(total number of people aged 1 or older who moved between March 2003 and March 2004 and percent distribution by age, race, and Hispanic origin; numbers in thousands)

	total		Asian	black	Hispanic	non-Hispanic white
	number	percent				
Total movers	**38,995**	**100.0%**	**5.1%**	**16.0%**	**17.7%**	**60.2%**
Aged 1 to 4	3,324	100.0	4.7	23.1	23.2	48.3
Aged 5 to 9	3,105	100.0	4.0	22.8	22.9	50.3
Aged 10 to 14	2,663	100.0	4.2	24.1	21.9	49.2
Aged 15 to 17	1,418	100.0	6.1	22.7	22.0	47.2
Aged 18 to 19	1,218	100.0	4.3	14.4	19.6	61.1
Aged 20 to 24	5,882	100.0	4.2	12.6	17.2	65.0
Aged 25 to 29	5,249	100.0	6.8	12.6	17.3	62.2
Aged 30 to 34	3,878	100.0	6.5	13.8	18.8	59.5
Aged 35 to 39	3,034	100.0	5.9	14.8	19.0	59.7
Aged 40 to 44	2,677	100.0	5.1	15.7	16.1	62.9
Aged 45 to 49	1,841	100.0	5.2	14.6	11.8	67.0
Aged 50 to 54	1,425	100.0	5.8	14.1	10.9	67.5
Aged 55 to 59	1,047	100.0	3.3	13.6	7.8	73.4
Aged 60 to 61	334	100.0	3.6	8.1	9.0	76.9
Aged 62 to 64	385	100.0	4.9	14.5	8.3	70.1
Aged 65 or older	1,513	100.0	4.2	8.1	7.9	79.4

Note: Percentages will not sum to 100 because Asians and blacks include those identifying themselves as being of the race alone and those identifying themselves as being of the race in combination with one or more other races, Hispanics may be of any race, and non-Hispanic whites are those identifying themselves as being white alone and not Hispanic.
Source: Bureau of the Census, Geographic Mobility: 2004, Detailed Tables, Internet site http://www.census.gov/population/www/ socdemo/migrate/cps2004.html; calculations by New Strategist

Table 6.49 Reasons for Moving by Homeownership Status, 2003

(number and percent distribution of total households with respondents who moved in the past 12 months by main reason for move and for choosing new neighborhood and house, by homeownership status, 2003; numbers in thousands)

	total	owners number	owners percent distribution	renters number	renters percent distribution
MAIN REASON FOR LEAVING PREVIOUS HOUSING UNIT					
Total movers	**17,866**	**5,971**	**100.0%**	**11,895**	**100.0%**
All reported reasons equal	261	60	1.0	201	1.7
Private displacement	139	14	0.2	125	1.1
Government displacement	49	12	0.2	37	0.3
Disaster loss (fire, flood, etc.)	110	32	0.5	78	0.7
New job or job transfer	1,739	493	8.3	1,246	10.5
To be closer to work/school/other	1,366	300	5.0	1,066	9.0
Other financial/employment reason	573	111	1.9	462	3.9
To establish own household	2,123	727	12.2	1,396	11.7
Needed larger house or apartment	1,835	689	11.5	1,146	9.6
Married, widowed, divorced, separated	1,156	428	7.2	728	6.1
Other family/personal reason	1,491	488	8.2	1,003	8.4
Wanted better home	1,342	453	7.6	889	7.5
Change from owner to renter/renter to owner	941	806	13.5	135	1.1
Wanted lower rent or maintenance	832	133	2.2	699	5.9
Other housing related reasons	834	210	3.5	624	5.2
Other	2,229	752	12.6	1,477	12.4
Not reported	846	264	4.4	582	4.9
MAIN REASON FOR CHOOSING PRESENT NEIGHBORHOOD					
Total movers	**17,866**	**5,971**	**100.0**	**11,895**	**100.0**
All reported reasons equal	444	153	2.6	291	2.4
Convenient to job	3,442	760	12.7	2,682	22.5
Convenient to friends or relatives	2,770	851	14.3	1,919	16.1
Convenient to leisure activities	391	131	2.2	260	2.2
Convenient to public transportation	199	22	0.4	177	1.5
Good schools	1,135	408	6.8	727	6.1
Other public services	198	36	0.6	162	1.4
Looks/design of neighborhood	2,475	1,079	18.1	1,396	11.7
House was most important consideration	2,646	1,261	21.1	1,385	11.6
Other	3,498	1,019	17.1	2,479	20.8
Not reported	669	249	4.2	420	3.5

(continued)

	total	owners		renters	
		number	percent distribution	number	percent distribution
MAIN REASON FOR CHOOSING PRESENT HOME					
Total movers	**17,866**	**5,971**	**100.0%**	**11,895**	**100.0%**
All reported reasons equal	587	254	4.3	333	2.8
Financial reasons	5,155	1,327	22.2	3,828	32.2
Room layout/design	3,026	1,354	22.7	1,672	14.1
Kitchen	78	32	0.5	46	0.4
Size	2,395	694	11.6	1,701	14.3
Exterior appearance	633	273	4.6	360	3.0
Yard/trees/view	840	421	7.1	419	3.5
Quality of construction	586	342	5.7	244	2.1
Only one available	928	94	1.6	834	7.0
Other	2,969	927	15.5	2,042	17.2
Not reported	670	252	4.2	418	3.5

Source: Bureau of the Census, American Housing Survey for the United States: 2003, *Current Housing Reports, Internet site http://www.census.gov/hhes/www/ahs.html; calculations by New Strategist*

Households Made Gains in Income between 1990 and 2003, Regardless of Race and Hispanic Origin

The median income of American households rose 6 percent between 1990 and 2003, to $43,318 after adjusting for inflation. Black households gained the most during those years, their median income rising 16 percent. Asians experienced only a 5 percent increase in median income between 1990 and 2003. Despite their relatively slow income growth, Asian households are most likely to have incomes of $100,000 or more, with 23 percent at that income level in 2003.

By age, household income peaks among Asian householders aged 55 to 59, at $70,366. Household income is lowest (below $17,000) among the youngest and the oldest black householders. By household type, incomes are greatest for Asian married couples, with a median of $70,548. They are lowest for Hispanic women living alone, at just $14,576.

Non-Hispanic whites account for the slim 51 percent majority of the nation's poor married couples, and for a smaller 38 percent of poor female- and male-headed families. Among poor married couples, Hispanics account for 31 percent. Among poor female-headed families, blacks account for more than one-third. Among the nation's 36 million poor people, non-Hispanic whites are a 44 percent minority. Blacks and Hispanics each account for one-fourth of the nation's poor people.

■ Although blacks and Hispanics are making income gains, their incomes are far below those of Asians and non-Hispanic whites. Hispanics trail because of their low educational level. Blacks are behind because married couples head relatively few black households.

Asian incomes are the highest

(median household income by race and Hispanic origin, 2003)

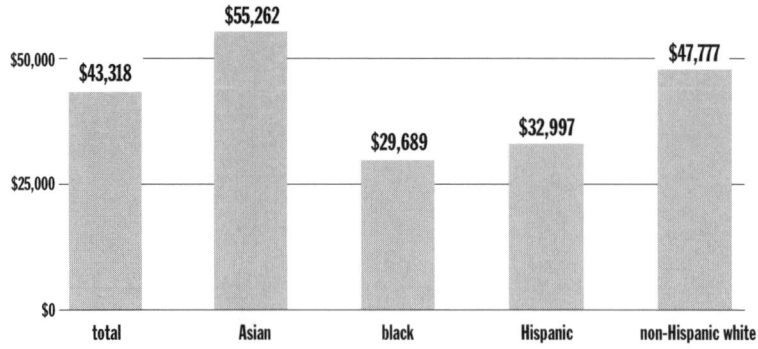

Table 6.50   Median Income of Households by Race and Hispanic Origin, 1990 to 2003

(median income of households by race and Hispanic origin, percent change in median for selected years, and index of median by race/Hispanic origin to total, 1990 to 2003; in 2003 dollars)

	total	Asian	black	Hispanic	non-Hispanic white
MEDIAN					
2003	$43,318	$55,262	$29,689	$32,997	$47,777
2002	43,381	53,483	29,845	33,861	47,974
2001	43,882	55,736	30,625	34,880	48,119
2000	44,853	59,559	31,690	35,429	48,734
1999	44,922	56,251	30,808	33,938	48,742
1998	43,825	52,562	28,572	31,929	47,831
1997	42,294	51,716	28,630	30,434	46,376
1996	41,431	50,517	27,411	29,073	45,277
1995	40,845	48,682	26,842	27,401	44,564
1994	39,613	49,703	25,816	28,756	43,127
1993	39,165	48,073	24,487	28,690	42,840
1992	39,364	48,570	24,098	29,035	42,774
1991	39,679	48,007	24,771	29,887	42,573
1990	40,865	52,475	25,488	30,475	43,597
Percent change					
2000 to 2003	–3.4%	–7.2%	–6.3%	–6.9%	–2.0%
1990 to 2003	6.0	5.3	16.5	8.3	9.6
INDEX					
2003	100	128	69	76	110
2002	100	123	69	78	111
2001	100	127	70	79	110
2000	100	133	71	79	109
1999	100	125	69	76	109
1998	100	120	65	73	109
1997	100	122	68	72	110
1996	100	122	66	70	109
1995	100	119	66	67	109
1994	100	125	65	73	109
1993	100	123	63	73	109
1992	100	123	61	74	109
1991	100	121	62	75	107
1990	100	128	62	75	107

Note: Data for Asians and blacks in 2002 and 2003 are for those identifying themselves as being of the race alone and those identifying themselves as being of the race in combination with other races. Data for non-Hispanic whites in 2002 and 2003 are for those identifying themselves as being white alone and not Hispanic. Hispanics may be of any race.
Source: Bureau of the Census, Current Population Surveys, Internet site http://www.census.gov/hhes/income/histinc/h05.html; calculations by New Strategist

Table 6.51 High-Income Households by Race and Hispanic Origin, 2003

(number and percent distribution of households with incomes of $100,000 or more by race and Hispanic origin, 2003; households in thousands as of 2004)

	total	Asian	black	Hispanic	non-Hispanic white
TOTAL HOUSEHOLDS	**112,000**	**4,235**	**13,969**	**11,693**	**81,148**
$100,000 or more	**16,945**	**973**	**946**	**871**	**14,031**
$100,000 to $149,999	10,719	594	679	572	8,797
$150,000 to $199,999	3,372	238	160	171	2,774
$200,000 to $249,999	1,307	70	61	58	1,105
$250,000 or more	1,547	71	46	70	1,355
PERCENT DISTRIBUTION BY RACE AND HISPANIC ORIGIN					
TOTAL HOUSEHOLDS	**100.0%**	**3.8%**	**12.5%**	**10.4%**	**72.5%**
$100,000 or more	**100.0**	**5.7**	**5.6**	**5.1**	**82.8**
$100,000 to $149,999	100.0	5.5	6.3	5.3	82.1
$150,000 to $199,999	100.0	7.1	4.7	5.1	82.3
$200,000 to $249,999	100.0	5.4	4.7	4.4	84.5
$250,000 or more	100.0	4.6	3.0	4.5	87.6
PERCENT DISTRIBUTION BY INCOME					
TOTAL HOUSEHOLDS	**100.0%**	**100.0%**	**100.0%**	**100.0%**	**100.0%**
$100,000 or more	**15.1**	**23.0**	**6.8**	**7.4**	**17.3**
$100,000 to $149,999	9.6	14.0	4.9	4.9	10.8
$150,000 to $199,999	3.0	5.6	1.1	1.5	3.4
$200,000 to $249,999	1.2	1.7	0.4	0.5	1.4
$250,000 or more	1.4	1.7	0.3	0.6	1.7

Note: Asians and blacks are those identifying themselves as being of the race alone and those identifying themselves as being of the race in combination with other races. Hispanics may be of any race. Non-Hispanic whites are those identifying themselves as being white alone and not Hispanic.
Source: Bureau of the Census, 2004 Current Population Survey, Internet site http://pubdb3.census.gov/macro/032004/hhinc/ new06_000.htm; calculations by New Strategist

Table 6.52 Household Income by Age of Householder, 2003

(number and percent distribution of total households by household income and age of householder, 2003; households in thousands as of 2004)

	total	15 to 24	25 to 34	35 to 44	45 to 54	55 to 64	aged 65 or older total	65 to 74	75 or older
Total households	**112,000**	**6,610**	**19,159**	**23,222**	**23,137**	**16,824**	**23,048**	**11,499**	**11,550**
Under $10,000	10,111	1,178	1,425	1,346	1,399	1,546	3,217	1,323	1,894
$10,000 to $19,999	15,174	1,227	2,002	1,898	1,694	1,805	6,550	2,502	4,047
$20,000 to $29,999	13,933	1,209	2,395	2,311	2,056	1,800	4,163	1,992	2,171
$30,000 to $39,999	12,583	951	2,593	2,433	2,217	1,818	2,570	1,426	1,143
$40,000 to $49,999	10,749	646	2,243	2,362	2,193	1,548	1,757	1,065	692
$50,000 to $59,999	9,151	438	1,890	2,275	1,956	1,405	1,187	734	453
$60,000 to $69,999	7,647	306	1,523	1,946	1,878	1,115	878	536	342
$70,000 to $79,999	6,471	193	1,289	1,661	1,707	1,033	589	401	189
$80,000 to $89,999	5,067	151	930	1,383	1,386	817	401	268	132
$90,000 to $99,999	4,168	93	713	1,152	1,163	682	366	242	125
$100,000 or more	16,945	219	2,157	4,454	5,490	3,254	1,371	1,010	362
Median income	$43,318	$27,053	$44,779	$55,044	$60,242	$49,215	$23,787	$29,640	$19,470

PERCENT DISTRIBUTION BY INCOME

	total	15 to 24	25 to 34	35 to 44	45 to 54	55 to 64	aged 65 or older total	65 to 74	75 or older
Total households	**100.0%**	**100.0%**	**100.0%**	**100.0%**	**100.0%**	**100.0%**	**100.0%**	**100.0%**	**100.0%**
Under $10,000	9.0	17.8	7.4	5.8	6.0	9.2	14.0	11.5	16.4
$10,000 to $19,999	13.5	18.6	10.4	8.2	7.3	10.7	28.4	21.8	35.0
$20,000 to $29,999	12.4	18.3	12.5	10.0	8.9	10.7	18.1	17.3	18.8
$30,000 to $39,999	11.2	14.4	13.5	10.5	9.6	10.8	11.2	12.4	9.9
$40,000 to $49,999	9.6	9.8	11.7	10.2	9.5	9.2	7.6	9.3	6.0
$50,000 to $59,999	8.2	6.6	9.9	9.8	8.5	8.4	5.2	6.4	3.9
$60,000 to $69,999	6.8	4.6	7.9	8.4	8.1	6.6	3.8	4.7	3.0
$70,000 to $79,999	5.8	2.9	6.7	7.2	7.4	6.1	2.6	3.5	1.6
$80,000 to $89,999	4.5	2.3	4.9	6.0	6.0	4.9	1.7	2.3	1.1
$90,000 to $99,999	3.7	1.4	3.7	5.0	5.0	4.1	1.6	2.1	1.1
$100,000 or more	15.1	3.3	11.3	19.2	23.7	19.3	5.9	8.8	3.1

Source: Bureau of the Census, 2004 Current Population Survey, Internet site http://pubdb3.census.gov/macro/032004/hhinc/new02_001.htm; calculations by New Strategist

Table 6.53 Median Household Income by Age, Race, and Hispanic Origin of Householder, 2003

(median income of households by age, race, and Hispanic origin of householder, and index of median to average by age, 2003)

	total	Asian	black	Hispanic	non-Hispanic white
Total households	**$43,318**	**$55,262**	**$29,689**	**$32,997**	**$47,777**
Under age 25	27,053	27,427	16,967	26,912	30,266
Aged 25 to 29	40,408	45,535	28,355	31,622	45,877
Aged 30 to 34	49,018	69,630	34,742	34,617	55,806
Aged 35 to 39	53,543	65,910	36,812	37,449	61,066
Aged 40 to 44	56,033	69,062	37,195	36,836	62,817
Aged 45 to 49	60,884	68,444	40,118	41,240	67,963
Aged 50 to 54	59,041	61,794	36,373	38,814	65,820
Aged 55 to 59	56,066	70,366	33,022	39,829	60,292
Aged 60 to 64	41,541	51,788	27,800	30,436	44,754
Aged 65 or older	23,787	19,734	16,736	17,771	24,910

INDEX OF MEDIAN INCOME BY RACE AND HISPANIC ORIGIN TO AVERAGE BY AGE

	total	Asian	black	Hispanic	non-Hispanic white
Total households	**100**	**128**	**69**	**76**	**110**
Under age 25	62	63	39	62	70
Aged 25 to 29	93	105	65	73	106
Aged 30 to 34	113	161	80	80	129
Aged 35 to 39	124	152	85	86	141
Aged 40 to 44	129	159	86	85	145
Aged 45 to 49	141	158	93	95	157
Aged 50 to 54	136	143	84	90	152
Aged 55 to 59	129	162	76	92	139
Aged 60 to 64	96	120	64	70	103
Aged 65 or older	55	46	39	41	58

Note: Data for Asians and blacks are for those identifying themselves as being of the race alone and those identifying themselves as being of the race in combination with other races. Data for non-Hispanic whites are for those identifying themselves as being white alone and not Hispanic. Hispanics may be of any race.
Source: Bureau of the Census, 2004 Current Population Survey, Internet site http://pubdb3.census.gov/macro/032004/hhinc/ new02_000.htm; calculations by New Strategist

Table 6.54 Household Income by Household Type, 2003

(number and percent distribution of total households by household income and household type, 2003; households in thousands as of 2004)

| | | family households | | | nonfamily households | | | |
| | | | | | female householder | | male householder | |
	total	married couples	female hh, no spouse present	male hh, no spouse present	total	living alone	total	living alone
Total households	**112,000**	**57,719**	**13,781**	**4,717**	**19,647**	**17,024**	**16,136**	**12,562**
Under $10,000	10,111	1,449	2,025	290	4,132	3,982	2,214	2,061
$10,000 to $19,999	15,174	3,801	2,646	558	5,209	4,960	2,961	2,674
$20,000 to $29,999	13,933	5,532	2,363	673	3,072	2,756	2,293	1,882
$30,000 to $39,999	12,583	5,590	1,978	698	2,158	1,829	2,159	1,738
$40,000 to $49,999	10,749	5,679	1,327	521	1,548	1,243	1,672	1,241
$50,000 to $59,999	9,151	5,375	956	476	1,042	763	1,301	924
$60,000 to $69,999	7,647	4,987	771	338	662	463	889	576
$70,000 to $79,999	6,471	4,549	520	244	496	332	664	390
$80,000 to $89,999	5,067	3,668	333	238	340	184	490	318
$90,000 to $99,999	4,168	3,221	228	163	239	99	317	158
$100,000 or more	16,945	13,866	634	518	748	413	1,178	599
Median income	$43,318	$62,405	$29,307	$41,959	$21,313	$18,676	$31,928	$27,438

PERCENT DISTRIBUTION BY INCOME

Total households	**100.0%**	**100.0%**	**100.0%**	**100.0%**	**100.0%**	**100.0%**	**100.0%**	**100.0%**
Under $10,000	9.0	2.5	14.7	6.1	21.0	23.4	13.7	16.4
$10,000 to $19,999	13.5	6.6	19.2	11.8	26.5	29.1	18.4	21.3
$20,000 to $29,999	12.4	9.6	17.1	14.3	15.6	16.2	14.2	15.0
$30,000 to $39,999	11.2	9.7	14.4	14.8	11.0	10.7	13.4	13.8
$40,000 to $49,999	9.6	9.8	9.6	11.0	7.9	7.3	10.4	9.9
$50,000 to $59,999	8.2	9.3	6.9	10.1	5.3	4.5	8.1	7.4
$60,000 to $69,999	6.8	8.6	5.6	7.2	3.4	2.7	5.5	4.6
$70,000 to $79,999	5.8	7.9	3.8	5.2	2.5	2.0	4.1	3.1
$80,000 to $89,999	4.5	6.4	2.4	5.0	1.7	1.1	3.0	2.5
$90,000 to $99,999	3.7	5.6	1.7	3.5	1.2	0.6	2.0	1.3
$100,000 or more	15.1	24.0	4.6	11.0	3.8	2.4	7.3	4.8

Source: Bureau of the Census, 2004 Current Population Survey, Internet site http://pubdb3.census.gov/macro/032004/hhinc/ new02_000.htm; calculations by New Strategist

Table 6.55 Median Household Income by Household Type, Race, and Hispanic Origin of Householder, 2003

(median household income by type of household, race, and Hispanic origin of householder; and index of race/Hispanic origin median to national median by household type, 2003)

	total	Asian	black	Hispanic	non-Hispanic white
Total households	**$43,318**	**$55,262**	**$29,689**	**$32,997**	**$47,777**
Married couples	62,405	70,548	52,671	40,675	66,677
Female-headed family, no spouse present	29,307	39,877	22,739	24,459	34,686
Male-headed family, no spouse present	41,959	52,768	35,660	37,834	45,416
Female-headed nonfamily	21,313	22,369	17,001	18,018	22,307
Women living alone	18,676	17,248	15,542	14,576	19,674
Male-headed nonfamily	31,928	36,311	24,495	26,450	34,280
Men living alone	27,438	32,059	21,304	20,571	30,156
INDEX					
Total households	**100**	**128**	**69**	**76**	**110**
Married couples	144	163	122	94	154
Female-headed family, no spouse present	68	92	52	56	80
Male-headed family, no spouse present	97	122	82	87	105
Female-headed nonfamily	49	52	39	42	51
Women living alone	43	40	36	34	45
Male-headed nonfamily	74	84	57	61	79
Men living alone	63	74	49	47	70

Note: The index is calculated by dividing the median income of each race/Hispanic origin household type by the national median and multiplying by 100. Data for Asians and blacks are for those identifying themselves as being of the race alone and those identifying themselves as being of the race in combination with other races. Data for non-Hispanic whites are for those identifying themselves as being white alone and not Hispanic. Hispanics may be of any race.
Source: Bureau of the Census, 2004 Current Population Survey, Internet site http://pubdb3.census.gov/macro/032004/hhinc/new01_000.htm; calculations by New Strategist

Table 6.56 Income of Men by Age, 2003

(number and percent distribution of men aged 15 or older by income and age, median income of men with income and of men working full-time, year-round, and percent working full-time, year-round, 2003; men in thousands as of 2004)

	total	under 25	25 to 34	35 to 44	45 to 54	55 to 64	65 or older
TOTAL MEN	**110,257**	**20,699**	**19,598**	**21,530**	**20,082**	**13,551**	**14,797**
Without income	**9,488**	**6,462**	**914**	**749**	**665**	**454**	**243**
With income	**100,769**	**14,237**	**18,684**	**20,781**	**19,417**	**13,097**	**14,554**
Under $10,000	16,018	7,133	1,970	1,787	1,681	1,268	2,178
$10,000 to $19,999	18,662	3,568	3,370	2,534	2,266	1,953	4,973
$20,000 to $29,999	15,777	2,037	3,690	3,081	2,340	1,828	2,800
$30,000 to $39,999	13,043	874	3,307	3,120	2,612	1,645	1,485
$40,000 to $49,999	9,942	314	2,286	2,658	2,428	1,411	847
$50,000 to $59,999	7,280	136	1,272	2,033	2,034	1,157	649
$60,000 to $69,999	5,181	63	953	1,422	1,430	874	438
$70,000 to $79,999	3,623	37	613	946	1,157	635	234
$80,000 to $89,999	2,524	10	365	717	762	488	182
$90,000 to $99,999	1,676	24	202	481	500	313	154
$100,000 or more	7,044	38	656	2,005	2,204	1,528	614
Median income of men with income	$29,931	$9,961	$30,562	$39,195	$42,079	$38,915	$20,363
Median income of men working full-time	41,503	21,580	35,245	44,588	50,076	51,965	53,696
Percent working full-time	53.3%	21.9%	71.1%	75.5%	74.3%	56.5%	10.1%
TOTAL MEN	**100.0%**	**100.0%**	**100.0%**	**100.0%**	**100.0%**	**100.0%**	**100.0%**
Without income	**8.6**	**31.2**	**4.7**	**3.5**	**3.3**	**3.4**	**1.6**
With income	**91.4**	**68.8**	**95.3**	**96.5**	**96.7**	**96.6**	**98.4**
Under $10,000	14.5	34.5	10.1	8.3	8.4	9.4	14.7
$10,000 to $19,999	16.9	17.2	17.2	11.8	11.3	14.4	33.6
$20,000 to $29,999	14.3	9.8	18.8	14.3	11.7	13.5	18.9
$30,000 to $39,999	11.8	4.2	16.9	14.5	13.0	12.1	10.0
$40,000 to $49,999	9.0	1.5	11.7	12.3	12.1	10.4	5.7
$50,000 to $59,999	6.6	0.7	6.5	9.4	10.1	8.5	4.4
$60,000 to $69,999	4.7	0.3	4.9	6.6	7.1	6.4	3.0
$70,000 to $79,999	3.3	0.2	3.1	4.4	5.8	4.7	1.6
$80,000 to $89,999	2.3	0.0	1.9	3.3	3.8	3.6	1.2
$90,000 to $99,999	1.5	0.1	1.0	2.2	2.5	2.3	1.0
$100,000 or more	6.4	0.2	3.3	9.3	11.0	11.3	4.1

Source: Bureau of the Census, 2004 Current Population Survey, Internet sites http://pubdb3.census.gov/macro/032004/perinc/ new01_010.htm and http://pubdb3.census.gov/macro/032004/perinc/new01_037.htm; calculations by New Strategist

Table 6.57 Income of Women by Age, 2003

(number and percent distribution of women aged 15 or older by income and age, median income of women with income and of women working full-time, year-round, and percent working full-time, year-round, 2003; women in thousands as of 2004)

	total	under 25	25 to 34	35 to 44	45 to 54	55 to 64	65 or older
TOTAL WOMEN	**117,327**	**20,009**	**19,603**	**22,043**	**20,987**	**14,824**	**19,862**
Without income	**14,614**	**6,415**	**2,447**	**2,033**	**1,684**	**1,400**	**637**
With income	**102,713**	**13,594**	**17,156**	**20,010**	**19,303**	**13,424**	**19,225**
Under $10,000	32,489	7,877	4,208	4,756	3,896	4,019	7,733
$10,000 to $19,999	23,652	3,231	3,543	3,852	3,567	2,595	6,864
$20,000 to $29,999	16,526	1,612	3,396	3,543	3,538	2,214	2,224
$30,000 to $39,999	11,444	601	2,676	2,726	2,772	1,559	1,112
$40,000 to $49,999	6,974	182	1,469	1,898	1,939	1,003	487
$50,000 to $59,999	3,984	45	698	1,088	1,175	690	287
$60,000 to $69,999	2,563	25	388	705	850	426	170
$70,000 to $79,999	1,602	6	267	444	476	312	98
$80,000 to $89,999	958	4	142	280	305	160	65
$90,000 to $99,999	556	4	82	168	174	82	46
$100,000 or more	1,964	8	289	545	614	368	140
Median income of women with income	$17,259	$7,435	$21,992	$23,472	$25,866	$20,368	$11,845
Median income of women working full-time	31,653	20,525	30,862	33,500	34,827	34,205	35,851
Percent working full-time	35.7%	16.2%	48.4%	50.4%	54.5%	38.4%	4.8%
TOTAL WOMEN	**100.0%**	**100.0%**	**100.0%**	**100.0%**	**100.0%**	**100.0%**	**100.0%**
Without income	**12.5**	**32.1**	**12.5**	**9.2**	**8.0**	**9.4**	**3.2**
With income	**87.5**	**67.9**	**87.5**	**90.8**	**92.0**	**90.6**	**96.8**
Under $10,000	27.7	39.4	21.5	21.6	18.6	27.1	38.9
$10,000 to $19,999	20.2	16.1	18.1	17.5	17.0	17.5	34.6
$20,000 to $29,999	14.1	8.1	17.3	16.1	16.9	14.9	11.2
$30,000 to $39,999	9.8	3.0	13.7	12.4	13.2	10.5	5.6
$40,000 to $49,999	5.9	0.9	7.5	8.6	9.2	6.8	2.5
$50,000 to $59,999	3.4	0.2	3.6	4.9	5.6	4.7	1.4
$60,000 to $69,999	2.2	0.1	2.0	3.2	4.1	2.9	0.9
$70,000 to $79,999	1.4	0.0	1.4	2.0	2.3	2.1	0.5
$80,000 to $89,999	0.8	0.0	0.7	1.3	1.5	1.1	0.3
$90,000 to $99,999	0.5	0.0	0.4	0.8	0.8	0.6	0.2
$100,000 or more	1.7	0.0	1.5	2.5	2.9	2.5	0.7

Source: Bureau of the Census, 2004 Current Population Survey, Internet sites http://pubdb3.census.gov/macro/032004/perinc/ new01_019.htm and http://pubdb3.census.gov/macro/032004/perinc/new01_046.htm; calculations by New Strategist

Table 6.58 Median Income of People Working Full-Time by Sex, 1990 to 2003

(median income of total people aged 15 or older working full-time, year-round by sex, and women's income as a percent of men's income, 1990 to 2003; percent change in income, 2000–03 and 1990–2003; in 2003 dollars)

	men	women	women's income as a percent of men's income
2003	$41,503	$31,653	76.3%
2002	41,435	31,680	76.5
2001	41,708	31,612	75.8
2000	41,543	31,109	74.9
1999	41,339	30,207	73.1
1998	40,858	30,267	74.1
1997	40,286	29,749	73.8
1996	39,150	29,107	74.3
1995	38,596	28,500	73.8
1994	38,812	28,564	73.6
1993	38,959	28,168	72.3
1992	39,616	28,387	71.7
1991	39,949	27,982	70.0
1990	39,549	28,102	71.1
Percent change			
2000 to 2003	–0.1%	1.7%	–
1990 to 2003	4.9	12.6	–

Note: (–) means not applicable.
Source: Bureau of the Census, Current Population Surveys, Internet site http://www.census.gov/hhes/income/histinc/p36b.html; calculations by New Strategist

Table 6.59 Median Earnings of People Working Full-Time by Education and Sex, 2003

(median earnings of total people aged 25 or older working full-time, year-round, by educational attainment and sex, and women's earnings as a percent of men's earnings, 2003)

	men	women	women's earnings as a percent of men's earnings
Total people	**$41,939**	**$31,565**	**75.3%**
Less than 9th grade	21,217	16,907	79.7
9th to 12th grade, no diploma	26,468	18,938	71.6
High school graduate	35,412	26,074	73.6
Some college, no degree	41,348	30,142	72.9
Associate's degree	42,871	32,253	75.2
Bachelor's degree or more	62,075	45,116	72.7

Source: Bureau of the Census, 2004 Current Population Survey, Internet site http://pubdb3.census.gov/macro/032004/perinc/new03_000.htm; calculations by New Strategist

Table 6.60 Poverty Status of Families, 1990 to 2003

(total number of families, and number and percent below poverty level by type of family and presence of children under age 18 at home, 1990 to 2003; percent change in numbers and percentage point change in rates, 2000–03 and 1990–2003; families in thousands as of March the following year)

| | total families | | | married couples | | | female hh, no spouse present | | | male hh, no spouse present | | |
| | | in poverty | | | in poverty | | | in poverty | | | in poverty | |
	total	number	percent	total	number	percent	total	number	percent	total	number	percent
Total families												
2003	76,232	7,607	10.0%	57,725	3,115	5.4%	13,791	3,856	28.0%	4,717	636	13.5%
2002	75,616	7,229	9.6	57,327	3,052	5.3	13,626	3,613	26.5	4,663	564	12.1
2001	74,340	6,813	9.2	56,755	2,760	4.9	13,146	3,470	26.4	4,440	583	13.1
2000	73,778	6,400	8.7	56,598	2,637	4.7	12,903	3,278	25.4	4,277	485	11.3
1999	73,206	6,792	9.3	56,290	2,748	4.9	12,818	3,559	27.8	4,099	485	11.8
1998	71,551	7,186	10.0	54,778	2,879	5.3	12,796	3,831	29.9	3,977	476	12.0
1997	70,884	7,324	10.3	54,321	2,821	5.2	12,652	3,995	31.6	3,911	507	13.0
1996	70,241	7,708	11.0	53,604	3,010	5.6	12,790	4,167	32.6	3,847	531	13.8
1995	69,597	7,532	10.8	53,570	2,982	5.6	12,514	4,057	32.4	3,513	493	14.0
1994	69,313	8,053	11.6	53,865	3,272	6.1	12,220	4,232	34.6	3,228	549	17.0
1993	68,506	8,393	12.3	53,181	3,481	6.5	12,411	4,424	35.6	2,914	488	16.8
1992	68,216	8,144	11.9	53,090	3,385	6.4	12,061	4,275	35.4	3,065	484	15.8
1991	67,175	7,712	11.5	52,457	3,158	6.0	11,693	4,161	35.6	3,025	392	13.0
1990	66,322	7,098	10.7	52,147	2,981	5.7	11,268	3,768	33.4	2,907	349	12.0
	percent change		percentage point change	percent change		percentage point change	percent change		percentage point change	percent change		percentage point change
2000 to 2003	3.3%	18.9%	1.3	2.0%	18.1%	0.7	6.9%	17.6%	2.6	10.3%	31.1%	2.2
1990 to 2003	14.9	7.2	−0.7	10.7	4.5	−0.3	22.4	2.3	−5.4	62.3	82.2	1.5

(continued)

Families with children

	total families			married couples			female lhh, no spouse present			male lhh, no spouse present		
		in poverty			in poverty			in poverty			in poverty	
	total	number	percent	total	number	percent	total	number	percent	total	number	percent
2003	39,029	5,772	14.8%	26,959	1,885	7.0%	9,614	3,416	35.5%	2,456	470	19.1%
2002	38,846	5,397	13.9	27,052	1,831	6.8	9,414	3,171	33.7	2,380	395	16.6
2001	38,427	5,138	13.4	26,931	1,643	6.1	9,171	3,083	33.6	2,325	412	17.7
2000	38,190	4,866	12.7	27,121	1,615	6.0	8,813	2,906	33.0	2,256	345	15.3
1999	37,688	5,210	13.8	26,694	1,711	6.4	8,793	3,139	35.7	2,200	360	16.3
1998	37,268	5,628	15.1	26,226	1,822	6.9	8,934	3,456	38.7	2,107	350	16.6
1997	37,427	5,884	15.7	26,430	1,863	7.1	8,822	3,614	41.0	2,175	407	18.7
1996	37,204	6,131	16.5	26,184	1,964	7.5	8,957	3,755	41.9	2,063	412	20.0
1995	36,719	5,976	16.3	26,034	1,961	7.5	8,751	3,634	41.5	1,934	381	19.7
1994	36,782	6,408	17.4	26,367	2,197	8.3	8,665	3,816	44.0	1,750	395	22.6
1993	36,456	6,751	18.5	26,121	2,363	9.0	8,758	4,034	46.1	1,577	354	22.5
1992	35,851	6,457	18.0	25,907	2,237	8.6	8,375	3,867	46.2	1,569	353	22.5
1991	34,862	6,170	17.7	25,357	2,106	8.3	7,991	3,767	47.1	1,513	297	19.6
1990	34,503	5,676	16.4	25,410	1,990	7.8	7,707	3,426	44.5	1,386	260	18.8
	percent change	percent change	percentage point change	percent change	percent change	percentage point change	percent change	percent change	percentage point change	percent change	percent change	percentage point change
2000 to 2003	2.2%	18.6%	2.1	-0.6%	16.7%	1.0	9.1%	17.5%	2.5	8.9%	36.2%	3.8
1990 to 2003	13.1	1.7	-1.6	6.1	-5.3	-0.8	24.7	-0.3	-9.0	77.2	80.8	0.3

Source: Bureau of the Census, Current Population Surveys, Internet site http://www.census.gov/hhes/www/poverty/histpov/hstpov4.html; calculations by New Strategist

Table 6.61 Families in Poverty by Family Type, Race, and Hispanic Origin, 2003

(number and percent of families in poverty, and percent distribution of families in poverty, by type of family and race and Hispanic origin of householder, 2003; families in thousands as of 2004)

	total	Asian	black	Hispanic	non-Hispanic white
NUMBER IN POVERTY					
Total families	**7,607**	**320**	**2,021**	**1,925**	**3,270**
Married couples	3,115	203	331	976	1,575
Female householders, no spouse present	3,856	89	1,496	792	1,455
Male householders, no spouse present	636	28	194	157	241
PERCENT IN POVERTY					
Total families	**10.0%**	**10.0%**	**22.1%**	**20.8%**	**6.1%**
Married couples	5.4	7.9	7.8	15.7	3.6
Female householders, no spouse present	28.0	23.5	36.8	37.0	20.4
Male householders, no spouse present	13.5	11.8	24.1	17.3	8.9
PERCENT DISTRIBUTION OF FAMILIES IN POVERTY BY RACE AND HISPANIC ORIGIN					
Total families	**100.0%**	**4.2%**	**26.6%**	**25.3%**	**43.0%**
Married couples	100.0	6.5	10.6	31.3	50.6
Female householders, no spouse present	100.0	2.3	38.8	20.5	37.7
Male householders, no spouse present	100.0	4.4	30.5	24.7	37.9
PERCENT DISTRIBUTION OF FAMILIES IN POVERTY BY FAMILY TYPE					
Total families	**100.0%**	**100.0%**	**100.0%**	**100.0%**	**100.0%**
Married couples	40.9	63.4	16.4	50.7	48.2
Female householders, no spouse present	50.7	27.8	74.0	41.1	44.5
Male householders, no spouse present	8.4	8.8	9.6	8.2	7.4

Note: Numbers will not add to total because Hispanics may be of any race and because not all races are shown. Data for Asians and blacks are for those identifying themselves as being of the race alone and those identifying themselves as being of the race in combination with other races. Data for non-Hispanic whites are for those identifying themselves as being white alone and not Hispanic.
Source: Bureau of the Census, 2004 Current Population Survey, Internet site http://pubdb3.census.gov/macro/032004/pov/ new04_100.htm.html

Table 6.62 Families with Children in Poverty by Family Type, Race, and Hispanic Origin, 2003

(number and percent of families with children under age 18 in poverty, and percent distribution of families with children in poverty, by type of family and race and Hispanic origin of householder, 2003; families in thousands as of 2004)

	total	Asian	black	Hispanic	non-Hispanic white
NUMBER IN POVERTY					
Total families with children	**5,772**	**199**	**1,698**	**1,629**	**2,185**
Married couples	1,885	121	210	789	746
Female householders, no spouse present	3,416	66	1,341	713	1,269
Male householders, no spouse present	470	12	146	127	170
PERCENT IN POVERTY					
Total families with children	**14.8%**	**10.9%**	**28.6%**	**25.2%**	**8.9%**
Married couples	7.0	8.0	9.1	18.4	4.0
Female householders, no spouse present	35.5	28.2	42.7	43.0	28.1
Male householders, no spouse present	19.1	15.2	30.7	24.9	12.5
PERCENT DISTRIBUTION OF FAMILIES IN POVERTY BY RACE AND HISPANIC ORIGIN					
Total families with children	**100.0%**	**3.4%**	**29.4%**	**28.2%**	**37.9%**
Married couples	100.0	6.4	11.1	41.9	39.6
Female householders, no spouse present	100.0	1.9	39.3	20.9	37.1
Male householders, no spouse present	100.0	2.6	31.1	27.0	36.2
PERCENT DISTRIBUTION OF FAMILIES IN POVERTY BY FAMILY TYPE					
Total families with children	**100.0%**	**100.0%**	**100.0%**	**100.0%**	**100.0%**
Married couples	32.7	60.8	12.4	48.4	34.1
Female householders, no spouse present	59.2	33.2	79.0	43.8	58.1
Male householders, no spouse present	8.1	6.0	8.6	7.8	7.8

Note: Numbers will not add to total because Hispanics may be of any race and because not all races are shown. Data for Asians and blacks are for those identifying themselves as being of the race alone and those identifying themselves as being of the race in combination with other races. Data for non-Hispanic whites are for those identifying themselves as being white alone and not Hispanic.
Source: Bureau of the Census, 2004 Current Population Survey, Internet site http://pubdb3.census.gov/macro/032004/pov/new04_100.htm.html

Table 6.63 Poverty Status by Sex and Age, 2003

(total number of people, and number and percent below poverty level by sex and age, 2003; people in thousands as of 2004)

		in poverty	
	total	number	percent
Total people	**287,699**	**35,861**	**12.5%**
Under age 18	72,999	12,866	17.6
Aged 18 to 24	27,824	4,596	16.5
Aged 25 to 34	39,201	5,037	12.8
Aged 35 to 44	43,573	4,164	9.6
Aged 45 to 54	41,068	3,136	7.6
Aged 55 to 59	16,158	1,322	8.2
Aged 60 to 64	12,217	1,188	9.7
Aged 65 or older	34,659	3,552	10.2
Total females	**146,768**	**20,078**	**13.7**
Under age 18	35,815	6,299	17.6
Aged 18 to 24	13,634	2,688	19.7
Aged 25 to 34	19,603	3,045	15.5
Aged 35 to 44	22,043	2,384	10.8
Aged 45 to 54	20,987	1,685	8.0
Aged 55 to 59	8,307	778	9.4
Aged 60 to 64	6,517	726	11.1
Aged 65 or older	19,862	2,473	12.5
Total males	**140,931**	**15,783**	**11.2**
Under age 18	37,184	6,567	17.7
Aged 18 to 24	14,189	1,908	13.4
Aged 25 to 34	19,598	1,991	10.2
Aged 35 to 44	21,530	1,779	8.3
Aged 45 to 54	20,082	1,451	7.2
Aged 55 to 59	7,851	545	6.9
Aged 60 to 64	5,699	463	8.1
Aged 65 or older	14,797	1,079	7.3

Source: Bureau of the Census, 2004 Current Population Survey, Internet site http://pubdb3.census.gov/macro/032004/pov/new01_100.htm

Table 6.64 People in Poverty by Age, Race, and Hispanic Origin, 2003

(number and percent of people in poverty and percent distribution of poor, by age, race, and Hispanic origin, 2003; people in thousands as of 2004)

	total	Asian	black	Hispanic	non-Hispanic white
NUMBER OF POOR					
Total people	**35,861**	**1,527**	**9,108**	**9,051**	**15,902**
Under age 18	12,866	420	4,108	4,077	4,233
Aged 18 to 24	4,596	202	1,062	1,043	2,242
Aged 25 to 34	5,037	308	1,133	1,589	1,949
Aged 35 to 44	4,164	175	914	1,058	1,980
Aged 45 to 54	3,136	167	722	541	1,675
Aged 55 to 59	1,322	51	247	168	826
Aged 60 to 64	1,188	52	233	169	719
Aged 65 or older	3,552	152	688	406	2,277
PERCENT IN POVERTY					
Total people	**12.5%**	**11.8%**	**24.3%**	**22.5%**	**8.2%**
Under age 18	17.6	12.7	33.6	29.7	9.8
Aged 18 to 24	16.5	16.0	26.6	21.0	12.9
Aged 25 to 34	12.8	13.1	21.8	21.4	8.2
Aged 35 to 44	9.6	8.2	16.5	17.6	6.7
Aged 45 to 54	7.6	9.8	15.0	13.8	5.5
Aged 55 to 59	8.2	8.1	15.8	13.1	6.6
Aged 60 to 64	9.7	12.1	18.5	19.3	7.5
Aged 65 tor older	10.2	14.2	23.5	19.5	8.0
PERCENT DISTRIBUTION OF POOR BY RACE AND HISPANIC ORIGIN					
Total people	**100.0%**	**4.3%**	**25.4%**	**25.2%**	**44.3%**
Under age 18	100.0	3.3	31.9	31.7	32.9
Aged 18 to 24	100.0	4.4	23.1	22.7	48.8
Aged 25 to 34	100.0	6.1	22.5	31.5	38.7
Aged 35 to 44	100.0	4.2	22.0	25.4	47.6
Aged 45 to 54	100.0	5.3	23.0	17.3	53.4
Aged 55 to 59	100.0	3.9	18.7	12.7	62.5
Aged 60 to 64	100.0	4.4	19.6	14.2	60.5
Aged 65 tor older	100.0	4.3	19.4	11.4	64.1

Note: Numbers will not add to total because Hispanics may be of any race and because not all races are shown. Data for Asians and blacks are for those identifying themselves as being of the race alone and those identifying themselves as being of the race in combination with other races. Data for non-Hispanic whites are for those identifying themselves as being white alone and not Hispanic.
Source: Bureau of the Census, 2004 Current Population Survey, Internet site http://pubdb3.census.gov/macro/032004/pov/new01_100.htm; calculations by New Strategist

Thirty-Five Percent of American Workers Are Managers or Professionals

Sixty-six percent of Americans aged 16 or older are in the labor force, including 73 percent of men and 59 percent of women. Among the nation's 147 million workers in 2004, 46 percent were women.

The largest share of workers—35 percent—are employed in managerial or professional occupations. Another 25 percent hold sales or office jobs. Sixteen percent of Americans are employed as service workers in jobs such as food preparation, personal care, and building maintenance.

Among all married couples, 56 percent are dual earners with both husband and wife in the labor force. Just 22 percent have only the husband in the labor force. Forty-two percent of households have two or more earners, while 21 percent have no earners—most of them the retired elderly.

It takes the average worker a median of 21 minutes to get to work each day. The median distance from home to work is 11 miles. Fully 79 percent of workers drive to work alone in their car. Only 4 percent use mass transit.

Between 2002 and 2012, the labor force will expand by 12 percent. The non-Hispanic white share of workers will decline during the decade from 71 to 65 percent. In 2012, Hispanics will account for 15 percent of workers, blacks for 12 percent, and Asians for 6 percent.

■ The labor force as a whole is becoming more diverse, but some occupations are far more diverse than others.

Most men and women work

(percent of people aged 16 or older in the civilian labor force, by sex, 2004)

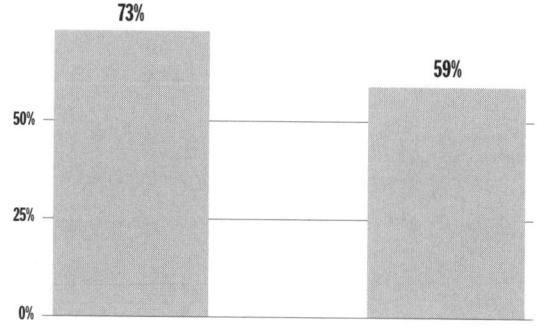

Table 6.65 Total Labor Force Participation Rate by Age and Sex, 2004

(percent of persons aged 16 or older in the civilian labor force, by age and sex, 2004)

	total	men	women
Total people	**66.0%**	**73.3%**	**59.2%**
Aged 16 to 19	43.9	43.9	43.8
Aged 20 to 24	75.0	58.4	70.5
Aged 25 to 29	82.0	90.9	73.1
Aged 30 to 34	83.4	92.9	74.0
Aged 35 to 39	83.5	92.7	74.5
Aged 40 to 44	83.8	91.2	76.7
Aged 45 to 49	83.7	89.3	78.2
Aged 50 to 54	79.8	85.4	74.5
Aged 55 to 59	71.1	77.6	65.0
Aged 60 to 64	50.9	57.0	45.4
Aged 65 or older	14.4	19.0	11.1
Aged 65 to 69	27.7	32.6	23.3
Aged 70 to 74	15.3	19.4	12.0
Aged 75 or older	6.1	9.0	4.3

Note: The civilian labor force equals the number of employed plus the number of unemployed.
Source: Bureau of Labor Statistics, 2004 Current Population Survey, http://www.bls.gov/cps/home.htm

Table 6.66 Employment Status of Total People by Sex and Age, 2004

(number and percent of people aged 16 or older in the civilian labor force by sex, age, and employment status, 2004; numbers in thousands)

		civilian labor force			unemployed	
	civilian non-institutional population	total	percent of population	employed	number	percent of labor force
Total people	**223,357**	**147,401**	**66.0%**	**139,252**	**8,149**	**5.5%**
Aged 16 to 19	16,222	7,114	43.9	5,907	1,208	17.0
Aged 20 to 24	20,197	15,154	75.0	13,723	1,431	9.4
Aged 25 to 34	38,939	32,207	82.7	30,423	1,784	5.5
Aged 35 to 44	43,226	36,158	83.6	34,580	1,578	4.4
Aged 45 to 54	41,245	33,758	81.8	32,469	1,288	3.8
Aged 55 to 64	28,919	18,013	62.3	17,331	682	3.8
Aged 65 or older	34,609	4,998	14.4	4,819	179	3.6
Total men	**107,710**	**78,980**	**73.3**	**74,525**	**4,456**	**5.6**
Aged 16 to 19	8,234	3,616	43.9	2,952	664	18.4
Aged 20 to 24	10,125	8,057	79.6	7,246	811	10.1
Aged 25 to 34	19,358	17,798	91.9	16,818	980	5.5
Aged 35 to 44	21,255	19,539	91.9	18,700	839	4.3
Aged 45 to 54	20,160	17,635	87.5	16,951	684	3.9
Aged 55 to 64	13,894	9,547	68.7	9,174	373	3.9
Aged 65 or older	14,684	2,787	19.0	2,683	104	3.7
Total women	**115,647**	**68,421**	**59.2**	**64,728**	**3,694**	**5.4**
Aged 16 to 19	7,989	3,498	43.8	2,955	543	15.5
Aged 20 to 24	10,072	7,097	70.5	6,477	619	8.7
Aged 25 to 34	19,581	14,409	73.6	13,605	804	5.6
Aged 35 to 44	21,970	16,619	75.6	15,880	739	4.4
Aged 45 to 54	21,085	16,123	76.5	15,518	605	3.7
Aged 55 to 64	15,025	8,466	56.3	8,157	309	3.6
Aged 65 or older	19,925	2,211	11.1	2,135	75	3.4

Note: The civilian labor force equals the number of the employed plus the number of the unemployed. The civilian population equals the number in the labor force plus the number not in the labor force.
Source: Bureau of Labor Statistics, 2004 Current Population Survey, Internet site http://www.bls.gov/cps/home.htm

Table 6.67 Total Workers by Occupation, 2004

(number and percent distribution of employed persons aged 16 or older in the civilian labor force, by occupation, 2004; numbers in thousands)

	total	percent distribution
TOTAL EMPLOYED	**139,252**	**100.0%**
Management, professional and related occupations	**48,532**	**34.9**
Management, business, and financial operations	20,235	14.5
Management occupations	14,555	10.5
Business and financial operations occupations	5,860	4.2
Professional and related occupations	28,297	20.3
Computer and mathematical occupations	3,140	2.3
Architecture and engineering occupations	2,760	2.0
Life, physical, and social science occupations	1,365	1.0
Community and social services occupations	2,170	1.6
Legal occupations	1,554	1.1
Education, training, and library occupations	7,900	5.7
Arts, design, entertainment, sports, and media occupations	2,687	1.9
Health care practitioner and technical occupations	6,721	4.8
Service occupations	**22,720**	**16.3**
Health care support occupations	2,921	2.1
Protective service occupations	2,847	2.0
Food preparation and serving-related occupations	7,279	5.2
Building and grounds cleaning and maintenance occupations	5,185	3.7
Personal care and service occupations	4,488	3.2
Sales and office occupations	**35,464**	**25.5**
Sales and related occupations	15,983	11.5
Office and administrative support occupations	19,481	14.0
Natural resources, construction, and maintenance occupations	**14,582**	**10.5**
Farming, fishing, and forestry occupations	991	0.7
Construction and extraction occupations	8,522	6.1
Installation, maintenance, and repair occupations	5,069	3.6
Production, transportation, and material moving occupations	**17,954**	**12.9**
Production occupations	9,462	6.8
Transportation and material moving occupations	8,491	6.1

Source: Bureau of Labor Statistics, 2004 Current Population Survey, Internet site http://www.bls.gov/cps/home.htm; calculations by New Strategist

Table 6.68 Total Workers by Industry, 2004

(number and percent distribution of employed people aged 16 or older in the civilian labor force, by industry, 2004; numbers in thousands)

	number	percent distribution
Total employed	**139,252**	**100.0%**
Agriculture, forestry, fishing, hunting	2,232	1.6
Mining	539	0.4
Construction	10,768	7.7
Manufacturing	16,484	11.8
Durable goods	10,329	7.4
Nondurable goods	6,155	4.4
Wholesale and retail trade	20,869	15.0
Wholesale trade	4,600	3.3
Retail trade	16,269	11.7
Transportation and utilities	7,013	5.0
Information	3,463	2.5
Financial activities	9,969	7.2
Professional and business services	14,108	10.1
Educational and health services	28,719	20.6
Leisure and hospitality	11,820	8.5
Other services	6,903	5.0
Other services, except private households	6,124	4.4
Private households	779	0.6
Public administration	6,365	4.6

Source: Bureau of Labor Statistics, 2004 Current Population Survey, Internet site http://www.bls.gov/cps/home.htm; calculations by New Strategist

Table 6.69 Total Workers by Full-Time and Part-Time Status, Age, and Sex, 2004

(number and percent distribution of employed people aged 16 or older by age, employment status, and sex, 2004; numbers in thousands)

	total			men			women		
	total	full-time	part-time	total	full-time	part-time	total	full-time	part-time
Total employed	**139,252**	**114,518**	**24,734**	**74,524**	**66,444**	**8,080**	**64,727**	**48,073**	**16,654**
Aged 16 to 19	5,906	1,770	4,136	2,952	1,068	1,884	2,955	703	2,252
Aged 20 to 24	13,724	9,701	4,023	7,246	5,566	1,680	6,478	4,135	2,343
Aged 25 to 54	97,471	86,077	11,394	52,468	49,964	2,504	45,003	36,113	8,890
Aged 55 or older	22,150	16,969	5,181	11,857	9,846	2,011	10,292	7,123	3,169

PERCENT DISTRIBUTION BY EMPLOYMENT STATUS

	total			men			women		
Total employed	**100.0%**	**82.2%**	**17.8%**	**100.0%**	**89.2%**	**10.8%**	**100.0%**	**74.3%**	**25.7%**
Aged 16 to 19	100.0	30.0	70.0	100.0	36.2	63.8	100.0	23.8	76.2
Aged 20 to 24	100.0	70.7	29.3	100.0	76.8	23.2	100.0	63.8	36.2
Aged 25 to 54	100.0	88.3	11.7	100.0	95.2	4.8	100.0	80.2	19.8
Aged 55 or older	100.0	76.6	23.4	100.0	83.0	17.0	100.0	69.2	30.8

PERCENT DISTRIBUTION BY AGE

	total			men			women		
Total employed	**100.0%**	**100.0%**	**100.0%**	**100.0%**	**100.0%**	**100.0%**	**100.0%**	**100.0%**	**100.0%**
Aged 16 to 19	4.2	1.5	16.7	4.0	1.6	23.3	4.6	1.5	13.5
Aged 20 to 24	9.9	8.5	16.3	9.7	8.4	20.8	10.0	8.6	14.1
Aged 25 to 54	70.0	75.2	46.1	70.4	75.2	31.0	69.5	75.1	53.4
Aged 55 or older	15.9	14.8	20.9	15.9	14.8	24.9	15.9	14.8	19.0

Source: Bureau of Labor Statistics, 2004 Current Population Survey, Internet site http://www.bls.gov/cps/home.htm

Table 6.70 Total Workers by Educational Attainment, 2004

(number and percent distribution of people aged 25 or older in the civilian labor force, by educational attainment, 2004; numbers in thousands)

	number	participation rate	percent distribution
Total aged 25 or older	**125,133**	**66.9%**	**100.0%**
Not a high school graduate	12,470	45.1	10.0
High school graduate only	37,834	63.2	30.2
Some college	22,298	70.3	17.8
Associate's degree	12,141	76.6	9.7
Bachelor's degree or more	40,390	77.9	32.3

Source: Bureau of Labor Statistics, 2004 Current Population Survey, Internet site http://www.bls.gov/cps/home.htm; calculations by New Strategist

Table 6.71 Total Workers by Job Tenure and Sex, 2004

(total number of employed wage and salary workers aged 16 or older and percent distribution by tenure with current employer, by sex, 2004; numbers in thousands)

	total	men	women
Total workers, number	**121,753**	**63,146**	**58,608**
Total workers, percent	**100.0%**	**100.0%**	**100.0%**
12 months or less	23.0	22.4	23.7
13 to 23 months	7.0	6.6	7.4
2 years	5.7	5.6	5.8
3 to 4 years	18.5	18.3	18.7
5 to 9 years	19.8	19.6	20.1
10 to 14 years	9.9	10.1	9.6
15 to 19 years	6.4	6.5	6.2
20 or more years	9.7	10.9	8.4

Source: Bureau of Labor Statistics, 2004 Current Population Survey, Internet site http://www.bls.gov/cps/home.htm; calculations by New Strategist

Table 6.72 Total Households by Number of Earners, 2004

(total number and percent distribution of households by number of earners per household, 2004; numbers in thousands)

	number	percent distribution
Total households	**112,000**	**100.0%**
No earners	23,932	21.4
One earner	40,769	36.4
Two or more earners	47,299	42.2
Two earners	37,917	33.9
Three earners	6,998	6.2
Four or more earners	2,384	2.1
Average number of earners per household	1.36	–

Note: (–) means not applicable.
Source: Bureau of the Census, 2004 Current Population Survey, Annual Social and Economic Supplement, Internet site http://pubdb3.census.gov/macro/032004/hhinc/new01_000.htm; calculations by New Strategist

Table 6.73 Total Married Couples by Labor Force Status of Husband and Wife, 2003

(number and percent distribution of married couples aged 20 or older by age of householder and labor force status of husband and wife, 2003; numbers in thousands)

	total	husband and/or wife in labor force			neither husband nor wife in labor force
		husband and wife	husband only	wife only	
Total couples	**57,245**	**31,909**	**12,415**	**3,552**	**9,369**
Aged 20 to 24	1,304	764	440	67	33
Aged 25 to 29	3,760	2,508	1,089	106	56
Aged 30 to 34	5,776	3,885	1,655	133	103
Aged 35 to 39	6,640	4,519	1,822	196	104
Aged 40 to 44	7,361	5,247	1,725	271	118
Aged 45 to 54	13,297	9,537	2,622	712	425
Aged 55 to 64	9,543	4,624	2,024	1,185	1,708
Aged 65 or older	9,565	820	1,038	882	6,824
Total couples	**100.0%**	**55.7%**	**21.7%**	**6.2%**	**16.4%**
Aged 20 to 24	100.0	58.6	33.7	5.1	2.5
Aged 25 to 29	100.0	66.7	29.0	2.8	1.5
Aged 30 to 34	100.0	67.3	28.7	2.3	1.8
Aged 35 to 39	100.0	68.1	27.4	3.0	1.6
Aged 40 to 44	100.0	71.3	23.4	3.7	1.6
Aged 45 to 54	100.0	71.7	19.7	5.4	3.2
Aged 55 to 64	100.0	48.5	21.2	12.4	17.9
Aged 65 or older	100.0	8.6	10.9	9.2	71.3

Source: Bureau of the Census, America's Families and Living Arrangements: 2003, detailed tables, Internet site http://www .census.gov/population/www/socdemo/hh-fam/cps2003.html; calculations by New Strategist

Table 6.74 Total Minimum Wage Workers by Sex, 2004

(number and percent distribution of wage and salary workers aged 16 or older paid hourly rates and those paid at or below minimum wage, by sex, 2004; numbers in thousands)

	total paid hourly rates	at or below minimum wage		
		total	at $5.15/hour	below $5.15/hour
Total workers aged 16 or older	**73,939**	**2,003**	**520**	**1,483**
Men	36,806	680	210	470
Women	37,133	1,323	310	1,013
PERCENT DISTRIBUTION BY SEX				
Total workers aged 16 or older	**100.0%**	**100.0%**	**100.0%**	**100.0%**
Men	49.8	33.9	40.4	31.7
Women	50.2	66.1	59.6	68.3
PERCENT DISTRIBUTION BY WAGE STATUS				
Total workers aged 16 or older	**100.0%**	**2.7%**	**0.7%**	**2.0%**
Men	100.0	1.8	0.6	1.3
Women	100.0	3.6	0.8	2.7

Source: Bureau of Labor Statistics, 2004 Current Population Survey, Internet site http://www.bls.gov/cps/home.htm

Table 6.75 Total Multiple Job Holders by Sex, 2004

(number and percent of employed people aged 16 or older who hold more than one job, by sex, 2004; numbers in thousands)

	number	percent
Total multiple job holders	**7,473**	**5.4%**
Men	3,835	5.1
Women	3,638	5.6

Source: Bureau of Labor Statistics, 2004 Current Population Survey, Internet site http://www.bls.gov/cps/home.htm

Table 6.76 Union Representation of Total Workers by Sex, 2004

(number of employed wage and salary workers aged 16 or older, number and percent represented by unions, and median weekly earnings of those working full-time by union representation status, by sex, 2004; number in thousands)

	total	men	women
Total employed	**123,554**	**64,145**	**59,408**
Number represented by unions	17,087	9,638	7,450
Percent represented by unions	13.8%	15.0%	12.5%
Median weekly earnings of full-time workers	**$638**	**$713**	**$573**
Workers represented by unions	776	828	719
Workers not represented by unions	612	685	541

Note: Workers represented by unions are either members of a labor union or similar employee association or workers who report no union affiliation but whose jobs are covered by a union or an employee association contract.
Source: Bureau of Labor Statistics, 2004 Current Population Survey, Internet site http://www.bls.gov/cps/home.htm

Table 6.77 Journey to Work by Total Workers, 2003

(number and percent distribution of total workers aged 16 or older by principal means of transportation to work last week, travel time from home to work, distance from home to work, and departure time to work, 2003; numbers in thousands)

	number	percent
Total workers	**115,342**	**100.0%**
Principal means of transportation to work		
Drives self	91,607	79.4
Carpool	10,057	8.7
Mass transportation	5,081	4.4
Taxicab	128	0.1
Bicycle or motorcycle	691	0.6
Walks only	3,171	2.7
Other means	1,072	0.9
Works at home	3,536	3.1
Travel time from home to work		
Less than 15 minutes	36,202	31.4
15 to 29 minutes	37,288	32.3
30 to 44 minutes	16,480	14.3
45 to 59 minutes	6,761	5.9
1 hour or more	5,237	4.5
Works at home	3,536	3.1
No fixed place of work	9,838	8.5
Median travel time (minutes)	21	–
Distance from home to work		
Less than 1 mile	4,513	3.9
1 to 4 miles	22,476	19.5
5 to 9 miles	22,455	19.5
10 to 19 miles	29,027	25.2
20 to 29 miles	12,816	11.1
30 miles or more	10,681	9.3
Works at home	3,536	3.1
No fixed place of work	9,838	8.5
Median distance (miles)	11	–
Departure time to work		
12:00 a.m. to 2:59 a.m.	658	0.6
3:00 a.m. to 5:59 a.m.	11,624	10.1
6:00 a.m. to 6:59 a.m.	20,291	17.6
7:00 a.m. to 7:29 a.m.	15,632	13.6
7:30 a.m. to 7:59 a.m.	14,279	12.4
8:00 a.m. to 8:29 a.m.	12,548	10.9
8:30 a.m. to 8:59 a.m.	5,936	5.1
9:00 a.m. to 9:59 a.m.	6,197	5.4
10:00 a.m. to 3:59 p.m.	10,460	9.1
4:00 p.m. to 11:59 p.m.	6,484	5.6

Note: Departure time numbers may not add to total because not reported is not shown and those who work at home are not included.98 (–) means not applicable.
Source: Bureau of the Census, American Housing Survey for the United States: 2003, Current Housing Reports, Internet site http://www.census.gov/hhes/www/ahs.html; calculations by New Strategist

Table 6.78 Labor Force Projections by Race and Hispanic Origin, 2002 and 2012

(number, percent distribution, and percent of people aged 16 or older in the civilian labor force by sex, race, and Hispanic origin, 2002 and 2012; percent change in number and percentage point change in rate 2002–12; numbers in thousands)

	number			percent distribution			participation rate		
	2002	2012	percent change 2002–12	2002	2012	percentage point change 2002–12	2002	2012	percentage point change 2002–12
Total in labor force	**144,863**	**162,269**	**12.0%**	**100.0%**	**100.0%**	–	**66.6%**	**67.2%**	**0.6**
Asian	5,949	8,971	50.8	4.1	5.5	1.4	66.3	68.7	2.4
Black	16,564	19,765	19.3	11.4	12.2	0.7	64.8	66.3	1.6
Hispanic	17,942	23,785	32.6	12.4	14.7	2.3	69.1	68.8	–0.3
Non-Hispanic white	103,348	106,237	2.8	71.3	65.5	–5.9	66.5	65.7	–0.8
Men in labor force	**77,500**	**85,252**	**10.0**	**100.0**	**100.0**	–	**74.1**	**73.1**	**–1.0**
Asian	3,215	4,941	53.7	4.1	5.8	1.6	75.6	77.3	1.7
Black	7,793	9,318	19.6	10.1	10.9	0.9	68.4	69.1	0.7
Hispanic	10,609	13,674	28.9	13.7	16.0	2.4	80.2	79.0	–1.2
Non-Hispanic white	55,340	56,849	2.7	71.4	66.7	–4.7	73.8	72.4	–1.4
Women in labor force	**67,363**	**77,017**	**14.3**	**100.0**	**100.0**	–	**59.6**	**61.6**	**2.0**
Asian	2,734	4,030	47.4	4.1	5.2	1.2	57.9	61.3	3.4
Black	8,771	10,447	19.1	13.0	13.6	0.5	61.8	64.0	2.2
Hispanic	7,332	10,111	37.9	10.9	13.1	2.2	57.5	58.6	1.0
Non-Hispanic white	48,008	49,388	2.9	71.3	64.1	–7.1	59.6	59.4	–0.3

Note: Asians and blacks are those identifying themselves as being of the race alone. Hispanics may be of any race. Non-Hispanic whites are those identifying themselves as being white alone and not Hispanic. (–) means not applicable.
Source: Bureau of Labor Statistics, "Labor Force Projections to 2012: The graying of the U.S. workforce," Monthly Labor Review, February 2004, Internet site http://www.bls.gov/opub/mlr/2004/02/art3exc.htm; calculations by New Strategist

Table 6.79 Labor Force Entrants and Leavers by Race and Hispanic Origin, 2002 to 2012

(number and percent distribution of people aged 16 or older in the civilian labor force in 2002 and 2012, and number and percent distribution of entrants, leavers, and stayers by race and Hispanic origin, 2002–12; numbers in thousands)

| | | 2002 to 2012 | | | |
	2002 labor force	entrants	leavers	stayers	2012 labor force
Total labor force	**144,863**	**40,461**	**23,055**	**121,808**	**162,269**
Race					
Asians	5,949	1,783	1,771	4,178	8,971
Blacks	16,564	5,538	2,338	14,226	19,765
Whites	120,150	31,019	20,811	99,339	130,358
Hispanic origin					
Hispanics	17,941	7,866	2,022	15,919	23,785
Non-Hispanics	126,922	32,595	21,034	105,889	138,484
PERCENT DISTRIBUTION					
Total labor force	**100.0%**	**100.0%**	**100.0%**	**100.0%**	**100.0%**
Race					
Asians	4.1	4.4	7.7	3.4	5.5
Blacks	11.4	13.7	10.1	11.7	12.2
Whites	82.9	76.7	90.3	81.6	80.3
Hispanic origin					
Hispanics	12.4	19.4	8.8	13.1	14.7
Non-Hispanics	87.6	80.6	91.2	86.9	85.3

Source: Bureau of Labor Statistics, "Labor Force Projections to 2012: The graying of the U.S. workforce," Monthly Labor Review, *February 2004, Internet site http://www.bls.gov/opub/mlr/2004/02/art3exc.htm; calculations by New Strategist*

Asians, Blacks, and Hispanics Account for a Large Share of Households

Because the Asian, black, and Hispanic populations are younger, on average, than the non-Hispanic white population, minorities account for a relatively large share of households headed by young adults. Asians, blacks, Hispanics, and other minorities account for 40 percent of householders under age 25 and more than one-third of householders aged 25 to 34. In contrast, among householders aged 65 or older, minorities account for only 17 percent.

The minority share of households varies greatly by household type. Asians, blacks, Hispanics, and other minorities head 48 percent of female-headed families, but only 23 percent of married couples. Because minority households are more likely than non-Hispanic white households to include children, their household size is above average. Asians, blacks, Hispanics, and other minorities head the 58 percent majority of the nation's households with seven or more people. They head only 21 percent of two-person households.

Sixty-eight percent of American children live with both parents, while 23 percent live with only their mother. Among children living with their mother only, most are black (37 percent) or Hispanic (19 percent).

■ With immigration adding substantially to U.S. population growth each year, the minority share of households will grow rapidly.

Minorities account for a large share of households headed by young adults

(percent distribution of households headed by people under age 25 and aged 65 or older, by race and Hispanic origin of householder, 2004)

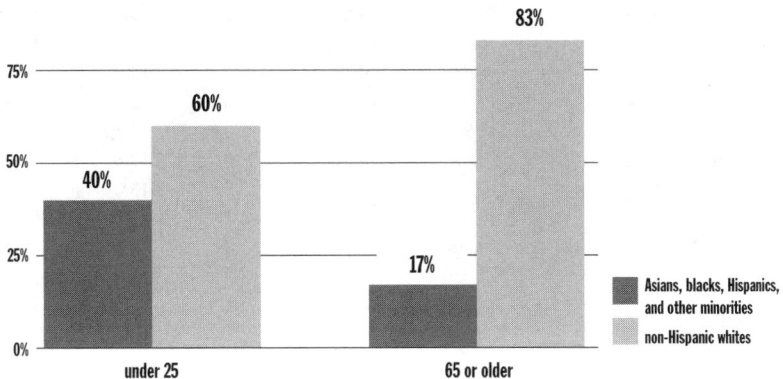

Table 6.80 Total Households by Age of Householder, 2004

(number and percent distribution of total households by age of householder, 2004, numbers in thousands)

	number	percent distribution
Total households	**112,000**	**100.0%**
Under age 25	6,610	5.9
Aged 25 to 29	8,737	7.8
Aged 30 to 34	10,421	9.3
Aged 35 to 39	10,997	9.8
Aged 40 to 44	12,225	10.9
Aged 45 to 49	12,360	11.0
Aged 50 to 54	10,777	9.6
Aged 55 to 59	9,504	8.5
Aged 60 to 64	7,320	6.5
Aged 65 to 69	6,121	5.5
Aged 70 to 74	5,377	4.8
Aged 75 or older	11,550	10.3

Source: Bureau of the Census, 2004 Current Population Survey Annual Social and Economic Supplement, Internet site http:// pubdb3.census.gov/macro/032004/hhinc/toc.htm; calculations by New Strategist

Table 6.81 Households by Age, Race, and Hispanic Origin of Householder, 2004

(number of total households and percent distribution by race and Hispanic origin of householder, by age of householder, 2004; numbers in thousands)

	total		Asian	black	Hispanic	non-Hispanic white
	number	percent				
Total households	**112,000**	**100.0%**	**3.8%**	**12.5%**	**10.4%**	**72.5%**
Under age 25	6,610	100.0	4.3	17.1	17.6	60.2
Aged 25 to 29	8,737	100.0	4.7	14.9	16.9	62.7
Aged 30 to 34	10,421	100.0	5.8	14.6	16.3	62.5
Aged 35 to 39	10,997	100.0	5.0	13.5	14.3	66.7
Aged 40 to 44	12,225	100.0	3.9	13.6	11.6	70.1
Aged 45 to 49	12,360	100.0	3.9	13.0	9.6	72.5
Aged 50 to 54	10,777	100.0	3.1	12.5	7.7	75.5
Aged 55 to 59	9,504	100.0	3.4	10.6	7.4	77.4
Aged 60 to 64	7,320	100.0	3.0	11.3	7.1	77.6
Aged 65 or older	23,048	100.0	2.3	9.0	4.8	83.1

Note: Percentages will not sum to total because Asians and blacks include those identifying themselves as being of the race alone and those identifying themselves as being of the race in combination with one or more other races, not all races are shown, and Hispanics may be of any race. Non-Hispanic whites include only those identifying themselves as being white alone and not Hispanic. Source: Bureau of the Census, 2004 Current Population Survey Annual Social and Economic Supplement, Internet site http:// pubdb3.census.gov/macro/032004/hhinc/toc.htm; calculations by New Strategist

Table 6.82 Total Households by Household Type, 2004

(number and percent distribution of total households by household type, 2004; numbers in thousands)

	number	percent distribution
TOTAL HOUSEHOLDS	**112,000**	**100.0%**
Family households	**76,217**	**68.1**
Married couples	57,719	51.5
Female householder, no spouse present	13,781	12.3
Male householder, no spouse present	4,717	4.2
Nonfamily households	**35,783**	**31.9**
Female householder	19,647	17.5
Living alone	17,024	15.2
Male householder	16,136	14.4
Living alone	12,562	11.2

Source: Bureau of the Census, 2004 Current Population Survey Annual Social and Economic Supplement, Internet site http://pubdb3.census.gov/macro/032004/hhinc/toc.htm; calculations by New Strategist

Table 6.83 Households by Type, Race, and Hispanic Origin of Householder, 2004

(number of total households and percent distribution by race and Hispanic origin of householder, by household type, 2004; numbers in thousands)

	total		Asian	black	Hispanic	non-Hispanic white
	number	percent				
TOTAL HOUSEHOLDS	**112,000**	**100.0%**	**3.8%**	**12.5%**	**10.4%**	**72.5%**
Family households	**76,217**	**100.0**	**4.2**	**12.0**	**12.2**	**70.9**
Married couples	57,719	100.0	4.5	7.4	10.8	76.6
Female householder, no spouse present	13,781	100.0	2.7	29.5	15.5	51.6
Male householder, no spouse present	4,717	100.0	5.1	17.0	19.2	57.5
Nonfamily households	**35,783**	**100.0**	**2.9**	**13.5**	**6.8**	**75.8**
Female householder	19,647	100.0	2.8	14.1	5.5	76.8
Living alone	17,024	100.0	2.6	14.7	5.1	76.8
Male householder	16,136	100.0	3.1	12.8	8.3	74.6
Living alone	12,562	100.0	3.0	13.8	7.1	74.8

Note: Percentages will not sum to total because Asians and blacks include those identifying themselves as being of the race alone and those identifying themselves as being of the race in combination with one or more other races, not all races are shown, and Hispanics may be of any race. Non-Hispanic whites include only those identifying themselves as being white alone and not Hispanic.
Source: Bureau of the Census, 2004 Current Population Survey Annual Social and Economic Supplement, Internet site http://pubdb3.census.gov/macro/032004/hhinc/toc.htm; calculations by New Strategist

Table 6.84 Households by Age of Householder and Type of Household, 2004

(number and percent distribution of households by age of householder and type of household, 2004; numbers in thousands)

| | | family households | | | nonfamily households | | | |
| | | | | | female-headed | | male-headed | |
	total	married couples	female hh, no spouse present	male hh, no spouse present	total	living alone	total	living alone
Total households	**112,000**	**57,719**	**13,781**	**4,717**	**19,647**	**17,024**	**16,136**	**12,562**
Under age 25	6,610	1,417	1,398	775	1,498	762	1,521	768
Aged 25 to 34	19,158	9,573	2,959	1,025	2,269	1,660	3,332	2,229
Aged 35 to 44	23,222	13,584	3,642	1,096	1,839	1,482	3,060	2,400
Aged 45 to 54	23,137	13,500	2,692	946	2,893	2,471	3,107	2,555
Aged 55 to 64	16,824	9,834	1,357	430	3,061	2,775	2,142	1,825
Aged 65 or older	23,048	9,812	1,733	444	8,085	7,873	2,974	2,785

PERCENT DISTRIBUTION BY HOUSEHOLD TYPE

Total households	**100.0%**	**51.5%**	**12.3%**	**4.2%**	**17.5%**	**15.2%**	**14.4%**	**11.2%**
Under age 25	100.0	21.4	21.1	11.7	22.7	11.5	23.0	11.6
Aged 25 to 34	100.0	50.0	15.4	5.4	11.8	8.7	17.4	11.6
Aged 35 to 44	100.0	58.5	15.7	4.7	7.9	6.4	13.2	10.3
Aged 45 to 54	100.0	58.3	11.6	4.1	12.5	10.7	13.4	11.0
Aged 55 to 64	100.0	58.5	8.1	2.6	18.2	16.5	12.7	10.8
Aged 65 or older	100.0	42.6	7.5	1.9	35.1	34.2	12.9	12.1

PERCENT DISTRIBUTION BY AGE

Total households	**100.0%**	**100.0%**	**100.0%**	**100.0%**	**100.0%**	**100.0%**	**100.0%**	**100.0%**
Under age 25	5.9	2.5	10.1	16.4	7.6	4.5	9.4	6.1
Aged 25 to 34	17.1	16.6	21.5	21.7	11.5	9.8	20.6	17.7
Aged 35 to 44	20.7	23.5	26.4	23.2	9.4	8.7	19.0	19.1
Aged 45 to 54	20.7	23.4	19.5	20.1	14.7	14.5	19.3	20.3
Aged 55 to 64	15.0	17.0	9.8	9.1	15.6	16.3	13.3	14.5
Aged 65 or older	20.6	17.0	12.6	9.4	41.2	46.2	18.4	22.2

Source: Bureau of the Census, 2004 Current Population Survey Annual Social and Economic Supplement, Internet site http:// pubdb3.census.gov/macro/032004/hhinc/toc.htm; calculations by New Strategist

Table 6.85 Total Households by Age of Householder, Type of Household, And Presence of Children, 2003

(number and percent distribution of households by age of householder, type of household, and presence of own children under age 18, and average age of householder, 2003; numbers in thousands)

	all households		married couples		female-headed families		male-headed families	
	total	with children	total	with children	total	with children	total	with children
Total households	**111,278**	**35,968**	**57,320**	**25,914**	**13,620**	**8,139**	**4,656**	**1,915**
Under age 20	916	132	75	40	251	71	266	20
Aged 20 to 24	5,695	1,823	1,304	805	1,132	878	523	140
Aged 25 to 29	8,535	3,930	3,760	2,433	1,391	1,247	508	250
Aged 30 to 34	10,521	6,180	5,776	4,498	1,501	1,395	503	287
Aged 35 to 39	11,486	7,532	6,640	5,521	1,826	1,674	498	337
Aged 40 to 44	12,583	7,521	7,361	5,697	1,826	1,428	589	395
Aged 45 to 49	11,957	5,257	7,085	4,110	1,505	889	529	258
Aged 50 to 54	10,666	2,377	6,212	1,850	1,139	387	393	140
Aged 55 to 64	16,260	1,040	9,543	842	1,305	126	413	72
Aged 65 or older	22,659	176	9,565	118	1,743	43	434	15
Average age of householder (years)	48.9	38.5	48.7	39.3	43.9	36.0	41.2	38.2

PERCENT OF HOUSEHOLDS WITH CHILDREN BY TYPE

	all households		married couples		female-headed families		male-headed families	
Total households	**100.0%**	**32.3%**	**100.0%**	**45.2%**	**100.0%**	**59.8%**	**100.0%**	**41.1%**
Under age 20	100.0	14.4	100.0	53.3	100.0	28.3	100.0	7.5
Aged 20 to 24	100.0	32.0	100.0	61.7	100.0	77.6	100.0	26.8
Aged 25 to 29	100.0	46.0	100.0	64.7	100.0	89.6	100.0	49.2
Aged 30 to 34	100.0	58.7	100.0	77.9	100.0	92.9	100.0	57.1
Aged 35 to 39	100.0	65.6	100.0	83.1	100.0	91.7	100.0	67.7
Aged 40 to 44	100.0	59.8	100.0	77.4	100.0	78.2	100.0	67.1
Aged 45 to 49	100.0	44.0	100.0	58.0	100.0	59.1	100.0	48.8
Aged 50 to 54	100.0	22.3	100.0	29.8	100.0	34.0	100.0	35.6
Aged 55 to 64	100.0	6.4	100.0	8.8	100.0	9.7	100.0	17.4

Source: Bureau of the Census, America's Families and Living Arrangements, 2003 Current Population Survey Annual Social and Economic Supplement; Internet site http://www.census.gov/population/www/socdemo/hh-fam/cps2003.html; calculations by New Strategist

Table 6.86 Total Households by Size, 2004

(number and percent distribution of total households by size, 2004; numbers in thousands)

	number	percent distribution
Total households	**112,000**	**100.0%**
One person	29,586	26.4
Two people	37,366	33.4
Three people	17,968	16.0
Four people	16,065	14.3
Five people	7,150	6.4
Six people	2,476	2.2
Seven or more people	1,388	1.2
Average number of persons per household	2.57	–

Note: (–) means not applicable.
Source: Bureau of the Census, 2004 Current Population Survey Annual Social and Economic Supplement, Internet site http:// pubdb3.census.gov/macro/032004/hhinc/toc.htm; calculations by New Strategist

Table 6.87 Households by Size, Race, and Hispanic Origin of Householder, 2004

(number of total households and percent distribution by race and Hispanic origin of householder, by household size, 2004; numbers in thousands)

	total		Asian	black	Hispanic	non-Hispanic white
	number	percent				
Total households	**112,000**	**100.0%**	**3.8%**	**12.5%**	**10.4%**	**72.5%**
One person	29,586	100.0	2.8	14.3	5.9	76.0
Two people	37,366	100.0	3.1	10.1	7.0	79.1
Three people	17,968	100.0	4.8	13.9	12.5	67.7
Four people	16,065	100.0	5.1	12.2	14.9	67.3
Five people	7,150	100.0	4.8	12.6	21.7	59.9
Six people	2,476	100.0	5.5	14.5	26.8	52.1
Seven or more people	1,388	100.0	7.1	17.4	32.9	41.8

Note: Percentages will not sum to total because Asians and blacks include those identifying themselves as being of the race alone and those identifying themselves as being of the race in combination with one or more other races, not all races are shown, and Hispanics may be of any race. Non-Hispanic whites include only those identifying themselves as being white alone and not Hispanic.
Source: Bureau of the Census, 2004 Current Population Survey Annual Social and Economic Supplement, Internet site http:// pubdb3.census.gov/macro/032004/hhinc/toc.htm; calculations by New Strategist

Table 6.88 People Living Alone by Sex and Age, 2004

(total number of people aged 15 or older, number and percent living alone, and percent distribution of people who live alone, by sex and age, 2004; numbers in thousands)

		living alone		
	total	number	percent distribution	share of total
Total people	**227,584**	**29,586**	**100.0%**	**13.0%**
Under age 25	40,708	1,530	5.2	3.8
Aged 25 to 34	39,201	3,888	13.1	9.9
Aged 35 to 44	43,573	3,882	13.1	8.9
Aged 45 to 54	41,069	5,026	17.0	12.2
Aged 55 to 64	28,375	4,600	15.5	16.2
Aged 65 to 74	18,238	4,197	14.2	23.0
Aged 75 or older	16,421	6,461	21.8	39.3
Total men	**110,257**	**12,562**	**100.0**	**11.4**
Under age 25	20,699	768	6.1	3.7
Aged 25 to 34	19,598	2,229	17.7	11.4
Aged 35 to 44	21,530	2,400	19.1	11.1
Aged 45 to 54	20,082	2,555	20.3	12.7
Aged 55 to 64	13,551	1,825	14.5	13.5
Aged 65 to 74	8,355	1,293	10.3	15.5
Aged 75 or older	6,441	1,492	11.9	23.2
Total women	**117,327**	**17,024**	**100.0**	**14.5**
Under age 25	20,009	762	4.5	3.8
Aged 25 to 34	19,603	1,659	9.7	8.5
Aged 35 to 44	22,043	1,482	8.7	6.7
Aged 45 to 54	20,987	2,471	14.5	11.8
Aged 55 to 64	14,824	2,775	16.3	18.7
Aged 65 to 74	9,883	2,904	17.1	29.4
Aged 75 or older	9,980	4,969	29.2	49.8

Source: Bureau of the Census, 2004 Current Population Survey Annual Social and Economic Supplement, Internet site http://pubdb3.census.gov/macro/032004/hhinc/toc.htm and http://pubdb3.census.gov/macro/032004/perinc/toc.htm; calculations by New Strategist

Table 6.89 Living Arrangements of Children, 2003

(number of total children under age 18 and percent distribution by living arrangement, 2003; numbers in thousands)

	number	percent distribution
Total children	**73,001**	**100.0%**
Living with both parents	49,903	68.4
Living with mother only	16,771	23.0
Never married	7,006	9.6
Divorced or separated	9,102	12.5
Widowed	663	0.9
Living with father only	3,324	4.6
Never married	1,172	1.6
Divorced or separated	1,979	2.7
Widowed	173	0.2
Living with neither parent	3,004	4.1

Source: Bureau of the Census, America's Families and Living Arrangements, 2003 Current Population Survey Annual Social and Economic Supplement; Internet site http://www.census.gov/population/www/socdemo/hh-fam/cps2003.html; calculations by New Strategist

Table 6.90 Children by Living Arrangement, Race, and Hispanic Origin, 2003

(total number of children under age 18 and percent distribution by living arrangement, race, and Hispanic origin, 2003; numbers in thousands)

	total		Asian	black	Hispanic	non-Hispanic white
	number	percent				
Total children	**73,001**	**100.0%**	**3.7%**	**16.7%**	**18.2%**	**59.9%**
Living with both parents	49,903	100.0	4.5	9.0	17.2	67.8
Living with mother only	16,771	100.0	1.7	36.5	19.5	41.3
Never married	7,006	100.0	1.4	52.4	21.3	24.8
Divorced or separated	9,102	100.0	1.8	25.2	17.9	53.5
Widowed	663	100.0	4.5	24.1	21.3	48.7
Living with father only	3,324	100.0	2.3	17.0	22.2	56.0
Never married	1,172	100.0	2.3	23.4	35.9	36.3
Divorced or separated	1,979	100.0	2.3	13.1	14.9	67.2
Widowed	173	100.0	1.7	18.5	12.1	61.3
Living with neither parent	3,004	100.0	2.9	34.1	23.4	38.3

Note: Percentages will not sum to total because Asians and blacks include those identifying themselves as being of the race alone and those identifying themselves as being of the race in combination with one or more other races, not all races are shown, and Hispanics may be of any race. Non-Hispanic whites include only those identifying themselves as being white alone and not Hispanic.
Source: Bureau of the Census, America's Families and Living Arrangements, 2003 Current Population Survey Annual Social and Economic Supplement; Internet site http://www.census.gov/population/www/socdemo/hh-fam/cps2003.html; calculations by New Strategist

Table 6.91 Total Men by Living Arrangement and Age, 2003

(number and percent distribution of total men aged 15 or older by living arrangement and age, 2003; numbers in thousands)

	total	under 25	25 to 29	30 to 34	35 to 44	45 to 54	55 to 64	65 or older
Total men	**108,696**	**20,194**	**9,366**	**10,177**	**21,702**	**19,578**	**13,158**	**14,521**
Married-couple householder or spouse	57,320	1,087	3,423	5,592	13,821	13,449	9,802	10,148
Other householder	20,676	2,295	2,161	2,193	4,365	3,894	2,437	3,333
Male family householder	4,656	788	508	503	1,087	923	413	434
Living alone	12,511	722	1,021	1,191	2,573	2,516	1,764	2,725
Living with nonrelatives	3,509	785	632	499	705	455	260	174
Nonhouseholder	30,700	16,812	3,783	2,392	3,516	2,235	920	1,041
Child of householder	18,391	13,318	1,742	967	1,429	749	168	17
Other relative of householder	5,552	1,697	795	443	764	677	407	768
Living with nonrelatives	6,757	1,797	1,246	982	1,323	809	345	256
Total men	**100.0%**	**100.0%**	**100.0%**	**100.0%**	**100.0%**	**100.0%**	**100.0%**	**100.0%**
Married-couple householder or spouse	52.7	5.4	36.5	54.9	63.7	68.7	74.5	69.9
Other householder	19.0	11.4	23.1	21.5	20.1	19.9	18.5	23.0
Male family householder	4.3	3.9	5.4	4.9	5.0	4.7	3.1	3.0
Living alone	11.5	3.6	10.9	11.7	11.9	12.9	13.4	18.8
Living with nonrelatives	3.2	3.9	6.7	4.9	3.2	2.3	2.0	1.2
Nonhouseholder	28.2	83.3	40.4	23.5	16.2	11.4	7.0	7.2
Child of householder	16.9	66.0	18.6	9.5	6.6	3.8	1.3	0.1
Other relative of householder	5.1	8.4	8.5	4.4	3.5	3.5	3.1	5.3
Living with nonrelatives	6.2	8.9	13.3	9.6	6.1	4.1	2.6	1.8

Source: Bureau of the Census, America's Families and Living Arrangements, 2003 Current Population Survey Annual Social and Economic Supplement; Internet site http://www.census.gov/population/www/socdemo/hh-fam/cps2003.html; calculations by New Strategist

Table 6.92 Total Women by Living Arrangement and Age, 2003

(number and percent distribution of total women aged 15 or older by living arrangement and age, 2003; numbers in thousands)

	total	under 25	25 to 29	30 to 34	35 to 44	45 to 54	55 to 64	65 or older
Total women	**116,361**	**19,838**	**9,330**	**10,329**	**22,322**	**20,617**	**14,229**	**19,695**
Married-couple householder or spouse	57,320	2,020	4,422	6,408	14,353	13,331	8,847	7,938
Other householder	33,281	2,936	2,615	2,553	5,703	5,433	4,281	9,763
Female family householder	13,620	1,383	1,392	1,501	3,653	2,644	1,305	1,743
Living alone	16,919	818	783	814	1,638	2,303	2,741	7,824
Living with nonrelatives	2,742	735	440	238	412	486	235	196
Nonhouseholder	25,759	14,885	2,294	1,370	2,267	1,852	1,101	1,996
Child of householder	14,666	11,848	986	511	710	429	162	23
Other relative of householder	5,851	1,277	394	273	671	781	639	1,818
Living with nonrelatives	5,242	1,760	914	586	886	642	300	155
Total women	**100.0%**	**100.0%**	**100.0%**	**100.0%**	**100.0%**	**100.0%**	**100.0%**	**100.0%**
Married-couple householder or spouse	49.3	10.2	47.4	62.0	64.3	64.7	62.2	40.3
Other householder	28.6	14.8	28.0	24.7	25.5	26.4	30.1	49.6
Female family householder	11.7	7.0	14.9	14.5	16.4	12.8	9.2	8.8
Living alone	14.5	4.1	8.4	7.9	7.3	11.2	19.3	39.7
Living with nonrelatives	2.4	3.7	4.7	2.3	1.8	2.4	1.7	1.0
Nonhouseholder	22.1	75.0	24.6	13.3	10.2	9.0	7.7	10.1
Child of householder	12.6	59.7	10.6	4.9	3.2	2.1	1.1	0.1
Other relative of householder	5.0	6.4	4.2	2.6	3.0	3.8	4.5	9.2
Living with nonrelatives	4.5	8.9	9.8	5.7	4.0	3.1	2.1	0.8

Source: Bureau of the Census, America's Families and Living Arrangements, 2003 Current Population Survey Annual Social and Economic Supplement; Internet site http://www.census.gov/population/www/socdemo/hh-fam/cps2003.html; calculations by New Strategist

Table 6.93 Marital Status of Total Men by Age, 2003

(number and percent distribution of total men aged 18 or older by age and marital status, 2003; numbers in thousands)

	total	never married	married, spouse present	married, spouse absent	separated	divorced	widowed
Total men	**102,313**	**28,577**	**58,575**	**1,641**	**1,871**	**8,957**	**2,692**
Aged 18 to 19	3,858	3,794	55	3	3	2	2
Aged 20 to 24	9,953	8,563	1,156	78	63	93	–
Aged 25 to 29	9,366	5,112	3,573	170	171	327	14
Aged 30 to 34	10,177	3,371	5,733	187	185	678	21
Aged 35 to 39	10,503	2,289	6,637	192	313	1,051	21
Aged 40 to 44	11,199	1,953	7,408	214	274	1,284	67
Aged 45 to 49	10,431	1,321	7,144	192	219	1,451	104
Aged 50 to 54	9,147	796	6,560	130	194	1,370	98
Aged 55 to 64	13,158	757	9,970	200	260	1,679	292
Aged 65 to 74	8,268	383	6,141	139	135	744	726
Aged 75 to 84	5,051	205	3,525	101	50	239	931
Aged 85 or older	1,202	34	675	34	5	38	416
Total men	**100.0%**	**27.9%**	**57.3%**	**1.6%**	**1.8%**	**8.8%**	**2.6%**
Aged 18 to 19	100.0	98.3	1.4	0.1	0.1	0.1	0.1
Aged 20 to 24	100.0	86.0	11.6	0.8	0.6	0.9	–
Aged 25 to 29	100.0	54.6	38.1	1.8	1.8	3.5	0.1
Aged 30 to 34	100.0	33.1	56.3	1.8	1.8	6.7	0.2
Aged 35 to 39	100.0	21.8	63.2	1.8	3.0	10.0	0.2
Aged 40 to 44	100.0	17.4	66.1	1.9	2.4	11.5	0.6
Aged 45 to 49	100.0	12.7	68.5	1.8	2.1	13.9	1.0
Aged 50 to 54	100.0	8.7	71.7	1.4	2.1	15.0	1.1
Aged 55 to 64	100.0	5.8	75.8	1.5	2.0	12.8	2.2
Aged 65 to 74	100.0	4.6	74.3	1.7	1.6	9.0	8.8
Aged 75 to 84	100.0	4.1	69.8	2.0	1.0	4.7	18.4
Aged 85 or older	100.0	2.8	56.2	2.8	0.4	3.2	34.6

Note: (–) means sample is too small to make a reliable estimate.
Source: Bureau of the Census, America's Families and Living Arrangements, 2003 Current Population Survey Annual Social and Economic Supplement; Internet site http://www.census.gov/population/www/socdemo/hh-fam/cps2003.html; calculations by New Strategist

Table 6.94 Marital Status of Total Women by Age, 2003

(number and percent distribution of total women aged 18 or older by age and marital status, 2003; numbers in thousands)

	total	never married	married, spouse present	married, spouse absent	separated	divorced	widowed
Total women	**110,115**	**23,333**	**58,559**	**1,482**	**2,793**	**12,660**	**11,288**
Aged 18 to 19	3,689	3,486	166	24	8	5	–
Aged 20 to 24	9,903	7,463	2,025	99	150	150	16
Aged 25 to 29	9,330	3,760	4,585	138	305	505	36
Aged 30 to 34	10,329	2,349	6,535	130	330	928	58
Aged 35 to 39	10,766	1,544	7,011	178	428	1,471	134
Aged 40 to 44	11,556	1,411	7,577	175	447	1,762	185
Aged 45 to 49	10,961	1,041	7,283	138	390	1,858	250
Aged 50 to 54	9,656	756	6,312	145	253	1,800	390
Aged 55 to 64	14,229	801	8,980	193	290	2,478	1,487
Aged 65 to 74	9,831	337	5,257	115	133	1,101	2,888
Aged 75 to 84	7,520	285	2,535	117	53	521	4,008
Aged 85 or older	2,344	98	294	29	6	81	1,836
Total women	**100.0%**	**21.2%**	**53.2%**	**1.3%**	**2.5%**	**11.5%**	**10.3%**
Aged 18 to 19	100.0	94.5	4.5	0.7	0.2	0.1	–
Aged 20 to 24	100.0	75.4	20.4	1.0	1.5	1.5	0.2
Aged 25 to 29	100.0	40.3	49.1	1.5	3.3	5.4	0.4
Aged 30 to 34	100.0	22.7	63.3	1.3	3.2	9.0	0.6
Aged 35 to 39	100.0	14.3	65.1	1.7	4.0	13.7	1.2
Aged 40 to 44	100.0	12.2	65.6	1.5	3.9	15.2	1.6
Aged 45 to 49	100.0	9.5	66.4	1.3	3.6	17.0	2.3
Aged 50 to 54	100.0	7.8	65.4	1.5	2.6	18.6	4.0
Aged 55 to 64	100.0	5.6	63.1	1.4	2.0	17.4	10.5
Aged 65 to 74	100.0	3.4	53.5	1.2	1.4	11.2	29.4
Aged 75 to 84	100.0	3.8	33.7	1.6	0.7	6.9	53.3
Aged 85 or older	100.0	4.2	12.5	1.2	0.3	3.5	78.3

Note: (–) means sample is too small to make a reliable estimate.
Source: Bureau of the Census, America's Families and Living Arrangements, 2003 Current Population Survey Annual Social and Economic Supplement; Internet site http://www.census.gov/population/www/socdemo/hh-fam/cps2003.html; calculations by New Strategist

Table 6.95 Race and Hispanic Origin Differences between Husband and Wife, 2003

(number and percent distribution of married-couple family groups by race and Hispanic origin differences between husband and wife, 2003; numbers in thousands)

	total couples		couples with children under 18	
	number	percent distribution	number	percent distribution
RACE DIFFERENCE				
Total married couples	**58,586**	**100.0%**	**26,445**	**100.0%**
Same-race couples	55,938	95.5	25,003	94.5
Both white only	49,725	84.9	21,826	82.5
Both black only	3,990	6.8	1,967	7.4
Both Asian only	2,223	3.8	1,210	4.6
Interracial couples	1,043	1.8	527	2.0
Black only/white only	416	0.7	224	0.8
Black only/Asian only	49	0.1	24	0.1
White only/Asian only	578	1.0	279	1.1
All remaining combinations	1,605	2.7	915	3.5
HISPANIC ORIGIN DIFFERENCE				
Total married couples	**58,586**	**100.0**	**26,445**	**100.0**
Both Hispanic	5,706	9.7	3,710	14.0
Neither Hispanic	50,992	87.0	21,632	81.8
One Hispanic, one non-Hispanic	1,888	3.2	1,102	4.2

Note: Race comparisons are regardless of Hispanic origin, and Hispanics may be of any race. Married-couple family groups include married-couple householders and married couples living in households headed by others.
Source: Bureau of the Census, America's Families and Living Arrangements: 2003, Current Population Reports P20–553, 2004; Internet site http://www.census.gov/population/www/socdemo/hh-fam.html; calculations by New Strategist

Table 6.96 Marital History of Total Men by Age, 2001

(number of total men aged 15 or older and percent distribution by marital history and age, 2001; numbers in thousands)

	total	15 to 19	20 to 24	25 to 29	30 to 34	35 to 39	40 to 49	50 to 59	60 to 69	70 or older
Total men, number	105,850	10,186	9,465	9,177	10,069	10,704	21,202	15,694	9,558	9,795
Total men, percent	100.0%	100.0%	100.0%	100.0%	100.0%	100.0%	100.0%	100.0%	100.0%	100.0%
Never married	30.9	99.1	83.9	50.8	29.5	21.5	14.2	6.3	4.3	3.3
Ever married	69.1	0.9	16.1	49.2	70.5	78.5	85.8	93.7	95.7	96.7
Married once	53.4	0.9	16.0	46.3	60.8	66.2	65.1	62.6	67.5	75.5
Still married	43.7	0.6	14.3	39.6	52.3	53.0	53.1	49.5	58.0	58.1
Married twice	12.5	0.0	0.1	2.8	8.7	10.9	17.1	23.2	21.3	16.5
Still married	9.9	0.0	0.1	2.6	7.4	9.1	13.8	17.6	17.0	12.2
Married three or more times	3.2	0.0	0.0	0.1	1.1	1.4	3.6	8.0	6.8	4.7
Still married	2.4	0.0	0.0	0.1	0.8	1.2	2.9	5.7	5.1	3.5
Ever divorced	21.0	0.1	1.0	7.5	15.4	22.9	29.5	40.8	30.9	18.6
Currently divorced	8.8	0.0	0.8	4.7	7.0	12.5	12.5	16.9	9.7	5.5
Ever widowed	3.6	0.0	0.0	0.1	0.3	0.5	1.3	2.9	7.6	23.1
Currently widowed	2.4	0.0	0.0	0.1	0.0	0.2	0.8	1.8	4.5	16.8

Source: Bureau of the Census, Number, Timing, and Duration of Marriages and Divorces: 2001, *Current Population Report P70-97, 2005; Internet site http://www.census.gov/population/www/socdemo/marr-div.html*

Table 6.97 Marital History of Total Women by Age, 2001

(number of total women aged 15 or older and percent distribution by marital history and age, 2001; numbers in thousands)

	total	15 to 19	20 to 24	25 to 29	30 to 34	35 to 39	40 to 49	50 to 59	60 to 69	70 or older
Total women, number	113,777	9,764	9,518	9,239	10,211	11,110	22,036	16,626	10,956	14,318
Total women, percent	100.0%	100.0%	100.0%	100.0%	100.0%	100.0%	100.0%	100.0%	100.0%	100.0%
Never married	24.6	96.3	72.4	37.3	21.7	15.6	10.5	6.4	4.1	3.3
Ever married	75.4	3.7	27.6	62.7	78.3	84.4	89.5	93.6	95.9	96.7
Married once	58.7	3.6	26.5	57.3	67.3	66.8	65.1	65.2	72.9	77.8
Still married	40.7	3.1	22.6	47.1	56.2	53.0	48.8	46.4	47.5	29.8
Married twice	13.6	0.1	1.1	5.1	10.0	15.7	19.8	22.1	17.4	15.5
Still married	9.1	0.1	0.8	4.1	7.9	12.0	14.5	15.3	10.6	6.1
Married three or more times	3.1	0.0	0.0	0.3	1.0	1.8	4.6	6.3	5.6	3.5
Still married	1.9	0.0	0.0	0.2	0.8	1.5	3.3	4.1	3.1	1.1
Ever divorced	23.1	0.2	2.6	11.9	18.6	28.1	35.4	38.9	28.4	17.7
Currently divorced	10.8	0.0	1.6	7.4	9.3	13.7	16.8	17.9	12.6	6.5
Ever widowed	11.6	0.0	0.3	0.5	0.6	1.1	3.5	9.5	23.3	56.3
Currently widowed	10.2	0.0	0.3	0.4	0.4	0.6	2.4	7.1	19.7	52.6

Source: Bureau of the Census, Number, Timing, and Duration of Marriages and Divorces: 2001, *Current Population Report P70-97, 2005; Internet site http://www.census.gov/population/www/socdemo/marr-div.html*

The United States Is Rapidly Becoming More Diverse

The U.S. population grew from 282 million in 2000 to 294 million in 2004, an increase of 4 percent. The non-Hispanic white share of the population fell from 69 to 67 percent during those years as minority populations grew much faster than the majority. Between 2000 and 2004, Hispanics (who may be of any race) surpassed blacks as the largest minority, growing to 41 million and accounting for 14 percent of the population. Blacks account for 13 percent of the population, Asians for 5 percent, and American Indians for less than 2 percent.

The United States is becoming more diverse because of immigration. Between 2000 and 2004, nearly 4 million immigrants came to the United States. This follows the decade of the 1990s, when immigration reached an all-time high of more than 9 million. Fully 34 million Americans are foreign-born, accounting for 12 percent of the total population. Among people aged 30 to 34, one in five is foreign-born.

More than one-third of the foreign-born live in the West, where they account for 20 percent of the population. Not surprisingly, the West is also the most diverse region, with non-Hispanic whites accounting for only 56 percent of the population.

Eighteen percent of U.S. residents speak a language other than English at home. The 61 percent majority of those speaking a language other than English at home are Spanish speakers. Among Spanish speakers, 49 percent say they speak English less than "very well."

■ The nation's growing diversity provides economic opportunity for immigrants and entrepreneurs alike, but it strains the political and social fabric of communities struggling to adapt to rapidly changing populations.

One-third of Americans are Asian, black, or Hispanic

(percent distribution of people by race and Hispanic origin, 2004)

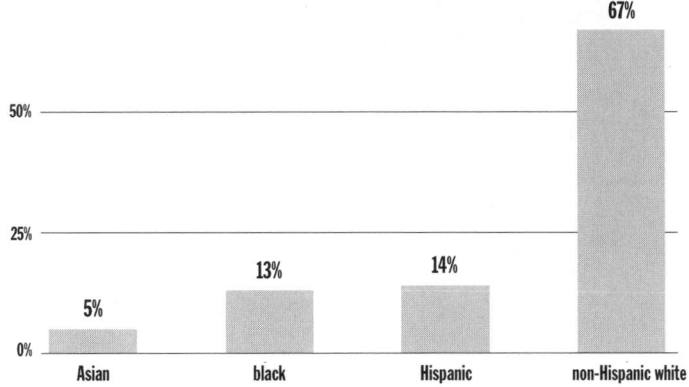

Table 6.98 Total Population by Race and Hispanic Origin, 2000 and 2004

(number and percent distribution of people by racial identification, 2000 and 2004; percent change, 2000–04)

	2004		2000		
	number	percent distribution	number	percent distribution	percent change 2000–04
Total population	**293,655,404**	**100.0%**	**282,192,162**	**100.0%**	**4.1%**
Race alone or in combination					
American Indian	4,409,446	1.5	4,236,378	1.5	4.1
Asian	13,956,612	4.8	12,121,816	4.3	15.1
Black	39,232,489	13.4	37,231,182	13.2	5.4
Native Hawaiian	976,395	0.3	910,932	0.3	7.2
White	239,880,132	81.7	231,978,329	82.2	3.4
Race alone					
American Indian	2,824,751	1.0	2,673,462	0.9	5.7
Asian	12,326,216	4.2	10,691,993	3.8	15.3
Black	37,502,320	12.8	35,812,716	12.7	4.7
Native Hawaiian	505,602	0.2	465,054	0.2	8.7
White	236,057,761	80.4	228,620,482	81.0	3.3
Two or more races	4,438,754	1.5	3,928,455	1.4	13.0
Total population	**293,655,404**	**100.0**	**282,192,162**	**100.0**	**4.1**
Hispanic	41,322,070	14.1	35,647,334	12.6	15.9
Not Hispanic	252,333,334	85.9	246,544,828	87.4	2.3

Note: Race alone or in combination figures will not add to total because they count the multiracial population more than once. American Indians include Alaska Natives. Native Hawaiians include other Pacific Islanders. Hispanics may be of any race. Source: Bureau of the Census, National Population Estimates, Internet site http://www.census.gov/popest/national/asrh/ NC-EST2004-srh.html; calculations by New Strategist

Table 6.99 Hispanic Origin Populations by Racial Identification, 2004

(number and percent distribution of people by racial identification and Hispanic origin, 2004)

	total	Hispanic	not Hispanic
Total people	**293,655,404**	**41,322,070**	**252,333,334**
Race alone or in combination			
American Indian	4,409,446	835,497	3,573,949
Asian	13,956,612	426,843	13,529,769
Black	39,232,489	1,806,345	37,426,144
Native Hawaiian	976,395	173,601	802,794
White	239,880,132	38,731,796	201,148,336
Race alone			
American Indian	2,824,751	618,003	2,206,748
Asian	12,326,216	257,792	12,068,424
Black	37,502,320	1,538,618	35,963,702
Native Hawaiian	505,602	107,441	398,161
White	236,057,761	38,216,940	197,840,821
Two or more races	4,438,754	583,276	3,855,478

PERCENT DISTRIBUTION BY RACE

Total people	**100.0%**	**100.0%**	**100.0%**
Race alone or in combination			
American Indian	1.5	1.0	1.4
Asian	4.8	2.0	5.4
Black	13.4	4.4	14.8
Native Hawaiian	0.3	0.4	0.3
White	81.7	93.7	79.7
Race alone			
American Indian	1.0	1.5	0.9
Asian	4.2	0.6	4.8
Black	12.8	3.7	14.3
Native Hawaiian	0.2	0.3	0.2
White	80.4	92.5	78.4
Two or more races	1.5	1.4	1.5

PERCENT DISTRIBUTION BY HISPANIC ORIGIN

Total people	**100.0%**	**14.1%**	**85.9%**
Race alone or in combination			
American Indian	100.0	9.7	81.1
Asian	100.0	6.0	96.9
Black	100.0	4.6	95.4
Native Hawaiian	100.0	17.8	82.2
White	100.0	16.1	83.9
Race alone			
American Indian	100.0	21.9	78.1
Asian	100.0	2.1	97.9
Black	100.0	4.1	95.9
Native Hawaiian	100.0	21.3	78.7
White	100.0	16.2	83.8
Two or more races	100.0	13.1	86.9

Note: Race alone or in combination figures will not add to total because they count the multiracial population more than once. American Indians include Alaska Natives. Native Hawaiians include other Pacific Islanders. Hispanics may be of any race.
Source: Bureau of the Census, National Population Estimates, Internet site http://www.census.gov/popest/national/asrh/ NC-EST2004-srh.html; calculations by New Strategist

Table 6.100   Total People in the Armed Forces, 2003

(number and percent distribution of people aged 18 or older who are in the armed forces or who are veterans, by sex and age, 2003)

	total	in armed forces	veteran
Total people aged 18 or older	**210,275,463**	**647,266**	**24,008,355**
Men	101,255,934	557,272	22,458,107
Aged 18 to 64	86,875,383	557,272	13,738,341
Aged 65 or older	14,380,551	0	8,719,766
Women	109,019,529	89,994	1,550,248
Aged 18 to 64	89,503,908	89,994	1,233,622
Aged 65 or older	19,515,621	0	316,626
Total people aged 18 or older	**100.0%**	**0.3%**	**11.4%**
Men	100.0	0.6	22.2
Aged 18 to 64	100.0	0.6	15.8
Aged 65 or older	100.0	0.0	60.6
Women	100.0	0.1	1.4
Aged 18 to 64	100.0	0.1	1.4
Aged 65 or older	100.0	0.0	1.6

Source: Bureau of the Census, 2003 American Community Survey, Internet site http://factfinder.census.gov/servlet/ DatasetMainPageServlet?_program=ACS&_lang=en&_ts=; calculations by New Strategist

Table 6.101   People in the Armed Forces by Race and Hispanic Origin, 2003

(number and percent distribution of people aged 18 to 64 in the armed forces, by race and Hispanic origin, 2003)

	total	American Indian	Asian	black	Hispanic	non-Hispanic white
Total people in armed forces	**647,266**	**3,187**	**21,393**	**99,495**	**53,266**	**458,950**
Men	557,272	2,876	17,731	78,124	46,689	401,961
Women	89,994	311	3,662	21,371	6,577	56,989

PERCENT DISTRIBUTION BY RACE AND HISPANIC ORIGIN

Total people in armed forces	**100.0%**	**0.5%**	**3.3%**	**15.4%**	**8.2%**	**70.9%**
Men	100.0	0.5	3.2	14.0	8.4	72.1
Women	100.0	0.3	4.1	23.7	7.3	63.3

Note: Numbers will not sum to total because not all races are shown, those identifying themselves as being of more than one race are not shown, and Hispanics may be of any race. Non-Hispanic whites include only those identifying themselves as white alone and not Hispanic.
Source: Bureau of the Census, 2003 American Community Survey, Internet site http://factfinder.census.gov/servlet/ DatasetMainPageServlet?_program=ACS&_lang=en&_ts=; calculations by New Strategist

Table 6.102 Total Population by Age, 2000 and 2004

(number of people by age, 2000 and 2004; percent change, 2000–04)

	2004	2000	percent change 2000–04
Total people	**293,655,404**	**282,192,162**	**4.1%**
Under age 5	20,071,268	19,187,336	4.6
Aged 5 to 9	19,605,572	20,486,569	–4.3
Aged 10 to 14	21,145,156	20,621,749	2.5
Aged 15 to 19	20,729,802	20,250,181	2.4
Aged 20 to 24	20,971,302	19,125,610	9.7
Aged 25 to 29	19,560,906	19,305,785	1.3
Aged 30 to 34	20,471,032	20,540,314	–0.3
Aged 35 to 39	21,052,318	22,660,105	–7.1
Aged 40 to 44	23,056,334	22,524,284	2.4
Aged 45 to 49	22,122,629	20,222,035	9.4
Aged 50 to 54	19,496,176	17,774,847	9.7
Aged 55 to 59	16,489,501	13,559,163	21.6
Aged 60 to 64	12,589,423	10,856,732	16.0
Aged 65 to 69	9,956,467	9,517,573	4.6
Aged 70 to 74	8,507,005	8,851,737	–3.9
Aged 75 to 79	7,410,757	7,435,575	–0.3
Aged 80 to 84	5,560,125	4,986,474	11.5
Aged 85 or older	4,859,631	4,286,093	13.4
Aged 18 or older	220,377,406	209,830,798	5.0
Aged 18 to 24	29,245,102	27,310,081	7.1
Aged 65 or older	36,293,985	35,077,452	3.5

Source: Bureau of the Census, National Population Estimates, Internet site http://www.census.gov/popest/national/asrh/ NC-EST2004-asrh.html; calculations by New Strategist

Table 6.103 Population by Age, Race, and Hispanic Origin, 2004

(total number of people and percent distribution by age, race, and Hispanic origin, 2004)

	total number	percent	American Indian	Asian	black	Hispanic	non-Hispanic white
Total people	**293,655,404**	**100.0%**	**1.5%**	**4.8%**	**13.4%**	**14.1%**	**67.4%**
Under age 5	20,071,268	100.0	1.3	5.2	17.0	21.8	56.0
Aged 5 to 9	19,605,572	100.0	1.9	5.1	16.7	19.8	58.4
Aged 10 to 14	21,145,156	100.0	2.0	4.6	17.2	17.9	59.9
Aged 15 to 19	20,729,802	100.0	2.0	4.6	16.2	16.1	62.6
Aged 20 to 24	20,971,302	100.0	1.9	5.1	15.2	18.0	61.2
Aged 25 to 29	19,560,906	100.0	1.7	6.1	14.3	20.0	59.3
Aged 30 to 34	20,471,032	100.0	1.5	6.6	13.7	18.1	61.4
Aged 35 to 39	21,052,318	100.0	1.5	5.6	13.4	15.5	65.1
Aged 40 to 44	23,056,334	100.0	1.5	4.8	12.9	12.5	69.2
Aged 45 to 49	22,122,629	100.0	1.4	4.5	12.3	10.3	72.2
Aged 50 to 54	19,496,176	100.0	1.4	4.4	11.5	8.9	74.5
Aged 55 to 59	16,489,501	100.0	1.3	4.0	10.2	7.9	77.1
Aged 60 to 64	12,589,423	100.0	1.2	3.7	9.8	7.3	78.5
Aged 65 to 69	9,956,467	100.0	1.1	3.7	9.8	7.2	78.7
Aged 70 to 74	8,507,005	100.0	0.9	3.4	9.0	6.5	80.5
Aged 75 to 79	7,410,757	100.0	0.8	2.9	8.0	5.6	83.0
Aged 80 to 84	5,560,125	100.0	0.7	2.5	7.3	4.8	85.0
Aged 85 or older	4,859,631	100.0	0.7	2.1	7.3	4.3	85.8
Aged 18 or older	220,377,406	100.0	1.4	4.7	12.2	12.4	70.2
Aged 18 to 24	29,245,102	100.0	1.9	5.0	15.4	17.4	61.7
Aged 65 or older	36,293,985	100.0	0.9	3.1	8.5	6.0	81.9

Note: Percentages will not sum to total because American Indians, Asians, and blacks include those identifying themselves as being of the race alone and those identifying themselves as being of the race in combination with one or more other races, not all races are shown, and Hispanics may be of any race. Non-Hispanic whites include only those identifying themselves as white alone and not Hispanic.
Source: Bureau of the Census, National Population Estimates, Internet site http://www.census.gov/popest/national/asrh/ NC-EST2004-sa.html; calculations by New Strategist

Table 6.104 Total Population by Age and Sex, 2004

(number of people by age and sex, and sex ratio by age, 2004)

	total	females	males	sex ratio
Total people	**293,655,404**	**149,117,996**	**144,537,408**	**97**
Under age 5	20,071,268	9,808,276	10,262,992	105
Aged 5 to 9	19,605,572	9,576,431	10,029,141	105
Aged 10 to 14	21,145,156	10,314,017	10,831,139	105
Aged 15 to 19	20,729,802	10,094,406	10,635,396	105
Aged 20 to 24	20,971,302	10,168,312	10,802,990	106
Aged 25 to 29	19,560,906	9,566,092	9,994,814	104
Aged 30 to 34	20,471,032	10,129,813	10,341,219	102
Aged 35 to 39	21,052,318	10,481,803	10,570,515	101
Aged 40 to 44	23,056,334	11,592,968	11,463,366	99
Aged 45 to 49	22,122,629	11,204,884	10,917,745	97
Aged 50 to 54	19,496,176	9,961,248	9,534,928	96
Aged 55 to 59	16,489,501	8,488,082	8,001,419	94
Aged 60 to 64	12,589,423	6,591,409	5,998,014	91
Aged 65 to 69	9,956,467	5,323,518	4,632,949	87
Aged 70 to 74	8,507,005	4,712,328	3,794,677	81
Aged 75 to 79	7,410,757	4,312,118	3,098,639	72
Aged 80 to 84	5,560,125	3,440,533	2,119,592	62
Aged 85 or older	4,859,631	3,351,758	1,507,873	45
Aged 18 or older	220,377,406	113,345,146	107,032,260	94
Aged 18 to 24	29,245,102	14,188,592	15,056,510	106
Aged 65 or older	36,293,985	21,140,255	15,153,730	72

Note: The sex ratio is the number of males divided by the number of females multiplied by 100.
Source: Bureau of the Census, National Population Estimates, Internet site http://www.census.gov/popest/national/asrh/
NC-EST2004-sa.html; calculations by New Strategist

Table 6.105 Total Population by Age, 2000 to 2020

(number of people by age, 2000 to 2020; percent change, 2000–10 and 2010–20; numbers in thousands)

				percent change	
	2000	**2010**	**2020**	**2000–10**	**2010–20**
Total people	**282,178**	**308,936**	**335,805**	**9.5%**	**8.7%**
Under age 5	19,212	21,426	22,932	11.5	7.0
Aged 5 to 9	20,481	20,706	22,564	1.1	9.0
Aged 10 to 14	20,594	19,767	21,914	–4.0	10.9
Aged 15 to 19	20,216	21,336	21,478	5.5	0.7
Aged 20 to 24	19,151	21,676	20,751	13.2	–4.3
Aged 25 to 29	19,253	21,375	22,361	11.0	4.6
Aged 30 to 34	20,574	20,271	22,704	–1.5	12.0
Aged 35 to 39	22,607	20,137	22,143	–10.9	10.0
Aged 40 to 44	22,529	20,984	20,673	–6.9	–1.5
Aged 45 to 49	20,226	22,654	20,219	12.0	–10.7
Aged 50 to 54	17,821	22,173	20,702	24.4	–6.6
Aged 55 to 59	13,567	19,507	21,876	43.8	12.1
Aged 60 to 64	10,866	16,679	20,856	53.5	25.0
Aged 65 to 69	9,528	12,172	17,618	27.8	44.7
Aged 70 to 74	8,845	9,097	14,161	2.9	55.7
Aged 75 to 79	7,436	7,186	9,450	–3.4	31.5
Aged 80 to 84	4,978	5,665	6,134	13.8	8.3
Aged 85 or older	4,295	6,123	7,269	42.6	18.7
Aged 18 or older	209,835	234,504	255,505	11.8	9.0
Aged 18 to 24	27,311	30,481	29,339	11.6	–3.7
Aged 65 or older	35,081	40,244	54,632	14.7	35.8

Source: Bureau of the Census, Internet site http://www.census.gov/ipc/www/usinterimproj/; calculations by New Strategist

Table 6.106 Total Population by Race and Hispanic Origin, 2020

(total number of people and percent distribution by race and Hispanic origin, 2020; numbers in thousands)

| | total | | Asian | black | Hispanic | non-Hispanic white |
	number	percent				
Total people	**335,805**	**100.0%**	**5.4%**	**13.5%**	**17.8%**	**61.3%**
Under age 5	22,932	100.0	4.6	15.4	24.3	51.9
Aged 5 to 9	22,564	100.0	4.6	15.6	23.5	52.8
Aged 10 to 14	21,914	100.0	4.8	15.4	23.2	53.4
Aged 15 to 19	21,478	100.0	5.0	15.1	23.0	54.0
Aged 20 to 24	20,751	100.0	5.2	15.0	22.4	54.8
Aged 25 to 29	22,361	100.0	5.3	15.7	21.1	55.8
Aged 30 to 34	22,704	100.0	5.7	15.3	19.0	58.0
Aged 35 to 39	22,143	100.0	6.2	14.5	18.6	58.9
Aged 40 to 44	20,673	100.0	6.8	13.9	19.7	58.1
Aged 45 to 49	20,219	100.0	7.4	13.2	18.8	59.4
Aged 50 to 54	20,702	100.0	6.4	12.7	16.0	63.7
Aged 55 to 59	21,876	100.0	5.4	12.2	13.1	68.1
Aged 60 to 64	20,856	100.0	5.0	11.5	10.8	71.4
Aged 65 or older	54,632	100.0	4.4	9.5	8.6	76.4

Note: Percentages will not sum to total because Hispanics may be of any race.
Source: Bureau of the Census, Internet site http://www.census.gov/ipc/www/usinterimproj/; calculations by New Strategist

Table 6.107 Total Population by Region, 2000 and 2004

(number of people by region, 2000 and 2004; percent change, 2000–04)

	2004	2000	percent change 2000–04
Total people	293,655,404	281,421,906	4.3%
Northeast	54,571,147	53,594,378	1.8
Midwest	65,729,852	64,392,776	2.1
South	105,944,965	100,236,820	5.7
West	67,409,440	63,197,932	6.7

Note: Total number of people in 2000 differs from the total in previous tables of this chapter because these are census counts from April 1, 2000, whereas the others are population estimates.
Source: Bureau of the Census, 2000 Census, Internet site http://factfinder.census.gov/servlet/DatasetMainPageServlet?_program=DEC&_lang=en&_ts=; and State Population Estimates, Internet site http://www.census.gov/popest/states/asrh/ SC-EST2004-04.html; calculations by New Strategist

Table 6.108 Population by Region, Race, and Hispanic Origin, 2004

(total number of people and percent distribution by region, race, and Hispanic origin, 2004)

	total		American Indian	Asian	black	Hispanic	non-Hispanic white
	number	percent					
Total people	293,655,404	100.0%	1.5%	4.8%	13.4%	14.1%	67.4%
Northeast	54,571,147	100.0	0.7	5.1	13.2	10.8	72.2
Midwest	65,729,852	100.0	1.1	2.5	10.9	5.6	80.3
South	105,944,965	100.0	1.3	2.6	19.8	13.2	63.8
West	67,409,440	100.0	2.8	10.0	5.7	26.3	56.5

Note: Percentages will not sum to total because American Indians, Asians, and blacks include those identifying themselves as being of the race alone and those identifying themselves as being of the race in combination with one or more other races, not all races are shown, and Hispanics may be of any race. Non-Hispanic whites include only those identifying themselves as being white alone and not Hispanic.
Source: Bureau of the Census, State Population Estimates, Internet site http://www.census.gov/popest/states/asrh/ SC-EST2004-04.html; calculations by New Strategist

Table 6.109 Total Population by State, 2000 and 2004

(number of people by state, 2000 and 2004; percent change, 2000–04)

	2004	2000	percent change 2000–04
Total people	**293,655,404**	**281,421,906**	**4.3%**
Alabama	4,530,182	4,447,100	1.9
Alaska	655,435	626,932	4.5
Arizona	5,743,834	5,130,632	12.0
Arkansas	2,752,629	2,673,400	3.0
California	35,893,799	33,871,648	6.0
Colorado	4,601,403	4,301,261	7.0
Connecticut	3,503,604	3,405,565	2.9
Delaware	830,364	783,600	6.0
District of Columbia	553,523	572,059	–3.2
Florida	17,397,161	15,982,378	8.9
Georgia	8,829,383	8,186,453	7.9
Hawaii	1,262,840	1,211,537	4.2
Idaho	1,393,262	1,293,953	7.7
Illinois	12,713,634	12,419,293	2.4
Indiana	6,237,569	6,080,485	2.6
Iowa	2,954,451	2,926,324	1.0
Kansas	2,735,502	2,688,418	1.8
Kentucky	4,145,922	4,041,769	2.6
Louisiana	4,515,770	4,468,976	1.0
Maine	1,317,253	1,274,923	3.3
Maryland	5,558,058	5,296,486	4.9
Massachusetts	6,416,505	6,349,097	1.1
Michigan	10,112,620	9,938,444	1.8
Minnesota	5,100,958	4,919,479	3.7
Mississippi	2,902,966	2,844,658	2.0
Missouri	5,754,618	5,595,211	2.8
Montana	926,865	902,195	2.7
Nebraska	1,747,214	1,711,263	2.1
Nevada	2,334,771	1,998,257	16.8
New Hampshire	1,299,500	1,235,786	5.2
New Jersey	8,698,879	8,414,350	3.4
New Mexico	1,903,289	1,819,046	4.6
New York	19,227,088	18,976,457	1.3
North Carolina	8,541,221	8,049,313	6.1
North Dakota	634,366	642,200	–1.2
Ohio	11,459,011	11,353,140	0.9
Oklahoma	3,523,553	3,450,654	2.1
Oregon	3,594,586	3,421,399	5.1

(continued)

	2004	2000	percent change 2000–04
Pennsylvania	12,406,292	12,281,054	1.0%
Rhode Island	1,080,632	1,048,319	3.1
South Carolina	4,198,068	4,012,012	4.6
South Dakota	770,883	754,844	2.1
Tennessee	5,900,962	5,689,283	3.7
Texas	22,490,022	20,851,820	7.9
Utah	2,389,039	2,233,169	7.0
Vermont	621,394	608,827	2.1
Virginia	7,459,827	7,078,515	5.4
Washington	6,203,788	5,894,121	5.3
West Virginia	1,815,354	1,808,344	0.4
Wisconsin	5,509,026	5,363,675	2.7
Wyoming	506,529	493,782	2.6

Note: Total number of people in 2000 differs from the total in previous tables of this chapter because these are census counts from April 1, 2000, whereas the others are population estimates.
Source: Bureau of the Census, 2000 Census, Internet site http://factfinder.census.gov/servlet/DatasetMainPageServlet?_ program=DEC&_lang=en&_ts=; and State Population Estimates, Internet site http://www.census.gov/popest/states/asrh/ SC-EST2004-04.html; calculations by New Strategist

Table 6.110 Population by State, Race, and Hispanic Origin, 2004

(total number of people and percent distribution by state, race, and Hispanic origin, 2004)

	total number	percent	American Indian	Asian	black	Hispanic	non-Hispanic white
Total people	**293,655,404**	**100.0%**	**1.5%**	**4.8%**	**13.4%**	**14.1%**	**67.4%**
Alabama	4,530,182	100.0	1.0	1.0	26.7	2.2	69.5
Alaska	655,435	100.0	18.9	5.8	4.5	4.9	66.9
Arizona	5,743,834	100.0	5.6	2.6	4.1	28.0	61.1
Arkansas	2,752,629	100.0	1.4	1.1	16.1	4.4	77.2
California	35,893,799	100.0	1.9	13.3	7.5	34.7	44.5
Colorado	4,601,403	100.0	1.9	3.1	4.7	19.1	72.5
Connecticut	3,503,604	100.0	0.8	3.4	10.8	10.6	75.9
Delaware	830,364	100.0	0.8	2.9	21.2	5.8	70.2
District of Columbia	553,523	100.0	0.8	3.5	58.6	8.5	30.3
Florida	17,397,161	100.0	0.8	2.4	16.2	19.0	62.8
Georgia	8,829,383	100.0	0.7	2.9	30.1	6.8	60.2
Hawaii	1,262,840	100.0	2.1	57.6	3.3	7.9	23.3
Idaho	1,393,262	100.0	2.1	1.5	0.8	8.9	87.2
Illinois	12,713,634	100.0	0.6	4.3	15.7	14.0	66.2
Indiana	6,237,569	100.0	0.7	1.4	9.3	4.3	84.6
Iowa	2,954,451	100.0	0.7	1.7	2.7	3.5	91.7
Kansas	2,735,502	100.0	1.7	2.4	6.6	8.1	81.9
Kentucky	4,145,922	100.0	0.6	1.1	8.0	1.9	88.7
Louisiana	4,515,770	100.0	1.0	1.6	33.4	2.8	61.8
Maine	1,317,253	100.0	1.0	1.0	1.0	0.9	96.1
Maryland	5,558,058	100.0	0.8	5.1	29.9	5.4	59.8
Massachusetts	6,416,505	100.0	0.6	5.0	7.5	7.7	80.8
Michigan	10,112,620	100.0	1.2	2.5	15.0	3.7	78.1
Minnesota	5,100,958	100.0	1.7	3.8	4.8	3.5	86.7
Mississippi	2,902,966	100.0	0.7	0.9	37.1	1.7	59.9
Missouri	5,754,618	100.0	1.1	1.6	12.0	2.6	83.1
Montana	926,865	100.0	7.5	0.8	0.6	2.4	89.1
Nebraska	1,747,214	100.0	1.3	1.8	4.8	6.9	85.7
Nevada	2,334,771	100.0	2.1	6.6	8.4	22.8	61.2
New Hampshire	1,299,500	100.0	0.6	2.0	1.3	2.1	94.3
New Jersey	8,698,879	100.0	0.6	7.4	15.2	14.9	63.8
New Mexico	1,903,289	100.0	10.9	1.6	2.8	43.3	43.5
New York	19,227,088	100.0	1.0	7.0	18.4	16.0	61.1
North Carolina	8,541,221	100.0	1.7	2.0	22.3	6.1	68.6
North Dakota	634,366	100.0	5.8	0.9	1.0	1.5	91.1
Ohio	11,459,011	100.0	0.7	1.6	12.6	2.2	83.3
Oklahoma	3,523,553	100.0	11.3	1.9	8.5	6.3	72.9
Oregon	3,594,586	100.0	2.5	4.2	2.3	9.5	82.0

(continued)

	total		American Indian	Asian	black	Hispanic	non-Hispanic white
	number	percent					
Pennsylvania	12,406,292	100.0%	0.5%	2.4%	11.1%	3.8%	82.9%
Rhode Island	1,080,632	100.0	1.1	3.0	7.0	10.3	80.5
South Carolina	4,198,068	100.0	0.7	1.3	29.8	3.1	65.6
South Dakota	770,883	100.0	9.4	0.9	1.1	2.0	87.1
Tennessee	5,900,962	100.0	0.7	1.4	17.2	2.8	78.1
Texas	22,490,022	100.0	1.1	3.5	12.1	34.6	49.8
Utah	2,389,039	100.0	1.8	2.4	1.3	10.6	83.8
Vermont	621,394	100.0	1.0	1.2	0.9	1.0	96.0
Virginia	7,459,827	100.0	0.8	5.0	20.6	5.7	68.7
Washington	6,203,788	100.0	2.7	7.5	4.4	8.5	77.5
West Virginia	1,815,354	100.0	0.6	0.7	3.6	0.8	94.4
Wisconsin	5,509,026	100.0	1.3	2.2	6.4	4.3	86.2
Wyoming	506,529	100.0	3.1	0.9	1.1	6.7	88.6

Note: Percentages will not sum to total because American Indians, Asians, and blacks include those identifying themselves as being of the race alone and those identifying themselves as being of the race in combination with one or more other races, not all races are shown, and Hispanics may be of any race. Non-Hispanic whites include only those identifying themselves as being white alone and not Hispanic.
Source: Bureau of the Census, State Population Estimates, Internet site http://www.census.gov/popest/states/asrh/ SC-EST2004-04.html; calculations by New Strategist

Table 6.111 Population by Metropolitan Area, Race, and Hispanic Origin, 2004

(total number of people and percent distribution for selected metropolitan areas by race and Hispanic origin, 2004)

	total	American Indian	Asian	black	Hispanic	non-Hispanic white
Albany–Schenectady–Troy, NY MSA	860,976	0.1%	2.4%	6.1%	3.0%	87.0%
Allentown–Bethlehem–Easton, PA MSA	650,230	0.1	2.1	4.0	9.8	83.9
Anchorage, AK MSA	265,176	6.0	6.7	5.7	6.9	67.6
Appleton–Oshkosh–Neenah, WI MSA	359,711	0.8	2.4	0.0	2.3	93.2
Atlanta, GA MSA	4,477,579	0.2	4.0	30.0	8.5	56.0
Augusta–Aiken, GA–SC MSA	476,167	0.1	1.5	34.9	2.6	59.7
Austin–San Marcos, TX MSA	1,373,125	0.5	4.1	7.4	29.0	57.9
Bakersfield, CA MSA	702,855	0.7	3.9	5.1	42.8	46.2
Baton Rouge, LA MSA	610,743	0.0	1.7	32.4	2.2	63.0
Beaumont–Port Arthur, TX MSA	366,244	0.4	2.4	24.4	8.7	63.5
Biloxi–Gulfport–Pascagoula, MS MSA	363,966	0.0	0.4	22.9	2.5	73.5
Binghamton, NY MSA	239,012	0.0	0.9	3.2	1.9	90.4
Birmingham, AL MSA	929,694	0.3	0.8	30.6	2.5	65.4
Boise City, ID MSA	479,284	1.4	1.6	0.5	10.1	85.3
Boston–Worcester–Lawrence, MA–NH–ME–CT CMSA	5,749,197	0.3	4.9	5.7	7.1	80.9
Brownsville–Harlingen–San Benito, TX MSA	367,603	0.1	0.8	0.2	85.9	13.0
Buffalo–Niagara Falls, NY MSA	1,119,037	0.5	1.5	11.9	3.0	82.2
Canton–Massillon, OH MSA	400,919	0.1	0.4	7.7	0.9	90.1
Charleston–North Charleston, SC MSA	563,828	0.2	1.5	30.0	2.8	64.1
Chicago, IL PMSA	8,388,723	0.2	5.4	18.1	19.4	56.1
Cleveland–Akron, OH CMSA	2,878,475	0.2	1.6	17.1	3.0	77.2
Colorado Springs, CO MSA	539,225	0.7	2.6	6.8	12.6	75.0
Columbia, SC MSA	543,126	0.3	1.7	33.1	2.0	61.9
Corpus Christi, TX MSA	381,422	0.5	1.3	3.3	56.4	37.2
Dallas–Fort Worth, TX CMSA	5,676,651	0.5	4.5	13.6	24.9	55.2
Davenport–Moline–Rock Island, IA–IL MSA	350,022	0.6	0.2	7.2	6.6	84.6
Dayton–Springfield, OH MSA	916,635	0.2	1.5	14.4	1.4	81.0
Daytona Beach, FL MSA	530,553	0.3	1.0	9.5	8.0	80.3
Denver–Boulder–Greeley, CO CMSA*	2,514,628	0.7	3.4	5.4	20.6	68.9
Des Moines, IA MSA	476,699	0.3	3.0	3.7	5.0	87.2
Detroit–Ann Arbor–Flint, MI CMSA	5,437,277	0.3	3.1	21.0	3.3	71.2
El Paso, TX MSA	700,225	0.5	1.1	2.6	81.2	14.6
Erie, PA MSA	267,426	0.2	0.5	6.6	2.4	89.1
Eugene–Springfield, OR MSA	324,176	1.7	2.8	1.2	5.4	87.6
Fayetteville, NC MSA	287,220	1.1	2.0	36.7	6.0	51.3
Fayetteville–Springdale–Rogers, AR MSA	345,308	2.3	2.0	1.1	12.0	81.6
Fort Myers–Cape Coral, FL MSA	508,634	0.1	1.2	7.2	13.0	77.1
Fort Pierce–Port St. Lucie, FL MSA	358,578	0.2	1.1	11.6	10.3	75.9
Fort Wayne, IN MSA	506,545	0.1	1.4	7.2	4.0	85.7

(continued)

	total	American Indian	Asian	black	Hispanic	non-Hispanic white
Fresno, CA MSA	978,274	1.3%	7.9%	4.3%	46.4%	39.1%
Grand Rapids–Muskegon–Holland, MI MSA	1,102,729	0.5	1.8	6.8	7.4	81.9
Greensboro–Winston-Salem–High Point, NC MSA	1,283,261	0.3	1.9	20.0	6.7	70.2
Greenville–Spartanburg–Anderson, SC MSA	976,678	0.1	1.5	16.9	3.9	76.3
Harrisburg–Lebanon–Carlisle, PA MSA	617,676	0.1	2.0	7.4	3.6	85.5
Hartford, CT MSA	1,163,367	0.1	2.7	9.7	10.7	75.0
Hickory–Morganton–Lenoir, NC MSA	345,590	0.0	2.7	6.6	5.6	84.5
Honolulu, HI MSA	868,751	0.1	49.0	2.2	7.1	19.1
Houston–Galveston–Brazoria, TX CMSA*	4,794,384	0.3	5.7	16.5	32.4	44.2
Huntsville, AL MSA	354,936	0.9	2.1	20.9	1.7	73.2
Indianapolis, IN MSA	1,664,412	0.1	1.6	13.5	3.7	79.2
Jackson, MS MSA	443,275	0.2	0.7	46.7	1.2	50.5
Jacksonville, FL MSA	1,182,453	0.3	2.9	21.9	4.8	68.7
Johnson City–Kingsport–Bristol, TN–VA MSA	482,047	0.6	0.7	1.1	1.4	95.3
Kalamazoo–Battle Creek, MI MSA	441,059	0.5	1.3	8.7	3.9	82.8
Kansas City, MO–KS MSA	1,823,092	0.4	1.9	12.4	6.4	77.5
Killeen–Temple, TX MSA	298,933	0.9	3.1	18.7	17.5	56.1
Knoxville, TN MSA	707,617	0.1	1.2	6.1	1.6	90.2
Lafayette, LA MSA	386,812	0.2	0.2	29.2	1.5	68.2
Lakeland–Winter Haven, FL MSA	511,565	0.0	1.3	14.0	12.4	71.6
Lancaster, PA MSA	473,104	0.0	1.8	2.4	6.6	88.0
Lansing–East Lansing, MI MSA	436,485	0.4	2.9	8.9	5.1	80.5
Lexington, KY MSA	478,625	0.1	1.8	9.5	3.3	84.3
Lincoln, NE MSA	249,670	0.7	3.2	2.3	4.1	88.0
Little Rock–North Little Rock, AR MSA	593,032	0.3	1.0	22.5	2.7	72.1
Los Angeles–Riverside–Orange County, CA CMSA	17,199,115	0.6	11.3	7.0	42.9	36.8
Lubbock, TX MSA	240,721	0.2	0.6	6.9	30.1	60.1
Macon, GA MSA	329,432	0.3	1.5	38.4	2.5	56.2
Madison, WI MSA	437,843	0.6	4.3	4.5	4.3	85.6
McAllen–Edinburg–Mission, TX MSA	651,974	0.5	0.6	0.0	89.3	9.5
Melbourne–Titusville–Palm Bay, FL MSA	509,248	0.2	1.7	9.0	5.8	82.0
Miami–Fort Lauderdale, FL CMSA	4,051,442	0.2	2.1	21.7	43.7	32.4
Milwaukee–Waukesha, WI PMSA	1,483,023	0.4	2.6	16.1	7.5	72.3
Mobile, AL MSA	547,153	1.3	1.3	27.8	0.5	68.3
Modesto, CA MSA	490,860	0.8	5.0	3.2	36.6	52.3
Montgomery, AL MSA	323,220	0.5	1.1	39.4	1.4	57.1
Nashville, TN MSA	1,275,212	0.3	2.0	15.6	4.6	76.7
New Orleans, LA MSA	1,313,694	0.4	2.4	38.1	4.9	53.4
New York–Northern New Jersey–Long Island, NY–NJ–CT–PA CMSA*	20,345,959	0.2	8.3	17.5	20.0	53.8
Oklahoma City, OK MSA	1,095,252	3.7	2.8	10.0	8.4	71.1
Orlando, FL MSA	1,831,212	0.6	3.4	14.7	20.2	60.3
Pensacola, FL MSA	410,542	0.4	2.1	16.7	2.2	75.8
Peoria–Pekin, IL MSA	337,020	0.0	1.4	9.3	1.8	86.3
Philadelphia–Wilmington–Atlantic City, PA–NJ–DE–MD CMSA*	5,383,262	0.2	4.2	19.5	6.1	69.0

(continued)

	total	American Indian	Asian	black	Hispanic	non-Hispanic white
Pittsburgh, PA MSA	2,260,551	0.0%	1.4%	8.4%	0.8%	88.7%
Portland, ME MSA	248,827	0.0	1.9	1.5	1.0	94.6
Providence–Fall River–Warwick, RI–MA MSA	1,165,549	0.3	2.7	5.2	9.7	81.4
Provo–Orem, UT MSA	395,173	0.3	2.0	0.5	8.3	87.8
Raleigh–Durham–Chapel Hill, NC MSA	1,278,372	0.3	3.6	22.5	8.4	64.6
Reading, PA MSA	378,456	0.0	0.7	2.9	11.9	82.5
Reno, NV MSA	375,344	1.8	5.1	2.2	19.5	69.7
Richmond–Petersburg, VA MSA	1,013,399	0.3	2.4	29.9	3.1	63.1
Rochester, NY MSA	1,057,917	0.1	2.2	10.2	4.5	81.8
Rockford, IL MSA	382,901	0.2	1.6	7.3	9.7	79.8
Sacramento, CA PMSA	1,803,160	1.3	10.8	8.0	16.1	61.5
Saginaw–Bay City–Midland, MI MSA	393,837	0.6	0.9	9.3	5.1	82.4
St. Louis, MO–IL MSA	2,620,334	0.1	1.7	18.6	1.8	76.7
Salinas, CA MSA	392,192	1.2	6.8	2.3	51.0	37.8
Salt Lake City–Ogden, UT MSA	1,384,041	0.5	2.4	1.2	12.8	80.9
San Antonio, TX MSA	1,683,872	0.5	1.7	6.4	53.4	37.5
San Diego, CA MSA	2,833,275	0.6	10.3	5.3	29.4	52.4
San Francisco–Oakland–San Jose, CA CMSA	6,951,260	0.6	21.0	6.6	21.2	47.8
San Luis Obispo–Atascadero– Paso Robles, CA MSA	238,502	0.6	3.2	0.8	17.0	76.7
Santa Barbara–Santa Maria–Lompoc, CA MSA	385,238	1.0	4.5	1.8	37.5	54.0
Sarasota–Bradenton, FL MSA	639,438	0.2	1.1	6.0	8.2	83.4
Savannah, GA MSA	299,920	0.1	1.9	35.1	2.5	60.1
Scranton–Wilkes-Barre–Hazleton, PA MSA	587,557	0.0	0.9	1.4	1.9	95.5
Seattle–Tacoma–Bremerton, WA CMSA*	3,184,924	0.9	9.8	5.1	6.9	73.6
Shreveport–Bossier City, LA MSA	387,312	0.2	1.0	36.8	2.3	57.4
South Bend, IN MSA	252,944	0.2	0.6	13.5	5.6	78.7
Spokane, WA MSA	420,592	1.9	1.8	1.6	3.1	89.6
Springfield, MA MSA	560,472	0.2	2.4	6.9	14.1	75.7
Springfield, MO MSA	332,918	0.8	1.1	1.2	1.9	93.4
Stockton–Lodi, CA MSA	632,143	0.8	14.2	7.5	33.9	42.4
Syracuse, NY MSA	707,901	0.4	1.7	6.4	2.1	87.4
Tallahassee, FL MSA	274,945	0.3	2.2	33.8	4.4	58.6
Tampa–St. Petersburg–Clearwater, FL MSA	2,537,586	0.3	2.3	10.8	12.6	72.9
Toledo, OH MSA	598,283	0.1	1.3	13.0	4.9	79.1
Tucson, AZ MSA	885,025	3.0	2.5	2.9	32.1	58.3
Tulsa, OK MSA	810,062	7.0	1.4	9.0	6.2	72.5
Utica–Rome, NY MSA	282,844	0.3	0.7	2.3	2.5	91.7
Visalia–Tulare–Porterville, CA MSA	395,493	1.2	3.5	1.7	54.6	38.5
West Palm Beach–Boca Raton, FL MSA	1,223,206	0.3	1.9	15.2	15.6	65.9
Wichita, KS MSA	546,308	0.8	3.5	7.1	9.0	77.2
York, PA MSA	393,426	0.2	1.1	3.5	3.6	90.5
Youngstown–Warren, OH MSA	566,597	0.0	0.6	10.2	1.8	86.9

Population figures are for only part of the metropolitan area.

Note: Some metropolitan areas are not shown because data are not available. Percentages will not sum to total because American Indians, Asians, and blacks include those identifying themselves as being of the race alone and those identifying themselves as being of the race in combination with one or more other races, not all races are shown, and Hispanics may be of any race. Non-Hispanic whites include only those identifying themselves as being white alone and not Hispanic. For the definition of CMSA, MSA, and PMSA, see the glossary.

Source: Bureau of the Census, 2004 American Community Survey, Internet site http://factfinder.census.gov/servlet/ DatasetMainPageServlet?_program=ACS&_lang=en&_ts=; calculations by New Strategist

Table 6.112 Immigration to the United States, 1901 to 2004

(number of immigrants granted permanent residence in the U.S. by single year, 2001 to 2004, and by decade, 1901 to 2000)

SINGLE YEAR	
Total, 2000 to 2004	**3,780,019**
2004	946,142
2003	705,827
2002	1,063,732
2001	1,064,318
DECADE	
1991–00	9,095,417
1981–90	7,338,062
1971–80	4,493,314
1961–70	3,321,677
1951–60	2,515,479
1941–50	1,035,039
1931–40	528,431
1921–30	4,107,209
1911–20	5,735,811
1901–10	8,795,386

Note: Immigrants are people granted legal permanent residence in the United States. They either arrive in the U.S. with immigrant visas issued abroad or adjust their status in the United States from temporary to permanent residence.
Source: Office of Immigration Statistics, 2004 Yearbook of Immigration Statistics, Internet site http://uscis.gov/graphics/shared/ statistics/yearbook/YrBk04Im.htm; calculations by New Strategist

Table 6.113   Immigrants by Country of Birth, 2004

(number and percent distribution of immigrants by world region and country of birth, 2004; for countries with at least 10,000 immigrants)

	number	percent distribution
IMMIGRANTS BY WORLD REGION		
Total immigrants	**946,142**	**100.0%**
Asia	330,004	34.9
Mexico	175,364	18.5
Europe	127,669	13.5
Caribbean	88,921	9.4
South America	71,785	7.6
Africa	66,309	7.0
Central America (excl. Mexico)	61,333	6.5
Canada	15,567	1.6
Oceania	5,960	0.6
Unknown	3,173	0.3
IMMIGRANTS BY COUNTRY		
Total immigrants	**946,142**	**100.0**
Mexico	175,364	18.5
India	70,116	7.4
Philippines	57,827	6.1
China, People's Republic	51,156	5.4
Vietnam	31,514	3.3
Dominican Republic	30,492	3.2
El Salvador	29,795	3.1
Cuba	20,488	2.2
Korea	19,766	2.1
Colombia	18,678	2.0
Guatemala	17,999	1.9
Canada	15,567	1.6
United Kingdom	14,915	1.6
Jamaica	14,414	1.5
Poland	14,250	1.5
Haiti	13,998	1.5
Ukraine	13,655	1.4
Russia	13,358	1.4
Pakistan	12,086	1.3
Peru	11,781	1.2
Bosnia-Herzegovina	10,552	1.1
Brazil	10,504	1.1
Iran	10,434	1.1
All other countries	267,433	28.3

Note: Immigrants are people granted legal permanent residence in the United States. They either arrive in the U.S. with immigrant visas issued abroad or adjust their status in the United States from temporary to permanent residence.
Source: Office of Immigration Statistics, 2004 Yearbook of Immigration Statistics, Internet site http://uscis.gov/graphics/shared/ statistics/yearbook/YrBk04Im.htm; calculations by New Strategist

Table 6.114 Foreign-Born Population by Age, 2004

(total number of people, number and percent distribution of foreign-born, and foreign-born share of total, by age, 2004; numbers in thousands)

	total	foreign-born number	foreign-born percent distribution	foreign-born share of total
Total people	**288,280**	**34,244**	**100.0%**	**11.9%**
Under age 5	19,932	334	1.0	1.7
Aged 5 to 9	19,646	709	2.1	3.6
Aged 10 to 14	21,118	1,113	3.3	5.3
Aged 15 to 19	20,369	1,677	4.9	8.2
Aged 20 to 24	20,339	2,884	8.4	14.2
Aged 25 to 29	19,008	3,751	11.0	19.7
Aged 30 to 34	20,193	4,033	11.8	20.0
Aged 35 to 39	20,791	3,873	11.3	18.6
Aged 40 to 44	22,782	3,686	10.8	16.2
Aged 45 to 49	21,823	3,049	8.9	14.0
Aged 50 to 54	19,246	2,267	6.6	11.8
Aged 55 to 59	16,158	1,811	5.3	11.2
Aged 60 to 64	12,217	1,360	4.0	11.1
Aged 65 or older	34,659	3,697	10.8	10.7

Source: Bureau of the Census, Foreign-born Population of the United States, Current Population Survey, March 2004, detailed tables (PPL-176), Internet site http://www.census.gov/population/www/socdemo/foreign/ppl-176.html; calculations by New Strategist

Table 6.115 Foreign-Born Population by Age and World Region of Birth, 2004

(number and percent distribution of foreign-born by age and world region of birth, 2004; numbers in thousands)

	total	Asia	Europe	Latin America	other areas
Total foreign-born	**34,244**	**8,685**	**4,661**	**18,314**	**2,584**
Under age 5	334	86	37	181	32
Aged 5 to 9	709	123	62	461	62
Aged 10 to 14	1,113	216	124	674	100
Aged 15 to 19	1,677	355	164	1,019	138
Aged 20 to 24	2,884	539	247	1,890	209
Aged 25 to 29	3,751	804	294	2,390	263
Aged 30 to 34	4,033	1,039	320	2,405	269
Aged 35 to 39	3,873	1,057	384	2,137	295
Aged 40 to 44	3,686	950	415	2,052	270
Aged 45 to 49	3,049	879	386	1,524	260
Aged 50 to 54	2,267	708	321	1,044	194
Aged 55 to 59	1,811	600	346	739	127
Aged 60 to 64	1,360	389	293	570	108
Aged 65 or older	3,697	940	1,269	1,228	259

PERCENT DISTRIBUTION BY WORLD REGION OF BIRTH

Total foreign-born	**100.0%**	**25.4%**	**13.6%**	**53.5%**	**7.5%**
Under age 5	100.0	25.7	11.1	54.2	9.6
Aged 5 to 9	100.0	17.3	8.7	65.0	8.7
Aged 10 to 14	100.0	19.4	11.1	60.6	9.0
Aged 15 to 19	100.0	21.2	9.8	60.8	8.2
Aged 20 to 24	100.0	18.7	8.6	65.5	7.2
Aged 25 to 29	100.0	21.4	7.8	63.7	7.0
Aged 30 to 34	100.0	25.8	7.9	59.6	6.7
Aged 35 to 39	100.0	27.3	9.9	55.2	7.6
Aged 40 to 44	100.0	25.8	11.3	55.7	7.3
Aged 45 to 49	100.0	28.8	12.7	50.0	8.5
Aged 50 to 54	100.0	31.2	14.2	46.1	8.6
Aged 55 to 59	100.0	33.1	19.1	40.8	7.0
Aged 60 to 64	100.0	28.6	21.5	41.9	7.9
Aged 65 or older	100.0	25.4	34.3	33.2	7.0

Source: Bureau of the Census, Foreign-born Population of the United States, Current Population Survey, March 2004, detailed tables (PPL-176), Internet site http://www.census.gov/population/www/socdemo/foreign/ppl-176.html; calculations by New Strategist

Table 6.116   Foreign-Born by U.S. Region of Residence, 2004

(number and percent distribution of total people and the foreign-born by U.S. region of residence and world region of birth, 2004; numbers in thousands)

	total	foreign-born				
		total	Asia	Europe	Latin America	other areas
Total people	**288,280**	**34,244**	**8,685**	**4,661**	**18,314**	**2,584**
Northeast	53,703	7,408	1,693	1,823	3,237	654
Midwest	64,784	3,684	1,183	694	1,365	443
South	103,545	10,175	1,882	865	6,661	768
West	66,247	12,978	3,927	1,280	7,051	720
PERCENT DISTRIBUTION BY FOREIGN-BORN STATUS						
Total people	**100.0%**	**11.9%**	**3.0%**	**1.6%**	**6.4%**	**0.9%**
Northeast	100.0	13.8	3.2	3.4	6.0	1.2
Midwest	100.0	5.7	1.8	1.1	2.1	0.7
South	100.0	9.8	1.8	0.8	6.4	0.7
West	100.0	19.6	5.9	1.9	10.6	1.1
PERCENT DISTRIBUTION BY U.S. REGION OF RESIDENCE						
Total people	**100.0%**	**100.0%**	**100.0%**	**100.0%**	**100.0%**	**100.0%**
Northeast	18.6	21.6	19.5	39.1	17.7	25.3
Midwest	22.5	10.8	13.6	14.9	7.5	17.1
South	35.9	29.7	21.7	18.6	36.4	29.7
West	23.0	37.9	45.2	27.5	38.5	27.9

Source: Bureau of the Census, Foreign-born Population of the United States, Current Population Survey, March 2004, detailed tables (PPL-176), Internet site http://www.census.gov/population/www/socdemo/foreign/ppl-176.html; calculations by New Strategist

Table 6.117 Foreign-Born by Citizenship Status, 2004

(number and percent distribution of foreign-born by world region of birth and citizenship status, 2004)

	total	naturalized citizen	not a citizen
Total foreign-born	**33,533,945**	**13,893,436**	**19,640,509**
Africa	1,039,489	396,724	642,765
Asia	9,146,958	4,916,520	4,230,438
Europe	4,775,586	2,732,626	2,042,960
Latin America	17,533,710	5,415,882	12,117,828
Caribbean	3,107,686	1,683,823	1,423,863
Central America	12,125,989	2,847,286	9,278,703
Mexico	10,010,902	2,238,740	7,772,162
Other Central America	2,115,087	608,546	1,506,541
South America	2,300,035	884,773	1,415,262
North America	846,882	366,665	480,217
Oceania	191,320	65,019	126,301
Total foreign-born	**100.0%**	**41.4%**	**58.6%**
Africa	100.0	38.2	61.8
Asia	100.0	53.8	46.2
Europe	100.0	57.2	42.8
Latin America	100.0	30.9	69.1
Caribbean	100.0	54.2	45.8
Central America	100.0	23.5	76.5
Mexico	100.0	22.4	77.6
Other Central America	100.0	28.8	71.2
South America	100.0	38.5	61.5
North America	100.0	43.3	56.7
Oceania	100.0	34.0	66.0

Source: Bureau of the Census, 2004 American Community Survey, Internet site http://factfinder.census.gov/servlet/ DatasetMainPageServlet?_lang=en&_ts=143469461584&_ds_name=ACS_2004_EST_G00_&_program=ACS; calculations by New Strategist

Table 6.118 Language Spoken at Home, 2003

(number and percent distribution of people aged 5 or older by language spoken at home, 2003; for languages spoken by at least 500,000 people)

	number	percent
Total people aged 5 or older	**263,230,104**	**100.0%**
English only	214,809,283	81.6
Language other than English	48,420,821	18.4
Language other than English	**48,420,821**	**100.0**
Spanish or Spanish Creole	29,698,115	61.3
Chinese	2,193,370	4.5
French (including Patois, Cajun)	1,378,825	2.8
Tagalog	1,261,746	2.6
Vietnamese	1,104,248	2.3
German	1,094,446	2.3
Korean	966,959	2.0
Italian	782,104	1.6
Russian	705,183	1.5
Polish	600,621	1.2
Portuguese	560,010	1.2
Arabic	558,105	1.2

Source: Bureau of the Census, 2003 American Community Survey Data Profile, Internet site http://www.census.gov/acs/www/Products/Profiles/Single/2003/ACS/Tabular/010/01000US2.htm; calculations by New Strategist

Table 6.119 Ability to Speak English by Language Spoken at Home, 2003

(number and percent distribution of people aged 5 or older who speak a language other than English at home by language spoken at home, and ability to speak English, 2003)

	number	percent distribution
Total, aged 5 or older	**263,230,104**	**100.0%**
Speak only English at home	214,809,283	81.6
Speak a language other than English at home	48,420,821	18.4
Speak English less than "very well"	22,001,256	8.4
Total who speak a language other than English at home	**48,420,821**	**100.0**
Speak Spanish at home	29,698,115	61.3
Speak other Indo-European language at home	9,509,828	19.6
Speak Asian or Pacific Island language at home	7,449,893	15.4
Speak other language at home	1,762,985	3.6
Speak Spanish at home	29,698,115	100.0
Speak English less than "very well"	14,432,957	48.6
Speak other Indo-European language at home	9,509,828	100.0
Speak English less than "very well"	3,275,644	34.4
Speak Asian or Pacific Island language at home	7,449,893	100.0
Speak English less than "very well"	3,749,195	50.3
Speak other language at home	1,762,985	100.0
Speak English less than "very well"	543,460	30.8

Source: Bureau of the Census, 2003 American Community Survey Data Profile, Internet site http://www.census.gov/acs/www/ Products/Profiles/Single/2003/ACS/Tabular/010/01000US2.htm; calculations by New Strategist

Table 6.120 People Who Speak a Language Other than English at Home, by State, 2003

(total number of people aged 5 or older and number and percent who speak a language other than English at home, by state, 2003)

	total aged 5 or older	speak a language other than English at home	
		number	percent
United States	**263,230,104**	**48,420,821**	**18.4%**
Alabama	4,087,909	138,663	3.4
Alaska	581,706	73,047	12.6
Arizona	5,031,761	1,328,297	26.4
Arkansas	2,460,507	113,149	4.6
California	32,115,612	13,102,411	40.8
Colorado	4,123,589	617,720	15.0
Connecticut	3,157,963	560,366	17.7
Delaware	738,327	74,973	10.2
District of Columbia	495,397	88,109	17.8
Florida	15,572,360	3,764,706	24.2
Georgia	7,779,928	821,758	10.6
Hawaii	1,136,645	268,087	23.6
Idaho	1,229,675	128,393	10.4
Illinois	11,442,014	2,313,351	20.2
Indiana	5,595,593	438,482	7.8
Iowa	2,660,537	149,998	5.6
Kansas	2,450,103	201,887	8.2
Kentucky	3,732,957	148,857	4.0
Louisiana	4,038,853	316,862	7.8
Maine	1,203,618	88,425	7.3
Maryland	5,006,754	652,545	13.0
Massachusetts	5,822,123	1,124,309	19.3
Michigan	9,178,031	786,842	8.6
Minnesota	4,591,314	424,029	9.2
Mississippi	2,577,551	78,378	3.0
Missouri	5,159,771	273,669	5.3
Montana	840,297	34,548	4.1
Nebraska	1,568,543	123,090	7.8
Nevada	2,045,157	490,928	24.0
New Hampshire	1,179,322	95,246	8.1
New Jersey	7,887,106	2,072,342	26.3
New Mexico	1,708,107	615,597	36.0
New York	17,394,711	4,778,534	27.5
North Carolina	7,557,056	621,011	8.2
North Dakota	572,574	32,895	5.7
Ohio	10,396,176	580,903	5.6
Oklahoma	3,162,666	217,707	6.9
Oregon	3,256,681	405,794	12.5

(continued)

	total aged 5 or older	speak a language other than English at home	
		number	percent
Pennsylvania	11,218,258	912,895	8.1%
Rhode Island	976,471	188,914	19.3
South Carolina	3,736,487	181,132	4.8
South Dakota	683,219	33,216	4.9
Tennessee	5,309,621	250,169	4.7
Texas	19,751,381	6,417,699	32.5
Utah	2,082,635	246,884	11.9
Vermont	567,271	29,059	5.1
Virginia	6,667,441	798,402	12.0
Washington	5,600,233	769,066	13.7
West Virginia	1,663,592	35,072	2.1
Wisconsin	4,978,150	389,410	7.8
Wyoming	456,351	22,995	5.0

Source: Bureau of the Census, 2003 American Community Survey, Internet site http://factfinder.census.gov/servlet/ DatasetMainPageServlet?_lang=en&_ts=143386397087&_ds_name=ACS_2003_EST_G00_&_program=; calculations by New Strategist

Spending Varies Greatly by Race and Hispanic Origin

Asian, black, Hispanic, and non-Hispanic white and "other" households spend differently for a variety of reasons. Household composition differs among the racial and ethnic groups, determining the number of earners in the home and household incomes. Educational attainment also varies by race and ethnicity, with better-educated groups earning and spending more.

Asian households spend the most—10 percent more than the average household. Non-Hispanic white and other households (which also include Asians), spend 6 percent more than average. Black households spend 30 percent less than average, while the spending of Hispanic households is 15 percent below average.

By product and service category, spending varies greatly among the racial and ethnic groups. Hispanics and blacks account for roughly 30 percent of the market for infants' clothes. (The two groups overlap somewhat because Hispanics may be of any race and some are black.) Hispanics and blacks also account for approximately 30 percent of the shoe market. Although Asians are the smallest minority examined by the Consumer Expenditure Survey, they account for a larger share of the education market than either blacks or Hispanics.

■ The racial and ethnic diversity of consumer markets is growing rapidly. Only by understanding the unique spending patterns of each group can businesses succeed in fulfilling consumer wants and needs.

Asians spend the most, blacks the least

(average annual spending of consumer units by race and Hispanic origin, 2003)

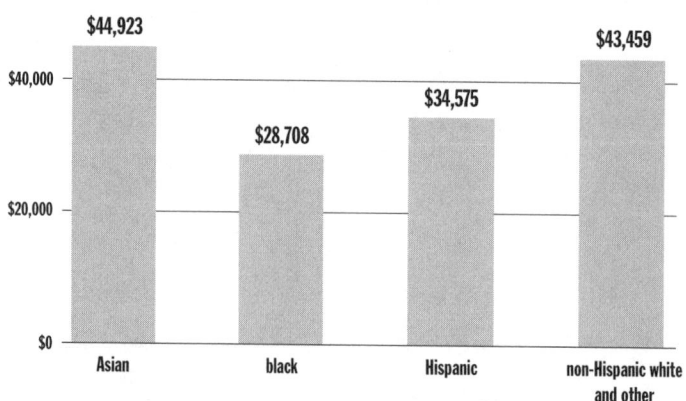

Table 6.121 Average Spending by Race and Hispanic Origin of Householder, 2003

(average annual spending of consumer units (CU) by product and service category and by race and Hispanic origin of consumer unit reference person, 2003)

	total consumer units	Asian	black	Hispanic	non-Hispanic white and other
Number of consumer units (000)	115,356	3,573	13,743	11,727	90,019
Number of persons per consumer unit	2.5	2.8	2.6	3.3	2.4
Average income before taxes	$51,128	$60,393	$34,485	$37,150	$55,463
Average annual spending	40,817	44,923	28,708	34,575	43,459
FOOD	5,340	6,285	4,007	5,717	5,486
Food at home	3,129	3,302	2,664	3,597	3,134
Cereals and bakery products	442	437	370	486	447
Cereals and cereal products	150	180	139	183	147
Bakery products	292	257	231	303	300
Meats, poultry, fish, and eggs	825	978	882	1,059	783
Beef	246	193	232	327	236
Pork	171	174	206	212	159
Other meats	102	81	90	113	102
Poultry	145	182	177	190	133
Fish and seafood	124	304	140	158	117
Eggs	37	43	36	59	34
Dairy products	328	247	227	374	337
Fresh milk and cream	127	112	94	160	127
Other dairy products	201	136	133	214	210
Fruits and vegetables	535	788	438	686	529
Fresh fruits	171	275	128	231	169
Fresh vegetables	172	322	133	240	168
Processed fruits	108	123	100	131	106
Processed vegetables	84	68	77	83	85
Other food at home	999	852	747	992	1,038
Sugar and other sweets	119	102	93	128	122
Fats and oils	86	63	80	97	85
Miscellaneous foods	490	400	360	452	514
Nonalcoholic beverages	268	248	202	289	275
Food prepared by consumer unit on trips	36	40	12	25	41
Food away from home	2,211	2,983	1,343	2,120	2,353
ALCOHOLIC BEVERAGES	391	308	169	315	437
HOUSING	13,432	16,326	10,622	12,300	14,005
Shelter	7,887	10,902	6,117	7,672	8,185
Owned dwellings	5,263	6,835	3,042	3,889	5,775
Mortgage interest and charges	2,954	4,348	1,848	2,471	3,182
Property taxes	1,344	1,713	748	779	1,507
Maintenance, repair, insurance, other expenses	965	774	446	638	1,086
Rented dwellings	2,179	3,661	2,946	3,560	1,889
Other lodging	445	406	129	224	521
Utilities, fuels, and public services	2,811	2,536	2,910	2,490	2,837
Natural gas	392	385	465	301	392
Electricity	1,028	780	1,094	860	1,039

(continued)

	total consumer units	Asian	black	Hispanic	non-Hispanic white and other
Fuel oil and other fuels	$110	$27	$46	$57	$126
Telephone	956	1,026	1,027	968	944
Water and other public services	326	318	278	305	336
Household services	**707**	**783**	**453**	**454**	**779**
Personal services	294	381	247	238	308
Other household services	414	403	206	216	471
Housekeeping supplies	**529**	**471**	**357**	**476**	**563**
Laundry and cleaning supplies	132	96	137	165	127
Other household products	263	228	168	199	287
Postage and stationery	133	146	53	111	148
Household furnishings and equipment	**1,497**	**1,634**	**785**	**1,208**	**1,642**
Household textiles	113	67	61	89	125
Furniture	401	334	234	403	426
Floor coverings	52	21	11	19	62
Major appliances	196	283	118	201	206
Small appliances, misc. housewares	88	128	43	82	95
Miscellaneous household equipment	648	802	318	415	729
APPAREL AND RELATED SERVICES	**1,640**	**1,736**	**1,601**	**1,756**	**1,631**
Men and boys	**372**	**342**	**292**	**435**	**374**
Men, aged 16 or older	282	290	181	307	294
Boys, aged 2 to 15	89	52	112	128	81
Women and girls	**634**	**609**	**565**	**564**	**655**
Women, aged 16 or older	529	538	446	438	554
Girls, aged 2 to 15	106	71	118	126	101
Children under age 2	**81**	**125**	**104**	**121**	**73**
Footwear	**294**	**292**	**440**	**368**	**262**
Other apparel products and services	**258**	**368**	**201**	**268**	**266**
TRANSPORTATION	**7,781**	**7,454**	**5,074**	**6,780**	**8,317**
Vehicle purchases	**3,732**	**2,992**	**2,097**	**3,063**	**4,063**
Cars and trucks, new	2,052	2,156	929	1,441	2,301
Cars and trucks, used	1,611	836	1,164	1,562	1,684
Other vehicles	68	–	4	60	79
Gasoline and motor oil	**1,333**	**1,313**	**1,016**	**1,328**	**1,381**
Other vehicle expenses	**2,331**	**2,383**	**1,728**	**2,057**	**2,458**
Vehicle finance charges	371	282	308	331	385
Maintenance and repairs	619	546	413	520	663
Vehicle insurance	905	989	730	812	944
Vehicle rentals, leases, licenses, other charges	436	565	278	393	466
Public transportation	**385**	**766**	**233**	**331**	**416**
HEALTH CARE	**2,416**	**1,955**	**1,309**	**1,439**	**2,711**
Health insurance	1,252	1,071	774	747	1,389
Medical services	591	476	229	365	675
Drugs	467	340	263	263	524
Medical supplies	107	69	43	65	122
ENTERTAINMENT	**2,060**	**1,713**	**1,007**	**1,245**	**2,326**
Fees and admissions	494	516	163	250	576
Television, radio, and sound equipment	730	621	616	621	761
Pets, toys, and playground equipment	378	197	123	194	441
Other entertainment products and services	457	378	105	179	546

(continued)

	total consumer units	Asian	black	Hispanic	non-Hispanic white and other
PERSONAL CARE PRODUCTS, SERVICES	$527	$520	$461	$490	$541
READING	127	111	52	48	149
EDUCATION	783	1,890	442	477	877
TOBACCO PRODUCTS, SMOKING SUPPLIES	290	119	180	171	322
MISCELLANEOUS	606	432	447	419	655
CASH CONTRIBUTIONS	1,370	1,311	832	594	1,552
PERSONAL INSURANCE AND PENSIONS	4,055	4,762	2,504	2,824	4,450
Life and other personal insurance	397	414	295	160	444
Pensions and Social Security	3,658	4,348	2,209	2,664	4,006
PERSONAL TAXES	2,532	2,882	966	680	3,013
Federal income taxes	1,843	1,993	592	413	2,221
State and local income taxes	502	650	317	197	570
Other taxes	187	240	57	70	222
GIFTS FOR NONHOUSEHOLD MEMBERS	1,007	1,342	524	745	1,115
Food	78	116	32	74	85
Alcoholic beverages	16	12	4	13	18
Housing	220	139	96	138	250
Housekeeping supplies	42	20	13	37	47
Household textiles	13	1	2	5	15
Appliances and misc. housewares	25	20	15	12	28
Major appliances	7	5	8	1	7
Small appliances and misc. housewares	18	15	7	11	21
Miscellaneous household equipment	57	50	15	31	66
Other housing	85	47	50	52	94
Apparel and services	225	179	222	187	231
Males, aged 2 or older	56	57	30	52	60
Females, aged 2 or older	80	53	93	51	82
Children under age 2	39	46	44	49	37
Other apparel products and services	50	24	54	35	52
Jewelry and watches	26	20	21	13	28
All other apparel products and services	25	4	33	21	24
Transportation	60	324	38	142	52
Health care	48	34	22	7	57
Entertainment	69	55	26	42	79
Toys, games, hobbies, and tricycles	26	13	13	13	30
Other entertainment	43	43	14	28	49
Personal care products and services	16	23	8	13	17
Reading	1	1	–	–	2
Education	200	388	45	98	237
All other gifts	74	71	30	33	86

Note: "Other" includes Alaska Natives, American Indians, Asians, Native Hawaiians, and other Pacific Islanders as well as those reporting more than one race. Spending by category will not add to total spending because gift spending is also included in the preceding product and service categories and personal taxes are omitted from the total. (–) means sample is too small to make a reliable estimate. The Bureau of Labor Statistics uses consumer unit rather than household as the sampling unit in the Consumer Expenditure Survey. For the definition of consumer unit, see the glossary.
Source: Bureau of Labor Statistics, 2003 Consumer Expenditure Survey, Internet site http://www.bls.gov/cex/

Table 6.122 Indexed Spending by Race and Hispanic Origin of Householder, 2003

(indexed average annual spending of consumer units by product and service category and race and Hispanic origin of consumer unit reference person, 2003)

	total consumer units	Asian	black	Hispanic	non-Hispanic white and other
Indexed income before taxes	**100**	**118**	**67**	**73**	**108**
Indexed average annual spending	**100**	**110**	**70**	**85**	**106**
FOOD	**100**	**118**	**75**	**107**	**103**
Food at home	**100**	**106**	**85**	**115**	**100**
Cereals and bakery products	100	99	84	110	101
Cereals and cereal products	100	120	93	122	98
Bakery products	100	88	79	104	103
Meats, poultry, fish, and eggs	100	119	107	128	95
Beef	100	78	94	133	96
Pork	100	102	120	124	93
Other meats	100	79	88	111	100
Poultry	100	126	122	131	92
Fish and seafood	100	245	113	127	94
Eggs	100	116	97	159	92
Dairy products	100	75	69	114	103
Fresh milk and cream	100	88	74	126	100
Other dairy products	100	68	66	106	104
Fruits and vegetables	100	147	82	128	99
Fresh fruits	100	161	75	135	99
Fresh vegetables	100	187	77	140	98
Processed fruits	100	114	93	121	98
Processed vegetables	100	81	92	99	101
Other food at home	100	85	75	99	104
Sugar and other sweets	100	86	78	108	103
Fats and oils	100	73	93	113	99
Miscellaneous foods	100	82	73	92	105
Nonalcoholic beverages	100	93	75	108	103
Food prepared by consumer unit on trips	100	111	33	69	114
Food away from home	**100**	**135**	**61**	**96**	**106**
ALCOHOLIC BEVERAGES	**100**	**79**	**43**	**81**	**112**
HOUSING	**100**	**122**	**79**	**92**	**104**
Shelter	**100**	**138**	**78**	**97**	**104**
Owned dwellings	100	130	58	74	110
Mortgage interest and charges	100	147	63	84	108
Property taxes	100	127	56	58	112
Maintenance, repair, insurance, other expenses	100	80	46	66	113
Rented dwellings	100	168	135	163	87
Other lodging	100	91	29	50	117
Utilities, fuels, and public services	**100**	**90**	**104**	**89**	**101**
Natural gas	100	98	119	77	100
Electricity	100	76	106	84	101

(continued)

	total consumer units	Asian	black	Hispanic	non-Hispanic white and other
Fuel oil and other fuels	100	25	42	52	115
Telephone	100	107	107	101	99
Water and other public services	100	98	85	94	103
Household services	**100**	**111**	**64**	**64**	**110**
Personal services	100	130	84	81	105
Other household services	100	97	50	52	114
Housekeeping supplies	**100**	**89**	**67**	**90**	**106**
Laundry and cleaning supplies	100	73	104	125	96
Other household products	100	87	64	76	109
Postage and stationery	100	110	40	83	111
Household furnishings and equipment	**100**	**109**	**52**	**81**	**110**
Household textiles	100	59	54	79	111
Furniture	100	83	58	100	106
Floor coverings	100	40	21	37	119
Major appliances	100	144	60	103	105
Small appliances, misc. housewares	100	145	49	93	108
Miscellaneous household equipment	100	124	49	64	113
APPAREL AND RELATED SERVICES	**100**	**106**	**98**	**107**	**99**
Men and boys	**100**	**92**	**78**	**117**	**101**
Men, aged 16 or older	100	103	64	109	104
Boys, aged 2 to 15	100	58	126	144	91
Women and girls	**100**	**96**	**89**	**89**	**103**
Women, aged 16 or older	100	102	84	83	105
Girls, aged 2 to 15	100	67	111	119	95
Children under age 2	**100**	**154**	**128**	**149**	**90**
Footwear	**100**	**99**	**150**	**125**	**89**
Other apparel products and services	**100**	**143**	**78**	**104**	**103**
TRANSPORTATION	**100**	**96**	**65**	**87**	**107**
Vehicle purchases	**100**	**80**	**56**	**82**	**109**
Cars and trucks, new	100	105	45	70	112
Cars and trucks, used	100	52	72	97	105
Other vehicles	100	–	6	88	116
Gasoline and motor oil	**100**	**98**	**76**	**100**	**104**
Other vehicle expenses	**100**	**102**	**74**	**88**	**105**
Vehicle finance charges	100	76	83	89	104
Maintenance and repairs	100	88	67	84	107
Vehicle insurance	100	109	81	90	104
Vehicle rentals, leases, licenses, other charges	100	130	64	90	107
Public transportation	**100**	**199**	**61**	**86**	**108**
HEALTH CARE	**100**	**81**	**54**	**60**	**112**
Health insurance	100	86	62	60	111
Medical services	100	81	39	62	114
Drugs	100	73	56	56	112
Medical supplies	100	64	40	61	114
ENTERTAINMENT	**100**	**83**	**49**	**60**	**113**
Fees and admissions	100	104	33	51	117
Television, radio, and sound equipment	100	85	84	85	104
Pets, toys, and playground equipment	100	52	33	51	117
Other entertainment products and services	100	83	23	39	119

(continued)

	total consumer units	Asian	black	Hispanic	non-Hispanic white and other
PERSONAL CARE PRODUCTS, SERVICES	100	99	87	93	103
READING	100	87	41	38	117
EDUCATION	100	241	56	61	112
TOBACCO PRODUCTS, SMOKING SUPPLIES	100	41	62	59	111
MISCELLANEOUS	100	71	74	69	108
CASH CONTRIBUTIONS	100	96	61	43	113
PERSONAL INSURANCE AND PENSIONS	100	117	62	70	110
Life and other personal insurance	100	104	74	40	112
Pensions and Social Security	100	119	60	73	110
PERSONAL TAXES	100	114	38	27	119
Federal income taxes	100	108	32	22	121
State and local income taxes	100	129	63	39	114
Other taxes	100	128	30	37	119
GIFTS FOR NONHOUSEHOLD MEMBERS	100	133	52	74	111
Food	100	149	41	95	109
Alcoholic beverages	100	75	25	81	113
Housing	100	63	44	63	114
Housekeeping supplies	100	48	31	88	112
Household textiles	100	8	15	38	115
Appliances and misc. housewares	100	80	60	48	112
Major appliances	100	71	114	14	100
Small appliances and misc. housewares	100	83	39	61	117
Miscellaneous household equipment	100	88	26	54	116
Other housing	100	55	59	61	111
Apparel and services	100	80	99	83	103
Males, aged 2 or older	100	102	54	93	107
Females, aged 2 or older	100	66	116	64	103
Children under age 2	100	118	113	126	95
Other apparel products and services	100	48	108	70	104
Jewelry and watches	100	77	81	50	108
All other apparel products and services	100	16	132	84	96
Transportation	100	540	63	237	87
Health care	100	71	46	15	119
Entertainment	100	80	38	61	114
Toys, games, hobbies, and tricycles	100	50	50	50	115
Other entertainment	100	100	33	65	114
Personal care products and services	100	144	50	81	106
Reading	100	100	–	–	200
Education	100	194	23	49	119
All other gifts	100	96	41	45	116

Note: The index is calculated by dividing the spending of each race/Hispanic origin group by average spending and multiplying by 100. An index of 125 indicates spending by the race/Hispanic origin group that is 25 percent above average. An index of 75 indicates spending that is 25 percent below average. "Other" includes Alaska Natives, American Indians, Asians, Native Hawaiians, and other Pacific Islanders as well as those reporting more than one race. (–) means sample is too small to make a reliable estimate. The Bureau of Labor Statistics uses consumer unit rather than household as the sampling unit in the Consumer Expenditure Survey. For the definition of consumer unit, see the glossary.
Source: Calculations by New Strategist based on the Bureau of Labor Statistics' 2003 Consumer Expenditure Survey, Internet site http://www.bls.gov/cex/

Table 6.123 Market Shares by Race and Hispanic Origin, 2003

(percentage of total annual spending accounted for by race and Hispanic origin groups, by product and service category, 2003)

	total consumer units	Asian	black	Hispanic	non-Hispanic white and other
Share of consumer units	100.0%	3.1%	11.9%	10.2%	78.0%
Share of income before taxes	100.0	3.7	8.0	7.4	84.7
Share of annual spending	100.0	3.4	8.4	8.6	83.1
FOOD	100.0	3.6	8.9	10.9	80.2
Food at home	100.0	3.3	10.1	11.7	78.2
Cereals and bakery products	100.0	3.1	10.0	11.2	78.9
Cereals and cereal products	100.0	3.7	11.0	12.4	76.5
Bakery products	100.0	2.7	9.4	10.5	80.2
Meats, poultry, fish, and eggs	100.0	3.7	12.7	13.0	74.1
Beef	100.0	2.4	11.2	13.5	74.9
Pork	100.0	3.2	14.4	12.6	72.6
Other meats	100.0	2.5	10.5	11.3	78.0
Poultry	100.0	3.9	14.5	13.3	71.6
Fish and seafood	100.0	7.6	13.5	13.0	73.6
Eggs	100.0	3.6	11.6	16.2	71.7
Dairy products	100.0	2.3	8.2	11.6	80.2
Fresh milk and cream	100.0	2.7	8.8	12.8	78.0
Other dairy products	100.0	2.1	7.9	10.8	81.5
Fruits and vegetables	100.0	4.6	9.8	13.0	77.2
Fresh fruits	100.0	5.0	8.9	13.7	77.1
Fresh vegetables	100.0	5.8	9.2	14.2	76.2
Processed fruits	100.0	3.5	11.0	12.3	76.6
Processed vegetables	100.0	2.5	10.9	10.0	79.0
Other food at home	100.0	2.6	8.9	10.1	81.1
Sugar and other sweets	100.0	2.7	9.3	10.9	80.0
Fats and oils	100.0	2.3	11.1	11.5	77.1
Miscellaneous foods	100.0	2.5	8.8	9.4	81.9
Nonalcoholic beverages	100.0	2.9	9.0	11.0	80.1
Food prepared by consumer unit on trips	100.0	3.4	4.0	7.1	88.9
Food away from home	100.0	4.2	7.2	9.7	83.0
ALCOHOLIC BEVERAGES	100.0	2.4	5.1	8.2	87.2
HOUSING	100.0	3.8	9.4	9.3	81.4
Shelter	100.0	4.3	9.2	9.9	81.0
Owned dwellings	100.0	4.0	6.9	7.5	85.6
Mortgage interest and charges	100.0	4.6	7.5	8.5	84.1
Property taxes	100.0	3.9	6.6	5.9	87.5
Maintenance, repair, insurance, other expenses	100.0	2.5	5.5	6.7	87.8
Rented dwellings	100.0	5.2	16.1	16.6	67.7
Other lodging	100.0	2.8	3.5	5.1	91.4
Utilities, fuels, and public services	100.0	2.8	12.3	9.0	78.8
Natural gas	100.0	3.0	14.1	7.8	78.0
Electricity	100.0	2.4	12.7	8.5	78.9

(continued)

	total consumer units	Asian	black	Hispanic	non-Hispanic white and other
Fuel oil and other fuels	100.0%	0.8%	5.0%	5.3%	89.4%
Telephone	100.0	3.3	12.8	10.3	77.1
Water and other public services	100.0	3.0	10.2	9.5	80.4
Household services	**100.0**	**3.4**	**7.6**	**6.5**	**86.0**
Personal services	100.0	4.0	10.0	8.2	81.8
Other household services	100.0	3.0	5.9	5.3	88.8
Housekeeping supplies	**100.0**	**2.8**	**8.0**	**9.1**	**83.1**
Laundry and cleaning supplies	100.0	2.3	12.4	12.7	75.1
Other household products	100.0	2.7	7.6	7.7	85.2
Postage and stationery	100.0	3.4	4.7	8.5	86.8
Household furnishings and equipment	**100.0**	**3.4**	**6.2**	**8.2**	**85.6**
Household textiles	100.0	1.8	6.4	8.0	86.3
Furniture	100.0	2.6	7.0	10.2	82.9
Floor coverings	100.0	1.3	2.5	3.7	93.0
Major appliances	100.0	4.5	7.2	10.4	82.0
Small appliances, misc. housewares	100.0	4.5	5.8	9.5	84.2
Miscellaneous household equipment	100.0	3.8	5.8	6.5	87.8
APPAREL AND RELATED SERVICES	**100.0**	**3.3**	**11.6**	**10.9**	**77.6**
Men and boys	**100.0**	**2.8**	**9.4**	**11.9**	**78.5**
Men, aged 16 or older	100.0	3.2	7.6	11.1	81.4
Boys, aged 2 to 15	100.0	1.8	15.0	14.6	71.0
Women and girls	**100.0**	**3.0**	**10.6**	**9.0**	**80.6**
Women, aged 16 or older	100.0	3.2	10.0	8.4	81.7
Girls, aged 2 to 15	100.0	2.1	13.3	12.1	74.4
Children under age 2	**100.0**	**4.8**	**15.3**	**15.2**	**70.3**
Footwear	**100.0**	**3.1**	**17.8**	**12.7**	**69.5**
Other apparel products and services	**100.0**	**4.4**	**9.3**	**10.6**	**80.5**
TRANSPORTATION	**100.0**	**3.0**	**7.8**	**8.9**	**83.4**
Vehicle purchases	**100.0**	**2.5**	**6.7**	**8.3**	**85.0**
Cars and trucks, new	100.0	3.3	5.4	7.1	87.5
Cars and trucks, used	100.0	1.6	8.6	9.9	81.6
Other vehicles	100.0	–	0.7	9.0	90.7
Gasoline and motor oil	**100.0**	**3.1**	**9.1**	**10.1**	**80.8**
Other vehicle expenses	**100.0**	**3.2**	**8.8**	**9.0**	**82.3**
Vehicle finance charges	100.0	2.4	9.9	9.1	81.0
Maintenance and repairs	100.0	2.7	7.9	8.5	83.6
Vehicle insurance	100.0	3.4	9.6	9.1	81.4
Vehicle rentals, leases, licenses, other charges	100.0	4.0	7.6	9.2	83.4
Public transportation	**100.0**	**6.2**	**7.2**	**8.7**	**84.3**
HEALTH CARE	**100.0**	**2.5**	**6.5**	**6.1**	**87.6**
Health insurance	100.0	2.6	7.4	6.1	86.6
Medical services	100.0	2.5	4.6	6.3	89.1
Drugs	100.0	2.3	6.7	5.7	87.6
Medical supplies	100.0	2.0	4.8	6.2	89.0
ENTERTAINMENT	**100.0**	**2.6**	**5.8**	**6.1**	**88.1**
Fees and admissions	100.0	3.2	3.9	5.1	91.0
Television, radio, and sound equipment	100.0	2.6	10.1	8.6	81.3
Pets, toys, and playground equipment	100.0	1.6	3.9	5.2	91.0
Other entertainment products and services	100.0	2.6	2.7	4.0	93.2

(continued)

	total consumer units	Asian	black	Hispanic	non-Hispanic white and other
PERSONAL CARE PRODUCTS, SERVICES	100.0%	3.1%	10.4%	9.5%	80.1%
READING	100.0	2.7	4.9	3.8	91.6
EDUCATION	100.0	7.5	6.7	6.2	87.4
TOBACCO PRODUCTS, SMOKING SUPPLIES	100.0	1.3	7.4	6.0	86.6
MISCELLANEOUS	100.0	2.2	8.8	7.0	84.3
CASH CONTRIBUTIONS	100.0	3.0	7.2	4.4	88.4
PERSONAL INSURANCE AND PENSIONS	100.0	3.6	7.4	7.1	85.6
Life and other personal insurance	100.0	3.2	8.9	4.1	87.3
Pensions and Social Security	100.0	3.7	7.2	7.4	85.5
PERSONAL TAXES	100.0	3.5	4.5	2.7	92.9
Federal income taxes	100.0	3.3	3.8	2.3	94.0
State and local income taxes	100.0	4.0	7.5	4.0	88.6
Other taxes	100.0	4.0	3.6	3.8	92.6
GIFTS FOR NONHOUSEHOLD MEMBERS	100.0	4.1	6.2	7.5	86.4
Food	100.0	4.6	4.9	9.6	85.0
Alcoholic beverages	100.0	2.3	3.0	8.3	87.8
Housing	100.0	2.0	5.2	6.4	88.7
Housekeeping supplies	100.0	1.5	3.7	9.0	87.3
Household textiles	100.0	0.2	1.8	3.9	90.0
Appliances and misc. housewares	100.0	2.5	7.1	4.9	87.4
Major appliances	100.0	2.2	13.6	1.5	78.0
Small appliances and misc. housewares	100.0	2.6	4.6	6.2	91.0
Miscellaneous household equipment	100.0	2.7	3.1	5.5	90.4
Other housing	100.0	1.7	7.0	6.2	86.3
Apparel and services	100.0	2.5	11.8	8.4	80.1
Males, aged 2 or older	100.0	3.2	6.4	9.4	83.6
Females, aged 2 or older	100.0	2.1	13.8	6.5	80.0
Children under age 2	100.0	3.7	13.4	12.8	74.0
Other apparel products and services	100.0	1.5	12.9	7.1	81.2
Jewelry and watches	100.0	2.4	9.6	5.1	84.0
All other apparel products and services	100.0	0.5	15.7	8.5	74.9
Transportation	100.0	16.7	7.5	24.1	67.6
Health care	100.0	2.2	5.5	1.5	92.7
Entertainment	100.0	2.5	4.5	6.2	89.3
Toys, games, hobbies, and tricycles	100.0	1.5	6.0	5.1	90.0
Other entertainment	100.0	3.1	3.9	6.6	88.9
Personal care products and services	100.0	4.5	6.0	8.3	82.9
Reading	100.0	3.1	–	–	–
Education	100.0	6.0	2.7	5.0	92.5
All other gifts	100.0	3.0	4.8	4.5	90.7

Note: Numbers may not add to total because of rounding. "Other" includes Alaska Natives, American Indians, Asians, Native Hawaiians, and other Pacific Islanders as well as those reporting more than one race. (–) means sample is too small to make a reliable estimate. The Bureau of Labor Statistics uses consumer unit rather than household as the sampling unit in the Consumer Expenditure Survey. For the definition of consumer unit, see the glossary.
Source: Calculations by New Strategist based on the Bureau of Labor Statistics' 2003 Consumer Expenditure Survey, Internet site http://www.bls.gov/cex/

The Median Net Worth of Americans Stood at $86,100 in 2001

The median net worth (assets minus debts) of American households varies sharply by race and Hispanic origin of householder. The median net worth of non-Hispanic white households stood at $120,900 in 2001 (the latest data available), while that of nonwhite and Hispanic households was a much smaller $17,100. The net worth of non-Hispanic white households is much higher than that of others because non-Hispanic whites are more likely to own a home. Home equity accounts for the largest share of Americans' net worth.

The average household had only $28,000 in financial assets in 2001, with transaction accounts (such as checking accounts) owned by the largest share. The 52 percent majority of households own retirement accounts, but they are worth a median of just $29,000.

Sixty-eight percent of households owned a home in 2001. The median value of the primary residence stood at $122,000. Three out of four households were in debt, owing a median of $38,775 in 2001. Mortgage debt accounts for the largest amount owed.

The 60 percent majority of workers neither owns an IRA nor participates in a 401(k)-type retirement plan. This explains why only 21 percent of workers say they are "very confident" they will have enough money to live comfortably throughout retirement.

■ Among Americans aged 65 or older, 91 percent receive Social Security benefits. Only 37 percent receive retirement income from pensions or IRAs.

Net worth varies sharply by race and Hispanic origin

(median net worth of total, non-Hispanic white, and nonwhite/Hispanic households, 2001)

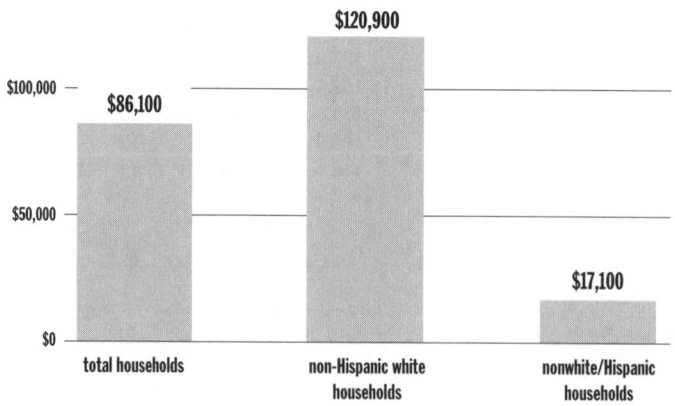

Table 6.124 Net Worth, Assets, and Debt of Households by Race and Hispanic Origin, 2001

(median net worth, median value of assets for owners, and median amount of debt for debtors, for households by race and Hispanic origin of householder, and index of race/Hispanic origin to total, 2001)

	total households	non-Hispanic whites		nonwhites/Hispanics	
		median	index	median	index
Median net worth	**$86,100**	**$120,900**	**140**	**$17,100**	**20**
Median value of financial assets	28,000	38,500	138	7,200	26
Median value of nonfinancial assets	113,500	131,500	116	58,200	51
Median amount of debt	38,775	44,478	115	20,000	52

Note: The index is calculated by dividing the race/Hispanic origin figure by the total figure and multiplying by 100.
Source: Federal Reserve Board, "Recent Changes in U.S. Family Finances: Evidence from the 1998 and 2001 Survey of Consumer Finances," Federal Reserve Bulletin, January 2003; calculations by New Strategist

Table 6.125 Financial Assets of Total Households, 2001

(percent of total households owning financial assets, and median value of assets for owners, 2001)

	percent owning asset	median value
Any financial asset	**93.1%**	**$28,000**
Transaction accounts	90.9	4,000
Certificates of deposit	15.7	15,000
Savings bonds	16.7	1,000
Bonds	3.0	43,500
Stocks	21.3	20,000
Mutual funds	17.7	35,000
Retirement accounts	52.2	29,000
Life insurance	28.0	10,000
Other managed assets	6.6	70,000
Other financial assets	9.3	4,000

Source: Federal Reserve Board, "Recent Changes in U.S. Family Finances: Evidence from the 1998 and 2001 Survey of Consumer Finances," Federal Reserve Bulletin, January 2003; calculations by New Strategist

Table 6.126 Nonfinancial Assets of Total Households, 2001

(percent of total households owning nonfinancial assets, and median value of assets for owners, 2001)

	percent owning asset	median value
Any nonfinancial asset	**90.7%**	**$113,500**
Vehicles	84.8	13,500
Primary residence	67.7	122,000
Other residential property	11.3	80,000
Nonresidential property	8.3	49,000
Business	11.8	100,000
Other nonfinancial asset	7.6	12,000

Source: Federal Reserve Board, "Recent Changes in U.S. Family Finances: Evidence from the 1998 and 2001 Survey of Consumer Finances," Federal Reserve Bulletin, *January 2003*

Table 6.127 Debt of Total Households, 2001

(percent of total households with debt, and median amount of debt for those with debts, 2001)

	percent with debt	median amount
Any debt	**75.1%**	**$38,775**
Home-secured	44.6	70,000
Other residential property	4.7	40,000
Installment loans	45.2	9,680
Other lines of credit	44.4	1,900
Credit card	1.5	3,900
Other debt	7.2	3,000

Source: Federal Reserve Board, "Recent Changes in U.S. Family Finances: Evidence from the 1998 and 2001 Survey of Consumer Finances," Federal Reserve Bulletin, *January 2003*

Table 6.128 Ownership of IRAs and 401(k)-Type Plans, 2002

(percent of total workers aged 21 to 64 owning IRAs and 401(k)-type plans, 2002)

	total workers
IRA or 401(k)-type plan	**40.4%**
IRA only	9.6
401(k)-type plan only	21.7
Both IRA and 401(k)-type plan	9.2
Neither IRA nor 401(k)-type plan	**59.6**

Source: Employee Benefit Research Institute, "401(k)-Type Plan and IRA Ownership," by Craig Copeland, EBRI Notes, Vol. 26, No. 1, January 2005; Internet site http://www.ebri.org/

Table 6.129 Retirement Confidence among Total Workers, 2003

(percent distribution of total workers aged 25 or older by degree of confidence in retirement savings and planning, 2003)

	very confident	somewhat confident	not too confident	not at all confident
Having enough money to live comfortably throughout retirement years	21%	45%	17%	16%
Having enough money to take care of basic expenses	33	45	10	11
Doing a good job of preparing financially for retirement	24	45	15	14
Not outliving retirement savings	20	42	16	17
Having enough money to take care of medical expenses	18	40	22	19
Having enough money to pay for long-term care	14	34	26	24

Source: The 2003 Minority Retirement Confidence Survey Summary of Findings, Employee Benefit Research Institute, American Savings Education Council, and Mathew Greenwald & Associates; Internet site http://www.ebri.org/surveys/rcs/2003/

Table 6.130 Sources of Income for Total People Aged 65 or Older, 2003

(number and percent of people aged 65 or older with income by selected source and average income for those with income, ranked by number receiving income, 2003; people in thousands as of 2004)

	number with income	percent with income	average amount received by those with income
Total people aged 65 or older with income	**33,779**	**100.0%**	**$14,664**
Social Security	30,882	91.4	10,258
Interest	18,407	54.5	1,642
Retirement income, including pensions	12,339	36.5	9,048
Dividends	6,855	20.3	1,822
Earnings	6,074	18.0	16,177
Rents, royalties, estates, or trusts	2,776	8.2	2,183
Survivor's benefits	1,736	5.1	6,233
SSI (Supplemental Security Income)	1,225	3.6	3,637
Veteran's benefits	940	2.8	4,982

Source: Bureau of the Census, 2004 Current Population Survey, Internet site http://pubdb3.census.gov/macro/032004/perinc/new09_001.htm; calculations by New Strategist

Attitudes and Behavior

The attitudes and lifestyles of Americans differ by race and Hispanic origin, although not as much as incomes, wealth, and education. Regardless of race or Hispanic origin, most of the population is at least somewhat religious, most are online, and most are busy trying to manage home and family life in just 24 hours a day.

The new time use survey of the Bureau of Labor Statistics reveals interesting differences in how people spend their day by race and Hispanic origin. Blacks, Hispanics, and whites spend the largest part of each day in personal care activities (including sleeping), followed by leisure activities and work. But whites spend more time eating and drinking than blacks or Hispanics do because the white population is older and more likely to be retired. Hispanics spend more time than others caring for household members because so many of their households include children. Blacks spend more time than Hispanics or whites in organizational, civic, and religious activities.

Blacks are most likely to identify themselves as "religious," with 49 percent doing so according to the American Religious Identification Survey. Regardless of race or Hispanic origin, most Americans use a computer and are online, according to the Pew Internet & American Life Project. Among voters in the 2004 presidential election, non-Hispanic whites accounted for fully 79 percent of those who went to the polls.

Most voters are non-Hispanic white

(percent distribution of voters by race and Hispanic origin, November 2004; shares do not add to 100 percent because not all races are shown and Hispanics may be of any race)

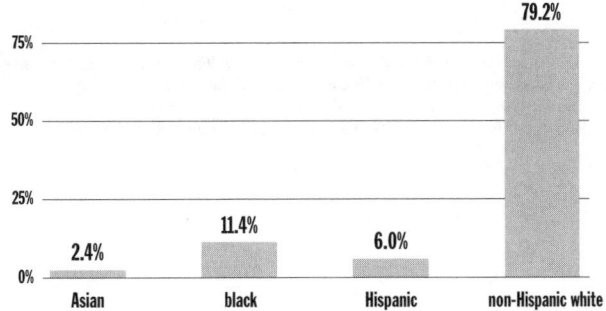

Table 7.1 Average Hours Per Day Spent in Primary Activities by Race and Hispanic Origin, 2003

(average number of hours per day spent in primary activities by people aged 15 or older by race and Hispanic origin, and index of hours to national average, 2003)

	total people	black	Hispanic	white
Hours				
Personal care activities	9.34	9.83	9.70	9.27
Eating and drinking	1.21	0.81	1.12	1.26
Household activities	1.83	1.30	1.82	1.93
Purchasing goods and services	0.81	0.70	0.81	0.83
Caring for and helping household members	0.55	0.54	0.72	0.54
Caring for and helping non-household members	0.29	0.37	0.21	0.28
Working and work-related activities	3.69	3.31	3.66	3.72
Educational activities	0.47	0.66	0.57	0.42
Organizational, civic, and religious activities	0.32	0.51	0.23	0.30
Leisure and sports	5.11	5.55	4.85	5.07
Telephone calls, mail, and e-mail	0.19	0.22	0.12	0.18
Other activities	0.19	0.20	0.19	0.19
Index				
Personal care activities	100	105	104	99
Eating and drinking	100	67	93	104
Household activities	100	71	99	105
Purchasing goods and services	100	86	100	102
Caring for and helping household members	100	98	131	98
Caring for and helping non-household members	100	128	72	97
Working and work-related activities	100	90	99	101
Educational activities	100	140	121	89
Organizational, civic, and religious activities	100	159	72	94
Leisure and sports	100	109	95	99
Telephone calls, mail, and e-mail	100	116	63	95
Other activities	100	105	100	100

Note: Primary activities are those respondents identified as their main activity. Other activities done simultaneously are not included. All major activities include related travel time. The index is calculated by dividing the hours spent by the race and Hispanic origin group per activity by the overall average for that activity and multiplying by 100.
Source: Bureau of Labor Statistics, American Time Use Survey, Internet site http://www.bls.gov/tus/home.htm; calculations by New Strategist

Table 7.2 Average Hours Per Day Men Spend in Primary Activities by Race and Hispanic Origin, 2003

(average number of hours per day spent in primary activities by men aged 15 or older by race and Hispanic origin, and index of hours to national average, 2003)

	men			
	total	black	Hispanic	white
Hours				
Personal care activities	9.13	9.41	9.64	9.08
Eating and drinking	1.24	0.84	1.15	1.29
Household activities	1.33	0.93	1.02	1.40
Purchasing goods and services	0.68	0.56	0.71	0.70
Caring for and helping household members	0.34	0.30	0.42	0.33
Caring for and helping nonhousehold members	0.26	0.43	0.21	0.24
Working and work-related activities	4.57	3.88	4.55	4.66
Educational activities	0.45	–	–	0.41
Organizational, civic, and religious activities	0.29	0.57	0.21	0.26
Leisure and sports	5.41	6.13	5.28	5.32
Telephone calls, mail, and e-mail	0.13	0.14	0.12	0.13
Other activities	0.18	0.18	0.19	0.18
Index				
Personal care activities	100	103	106	99
Eating and drinking	100	68	93	104
Household activities	100	70	77	105
Purchasing goods and services	100	82	104	103
Caring for and helping household members	100	88	124	97
Caring for and helping nonhousehold members	100	165	81	92
Working and work-related activities	100	85	100	102
Educational activities	100	–	–	91
Organizational, civic, and religious activities	100	197	72	90
Leisure and sports	100	113	98	98
Telephone calls, mail, and e-mail	100	108	92	100
Other activities	100	100	106	100

Note: Primary activities are those respondents identified as their main activity. Other activities done simultaneously are not included. All major activities include related travel time. The index is calculated by dividing the hours spent by the race and Hispanic origin group per activity by the overall average for that activity and multiplying by 100. (–) means sample is too small to make a reliable estimate.
Source: Bureau of Labor Statistics, American Time Use Survey, Internet site http://www.bls.gov/tus/home.htm; calculations by New Strategist

Table 7.3 Average Hours Per Day Women Spend in Primary Activities by Race and Hispanic Origin, 2003

(average number of hours per day spent in primary activities by women aged 15 or older by race and Hispanic origin, and index of hours to national average, 2003)

	women			
	total	black	Hispanic	white
Hours				
Personal care activities	9.54	10.17	9.77	9.45
Eating and drinking	1.18	0.79	1.08	1.23
Household activities	2.30	1.59	2.67	2.43
Purchasing goods and services	0.94	0.82	0.91	0.96
Caring for and helping household members	0.75	0.72	1.02	0.74
Caring for and helping nonhousehold members	0.31	0.32	0.22	0.31
Working and work-related activities	2.87	2.86	2.74	2.83
Educational activities	0.50	0.68	0.63	0.44
Organizational, civic, and religious activities	0.35	0.47	0.25	0.33
Leisure and sports	4.83	5.09	4.41	4.83
Telephone calls, mail, and e-mail	0.24	0.29	0.12	0.24
Other activities	0.20	0.22	0.19	0.20
Index				
Personal care activities	100	107	102	99
Eating and drinking	100	67	92	104
Household activities	100	69	116	106
Purchasing goods and services	100	87	97	102
Caring for and helping household members	100	96	136	99
Caring for and helping nonhousehold members	100	103	71	100
Working and work-related activities	100	100	95	99
Educational activities	100	136	126	88
Organizational, civic, and religious activities	100	134	71	94
Leisure and sports	100	105	91	100
Telephone calls, mail, and e-mail	100	121	50	100
Other activities	100	110	95	100

Note: Primary activities are those respondents identified as their main activity. Other activities done simultaneously are not included. All major activities include related travel time. The index is calculated by dividing the hours spent by the race and Hispanic origin group per activity by the overall average for that activity and multiplying by 100.
Source: Bureau of Labor Statistics, American Time Use Survey, Internet site http://www.bls.gov/tus/home.htm; calculations by New Strategist

Table 7.4 Religious Groups by Race and Hispanic Origin, 2001

(total number of adults identifying themselves as belonging to selected religious groups and percent distribution by race and Hispanic origin, 2001; numbers in thousands)

	number	percent distribution by race and Hispanic origin				
		Asian	non-Hispanic black	Hispanic	non-Hispanic white	other
Total U.S. adults	**208,000**	**3%**	**10%**	**12%**	**70%**	**5%**
Catholic	50,873	3	3	29	64	2
Baptist	33,830	1	29	3	64	2
No religion	29,481	5	8	11	73	4
Christian	14,190	3	12	14	67	3
Methodist	14,140	1	11	1	86	1
Lutheran	9,580	0	1	1	96	1
Presbyterian	5,596	2	3	3	91	1
Protestant	4,647	0	4	6	87	3
Pentecostal	4,407	0	22	17	58	3
Episcopalian/Anglican	3,451	1	9	0	89	1
Jewish	2,831	1	1	5	92	1
Mormon	2,787	0	0	8	91	1
Churches of Christ	2,503	1	6	2	89	2
Nondenominational	2,489	1	11	13	73	2
Congregational/UCC	1,378	0	0	5	93	2
Jehovah's Witnesses	1,331	0	37	14	46	3
Assemblies of God	1,105	5	5	8	80	2
Muslim/Islamic	1,104	34	27	10	15	14
Buddhist	1,082	61	4	2	32	1
Evangelical/born again	1,032	0	3	20	77	0
Church of God	944	0	12	4	84	0
Seventh Day Adventist	724	0	26	7	67	0

(continued)

	number	percent distribution by religious group				
		Asian	non-Hispanic black	Hispanic	non-Hispanic white	other
Total U.S. adults	**100.0%**	**100.0%**	**100.0%**	**100.0%**	**100.0%**	**100.0%**
Catholic	24.5	24.5	7.3	59.1	22.4	9.8
Baptist	16.3	5.4	47.2	4.1	14.9	6.5
No religion	14.2	23.6	11.3	13.0	14.8	11.3
Christian	6.8	6.8	8.2	8.0	6.5	4.1
Methodist	6.8	2.3	7.5	0.6	8.4	1.4
Lutheran	4.6	0.0	0.5	0.4	6.3	0.9
Presbyterian	2.7	1.8	0.8	0.7	3.5	0.5
Protestant	2.2	0.0	0.9	1.1	2.8	1.3
Pentecostal	2.1	0.0	4.7	3.0	1.8	1.3
Episcopalian/Anglican	1.7	0.6	1.5	0.0	2.1	0.3
Jewish	1.4	0.5	0.1	0.6	1.8	0.3
Mormon	1.3	0.0	0.0	0.9	1.7	0.3
Churches of Christ	1.2	0.4	0.7	0.2	1.5	0.5
Nondenominational	1.2	0.4	1.3	1.3	1.2	0.5
Congregational/UCC	0.7	0.0	0.0	0.3	0.9	0.3
Jehovah's Witnesses	0.6	0.0	2.4	0.7	0.4	0.4
Assemblies of God	0.5	0.9	0.3	0.4	0.6	0.2
Muslim/Islamic	0.5	6.0	1.4	0.4	0.1	1.5
Buddhist	0.5	10.6	0.2	0.1	0.2	0.1
Evangelical/born again	0.5	0.0	0.1	0.8	0.5	0.0
Church of God	0.5	0.0	0.5	0.2	0.5	0.0
Seventh Day Adventist	0.3	0.0	0.9	0.2	0.3	0.0

Note: Figures will not add to total because not all religions are shown.
Source: American Religious Identification Survey 2001, Barry A. Kosmin, Egon Mayer, and Ariela Keysar. For further details see:
Barry A. Kosmin and Ariela Keysar, Religion in a Free Market, *Paramount Market Publishing, Inc. Ithaca, NY, 2006.*

Table 7.5 Attitude toward Religion by Race and Hispanic Origin, 2001

"When it comes to your outlook, do you regard yourself as…"

(percent distribution of people aged 18 or older by response, by race and Hispanic origin, 2001)

	total	Asian	black	Hispanic	non-Hispanic white
Total people	**100%**	**100%**	**100%**	**100%**	**100%**
Religious	37	28	49	30	37
Somewhat religious	38	34	32	45	40
Somewhat secular	6	9	5	5	7
Secular	10	21	7	12	10
Don't know, refused	9	8	7	8	6

Source: American Religious Identification Survey 2001, Barry A. Kosmin, Egon Mayer, and Ariela Keysar. For further details see: Barry A. Kosmin and Ariela Keysar, Religion in a Free Market, *Paramount Market Publishing, Inc. Ithaca, NY, 2006.*

Table 7.6 Computer and Internet Use by Race and Hispanic Origin, 2000 and 2005

(percent of people aged 18 or older who use a computer, use the Internet, and were online yesterday, by race and Hispanic origin, 2000 and 2005; percentage point change in use, 2000–05)

	2005	2000	percentage point change 2000–05
USE COMPUTER			
Total people	**72%**	**62%**	**10**
Black	64	51	13
Hispanic	76	58	18
White	73	63	10
USE INTERNET			
Total people	**68**	**46**	**22**
Black	57	35	22
Hispanic	70	40	30
White	70	48	22
ONLINE YESTERDAY (AMONG INTERNET USERS)			
Total people	**60**	**60**	**0**
Black	39	37	2
Hispanic	51	51	0
White	64	62	2

Source: Pew Internet & American Life Project, Internet site http://www.pewinternet.org/trends.asp#demographics; calculations by New Strategist

Table 7.7 Voting in Presidential Elections by Race and Hispanic Origin, 1980 to 2004

(percent of people who reported voting in presidential elections by race and Hispanic origin, and percentage point change, 1980 to 2004)

	total	Asian	black	Hispanic	non-Hispanic white
2004	58.3%	30.7%	56.1%	28.0%	65.8%
2000	54.7	25.4	53.5	27.5	60.4
1996	54.2	25.7	50.6	26.7	59.6
1992	61.3	27.3	54.0	28.9	66.9
1988	57.4	–	51.5	28.8	61.8
1984	59.9	–	55.8	32.6	63.3
1980	59.2	–	50.5	29.9	62.8
Percentage point change					
1980 to 2004	–0.9	–	5.6	–1.9	3.0

Note: (–) means data not available.
Source: Bureau of the Census, Voting and Registration in the Election of November 2004, Detailed Tables, Internet site http://www.census.gov/population/www/socdemo/voting/cps2004.html; and Historical Time Series Tables, http://www.census.gov/population/www/socdemo/voting.html; calculations by New Strategist

Table 7.8 Number of Voters by Age, Race, and Hispanic Origin, November 2004

(total number of people aged 18 or older, number and percent voting, and percent of citizens voting, by age, race, and Hispanic origin, 2004 presidential election; numbers in thousands)

| | | voted | | percent of |
	total	number	percent	citizens voting
Total people	**215,694**	**125,736**	**58.3%**	**63.8%**
Aged 18 to 24	27,808	11,639	41.9	46.7
Aged 25 to 44	82,133	42,845	52.2	60.1
Aged 45 to 64	71,014	47,327	66.6	70.4
Aged 65 to 74	18,363	13,010	70.8	73.3
Aged 75 or older	16,375	10,915	66.7	68.5
Asian				
Total people	**9,721**	**2,980**	**30.7**	**44.6**
Aged 18 to 24	1,233	302	24.5	34.5
Aged 25 to 44	4,560	1,158	25.4	41.4
Aged 45 to 64	2,850	1,106	38.8	51.4
Aged 65 to 74	610	266	43.6	54.1
Aged 75 or older	468	148	31.5	39.7
Black				
Total people	**25,510**	**14,324**	**56.1**	**59.9**
Aged 18 to 24	4,126	1,817	44.0	47.0
Aged 25 to 44	10,618	5,729	54.0	59.1
Aged 45 to 64	7,819	4,890	62.5	65.3
Aged 65 to 74	1,754	1,162	66.2	68.6
Aged 75 or older	1,193	726	60.9	61.9
Hispanic				
Total people	**27,129**	**7,587**	**28.0**	**47.2**
Aged 18 to 24	4,917	1,003	20.4	33.0
Aged 25 to 44	13,715	3,152	23.0	45.2
Aged 45 to 64	6,347	2,444	38.5	56.2
Aged 65 to 74	1,305	610	46.8	57.9
Aged 75 or older	846	378	44.7	55.6
Non-Hispanic white				
Total people	**151,410**	**99,567**	**65.8**	**67.2**
Aged 18 to 24	17,255	8,368	48.5	49.8
Aged 25 to 44	52,578	32,384	61.6	63.5
Aged 45 to 64	53,295	38,393	72.0	73.2
Aged 65 to 74	14,531	10,830	74.5	75.5
Aged 75 or older	13,751	9,591	69.7	70.6

Note: Asians and blacks are those identifying themselves as being of the race alone and those identifying themselves as being of the race in combination with one or more other races. Non-Hispanic whites are those identifying themselves as being white alone and not Hispanic. Numbers by race and Hispanic origin will not sum to total because not all races are shown and Hispanics may be of any race.
Source: Bureau of the Census, Voting and Registration in the Election of November 2004, Detailed Tables, Internet site http:// www.census.gov/population/www/socdemo/voting/cps2004.html; calculations by New Strategist

Table 7.9 Share of Voters by Age, Race, and Hispanic Origin, November 2004

(total number of voters and percent distribution by age, race, and Hispanic origin, 2004 presidential election; numbers in thousands)

	total		Asian	black	Hispanic	non-Hispanic white
	number	percent				
Total voters	**125,736**	**100.0%**	**2.4%**	**11.4%**	**6.0%**	**79.2%**
Aged 18 to 24	11,639	100.0	2.6	15.6	8.6	71.9
Aged 25 to 44	42,845	100.0	2.7	13.4	7.4	75.6
Aged 45 to 64	47,327	100.0	2.3	10.3	5.2	81.1
Aged 65 to 74	13,010	100.0	2.0	8.9	4.7	83.2
Aged 75 or older	10,915	100.0	1.4	6.7	3.5	87.9

Note: Asians and blacks are those identifying themselves as being of the race alone and those identifying themselves as being of the race in combination with one or more other races. Non-Hispanic whites are those identifying themselves as being white alone and not Hispanic. Percentages by race and Hispanic origin will not sum to total because not all races are shown and Hispanics may be of any race.

Source: Bureau of the Census, Voting and Registration in the Election of November 2004, Detailed Tables, Internet site http:// www.census.gov/population/www/socdemo/voting/cps2004.html; calculations by New Strategist

Table 7.10 Reasons for Not Voting by Race and Hispanic Origin, 2004

(number of people aged 18 or older, number registered to vote, number voting, number registered who did not vote, and percent distribution by reason for not voting, by race and Hispanic origin, 2004 presidential election; numbers in thousands)

	total	Asian	black	Hispanic	non-Hispanic white
Total aged 18 or older	**215,694**	**9,721**	**25,510**	**27,129**	**151,410**
Total registered to vote	142,070	3,508	16,408	9,308	111,318
Total voting	125,736	2,980	14,324	7,587	99,567
Total registered who did not vote, number	**16,334**	**528**	**2,084**	**1,721**	**11,752**
Total registered who did not vote, percent	**100.0%**	**100.0%**	**100.0%**	**100.0%**	**100.0%**
Reason for not voting					
Illness or disability	15.4	7.2	16.5	10.7	16.2
Out of town	9.0	10.5	5.9	6.3	9.9
Forgot to vote	3.4	2.1	3.9	6.1	3.0
Not interested	10.7	7.7	9.9	10.5	10.8
Too busy, conflicting schedule	19.9	31.2	20.6	23.5	18.9
Transportation problems	2.1	1.2	4.1	1.6	1.9
Did not like candidates or campaign issues	9.9	5.4	6.6	7.3	11.1
Registration problems	6.8	5.7	7.3	10.9	6.2
Bad weather conditions	0.5	1.3	0.3	0.2	0.5
Inconvenient polling place	3.0	5.0	2.6	1.5	3.2
Other reason	10.9	13.7	9.5	11.6	10.8
Don't know/refused	8.5	9.1	12.9	9.8	7.6

Note: Asians and blacks are those identifying themselves as being of the race alone and those identifying themselves as being of the race in combination with one or more other races. Non-Hispanic whites are those identifying themselves as being white alone and not Hispanic. Numbers by race and Hispanic origin will not sum to total because not all races are shown and Hispanics may be of any race.
Source: Bureau of the Census, Voting and Registration in the Election of November 2004, detailed tables Internet site http:// www.census.gov/population/www/socdemo/voting/cps2004.html; calculations by New Strategist

Table 7.11 Volunteering by Race and Hispanic Origin, 2004

(total number of people aged 16 or older, number and percent who performed unpaid volunteer work for an organization during the past year, and percent distribution of volunteers, by race and Hispanic origin, 2004; numbers in thousands)

| | | volunteers | | |
	total	number	percent who volunteer	percent distribution
Total people	**223,941**	**64,542**	**28.8%**	**100.0%**
Asian	9,506	1,832	19.3	2.8
Black	26,163	5,435	20.8	8.4
Hispanic	28,338	4,102	14.5	6.4
White	183,022	55,892	30.5	86.6

Note: Numbers will not sum to total because not all races are shown and Hispanics may be of any race.
Source: Bureau of Labor Statistics, Volunteering in the United States, 2004, Internet site http://www.bls.gov/news.release/volun.toc.htm

Table 7.12 Attendance at Arts Events by Race and Hispanic Origin, 2002

(percent of people aged 18 or older who attended, visited, and read selected arts during the past year, and share of total audience, by race and Hispanic origin, 2002)

	total	black	Hispanic	non-Hispanic white	other
PERCENT ATTENDING, VISITING, READING					
Any listed activity	**39.0%**	**27.8%**	**23.1%**	**43.6%**	**41.8%**
Attended jazz performance	10.8	12.7	6.2	11.4	7.3
Attended classical music performance	11.6	4.5	5.5	13.7	10.3
Attended opera	3.2	1.1	1.8	3.8	2.5
Attended musical	17.1	10.3	6.9	20.1	11.9
Attended nonmusical play	12.3	7.1	6.2	14.2	10.0
Attended ballet	3.9	1.5	1.6	4.7	2.3
Visited art museum or gallery	26.5	14.8	16.1	29.5	32.7
Attended dance performance (except ballet)	6.3	4.2	5.6	6.9	5.1
Read literature (novels, poetry, or plays)	46.7	37.1	26.5	51.4	43.7
Visited historic site	31.6	17.9	17.2	36.0	30.4
Attended art or craft fair or festival	33.4	19.7	20.3	38.0	25.8
SHARE OF AUDIENCE					
Any listed activity	**100.0%**	**8.1%**	**6.5%**	**80.5%**	**4.9%**
Attended jazz performance	100.0	13.5	6.3	77.0	3.1
Attended classical music performance	100.0	4.5	5.2	86.2	4.1
Attended opera	100.0	3.8	6.1	86.4	3.6
Attended musical	100.0	6.9	4.5	85.4	3.2
Attended nonmusical play	100.0	6.6	5.5	84.1	3.7
Attended ballet	100.0	4.5	4.6	88.2	2.7
Visited art museum or gallery	100.0	6.4	6.7	81.2	5.7
Attended dance performance (except ballet)	100.0	7.6	9.7	79.0	3.7
Read literature (novels, poetry, or plays)	100.0	9.1	6.2	80.3	4.3
Visited historic site	100.0	6.5	6.0	83.1	4.4
Attended art or craft fair or festival	100.0	6.8	6.7	83.0	3.5

Note: Other includes Asians and American Indians.
Source: National Endowment for the Arts, 2002 Survey of Public Participation in the Arts: Summary Report, Research Division Report No. 45, Internet site http://www.nea.gov/pub/ResearchReports_chrono.html

Table 7.13 Personal Participation in the Arts by Race and Hispanic Origin, 2002

(percent of people aged 18 or older who personally participated in the arts during the past year, and share of total participants, by race and Hispanic origin, 2002)

	total	black	Hispanic	non-Hispanic white	other
PERCENT PERSONALLY PARTICPATING IN					
Jazz performance	1.3%	1.2%	0.5%	1.5%	0.5%
Classical music performance	1.8	0.4	0.7	2.1	2.3
Opera	0.7	0.4	0.4	0.8	1.0
Choir or chorale	4.8	9.1	2.9	4.5	3.5
Nonmusical play	2.4	1.4	0.8	2.8	1.1
Act in play	1.4	2.2	1.3	1.3	1.1
Ballet	0.3	0.4	0.2	0.4	0.3
Dance (except ballet)	4.2	3.5	4.2	4.1	5.8
Music composition	2.3	3.0	0.6	2.5	2.3
Painting, drawing, sculpture, or printmaking	8.6	5.6	6.8	9.4	7.4
Writing	7.0	7.4	4.0	7.6	5.3
Photography	11.5	7.6	6.7	12.8	11.9
Pottery, jewelry, leatherwork, or metalwork	6.9	4.1	5.1	7.6	6.5
Sewing, weaving, crocheting, quilting, or needlepoint	16.0	9.4	12.5	17.6	14.9
Own original pieces of art	19.3	8.8	7.0	23.1	14.5
Purchased art recently	29.5	35.9	37.5	28.9	26.3
SHARE OF PARTICIPANTS					
Jazz performance	100.0%	10.8%	4.6%	83.0%	1.6%
Classical music performance	100.0	2.4	4.4	87.1	6.0
Opera	100.0	6.2	6.7	80.8	6.4
Choir or chorale	100.0	22.0	6.6	68.1	3.4
Musical play	100.0	6.6	3.8	87.4	2.2
Nonmusical play	100.0	17.6	10.4	68.4	3.6
Ballet	100.0	13.1	6.6	76.5	3.7
Dance (except ballet)	100.0	9.7	11.2	72.7	6.4
Music composition	100.0	14.6	3.0	78.0	4.4
Painting, drawing, sculpture, or printmaking	100.0	7.4	8.7	79.9	3.9
Writing	100.0	12.1	6.3	78.2	3.4
Photography	100.0	7.6	6.5	81.2	4.7
Pottery, jewelry, leatherwork, or metalwork	100.0	6.9	8.2	80.6	4.3
Sewing, weaving, crocheting, quilting, or needlepoint	100.0	6.8	8.6	80.3	4.3
Own original pieces of art	100.0	5.3	4.0	87.3	3.4
Purchased art recently	100.0	6.4	5.1	85.4	3.1

Note: Other includes Asians and American Indians.
Source: National Endowment for the Arts, 2002 Survey of Public Participation in the Arts: Summary Report, Research Division Report No. 45, Internet site http://www.nea.gov/pub/ResearchReports_chrono.html

Table 7.14 Participation in the Arts through Media by Race and Hispanic Origin, 2002

(percent of people aged 18 or older who participated in the arts through media during the past year, and share of total participants, by race and Hispanic Origin, 2002)

	total	black	Hispanic	non-Hispanic white	other
PERCENT PARTICIPATING IN MEDIA					
Jazz					
Television	16.4%	25.9%	12.4%	15.6%	15.2%
Radio	23.5	33.4	14.0	23.5	22.3
Recordings	17.2	23.6	9.1	17.4	18.7
Classical music					
Television	18.1	10.2	11.4	20.1	22.1
Radio	23.9	12.9	15.5	26.9	24.7
Recordings	19.3	8.5	9.0	22.5	20.7
Opera					
Television	5.8	4.6	5.5	5.7	9.5
Radio	5.7	3.8	3.6	6.2	6.8
Recordings	5.5	2.5	3.0	6.3	7.1
Musical play					
Television	11.7	9.7	6.7	12.7	13.3
Radio	2.4	1.3	2.4	2.4	4.7
Recordings	4.3	1.3	1.9	5.0	6.4
Nonmusical play					
Television	9.4	8.8	7.7	9.7	11.0
Radio	2.1	2.3	1.4	2.2	1.7
Dance (on television)	**12.6**	**10.0**	**11.3**	**13.2**	**12.6**
Artists, art work, or art museums (on television)	25.0	18.2	17.9	27.2	22.9

(continued)

	total	black	Hispanic	non-Hispanic white	other
SHARE OF AUDIENCE					
Jazz					
Television	100.0%	18.1%	8.3%	69.3%	4.3%
Radio	100.0	16.3	6.5	72.8	4.4
Recordings	100.0	15.7	5.8	73.5	5.0
Classical music					
Television	100.0	6.5	6.9	80.9	5.7
Radio	100.0	6.2	7.1	81.9	4.7
Recordings	100.0	5.1	5.2	84.9	4.9
Opera					
Television	100.0	9.2	10.5	72.7	7.6
Radio	100.0	7.7	6.9	79.9	5.5
Recordings	100.0	5.2	5.9	83.0	5.9
Musical play					
Television	100.0	9.5	6.3	79.0	5.2
Radio	100.0	6.4	10.8	73.7	9.1
Recordings	100.0	3.6	5.0	84.6	6.9
Non-musical play					
Television	100.0	10.7	9.0	75.0	5.4
Radio	100.0	12.8	7.6	75.9	3.7
Dance (on television)	**100.0**	**9.1**	**9.9**	**76.4**	**4.6**
Artists, art work, or art museums (on television)	100.0	8.4	7.9	79.5	4.2

Note: Other includes Asians and American Indians.
Source: National Endowment for the Arts, 2002 Survey of Public Participation in the Arts: Summary Report, Research Division Report No. 45, Internet site http://www.nea.gov/pub/ResearchReports_chrono.html

Table 7.15 Participation in Selected Leisure Activities by Race and Hispanic Origin, 2002

(percent of people aged 18 or older who participated in selected leisure activities during the past year, and share of total participants, by race and Hispanic origin, 2002)

	total	black	Hispanic	non-Hispanic white	other
PERCENT PARTICIPATING OR ATTENDING					
Go to the movies	60.0%	49.2%	52.5%	63.0%	58.1%
Attend sports events (except youth sports)	35.0	27.0	26.4	38.4	22.3
Go to an amusement park or carnival	41.7	36.6	38.9	42.8	43.9
Jog, lift weights, walk, or participate in any other exercise routine	55.1	46.1	40.1	59.1	50.4
Participate in sports, such as golf, bowling, skiing, or basketball	30.4	23.1	22.3	33.0	26.9
Participate in outdoor activities such as camping, hiking, or canoeing	30.9	8.2	14.9	37.3	23.9
Perform volunteer or charity work	29.0	22.7	15.3	32.5	22.5
Participate in home improvement or repair to own home	42.4	26.3	28.0	47.7	33.8
Garden indoors or outdoors	47.3	30.3	34.8	52.3	41.3
SHARE OF PARTICIPANTS OR ATTENDEES					
Go to the movies	100.0%	9.4%	9.6%	76.5%	4.5%
Attend sports events (except youth sports)	100.0	8.9	8.3	79.9	2.9
Go to an amusement park or carnival	100.0	10.1	10.3	74.8	4.8
Jog, lift weights, walk, or participate in any other exercise routine	100.0	9.6	8.0	78.2	4.2
Participate in sports, such as golf, bowling, skiing, or basketball	100.0	8.7	8.1	79.1	4.1
Participate in outdoor activities such as camping, hiking, or canoeing	100.0	3.1	5.3	88.1	3.5
Perform volunteer or charity work	100.0	9.0	5.8	81.6	3.5
Participate in home improvement or repair to own home	100.0	7.1	7.3	82.0	3.7
Garden indoors or outdoors	100.0	7.4	8.1	80.5	4.0

Note: Other includes Asians and American Indians.
Source: National Endowment for the Arts, 2002 Survey of Public Participation in the Arts: Summary Report, Research Division Report No. 45, Internet site http://www.nea.gov/pub/ResearchReports_chrono.html

Glossary

adjusted for inflation Income or a change in income that has been adjusted for the rise in the cost of living, or the consumer price index (CPI-U-RS).

age Classification by age is based on the age of the person at his or her last birthday.

American Community Survey The ACS is an on-going nationwide survey of 250,000 households per month, providing detailed demographic data at the community level. Designed to replace the census long-form questionnaire, the ACS includes more than 60 questions that formerly appeared on the long form, such as language spoken at home, income, and education. ACS data are available for the nation, regions, states, counties, metropolitan areas, and many places.

American Housing Survey The AHS collects national and metropolitan-level data on the nation's housing, including apartments, single-family homes, and mobile homes. The nationally representative survey, with a sample of 55,000 households, is conducted by the Census Bureau for the Department of Housing and Urban Development every other year.

American Indians In this book, American Indians include Alaska Natives (Eskimos and Aleuts) unless those groups are shown separately. Beginning with the 2000 census and in 2003 for government surveys, American Indians can identify themselves as being American Indian and no other race (called "American Indian alone") or as being American Indian in combination with one or more other races (called "American Indian in combination"). The combination of the two groups is termed "American Indian alone or in combination." In this book, the "American Indian alone or in combination" population is shown whenever possible.

American Religious Identification Survey The 2001 ARIS, sponsored by the Graduate Center of the City University of New York, was based on a random telephone survey of 50,281 households in the continental U.S. Interviewers asked respondents aged 18 or older for their demographic characteristics and their religion. The 2001 ARIS updates the 1990 National Survey of Religious Identification.

American Time Use Survey Under contract with the Bureau of Labor Statistics, the Census Bureau collects ATUS information, revealing how people spend their time. The ATUS sample is drawn from U.S. households that have completed their final month of interviews for the Current Population Survey. One individual from each selected household is chosen to participate in the ATUS. Respondents are interviewed by telephone only once about their time use on the previous day. In 2003, the sample consisted of approximately 3,000 cases each month, which yielded about 1,700 completed interviews.

Asian The term "Asian" includes Native Hawaiians and other Pacific Islanders unless those groups are shown separately. Middle Eastern nations—such as Israel, Jordan, Iran, and Iraq—are considered part of the Asian world region. Therefore, immigrants from the Middle East are counted as Asians in the immigration and foreign-born tables. Beginning with the 2000 census and in 2003 for government surveys, Asians can identify themselves as being Asian and no other race (called "Asian alone") or as being Asian in combination with one or more other races (called "Asian in combination"). The combination of the two groups is termed "Asian alone or in combination." In this book, the "Asian alone or in combination" population is shown whenever possible.

baby boom Americans born between 1946 and 1964.

baby bust Americans born between 1965 and 1976, also known as Generation X.

black The black racial category includes those who identified themselves as "black" or "African American." Beginning with the 2000 census and in 2003 for government surveys, blacks can identify themselves as being black and no other race (called "black alone") or as being black in combination with one or more other races (called "black in combination"). The combination of the two groups is termed "black alone or in combination." In this book, the "black alone or in combination" population is shown whenever possible.

central cities The largest city in a metropolitan area is called the central city. The balance of the metropolitan area outside the central city is regarded as the "suburbs."

consolidated metropolitan statistical area or CMSA An area that meets the requirements for recognition as an MSA (metropolitan statistical area) and also has a population of 1 million or more may be recognized as a consolidated metropolitan statistical area (or CMSA) if it includes separate component areas that meet the statistical criteria specified in the standards for metropolitan areas, and if local opinion indicates there is support for the component areas. The components of CMSAs are called primary metropolitan statistical areas (or PMSAs).

Consumer Expenditure Survey The CEX is an ongoing study of the day-to-day spending of American households administered by the Bureau of Labor Statistics. The CEX includes an interview survey and a diary survey. The average spending figures shown in this book are the integrated data from both the diary and interview components of the survey. Two separate, nationally representative samples are used for the interview and diary surveys. For the interview survey, about 7,500 consumer units are interviewed on a rotating panel basis each quarter for five consecutive quarters. For the diary survey, 7,500 consumer units keep weekly diaries of spending for two consecutive weeks.

consumer unit *(on spending tables only)* For convenience, the terms consumer unit and households are used interchangeably in the spending section of this book, although consumer units are somewhat different from the Census Bureau's households. Consumer units are all related members of a household, or financially independent members of a household. A household may include more than one consumer unit.

Current Population Survey The CPS is a nationally representative survey of the civilian noninstitutional population aged 15 or older. It is taken monthly by the Census Bureau for the Bureau of Labor Statistics, collecting information from more than 50,000 households on employment and unemployment. In March of each year, the survey includes the Annual Social and Economic Supplement (formerly called the Annual Demographic Survey), which is the source of most national data on the characteristics of Americans, such as educational attainment, living arrangements, and incomes.

disability The National Health Interview Survey estimates the number of people aged 18 or older who have difficulty in physical functioning, probing whether respondents could perform nine activities by themselves without using special equipment. The categories are walking a quarter mile; standing for two hours; sitting for two hours; walking up 10 steps without resting; stooping, bending, kneeling; reaching over one's head; grasping or handling small objects; carrying a 10-pound object; and pushing/pulling a large object. Adults who reported that any of these activities was very difficult or they could not do it at all were defined as having physical difficulties.

dual-earner couple A married couple in which both the householder and the householder's spouse are in the labor force.

earnings A type of income, earnings is the amount of money a person receives from his or her job. *See also* Income.

employed All civilians who did any work as a paid employee or farmer/self-employed worker, or who worked 15 hours or more as an unpaid farm worker or in a family-owned business, during the reference period. All those who have jobs but who are temporarily absent from their jobs due to illness, bad weather, vacation, labor management dispute, or personal reasons are considered employed.

expenditure The transaction cost including excise and sales taxes of goods and services acquired during the survey period. The full cost of each purchase is recorded even though full payment may not have been made at the date of purchase. Average expenditure figures may be artificially low for infrequently purchased items such as cars because figures are calculated using all consumer units within a demographic segment rather than just purchasers. Expenditure estimates include money spent on gifts for others.

family A group of two or more people (one of whom is the householder) related by birth, marriage, or adoption and living in the same household.

family household A household maintained by a householder who lives with one or more people related to him or her by blood, marriage, or adoption.

female/male householder A woman or man who maintains a household without a spouse present. May head family or nonfamily households.

foreign-born population People who are not U.S. citizens at birth.

full-time employment Full-time is 35 or more hours of work per week during a majority of the weeks worked.

full-time, year-round Indicates 50 or more weeks of full-time employment during the previous calendar year.

generation X Americans born between 1965 and 1976, also known as the baby-bust generation.

Hispanic Because Hispanic is an ethnic origin rather than a race, Hispanics may be of any race. While most Hispanics are white, there are black, Asian, American Indian, and even Native Hawaiian Hispanics.

household All the persons who occupy a housing unit. A household includes the related family members and all the unrelated persons, if any, such as lodgers, foster children, wards, or employees who share the housing unit. A person living alone is counted as a household. A group of unrelated people who share a housing unit as roommates or unmarried partners is also counted as a household. Households do not include group quarters such as college dormitories, prisons, or nursing homes.

household, race/ethnicity of Households are categorized according to the race or ethnicity of the householder only.

householder The householder is the person (or one of the persons) in whose name the housing unit is owned or rented or, if there is no such person, any adult member. With married couples, the householder may be either the husband or wife. The householder is the reference person for the household.

householder, age of The age of the householder is used to categorize households into age groups such as those used in this book. Married couples, for example, are classified according to the age of either the husband or wife, depending on which one identified him or herself as the householder.

housing unit A housing unit is a house, an apartment, a group of rooms, or a single room occupied or intended for occupancy as separate living quarters. Separate living quarters are those in which the occupants do not live and eat with any other persons in the structure and that have direct access from the outside of the building or through a common hall that is used or intended for use by the occupants of another unit or by the general public. The occupants may be a single family, one person living alone, two or more families living together, or any other group of related or unrelated persons who share living arrangements.

housing value The respondent's estimate of how much his or her house and lot would sell for if it were for sale.

immigrants Aliens admitted for legal permanent residence in the United States.

income Money received in the preceding calendar year by each person aged 15 or older from each of the following sources: (1) earnings from longest job (or self-employment); (2) earnings from jobs other than longest job; (3) unemployment compensation; (4) workers' compensation; (5) Social Security; (6) Supplemental Security income; (7) public assistance; (8) veterans' payments; (9) survivor benefits; (10) disability benefits; (11) retirement pensions; (12) interest; (13) dividends; (14) rents and royalties or estates and trusts; (15) educational assistance; (16) alimony; (17) child support; (18) financial assistance from outside the household, and other periodic income. Income is reported in several ways in this book. Household income is the combined income of all household members. Income of persons is all income accruing to a person from all sources. Earnings are the money a person receives from his or her job.

industry Refers to the industry in which a person worked longest in the preceding calendar year.

job tenure The length of time a person has been employed continuously by the same employer.

labor force The labor force tables in this book show the civilian labor force only. The labor force includes both the employed and the unemployed (people who are looking for work). People are counted as in the labor force if they were working or looking for work during the reference week in which the Census Bureau fields the Current Population Survey.

labor force participation rate The percent of the civilian noninstitutional population that is in the civilian labor force, which includes both the employed and the unemployed.

married-couple family group Married couples who may or may not be householders. Those who are householders are "married-couple households." Those who are not householders are married couples living in a household headed by someone else, such as a parent of the husband or wife. Because married-couple family groups include married-couple households, the number of married-couple family groups will always outnumber married-couple households.

married couples with or without children under age 18 Refers to married couples with or without own children under age 18 living in the same household. Couples without children under age 18 may be parents of grown children who live elsewhere, or they could be childless couples.

median The median is the amount that divides the population or households into two equal portions: one below and one above the median. Medians can be calculated for income, age, and many other characteristics.

median income The amount that divides the income distribution into two equal groups, half having incomes above the median, half having incomes below the median. The medians for households or families are based on all households or families. The median for persons are based on all persons aged 15 or older with income.

metropolitan statistical area (or MSA) To be defined as an MSA, an area must include a city with 50,000 or more inhabitants, or a Census Bureau-defined urbanized area of at least 50,000 inhabitants and a total metropolitan population of at least 100,000 (75,000 in New England). The county (or counties) that contains the largest city becomes the "central county" (counties), along with any adjacent counties that have at least 50 percent of their population in the urbanized area surrounding the largest city. Additional "outlying counties" are included in the MSA if they meet specified requirements of commuting to the central counties and other selected requirements of metropolitan character (such as population density and percent urban). In New England, MSAs are defined in terms of cities and towns rather than counties. For this reason, the concept of NECMA is used to define metropolitan areas in the New England division.

millennial generation Americans born between 1977 and 1994.

mobility status People are classified according to their mobility status on the basis of a comparison between their place of residence at the time of the March Current Population Survey and their place of residence in March of the previous year. Nonmovers are people living in the same house at the end of the period as at the beginning of the period. Movers are people living in a different house at the end of the period than at the beginning of the period. Movers from abroad are either citizens or aliens whose place of residence is outside the United States at the beginning of the period, that is, in an outlying area under the jurisdiction of the United States or in a foreign country. The mobility status for children is fully allocated from the mother if she is in the household; otherwise it is allocated from the householder.

National Ambulatory Medical Care Survey The NAMCS is an annual survey of visits to nonfederally employed office-based physicians who are primarily engaged in direct patient care. Data are collected from physicians rather than patients, with each physician assigned a one-week reporting period. During that week, a systematic random sample of visit characteristics are recorded by the physician or office staff.

National Health and Nutrition Examination Survey The NHANES is a continuous survey of a representative sample of the U.S. civilian noninstitutionalized population. Respondents are interviewed at home about their health and nutrition, and the interview is followed up by a physical examination that measures such things as height and weight in mobile examination centers.

National Health Interview Survey The NHIS is a continuing nationwide sample survey of the civilian noninstitutional population of the U.S. conducted by the Census Bureau for the National Center for Health Statistics. In interviews each year, data are collected from more than 100,000 people about their illnesses, injuries, impairments, chronic and acute conditions, activity limitations, and use of health services.

National Household Education Survey The NHES, sponsored by the National Center for Education Statistics, provides descriptive data on the educational activities of the U.S. population, including after-school care and adult education. The NHES is a system of telephone surveys of a representative sample of 45,000 to 60,000 households in the U.S conducted in 1991, 1993, 1995, 1996, 1999, 2001, and 2003.

Native Hawaiian and other Pacific Islander The 2000 census identified this group for the first time as a separate racial category from Asians. In most survey data, however, the population is included with Asians.

nonfamily household A household maintained by a householder who lives alone or who lives with people to whom he or she is not related.

nonfamily householder A householder who lives alone or with nonrelatives.

non-Hispanic People who do not identify themselves as Hispanic are classified as non-Hispanic. Non-Hispanics may be of any race.

non-Hispanic white People who identify their race as white alone and who do not indicate their ethnicity as Hispanic.

nonmetropolitan area Counties that are not classified as metropolitan areas.

occupation Occupational classification is based on the kind of work a person did at his or her job during the previous calendar year. If a person changed jobs during the year, the data refer to the occupation of the job held the longest during that year.

occupied housing units A housing unit is classified as occupied if a person or group of people is living in it or if the occupants are only temporarily absent—on vacation, example. By definition, the count of occupied housing units is the same as the count of households.

outside central city The portion of a metropolitan county or counties that falls outside of the central city or cities; generally regarded as the suburbs.

own children Own children are sons and daughters, including stepchildren and adopted children, of the householder. The totals include never-married children living away from home in college dormitories.

owner occupied A housing unit is "owner occupied" if the owner lives in the unit, even if it is mortgaged or not fully paid for. A cooperative or condominium unit is "owner occupied" only if the owner lives in it. All other occupied units are classified as "renter occupied."

part-time employment Part-time is less than 35 hours of work per week in a majority of the weeks worked during the year.

percent change The change (either positive or negative) in a measure that is expressed as a proportion of the starting measure. When median income changes from $20,000 to $25,000, for example, this is a 25 percent increase.

percentage point change The change (either positive or negative) in a value which is already expressed as a percentage. When a labor force participation rate changes from 70 percent of 75 percent, for example, this is a 5 percentage point increase.

poverty level The official income threshold below which families and people are classified as living in poverty. The threshold rises each year with inflation and varies depending on family size and age of householder.

primary metropolitan statistical area (or PMSA) PMSAs are metropolitan statistical areas that are components of consolidated metropolitan statistical areas (CMSAs). If an area qualifies as a metropolitan statistical area and has a population of 1,000,000 or more, two or more PMSAs may be defined within it if statistical criteria are met and local opinion favors the designation.

proportion or share The value of a part expressed as a percentage of the whole. If there are 4 million people aged 25 and 3 million of them are white, then the white proportion is 75 percent.

race Race is self-reported and, beginning with the 2000 census and 2003 for government surveys, can be defined in three ways. The "race alone" population comprises people who identify themselves as only one race. The "race in combination" population comprises people who identify themselves as more than one race, such as white and black. The "race, alone or in combination" population includes both those who identify themselves as one race and those who identify themselves as more than one race. In this book, the "race alone or in combination" population is shown whenever possible.

regions The four major regions and nine census divisions of the United States are the state groupings as shown below:

Northeast:
—New England: Connecticut, Maine, Massachusetts, New Hampshire, Rhode Island, and Vermont
—Middle Atlantic: New Jersey, New York, and Pennsylvania

Midwest:
—East North Central: Illinois, Indiana, Michigan, Ohio, and Wisconsin
—West North Central: Iowa, Kansas, Minnesota, Missouri, Nebraska, North Dakota, and South Dakota

South:
—South Atlantic: Delaware, District of Columbia, Florida, Georgia, Maryland, North Carolina, South Carolina, Virginia, and West Virginia
—East South Central: Alabama, Kentucky, Mississippi, and Tennessee
—West South Central: Arkansas, Louisiana, Oklahoma, and Texas

West:
—Mountain: Arizona, Colorado, Idaho, Montana, Nevada, New Mexico, Utah, and Wyoming
—Pacific: Alaska, California, Hawaii, Oregon, and Washington

renter occupied *See* Owner occupied.

Retirement Confidence Survey The RCS, sponsored by the Employee Benefit Research Institute (EBRI), the American Savings Education Council (ASEC), and Mathew Greenwald & Associates (Greenwald), is an annual survey of a nationally representative sample of 1,000 people aged 25 or older. Respondents are asked a core set of questions that have been asked since 1996, measuring attitudes and behavior towards retirement. Additional questions are also asked about current retirement issues such as 401(k) participation.

rounding Percentages are rounded to the nearest tenth of a percent; therefore, the percentages in a distribution do not always add exactly to 100.0 percent. The totals, however, are always shown as 100.0. Moreover, individual figures are rounded to the nearest thousand without being adjusted to group totals, which are independently rounded; percentages are based on the unrounded numbers.

self-employment A person is categorized as self-employed if he or she was self-employed in the job held longest during the reference period. Persons who report self-employment from a second job are excluded, but those who report wage-and-salary income from a second job are included. Unpaid workers in family businesses are excluded. Self-employment statistics include only nonagricultural workers and exclude people who work for themselves in incorporated business.

sex ratio The number of men per 100 women.

suburbs *See* Outside central city.

Survey of Consumer Finances The Survey of Consumer Finances is a triennial survey taken by the Federal Reserve Board. It collects data on the assets, debts, and net worth of American households. In the 2001 survey, the Federal Reserve Board interviewed a representative sample of 4,449 households.

Survey of Public Participation in the Arts Initiated in 1982 by the National Endowment for the Arts, this survey examines the public's participation in the performing arts, visual arts, historic site visits, music, and literature. The 2002 survey is the fifth (earlier surveys were in 1982, 1985, 1992, and 1997) and was conducted as a supplement to the Current Population Survey. More than 17,000 respondents to the August 2002 Current Population Survey were asked about their arts participation and involvement.

unemployed Unemployed people are those who, during the survey period, had no employment but were available and looking for work. Those who were laid off from their jobs and were waiting to be recalled are also classified as unemployed.

white The "white" racial category includes many Hispanics (who may be of any race) unless the term "non-Hispanic white" is used. In this book, the non-Hispanic white population is shown whenever possible.

Bibliography

Bureau of Labor Statistics

Internet site http://www.bls.gov/

—2003 Consumer Expenditure Survey, Internet site http://www.bls.gov/cex

—American Time Use Survey, Internet site http://www.bls.gov/tus/home.htm

—Current Population Survey, Internet site http://www.bls.gov/cps/home.htm

—*Employee Tenure*, Internet site http://www.bls.gov/news.release/tenure.toc.htm

—*Monthly Labor Review*, February 2004, Internet site http://www.bls.gov/opub/mlr/2004/02/art3exc.htm

—*Volunteering in the United States*, 2004, Internet site http://www.bls.gov/news.release/volun.toc.htm

Bureau of the Census

Internet site http://www.census.gov/

—American Community Survey, Internet site http://factfinder.census.gov/servlet/Dataset-MainPageServlet?_program=ACS&_lang=en&_ts=

—*American Housing Survey for the United States: 2003*, Current Housing Reports, Internet site http://www.census.gov/hhes/www/ahs.html

—America's Families and Living Arrangements: 2003, detailed tables, Internet site http://www.census.gov/population/www/socdemo/hh-fam/cps2003.html

—Census 2000, Internet site http://www.census.gov/main/www/cen2000.html

—Current Population Survey, Annual Social and Economic Supplement, Internet site http://www.census.gov/hhes/income/dinctabs.html

—Current Population Survey, Historical Income Tables, Internet site http://www.census.gov/hhes/income/histinc/histinctb.html

—Current Population Survey, Historical Poverty Tables, Internet site http://www.census.gov/hhes/income/histinc/histpovtb.html

—Educational Attainment in the United States: 2004, detailed tables, Internet site http://www.census.gov/population/www/socdemo/education/cps2004.html

—Foreign-Born Population in the United States, Current Population Survey—March 2004, Detailed Tables, (PPL-176), Internet site http://www.census.gov/population/www/socdemo/foreign/ppl-176.html

—Geographic Mobility: 2004, detailed tables, Internet site http://www.census.gov/population/www/socdemo/migrate/cps2004.html

—National Population Estimates, Internet site http://www.census.gov/popest/national/asrh/NC-EST2004-sa.html

—*Number, Timing, and Duration of Marriages and Divorces: 2001*, Current Population Report P70-97, 2005, Internet site http://www.census.gov/population/www/socdemo/marr-div.html

—Population Estimates by State, Internet site http://www.census.gov/popest/states/asrh/SC-est2004-02.html

—School Enrollment: Social and Economic Characteristics of Students: October 2003, Internet site http://www.census.gov/population/www/socdemo/school/cps2003.html

—*Statistical Abstract of the United States: 2004–2005*, Internet site http://www.census.gov/prod/www/statistical-abstract-04.html

—U.S. Interim Projections by Age, Sex, Race, and Hispanic Origin, Internet site http://www.census.gov/ipc/www/usinterimproj/

—Voting and Registration, Historical Time Series Tables, Internet site http://www.census.gov/population/www/socdemo/voting.html

—Voting and Registration in the Election of November 2004, detailed tables, Internet site http://www.census.gov/population/www/socdemo/voting/cps2004.html

Employee Benefit Research Institute

Internet site http://www.ebri.org/

—"401(k)-Type Plan and IRA Ownership," Craig Copeland, *Notes*, Vol. 26, No. 1, January 2005, Internet site http://www.ebri.org/store/notes.htm

Employee Benefit Research Institute, American Savings Education Council, and Mathew Greenwald & Associates

Internet site http://www.ebri.org/

—*The 2003 Minority Retirement Confidence Survey Summary of Findings*, Internet site http://www.ebri.org/surveys/rcs/2003/

Federal Reserve Board

Internet site http://www.federalreserve.gov/

—"Recent Changes in U.S. Family Finances: Evidence from the 1998 and 2001 Survey of Consumer Finances," *Federal Reserve Bulletin*, January 2003, Internet site http://www.federalreserve.gov/pubs/oss/oss2/2001/scf2001home.html

Graduate Center of the City University of New York

Internet site http://www.gc.cuny.edu/index.htm

—American Religious Identification Survey 2001, Egon Mayer, Barry A. Kosmin, and Ariela Keysar, Internet site http://www.gc.cuny.edu/studies/aris_index.htm

National Center for Education Statistics

Internet site http://nces.ed.gov/

—Adult Education and Lifelong Learning Survey of the National Household Education Surveys Program, Internet site http://nces.ed.gov/programs/coe/2003/section1/tables/t08_2.asp

—*Digest of Education Statistics 2003*, Internet site http://nces.ed.gov//programs/digest/

—Projections of Education Statistics to 2013, Internet site http://nces.ed.gov//programs/projections/tables.asp

National Center for Health Statistics

Internet site http://www.cdc.gov/nchs/

—*Births: Final Data for 2003*, National Vital Statistics Reports, Vol. 54, No. 2, 2005, Internet site http://www.cdc.gov/nchs/products/pubs/pubd/nvsr/54/54-pre.htm

—*Deaths: Final Data for 2002*, National Vital Statistics Reports, Vol. 53, No. 5, 2004, Internet site http://www.cdc.gov/nchs/about/major/dvs/mortdata.htm

—*Health Characteristics of the American Indian and Alaska Native Adult Population: United States, 1999–2003*, Advance Data, No. 356, 2005; Internet site http://www.cdc.gov/nchs/nhis.htm

—*Health, United States, 2004*, Internet site http://www.cdc.gov/nchs/hus.htm

—*Mean Body Weight, Height, and Body Mass Index, United States 1960–2002*, Advance Data, No. 347, 2004, Internet site http://www.cdc.gov/nchs/pressroom/04news/americans.htm

—*National Ambulatory Medical Care Survey: 2002 Summary*, Advance Data No. 346, 2004;

Internet site http://www.cdc.gov/nchs/about/major/ahcd/adata.htm
—*Summary Health Statistics for U.S. Adults: National Health Interview Survey, 2003*, Series 10, No. 225, 2005; Internet site http://www.cdc.gov/nchs/nhis.htm
—*Summary Health Statistics for U.S. Children: National Health Interview Survey, 2003*, Series 10, No. 223, 2005; Internet site http://www.cdc.gov/nchs/nhis.htm

National Endowment for the Arts
Internet site http://www.arts.endow.gov/
—*2002 Survey of Public Participation in the Arts: Summary Report*, Research Division Report No. 45, Internet site http://www.nea.gov/pub/ResearchReports_chrono.html

Office of Immigration Statistics
Internet site http://uscis.gov/graphics/shared/statistics/index.htm
—*2004 Yearbook of Immigration Statistic*, Internet site http://uscis.gov/graphics/shared/statistics/yearbook/YrBk04Im.htm

Pew Internet & American Life Project
Internet site http://www.pewinternet.org
—Latest Trends, Internet site http://www.pewinternet.org/trends.asp#usage

Index

families with children in college.
Asian, 70
black, 178
Hispanic, 291
non-Hispanic white, 422
total, 519
female-headed families. *See also* Male-headed families *and* Married couples.
American Indian, 41–42
Asian, 132–133, 136, 585
black, 245–246, 249, 585
foreign-born, 367
Hispanic, 366–368, 371, 585
homeownership of, 94–95, 204, 317, 446, 543–544
in poverty, 35, 108, 222, 338, 459, 564–567
income of, 101, 216, 329, 453, 559–560
non-Hispanic white, 474–475, 478, 585
total, 585–587
food, spending on
by Asians, 166, 625, 628, 631
by blacks, 272, 625, 628, 631
by Hispanics, 405, 625, 628, 631
by non-Hispanic whites, 501, 625, 628, 631
total, 625, 628, 631
foreign-born
Asian, 102, 106, 110, 162, 617–619
by age, 162, 398–400, 616–617
by educational attainment, 286
by region of birth, 399–401
by region of residence, 162, 401, 618
by sex, 399–400
earnings of, 106, 334–335
European, 617–619
households headed by, 367
income of, 102, 330
Latin American, 286, 330, 334–335, 341, 367, 398–401, 617–619
poverty of, 110, 341
year of arrival, 399–400
full-time workers
Asian, 123
black, 237
Hispanic, 358
income of, 103–105, 217–219, 331–333, 454–456, 561–563
total, 575
white, 467

gardening, 656
gifts for nonhousehold members, spending on
by Asians, 168, 626, 629, 632
by blacks, 274, 626, 629, 632
by Hispanics, 407, 626, 629, 632
by non-Hispanic whites, 503, 626, 629, 632
total, 626, 629, 632

health care, spending on
by Asians, 167, 626, 629, 632
by blacks, 273, 626, 629, 632
by Hispanics, 406, 626, 629, 632
by non-Hispanic whites, 502, 626, 629, 632
total, 626, 629, 632
health care visits. *See* Physician office visits.

health conditions
American Indian, 23–24
Asian, 89–90
black, 197
Hispanic, 310–311
non-Hispanic white, 440–441
of adults, 23, 89, 197, 310, 440, 536
of children, 24, 90, 198, 311, 441, 537
total, 536–537
health insurance
spending on, 167, 273, 406, 502, 626, 629, 632
status of Asians, 86–88, 535
status of blacks, 194–196, 535
status of Hispanics, 307–309, 535
status of non-Hispanic whites, 437–439, 535
status of total, 532–535
health status
American Indian, 17
Asian, 80
black, 188
Hispanic, 300
non-Hispanic white, 431
hearing problems
American Indians with, 23
Asians with, 89
blacks with, 197
Hispanics with, 310
non-Hispanic whites with, 440
total with, 536
heart disease
American Indians with, 23
as cause of death, 26, 92, 200, 313, 443, 539
Asians with, 89
blacks with, 197
Hispanics with, 310
non-Hispanic whites with, 440
total with, 536
Hispanic origin
of American Indians, 46
of Asians, 144
of blacks, 257
of whites, 486
of total, 598–599
homeownership
American Indian, 28–29, 541, 545
Asian, 94–96, 541, 544–545
black, 202–205, 541, 544–545
by age, 203, 316, 542
by household type, 94–95, 204, 317, 446, 543–544
by region, 28–29, 95–96, 205, 318, 447, 544–545
Hispanic, 315–318, 541, 544–545
non-Hispanic white, 445–447, 541, 544–545
total, 541–545
homes, as asset, 277, 410, 506, 636
homicide, as cause of death, 26, 200, 313
households
American Indian, 41
Asian, 131–136, 584–585, 588
black, 245–249, 584–585, 588
by age, 41, 131, 133, 135–136, 245–246, 248–249, 366, 368, 370–371, 474–475, 477–478, 584, 586–587, 589
by number of earners, 125, 238, 359, 469, 576